Public Interest Considerations in US Merger Control

Public Interest Considerations in US Merger Control

An Assessment of National Security and Sectoral Regulators

IOANNIS KOKKORIS
*Professor of Competition Law and Economics,
Queen Mary University London, UK*

OXFORD
UNIVERSITY PRESS

Great Clarendon Street, Oxford, OX2 6DP,
United Kingdom

Oxford University Press is a department of the University of Oxford.
It furthers the University's objective of excellence in research, scholarship,
and education by publishing worldwide. Oxford is a registered trade mark of
Oxford University Press in the UK and in certain other countries

© Ioannis Kokkoris 2024

The moral rights of the author have been asserted

First Edition published in 2024

All rights reserved. No part of this publication may be reproduced, stored in
a retrieval system, or transmitted, in any form or by any means, without the
prior permission in writing of Oxford University Press, or as expressly permitted
by law, by licence or under terms agreed with the appropriate reprographics
rights organization. Enquiries concerning reproduction outside the scope of the
above should be sent to the Rights Department, Oxford University Press, at the
address above

You must not circulate this work in any other form
and you must impose this same condition on any acquirer

Public sector information reproduced under Open Government Licence v3.0
(http://www.nationalarchives.gov.uk/doc/open-government-licence/open-government-licence.htm)

Published in the United States of America by Oxford University Press
198 Madison Avenue, New York, NY 10016, United States of America

British Library Cataloguing in Publication Data
Data available

Library of Congress Control Number: 2023941943

ISBN 978-0-19-286445-1

DOI: 10.1093/ocl/9780192864451.001.0001

Printed and bound by
CPI Group (UK) Ltd, Croydon, CR0 4YY

Links to third party websites are provided by Oxford in good faith and
for information only. Oxford disclaims any responsibility for the materials
contained in any third party website referenced in this work.

Preface

The book describes the extensive US regulatory framework that is relevant for merger control and the possibility of parallel reviews of the same transaction depending on the sector that the transaction relates to. After assessing legislative developments and a plethora of precedents, the book argues that the US regime is at times convoluted when it comes to merger control. Assessment of transactions based on these considerations is at times at odds with the assessment of the same transactions based on competition law considerations. This book will present a detailed account of the relevant US regulatory framework and assess the different approach that regulatory authorities in the US take.

The book will discuss the approach of the Committee on Foreign Investment in the United States (CFIUS), the Federal Communications Commission, the Surface Transportation Board, the Department of Transportation, the Federal Energy Regulatory Commission, the Office of the Comptroller General, the Federal Deposit Insurance Corporation, and the Board of Governors of the Federal Reserve System. The analysis will focus on the composition, legislation, and the relevant public interest considerations that each regulatory authority takes into account, the respective decision-making process, and will present some seminal cases that illustrate not only the enforcement approach of each regulatory authority but also the possibility for discrepancy between the competition law-based assessment on the one hand and the national security and public interest-based assessment on the other.

In order to do so, the book will closely scrutinize the US merger control enforcement in all its variants and in different regulated sectors and discuss the approach of the authorities involved as they are focusing on competition considerations (such as the impact of the transaction on consumer welfare), as well as non-competition considerations, taking into account social and economic values (such as national security and public interest).

The book will start by introducing the institutional context of merger control assessment in the US and focus on the Federal Trade Commission (FTC) and the Department of Justice (DOJ) assessment of concentrations. It will then discuss the concept of national security and will present the relevant regulatory framework. It will also analyse the role of the CFIUS, as well as its enforcement record and the considerations that national security concerns imply for the assessment of concentrations. The book will then discuss the assessment of concentrations by various sectoral regulators based on the public interest standard. In these sectors, a transaction is likely to be assessed under a public interest test by the relevant sectoral regulatory authority and at the same time under the substantial lessening to competition test by the FTC/DOJ. This overlapping assessment approach can lead at times, as the book will illustrate, to contradictory outcomes. Furthermore, depending on the sector in question, the outcome of the public interest assessment may supersede that of the competition law assessment, an outcome that in itself can lead to ineffective competitive dynamics in the sectoral market. Finally, the book will discuss cases where the FTC/DOJ sought to overturn decisions by the sectoral regulators on certain mergers and acquisition transactions in the courts.

A balanced approach must be taken to resolve this conundrum created by this concurrent jurisdiction in the above-mentioned sectors. If some measures are not introduced to mitigate the overlap between authorities, it is very likely that we will continue witnessing how these markets become more concentrated. Most importantly, such a divergence will impede the attainment of a sector-wide coherent enforcement policy. This book has established that when deciding a merger under public interest considerations the relevant regulator seems to enjoy unlimited discretion. Whether a transaction induces national security or public interest concerns, it is crucial that the parties can predict the outcomes of the authorities' assessments based on the analysis of objective factors. In short, more transparency, accountability, and efficiency in the merger review process across all regulated sectors in the US would be advisable and welcome.

I would like to acknowledge the commitment and dedication shown by Dr Claudia Lemus, my colleague at QMUL. In addition to Claudia, I was blessed with a stellar group of research assistants including Massimiliano Trovato, Stefanos Merikas, Athanassios Skourtis, Micaela Duffau, and Anton Dinev.

I would also like to express my gratitude to Imogen Hill, Charlotte Kershaw, and the whole team at Oxford University Press for their foresightedness and continuous support in this book.

Professor Ioannis Kokkoris
London
October 2023

Contents

Table of Cases	xiii
Table of Legislation	xix
List of Abbreviations	xxv

Competition Law and Public Interest Considerations	1
1. The US Merger Control Regime	5
1.1 A Brief Historical Overview	5
1.2 The Merger Guidelines	10
1.3 The Hart-Scott-Rodino Antitrust Improvements Act	18
1.4 Institutional Setting	19
1.4.1 The Antitrust Division (Department of Justice)	19
1.4.2 The Federal Trade Commission	19
1.4.3 The State Authorities	22
1.4.4 Private Plaintiffs	23
1.5 Merger Review Assessment	25
1.5.1 Procedural Process	25
1.5.2 Substantive Assessment	27
1.5.3 Settlements	30
1.5.4 Judicial Review	32
1.6 Concluding Remarks	34
2. National Security Assessment	35
2.1 Geopolitical Developments	35
2.2 Concept of National Security	36
2.3 Committee on Foreign Investment in the US (CFIUS)	37
2.3.1 Composition and Legislation	37
2.3.2 Filing Instructions and Process Overview	39
2.4 Enforcement Record	43
2.4.1 Lessons Drawn from the CFIUS National Security Assessment	49
2.4.2 Analysis of Some Seminal Cases	51
2.4.2.1 Verio—NTT Communications	52
2.4.2.2 SoftBank—Sprint Nextel	53
2.4.2.3 Smithfield Foods—Shuanghui International Holdings	54
2.4.2.4 ChemChina—Syngenta	55
2.4.2.5 Chicago Stock Exchange—Chongqing Casin Enterprise Group	56
2.4.2.6 Alibaba—MoneyGram	57
2.4.2.7 Aleris—Zhongwang	58
2.4.2.8 Cree—Infineon	59
2.4.2.9 NavInfo—HERE	59
2.4.2.10 Ekso—Zhejiang & Shaoxing	60
2.4.2.11 Magnachip	62

viii CONTENTS

2.4.3 Transactions Blocked by US Presidents	63
2.4.3.1 George H. W. Bush administration	63
2.4.3.1.1 China National Aero-Technology Import and Export Corp.	63
2.4.3.2 Barack H. Obama administration	64
2.4.3.2.1 Ralls Corporation (2012)	64
2.4.4 A Brief Historical Overview	66
2.4.4.1 Aixtron (2016)	66
2.4.4.2 Donald Trump administration	68
2.4.4.2.1 Lattice Semiconductor (2017)	69
2.4.4.2.2 Qualcomm (2018)	70
2.4.4.2.3 StayNTouch, Inc. (2020)	71
2.4.4.2.4 Infineon (2020)	72
2.4.4.3 Joe Biden administration	72
2.4.5 National Security Concerns and State-Owned Enterprises (SOEs)	72
2.4.5.1 LENOVO—IBM (2005)	74
2.4.5.2 CNOOC—UNOCAL (2005)	74
2.4.5.3 BAIN—3Com/HUAWEI Technologies Co (2007)	75
2.5 Proposals for Changes to the CFIUS	76
2.5.1 National Defence Authorization Act for Fiscal Year 2018, HR 2810	76
2.5.2 Foreign Investment and Economic Security Act of 2017, HR 2932	77
2.5.3 Section 616: The Food Security is National Security Act of 2017	77
2.5.4 Section 1722: The True Reciprocity Investment Act of 2017	77
2.5.5 Section 2987/HR 5515: The Foreign Investment Risk Review Modernization Act of 2018 (FIRRMA)	78
2.6 Concluding Remarks	80
3. Public Interest Assessment and the Federal Communications Commission (FCC)	83
3.1 The Federal Communications Commission (FCC)	83
3.1.1 Composition and Legislation	84
3.1.2 Filing Instructions and Process Overview	85
3.2 The 'Public Interest' Standard	87
3.3 Challenges of Concurrent Jurisdiction	90
3.4 Enforcement Record	91
3.4.1 Analysis of Some Seminal Cases	92
3.4.1.1 Transactions where FTC/DOJ and FCC diverged on the remedies needed to clear a transaction	92
3.4.1.1.1 Bell Atlantic—NYNEX	92
3.4.1.1.2 SBC—Ameritech	94
3.4.1.1.3 AT&T—TCI	96
3.4.1.1.4 Bell Atlantic—GTE	97
3.4.1.1.5 Verizon—MCI	99
3.4.1.1.6 Comcast—NBCU	100
3.4.1.1.7 Sinclair—Tribune	101
3.4.1.2 Transactions where FTC/DOJ and FCC converged on the assessment	103
3.4.1.2.1 AOL—Time Warner	103
3.4.1.2.2 News Corp—DirecTV	105
3.4.1.2.3 AT&T—DirecTV	106

3.4.1.2.4 Altice—Cablevision	107
3.4.1.2.5 Nexstar—Media General	109
3.4.1.2.6 CenturyLink—Level 3	111
3.4.1.2.7 T-Mobile—Sprint	112
3.4.1.2.8 AT&T—Time Warner	113
3.4.1.2.9 Nexstar—Tribune	115
3.4.1.2.10 Verizon—TracFone	116
3.5 Some Implications of the Analysis	118
3.6 Concluding Remarks	120
4. Public Interest Assessment and the Federal Energy Regulatory Commission (FERC)	**123**
4.1 The Federal Energy Regulatory Commission (FERC)	123
4.1.1 Composition and Legislation	123
4.1.2 Filing Instructions and Process Overview	128
4.2 The 'Public Interest' Standard	131
4.3 Challenges of Concurrent Jurisdiction	133
4.4 Enforcement Record	135
4.4.1 Analysis of Some Seminal Cases	136
4.4.1.1 Transactions assessed by the sectoral regulator	137
4.4.1.1.1 PacifiCorp—UP&L	137
4.4.1.1.2 Northeast Utilities—Public Service Company of New Hampshire	138
4.4.1.2 Transactions with diverging remedies between the FERC and the DOJ	139
4.4.1.2.1 American Electric Power Company—Central and South West Corporation	139
4.4.1.2.2 Pacific Enterprises—Enova	141
4.4.1.2.3 Dominion—CNG	143
4.4.1.2.4 Exelon—PSEG	144
4.4.1.2.5 Duke—Progress	147
4.4.1.2.6 Exelon—Constellation	148
4.4.1.2.7 Dominion—SCANA and SCE&G	149
4.5 Some Implications of the Analysis	150
4.6 Concluding Remarks	152
5. Public Interest Assessment and the Surface Transportation Board (STB)	**153**
5.1 The Surface Transportation Board (STB)	153
5.1.1 Composition and Legislation	154
5.1.2 Filing Instructions and Process Overview	157
5.2 The 'Public Interest' Standard	160
5.3 Challenges of Concurrent Jurisdiction	163
5.4 Enforcement Record	164
5.4.1 Analysis of Some Seminal Cases	164
5.4.1.1 Divergence in the approach of STB and DOJ	166
5.4.1.1.1 Pennsylvania Railroad—New York Central Railroad	166
5.4.1.1.2 Seaboard Air Line—Atlantic Coast Line	168
5.4.1.1.3 Great Northern—Northern Pacific (The Northern Lines)	170
5.4.1.1.4 Union Pacific—Missouri Pacific—Western Pacific	171

X CONTENTS

	5.4.1.1.5 Union Pacific—Southern Pacific	173
	5.4.1.1.6 Peter Pan—Greyhound	175
	5.4.1.1.7 CSX/NS Acquisition of CONRAIL	176
	5.4.1.1.8 Canadian Pacific—Kansas City Southern	178
5.4.1.2	Convergence in the approach of STB and DOJ but using contradictory analysis	180
	5.4.1.2.1 Averitt Express and others—Pooling Agreement	180
	5.4.1.2.2 Canadian Pacific—Norfolk Southern	182
	5.4.1.2.3 Southern Pacific—Santa Fe	184
	5.4.1.2.4 Norfolk Southern—Conrail	185
	5.4.1.2.5 CSX—Pan Am Railway	187
5.5	Some Implications of the Analysis	188
5.6	Concluding Remarks	190

6. **Public Interest Assessment and the Department of Transportation (DOT)**   193

6.1	The Department of Transportation (DOT)	193
	6.1.1 Composition and Legislation	194
	6.1.2 Filing Instructions and Process Overview	198
	6.1.2.1 Assessment of Alliances	198
	6.1.2.2 Assessment of Mergers	199
6.2	The 'Public Interest' Standard	201
6.3	Challenges of Concurrent Jurisdiction	203
6.4	Enforcement Record	204
	6.4.1 Analysis of Some Seminal Cases	204
	6.4.1.1 Transactions where the DOT and the DOJ diverged on the outcome	206
	6.4.1.1.1 Northwest—Republic	206
	6.4.1.1.2 Ozark—TWA	208
	6.4.1.2 Transactions on slot allocation where there is convergence between the DOT and the DOJ	209
	6.4.1.2.1 Delta—US Airways slot swap	209
	6.4.1.2.2 United Airlines—Delta (Newark slots)	211
	6.4.1.3 Transactions assessed solely by the DOJ	212
	6.4.1.3.1 Delta Air Lines—Northwest Airlines Corporation	212
	6.4.1.3.2 United—Continental	213
	6.4.1.3.3 American—US Airways	214
	6.4.1.4 International Airline Alliances with Antitrust Immunity	217
	6.4.1.4.1 Delta—Swissair—Sabena—Austrian Airlines alliance	217
	6.4.1.4.2 American Airlines—TACA	218
	6.4.1.4.3 Continental—United—Star	219
	6.4.1.4.4 Delta—Aerovias de Mexico SA de CV	221
	6.4.1.4.5 American Airlines—JetBlue	223
6.5	Some Implications of the Analysis	224
6.6	Concluding Remarks	227

7. Public Interest Assessment and the Federal Reserve Board (FRB),
the Office of the Comptroller of the Currency (OCC), and the
Federal Deposit Insurance Corporation (FDIC)   229
  7.1 The Regulators   229
    7.1.1 Composition and Legislation   230
      7.1.1.1 Federal Reserve Board (FRB)   232
      7.1.1.2 Office of the Comptroller of the Currency (OCC)   233
      7.1.1.3 The Federal Deposit Insurance Corporation (FDIC)   233
    7.1.2 Filing Instructions and Process Overview   234
  7.2 The 'Public Interest' Standard   239
  7.3 Challenges of Concurrent Jurisdiction   242
  7.4 Enforcement Record   245
    7.4.1 Analysis of Some Seminal Cases   247
      7.4.1.1 Transactions decided by the sectoral regulators   247
        7.4.1.1.1 Community Bankshares—Citizens   247
        7.4.1.1.2 First Financial Bancorp—MainSource Financial Group   248
        7.4.1.1.3 Philadelphia National Bank—Girard Trust Corn   249
      7.4.1.2 Transactions where the sectoral regulators and the DOJ diverged   251
        7.4.1.2.1 National Bank of Commerce—Washington Trust Bank   251
        7.4.1.2.2 First National State Bancorporation
(FNSB Central—South)   252
        7.4.1.2.3 First National Bank of Logan—Zions First
National Bank   254
        7.4.1.2.4 Indiana Bancorporation—Financial Incorporated,
Fort Wayne, Indiana   255
        7.4.1.2.5 National Bank and Trust Company of Norwich—
National Bank of Oxford   256
        7.4.1.2.6 First Hawaiian—First Interstate of Hawaii   257
        7.4.1.2.7 Fleet/Norstar—New Maine National Bank   258
        7.4.1.2.8 Society—Ameritrust   259
        7.4.1.2.9 First Busey Corporation—Main Street Trust   260
        7.4.1.2.10 Alaska Mutual Bancorporation—United
Bancorporation Alaska   261
        7.4.1.2.11 Continental Illinois—Grand Canyon   264
  7.5 Some Implications of the Analysis   265
  7.6 Concluding Remarks   268

Conclusion   271

Index   277

Table of Cases

EUROPEAN COMMISSION

Case No COMP/M.5830 Olympic/Aegean, Commission Decision of 26 January 2011 ...... 196n.82
Case No COMP/M.6796 Olympic/Aegean II, Commission Decision of 9 October 2013..... 196n.81
Case M.7932 Dow–DuPont C(2017) 1946 .... 85n.13

US CASES

Alaska Mutual Bancorporation, 73 Fed Res Bull 921 (1987).......... 257n.218, 257n.221, 262n.275
American Electric Power Company and Central and South West Corporation,
    90 FERC 61242, 61799 (15 March 2000) 138n.128
Ash Grove Cement Co v FTC 577 F 2d 1368 (9th Cir 1978) 19–20n.112
AT&T–TCI, Memorandum Opinion and Order, CS-Docket 98-178 ......95–96nn.97–98, 118n.251
Averitt Express Inc, STB Docket No MC-F-21023, 2008 WL 258338
    (Surface Transp Bd (31 January 2008) 178n.180
Bank of New Bern v Wachovia Bank & Trust Co NA, 353 F Supp 643 (EDNC 1972) 236, 236n.99
Brown Shoe Co v United States 370 US 294 (1962) 8n.26
Brunswick Corp v Pueblo Bowl-o-Matt Inc 429 US 477 (1977) 24n.148, 24nn.151–52
Cadence Bancorporation, FRB Order No 2018-26 (7 December 2018) 244n.140
California v American Stores Co 495 US 271 (1990) 23n.144
Coal Rate Guidelines, Nationwide, 1 ICC 2d 520 (1985)............................. 182n.207
Commonwealth Edison Co, 36 FPC 927 (1966)..................................... 130n.77
Community Bankshares Inc 93 Fed Res Bull C59 (2007) 242n.132, 261n.253
Delta Air Lines Inc and US Airways Inc v FAA and DOT No 10-1153, Doc 1259764, 3
    (DC Cir 2010).. 206n.153
Delta-Swissair-Sabena-Austrian, Docket OST-95-618-39, 17 (28 May 1996) 213n.212
Department of Transportation, Final Order, American Airlines Inc and the TACA
    Group Reciprocal Code-Share Services Proceeding, Docket OST-96-1700,134,
    1 (20 May 1998) 199n.103, 214n.218, 216nn.230–31, 216n.234, 222n.275
Department of Transportation, Final Order, Docket OST-2008-234 at 18
    (10 July 2009) 217n.238, 223n.286
Department of Transportation, Final Order, Joint Application of Air Canada, the
    Austrian Group, British Midland Airways Ltd, Continental Airlines Inc, Deutsche
    Lufthansa AG, Polskie Linie Lotnicze Lot SA, Scandinavian Airlines System,
    Swiss International Air Lines Ltd, Tap Air Portugal, and United Air Lines Inc,
    Docket OST-2008-234, 1 (10 July 2009) 199n.104, 222n.276, 222n.278
Department of Transportation, Final Order, Joint Application of Delta Air Lines Inc and
    Aerovias de Mexico SA de CV, Docket OST-2015-0070, 1 (14 December 2016) 218n.244
Department of Transportation, Final Order, Joint Application of Delta Air Lines, Inc. and
    Aerovias de Mexico, S. A. DE C.V., Docket OST-2015-0070 at 1 (December 14, 2016)..... 222n.280
Dominion Resources, FTC Docket C-3901 (9 December 1999) 141n.147, 149n.209
DOT Notice Providing Access to Documents, Expanded Star Application, Docket
    DOT-OST-2008-0234-0006, issued 24 July 2008 .... 194n.63
DOT Order 2008-11-8, Expanded Star Application, Docket DOT-OST-2008-0234-0067,
    issued 12 November 2008 .... 194n.62
DOT, Joint Application of Delta Air Lines NC, Swissair, Swiss Air Transport Company Ltd,
    Sabena SA, Sabena Belgium World Airlines, and Austrian Airlines, for approval of
    and Antitrust Immunity for Alliance Agreements Pursuant to 49 USC §§ 41308
    and 41309, Order 96-6-33, Docket OST-95-618-47 (17 June 1996).........213n.208, 214n.214,
                               214n.217, 222n.277, 222n.279

xiv TABLE OF CASES

Duke Energy Corporation & Progress Energy Inc, 139 FERC, 61,194 (2012) 144n.170, 145n.172, 148n.200, 149n.206

Electricity Consumers Resource Council v FERC, 747 F 2d 1511 (DC Cir 1984) 136n.117

Exelon Corporation, 138 FERC 61,167 (2012) . . . 143n.163, 145n.176, 148n.197, 148n.201, 149n.210

FCC v RCA Communications 346 US 86 (1953) 89n.48

Federal Reserve System, FRB Order No 2018-07 . . . . 243n.138, 262n.282

Federal Reserve System, Orders Approving the Merger of Robertson Holding
    Company LP, Unified Shares LLC, and Commercial Bancgroup Inc,
    FRB Order No 2017-36 (15 December 2017) 244n.140

FERC, 'Final Rule to advance the formation of Regional Transmission
    Organizations (RTOs)' 18 CFR pt 35, Docket No RM 99–2-000; Order No 2000,
    95–96 (20 December 1999) 137nn.125–26

FERC, 'Order Authorizing Disposition and Merger' Docket No EC18–60-000
    (12 July 2018) 1 . . . . .147n.185, 147n.190, 147–48nn.192–93, 148n.198

FERC, 'Order Conditionally Approving Disposition of Facilities, Dismissing Complaint
    as Moot, and Denying Request for Consolidation' Enova Corporation and
    Pacific Enterprises, Docket No EL97–15-001 (25 June 1997) III.C.1.d 139n.137, 149n.208

FERC, 'Regional Transmission Organizations' Order No 2000, Docket
    No RM99–2-000 (20 December 1999) 137n.125, 149n.205

Final Order, American Airlines-TACA Group, Docket OST-96-1700-134, 15
    (20 May 1998) 215n.227

Finance Docket 33388, Comments of the United States Department of Agriculture
    (21 October 1997) 13, 15 175

First Bancorporation of NH Inc, 64 Fed Res Bull 967 (1978) 249n.172

First Busey Corporation and Main Street Trust Inc, 93 Fed Res Bull
    C90 (2007) 256n.213, 256n.216, 262n.281, 263n.287

First Hawaiian Inc 77 Fed Res Bull 52 (1991) 252n.191, 261n.251, 261n.255, 261n.264, 261n.271, 263n.284

FRB Order No 2019-01 (10 January 2019) 244n.141

FRB Order No 2019-02 (23 January 2019) 244n.141

FRB Order No 2019-03 (5 February 2019) 244n.141

FRB Order No 2019-04 (27 February 2019) 244n.141

FRB Order No 2019-05 (6 March 2019) 244n.141

FRB Order No 2019-06 (11 March 2019) 244n.141

FTC v Actavis 570 US 136 (2013) 10n.36

FTC v Tenet Health Care Corp 186 F 3d 1045 (8th Cir 1999) 14–15n.76

FTC v Western Meat Co 272 US 554 (1926) 7n.20

FTC, 'China National Chemical Corporation and others' Decision and Order,
    Docket No C-4610 (16 June 2017) 56n.103

FTC, Early Termination Notices, Transaction No 20201618 (24 November 2020) 116n.238

Gozlon-Peretz v United States 498 US 395, 406 (1991) 152n.11

Illinois Brick Co v Illinois 431 US 720 (1977) 24n.155

Indiana Bancorp, Fed Res Bull 913 (1983) 250n.183, 261n.269, 262n.274

Individual Merger Cases (FR 2060; OMB No 7100- 0232) 249n.171

Interstate Commerce Commission, Finance Docket No 30,400 (March 1984) . . . 182n.203, 187n.253

Joint Application of Delta Air Lines Inc, Swissair Ltd, Sabena SA, Austrian Airlines AG,
    Docket OST-95-618-44, 6–7 . . . . 214n.216

Kansas v Utilicorp United Inc 497 US 199 (1990) 24n.155

McLean Trucking Co v United States 321 US 67 (1944) 166n.113, 167, 168, 170, 187, 187n.248

Memorandum Opinion and Order in the Matter of Entercom Communications and
    CBS Radio Seek Approval to Transfer Control of and Assign FCC Authorizations
    and Licenses (MB Docket No 17-85, 2017) 88n.46

Minneapolis & St Louis Ry v United States 361 US 173 (1959) 187n.248

Missouri-Kansas-Texas R Co v United States 632 F 2d 392 (5th Cir 1980),
    451 US 1017 (1981) 160n.81

Morales v Trans World Airlines Inc 504 US 374, 385 (1992) 152n.11

National Petroleum Refiners Association v FTC 340 F Supp 1343 (DDC 1972) 21n.128

TABLE OF CASES XV

NCNB and C&S/ Sovran case 239n.125
Norfolk & Western Ry, Merger, 307 ICC 40, 440 (1959) 164n.97
Northeast Utils Serv Co v FERC, 993 F 2d 937 (1st Cir 1993) 136n.114, 136n.117, 148n.204
Northern Securities Co v United States 193 US 197 (1904) 7n.14
Northwest-Republic Acquisition Case, DOT Docket No 43,754 . . . . 203n.128, 221n.263
Old Stone Corporation, 62 Fed Res Bull 1055 (1976) 249n.172
Ozarks Inc, FRB Order No 2016- 11 (28 June 2016) 244n.140
PacifiCorp—UP&L 45 FERC 61095 (1989) 135n.111
Pennsylvania v Playmobil USA Inc 1995-2 Trade Cas (CCH) 71,215 (MD Pa 1995) 23n.140
Ring v Arizona 536 US 584 (2002) 245n.149
SBC Commc'ns Inc v FCC 56 F3d 1484 (DC Cir 1995) 88n.45
SBC–Ameritech, Memorandum Opinion and Order, Docket 98-141 . . . .117n.246, 118n.250, 119n.262
Seaboard Air Line R Co v United States 382 US 154 (1965) 167n.118
Seaboard Air Line RR-Control-Atlantic Coast Line RR, ICC, Finance Docket No 21215,
        60 (2 December 1963) 166n.110, 186n.233, 186n.237, 187n.245, 187n.250, 187n.254
Southern Pacific Transp Co v ICC 736 F 2d 708 (DC Cir 1984) 160n.83, 170n.132
Standard Oil v United States 221 US 1 (1911) 7n.15, 7n.16
STB, Docket No FD 36472 (14 April 2022) 185n.224, 185n.228
STB, Docket No FD 36500 (14 March 2023) 18 . . . . 176n.171, 177n.178
STB, Docket No MC-F-20908 (21 April 1998) 173n.152, 187n.242
STB, Finance Docket 33388_ 0, CSX Corporation, Norfolk Southern Corporation
        Control, Conrail Inc., Decision (23 July 1998) 50, 250–51 . . . . 175n.165
STB, Finance Docket No 3276 . . . . 182n.209, 186n.236, 186n.238, 187n.241
STB, Finance Docket No 36004 . . . . 180n.192, 180n.194, 181n.195, 181n.196, 188n.255
Synovus Financial Corp and Synovus Bank Columbus, FRB Order No 2018-25
        (7 December 2018) 244n.140
TWA-Ozark Acquisition Case, DOT Order No 86-9-29, 2 (12 September 1986) 204n.133, 221n.264
Union Pacific And others: Control and Merger-Southern Pacific and others
        (Houston Gulf Coast Oversight) Decision No 1, served 31 March 1998,
        published at 63 Fed Reg 16,628 (3 April 1998) 172n.146
Union Pacific Corp—Control and Merger—Southern Pacific Rail Corp, Finance
        Docket No 32760 (UP/SP Merger), Decision No 44 (STB served 12 August 1996),
        Decision No 44, decided on 6 August 1996, 98–99 . . . . . 159n.73, 171n.136, 171n.139, 172nn.143–45
United States and Others v American Airlines and JetBlue Airways Case 1:21-cv-11558
        (D Mass 2021) 219n.253
United States and Others v JetBlue Airways and Spirit Airlines Case 1:23-cv-10511
        (D Mass 2023) 220n.257
United States Department of Justice on the Order to Show Cause, 'American Airlines Inc
        and the TACA Group Reciprocal Code-Share Services Proceeding' Docket
        OST-96-1700-99, 2 (28 January1998) 215n.221
United States Department of Justice on the Show Cause Order, Joint Application of
        Air Canada, the Austrian Group, British Midland Airways Ltd, Continental Airlines Inc,
        Deutsche Lufthansa AG, Polskie Linie Lotniecze Lot SA, Scandinavian Airlines
        System, Swiss International Air Lines Ltd, Tap Air Portugal, and United Air Lines Inc,
        Docket OST-2008-234, 6 (26 June 2009) 216n.230, 216n.232, 216n.233
United States District Court Southern District Court of New York and Others v
        Deutsche Telekom AG and Others, 19 Civ 5434 (VM) 112n.212
United States of America v AT&T Inc and Others, Civil Case No 17-2511 (RJL)
        (12 June 2018) 113n.220
United States of America v Exelon Corporation and Public Service Enterprise Group
        Incorporated 71 FR 49477 (23 August 2006) 142n.159, 148n.199, 148n.203, 149n.207
United States v American Naval Stores Co 172 F 455 (CCSD Ga 1909) 6n.7
United States v American Tobacco Co 221 US 106 (1911) 7n.15
United States v Baker Hughes Inc 908 F 2d 981 (DC Cir 1990) 10n.39, 33n.212
United States v Bell Atlantic Corp and Others Civil Action No 1:99CV01119,
        Final Judgment (DDC filed 9 December 1999) 96–97nn.102–3
United States v Columbia Steel Co 334 US 495 (1948) 8n.24

xvi TABLE OF CASES

United States v Deutsche Telecom AG, No 19-cv-02232 (DDC 26, July 2019)
  ECF No 2-2 (DOJ Proposed Final Judgment)...................................... 112n.210
United States v E.I. du Pont de Nemours & Co 353 US 586 (1957)......................... 7n.15
United States v Engelhard Corp 126 F 3d 1302 (11th Cir 1997) 10n.39
United States v Enova Corp No 98-cv-583 (DDC) (filed 9 March 1998)................... 140n.139
United States v Exelon Corp 2012 WL 3018030 (DDC 23 May 2012)
  (No 1:11-cv-02276), 76 FR 81,528 (28 December 2012) 145n.175, 146n.181
United States v First City National Bank of Houston 386 US 361 (1967).................. 237n.106
United States v First Hawaiian Inc, Competitive Impact Statement
  (D Hawaii 1991) 252n.195, 253nn.197–98
United States v First National Bank & Trust Co of Lexington, 376 US 655 (1964) 227n.14
United States v First National State Bancorporation 499 F Supp 793
  (DNJ 1980) 247n.163, 248n.169, 261n.250, 261n.257, 261n.261, 261n.267
United States v Fleet Norstar Financial Group Inc Competitive Impact Statement
  (ND Maine, 10 July 1991) 253n.199, 254nn.203–4, 261n.252, 261n.256, 261n.265, 261n.272
United States v General Dynamics Corp 415 US 486 (1974)............................9nn.32–33
United States v Marine Bancorporation Inc 418 US 602 (1974) 246n.154, 248n.168,
                                                            261n.249, 261n.258, 261n.260
United States v National Bank and Trust Company of Norwich and National Bank
  of Oxford, 1984-2 Trade Cases 66,074 (ND New York 1984) 252n.190, 261n.254,
                                                            261n.263, 261n.270, 263n.285
United States v National Bank and Trust Company of Norwich and
  National Bank of Oxford, Complaint (ND New York 1983) 251n.187
United States v Nexstar Media and Tribune Media, Case 1:19-cv-02295-DLF
  (DDC 2 February 2020).. 115n.235
United States v Oracle Corp 331 F Supp 2d 1098 (ND Cal 2004) 33n.210
United States v Penn-Olin Chem Co and Others 378 US 158, 171 (1964)................. 28n.178
United States v Philadelphia National Bank 374 US 321 (1963)............................ 8n.28
United States v Philadelphia National Bank 374 US 321 (1963) 227n.14, 243n.133,
                                                            245n.145, 260n.248, 261n.259
United States v Society Corp (ND Ohio, 4 June 1992) 255n.211, 261n.266,
                                                            261n.273, 263n.283, 263n.286
United States v Society Corp, Competitive Impact Statement (ND Ohio, 13 March 1992) 255n.209
United States v Sungard Data Systems Inc 172 F Supp 2d 172 (DDC 2001) 33n.210
United States v Third National Bank in Nashville 390 US 171, 184 (1968) 236n.93
United States v United Continental No 2:33-av-00001 (DNJ 2015).... 207n.159, 207n.162, 223n.282
United States v United States Steel Corp 251 US 417 (1920) 8n.23
United States v US Airways Grp Inc 38 F Supp 3d 69 (DDC 2014) (No 1:13-CV-01236)
  ECF No 148...................210n.180, 210n.186, 212n.198, 221n.263, 221n.269, 221n.272
United States v Verizon Communications, Civil Action No 1:05CV02103,
  Final Judgment (DDC filed 27 October 2005) 98n.118
United States v Von's Grocery Co 384 US 270 (1966)............................ 8–9n.30, 9n.31
United States v Waste Management Inc 743 F 2d 976 (2d Cir 1984)...................... 10n.39
United States v Zions Utah Bancorporation C79-0769A (D Utah 1980)........249n.175, 250n.179,
                                                            261n.262, 261n.268
UPC-Control, 366 ICC, 487, 533, 642 ....169n.128, 170n.131, 186n.235, 187n.240,
                                                            187nn.247–48, 187n.252
Verizon–TracFone, GN Docket No 21-112 (19 November 2021) 2 .... 116n.239, 116n.241

FEDERAL COMMUNICATIONS COMMISSION

Altice–Cablevision, 31 FCC Rcd 4365 (2016).................106n.169, 107, 107n.174, 107n.177,
                                                            107n.180, 108, 109n.194
AOL–Time Warner, 16 FCC Rcd 6547....103n.145, 103n.147, 103–4n.150, 104nn.152–54, 117n.243
Applications of AT&T Inc and CellCo Partnership d/b/a Verizon Wireless for Consent
  to Assign or Transfer Control of Licences and Authorizations and Modify a
  Spectrum Leasing Arrangement, Memorandum Opinion and Order,
  25 FCC Rcd 8704, 8747 101 (2010) 106n.169

TABLE OF CASES xvii

Applications of AT&T Wireless Services Inc and Cingular Wireless Corporation for
    Consent to Transfer Control of Licences and Authorizations and others,
    Memorandum Opinion and Order, 19 FCC Rcd 21522, 21545–46 43 (2004) 106n.169
Applications of Nextel Partners Inc Transferor, and Nextel WIP Corp and Sprint
    Nextel Corporation, Transferees, for Consent to Transfer Control of Licences and
    Authorizations, Memorandum Opinion and Order, 21 FCC Rcd 7358, 7361 9 (2006) 106n.169
AT&T–DirecTV, 30 FCC Rcd 9131 (2015) 105n.165, 106n.171, 118n.256, 119n.260
Bell Atlantic–GTE, 15 FCC Rcd 14032 (2000) 96n.99, 97n.104, 97n.111, 98n.115, 118n.253
Bell Atlantic–NYNEX, 12 FCC Rcd 19985 (1997) 93n.76, 117n.242, 117n.244, 118n.248
CenturyLink–Level 3, 32 FCC Rcd 9581 . . . . 110n.198, 110n.201, 111n.204, 118n.258
Federal Communications Commission, FCC 11-4, Docket No 10-56 . . . . .100n.128, 118n.255, 119n.261
GM–Hughes–News Corp, 19 FCC Rcd 473 . . . . 104n.157, 105n.160, 119n.259
Nexstar–Media General 32 FCC Rcd 183 (2017) 3. . . . . 108n.186, 108n.189, 109n.193
Nexstar–Tribune 34 FCC Rcd 8436 . . . . 115n.229
SBC–Ameritech 14 FCCR 14712 (1999) 88n.37, 94n.85, 95n.91
SBC–Ameritech, 19 FCC Rcd 9308 . . . . .94nn.88–89
SBC Communications Inc and AT&T Corp Applications for Approval of Transfer of
    Control, Memorandum Opinion and Order, 20 FCC Rcd 18290, 18303 19 (2005). 106n.169
Sinclair Broadcast Group–Tribune Media Company, Hearing Designation Order,
    33 FCC Rcd 6830 (2018) 101n.135, 101n.139
Suddenlink–Altice order, 30 FCC Rcd 14358 . . . . 107n.176
T-Mobile–Sprint, Memorandum Opinion and Order, FCC-19-103, WC-Docket
    No 18-197 . . . . .112nn.210–11
United States v Ray and Graycom, Case 1:18-cv-02951 DDC (5 June 2019);
    33 FCC Rcd 12349 . . . . 116n.236
Verizon–Frontier order, 25 FCC Rcd at 5981–83 . . . . 107n.179
Verizon–MCI, 20 FCC Rcd 18433 . . . . 98nn.118–19, 99n.121, 118n.254

Table of Legislation

UNITED STATES

Code of Federal Regulations

12 CFR
§ 5.33 229
§ 25.24 .... 229n.33
§ 303.2............................. 233n.67
§ 303.2(r) 233n.67
§ 303.7 .... 233n.66
§ 303.64 .... 233n.67
§ 303.65 .... 233n.66

14 CFR
§ 204.5 .... 192–93n.46
§ 298.53 .... 191n.24
§ 302.12 .... 194n.63
§ 303.06 .... 195n.73

16 CFR
§ 1.11 .... 21n.126
§ 1.16 .... 21n.126
§ 3................................ 27n.175
§§ 801–803.10(b) 128n.69
§ 803.20 .... 195n.76

18 CFR
§ 33.1(b)(4) 123n.12
§ 33.1(c)........................... 123n.20
§ 33.1(c) (12)–(16) 123n.20
§ 388.112 .... 126n.43

28 CFR
§ 50.6 178–79

31 CFR
Pts 800–801....................... 39n.26
§ 800.243 .... 38n.18
§ 800.302 .... 61n.145
§ 800.302(f)(6) 61n.145
§ 800.302(f)(7) 61n.145
Pt 801............................. 78n.272
§ 801.302 .... 62n.146
§801.402........................... 78n.272
§ 801.501 .... 78n.272
§ 801.503 .... 78n.272

47 CFR............................. 87–88
§ 25.201 .... 104n.156
§ 73.3555 .... 84n.8
§ 73.3555(a)......................... 84
§ 73.3555(b)......................... 84
§ 73.3555(c)......................... 84
§ 73.3555(d) 84

49 CFR
§ 1180............................. 159n.67

§ 1180.1 .... 154n.30
§ 1180.1(a)....................... 160n.76
§ 1180.1(c)....................... 160n.78
§ 1180.2 .... 155n.38
§ 1180.2(a)....................... 155n.39
§ 1180.2(b)....................... 156n.40
§ 1180.2(d)....................... 156n.42
§ 1180.2(d)(2) 161n.88
§ 1180.2(I)....................... 156n.41
§ 1180.4(g)(2)(iii)................ 156n.42

Electronic Code of Federal
   Regulations (e-CFR) 84

United States Code

5 USC
§ 18.............................. 84n.5
§ 551(4) 21n.125
§ 553(b)(1)–(3)................... 21n.125

12 USC
§§ 215–215b 226n.5
§ 1242(c)(3)–(4) 228n.28
§§ 1461–1700 .... 228n.23
§ 1811............................ 235n.90
§ 1816............................ 235n.91
§ 1817(j)......................... 228n.24
§ 1828(c) .... .226n.6, 226n.10,
                      227n.15, 230n.41
§ 1828(c)(1)(2) 237n.107, 239n.121
§ 1828(c)(5)...... 227n.18, 227n.21, 236n.98
§ 1828(c)(5)(B) 236n.97
§ 1828(i)(4) 227n.13
§ 1842........................... 259n.236
§ 1842(c) 228n.22
§§ 2901–2905 .... 236n.94
§ 2903........................... 227n.20
§ 2903(a)(2)........................ 229

15 USC
§ 1.............................. 128n.71
§ 1 ff 19n.105
§§ 15c–15h 22n.132
§ 16(b)–(h) 87n.29
§§ 17–19......................... 226n.4
§ 18......... 18n.96, 84n.6, 86n.20, 86n.24,
        87n.28, 90n.58, 128n.67, 128n.71,
      190nn.12–13, 192nn.42–43, 195n.74
§ 18a........... 18n.101, 26n.162, 128n.69
§ 18a(a) 18n.100, 86n.25, 128n.68
§ 18a(b) 26n.165, 129n.75, 195n.75
§ 18a(b)(1)(B) 86n.25

XX TABLE OF LEGISLATION

§ 18a(b)(2) 26n.166, 86n.25
§ 18a(d)(1) 18n.101
§ 18a(e) 26n.165, 26n.170, 129n.75
§ 18a(e)(1) 87n.26
§ 18a(e)(2) 87n.26
§ 18a(f) 195n.78
§ 21 . . . . 190n.12, 192n.43, 226n.4
§ 21(a) 84n.6, 86n.20
§ 25 . . . . 26n.167
§ 26 . . . . 22n.132
§§ 41–58 . . . . 21n.121
§ 45 . . . . 20n.118
§ 45(a) 20n.118, 21n.124
§ 45(a)(6) 21n.121
§ 45(b)-(c) 27n.175
§ 46(b) 19–20n.112
§ 46(f) 19–20n.112
§ 46(g) 21n.125
§ 53 . . . . 26n.167
§ 53(b) 27n.176, 128n.73
§ 79(i) 124n.27
§ 79(j) 124n.28
§§ 717–717z 126n.40
§ 3301 . . . . 125n.37
§§ 3301–32 . . . . 125n.36

16 USC

§ 796(22) 123n.15
§ 796(23) 123n.14
§ 824(a) 125n.31
§ 824(d) 125n.31
§ 824a-3(a)(2) 125n.32
§ 824a-3(b) 125n.33
§ 824b 131n.86
§ 824b(a) 122n.7
§ 824b(a)(1) 122n.9
§ 824b(a)(1)(A)-(D) 122n.10
§ 824b(a)(2) 123n.11
§ 824b(a)(4) 130nn.82–83
§ 824b(a)(5) 128n.64
§ 824b(a)(6) 123n.12
§ 824I 123n.17

28 USC

§ 517 . . . . 23n.145

31 USC

§ 3733 . . . . 234n.77

42 USC

§§ 15801–16524 . . . . 122n.8
§ 16451(5) 123n.12, 123n.16
§ 16451(7) 123n.12
§ 16451(8) 123n.12
§ 16451(9) 123n.13
§ 16451(14) 123n.12
§§ 3701-96c 22n.133

45 USC

§§ 701–748 . . . . . 174n.157, 183n.214, 183n.215
§§ 761–767c 183n.216
§§ 1101–1116 . . . . 183n.216

47 USC

§§ 34–39 . . . . 84n.3
§ 214 . . . . 84n.3
§ 214(c) 90n.61
§ 303(r) 90n.61
§ 309(e) 88n.46
§ 310 . . . . 84n.3
§ 310(d) 84n.4, 87n.34

49 USC 158–59

§ 5(2)(b) 153n.12, 153n.16
§ 5(2)(c)(1) 158n.61
§ 5(11) 153n.14
§§ 12–27 . . . . 152n.6
§ 1301 . . . . 154n.23
§ 1384 . . . . 191n.31
§ 10101 155–56
§ 10501(b) 154n.25
§ 10501(b)(2) 154n.24
§ 10502 155–56
§ 10502(a) 156n.43
§ 10502(b)(g) 157n.47
§ 10706 154
§ 10706(a)(5) 154n.26
§ 11321 154
§ 11321 ff 159n.66
§ 11321(a) 154n.25
§§ 11321–11328 . . . . 157n.48, 159n.69
§ 11323 155–56
§§ 11323–25 . . . . 155n.36
§ 11324 . . . . 154nn.28–29
§ 11324(a) 159n.70
§ 11324(b) 159n.71
§ 11324(c) 160n.77, 176n.170
§ 14302 . . . . 173, 178
§ 14303 . . . . 154n.31
§ 14303(b) 155n.32
§ 14303(f) 155n.33
§ 40101 . . . . 192n.44, 202n.117
§ 40102(15) 193n.55
§ 40103 . . . . 192n.44
§ 40109(c) 191n.23
§ 41102 . . . . 191n.20, 192–93n.46
§ 41103 . . . . 192–93n.46
§ 41104 . . . . 196n.84
§ 41105 . . . . 191n.19, 193n.48, 193n.50
§ 41105(a) 191n.21
§ 41105(b)(2) 191n.22
§ 41110 . . . . 192–93n.46
§ 41308 . . . . 193–94, 213n.208
§ 41308(b) 194n.61
§ 41308(c) 194n.59
§ 41309 . . . . 193–94, 213n.208
§ 41309(b) 194n.61
§ 41309(b)(1)(A) 198n.95
§ 41309(c)(2) 194n.60
§ 41710 . . . . 194n.65
§ 41712 . . . . 192n.41
§ 41714 . . . . 198n.99
§ 41720 219–20

TABLE OF LEGISLATION

§ 44702.......................... 196n.85
Appendix
 § 1301....................... 193n.53
 § 1378(b)(1)(A) 191n.33
 § 1378(b)(1)(B)............192nn.35–36
 § 1384...................... 192n.37
 § 1508(b) 193n.54
 § 1551(b)(1)(C)................ 192n.38
50 USC
 § 4565.......................... 36n.6
 § 4565(a)(5)..................... 36n.7
 § 4565(b)(1)(C)(v) 40n.30
 § 4565(b)(2)(C)(ii)(I).............. 40n.32
 § 4565(c)(2)(C).................. 39n.24
Appendix
 § 2170(a)(3)................... 38n.17

Statutes

Administrative Procedure Act
 (APA)..................... 21n.125, 194
Airline Deregulation Act of 1978
 Pub L No 95-504, 92 Stat
 1705 (1978) 191–92, 191n.30
Antitrust Procedures and Penalties
 Act (Tunney Act) 31n.196
Bank Control Act (Control Act) 228
Bank Holding Company Act
 of 1956 (BHCA) 227–29, 231, 236n.94
 s 3 ....243, 259
Bank Merger Act of 1966 236
Bank Merger Act of 1960, Pub L
 No 86-463, 74 Stat 129 (1960)..... 226–28,
    226n.10, 229–30, 236n.96, 244–46
Bank Service Company Act
 (12 USC 1861–1867) 231n.52
Banking Act of 1933, ch 89, Pub L
 No 73-66, 48 Stat 162 .... 226n.6
Banking Act of 1935, 49 Stat 684....... 235n.90
Bankruptcy Act
 s 77 165
Cable Television Consumer
 Protection and Competition Act
 of 1992, Pub L No 102-385,
 106 Stat 1460 (1992)............. 87n.36
Celler-Kefauver Act 8
Civil Aeronautics Act of 1938, Pub L
 No 75-706, 52 Stat 973 .... 191n.25
Clayton Antitrust Act of 1914, 38
 Stat 730 (1914) 7, 8, 9–10, 19,
   20–21, 22–23, 34, 84n.5, 170, 183–84,
   191–93, 191n.28, 194–95, 226, 260–61
 s 5 .... 32n.207
 s 7 .... 7n.18, 8–9, 18, 23–24, 25, 28n.177,
   33, 84n.5, 86–87, 128n.67, 128n.70,
   164, 167, 190n.13, 192n.42, 244–45,
   246, 248, 249–50, 251–52, 254
 s 7A............................. 18n.101
 s 7A(e) 3n.11

s 11 ....84, 86–87
s 17 .... 7n.19
Clayton Act of 1982, 15 USC 12–27 .... 191n.34
Commission Regulations, 94 FERC
 § 61289 (2001)
 Pt 33 .... 126n.42
Communications Act of 1934,
 48 Stat 1093 (1934)......84, 86–87, 94, 107
 s 2(a).......................... 85–86n.15
 s 308(b) 107
 s 309(d) 101n.139, 102n.142
 s 310(d) 84
 s 621(a)(1) 87n.33
 s 621(b)(1)...................... 87n.33
Community Reinvestment Act
 of 1977, Pub L No 95-128 § 804,
 91 Stat 1111, 1148...... 227n.20, 228–29,
   231, 236n.94, 237, 237n.102, 239n.121,
   244, 256–57, 259–60, 262–64
Constitution
 Art 1 s 8, cl 3 .... 6n.11
Creating Helpful Incentives to Produce
 Semiconductors (CHIPS) Act..... 80n.287
Crime Control Act of 1976, 90 Stat
 2407, 2415 .... 22n.133
 s 116 .... 22n.133
Defence Production Act of 1950............80
 s 721 .... 35n.4, 49n.62
 s 721(f)..................... 49–50n.64
Department of Energy Organization Act.....121–22
Emergency Railroad Transportation
 Act of 133, 48 Stat 211 (1933) 158
Emergency Rail Services Act of 1970 183
Energy Policy Act of 2005, Pub L
 No 109-58, 1289, 119 Stat 594,
 982-83 (2005) 122n.8, 124–25, 130n.82
Enterprise Act of 2002
 s 45 ....258–59n.232
 s 56 .... 258n.231
 s 58 258–59
False Claims Act 234n.77
Federal Aviation Act of 1958, Pub L
 No 85-726, 72 Stat 31 .... 191n.25
 s 411 219
Federal Deposit Insurance Act
 of 1950, Pub L No 81-797,
 64 Stat 873, 892 .... 226, 235n.90
 s 2 .... 226n.6
 s 18(c).....................229–30, 231, 243
Federal Power Act of 1935.........121–22, 132
 s 203 ....128, 135–36
 s 203(a)(1) 122, 124–25, 130–31, 133n.96, 147
 s 203(a)(1)(A) 123–24
 s 203(a)(1)(B) 124–25
 s 203(a)(2) 122–23, 124–25, 130–31, 147
Federal Reserve Act of June 13, 1933,
 48 Stat. 162..................... 235n.90
 s 9 243

xxii TABLE OF LEGISLATION

Federal Trade Commission
    Act (FTCA) 7, 19–22
    s 5 . . . . .19–20, 27–28
    s 5(a)(6) 21n.121
    s 6 21–22
    s 6(b) 19–20n.112, 21n.124
    s 6(f) 19–20n.112
    s 6(g) 21n.125
    s 13(b) 128n.73
Freedom of Information Act (FOIA Act) 126
Food Security is National Security
    Act of 2017
    s 616 77–78
Foreign Adversary Risk
    Management (FARM) Act 78n.266
    s 2931 . . . . 55n.100, 78n.266
Foreign Investment and Economic
    Security Act of 2017 77
Foreign Investment and National Security
    Act of 2007 (FINSA) 36n.7, 38–39, 41
Foreign Investment Risk Review
    Modernization Act of 2018
    (FIRRMA) 37, 38–39, 40, 40n.33,
               49–51, 52, 69, 76, 78–80, 78n.269
    s 1703, § (A)(i)(ii) 79nn.273–74
    s 1706 . . . . 40n.30
    s 1706, § (v)(IV)(bb)(AA)(cc) 79n.282
    s 1709 . . . . 40n.32
    s 1727 . . . . 79n.273
    s 2987 78–80
Gramm-Leach-Bliley Act of 1999 (GLBA) 235
Hart-Scott-Rodino Antitrust
    Improvements Act of 1976, Pub L
    No 94-435, 90 Stat 1383 (1976) . . . 18, 18n.100,
               18n.101, 22n.132, 23–24, 25n.157,
             26–27, 30, 48n.59, 86–87, 126, 128,
             129n.75, 147, 195, 234n.76, 235
Home Owners' Loan Act (HOLA) 228
ICC Termination Act of 1995 (ICCTA),
    Pub L No 104-88, 109 Stat 803 . . . . 153n.20
Intelligence Reform and Terrorism
    Prevention Act of 2004
    s 7120 . . . . 49–50n.64
International Air Transportation
    Act of 1979, Pub L No 96-192,
    94 Stat 35 (1980) 190n.14, 193n.47
Interstate Commerce Act
    of 1887 (ICA) 152, 153, 170
    s 5 153
    s 5(2) 152, 158n.56
    s 5(6) 158n.58
Motor Carrier Act of 1980 (MCA) 152, 153n.19
National Bank Consolidation Act
    of 1918, Pub L No 65-240,
    40 Stat 1043, 1043–44 . . . . 226n.5
National Defense Authorization Act of 2019 78

National Defence Authorization Act
    for Fiscal Year of 2018 77
    s 1069 . . . . 77n.259
    s 1612 . . . . 77n.263
    s 1071 . . . . 77n.260
    s 1711 . . . . 77n.261
    s 1712 . . . . 77n.262
Natural Gas Act 121–22
    s 7(c) 126n.39
Natural Gas Policy Act of 1978 (NGPA) 125
Natural Gas Wellhead Decontrol Act 125
Northeast Rail Service Act (NERSA) 183–84
NY Laws 1908
    Ch 125, § 5 . . . . 235n.87
Public Law No 89-670
    s 3(a) 190n.9, 190n.15
Public Utility Act of 1935, Pub L
    No 74-333, 49 Stat 803 (1935) 122n.4
Public Utility Holding Company Act
    of 1935 (PUHCA) 124n.23
    s 9(a)(2) 124–25
Public Utility Regulatory Policy Act
    of 1978 (PURPA) 125
Railroad Revitalization and Regulatory
    Reform Act of 1976, Pub L No 94-210,
    S 2718, 90 Stat 31 (4R Act) 153, 158–59
    s 5(3) 158–59n.64
Reed-Bulwinkle Act 153
Regional Rail Reorganization Act
    of 1973 (3-R Act) 183
Riegle-Neal Amendments Act of 1997,
    Pub L No 105-24, 111 Stat
    238 (1997) 228n.25
Riegle-Neal Interstate Banking and
    Branching Efficiency Act of 1994 228
Security and Exchange Act of 1934 . . . . . 124n.27
    s 14(a) 126n.27
Sherman Act 1890 . . . . 1n.4, 5–8, 13–14, 19,
                    20–21, 22–23, 27–28,
                  152, 166–67, 191n.32
    ss 1–7 . . . . 6n.6
    s 1 . . . . 7n.16, 22–23, 128n.71
    s 2 22–23
Sherman Act, 15 USC 1–7 (1982) 191n.32
Staggers Rail Act of 1980 . . . . .153n.19,
                  158–59, 170n.134
    s 228(a)(2) 159n.65
Strategic Competition Act of 2021 80
Sunset Act of 1984, Pub L No 98-444,
    98 Stat 1704 . . . . 191n.26, 192n.39
Surface Transportation Board
    Reauthorization Act of 2015,
    Pub L No 114-110 (2015) 154n.21
    s 12(a) 155n.34
Telecommunications Act of 1996, Pub L
    No 104-104, 110 Stat 56 (1996) 87n.36

TABLE OF LEGISLATION · xxiii

Transportation Act of 1920,
 41 Stat 456 (1920) 152n.8, 158n.57,
  164, 188n.257
 Ch 91 § 407 . . . . 158n.56, 158n.58
Transportation Act of 1940,
 54 Stat 906 (1940) 158, 168
True Reciprocity Investment Act
 of 2017
 s 1722 78
US Innovation and Competition Act
 s 138 . . . . 80n.283
Wheeler-Lea Act 21n.121

Guidelines

NAAG Horizontal Merger Guidelines 22n.136
NAAG Vertical Restraint Guidelines
 § 2.1 . . . . 22n.136
US Department of Justice Merger
 Guidelines (1982) 11, 12n.48
 § III.C.1.a 11n.47
 § 1 . . . . 11n.44
 § 3.5 . . . . 12n.51

US Department of Justice Merger
 Guidelines (1984) 12n.52, 14, 16–17
 § 3.12 . . . . 12n.52
US Department of Justice & Federal
 Trade Commission, Merger
 Guidelines (1992) 13, 14, 127n.50,
  127n.55, 143
 § 4 . . . . 13n.61
US Department of Justice & Federal
 Trade Commission, Horizontal
 Merger Guidelines (rev 1997) 14n.71
 § 4 . . . . 14n.75
US Department of Justice & Federal Trade
 Commission, Horizontal Merger
 Guidelines (2010) 15–16, 129, 139, 157
 §§ 1–2 . . . . 15n.78
 §§ 4–11 . . . . 15n.77
 § 4 . . . . 15n.79, 15n.81
 § 6.1 . . . . 15n.83, 16nn.86–87
 § 6.2 . . . . 16n.86
 § 6.3 . . . . 16n.86
 § 6.4 . . . . 16n.86

List of Abbreviations

ALJ	administrative law judge
AM	amplitude modulation
BHCA	Bank Holding Company Act
CAS	competitive analysis screen
CEO	chief executive officer
CFIUS	Committee on Foreign Investment in the United States
CID	civil investigative demand
CRA	Community Reinvestment Act
DMAs	designated market areas
DNI	Director of National Intelligence
DOJ	Department of Justice
DOT	Department of Transportation
DSL	digital subscriber line
EWG	exempt wholesale generators
EU	European Union
FCC	Federal Communications Commission
FDI	foreign direct investment
FDIA	Federal Deposit Insurance Act
FDIC	Federal Deposit Insurance Corporation
FERC	Federal Energy Regulatory Commission
FIRRMA	Foreign Investment Risk Review Modernization Act of 2018
FM	frequency modulation
FOIA 2000	Freedom of Information Act 2000
FPA	Federal Power Act
FPC	Federal Power Commission
FRB	Federal Reserve Board
FSS	fixed satellite services
FTC	Federal Trade Commission
FTCA	Federal Trade Commission Act
FUCOs	foreign utility companies
HHI	Herfindahl–Hirschman Index
HMT	hypothetical monopolist test
HOLA	Home Owners' Loan Act
HSR	Hart-Scott-Rodino Antitrust Improvements Act
IM	instant messaging
ISO	independent system operator
ISPs	internet service providers
LEC	local exchange carrier
LFAs	local franchising authorities
LMI	low and moderate income
M&A	mergers and acquisition

xxvi LIST OF ABBREVIATIONS

MSAs	metropolitan statistical areas
MTAs	main trading areas
MVNO	mobile virtual network operator
MVPDs	multi-channel video programming distributors
NAAG	National Association of Attorneys General
NGPA 1978	Natural Gas Policy Act of 1978
OCC	Office of the Comptroller of the Currency
OVDs	online video programming distributors
PCSs	personal communications services
PUCs	state public utility commissions
PUHCA 1935	Public Utility Holding Company Act of 1935
PURPA 1978	Public Utility Regulatory Policy Act of 1978
QFs	qualifying facilities
RBOCs	regional Bell operating companies
RSAs	rural service areas
RSNs	regional sports networks
RTO	regional transmission organization
SEC	Securities and Exchange Commission
SSNIP test	small but significant non-transitory increase in price test
STB	Surface Transportation Board
SVDOs	subscription video on demand services
UK	United Kingdom
UNEs	unbundled network elements
UPP test	upward pricing pressure test
US	United States

Competition Law and Public Interest Considerations

Competition law cannot be analysed in a vacuum, since it is subject to wider policy considerations as well as political influence, especially in certain sectors of the economy such as energy, banking and financial services, telecoms, rail, and air transport. Competition law is also influenced by considerations of national security that are closely intertwined with foreign direct investment (FDI). However, these may vary from one sector to another. A visible way of how politics influence competition enforcement concerns 'the manner in which the application of competition law is handled and the way competition cases are decided'.[1] It follows, then, that there is a double role of politics in the US competition law enforcement, namely in the legislative process as well as in the enforcement of US competition and regulatory authorities.[2] According to Doern and Wilks, there are three modes in which such political expression could exist: 'the core of competition policy and its objectives; the extent and nature of non-competition policy goals that are allowed by statute to be considered in decision-making; and exemption provisions'.[3]

The approach to competition enforcement and to merger control in the United States (US) is to achieve efficiency.[4] In principle, US competition agencies[5] do not consider

---

[1] Eyad Maher Dabbah, *International and Comparative Competition Law* (CUP 2010) 57.

[2] ibid 256.

[3] B Doern and S Wilks, *Comparative Competition Policy* (OUP 1996) 15.

[4] OECD, 'Public Interest Considerations in Merger Control: Note by the United States' (2016) DAF/COMP/WP3/WD(2016)10 2 https://one.oecd.org/document/DAF/COMP/WP3/WD(2016)10/En/pdf. Consumer welfare is the dominant paradigm that emerged in US antitrust law in the 1970s. It is not the purpose of the book to engage in detail with the emergence of consumer welfare as the prevalent aim in US antitrust, as the presentation of the historical context and the development of the concept of consumer welfare has been well documented in literature; cf eg Barak Orbach, 'How Antitrust Lost Its Goal' (2013) 81(5) Fordham Law Review 2253, 2257 ff, 2268 ff. It has been pointed out that the link made by Robert Bork, *The Antitrust Paradox* (Free Press 1993) between the intent of the historical legislator with regard to the Sherman Act (Act) and consumer welfare as the intended aim of the Act is more than doubtful. Nevertheless, US courts and primarily the Supreme Court seem to have been willing to adopt consumer welfare as the new paradigm in US antitrust; cf Kenneth Heyer, 'Consumer Welfare and the Legacy of Robert Bork' (2014) 57(S3) Journal of Law & Economics S19, and Orbach ibid. See also Ioannis Kokkoris and Athanassios Skourtis, 'Is Consumer Welfare Still Fit for Purpose in the EU Competition Regime?' in Ioannis Kokkoris and Claudia Lemus (eds), *Research Handbook on the Law and Economics of Competition Enforcement* (Edward Elgar Publishing 2022) 410. Consumer welfare has been credited with a switch to an approach that has moved away from adhering to structuralist considerations and bringing competitive assessment closer to market actuality. Notwithstanding the ongoing discussion regarding the contours of the paradigm, consumer welfare has brought to the fore of competition law enforcement the focus on economic goals and has thus rationalized to a significant extent the identification of harm to competition in enforcement particularly in light of the measurability and hence predictability that it entails.

[5] Technically, only the Federal Trade Commission (FTC) is an independent agency, while the Antitrust Division of the US Department of Justice (DOJ) is part of the executive branch of government. However, for the purposes of this book they are referred altogether as 'agencies'.

2 COMPETITION LAW AND PUBLIC INTEREST CONSIDERATIONS

public interest factors in the enforcement of the antitrust laws. They note that decisions should be based solely on the competitive effects and consumer benefits of the transaction under review.[6] It was even explained by academics at the beginning of the 1960s that 'using antitrust law to achieve non-competition goals, which often resulted in the protection of inefficient competitors, was inimical to consumer welfare and was not Congress's intent in enacting the U.S. statutes'.[7]

In this same line of argument, it should be noted that the Sherman Act's[8] intention was not to achieve 'broad non-commercial goals', but rather to create an illegality test, which relies on the effect upon commerce, and not upon a social or political objective.[9] Notwithstanding how straightforward this aim seems to be, there are still aspects of the regime that supports former US President Franklin Roosevelt's warning that

> [t]he liberty of democracy can be threatened if the people tolerate the growth of private power to a point where it becomes stronger than their democratic state itself ... For this reason, the primary concern of competition law should not be to achieve economic goals but rather safeguard important social and economic values.[10]

These aspects of the merger control regime in the US have developed over time and have adapted to the realities of economic and political developments over the last few decades. This has led to the expansion of considerations that the regime takes into account in assessing mergers and acquisition (M&A) transactions.

The overall objective of this book is to assess whether US government and regulatory authorities in a variety of sectors assess M&A transactions by looking at the impact of these transactions on public interest considerations. The Federal Trade Commission (FTC) and/or Department of Justice (DOJ) approach to the assessment of transactions brings to light areas of convergence and divergence between these two competition authorities and authorities such as the Committee on Foreign Investment in the United States, the Federal Communications Commission, and other sector regulatory authorities in the US. The book will closely scrutinize the US merger control enforcement in all its variants and in different industry sectors and discuss the approach of the authorities involved as they are focusing on competition considerations, such as the impact of the transaction on consumer welfare, as well as non-competition considerations such as public interest, taking into account social and economic values, including national security and other aspects of public interest aspects relevant for the regulated sectors.

The public interest approach of the sectoral regulators varies between the sectoral regulators. The Federal Communications Commission (FCC) focuses inter alia on public interest, convenience, and necessity. The Federal Energy Regulatory Commission (FERC) focuses inter alia on the impact on the applicants' operating costs

---

[6] OECD (n 4) 2.
[7] ibid 4.
[8] First legislation regulating competition among companies in the US.
[9] OECD (n 4) 4.
[10] Dabbah (n 1) 42.

and the rate levels. The Department of Transportation (DOT) has placed emphasis inter alia on safety; improving relations between air carriers; encouraging fair wages and working conditions, whereas the Surface Transportation Board (STB) focuses inter alia on the needs of rail transportation; the effect on rail and intermodal competition; the environmental impact; the cost of facility rehabilitation; the rationalization of the system; and the impact on shippers. Finally, the banking regulators focus inter alia on the transaction meeting the convenience and needs of the community to be served.

In the regulated sectors, a transaction is likely to be assessed under a public interest test by the relevant sectoral regulatory authority and at the same time under the substantial lessening to competition test by the FTC/DOJ. This overlapping assessment approach can lead at times, as the book will illustrate, to contradictory outcomes. Furthermore, depending on the sector in question, the outcome of the public interest assessment may supersede that of the competition law assessment, an outcome that in itself can lead to ineffective competitive dynamics in the sectoral market. The book will discuss cases where the FTC/DOJ has sought to overturn decisions by the sectoral regulators on certain M&A transactions in the courts.

The book will focus on the role that public interest considerations play in the US merger control regime[11] and assess the different approach that competition and regulatory authorities in the US take. The approach is a comparative one. The book describes the extensive US regulatory framework that is relevant for merger control and the possibility of parallel reviews of the same transaction depending on the sector that the transaction relates to. The book argues that the US regime is at times convoluted when it comes to merger control incorporating public interest considerations such as: (i) national security and (ii) public interest facets in regulated sectors. Assessment of transactions based on these considerations is at times at odds with the assessment of the same transactions based on competition law considerations.

The structure of the book is self-explanatory. It will start by introducing the institutional context of merger control assessment in the US as it is applied by the FTC and the DOJ. It will then discuss the concept of national security and will present the relevant regulatory framework. It will analyse the role of the Committee on Foreign Investment

---

[11] That is, the competition assessment of mergers and/or acquisitions or other types of transactions where companies change control status. The Hart-Scott-Rodino Act specifies what types of transactions ('concentrations') need to be notified to FTC and/or DOJ for competition (or antitrust) approval. The Act requires that parties to certain mergers or acquisitions notify the Federal Trade Commission and the Department of Justice (the 'enforcement agencies') before consummating the proposed acquisition. In general, the Act requires that certain proposed acquisitions of voting securities, non-corporate interests (NCI) or assets be reported to the FTC and the DOJ prior to consummation. The parties must then wait a specified period, usually thirty days (fifteen days in the case of a cash tender offer or a bankruptcy sale), before they may complete the transaction. If either agency determines during the waiting period that further inquiry is necessary, it is authorized by s 7A(e) of the Clayton Act to request additional information or documentary materials from the parties to a reported transaction (a 'second request'). A second request extends the waiting period for a specified period, usually thirty days (ten days in the case of a cash tender offer or a bankruptcy sale), after all parties have complied with the request (or, in the case of a tender offer or a bankruptcy sale, after the acquiring person complies). FTC, 'HSR Premerger Notification Program Introductory Guide I' https://www.ftc.gov/sites/default/files/attachments/premerger-introductory-guides/guide1.pdf. See further Competition Commission and the Office of Fair Trading, 'Merger Assessment Guidelines' (2010) CC2 (Revised)/OFT1254, paras 3.1.3 and 3.2.2. Under both US and UK regimes the authorities can have jurisdiction on a transaction based on assets and/or turnover that the parties have in the UK/US.

4 COMPETITION LAW AND PUBLIC INTEREST CONSIDERATIONS

in the United States (CFIUS), as well as its enforcement record and the considerations that national security concerns imply for the assessment of concentrations.

The book will then discuss the assessment of concentrations by various sectoral regulators based on the public interest standard. In these sectors, a transaction is likely to be assessed under a public interest test by the relevant sectoral regulatory authority and at the same time under the substantial lessening to competition test by the FTC/DOJ. This overlapping assessment approach can lead, at times, as the book will illustrate, to contradictory outcomes. Furthermore, depending on the sector in question, the outcome of the public interest assessment may supersede that of the competition law assessment, an outcome that can lead to ineffective competitive dynamics in the sectoral market. The book will emphasize the cases where the FTC/DOJ sought to overturn decisions by the sectoral regulators on certain transactions in the courts.

The book will discuss in separate chapters the regulatory framework and enforcement record of the assessment of M&As of the STB, the FERC, the DOT, the FCC, the Office of the Comptroller General, the Federal Deposit Insurance Corporation, and the Board of Governors of the Federal Reserve System. The analysis will focus on the structure, legislation, and the relevant public interest considerations that each regulatory authority considers, the respective decision-making process and will present some seminal cases that illustrate not only the enforcement approach of each regulatory authority but also the possibility for discrepancy between the competition law-based assessment and the public interest-based assessment.

1
The US Merger Control Regime

1.1 A Brief Historical Overview

In seeking to provide a comprehensive study of merger control assessment in the US, it is important to trace its origins and its development over time. Such an endeavour would facilitate an understanding of the institutional and legislative context in which merger control has evolved, the unique features of this regime, its advantages, and disadvantages, and, most importantly, the interaction of the various enforcers in assessing the same transaction pursuant to their own respective substantive rules. The simultaneous assessment of transactions by various agencies can lead to diverging assessments and contradictory decisions (eg on remedies, on prohibition, and on clearance).

After the end of the Civil War in 1865, American society shifted from agrarian to urban; this was a transformation period in which a few companies and persons accumulated economic power and capital. This led to the creation of 'trusts'.[1] In 1879, the first trust was formed—the Standard Oil Trust—which enjoyed control over the whole oil industry, from the production process to the sale of the final products.[2] A salient feature of the dominance acquired by this trust was that just three years after its creation, John D. Rockefeller, its owner, owned twenty-one refineries,[3] as well as to use business tactics such as price and output fixing, while avoiding any negative repercussions that could potentially have originated from his relying on such practices.[4] In an attempt to counteract such conducts, Ohio Senator John Sherman presented the first competition law or 'antitrust law', named the Sherman Act, which was passed by the US Congress in 1890.[5]

---

[1] C Paul Rogers III, 'A Concise History of Corporate Mergers and the Antitrust Laws in the United States' (2013) 24(2) National Law School of India Review 10, 11.

[2] Ross Barrett, 'Picturing a Crude Past: Primitivism, Public Art, and Corporate Oil Promotion in the United States' (2012) 46(2) Journal of American Studies 395, 406.

[3] Harold F Williamson and Arnold R Daum, *The American Petroleum Industry: The Age of Illumination, 1859–1899* (Northwestern University Press 1959).

[4] Rogers (n 1) 11.

[5] For a further discussion about the circumstances that surrounded the enactment of the Sherman Act see Richard N Langlois, 'Hunting the Big Five: Twenty-First Century Antitrust in Historical Perspective' (2019) 23(3) Independent Review 411, 414–15; Peter R Dickson and Philippa K Wells, 'The Dubious Origins of the Sherman Antitrust Act: The Mouse That Roared' (2001) 20(1) Journal of Public Policy & Marketing 3. See also Daniel Sokol, 'Antitrust, Institutions, and Merger Control' (2010) 17(4) George Mason Law Review 1055, 1073 http://scholars hip.law.ufl.edu/facultypub/228, indicating that the Sherman Act was the result of political choice between the interests of small producers and those of large corporations. For more literature about this political bargaining process see Thomas J DiLorenzo, 'The Origins of Antitrust: An Interest-Group Perspective' (1985) 5(1) International Review of Law & Economics 73, 75; Fred S McChesney, 'Economics Versus Politics in Antitrust' (1999) 23(1) Harvard Journal of Law & Public Policy 133, 136.

6 THE US MERGER CONTROL REGIME

According to the text of the Sherman Act, any type of contract, combination, or conspiracy 'in restraint of trade or commerce', or 'monopolization', or attempt to monopolize trade or commerce was forbidden.[6] The adoption of the Sherman Act signalled that Congress had embedded an antitrust enforcement model that required the identification of an illegal act, instead of adopting a corporate-regulatory model that inspected the effects of capital-concentrating generated by incorporation laws.[7] In addition, the wording 'restraint of trade' was so open that a divergent number of interpretations emerged around it, provoking an enforcement that was tailored by every administration according to its own views.[8] This vagueness brought some more unintended consequences. Among them was that control of business concentrations was outside the remit/scope of the Sherman Act, resulting in an unprecedented number of 4,227 firms in the economy, which after a significant degree of consolidation merged into 257 between 1897 and 1904. By 1904, a projected number of 318 trusts controlled a significant portion of the US manufacturing assets.[9] With the aim of ameliorating this impressive consolidation process, in 1903 the Bureau of Corporations was created with the power to investigate and report on interstate corporations; yet it did not have any regulatory authority to intervene in the developing consolidation trend.[10] In light of this unmanageable consolidation phenomenon, the Department of Justice (DOJ) was also forced to act by choosing to challenge a horizontal transaction in the sugar industry. This case reached the Supreme Court, which ruled that manufacturing was not part of trade and commerce, a decision that was interpreted as if the federal government did not have the power to prosecute corporations in the manufacturing sector.[11] The judgment of the Supreme Court incentivized small businesses to merge into larger ones and influenced the enforcement of the Sherman Act against small producers and labour unions.[12] Indeed, amidst the first thirteen successful antitrust enforcement cases under the Sherman Act, twelve involved labour union combinations.[13]

Remarkably, in 1904, there was an upheaval when the Supreme Court proscribed the consolidation of railroad companies through a holding company, the Northern

---

[6] 26 Stat 209, 15 USC §§ 1–7 (1890).

[7] Daniel A Crane, *The Institutional Structure of Antitrust Enforcement* (OUP 2011) 13; Daniel A Crane, 'Antitrust Federalism' (2008) 96 California Law Review 1, 2. This wrongdoing approach was methodically captured by the court in American Naval Stores: 'Since the size of the business it not necessarily illegal, it is the crushing of competition, by means of force, threats, intimidations, fraud or artful and deceitful means and practices, which violates the law ... The size of the business, and the gaining of business popularity, fair dealing, sagacity, foresight, and honest business methods, even if it should result in acquiring the business of competitors, would not make an illegal monopoly.' See *United States v American Naval Stores Co* 172 F 455, 458 (CCSD Ga 1909).

[8] Langlois (n 5) 415; see also Alison Jones and William E Kovacic, 'Identifying Anticompetitive Agreements in the United States and the European Union: Developing a Coherent Antitrust Analytical Framework' (2017) 62(2) Antitrust Bulletin 255, noting that the antitrust legislation in the US does not provide a precise definition of core concepts such as 'restraint of trade' or 'monopolization', and that the Supreme Court has been charged with the task of developing the respective meanings through jurisprudence.

[9] Jesse W Markham, 'Survey of the Evidence and Findings on Mergers' in Jesse W Markham, *Business Concentration and Price Policy* (National Bureau of Economic Research Inc 1955) 141–212, 157.

[10] Act of 14 February 1903, 32 Stat 827.

[11] Charles W McCurdy, 'The Knight Sugar Decision of 1895 and the Modernization of American Corporation Law, 1869–1903' (1979) 53(3) The Business History Review 304, 328–30. The US Constitution (art 1, s 8, cl 3) was indeed related to determining powers in relation to regulation between Congress and the States.

[12] Langlois (n 5) 415.

[13] Herbert Hovenkamp, *Enterprise and American Law, 1836–1937* (Harvard UP 1991) 229.

Securities Company, which was used to reduce competition among them.[14] This decision showed the efficacy of the Sherman Act in hindering the consolidation process observed hitherto. This approach was successfully applied again in 1911, when three additional merger plans between large enterprises operating in different sectors were also impeded.[15]

Nevertheless, in the Standard Oil Co v United States case, the Supreme Court established the rule of reason as the standard to be used in dealing with the Sherman Act's prohibition on contracts in restraint of trade, by replacing the absolute prohibition on restraints of trade with a prohibition applicable to just those restraints considered to be 'unreasonable' in the context of a particular case.[16] Thus, the rule of reason approach was perceived as incapable of preventing the amalgamation of big companies unless anti-competitive tactics were used to nudge market power. The Cummins Report stated that 'whenever the rule [of reason] is invoked the court does not administer the law, but makes the law', adding that it was 'inconceivable that in a country governed by a written Constitution and statute law the courts can be permitted to test each restraint of trade by the economic standard which the individual members of the court may happen to approve'.[17]

Therefore, based on the assumption that it was necessary to reinforce the Sherman Act, in 1914 Congress passed the Clayton Act and the Federal Trade Commission Act (FTCA). In particular, section 7 of the Clayton Act was conceived as an effective tool for preventing anti-competitive mergers.[18] Additionally, section 6 addressed the limitation on labour organizations by declaring that 'the labor of a human being is not a commodity or article of commerce'.[19] In spite of the big enforcement efforts seen after the Clayton Act was enacted, in 1926 the Supreme Court clarified that the new law applied only to acquisitions of stock of other companies, leaving outside of its scope any other type of acquisitions such as acquisition of assets.[20] As a result, in the period from 1926 to 1930, over 4,800 companies were bought without scrutiny.[21]

---

[14] *Northern Securities Co v United States* 193 US 197 (1904).

[15] See *Standard Oil v United States* 221 US 1 (1911); *United States v American Tobacco Co* 221 US 106 (1911); and *United States v E.I. du Pont de Nemours & Co* 353 US 586 (1957).

[16] *Standard Oil v United States* (n 15) 60, indicating that: 'The standard of reason ... was intended to be the measure used for the purpose of determining whether in a given case a particular act had or had not brought the wrong against which [s One of the Sherman Act] provided.'

[17] See Control of Corporations, Persons and Firms Engaged in Interstate Commerce, S Rep No 1326, 62d Cong, 3d Sess 1 (1913) (Cummins Report).

[18] 38 Stat 730 (1914). The original version of the Clayton Act, s 7 indicated: 'That no corporation engaged in commerce shall acquire, directly or indirectly, the whole or any part of the stock or other share of capital of another corporation engaged also in commerce where the effect of such acquisition may be to substantially lessen competition between the corporation whose stock is so acquired and the corporation making the acquisition, or to restrain such commerce in any section or community, or tend to create a monopoly in any line of commerce.'

[19] Clayton Act 1914, § 17.

[20] *FTC v Western Meat Co* 272 US 554 (1926). See also Derek C Bok, 'Section 7 of the Clayton Act and the Merging of Law and Economics' (1960) 74(2) Harvard Law Review 226,, 230. It has also been reported that in response to the fears expressed by the business community that the act would put them in prison for carrying out ordinary business activities, Congress removed the criminal sanctions from the proposal and included a vague description of anti-competitive practices. See Thomas McCraw, *Prophets of Regulation: Charles Francis Adams, Louis D. Brandeis, James M. Landis, Alfred E. Kahn*' (Harvard Business School Press 1984) 120–21.

[21] J Keith Butters, John Lintner, and William Lucius Cary, *Effects of Taxation: Corporate Mergers* (HUP 1951) 292.

8   THE US MERGER CONTROL REGIME

Prior to the Celler-Kefauver Act, which was enacted in 1950,[22] expanding the scope of section 7 of the Clayton Act by including the acquisitions of assets, two important judicial decisions triggered such a reform. First, in the *US Steel* case the Supreme Court ruled that the mere size of the companies did not amount to an offense under the Sherman Act and that the Clayton Act required a 'substantial likelihood' of less competition because of the merger.[23] Secondly, in the *Columbia Steel* case the Supreme Court asserted that the acquisition of the assets of the second largest steel fabricator in the western part of the country by the nation's largest steel producer did not infringe the Sherman Act, although the transaction had taken place in an already highly concentrated market.[24]

The enactment of the Celler-Kefauver Act facilitated a prolific period of merger enforcement actions between 1950 and 1960.[25] This trend was reinforced with the decision that the Supreme Court took in the seminal *Brown Shoe* case,[26] which was the first case that reached Supreme Court under the amended version of the Clayton Act. In this case, the merging parties manufactured and distributed shoes, and after analysing the market composition, the Supreme Court concluded that in forty-seven cities where the parties were present, the combined market share would exceed 5 per cent; therefore, the transaction was seen as 'likely to lessen competition', even though the market was fragmented, and was prohibited as a result.[27]

Later, this doctrine was expanded in the landmark *Philadelphia National Bank* case, whereby the Supreme Court established a presumption of illegality when a merger produces 'a firm controlling an undue percentage share of the relevant market, and results in a significant increase in the concentration of firms in that market'.[28] The economic theory used to support this presumption suggests that '[c]ompetition is likely to be greatest when there are many sellers, none of which has any significant market share'.[29] Following a sequence of more prohibitions, in 1966 the Supreme Court censured the Von's Grocery merger, in which the amalgamation of the third and sixth largest grocery chains in Los Angeles would have resulted in a combined share of only 7.5 per cent. This decision raised some concerns about the accuracy of the market share presumption doctrine, which was portrayed as a 'populist' approach conceived to protect small businesses rather than competition.[30] Perhaps one of the most significant signs of this

---

[22] Celler-Kefauver Act, ch 1184 Pub L No 81-899, 64 Stat 1125 (1950) (Current version at 15 USC §§ 18, 21 (2006)).

[23] *United States v United States Steel Corp* 251 US 417 (1920).

[24] *United States v Columbia Steel Co* 334 US 495 (1948).

[25] Rogers (n 1) 16.

[26] *Brown Shoe Co v United States* 370 US 294 (1962).

[27] ibid. See Peter W Rodino Jr, 'The Future of Antitrust: Ideology Vs. Legislative Intent' (1990) 35(3) The Antitrust Bulletin 575,, 586–87; Lawrence A Sullivan and Warren S Grimes, 'The Law of Antitrust: An Integrated Handbook' 599 (West Group 2000); Robert H Lande, 'Wealth Transfers as the Original and Primary Concerns of Antitrust: The Efficiency View Challenged' (1982) 34 Hastings Law Journal 65, 130–40.

[28] *United States v Philadelphia National Bank* 374 US 321 (1963).

[29] ibid.

[30] This point was made clear in the merger decision as follows: 'A Third aspect of this merger is that it creates a large national chain which is integrated with a manufacturing operation. The retail outlets of integrated companies, by eliminating wholesalers and by increasing the volume of purchases from the manufacturing division of the enterprise, can market their own brands at prices below those of competing independent retailers. Of course, some of the results of large integrated or chain operations are beneficial to consumers. Their expansion is not

controversial philosophy was the dissent expressed in Von's Grocery by Justice Stewart who wrote: '[T]he sole consistency is that in litigation under Section 7, the Government always wins.'[31]

In 1974, the Supreme Court revisited the market share presumption doctrine discussed above and in the General Dynamics merger case, involving two coal companies, the concerns raised by the DOJ about the increase of the market shares of the acquiring company, were disregarded. On this occasion, the Court stated that just looking at the market concentration measures to derive the likely competitive effects of the deal was an insufficient assessment of future market power, leaving aside the market share presumption applied until then by instead considering other aspects such as the coal reserves of the acquired company.[32] The Court noted that 'its (General Dynamics) current and future power to compete for subsequent long-term contracts were severely limited by its scarce uncommitted resources.'[33]

This was the last merger case to be decided on its merits by the Supreme Court, as only a limited number of merger cases reach the Supreme Court.[34] In this context, it emerges that firm size was the major concern that was the driving force for the implementation of antitrust law and merger control in the US. Another important aspect that will underpin the discussion that follows is the breadth and vagueness of the terms contained in the Clayton Act and the corresponding lack of guidance. It is remarkable to observe the unrestrained discretion that was given to the courts to decide on what constitutes an anti-competitive merger and to decide how the statute was meant to be applied. Kauper's indication of merger law is pertinent: the task of '[p]utting flesh on this skeleton [the Clayton Act] was left to the federal courts.'[35] It is no surprise that judicial interpretation have struggled to discern a consistent standard and have evolved over

---

rendered unlawful by the mere fact that small independent stores may be adversely affected ... But we cannot fail to recognize Congress' desire to protect competition through the protection of viable, small, locally owned businesses. Congress appreciated that occasional higher costs and prices might result from the maintenance of fragmented industries and markets. It resolved these competing considerations in favor of decentralization.' *United States v Von's Grocery Co* 384 US 270, 344 (1966). For a good discussion about the doctrine that was initiated in *Brown Shoe* and strictly applied in *Von's Grocery* see Robert H Lande, 'Resurrecting Incipiency: From Von's Grocery to Consumer Choice' (2001) 68(3) Antitrust Law Journal 875; Eleanor M Fox and Lawrence A Sullivan, 'Retrospective and Prospective: Where Are We Coming From? Where Are We Going?' in Harry First, Eleanor M Fox, and Robert Pitofsky (eds), *Revitalizing Antitrust in its Second Century* (Quorum Books 1991).

[31] *United States v Von's Grocery Co* (n 30) 301 (Stewart J dissenting).

[32] *United States v General Dynamics Corp* 415 US 486 (1974). See C Paul Rogers III, 'Perspectives on Corporate Mergers and the Antitrust Laws' (1981) 12 Loyola University Chicago Law Journal 301, 306–309; William J Baer, 'Surf's Up: Antitrust Enforcement and Consumer Interests in a Merger Wave' (1996) 30(2) Journal of Consumer Affairs 292, 306.

[33] United States v General Dynamics Corp (n 32) 503.

[34] Carl Shapiro, 'Protecting Competition in the American Economy: Merger Control, Tech Titans, Labor Markets' (2019) 33(3) Journal of Economic Perspectives 69, 74; Stephen Calkins, 'In Praise of Antitrust Litigation: The Second Annual Bernstein Lecture' 72 St John's Law Review 1 (1998); Herbert Hovenkamp, *The Antitrust Enterprise: Principle and Execution* (HUP 2008) 208; Louis Kaplow and Carl Shapiro, 'Antitrust' in A Mitchell Polinsky and Steven Shavell (eds), *Handbook of Law and Economics*, vol 2 (Elsevier 2007) 1073, 1161. (This chapter will study in more detail the reasons for, as well as the implications of, the absence of the US Supreme Court decisions at a later stage.)

[35] Thomas E Kauper, 'Merger Control in the United States and the European Union: Some Observations' (2000) 74 St John's Law Review 305, 310.

10   THE US MERGER CONTROL REGIME

time.[36] Seeking to find a consistent theory to ascertain the likely competitive effects of a merger with the underlying duty to preclude additional increases in concentration, the Supreme Court created stringent presumptions based just on concentration levels. The challenge of creating a coherent merger control, combined with the fact that since the middle of the 1970s the Supreme Court has not provided further merger guidance, had influenced the need for merger guidelines to fill the gaps in the merger statute and to attain a stable doctrine, as the next part of this chapter explores in more detail.[37]

1.2 The Merger Guidelines

As indicated earlier, the evolving and unpredictable judicial guidance offered by the Supreme Court during the 1950s, 1960s, and early 1970s signalled the need for a more consistent regulation of the merger review process. Trying to address this issue, at least partially, in 1968 the DOJ issued its first Merger Guidelines, which were non-binding, and described how merger assessment would take place, by pointing to the types of transactions likely to be challenged.[38] Although the initial intention of the Merger Guidelines was to make public how the antitrust agencies would assess a transaction, progressively these guidelines became the cornerstone of merger analysis, not just for the enforcement agencies but also for merging parties, courts, and other agencies.[39]

The assessment of mergers in these first DOJ 1968 Merger Guidelines embraced the enforcement approach adopted by the Supreme Court during the 1960s and 1970s, which relied heavily on the market shares of the merging parties. As an illustration, the DOJ specified that merging parties could expect their transactions to be subject to challenge if they had a 5 per cent market share each or if the transaction involved one party with a 20 per cent market share and the other with at least a 2 per cent.[40] Another transaction that could potentially be challenged was one in which the collective market

---

[36] Judges themselves have recognized the complexity that trying to administer antitrust standards entails [or involves]. As an illustration, in *FTC v Actavis* 570 US 136, 173 (2013) it was stated: 'Good luck to the district courts that must, when faced with a patent settlement, weigh the "likely anticompetitive effects, redeeming virtues, market power, and potentially offsetting legal considerations present in the circumstances".'

[37] Commissioner Phillip Elman observed that: 'Where controlling legal principles have not yet crystallized ... [guidelines] may often provide a useful alternative or supplement to the traditional case-by-case adjudicative approach as a method of formulating legal doctrines and standards.' See Philip Elman, 'Rulemaking Procedures in the FTC's Enforcement of the Merger Law' (1964) 78 Harvard Law Review 385, 386.

[38] Rogers (n 1) 21; Hillary Greene, 'Agency Character and the Character of Agency Guidelines: An Historical and Institutional Perspective' (2005) 72(3) Antitrust Law Journal 1039, 1040; Giancarlo Piscitelli, 'Public Interest in Merger Control Systems in the EU and US: A Comparative Analysis of the Uneasy Relationship between Merger Control and Public Interest' (2019) 3 European Competition & Regulatory Law Review 380, 386.

[39] Kaplow and Shapiro (n 34) 1162; Antitrust Modernization Commission, 'Report and Recommendations' (2007) 48 https://govinfo.library.unt.edu/amc/report_recommendation/amc_final_report.pdf; Spencer W Waller, 'Prosecution by Regulation: The Changing Nature of Antitrust Enforcement' (1998) 77 Oregon Law Review 1383, 1405–406; Lawrence M Frankel, 'The Flawed Institutional Design of U.S. Merger Review: Stacking the Deck Against Enforcement' (2008) Utah Law Review 159, 162; Hillary Greene, 'Guideline Institutionalization: The Role of Merger Guidelines in Antitrust Discourse' (2006) 48 William & Mary Law Review 771. Also, as an illustration, the Merger Guidelines have expressly been applied by lower courts in the following cases: *United States v Engelhard Corp* 126 F 3d 1302, 1304 (11th Cir 1997); *United States v Baker Hughes Inc* 908 F 2d 981, 983 (DC Cir 1990); *United States v Waste Management Inc* 743 F 2d 976, 982 (2d Cir 1984).

[40] Shapiro (n 34) 73.

share of the four largest companies was at least 75 per cent, and the market share of the acquiring company was 15 per cent and that of the acquired company was at least 1 per cent.[41] This policy on merger enforcement was based on very low thresholds that signalled potential harm to consumers and competition.

The above-mentioned policy was changed in 1982 when the DOJ promulgated new merger guidelines. Among the factors that influenced the adoption of a renewed merger analytical framework was that early in the 1970s imports started to play a significant role in the US economy and an increasing number of foreign companies began to operate in the domestic manufacturing sector.[42] According to Fox, these concerns about foreign competition were exacerbated by the high levels of inflation, low levels of productivity and weak economic performance observed in the US during this period.[43] The combination of all of these factors resulted in a new way of thinking in which less weight was given to market shares and higher thresholds were adopted as indicators of potential anti-competitive effects. This new model put more emphasis on using merger control as a tool to inhibit market power and its exercise rather than on using it as a device to establish structural presumptions.[44] The 1982 Guidelines introduced the well-known hypothetical monopolist test (HMT) as an analytical instrument for defining the relevant market, which focuses on the question involving a hypothetical increase in price.[45] These guidelines also presented the Herfindahl–Hirschman Index (HHI) as a tool to measure market concentration.[46] Changes in this index as a result of a merger, were used to establish enforcement thresholds. At the same time, the 1982 guidelines listed some factors as predictors of coordinated effects and discussed the potential competitive implications of a merger.[47] The reformulation of the analytical framework contained in the 1982 Merger Guidelines represented a remarkable departure from the approach seen in the previous guidelines, by leaving behind a static analysis underpinned by just market shares around which stringent presumptions of illegality were shaped and introducing antitrust analytical tools that are now used worldwide. The 1982 Merger Guidelines have been subject to further revisions, as we will see below.

The most immediate revision took place in 1984 in relation to the analysis of efficiency claims that was introduced by the 1982 Merger Guidelines as follows:

---

[41] Carl Shapiro, 'The 2010 Horizontal Merger Guidelines: From Hedgehog to Fox in Forty Years' (2010) 77(1) Antitrust Law Journal 49, 50–51.

[42] Baer (n 32) 309.

[43] Eleanor M Fox, 'The Modernization of Antitrust: A New Equilibrium' (1981) 66 Cornell Law Review 1140.

[44] US Department of Justice Merger Guidelines (1982) § 1.

[45] For a good explanation about the HMT test see Malcolm B Coate and Jeffrey H Fischer, 'A Practical Guide to the Hypothetical Monopolist Test for Market Definition' (2008) 4(4) Journal of Competition Law & Economics 1031, doi:10.1093/joclec/nhn007; Gregory J Werden, 'The 1982 Merger Guidelines and the Ascent of the Hypothetical Monopolist Paradigm' (2002) 71 Antitrust Law Journal 253, 254–57.

[46] Charles R Laine, 'The Herfindahl-Hirschman Index: A Concentration Measure Taking the Consumer's Point of View' (1995) 40(2) The Antitrust Bulletin 423. Doi:10.1177/0003603X9504000206; Donald I Baker and William Blumenthal, 'Demystifying the Herfindahl-Hirschman Index' (1984) 19(2) Mergers and Acquisitions 42.

[47] The guidelines indicated that in assessing coordinated effects, product differentiation 'will be taken into account only in relatively extreme cases'. See US Department of Justice Merger Guidelines (1982) § III.C.1.a. See also Shapiro (n 41) 53.

12 THE US MERGER CONTROL REGIME

> Except in extraordinary cases, the Department [of Justice] will not consider a claim of specific efficiencies as a mitigating factor for a merger that would otherwise be challenged. Plausible efficiencies are far easier to allege than to prove. Moreover, even if the existence of efficiencies were clear, their magnitudes would be extremely difficult to determine.[48]

The amendment consisted of eliminating the phrases 'except in extraordinary cases' and 'easier to allege than to prove' and instead stating that to substantiate an efficiency claim it was necessary to provide 'clear and convincing evidence'.[49] Moreover, the 1984 revision removed the requirement that the parties had to prove that the efficiencies were 'already enjoyed by one of more firms in the industry'.[50] The reform clarified that just those efficiencies that could not be achieved otherwise would be taken into consideration, and that the magnitude of the risk would dictate the scope of the net efficiencies.[51] Finally, the 1984 Guidelines introduced the concept of 'leading firm proviso', an approximation of what are now known as unilateral effects, whose intended purpose was to avert 'mergers that may create or enhance the market power of a single dominant firm'.[52]

The next revision was made in 1992, in the context of a decline in the number of merger enforcement actions, which between 1982 and 1986 accounted for only 0.7 per cent of the proposed mergers compared to 2.5 per cent between 1979 and 1980.[53] The 'merger-mania' (as described by Pitofsky) observed in this period was influenced by the unprecedented growth in imports, which moved from US$40 billion in 1970 to US$495 billion in 1990,[54] a fact that motivated a relaxation of the merger rules and, more specifically, led to the new merger guidelines being ignored both by merging parties and agencies.[55] It has been argued that another cause of the decline in merger enforcement was the approach adopted by the Reagan administration, which incorporated the view that mergers would rarely result in a decrease in competition.[56] This view comprised the presumption that merger enforcement would do more harm than good.[57] In the words of Robert Pitofsky:

---

[48] US Department of Justice *Merger Guidelines* (1982).

[49] ibid § 3.5.

[50] William J Kolasky and Andrew R Dick, 'The Merger Guidelines and the Integration of Efficiencies into Antitrust Review of Horizontal Mergers' (2003) 71(1) Antitrust Law Journal 207, 220–21.

[51] US Department of Justice *Merger Guidelines* (1982) § 3.5.

[52] US Department of Justice *Merger Guidelines* (1984) § 3.12. The 1984 Guidelines stated that 'the Department is likely to challenge the merger of any firm with a market share of at least one percent with the leading firm in the market, provided the leading firm has a market share that is at least 35 percent'.

[53] Robert Pitofsky, 'Proposals for Revised United States Merger Enforcement in a Global Economy' (1992) 81 Georgetown Law Journal 195, fn 4.

[54] ibid.

[55] Thomas G Krattenmaker and Robert Pitofsky, 'Antitrust Merger Policy and the Reagan Administration' (1988) 33 Antitrust Bulletin 211, 218.

[56] John J Flynn, '"Reaganomics" and Antitrust Enforcement: A Jurisprudential Critique' (1983) 2 Utah Law Review 269.

[57] Baer (n 32) 311.

[A]ntitrust in the 1980s came under the influence of an economic orthodoxy that viewed government regulation as a source of much mischief. That orthodoxy depended upon the validity of premises like the contention that only economic efficiency mattered (and then only economy-wide efficiency), efficiency could be presumed from all transactions not aggregating substantial market power (or else why would the transaction happened at all), the free market was almost invariably an effective allocator of national resources, and in any event the free market was a far better instrument for regulation than any band of bureaucrats.[58]

In 1992, the Federal Trade Commission (FTC) and the DOJ jointly issued new merger guidelines that reaffirmed the position of recalibrating the importance of market shares in the assessment of a merger by transferring more attention to the extent to which the deal would cause a change in the competition landscape.[59] In consequence, the concept of unilateral effects was introduced into the analytical framework, moving away from the strictly applied approach of loss of competition between the merging parties and the configuration of the market.[60] In terms of efficiencies, although the revision did not entail a dramatic change, it provided more detailed guidance by, for instance, stating that even the greatest 'efficiencies almost never justify a merger to monopoly or near monopoly'.[61] A significant contribution of the 1992 Guidelines was that they set the criteria for the analysis of entry, which must be 'timely, likely and sufficient' to be able to alleviate the competitive concerns of a deal.[62]

Furthermore, the antitrust enforcement philosophy was transformed by acknowledging that government intervention did not always mean harm and that merger control was a tool to advance consumer welfare.[63] As Kokkoris and Skourtis note,[64] consumer welfare as a dominant paradigm emerged in US antitrust in the 1970s. It is not the purpose of the present chapter to engage in detail with the emergence of consumer welfare as the prevalent aim in US antitrust, as the presentation of the historical context and the development of the concept of consumer welfare as well as the controversy surrounding the emergence of the latter to dominance has been well documented in literature.[65] It has been pointed out that the link made by Robert Bork[66] between the intent of the historical legislator with regard to the Sherman Act (Act) and consumer

---

[58] Robert Pitofsky, 'Antitrust Policy in a Clinton Administration' (1993) 62 Antitrust Law Journal 217.

[59] Shapiro (n 34) 74.

[60] ibid; Jonathan B Baker, Why Did the Antitrust Agencies Embrace Unilateral Effects? (2003) 12 George Mason Law Review 31, 33–45; Gregory J Werden and Luke M Froeb, 'Unilateral Competitive Effects of Horizontal Mergers' in Paolo Buccirossi (ed), *Handbook of Antitrust Economics* (MIT Press 2008) 43.

[61] US Department of Justice & Federal Trade Commission, *Merger Guidelines* (1992) § 4.

[62] Shapiro (n 41) 54.

[63] Baer (n 32) 312; Debra A Valentine and Raj De, 'Transatlantic Similarities and Differences in Merger Policy: How the United States and the European Union Evaluate Transactions' (2002) 37(4) Business Economics 33, 36.

[64] Ioannis Kokkoris and Athanassios Skourtis, 'Is Consumer Welfare Still Fit for Purpose in the EU Competition Regime?' in Ioannis Kokkoris and Claudia Lemus (eds), *Research Handbook on the Law and Economics of Competition Enforcement* (Edward Elgar Publishing 2022) 410.

[65] cf eg Barak Orbach, 'How Antitrust Lost Its Goal' (2013) 81(5) Fordham Law Review 2253, 2257 ff, 2268 ff.

[66] Robert Bork, *The Antitrust Paradox* (Free Press 1993).

14 THE US MERGER CONTROL REGIME

welfare as the intended aim of the Act is more than doubtful.[67] Nevertheless, US courts and primarily the Supreme Court seem to have been willing to adopt consumer welfare as the new paradigm in US antitrust.[68]

The consumer welfare criterion involves a certain controversy surrounding its proper definition as an antitrust goal. The resulting perceived lack of clarity regarding its meaning is accentuated through inconsistent judicial application both terminologically and substantively.[69] Following the emergence of the standard in US antitrust, uncertainty has reigned with regard to the correspondence of the legal concept to an economic counterpart and whether it should be identified as consumer surplus or total surplus.[70]

In 1997, a new revision focused on the handling of merger efficiencies, for which a test comprising three steps was suggested.[71] The first step consisted of confirming whether the analytical process applied is valid, the second whether the efficiencies are verifiable and the third whether they are merger specific.[72] Once these three steps have been completed, it is possible to establish to what degree the alleged efficiencies will be taken into consideration in merger assessment. In other words, if the efficiencies satisfy the three steps of the so-called cognizability test it is more likely that they can be balanced against the anti-competitive price effects of the transaction. If one or more of the factors are not proven, the chances that they can be used as part of the competitive analysis are reduced.[73] At the same time, the 1997 revision confirmed what the 1984 and 1992 Guidelines had stated about the nature of mergers, which is 'their potential to generate ... efficiencies', and explained that efficiencies increased the competitiveness of firms by 'increasing their incentive and ability to compete',[74] not just in terms of lower prices but also in relation to 'improved quality, enhanced service, or new products'.[75] In a footnote, the revised guidelines also acknowledged that some efficiencies may involve some degree of anti-competitive harm and that such an undesirable outcome would be justified as long as the efficiencies are greater than the harm, and the harm is unavoidable.[76]

---

[67] Orbach (n 65) 2275.

[68] ibid 2257 ff; Kenneth Heyer, 'Consumer Welfare and the Legacy of Robert Bork' (2014) 57(S3) Journal of Law & Economics S19.

[69] cf Maurice E Stucke, 'Reconsidering Antitrust's Goals' (2012) 53 Boston College Law Review 551, 571 fn 133.

[70] See eg Autoriteit Consument & Markt, 'Behavioural Economics and Competition Policy' (2013) 8 fn 10; Gregory Werden, 'Consumer Welfare and Competition Policy' in Josef Drexl, Wolfgang Kerber, and Rupprecht Podszun (eds), Competition Policy and the Economic Approach. Foundations and Limitations (Edward Elgar Publishing 2011) 11 ff. Commentators have further stressed that in the context of US antitrust and despite the contribution of the adoption of the consumer welfare standard to the improvement, clarification and rationalization of antitrust law, the paradigm in question is 'a far more technical and complicated concept than meets the eye.' See Sean Sullivan, 'Antitrust Amorphisms' CPI Antitrust Chronicle (November 2019) 5.

[71] US Department of Justice & Federal Trade Commission, Horizontal Merger Guidelines (rev 1997).

[72] ibid.

[73] For a good discussion about the cognizability test see Malcolm B Coate, 'Efficiencies in Merger Analysis: An Institutional View' (2005) 13 Supreme Court Economic Review 189, 193; see also Kolasky and Dick (n 50) 227–31.

[74] US Department of Justice Press Release, 'Justice Department and Federal Trade Commission Announce Revisions to Merger Guidelines' (8 April 1997).

[75] US Department of Justice & Federal Trade Commission, Horizontal Merger Guidelines (rev 1997) § 4.

[76] See Kolasky and Dick (n 50) 231. This situation is well illustrated in the FTC v Tenet Health Care Corp. merger case, where the Court of Appeals reversed the preliminary injunction granted by the Eighth Circuit preventing the merger of the only two general-care hospitals in Poplar Bluff, Missouri. The Appeals Court indicated that although the transaction 'reaped the benefit of a price war in a small corner of the health care market in the southeastern

In 2010, the DOJ and the FTC jointly issued an important revision of the Merger Guidelines. Remarkably, the agencies disowned the following sequential approach adopted previously in assessing mergers: (1) market definition and concentration; (2) competitive effects; (3) entry; (4) efficiencies; and (5) failing firm defence.[77] The 2010 revision highlighted that at the core of the merger analysis was the analysis of the competitive effects, and an entire section was devoted to examining the theories of harm that the agencies would apply, to describing the types of evidence on which the theories of harm would rest, and to explaining how the analysis would be constructed.[78] In doing so, the role of market definition in merger assessment was clarified and depicted as a factor that was closely interlinked with the competitive effects rather than as an independent and separate step in the assessment. In this respect, section 4 stated: 'Evidence of competitive effects can inform market definition, just as market definition can be informative regarding competitive effects.'[79] Furthermore, the 2010 Guidelines expressed that in those cases where there was a more accurate tool to 'more directly predict the competitive effects of a merger' than market definition, the antitrust agencies could choose not to apply the latter.[80] By looking at the competitive effects, the Guidelines also emphasized that market shares and market concentration are good indicators but cannot be used in isolation to exert definite outcomes.[81]

Another significant contribution of the 2010 Guidelines was the introduction of the upward pricing pressure test (UPP test),[82] which, unlike the small but significant non-transitory increase in price (SSNIP) test, was not presented as a formal screen but as a methodological option to be applied: '[I]n some cases, where sufficient information is available, the Agencies assess the value of diverted sales between the parties to the consolidation and between them and other competitors, which can serve as an indicator of the upward pricing pressure on the first product resulting from the merger.'[83] Regarding efficiencies, the new Guidelines expressly recognized that a merger can offer 'lower prices, improved quality, enhanced services, or new products,'[84] and delineated the role

---

Missouri', the harm was compensated by the improved quality of the services that the merger entity was able to offer. See 186 F 3d 1045 (8th Cir 1999) 1054.

[77] US Department of Justice & Federal Trade Commission, *Horizontal Merger Guidelines* (2010) §§ 4–11; Shapiro (n 41) 56; Michael A Salinger, 'The 2010 Revised Merger Guidelines and Modern Industrial Economics' (2011) 39(1–2) Review of Industrial Organization 159, 161.

[78] US Department of Justice & Federal Trade Commission, *Horizontal Merger Guidelines* (2010) §§ 1–2; Shapiro (n 41) 56.

[79] US Department of Justice & Federal Trade Commission, *Horizontal Merger Guidelines* (2010) § 4.

[80] ibid.

[81] Section 4 of the 2010 Guidelines indicate that: 'The measurement of market shares and market concentration is not and end in itself but, is useful to the extent it illuminates the merger's likely competitive effects.' The reduced emphasis on market shares is also observed in Section 6 of the Guidelines stating that: 'The Agencies consider any reasonably available and reliable information to evaluate the extent of direct competition between the products sold by the merging parties. This includes documentary and testimonial evidence from discount approval processes, customer switching patterns, and customer surveys.' The Guidelines described the information gathering process and interpretation of this evidence.

[82] For a good explanation of the UPP test see Joseph Farrell and Carl Shapiro, 'Antitrust Treatment of Horizontal Mergers: An Alternative to Market Definition' (2010) 10(1) Berkeley Electronic Journal of Theoretical Economics 1. See also James A Keyte and Kenneth B Schwartz, ' "Tally-Ho!": UPP and the 2010 Horizontal Merger Guidelines' (2011) 77(2) Antitrust Law Journal 587, 600–22.

[83] US Department of Justice & Federal Trade Commission, *Horizontal Merger Guidelines* (2010) § 6.1.

[84] ibid § 10.

16 THE US MERGER CONTROL REGIME

of the efficiencies defence according to the anti-competitive risks by stating that, '[t]he greater the potential adverse competitive effect, the greater must be the cognizable efficiencies, and the more they must be passed through to consumers'.[85] This revision paid special attention to the unilateral effects concerns that could arise in differentiated product markets and provided an approach to determine the closeness of competition (known as diversion) between the merging parties by looking at pricing, negotiation and innovation models.[86] Hence, the Guidelines presented the approach that the agencies had previously put into practice in relation to diversion as follows: 'Diversion ratios between products sold by one merging firm and products sold by the other merging firm can be very informative for assessing unilateral price effects, with higher diversion ratios indicating a greater likelihood of such effects. Diversion ratios between products sold by merging firms and those by non-merging firms have at most secondary predictive value.'[87]

In 2020, the DOJ and FTC released the most updated version of the Vertical Merger Guidelines,[88] which, since the 1984 Merger Guidelines, when some aspects of non-horizontal transactions were introduced, had not been further revised. The antitrust agencies recognized the need to revisit the scrutiny of vertical mergers, as in the words of FTC Chairman Joseph Simons 'anticompetitive vertical mergers are not unicorns, and there should not be a presumption that all vertical mergers are benign'.[89] The 2020 Guidelines indicate that antitrust agencies will be concerned with vertical integrations that might cause harm by foreclosing the markets, raising rivals' costs, accessing competitively sensitive information, and increasing the risk of marketplace coordination.[90] As a novelty, the Guidelines introduced diagonal mergers and mergers of complements as new types of deals that will be subject to scrutiny.[91] At the same time, the Guidelines recognize that vertical integration can provide some benefits such as

[85] ibid. See also Roger D Blair and Jessica S Haynes, 'The Efficiencies Defense in the 2010 Horizontal Merger Guidelines' (2011) 38(1–2) Review of Industrial Organization 57, 58–60.

[86] US Department of Justice & Federal Trade Commission, *Horizontal Merger Guidelines* (2010); §§ 6.1 and 6.2 deal with pricing and bidding competition among suppliers of differentiated products, § 6.3 addresses capacity and output for homogeneous products, and § 6.4 describes a type of analysis based on innovation and product variety. For a good explanation see Malcolm B Coate and Shawn W Ulrick, 'Unilateral Effects Analysis in Differentiated Product Markets: Guidelines, Policy, and Change' (2016) 48 Review of Industrial Organization 45.

[87] US Department of Justice & Federal Trade Commission, *Horizontal Merger Guidelines* (2010) § 6.1.

[88] See Prepared Statement of Federal Trade Commission Acting Chairwoman Rebecca Kelly Slaughter, Before the Subcommittee on Antitrust, Commercial and Administrative Law Of the Judiciary Committee: United States House of Representatives, 'Reviving Competition, Part 3: Strengthening the Laws to Address Monopoly Power' (18 March 2021) https://www.ftc.gov/system/files/documents/public_statements/1588320/p180101_prepared_statement_of_ftc_acting_chairwoman_slaughter.pdf (accessed 9 November 2022).

[89] FTC Chairman Joseph Simons, Fordham Speech on Hearings Output (Sept. 13, 2019) https://www.ftc.gov/system/files/documents/public_statements/1544082/simons_-_fordham_speech_on_hearings_output_9-13-19.pdf (accessed 9 November 2022).

[90] For a good explanation of the analysis of vertical mergers using the general approach to input foreclosure and raising rivals' costs as described in the 2020 *Vertical Merger Guidelines* see Carl Shapiro, 'Vertical Mergers and Input Foreclosure Lessons from the AT&T/Time Warner Case' (2021) 59 Review of Industrial Organization 303 https://doi.org/10.1007/s11151-021-09826-x.

[91] US Department of Justice Press Release, 'Department of Justice and Federal Trade Commission Issue New Vertical Merger Guidelines' (30 June 2020). See also James A Fishkin, Rani A Habash, and Dennis S Schmelzer, 'The US DoJ and FTC Issue a Revised Version of the Vertical Merger Guidelines' *e-Competitions* (2020) https://www.concurrences.com/en/bulletin/news-issues/june-2020/the-us-doj-and-ftc-issue-a-revised-version-of-the-vertical-merger-guidelines.

restructuring production, inventory management and distribution, enabling the creation of new products, and cost savings.[92] Interestingly, on 15 September 2021 the FTC announced its withdrawal of the 2020 Guidelines after recognizing that the listed procompetitive benefits were not properly supported by law, sound economic theories, or market realities.[93] In Lina Khan's separate statement, she outlined that, 'in particular, the 2020 VMGs contravene statutory text, improperly suggesting that efficiencies or "procompetitive effects" may rescue an otherwise unlawful transaction.'[94]

The analysis above has shown the importance of the merger guidelines, which beyond being a public statement that reflects the antitrust agencies' enforcement practices, also serve as an invaluable tool for practitioners, courts, companies, and sectoral agencies.[95] Their importance has surpassed the domestic boundaries and has impacted the global antitrust community, which has benefitted from the use of critical antitrust analytical tools, such as the HMT, HHI, SSNIP and UPP tests. Also, the regular revisions of the guidelines have revealed the need for refreshing the economic and legal analysis applied when reviewing merger cases, adapting to the new business models, and employing the experience that antitrust agencies have gained with time. Yet even if this evolution appears to be appropriate, it also casts doubt on whether the desire to use the merger guidelines to provide helpful context for the enforcement of the merger statute and to attain an effective regime has been achieved.

Moreover, despite the importance of the merger guidelines and the intentions of the federal agencies in applying them, the enforcement levels have exposed the tensions between the goals of antitrust enforcers and those of other policy-makers, in which the views of the latter seem to have a prevailing position over the former. The following chapters of this book will explore these tensions and identify areas of convergence and divergence in the enforcement approach of DOJ/FTC and sectoral regulators.

Having explored the scope, relevance, and evolution of the merger guidelines, the next part focuses on the enactment of the Hart-Scott-Rodino Antitrust Improvements Act, which has brought about wide implications for merger enforcement.

---

[92] Craig Waldman and Michael A Gleason, 'A Dealmaker's Guide to the Final DOJ/FTC Vertical Merger Guidelines' *The M&A Lawyer* (July/August 2020) https://www.jonesday.com/en/insights/2020/08/a-dealmakers-guide-to-the-final-doj-ftc-vertical-merger (accessed 9 November 2022).

[93] Federal Trade Commission Withdraws Vertical Merger Guidelines and Commentary (15 September 2021) https://www.ftc.gov/news-events/press-releases/2021/09/federal-trade-commission-withdraws-vertical-merger-guidelines (accessed 9 November 2022). For some reactions to the FTC's withdrawal decision see Carl Shapiro and Herbert Hovenkamp, 'How Will the FTC Evaluate Vertical Mergers?' *Promarket* (23 September 2021) https://promarket.org/2021/09/23/ftc-vertical-mergers-antitrust-shapiro-hovenkamp/ (accessed 9 November 2022); Hal Singer and Marshall Steinbaum, 'Missing the Forest for the Trees: A Reply to Hovenkamp and Shapiro' *Promarket* (27 September 2021) https://promarket.org/2021/09/27/ftc-vertical-mergers-guidelines-hovenkamp-shapiro-singer-steinbaum-response/ (accessed 9 November 2022).

[94] Federal Trade Commission, 'Remarks of Chair Lina M. Khan Regarding the Proposed Rescission of the FTC's Approval of the 2020 Vertical Merger Guidelines Commission File No P810034' (15 September 2021) https://www.ftc.gov/system/files/documents/public_statements/1596392/remarks_of_chair_lina_m_khan_regarding_the_proposed_rescission_of_the_ftcs_approval_of_the_2020_vmgs.pdf (accessed 9 November 2022).

[95] As an illustration, Williamson highlighted the immense contribution made by the 1968 Merger Guidelines noting that: 'With the benefit of hindsight, the field of industrial organization and the enforcement of antitrust were in crisis in the 1960s. Price-theoretic reasoning, with emphasis on monopoly and the real and imagined consequences of barriers to entry, carried the day.' See Oliver E Williamson, 'Economics and Antitrust Enforcement: Transition Years' (2003) 17 Antitrust 61, 61.

18 THE US MERGER CONTROL REGIME

1.3 The Hart-Scott-Rodino Antitrust Improvements Act

In 1976, the Hart-Scott-Rodino Antitrust Improvements Act (HSR) was enacted incorporating important transformations in the merger enforcement regime. Inter alia, it removed the need to prove anti-competitive conduct to prohibit a merger under section 7 of the Clayton Act.[96] Put differently, it introduced a prophylactic approach in which the assessment of a merger focuses on identifying the potential occurrence of anti-competitive conduct. This change addressed the time-consuming and resource-intensive endeavours that before 1976 characterized overwhelmingly long merger trials, which often lasted for many years.[97] At the same time, it remedied the trend observed during the 1960s and early 1970s of reversing those transactions the violation of which was declared after their consummation,[98] resulting in a high number of very complex divestitures.[99] Then, a pre-merger notification obligation was imposed on merging parties in relation to certain covered transactions—mergers of very large size-[100] and the federal antitrust agencies were entitled to request the necessary information to assess their effects before consummation.[101] This request for information was reinforced with the possibility of issuing a second information request, meaning that merging parties could not conclude/complete the transaction until the agency declared that the information obligation had been satisfied.[102] The HSR Act gave the DOJ the authority to issue civil investigative demands, thereby giving both the DOJ and the FTC equal authority to review mergers under the HSR Act.[103] Also, as will be presented in the next section, which covers the institutional setting, the HSR Act entrusted the State Attorney General with the authority to sue as *parens patriae* on behalf of natural persons.[104]

---

[96] 15 USC § 18.

[97] Crane, 'Antitrust Federalism' (n 7) 54.

[98] See S Rept No 94-803 (1976) 61–62.

[99] See HR Rept No 94-1373 (1976) 8. It has been indicated that before the enactment of the HSR Act, merging parties expeditiously consummated the mergers that after litigation were enjoined, sometimes a decade later, making practical divestiture difficult or impossible. See Kaplow and Shapiro (n 34) 1159.

[100] The Hart-Scott-Rodino Antitrust Improvements Act of 1976 requires merging firms to provide notification to the federal agencies prior to closing mergers that meet certain size thresholds. See 15 USC § 18a(a).

[101] Pub L No 94-435, 90 Stat 1383 (1976). The pre-merger notification provisions are contained in s 7A of the Clayton Act. See 15 USC § 18a (1994). See also 15 USC § 18a(d)(1).

[102] Some commentators have referred to this agencies' power as 'de facto injunctions' or 'automatic stay of a transaction'. See Edward T Swaine, '"Competition, Not Competitors", Nor Canards: Ways of Criticizing the Commission' (2002) 23(3) University of Pennsylvania Journal of International & Economic Law 597, 632; Joe Sims and Deborah P Herman, 'The Effect of Twenty Years of Hart-Scott-Rodino on Merger Practice: A Case Study in the Law of Unintended Consequences Applied to Antitrust Legislation' (1997) 65 Antitrust Law Journal 865, 881.

[103] Hart-Scott-Rodino Antitrust Improvements Act of 1976 (HSR Act) (Pub L No 94-435); see ABA Section of Antitrust Law, *The Merger Review Process: A Step-by-Step Guide to U.S. and Foreign Merger Review* (2006) 22–30.

[104] Pub L No 94-435, 90 Stat 1383 (1976).

1.4 Institutional Setting

1.4.1 The Antitrust Division (Department of Justice)

In 1903, the Assistant Attorney General for Antitrust position was created in the DOJ,[105] and in 1933 the Antitrust Division was converted into an independent unit within the DOJ.[106] The DOJ is an executive agency, whose Antitrust Division is supervised by an Assistant Attorney who is nominated by the President and confirmed by the Senate.[107] The Antitrust Division has specialized sections, among which are the economic section, the appellate section, the competition policy and advocacy section, the international section, and the executive office.[108] In the development of antitrust policy the Antitrust Division has played a significant role in enforcing the antitrust laws, providing guidance through different means and promoting competition reflections to be integrated as part of future national economic policies.[109] Congress oversees the conduct of the Antitrust Division, approves the organizational structure, and challenges its policies.[110] Specifically, the DOJ enforces the Sherman Act and the Clayton Act through civil actions and criminally prosecutes hard core offences under the Sherman Act.[111] In other words, the DOJ enforces the Sherman Act civilly and criminally, and the Clayton Act civilly.

1.4.2 The Federal Trade Commission

In 1914, the FTC was created as an independent expert agency on competition policy, replacing the Bureau of Corporations, and it was bestowed with antitrust enforcement authority.[112] According to Crane, Congress saw the Commission as 'an indispensable

---

[105] The Assistant Attorney for Antitrust position's main task was to deal with all lawsuits filed under the antitrust and interstate commerce laws. See Antitrust Division Manual (5th edn) Chapter 1: Organization and Functions of the Antitrust Division https://www.justice.gov/atr/file/761166/download (accessed 11 November 2022).

[106] Act of 2 July 1890, 51 Cong Ch 647, 26 Stat 209 (codified as amended at 15 USC § 1 ff).

[107] Antitrust Division Manual (n 105).

[108] ibid. The Antitrust Division has five criminal offices that are responsible for conducting criminal investigations and litigation, and some of them also conduct civil merger and non-merger matters. These criminal offices deal with all stages of the enforcement process: investigation, litigation, settlement, and sentencing. They also interact with US Attorneys, State Attorneys General, and other law enforcement agencies.

[109] Ira M Millstein and others, 'Report of the ABA Antitrust Law Section Task Force on the Antitrust Division of the U.S. Department of Justice' (1998) 58(3) Antitrust Law Journal 737, 754.

[110] Congress has challenged merger enforcement policies. See eg Statement of Peter Rodino, 'Oversight and Authorization Hearings into the Policies and Enforcement Record of the Antitrust Division (DOJ): Hearings before the Subcommission on Monopoly and Commercial Law of the House of Comm. on the Judiciary' 99th Cong 2d Sess (26 February 1986).

[111] Antitrust Modernization Commission (n 39) 129.

[112] FTCA §§ 6(b), (f), as amended 15 USC §§ 46(b), (f). The FTC's powers were described by a court as broad investigatory powers that 'can be used for a variety of purposes, including promulgation of new rules, reporting to Congress, disseminating economic knowledge to the public, or … to enable the Commission to better administer the statute over which it has jurisdiction'. See *Ash Grove Cement Co v FTC* 577 F 2d 1368, 1375 (9th Cir 1978).

20 THE US MERGER CONTROL REGIME

instrument of information and publicity, as a clearinghouse for the facts by which both the public mind and the managers of great business undertakings should be guided'.[113] Congress held this view as there was a sense of defeat that the common law approach that had been adopted until then was delivering an inconsistent and unpredictable body of law, so the creation of the FTC was envisaged to progress antitrust inside and outside the courts.[114] What was intended with the creation of the FTC was to run an expert-agency model to try to retrieve the unlimited power to steer merger policy back from the courts.[115] Rather than intending to replace the authority of the Attorney General by establishing the FTC, Congress sought to complement it.[116] In this regard, it has been noted that some law-makers feared that by placing all enforcement powers in the hands of the DOJ the risks of having 'periodic policy defaults' would be higher.[117] Hence, the FTC was empowered to prevent 'unfair methods of competition' under section 5 of the FTCA, through quasi-judicial powers to file complaints, hearings to determine whether violations of the FTCA were occurring, and cease and desist orders to terminate such violations.[118]

Like the Sherman Act and the Clayton Act, the FTCA is afflicted by vague and broad terms;[119] for instance, the statute does not define what constitutes an unfair practice, leaving the entire task of defining and interpreting it to the FTC.[120] Later, in 1938, the Wheeler-Lea Amendment was passed with the key aim of widening the FTC's area of concern by adding the words 'unfair or deceptive acts or practices', clarifying that the Commission can protect consumers directly and through the protection of competition.[121]

---

[113] Daniel A Crane, 'Debunking Humphrey's Executor' (2015) 83 George Washington Law Review 1835, 1859. William E Kovacic, 'The Quality of Appointments and the Capability of the Federal Trade Commission' (1997) 49 Administrative Law Review 915, 919, has noted that the law-makers expected the FCT to be 'unusually expert'.

[114] Crane, 'Debunking Humphrey's Executor' (n 113) 1859, informing that prior to the approval of the FTCA, President Woodrow Wilson expressed his vision that the FTC could 'provide clear rules and direction for business that courts had been incapable of providing'. Crane referred to Woodrow Wilson, 'Address to a Joint Session of Congress on Trusts and Monopolies' *American Presidency Project* (20 January 1914), archived at https://perma.cc/683G-WWVS.

[115] Among the discussions within Congress in relation to the creation of the FTC, Senator Albert Cummins indicated: '[I] would rather take my chance with a commission at all times under the power of Congress, at all times under the eye of the people ... than ... upon the abstract propositions, even though they be full of importance, argued in the comparative seclusion of the courts.' See Federal Trade Commission, 63d Cong, 3d Sess, in 51 Cong Rec 13047 (1914).

[116] Daniel Crane has noted that: 'The FTC was designed as a complement to, not as a substitute for, the Justice Department. The FTC Act's legislative history evidence a Congressional intent that "[f]ar from being regarded as a rival of the Justice Department ... the [FTC] was envisioned as an aid to them". See Crane, 'The Institutional Structure' (n 7) 130.

[117] William E Kovacic, 'Downsizing Antitrust: Is it Time to End Dual Federal Enforcement?' (1996) 41(3) Antitrust Bulletin 505, 523.

[118] 15 USC § 45, 45(a).

[119] William L Wilkie, 'Special Section Commemorating the 100th Anniversary of the U.S. Federal Trade Commission' (2014) 33(2) Journal of Public Policy & Marketing 188.

[120] The Committee, which was set up to revise the need for a new legislation, indicated the reason for omitting a narrow definition as follows: 'The committee gave careful consideration to the question as to whether it would attempt to define the many and variable unfair practices which prevail in commerce and to forbid [them] or whether it would, by a general declaration condemning unfair practices, leave it to the commission to determine what practices were unfair. It concluded that the latter course would be the better, for the reason ... that there were too many unfair practices to define, and after writing 20 of them into the law it would be quite possible to invent others.' See Federal Trade Commission, S Rep No 597, 63d Cong, 2d Sess 13 (1914).

[121] 52 Stat 111 codified as amended at 15 USC §§ 41–58. The Wheeler-Lea Act added the words 'unfair or deceptive acts or practices' to the language of s 5(a)(6), 15 USC § 45 (a)(6) (1970).

1.4 INSTITUTIONAL SETTING 21

The FTC is composed of five Commissioners, and no more than three of them can be from the same political party. The President nominates the Commissioners, and the Senate confirms their nominations for alternate seven-year terms. It is possible that the Commissioners have been appointed by different presidential administrations,[122] which reflects the intention to ensure a degree of independence. The FTC has three main Bureaus, Competition, Consumer Protection, and Economics.[123] As this chapter has described in section 1.4.2 above, the FTC enjoys the authority to interpret and pro-scribe 'unfair methods of competition'. It is also important to note that the FTC has also received the authority to collect confidential business information and carry out industry studies,[124] and that section 6 of the FTCA granted the FTC broad investiga-tory powers, described as the power '[f]rom time to time to ... to make rules and re-gulations for the purpose of carrying out the provisions'.[125] In 1962, the FTC adopted a methodology describing the enforcement of its trade regulation rules, which, instead of showing that the act was an unfair trade practice, as specified by the FTCA, stated that it would only require proof that the act violated the rule.[126] Although it is beyond the scope of this book to assess whether the FTC has exhausted its rule-making powers, it is worth mentioning that when, on occasion, the FTC has tried to issue substantive rules, it has not always received Congress support[127] and, most importantly, since the District Court decision in *National Petroleum Refiners Association v FTC*, where it was declared that the FTC does not have statutory authority to promulgate substantive rules in connection with its investigatory responsibilities, the FTC's rule-making attempts have decreased to almost none.[128] Therefore, a cluster of scholars have claimed that the Commission has neglected the use of such a power to ascertain positively what conduct or practices constitute an 'unfair method of competition', by relying heavily on adjudi-cation instead.[129] Yet, even if the FTC is still trying to exercise its rule-making power,

---

[122] Greene (n 38) 1052.

[123] Wilkie (n 119).

[124] FTCA § 6(b) as amended 15 USC § 45(a).

[125] 15 USC § 46(g); 60 Stat 237 (1946) codified as amended in various sections of Title 5. The FTC's rule-making authority has been supported under the argument that the world 'rules' in section 6(g) is properly defined as in the Administrative Procedure Act (APA): '[T]he whole or part of an agency statement of general or particular applic-ability and future effect designed to implement, interpret, or prescribe law or policy.' See 5 USC § 551(4) (1970). APA demands that rule-makers give notice of the proposed rule including: '(1) a statement of the time, place, and nature of public rule making proceedings; (2) reference to the legal authority under which the rule is proposed; and (3) either the terms or substance of the proposed rule or a description of the subjects and issues involved.' See 5 USC § 553 (b)(1)–(3). Also, for a good discussion about the rule-making authority, see Rohit Chopra and Lina Khan, 'The Case for "Unfair Methods of Competition" Rulemaking' (2020) 87(2) The University of Chicago Law Review 357, 366–79.

[126] 27 FR 4609 (1962). See 16 CFR §§ 1.11.16 (1972).

[127] 'Denial of FTC Rulemaking Powers' (1973) 1 Duke Law Journal 336, 343.

[128] 340 F Supp 1343 (DDC 1972), noted in (1973) 18 S Dakota Law Review 243.

[129] Jan M Rybnicek and Joshua D Wright, 'Defining Section 5 of the FTC Act: The Failure of the Common Law Method and the Case for Formal Agency Guidelines' (2014) 21 George Mason Law Review 1287, 1304; David L Shapiro, 'The Choice of Rulemaking or Adjudication in the Development of Administrative Policy' (1965) 78 Harvard Law Review 921; Richard K Berg, 'Re-examining Policy Procedures: The Choice Between Rulemaking & Adjudication' (1986) 38 Admin Law Review 149; 'Report of the American Bar Association Section of Antitrust Law Special Committee to Study the Role of the Federal Trade Commission' (1989) 58 Antitrust Law Journal, 37th Annual Spring Meeting: Part I (5–7 April 1989) 43, 89.

22   THE US MERGER CONTROL REGIME

the heated controversy about its authority to promulgate not just procedural but substantive rules remains current.

1.4.3 The State Authorities

The US States have the authority to enforce their own antitrust laws.[130] Indeed, it has been reported that by the time the Sherman Act was enacted in 1890, twenty-six states had an antitrust statutes that resembled sections 1 and 2 of the Sherman Act and, as declared by Senator Sherman, the act that bears his name was intended 'to supplement the enforcement of' state laws.[131] Thus, the Clayton Act initially permitted State Attorneys General to pursue their own injunctive federal antitrust claims and in 1976 Congress also authorized them to file federal *parens patriae* suits on behalf of citizens seeking damages caused by violations of the Sherman Act, and requested the DOJ to share investigative information with the State Attorneys General.[132] Also in 1976, the Crime Control Act provided states with financial assistance to investigate and enforce the federal antitrust laws.[133] It is important to note that when states pass their own antitrust laws they cannot make lawful a conduct that Congress has declared unlawful, but they can do the opposite; that is to say, they can proscribe a conduct that has not been considered illicit by Congress.[134] Another relevant aspect is that states are entitled to enforce state antitrust laws even if the antitrust federal agencies have decided not to proceed.[135] Likewise, states, through the National Association of Attorneys General (NAAG), have adopted their own respective guidelines.[136] In comparing states' guidelines with the guidelines adopted by the antitrust federal agencies, it can be seen that states tend to define the relevant market more narrowly, disregard efficiencies as a meaningful tool capable of counterbalancing market concentration, and minimize the

[130] See Douglas H Ginsburg, 'Comparing Antitrust Enforcement in the United States and Europe' (2005) 1(3) Journal of Competition Law and Economics 427, 429, doi:10.1093/joclec/nhi017.

[131] See 21 Cong Rec 2457 (1890). Many state statutes provide that they need to be interpreted consistently with federal precedent, see Barry Hawk and Laraine Laudati, 'Antitrust Federalism in the United States and Decentralization of Competition Law Enforcement in the European Union: A Comparison' (1996) 20 Fordham International Law Journal 18, 21.

[132] 15 USC §§ 26; 15 USC §§15c–h; The Hart-Scott-Rodino Act of 1976. It has been reported that fifty states and the District of Columbia are authorized to bring *parens patriae* lawsuits; see Antitrust Modernization Commission (n 39) 127. State statutes are reprinted in 6 Trade Reg Rep (CCH) paras 30,202,03-35,585 (2003). The *parens patriae* doctrine or 'parent of the country' was transplanted from England, referring to the 'king's power as guardian of persons under legal disabilities to act for themselves'. See Jack Ratliff, 'Parens Patriae: An Overview' (2000) 74 Tulane Law Review 1847. For a description of the history and implementation of the statutory *parens patriae* authority, see Susan Beth Farmer, 'More Lessons from the Laboratories: Cy Press Distributions in Parens Patriae Antitrust Actions Brought by State Attorneys General' (1999) 68 Fordham Law Review 361, 376–91.

[133] Crime Control Act of 1976, Pub L No 94-503, § 116, 90 Stat 2407, 2415 (codified as amended at 42 USC §§ 3701-96c (2000)). Folsom has informed that with the seed money states established antitrust divisions or units, see Ralph H Folsom, 'State Antitrust Remedies: Lessons from the Laboratories' (1990) 35 Antitrust Bulletin 941, 950, 955.

[134] Douglas H Ginsburg, 'Comparing Antitrust Enforcement in the United States and Europe' (2005) 1(3) Journal of Competition Law and Economics 427, 430.

[135] Antitrust Modernization Commission (n 39) 127.

[136] See National Association of Attorneys General, *NAAG Vertical Restraint Guidelines* § 2.1, Antitrust & Trade Reg Rep 49 (BNA) No 1243, 996 (5 December 1985); *NAAG Horizontal Merger Guidelines* 4 Trade Reg Rep (CCH) para 13,405 (1987).

importance of entry into the market as a key element in the merger assessment.[137] It has also been noticed that when looking at mergers, states try to coordinate amongst themselves, identifying which state could lead the merger review process,[138] and are more inclined to give more prevalence to public interest considerations such as job losses or the protection of small businesses.[139]

Hence, the antitrust enforcement process can start with an action under federal or state law, or both. Specifically, under the *parens patriae* doctrine State Attorneys General may pursue direct damages on behalf of natural persons and injunctive relief under federal law.[140] According to states' provisions, State Attorneys General can file civil or criminal suits, and may have the authority to recover indirect damages on behalf of consumers and the state.[141] In addition, all State Attorneys General can seek direct damages on behalf of state agencies.[142] Unlike the State Attorneys General, the DOJ does not have the authority to recover damages on behalf of parties who have suffered a loss.[143] Importantly, when seeking to block a merger before a federal court, states need to observe the federal antitrust statutes and the jurisprudence.[144]

1.4.4 Private Plaintiffs

As discussed above, states have jurisdiction to enact their own antitrust statutes and State Attorneys General can enforce them. This enforcement authority is shared with private plaintiffs such as businesses and consumers.[145] States and private plaintiffs are both non-federal institutions that are part of the US antitrust enforcement regime.[146] A private party is entitled to challenge a merger under section 7 of the Clayton Act[147] even if the antitrust federal agency has decided to clear the deal. The involvement of private parties in merger enforcement was so common, that before the enactment of

---

[137] Douglas H Ginsburg and Scott H Angstreich, 'Multinational Merger Review: Lessons from Our Federalism' (2000) 68 Antitrust Law Journal 219, 228.

[138] Eleanor M Fox, 'Can We Control Merger Control? An Experiment' in Sebastian O'Meara (ed), *Policy Directions for Global Merger Review* (Global Forum for Competition and Trade Policy 1998). In 1983, the National Association of Attorneys General Antitrust Committee established the Multistate Antitrust Task Force with the aim of drafting guidelines and *amicus* briefs and to coordinate multistate investigations and litigation. See ABA Section of Antitrust, *Antitrust Law Developments* (5th edn, American Bar Association 2002) 824–25.

[139] Jonathan Rose, 'State Antitrust Enforcement, Mergers, and Politics' (1994) 41 Wayne Law Review 71, 87–103; David A Zimmerman, 'Why State Attorneys General Should Have a Limited Role in Enforcing the Federal Antitrust Law of Mergers' (1999) 48 Emory Law Journal 337, 349–59; Kevin J O'Connor, 'Federalist Lessons for International Antitrust Convergence' (2002) 70(2) Antitrust Law Journal 413, 422–23.

[140] See *Pennsylvania v Playmobil USA Inc* 1995-2 Trade Cas (CCH) 71,215 (MD Pa 1995).

[141] See ABA Section of Antitrust Law, *Antitrust Law Developments*, vol IV (4th edn, American Bar Association, 1997) 743.

[142] ibid.

[143] ibid 687–724.

[144] See *California v American Stores Co* 495 US 271 (1990).

[145] ABA Section of Antitrust Law, *State Antitrust Practices and Statutes* (American Bar Association 1990) 44–53. In any antitrust case pending in a federal court, the Antitrust Division has the authority to submit a statement of interest that allows the Attorney General to ask any officer of the DOJ to attend to the interests of the United States. See 28 USC § 517.

[146] See William E Kovacic, 'The Influence of Economics on Antitrust Law' (1992) 30 Economics Inquiry 294, 295.

[147] Matters of standing have been addressed further below.

24 THE US MERGER CONTROL REGIME

the HSR Act, most mergers were civilly litigated; parties tried to exert a fair divestiture remedy and injured parties sought private damages.[148] Nonetheless, this tendency was altered with the enactment of the HSR, which, despite not expressly prohibiting private plaintiffs, brought as an unintended consequence a decline in private merger challenges.[149] This decline resulted from the authority granted to federal agencies to issue second requests for information, which, as will be explained in more detail later, led to a considerable number of mergers being settled, leaving private parties in a position where it was counterproductive to challenge all of them.[150]

Another aspect that had broad implications for private enforcement was the introduction of the doctrine of 'standing'. According to the Supreme Court, a plaintiff bears not just the burden of alleging that they have suffered harm due to illegal conduct, but also of contending and eventually proving that they have suffered an 'antitrust injury, that is to say an injury of the type that the antitrust laws were intended to prevent and that flows from that which makes defendants' acts unlawful,[151] meaning that the plaintiff is able to show harm to 'competition, not competitors'.[152] This requirement has influenced the choice of private parties in challenging mergers.[153] Moreover, Kaplow and Shapiro have explained that under the antitrust injury doctrine, competitors will not challenge mergers frequently because they 'tend to be injured by pro-competitive mergers that lead to lower prices (deemed not to be the sort of injury that the antitrust laws were enacted to prevent).[154] Building on this doctrine, in the *Illinois Brick Co. v Illinois*, the 'indirect purchaser' rule was established, according to which the standing to claim an anti-competitive overcharge rests only on the first entity to pay the overcharge, denying indirect purchasers the possibility of pursuing an action.[155] A couple of other factors have also played an important role in deterring private parties from challenging mergers: the first is the cost of litigation, which could be distributed through a collective action but the complexity which discourages its use; and the second is the risk of retaliation, particularly when an important supplier is one of the merging parties.[156]

The combination of all the above aspects has resulted in an effective hurdle to private enforcement. In particular, the 'antitrust injury' doctrine that instituted the reasoning that sufficient evidence of the plaintiff's injury is compelled to establish the adverse effect of the defendant's conduct on competition and consumers has implied that most

---

[148] See eg *Brunswick Corp v Pueblo Bowl-o-Matt Inc* 429 US 477, 480 (1977).

[149] Crane, 'Antitrust Federalism' (n 7) 55.

[150] ibid 56.

[151] *Brunswick v Pueblo Bowl-O-Mat* (n 148). For an interesting discussion about the 'antitrust injury' doctrine, see Ronald W Davis, 'Standing on Shaky Ground: The Strangely Elusive Doctrine of Antitrust Injury' (2003) 70(3) Antitrust Law Journal 697. See also John E Lopatka and William H Page, 'Antitrust Injury and the Evolution of Antitrust Law' (2002) Antitrust 20; Robert P Taylor, 'Antitrust Standing: Its Growing—or More Accurately—Its Shrinking Dimensions' (1986) 55 Antitrust Law Journal 515; Jonathan M Jacobson and Tracy Greer, 'Twenty-One Years of Antitrust Injury: Down the Alley with Brunswick v. Pueblo Bowl-O-Mat' (1998) 66(2) Antitrust Law Journal 273.

[152] *Brunswick v Pueblo Bowl-O-Mat* (n 148) 488.

[153] See Paul J Stancil, 'Atomism and the Private Merger Challenge' (2005) 78 Temple Law Review 949, 972–74.

[154] Kaplow and Shapiro (n 34) 1158.

[155] *Illinois Brick Co v Illinois* 431 US 720 (1977). See also *Kansas v Utilicorp United Inc* 497 US 199 (1990).

[156] Frankel (n 39) 171.

plaintiffs who fail to demonstrate with sufficiency the alleged harm do not have a chance to win in court.

This section has briefly described the institutional design of the dual enforcement by the federal government: the DOJ and the FTC, sketching the reasons for their creation, composition, and authority over merger review. A similar exercise was undertaken in relation to states that are part of the US antitrust enforcement structure, which are governed by the antitrust federal statutes as well as their own, and have a broad range of powers, from filing civil and criminal proceedings to claiming damages on behalf of third parties. It has also been established that the coercive second request for information and the 'antitrust injury' doctrine have halted private enforcement of section 7 of the Clayton Act. At this point it is necessary to indicate that in addition to the federal and non-federal enforcers with the authority to review mergers, some regulatory agencies also have jurisdiction to assess them in parallel to that of the federal enforcers. However, considering that the main purpose of this book is to examine and compare the concurrent merger assessment between the federal agencies and the regulatory agencies, a separate chapter has been devoted to explaining the institutional setting of each regulator, their respective legal frameworks, and their respective review processes. The next part provides an analysis of the merger review process conducted by the antitrust federal agencies.

1.5 Merger Review Assessment

1.5.1 Procedural Process

It is important to describe at this stage the main steps and requirements of the procedural process before the FTC/DOJ. A similar analysis of the main procedural steps and requirements will be made for each of the sectoral regulators discussed herein. This analysis will provide useful context for the discussion that will follow in this book on the areas of divergence/convergence in the enforcement approach that the two antitrust agencies and the sectoral regulators take.

It has been established that the HSR Act granted responsibility to review mergers to the DOJ and the FTC.[157] Thus, both agencies are competent to assess them and therefore merging parties need to notify both enforcers of their intended deals and do not have the discretion to select the agency they prefer. Given this shared authority, the DOJ and the FTC have developed a so-called 'clearance' procedure aimed at ensuring that just one of them will review the notified transaction.[158] This clearance process implies that one agency requests authority while the other clears the request, and that no information from the merging parties can be demanded until clearance has been

---

[157] Hart-Scott-Rodino Antitrust Improvements Act of 1976 (HSR Act) (Pub L No 94-435).
[158] See ABA Section of Antitrust Law (n 138) 727.

granted.[159] This clearance system has been largely underpinned by the knowledge that each federal agency has on specific industries; for instance, the DOJ has extensive expertise on the airlines and banking sectors, so usually transactions taking place in these industries will be reviewed by it.[160] Usually, clearance is a quick process and, occasionally, when there is a dispute, the agency that is claiming authority signs a memo stating the expertise it enjoys in the sector in which the merging parties are involved; then the dispute is solved by senior members of staff of both agencies. Seldom is a clearance request decided by the chairman of the FTC and the Assistant Attorney General for antitrust.[161]

Since the HSR Act was put into effect, acquisition thresholds have determined which transactions will be captured by the statute.[162] As an illustration, as of 2022, the revised thresholds for merger control filings under the HSR Act require notification when cumulatively one party has assets or sales of at least US$20.2 million (the 2021 threshold was US$18.4 million), the other party has at least US$202 million in assets or sales, and the acquired stock or assets are worth more than US$101 million but no more than US$403.9 million.[163] At the same time, the merging parties may file once there is a letter of intent involving the future transaction and they need to complete the HSR notification form to officially initiate the merger review process.[164] The HSR Act provides the procedure that the federal agencies need to follow once a merger that has met the threshold is notified to them. According to the Act, the federal agencies have thirty calendar days after the notification of the proposed transaction to investigate and resolve whether the merger can proceed or whether a second request for information should be issued.[165] The merging parties will know that their merger can proceed when the federal enforcers choose not to challenge it.[166] This point is relevant as the federal enforcers cannot simply decide to prohibit the merger; rather, it is up to the courts to make such a decision once the agencies have filed an injunction request, as will be explained in more detail below.[167]

Another important implication is that judicial review is only available to correct an agency decision that a merger is anti-competitive (false negative),[168] so a decision of approval would go unchecked (false positive).[169] If a second request is issued, the parties cannot consummate the merger until the agency is satisfied with their compliance with the information request.[170] Some commentators have argued that because the US

---

[159] Antitrust Modernization Commission (n 39) 133.

[160] ABA Section of Antitrust Law (n 103) appendix 9.

[161] The Antitrust Modernization Commission (n 39) 134–36 noted that this clearance process, particularly when it is disputed, can cause significant delays.

[162] HSR is codified as amended at 15 USC § 18a.

[163] See 87 FR 3540-1.

[164] Valentine and De (n 63) 39, describing the HSR form as very simple and easy to complete.

[165] 15 USC § 18a(b), (e).

[166] See 15 USC § 18 a(b)(2) (1994). The federal enforcers normally do not explain why they have decided not to challenge a proposed merger. See Warren S Grimes, 'Transparency in Federal Antitrust Enforcement' (2003) 51 Buffalo Law Review 937.

[167] 15 USC §§ 25, 53.

[168] False positives refer to finding violations of competition law when a conduct is pro-competitive or competitive-neutral.

[169] Frankel (n 39) 172.

[170] 15 USC § 18a (e).

antitrust agencies have just twenty calendar days to make a decision following the parties' full compliance with a second request for information, this deadline has incentivized the demand for vast amounts of information, making the merger process unduly prolonged and expensive.[171] During the investigatory stage, the merging parties usually present their own studies and expert opinions, which are known as 'white papers'.[172] In sum, a notified transaction under the HSR Act can have different outcomes. It can be approved, or in other words, not challenged and in such a case it will not be subject to judicial review; it can be subject to a second request; the parties can enter into negotiations to try to find a remedy capable of overcoming the competition concerns raised by the transaction; it can be challenged—an injunction can be sought from a court to block the merger; or it can be abandoned if the merging parties decide not to progress with it.[173]

A distinctive procedure is followed when the FTC acts under section 5 of the FTCA, which proscribes '[u]nfair methods of competition'. This action takes place through internal administrative litigation, known as the Part III proceedings, before an administrative law judge (ALJ). The procedure starts with an administrative complaint, which requires a 'reason to believe' that an antitrust violation has occurred, which goes to an ALJ, acting like a federal court judge, who will be in charge of an administrative litigation procedure.[174] The decision made by this judge is reviewed by the five FTC Commissioners, who will issue a reasoned opinion that can be directly appealed by the defendant before a federal court of appeal.[175] The FTC may apply for a preliminary or permanent injunction in the federal court.[176]

1.5.2 Substantive Assessment

Merger control in the US is governed by three main statutes: (i) the Sherman Act, whose section 1 prohibits any 'contract, combination ... or conspiracy in restraint of trade'; (ii) section 7 of the Clayton Act, which prohibits acquisitions of stock or assets whose effect 'may be substantially to lessen competition, or to tend to create a monopoly'; and

---

[171] Valentine and De (n 63) 40; James S Venit and William J Kolasky, 'Substantive Convergence and Procedural Dissonance in Merger Review' in Simon J Evenett, Alexander Lehmann, and Benn Steil (eds), 'Antitrust Goes Global: What Future for Transatlantic Cooperation?' (Brookings Institution 2000) 94; Antitrust Modernization Commission (n 39) 152.

[172] Frankel (n 39) 168.

[173] Merging parties usually desist when the chances of success are low or when there are expected delays. It has also been noted by Kaplow and Shapiro (n 34) 1159, that it is difficult to calculate the number of mergers that are not filed because of the same reasons.

[174] See OECD, 'The Standard of Review by Courts in Competition Cases – Note by the United States' (2019) DAF/COMP/WP3/WD(2019)22 4-5 https://www.ftc.gov/system/files/attachments/us-submissions-oecd-2010-present-other-international-competition-fora/standard_of_review_us-oecd.pdf (accessed 23 November 2022), describing that 'the ALJ oversees discovery, makes evidentiary rulings, conducts a trial, renders an initial decision, and drafts a written opinion containing the factual and the legal basis for the decision'.

[175] 15 USC §45(b)-(c); 16 CFR § 3 (2006). The five Commissioners review the legal and factual aspects of the case on a *de novo* basis.

[176] 15 USC § 53(b). The appellate court reviews questions of law *de novo* without interfering with factual determinations of the FTC that are supported by substantial evidence.

28 THE US MERGER CONTROL REGIME

(iii) the FTCA section 5's prohibition on any 'unfair method of competition'. One commonality in the application of any of these three statutes is that the federal enforcers are driven solely by an economic-based approach, in which the incorporation of public considerations is far-fetched. Such an approach is grounded on different aspects. First, none of the statutes contains a public interest clause.[177] Secondly, given the broadness of their wording, the courts have shaped their meaning by stressing the supremacy of the purely economic view, as stated in the *United States v Penn-Olin* merger case.[178] Thirdly, a cluster of academics have supported the notion that competition analysis should embrace only an economic approach, arguing that 'the Sherman Act is not intended to achieve ... broad non-commercial goals'.[179] Both agencies have been influenced by these aspects and, therefore, have decided not to incorporate non-competition considerations in the competition analysis as that, in their words, 'can lead to poor outcomes to the detriment of both businesses and consumers'.[180]

Despite this rigid acceptance of the 'more economic-based approach', there is a growing number of voices postulating more ambitious theories of harm in which public interest merits accommodation in the analysis of mergers. As an illustration, some scholars have presented some evidence that the approval of vertical mergers between insurers and drug suppliers in the US health sector, in which data plays a significant role, has allowed discrimination against those identified as unprofitable, and therefore vulnerable, customers expanding the gap between socio-economic groups.[181] Indeed, President Joe Biden, in his most recent executive order on promoting competition in the American economy, has encouraged the DOJ and the FTC to review their merger guidelines.[182] The effects of monopsony in labour markets has also received great attention,[183] with preliminary findings pointing to a correlation between the text

[177] See Piscitelli (n 38), explaining that Section 7 of the Clayton Act did not provide any guidance about the substantive assessment to be applied in merger control, which has been construed by the jurisprudence of federal courts.

[178] *United States v Penn-Olin Chem Co and Others* 378 US 158, 171 (1964).

[179] Robert H Bork, 'Legislative Intent and the Policy of the Sherman Act' (1966) 9 Journal of Law & Economics 7, 13.

[180] Edith Ramirez, 'Core Competition Agency Principles: Lessons Learned at the FTC' Keynote Address by FTC Chairwoman (22 March 2014) https://www.ftc.gov/system/files/documents/public_statements/314 151/140522abachinakeynote.pdf (accessed 17 November 2022). See also Bill Baer, 'International Antitrust Enforcement: Progress Made; Work to be Done' Keynote Address by DOJ Assistant Attorney General of the Antitrust Division (12 September 2014) https://www.justice.gov/atr/file/517736/download (accessed 17 November 2022), stating that: 'We agree that non-competition factors, such as the pursuit of industrial or domestic policy goals, play no role in sound competition enforcement.'

[181] Theodosia Stavroulaki, 'Mergers that Harm Our Health' (2022) 19(1) Berkeley Business Law Journal 89, 98. Khan and Vaheesan have examined the rising concentration levels in the health care system in the United States indicating that a lenient antitrust approach has created market failures, it has been inadequate to preserve a competitive market and has eventually led to high inequality. See also Lina Khan and Sandeep Vaheesan, 'Market Power and Inequality: The Antitrust Counterrevolution and Its Discontents' (2017) 11 Harvard Law & Policy Review 235, 268.

[182] The White House, 'FACT SHEET: Executive Order on Promoting Competition in the American Economy' Statements and Releases (9 July 2021) https://www.whitehouse.gov/briefing-room/statements-releases/2021/07/09/fact-sheet-executive-order-on-promoting-competition-in-the-american-economy/ (accessed 17 November 2022). The executive order indicates that increased concentration and decreased competition has widened 'racial, income, and wealth inequality'.

[183] In relation to labour markets see José Azar and others, whose study suggests that in concentrated markets the labour market power seems to increase. See José Azar, Ioana Marinescu, Marshall Steinbaum, and Bledi Taska, 'Concentration in US Labor Markets: Evidence from Online Vacancy Data' (2020) 66 Labour Economics 101886. The following studies show a decline in real increases in wages: Lawrence Mishel and Ross Eisenbrey,

of US antitrust law and the enforcement practice with economic inequality, market concentration, and the stagnation of wages.[184] Thus, the number of calls for stricter antitrust enforcement to counter employer monopsony power in labour markets is growing.[185] In line with this research and the enforcement efforts, in September 2020, the FTC announced a revamped 'Merger Retrospective Program' aimed at building on the studies that suggest that mergers create labour market monopsony power and, based on the findings, test whether the antitrust analytical tools used hitherto are sufficient or whether it is necessary to improve them.[186]

Congress has not been unresponsive to this new advent either and recently a significant number of bills have been presented seeking to curb the market power enjoyed by big businesses. An interesting aspect is that with more frequency non-economic factors are invoked to justify the need for those legislative initiatives.[187] While it is still too early to predict whether there will be a departure from the rigorous view that forecloses the possibility of including different facets of public interest in the substantive analysis of mergers carried out by the federal agencies, following the developments in US and EU in relation to enforcement priorities in data markets, and sustainability considerations,[188] it is safe to anticipate that the centrality of a purely economic approach, which has reigned until now, in which predictive rules such as market shares and concentration data are so determinant, might be subject to some adjustments. Until then, the trend of negotiated settlements in merger cases might continue its trajectory, as will be further elaborated below.

'How to Raise Wages: Policies that Work and Policies that Don't' (2015) 45(1) Stetson Law Review 43. See also Efraim Benmelech, Nittai K Bergman, and Hyunseob Kim, 'Strong Employers and Weak Employees: How Does Employer Concentration Affect Wages?' (2022) 57(S) Journal of Human Resources S200; David Autor and others, 'The Fall of the Labor Share and the Rise of Superstar Firms' (2020) 135(2) Quarterly Journal of Economics 645; Wyatt J Brooks and others, 'Exploitation of Labor? Classical Monopsony Power and Labor's Share' (2021) 150 Journal of Development Economics 102627. On policy implications see Suresh Naidu, Eric A Posner, and E Glen Weyl, 'Antitrust Remedies for Labor Market Power' (2018) 132 Harvard Law Review 537; Ioana E Marinescu and Herbert Hovenkamp, 'Anticompetitive Mergers in Labor Markets' (2019) 94 Indiana Law Journal 1.

[184] Amit Zac and others, 'Competition Law and Income Inequality: A Panel Data Econometric Approach' (2021) https://ssrn.com/abstract=3402436.

[185] Eric A Posner and Glen Weyl, *Radical Markets: Uprooting Capitalism and Democracy for a Just Society* (PUP 2018) 200.

[186] Federal Trade Commission, 'FTC's Bureau of Economics to Expand Merger Retrospective Program' (17 September 2020) https://www.ftc.gov/news-events/press-releases/2020/09/ftcs-bureau-economics-expand-merger-retrospective-program (accessed 17 November 2022).

[187] As an illustration, Representative David Cicilline of Rhode Island indicated that the legislative proposals are needed because dominant platforms '[a]re in a unique position to pick winners and losers, destroy small businesses, raise prices on consumers and put folks out of work'. See 'House Lawmakers Release Anti-Monopoly Agenda for "A Stronger Online Economy: Opportunity, Innovation, Choice"' (11 June 2021) https://appliedantitrust.com/00_basic_materials/hipster_antitrust/A-Better-Deal-on-Competition-and-Costs.pdf (accessed 27 October 2023). US Senate Democrats have also stated that: '[l]arge mergers that would harm consumers and workers via higher prices and lower wages should be blocked'. See Policy Statement, Democratic Party, 'A Better Deal: cracking Down on Corporate Monopolies' (24 July 2017) https://www.democrats.senate.gov/imo/media/doc/2017/07/A-Better-Deal-on-Competition-and-Costs-1.pdf (accessed 17 November 2021).

[188] OECD, 'Environmental Considerations in Competition Enforcement' (2021) https://www.oecd.org/daf/competition/environmental-considerations-in-competition-enforcement-2021.pdf; Jurgita Malinauskaite, 'Competition Law and Sustainability: EU and National Perspectives' (2022) 13(5) Journal of European Competition Law & Practice 336.

1.5.3 Settlements

When the federal agencies are confronted with the possibility that a merger is a potential threat to competition, in deciding whether to initiate an enforcement action, they evaluate their chances of having a favourable court decision and the litigation costs.[189] It is also possible that the expected harm might affect a particular geographic or product market.[190] In such cases, the antitrust agencies might find it appropriate to negotiate a remedy that would offset the concerns posed by the transaction without incurring high litigation costs and high levels of uncertainty, allowing the merger to ensue with consent decrees or orders. Nevertheless, it has been indicated that since the enactment of the HSR Act, which introduced an automatic stay triggered by a second request for information, the federal agencies have relied heavily on the negotiation of remedies—which are sometimes unnecessary or unsuitable—that the merging parties choose to accept regardless of the strength of the case.[191] Adding to this point, it has been argued that the agencies have significant negotiating leverage because they know that merging parties cannot bear delays,[192] which has resulted in remedies being imposed that through litigation would be unlikely to be considered.[193] Controversy has arisen with respect to the negotiating power allegedly enjoyed by the agencies, with some claiming that enforcers choose to reconcile making important concessions given the lack of resources, especially and because courts regularly rule against those who bear the burden of proof.[194]

One further consideration in relation to the implications of the use of settlements is that there is an asymmetry of information elicited from the fact that the federal enforcers typically do not release any information or analysis where a negotiated settlement is agreed, giving the agencies the advantage of being able to use the information collected in previous negotiations that the merging parties cannot access.[195] The DOJ needs to observe some obligations when ending a procedure with a consent decree.

---

[189] Frankel (n 39) 168 has referred to these as subsidiary considerations.

[190] Kaplow and Shapiro (n 34) 1159.

[191] Joe Sims and Michael McFalls, 'Negotiated Merger Remedies: How Well Do They Solve Competition Problems' (2001) 69 George Washington Law Review 932, 935–936. Also, a study carried out by Kwoka found that the remedies frequently imposed to mitigate the anti-competitive concerns raised by some mergers did not serve the purpose. See John E Kwoka Jr, 'Does Merger Control Work? A Retrospective on U.S. Enforcement Actions and Merger Outcomes' (2013) 78(3) Antitrust Law Journal 619, 641. Likewise, according to the statistics presented by the DOJ, in the period from 1999 to 2005 a total number of 248 second requests were issued from which 55 resulted in the filing of a complaint, and just four terminated in trial. See Department of Justice, Antitrust Division, Background Information on the 2006 Amendments to the Merger Review Process Initiative 8–9 (14 December 2006) http://usdoj.gov/atr/public/220241.htm (accessed 19 November 2022).

[192] Sims and McFalls (n 191) 938.

[193] ibid 941–42.

[194] Hovenkamp (n 34) 207, 146; Jonathan B Baker and Carl Shapiro, 'Reinvigorating Horizontal Merger Enforcement' in Robert Pitofsky (ed), *How the Chicago School Overshot the Mark: The Effect of Conservative Economic Analysis on U.S. Antitrust* (OUP 2008) 235; Frankel (n 39) 180; Shapiro (n 34) 75, noting that antitrust authorities are cautious in selecting the mergers they challenge because it has been difficult for them to prevail in Court. See also Antitrust Modernization Commission (n 39) 152, noting that filing fees represent a significant part of the federal agencies' budgets.

[195] Grimes (n 166); Sims and McFalls (n 191) 942.

1.5 MERGER REVIEW ASSESSMENT   31

Under the Antitrust Procedures and Penalties Act (the Tunney Act),[196] the DOJ must file a complaint before a federal district court, in which the relevant markets and the theories of harm at stake are described, together with a Competitive Impact Statement and a suggested final judgment, which, after a public comment period, the DOJ will request the court to enter.[197] Yet even if district courts oversee the terms of the consent decrees, the standard of review applied is solely based on the agreement being in the public interest and remedies the alleged harm, lacking the authority to refuse a settlement on aspects of the merger that the DOJ has not found concerning.[198]

Some statistics [can] shed some light on the preferential use of consent decrees by the federal agencies. Since the first consent decree was agreed in 1906, their progressive use shows that by the 1950s the DOJ had settled 87 per cent of all civil antitrust cases, by the 1980s 97 per cent, and by the 1990s 93 per cent.[199] In relation to the FTC, it has been reported that since 1995, 93 per cent of its competition cases have been settled.[200] The fact that many merger cases are concluded with a consent decree after confidential negotiations without records and judicial oversight implies that, in effect, the antitrust agencies are exerting a great influence on merger policy.[201] Thus, as the use of consent agreements means that fewer cases are litigated, courts are deprived of the opportunity to review the enforcement activities of the agencies and to develop the common law through adjudication.[202] Moreover, the extensive use of close negotiations erodes the levels of transparency of the enforcement policies and reduces the levels of predictability amongst the business community.[203] In addition, the extensive use of these remedial options affects the ability of the agencies to develop investigative skills, which are essential when dealing with traditional markets but even more crucial when facing the intricate digital markets.[204] Thus, if the argument that the agencies are inclined to negotiate because of the insufficiency of resources is correct, maybe it is time to fund

---

[196] Antitrust Procedures and Penalties Act (Tunney Act) Pub L No 93-528, 88 Stat 1706 (1974).

[197] OECD (n 174) 5–6.

[198] ibid 6.

[199] See Douglas H Ginsburg and Joshua D Wright, 'Antitrust Settlements: The Culture of Consent' in Nicolas Charbit and others (eds), *William E Kovacic—An Antitrust Tribute: Liber Amicorum*, vol I (Concurrences 2013) 177.

[200] ibid.

[201] See A Douglas Melamed, 'Antitrust: The New Regulation' (1995) 10 Antitrust 13, describing antitrust enforcement as having 'moved markedly along the continuum from the Law Enforcement Model toward the Regulatory Model'. As an illustration, it has been reported that in 2006 just 1.7 per cent of the notified mergers were subject to judicial review. See Rogers (n 1) 25–26. See also Shapiro (n 34) 73, asserting that very few merger cases are litigated and most of them can proceed after agreeing a remedy, usually an asset divestiture; William J Baer and Ronald C Redcay, 'Solving Competition Problems in Merger Control: The Requirements for an Effective Divestiture Remedy' (2001) 69 George Washington Law Review 915, 915 reporting that between 1998–99 a number of 111 mergers were negotiated with a divestiture out of 161 challenged; William Blumenthal, 'Twenty Years of Hart-Scott-Rodino Merger Enforcement' (1997) 65 Antitrust Law Journal 813, 821, suggesting a 'dissonance over whether the agencies are really law enforcers or regulators in the world as it has evolved in the wake of the [HSR] Act'.

[202] Kovacic (n 117) 516.

[203] Kovacic argues that the expanded use of consent decrees magnifies the discretion of the enforcement agencies (ibid 537–38).

[204] See Ginsburg and Wright (n 199) 181.

32 THE US MERGER CONTROL REGIME

them properly,[205] as they bear the burden of proof before the courts; the next section will dig deeper into the matter.

1.5.4 Judicial Review

Contrary to the ample discretion that the antitrust agencies have to approve mergers or to accept remedies, they need judicial authorization to block a merger. In seeking a federal court order to prohibit a merger that may substantially reduce competition, the agencies need to file an injunction, which can be permanent or preliminary. When a preliminary injunction is granted, that means that a merger cannot be consummated until a final decision is made, but if the agency fails to secure the injunction, that provokes different outcomes for each agency: (i) for the DOJ it signifies that the transaction can move forward and no further litigation is expected, and (ii) for the FTC it indicates that the transaction can be completed but litigation can continue until administrative litigation through the Part III proceedings is exhausted (that often takes one year).[206] Here it is important to clarify that even if the FTC is entitled to request preliminary and permanent injunctions concurrently, often, if not always, the agency only seeks a preliminary injunction before the federal district court given that the Commission has the possibility to litigate the case afterwards. By contrast, the DOJ usually pursues preliminary and permanent injunctions concurrently, which, if granted, suggests that the merging parties might abandon the deal, but, if denied, clearly indicates that the transaction can be consummated without further litigation (unless the DOJ appeals, which is unlikely).[207] In practice, when the DOJ files a preliminary injunction, a trial is scheduled where a hearing for both the preliminary and permanent injunctions takes place.[208] As has been indicated, the merging parties cannot choose the federal enforcer of their preference, which has significant implications for the success of a deal. This is, if the transaction is reviewed by the DOJ and the agency fails to obtain an injunction, then the merging parties can almost automatically consummate the deal. The same is not true for those merging parties whose transaction is reviewed by the FTC: even if

---

[205] In June 2021, a bill was presented to Congress by the Republicans Representatives Mike Lee and Chuck Grassley that suggests transferring the FTC antitrust authority to the DOJ and increasing the budget of the DOJ to US$600 million. See House of Representatives, *Tougher Enforcement Against Monopolist Act (TEAM Act)* (2021) https://www.lee.senate.gov/services/files/23028e91-a982-43d0-9324-f6849c7522fc (accessed 19 November 2022). Another bill, the Merger Filing Fee Modernization Act, was presented to Congress proposing to raise antitrust enforcement resources by increasing pre-merger filing fees. See House of Representatives, *Merger Filing Fee Modernization Act* (2021) https://cicilline.house.gov/sites/cicilline.house.gov/files/documents/Merger%20 Filing%20Fee%20Modernization%20Act%20of%202021%20-%20Bill%20Text%20%281%29.pdf (accessed 19 November 2022).

[206] See Antitrust Modernization Commission (n 39) 130 fns 62–63. Part III proceedings have been explained earlier in the section explaining the procedural process under Merger review assessment.

[207] See Antitrust Modernization Commission (n 39) 130 fns 62–63. The DOJ seeks injunction based on s 15 of the Clayton Act. See also Kirkwood and Zerbe reporting that in fifteen years since the publication of the 1992 *Merger Guidelines* there have been just six appellate merger decisions. John B Kirkwood and Richard O Zerbe, 'The Path to Profitability: Reinvigorating the Neglected Phase of Merger Analysis' (2009) 17(1) George Mason Law Review 39.

[208] See Antitrust Modernization Commission (n 39) 149.

a preliminary injunction has been denied, the merging parties need to face administrative litigation; the deal can be terminated up until a final decision is made but there remains the risk of having a prohibition decision.

Further differences are present in the judicial review process depending on the federal agency that is requesting an injunction. For instance, the DOJ must demonstrate that the merger would violate section 7 of the Clayton Act by a preponderance of evidence, which indicates that the agency needs to show that it is reasonable to expect that the deal would cause anti-competitive harm.[209] In other words, the DOJ has 'the burden of proving a violation of section 7 by a preponderance of the evidence'.[210] By contrast, the FTC only needs to show that there are considerable inquiries that deserve litigation to obtain a preliminary injunction.[211] Another issue that seems to be less recurrent and perhaps more debatable is that when the burden of proof shifts to the merging parties, especially when the FTC oversees the merger review, they carry the task of providing significant evidence about industry conditions, technical barriers, and past entry patterns, given that the FTC has not sufficiently defined the relevant market, as indicated earlier.[212]

The general district court judges, besides deciding on any motion to dismiss the complaint, also grant subpoenas for documents and sworn testimony, and the cross-examination of the parties' witnesses.[213] Here it is important to indicate that the federal agencies have also the authority to seek access to documents and testimony from witnesses, suspects, and targets under a civil investigative demand (CID), which is a form of administrative subpoena but less demanding, and available just in support of civil charges, that are not subject to court approval unless the affected party filed a 'motion to quash', alleging that the scope of the CID is disproportionately burdensome and very difficult to satisfy.[214] Once the district court has issued a final decision, the merging parties and the antitrust agencies can appeal to the appellate court within the circuit

---

[209] James Rill and Jaimee Lederman, 'Evidence in Judicial Review of U.S. Federal Trade Commission and U.S. Department of Justice Merger Cases' in Claus-Dieter Ehlermann and Mel Marquis (eds), *European Competition Law Annual 2009* (Hart Publishing 2011) 601.

[210] *United States v Oracle Corp* 331 F Supp 2d 1098, 1109 (ND Cal 2004); *United States v Sungard Data Systems Inc* 172 F Supp 2d 172, 180 (DDC 2001).

[211] Rill and Lederman (n 209) 603, fn 4, describing that the courts have recognized that it was the Congress desire to provide the FTC with a different standard of review governing their actions as the traditional standard was not 'appropriate for the implementation of a federal statute by an independent regulatory agency where the standards of the public interest measure the propriety and the need for injunctive relief' instead the following standard was introduced: 'whether the FTC raises questions that are so serious, substantial, difficult, and doubtful as to make them fair ground for through investigation'.

[212] See *United States v Baker Hughes Inc* (n 39) 982–83, stating that: 'By showing that a transaction will lead to undue concentration in the market for a particular product in a particular geographic area, the government establishes a presumption that the transaction will substantially lessen competition. The burden of producing evidence to rebut this presumption then shifts to the defendant. If the defendant successfully rebuts the presumption, the burden of producing additional evidence of anticompetitive effect shifts to the government, and mergers with the ultimate burden of persuasion, which remains with the government at all times.' See also Rill and Lederman (n 209) 601, fn 11.

[213] OECD (n 174) 2.

[214] See Douglas H Ginsburg and Joshua D Wright, 'Antitrust Settlements: The Culture of Consent' (2013) George Mason University Law and Economics, Research Paper Series 13–18, 8 at 15 (2013). See also Nick Oberheiden, 'Seven Critical Steps to Follow if You Receive a Civil Investigative Demand' *The National Law Review* (25 March 2021) https://www.natlawreview.com/article/seven-critical-steps-to-follow-if-you-receive-civil-investigative-demand (accessed 26 November 2022).

34 THE US MERGER CONTROL REGIME

of that district court, under a *de novo* standard that means that no deference is given to the district court.[215] The US Supreme Court has the authority to review the appellate court's decision, which, following a petition from the interested parties, will be heard if the case involves matters of the utmost relevance.[216] Despite the important role played by courts in merger enforcement, their involvement is scant given the very few deals that are subject to enforcement action.[217]

1.6 Concluding Remarks

This chapter has discussed the origins and development of merger control assessment in the US. The chapter elaborated on the breadth and vagueness of the Clayton Act, arguing that the merger guidelines adopted by the federal antitrust agencies have tried to overcome this issue. A central feature that emerges from this chapter is that there is a clash between the aims of the antitrust enforcers, reflected in their merger guidelines, and those of other policy-makers. Further, it has illustrated the various enforcement institutions and assessment processes. The main lesson we draw is that the shared jurisdiction amongst the DOJ, the FTC, and State Attorneys General is a very complex structure that merging parties need to navigate.

As we shall see in the following chapters, the presence of sectoral regulators applying divergent standards to the antitrust agencies adds to the complexity of the merger review process. The next chapter will focus on the assessment of the implications of a transaction for national security and will discuss the scope of the Committee on Foreign Investment in the US (CFIUS), as well as its enforcement record.

---

[215] OECD (n 174) 3, 4, 7. At the appellate level, the DOJ Antitrust Division can intervene as *amicus curiae* (a friend of the court).

[216] ibid 4.

[217] As an illustration, in 2017, a total number of 2,052 transactions were notified, of which 51 were investigated in-depth and 21 were subject to an enforcement action. See Shapiro (n 34) 73.

2

National Security Assessment

2.1 Geopolitical Developments

As the multilateral approach to international trade has lost its appeal in recent years, foreign direct investments (FDIs) in strategic industries or companies are increasingly subject to non-competition scrutiny based on public interest considerations.[1] One of the public interest considerations is that of national security, on which this chapter will now focus.

While such considerations are not new to merger control, their potential to introduce or complement wider industrial policy or other priorities that are unrelated to competition law has brought them back to prominence in many jurisdictions across the globe. This trend is visible not only in developing economies, which have traditionally been more prone to protectionism,[2] but also in the historical proponents of free and open market economy such as the United States and the European Union.

US law generally does not restrict foreign ownership of, or investment in, US companies.[3] However, cross-border mergers may require not only an antitrust review but also a review by the Committee for Foreign Investment in the US (CFIUS), to assess if they are harmful to national interests or national security.[4]

Notwithstanding that US policy has been open to FDIs, there have been many cases over the last forty years where the attempts by foreign companies to invest have been assessed with caution by the CFIUS in relation to the impact of these transactions on national security, a concept as ambiguous as, if not more, than the impact of the transaction on competition.[5]

---

[1] This chapter draws from Ioannis Kokkoris, 'Assessment of National Security Concerns in the Acquisition of U.S. and U.K. Assets' (2022) 12 Journal of National Security Law and Policy 349 https://jnslp.com/2022/02/19/assessment-of-national-security-concerns-in-the-acquisition-of-u-s-and-u-k-assets/ (accessed 15 November 2022)

[2] cf eg MOFCOMS's assessment of Samsung/Seagate http://english.mofcom.gov.cn/article/policyrelease/buwei/201510/20151001148014.shtml (accessed 15 November 2022); Western Digital/Hitachi http://english.mofcom.gov.cn/article/policyrelease/buwei/201510/20151001148009.shtml (accessed 15 November 2022); Russian FAS assessment of Bayer/Monsanto https://en.fas.gov.ru/press-center/news/detail.html?id=52952 (accessed 15 November 2022).

[3] Marvin Goldman, 'United States: Doing Business in the USA: Regulation of Foreign Investment' *Mondaq* (20 December 2006) http://www.mondaq.com/unitedstates/x/45120/Compliance/Doing+Business+In+The+USA+Regulation+Of+Foreign+Investment (accessed 9 November 2022).

[4] See US Department of the Treasury, 'CFIUS Laws and Guidance' https://home.treasury.gov/policy-issues/international/the-committee-on-foreign-investment-in-the-united-states-cfius/cfius-laws-and-guidance (accessed 9 November 2022): 'CFIUS operates pursuant to section 721 of the Defence Production Act of 1950, as amended (section 721), and as implemented by Executive Order 11858, as amended, and the regulations at chapter VIII of title 31 of the Code of Federal Regulations ... The authority of the President to suspend or prohibit certain transactions was initially provided by the addition of section 721 to the Defence Production Act of 1950 by a 1988 amendment commonly known as the Exon-Florio amendment.'

[5] The high degree of difficulty inherent to a competition assessment coupled with the uncertainty linked to a future-oriented exercise (prognosis) is undeniable.

36 NATIONAL SECURITY ASSESSMENT

The chapter will discuss the boundaries of US merger control set by national security concerns, as these have been exemplified in the decisional practice of the competent authorities. The chapter will first discuss the concept of national security and will then present an overview of the existing legal framework for considering national security when reviewing mergers and acquisitions in strategic industries or companies, as these are proscribed in the legislation. The chapter will provide a critical perspective of the structure of the CFIUS, its enforcement record, and the approach the CFIUS takes in assessing national security concerns. The analysis will then turn to the main precedents where issues of national security were raised and will discuss how the CFIUS and the President of the US assess such transactions from a national security angle and any lessons that can be drawn for the future enforcement trend of the CFIUS.

2.2 Concept of National Security

According to the Exon-Florio amendment (Exon-Florio),[6] which codified the process the CFIUS uses to review foreign investment transactions, 'the term "national security" shall be construed so as to include those issues relating to "homeland security", including its application to critical infrastructure'. The latter term in this definition implies 'systems and assets, whether physical or virtual, so vital to the United States that the incapacity or destruction of such systems or assets would have a debilitating impact on national security'. However, the scope of such a scenario has never been precisely defined since national security considerations are not listed, and thus are currently subject to different interpretations even within Congress.[7] Instead of offering a clear-cut definition, the law regulating foreign investments in the US defines 'national security sensitive industries' as those that implicate 'critical infrastructure', 'critical technology', 'critical resources', and the presence of any other factors the executive branch deems appropriate.[8] Such an open-ended and broad definition results in ambiguity and legal uncertainty, and grants political actors the ability to block proposed transactions under the pretence of national security concerns.

The lack of transparency and certainty related to the notion of national security that is observed in the US regulatory regime is a common finding amongst national security regimes globally, with different jurisdictions adopting a different degree of transparency and certainty.[9] It is understandable that the concept of national security needs to

---

[6] 50 USC 4565. The actual introduction of national security into the US regime came a few years before, on 7 May 1975, when the CFIUS was established by Executive Order 11858, 40 FR 20263.

[7] The Foreign Investment and National Security Act of 2007 (FINSA) tried to fill the gap by including threats to homeland security and critical infrastructure as part of the definition of national security. 50 USC 4565(a)(5).

[8] Chase Kaniecki and others, 'Foreign Investment Review: USA' in 'Getting the Deal Through' *Lexology* (2023) https://www.clearygottlieb.com/-/media/files/2023-foreign-investment-review---usa.pdf (accessed 30 April 2023).

[9] For a comparative perspective of the approach different jurisdictions follow in assessing national security cf Ioannis Kokkoris, *National Security Considerations in Assessing FDI and Its Relevance for Merger Control* (OUP 2023).

have some vagueness in order to allow governments quickly to adapt the enforcement approach to the developing national security priorities.

The Foreign Investment Risk Review Modernization Act of 2018 (FIRRMA) has tried to address some of the lack of transparency and certainty by providing some examples of businesses that involve national security considerations, that is, for 'critical technology' (defence articles, defence services, nuclear-related facilities), for 'critical infrastructure' (telecoms, power, oil and gas, water, finance), and for 'sensitive personal data' (health data, geo location, biometric enrolment, etc.).

After assessing how the notion of national security is described in the US regulatory framework, this chapter turns its focus onto the CFIUS and will discuss in detail the structure of the CFIUS, and the main legislative texts and the process that the CFIUS follows in assessing national security concerns. This will lay the groundwork to focus next on the enforcement record of the CFIUS.

2.3 Committee on Foreign Investment in the US (CFIUS)

2.3.1 Composition and Legislation

The CFIUS, established by Executive Order 11858 in 1975,[10] is an interagency body, which consists of nine cabinet members, comprising the Departments of the treasury (chair), justice, homeland security, commerce, defence, state, energy, and the Offices of the US Trade Representative, and Science & Technology Policy.[11] The Secretary of Labor and the Director of National Intelligence (DNI) serve as ex officio members.[12] Notices to the CFIUS for the assessment of transactions are received by the director of the Office of Investment Review and Investigation in the Department of the Treasury.[13]

The 1975 executive order added five executive office members to the CFIUS in order to 'observe and, as appropriate, participate in and report to the President':[14] the director of the Office of Management and Budget; the chairman of the Council of Economic Advisors; the assistant to the President for National Security Affairs; the assistant to the President for Economic Policy; and the assistant to the President for Homeland Security and Counterterrorism. The President can also appoint members on a temporary basis to the Committee.[15]

The law 'requires CFIUS to review all "covered" foreign investment transactions to determine whether the transaction threatens to impair the national security, or the

---

[10] Executive Order 11858, 40 FR 20263 (7 May 1975).

[11] US Department of the Treasury, 'CFIUS Overview' https://home.treasury.gov/policy-issues/international/the-committee-on-foreign-investment-in-the-united-states-cfius/cfius-overview (accessed 9 November 2022).

[12] Congressional Research Service, 'The Committee on Foreign Investment in the United States (CFIUS)' RL33388 (26 February 2020)10 https://crsreports.congress.gov/product/pdf/RL/RL33388 (accessed 9 November 2022).

[13] US Department of the Treasury (n 11).

[14] This refers to the President of the United States.

[15] Congressional Research Service (n 12) 24.

38 NATIONAL SECURITY ASSESSMENT

foreign entity is controlled by a foreign government, or it would result in control of any "critical infrastructure that could impair national security".[16] A 'covered transaction' is defined as 'any merger, acquisition, or takeover ... by or with any foreign person which could result in foreign control of any person engaged in interstate commerce in the United States'.[17] Transactions that lead to a smaller than 7 per cent shareholding, bought on a stock exchange or other open market, and which are aimed at being merely a passive investment[18] can be excluded from the CFIUS review.

The CFIUS is required on an annual basis[19] to assess whether there is credible evidence of: (i) a coordinated strategy by one or more countries to acquire US companies involved in research, development, or production of 'critical technologies'; or (ii) industrial espionage activities assisted by foreign governments against US companies aimed at obtaining commercial secrets related to such critical technologies.[20]

President Trump in 2018 enacted the FIRRMA into law,[21] which broadened the scope of the CFIUS by explicitly adding four new types of 'covered transactions':

(i) a purchase, lease, or concession by or to a foreign person of real estate located in proximity to sensitive government facilities;

(ii) 'other investments' in certain US businesses that afford a foreign person access to material non-public technical information in the possession of the US business, membership on the board of directors, or other decision-making rights, other than through voting of shares;

(iii) any change in a foreign investor's rights resulting in foreign control of a US business or an 'other investment' in certain US businesses; and

(iv) any other transaction, transfer, agreement, or arrangement designed to circumvent CFIUS jurisdiction.

The amendments brought in by the FIRRMA have been called 'the most substantial changes to the CFIUS to have come with the Congress and the White House working in unison'.[22]

The authority of the President to suspend or prohibit certain transactions was initially provided by the addition of the Exon-Florio amendment in 1988, which was

---

[16] ibid.

[17] 50 USC App 2170(a)(3).

[18] See 31 CFR § 800.243. The term 'passive investment' denotes an investment strategy where the investor does not seek an active management/control status in the company where it holds the shareholding. David Easley and others, 'The Active World of Passive Investing' (2021) 25(5) Review of Finance 1433 https://www.clm.com/the-expanding-scope-of-cfiuss-jurisdiction-and-mandatory-reporting/.

[19] Through its Annual Report issued to the Congress.

[20] CFIUS, 'Annual Report to Congress' (CY 2015) 27–31 https://home.treasury.gov/system/files/206/Unclassified-CFIUS-Annual-Report-report-period-CY-2015.pdf (accessed 15 September 2023). The 2015 report concluded that there is a high likelihood of espionage activity but, given the report's unclassified nature, declines to provide an assessment of whether a 'coordinated strategy' exists.

[21] Effective since 13 August 2018.

[22] Harry G Broadman, 'U.S. Foreign Investment Policy Gets a Tougher but More Transparent CFIUS' Forbes (4 January 2019) https://www.forbes.com/sites/harrybroadman/2019/01/04/u-s-foreign-investment-policy-gets-a-tougher-but-more-transparent-cfius (accessed 15 November 2022).

2.3 COMMITTEE ON FOREIGN INVESTMENT IN THE US (CFIUS)   39

substantially revised by FINSA in 2007[23] and by the FIRRMA in 2018. Moreover, the FIRRMA also introduced a relevant change, since henceforth it is permitted to share

> [i]nformation important to the national security analysis or actions of the Committee [CFIUS] to any domestic governmental entity, or to any foreign governmental entity of a United States ally or partner, under the exclusive direction and authorization of the chairperson, only to the extent necessary for national security purposes, and subject to appropriate confidentiality and classification requirements.[24]

The disclosure of information appears to be relatively wide since the FIRRMA states that information sharing could be to any domestic or foreign 'governmental entity of a United States ally or partner'. The definitions of 'ally' and 'partner' have not been included either in the FIRRMA or in any other legislative text.

As the chapter analyses in the following sections, the CFIUS assessment process is not impervious to the political agenda of the US administration. However, there are commentators who argue that the CFIUS assessment process in principle seems to be isolated from politics,[25] as the CFIUS never discloses whether a transaction is pending review, not even in cases where the parties disclose this information to the press. The POTUS is entitled to be the decision-maker on the approval of concentrations—when the CFIUS delegates such decision-making to the POTUS.

2.3.2 Filing Instructions and Process Overview

The regulations governing the CFIUS review process[26] were wholly revised by the Final Rule published by the Department of the Treasury, which became effective on 22 December 2008.[27]

Over the years, the CFIUS process evolved and currently includes an informal stage with no deadline that comprises an unofficial CFIUS determination prior to the formal filing.[28] The parties to a transaction are encouraged to file a draft notice and other appropriate documents describing the transaction. This informal review, which is not subject to a binding timetable and can last for a significant length of time, serves the interests of the CFIUS (which manages to achieve a better understanding of the transaction), as well as the companies involved in the proposed transaction. It is worth noting that Treasury Department officials have acknowledged that this informal contact enabled 'CFIUS staff to identify potential issues before the review process formally

---

[23] Effective since 24 October 2007.

[24] 50 USC 4565(c)(2)(C).

[25] Neal Wolin, 'Wolin on CFIUS' (2018) 14 Brunswick Review 18 https://www.brunswickgroup.com/neal-wolin-on-cfius-committee-on-foreign-investment-in-the-united-states-i7159/ (accessed 8 September 2022).

[26] Codified at 31 CFR Parts 800–801.

[27] 73 FR 70702.

[28] Congressional Research Service (n 12) 11.

40 NATIONAL SECURITY ASSESSMENT

begins'.[29] Once this informal stage has been completed, it is followed by the formal stages of the CFIUS assessment.

The FIRRMA provides for an abbreviated filing or 'light filing' process through a new 'declaration' procedure,[30] where the CFIUS has thirty (30) days to review the declaration and to determine if the transaction involves a foreign person/entity in which a foreign government has a substantial interest.[31] The national security review must be completed within forty-five days of the filing of the declaration, and entails also a review by the DNI, who can send requests for information to different government departments. Notably, the majority of transactions are cleared at the initial stage.

The CFIUS may initiate a forty-five-day investigation of the transaction, which could be extended for an additional fifteen-day period under extraordinary circumstances[32] if the following conditions hold cumulatively:[33]

(i) CFIUS believes that the transaction threatens the national security and the threat has not been mitigated through an agreement with the parties;

(ii) the lead CFIUS agency reviewing the transaction recommends that an investigation be conducted;

(iii) the transaction is a 'foreign government-controlled transaction';[34] or

(iv) the transaction would result in foreign control of any 'critical infrastructure' of the US.[35]

Should such national security investigation take place because the national security concerns are not addressed, the CFIUS, acting on behalf of the President of the US and based on a 'risk-based analysis' of the threat posed by the transaction,[36] has the authority to negotiate, impose, or enforce any conditions on the parties in order to mitigate any threat to US national security.[37] These conditions are often instrumented as contracts 'between the US government and the transaction parties and typically contain[s] enforcement clauses'.[38] The US government has stated that these contracts impose 'strict compliance backed by the threat of court-imposed injunctive relief to compel performance. However ... CFIUS agencies are reportedly seeking very high

---

[29] Senate Hearing 109-782, Briefing on the Dubai Ports World Deal before the Senate Armed Services Committee, Statement of Robert Kimmitt (23 February 2006) https://www.govinfo.gov/content/pkg/CHRG-109shrg32744/html/CHRG-109shrg32744.htm.

[30] FIRRMA § 1706, introducing 50 USC 4565(b)(1)(C)(v).

[31] Congressional Research Service (n 12) 19.

[32] FIRRMA § 1709. What constitutes extraordinary circumstances will be defined by regulation; see 50 USC 4565(b)(2)(C)(ii)(I).

[33] FIRRMA revised the procedures and timetables governing filings with the CFIUS. Under this new law, unless investors choose to file a formal 'long-form' notice with the CFIUS, they are obligated to file a 'short-form' declaration forty-five days before the transaction is completed.

[34] CFIUS will continue to consider all relevant facts and circumstances, rather than applying a bright-line test to determine whether a transaction results in foreign control. See CFIUS reform (14 November 2008).

[35] Exon-Florio amendment.

[36] Daniel C Schwartz and Jennifer K Mammen, 'The Role of CFIUS in International Business Transactions' (2017) 2 International Business Law Journal 115.

[37] Congressional Research Service (n 12) 13.

[38] Jeanne Archibald and Jeremy Zucker, 'Exon-Florio "Safe Harbour" Threatened' European Lawyer (May 2007) 14 https://www.hoganlovells.com/~/media/hogan-lovells/pdf/publication/europeanlawyermay_pdf.pdf.

monetary penalties for breaches'.[39] It should be noted that there are a great number of deals that do not proceed due to national security concerns and the required conditions imposed by the CFIUS, but only a small percentage will become publicly known.[40]

At the end of the investigation, if a CFIUS member recommends that the transaction be prohibited or that a presidential determination is appropriate, it may refer the matter to the POTUS, who has fifteen days to make a decision.[41] The POTUS has the authority—granted by FINSA—to block transactions that threaten to impair the national security. However, the POTUS is under no obligation to follow the recommendation of the CFIUS to suspend or prohibit a transaction. The President must conclude that US laws are inadequate to protect the national security and must have 'credible evidence' that the transaction will impair national security.[42]

In deciding whether to block a transaction, the POTUS can take into account a non-exhaustive list of twelve criteria:

(i) domestic production needed for projected national defence requirements;
(ii) capability and capacity of domestic industries to meet national defence requirements, including the availability of human resources, products, technology, materials, and other supplies and services;
(iii) control of domestic industries and commercial activity by foreign citizens to the extent that it affects the capability and capacity of the US to meet the requirements of national security;
(iv) potential effects of the transactions on the sales of military goods, equipment, or technology to a country that supports terrorism or proliferates missile technology or chemical and biological weapons; and transactions identified by the Secretary of Defence as 'posing a regional military threat' to the interests of the US;
(v) potential effects of the transaction on US technological leadership in areas affecting US national security;
(vi) whether semiconductor deals have a security-related impact on critical infrastructure in the US;
(vii) potential effects on US critical infrastructure, including major energy assets;
(viii) potential effects on US critical technologies;
(ix) whether the transaction is a foreign government-controlled transaction;

---

[39] ibid.

[40] Wolin (n 25).

[41] According to Executive Order 11858, s 6, '(a) any member of the CFIUS may conduct its own enquiry with respect to the potential national security risk posed by a transaction, but communication with the parties to a transaction shall occur through or in the presence of the lead agency, or the chairperson if no lead agency has been designated.

(b) The CFIUS shall undertake an investigation of a transaction in any case, in addition to the circumstances described in the Act, in which following a review a member of the CFIUS advises the chairperson that the member believes that the transaction threatens to impair the national security of the US and that the threat has not been mitigated'.

[42] Congressional Research Service (n 12) 13.

42 NATIONAL SECURITY ASSESSMENT

> (x) in cases involving a government-controlled transaction, a review of
> (A) the adherence of the foreign country to non-proliferation control regimes;
> (B) the foreign country's record on cooperating in counter-terrorism efforts;
> (C) the potential for transhipment or diversion of technologies with military applications;
> (xi) long-term projection of the US requirements for sources of energy and other critical resources and materials; and
> (xii) such other factors as the President or the CFIUS determine to be appropriate.[43][44]

However, it should be noted that none of them has actually been invoked explicitly in any of the executive orders from the five deals that have been blocked by US Presidents so far. Instead, they were mentioned only in some of the press releases from the President's staff in the context of each transaction.[45]

Notwithstanding that the CFIUS process is a voluntary one, the advantage of filing a notice before the CFIUS outweighs the risk of not doing so. This is because a transaction that has been reviewed by the CFIUS is then placed under a 'safe harbour', which means that it cannot be challenged as infringing the Exon-Florio thereafter.[46] Conversely, not filing a foreign transaction before the CFIUS puts the transaction at an open-ended risk, since it could be deemed contrary to national security, thus having a sword of Damocles hanging over it at any time after its completion.

After presenting the CFIUS' architecture and process, this chapter turns now to discussing the CFIUS' track record, aiming on the one hand at providing an overview of the trend the CFIUS has followed over the years, and how this enforcement trend has evolved over time as different national security concerns were prioritized over others. On the other hand, the analysis below aims at critically assessing the CFIUS' enforcement record in order to draw some conclusions as to the national security priorities of the US regime.

---

[43] The last requirement under factor iv and factors vi–xii were added by PL 110-49.

[44] Congressional Research Service (n 12) 18–19.

[45] As an example see, among many others, Treasury Secretary Mnuchin's comments regarding the *Lattice Semiconductor* deal: Herbert Smith Freehills, 'President Trump Blocks Chinese Firm's Acquisition of U.S. Semiconductor Company' (19 September 2017) https://www.herbertsmithfreehills.com/latest-thinking/presid ent-trump-blocks-chinese-firms-acquisition-of-us-semiconductor-company (accessed 15 November 2022); or the CFIUS statements regarding the *Qualcomm/Broadcom* deal: 'President Trump halts Broadcom takeover of Qualcomm' *Reuters* (12 March 2018) https://www.reuters.com/article/us-qualcomm-m-a-broadcom-merger/ president-trump-halts-broadcom-takeover-of-qualcomm-idUSKCN1GO1Q4.

[46] Archibald and Zucker (n 38) 15. See also Gregory Husisian, 'The Future of CFIUS Reviews under the Trump Administration' (2017) 23(2) International Trade Law and Regulation 68, 69; however, it should be noted that '[a]lthough it is possible the new administration [Trump's] might try to undo previously approved transactions, it is unlikely. The statute provides for undoing previous approvals only if information submitted turns out to be false, misleading or to have had material omissions' (ibid 74).

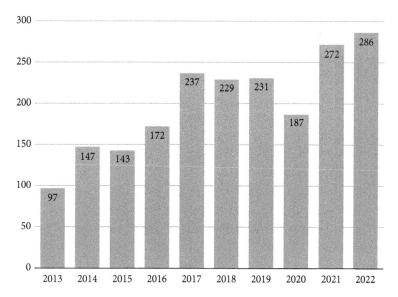

Figure 2.1 Growth in CFIUS notices filed (2013–2022)
Source: CFIUS Annual Report CY 2022, 21

2.4 Enforcement Record

There were a series of events[47] that drew the attention of the Members of Congress and the public to the CFIUS' procedures and led to the expansion of the CFIUS' powers.[48] Even though political initiatives have led to legislation and executive orders, which created a legal framework for the CFIUS to review proposed transactions, the CFIUS has been criticized for operating 'in the shadows', far from the public eye,[49] and its 'reviews have always been something of a black box'.[50] Since 2008, the CFIUS has been publishing Annual Reports showcasing its enforcement record. The number of cases that fall under the scrutiny of the CFIUS increased almost every year. For instance, in 2017, as evidenced in Figure 2.1, there was a significant change, as nearly 250 cases were reviewed, an increase of approximately 40 per cent over the high-water mark that occurred in 2016;[51] the trajectory stalled in 2018 and 2019, and there was a dip in 2020 in the wake of the Covid-19 pandemic, but in 2021 the numbers started growing again, reaching 272 filings and eventually 286 filings in 2022. Figure 2.1 presents an important observation. The number of notices filed in 2022 was almost three times higher than

---

[47] These events included the 11 September 2001, terrorist attacks and the proposed acquisition of commercial operations at six US ports by Dubai Ports World in 2006.
[48] Congressional Research Service (n 12) 4–5, 9, 17.
[49] Archibald and Zucker (n 38).
[50] Husisian (n 46) 68.
[51] Wilson Sonsini Goodrich & Rosati Professional Corporation, 'CFIUS in 2017: A Momentous Year' *Newsletter* (4 January 2018) < https://www.wsgr.com/publications/PDFSearch/CFIUS-Report/2017/CFIUS-YIR-2017.pdf> accessed 9 November 2022 (accessed 9 November 2022).

44 NATIONAL SECURITY ASSESSMENT

those in 2012, a clear indication of the strengthening of the regime as well as of its enhanced protectionism.

Furthermore, Table 2.1 illustrates a second important observation. There is a gradual change in the countries whence firms acquiring US domestic assets originate and which therefore notify the CFIUS of their transactions. As former Deputy US Treasury Secretary Neal Wolin explains, '[p]reviously, there were many transactions from the UK, from Canada and from other NATO allies. And increasingly there are now transactions that originate from other countries that have more complicated national security relationships with the US'.[52] Singapore and China were the top two countries where acquirers of US assets were domiciled in 2022, with more than double the transactions originating from the usual suspects—the UK, Canada, and Japan. If we consider the entire decade, China is by far the top country, with 365 transactions—or 18 per cent of the total—and almost double those of Japan and Canada, the immediate followers, combined.

The debate concerning the CFIUS' approach and scope of intervention is intense. There are those who argue that the CFIUS' involvement in deals is increasing year after year, a view supported by the data illustrated in Figure 2.1. On the other hand, there are commentators who strongly argue that the CFIUS attempts to mitigate national security issues and 'get to a place where the deal can be approved with modifications'.[53] In particular, Wolin firmly sustains that '[t]he basic policy judgment of the Obama administration, and of many administrations before it, was favourably disposed to inward foreign investment because it is good for the US economy'.[54] It is only by means of the analysis of case law in the next section of this book, that one can get a flavour of the CFIUS' criteria and enforcement trend. Before we embark on this analysis it is important to outline the concept of national security and discuss whether there is sufficient clarity in the concept so as to provide the much needed transparency and certainty to the legal and the investment communities.

The CFIUS enforcement record provides a somewhat clearer picture of the sectors of interest from a national security perspective. The majority of the reviewed transactions involve 'dual-use technologies or artificial intelligence or semiconductors or big sets of personal data ... [a]nd those transactions have tended to raise greater national security sensitivity'.[55] As Figure 2.2 illustrates, finance, information, and services are the sectors which most covered transactions relate to.Figure 2.2 shows the constant increase in the number of cases that fell under the scrutiny of the CFIUS between 2013 and 2022 in all sectors, with 2016 being a year of substantial increase. In 2017 this pattern changed, when the finance, information, and services sector drastically fell. In 2018, the same situation was observed in the mining, utilities, and construction sector, and in 2019,

[52] Wolin (n 25).
[53] Wolin (n 25).
[54] ibid.
[55] ibid.

2.4 ENFORCEMENT RECORD 45

Table 2.1 Covered Transactions by Acquirer Home Country or Economy (2013–2022)

Country / Economy	2013	2014	2015	2016	2017	2018	2019	2020	2021	2022	Total
Australia	0	4	4	4	5	4	11	10	4	6	52
Austria	0	0	0	1	2	1	4	0	3	4	15
Bahamas	0	0	0	0	0	0	1	0	0	0	1
Bahrain	0	0	0	0	0	0	0	0	0	1	1
Belgium	0	0	1	0	3	1	0	0	1	1	7
Bermuda	0	0	0	1	0	2	2	1	0	1	7
Brazil	1	0	0	1	1	0	0	2	2	3	10
British Virgin Islands	0	1	0	6	4	0	0	1	1	4	17
Canada	12	15	22	22	22	29	23	11	28	17	201
Cayman Islands	1	3	8	5	8	2	2	5	18	10	62
Chile	1	0	0	0	0	0	0	1	1	1	4
China	21	24	29	54	60	55	25	17	44	36	365
Colombia	0	0	0	0	0	0	1	0	0	0	1
Croatia	0	0	0	0	0	0	0	0	0	1	1
Czech Republic	0	0	0	0	0	0	0	1	3	2	6
Denmark	0	0	1	0	0	3	2	2	5	2	15
Dominican Republic	0	0	0	0	0	0	0	0	0	1	1
Finland	0	1	2	3	0	0	0	2	1	2	11
Fiji	0	0	0	0	0	2	0	0	0	0	2
France	7	6	8	8	14	21	13	11	13	14	115
Germany	4	9	1	6	7	12	13	7	10	10	79
Guernsey	0	0	0	0	1	1	4	3	3	6	18
Hong Kong	1	6	2	3	0	0	4	3	0	0	19
Hungary	0	0	0	0	1	0	0	0	0	0	1
India	1	2	0	1	3	4	3	6	1	3	24
Indonesia	0	1	2	0	0	0	0	0	0	0	3
Ireland	1	1	2	3	3	9	1	2	2	9	33
Isle of Man	0	0	0	0	0	0	0	0	0	1	1
Israel	1	5	3	3	4	5	2	6	12	9	50
Italy	0	0	2	0	2	3	3	3	4	3	20
Japan	18	10	12	13	20	31	46	19	26	15	210
Jersey	0	0	0	1	3	1	0	3	2	2	12
Kuwait	0	0	0	1	2	0	0	1	0	2	6
Lebanon	0	0	0	1	0	0	0	1	2	0	4
Liechtenstein	0	1	0	0	1	0	0	0	1	1	4
Luxembourg	1	0	2	5	2	0	1	5	4	5	25
Malaysia	0	0	0	0	0	1	0	1	0	0	2
Malta	0	0	0	1	0	0	0	0	0	1	2
Mauritius	0	0	0	0	0	0	0	0	0	1	1
Mexico	2	0	0	1	2	0	0	0	2	2	9

(continued)

46 NATIONAL SECURITY ASSESSMENT

Table 2.1 Continued

Country / Economy	2013	2014	2015	2016	2017	2018	2019	2020	2021	2022	Total
Netherlands	1	8	5	3	7	5	6	6	5	1	47
New Zealand	0	0	0	0	0	0	0	0	0	3	3
Norway	1	1	0	2	2	0	0	1	2	1	10
Philippines	0	0	0	0	0	0	0	1	0	0	1
Papua New Guinea	0	0	0	0	1	0	0	0	0	0	1
Portugal	0	0	1	0	5	0	1	4	7	2	20
Qatar	0	1	0	0	0	1	1	2	2	1	8
Russian Federation	1	1	0	0	3	6	1	0	7	1	20
Saudi Arabia	2	1	1	0	1	1	3	0	3	4	16
Seychelles	0	0	0	1	0	0	0	0	0	0	1
Singapore	3	6	3	2	6	5	10	10	13	37	95
South Africa	0	0	2	0	2	1	0	1	1	1	8
South Korea	1	7	1	7	6	4	10	2	13	14	65
Spain	1	2	2	1	1	2	2	3	0	4	18
Sweden	2	2	3	1	6	9	7	10	5	9	54
Switzerland	3	7	2	0	7	2	4	2	1	1	29
Taiwan	1	0	0	1	0	4	4	4	4	3	21
Thailand	0	0	0	0	0	0	1	0	2	2	5
Turkey	0	0	2	2	0	2	2	1	0	1	10
Ukraine	0	0	0	0	0	0	0	0	1	1	2
United Arab Emirates	2	1	1	1	2	3	4	2	0	6	22
United Kingdom	7	21	19	7	18	5	13	14	13	18	135
Vietnam	0	0	0	0	0	0	1	0	0	0	1
Total	97	147	143	172	237	229	231	187	272	286	2001

Source: CFIUS, Annual Reports (CY 2015, 16–17; CY 2018, 20–21; CY 2021, 32–33; CY 2022, 39–40)

the most drastic drop took place in the manufacturing sector. In 2020, the pattern was reversed in the finance, information, and services sector when a dramatic rise in the number of covered notices took place as Figure 2.2 shows.[56]

Figure 2.3 presents the same data from a different perspective, as it focuses on the shares of transactions by sectors. It evidences that finance, information, and services have generated more than half the activity in both 2021 and 2022, a noticeable increase from a third in 2013, and about a quarter in 2014. Manufacturing has experienced the inverse trend, falling from almost half of the transactions in 2014 and 2015 to less than 30 per cent in the last two years. The remaining two sectors—mining, utilities, and construction; and wholesale and retail trade and transportation—have recorded similar reductions over the decade considered, from 21 to 13 per cent and from 10 to 6 per cent, respectively.

[56] Wilson Sonsini Goodrich & Rosati (n 51).

2.4 ENFORCEMENT RECORD   47

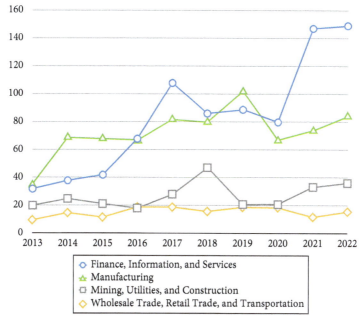

Figure 2.2 Covered notices by sector (2013–2022)
Source: CFIUS Annual Report CY 2022, 24
Note: The data does not include real estate notices filed under 31 CFR Part 802.

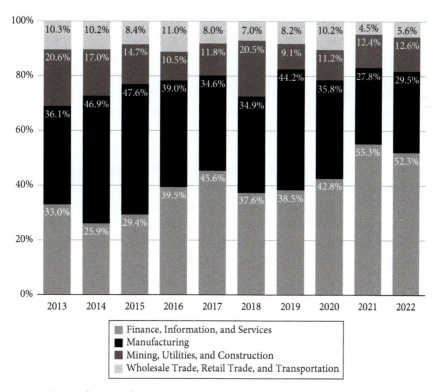

Figure 2.3 Covered notices by sector as a percentage of all covered notices (2013–2022)
Source: CFIUS Annual Report CY 2022, 24
Note: The data does not include real estate notices filed under 31 CFR Part 802.

48   NATIONAL SECURITY ASSESSMENT

Table 2.2 Covered transactions, withdrawals, and presidential decisions (2013–2022)

Year	Filed	Withdrawn (during Review)	Investigated	Withdrawn (during Investigation)	Presidential decisions
2013	97	3	49	5	0
2014	147	3	52	9	0
2015	143	3	67	10	0
2016	172	6	79	21	1
2017	237	4	172	70	1
2018	229	2	158	64	1
2019	231	0	113	30	1
2020	187	1	88	28	1
2021	272	2	130	72	0
2022	286	1	162	87	0
Total	2001	25	1070	396	5

Source: CFIUS Annual Report CY 2022, 21

Finally, Table 2.2 shows the number of deals that were submitted to the CFIUS' scrutiny between 2013 and 2022. The table also shows how many of these deals triggered a subsequent investigation, as well as the respective outcomes: withdrawals, or rejections.[57]

Out of 2,001 covered notices filed, and over 1,000 transactions investigated by the CFIUS, only five transactions were rejected in the entire period examined—one each year between 2016 and 2020. In spite of the onerous nature of the CFIUS review, and of its uncertain outcome, this ratio of about 0.25 per cent of CFIUS annual reviews leading to rejection is actually encouraging for foreign companies looking to invest in the US.[58] However, if the number of transactions that were abandoned because of national security concerns is taken into account, then the proportion increases to approximately 21 per cent (or about 37 per cent if we only consider the investigation phase, at which stage virtually all withdrawals take place).[59] This percentage is much higher than the number of transactions blocked in the EU or US on competition law grounds.

After discussing the enforcement trend and record of the CFIUS, the chapter will discuss below some lessons that can be drawn from the assessment of national security concerns raised by the CFIUS.

[57] ibid.

[58] In CY 2015, 1,801 transactions were reported under the HSR Act. The DOJ brought 22 merger enforcement challenges, from which in only 3 it initiated administrative litigation (less than 0.2 per cent transactions where the competition authorities were against the deal occurring). See https://www.ftc.gov/policy/reports/policy-reports/annual-competition-reports (accessed 15 November 2022).

[59] For an overview of the reasons leading the parties to withdraw their notices, see CFIUS, 'Annual Report to Congress' (CY 2022) 44 https://home.treasury.gov/system/files/206/CFIUS%20-%20Annual%20Report%20to%20Congress%20CY%202022_0.pdf (accessed 15 September 2023). It should, however, be noted that in the majority of cases the parties filed new notices following the withdrawal of the earlier ones.

2.4.1 Lessons Drawn from the CFIUS National Security Assessment

Throughout the CFIUS assessment process, the analysis of the capability or intention of a foreign entity to cause national security harm is at the core of the CFIUS assessment of the transaction. The focus is on whether the nature of the US business can lead to an impairment of US national security.

The CFIUS assessment is grounded on information provided by the parties, public and government sources, including the classified 'National Security Threat Assessment' that, as required by section 721 of the Defence Production Act of 1950, as amended, the DNI prepares for the CFIUS within twenty days after a notice of a transaction is accepted.[60] However, it must be stressed that the requirement is not only that the transaction imposes a mere threat, but that it can also lead to a vulnerability in US national security.[61] There is a statutory list of national security factors included in section 721(f),[62] which focus on the nature of the US business over which control is being acquired,[63] as well as on the identity of the foreign person/entity acquiring control of a US business.[64]

---

[60] 73 FR 70702; see also Department of Defence, 'DoD Instruction 2000.25: DoD Procedures for Reviewing and Monitoring Transactions Filed with the Committee on Foreign Investment in the United States' 11 https://www.esd.whs.mil/Portals/54/Documents/DD/issuances/dodi/200025p.pdf (accessed 8 September 2022).

[61] David N Fagan, 'The US Regulatory and Institutional Framework for FDI' in Karl P Sauvant (ed), *Investing in the United States: Is the US Ready for FDI from China?* (Edward Elgar Publishing 2009) 59.

[62] CFIUS operates pursuant to s 721 of the Defence Production Act of 1950, as amended.

[63] Transactions that the CFIUS has reviewed that have presented national security considerations usually involve foreign control of US businesses that provide products and services to agencies of the US government and state and local authorities.

[64] Section 721(f) comprises the following factors: '(1) domestic production needed for projected national defense requirements, (2) the capability and capacity of domestic industries to meet national defense requirements, including the availability of human resources, products, technology, materials, and other supplies and services, (3) the control of domestic industries and commercial activity by foreign citizens as it affects the capability and capacity of the United States to meet the requirements of national security, (4) the potential effects of the proposed or pending transaction on sales of military goods, equipment, or technology to any country—

  (A) identified by the Secretary of State—

    (i) ... as a country that supports terrorism;

    (ii) ... as a country of concern regarding missile proliferation; or

    (iii) ... as a country of concern regarding the proliferation of chemical and biological weapons;

  (B) identified by the Secretary of Defense as posing a potential regional military threat to the interests of the United States; or'

  (C) listed under ... the 'Nuclear Non-Proliferation-Special Country List' ... or any successor list;

    (5) the potential effects of the proposed or pending transaction on United States international technological leadership in areas affecting United States national security;

    (6) the potential national security-related effects on United States critical infrastructure, including major energy assets;

    (7) the potential national security-related effects on United States critical technologies;

    (8) whether the covered transaction is a foreign government-controlled transaction ...

    (9) as appropriate, and particularly with respect to transactions requiring an investigation ... a review of the current assessment of—

  (A) the adherence of the subject country to non-proliferation control regimes, including treaties and multilateral supply guidelines, which shall draw on, but not be limited to, the annual report on 'Adherence to and Compliance with Arms Control, Nonproliferation and Disarmament Agreements and Commitments' required by section 403 of the Arms Control and Disarmament Act;

50 NATIONAL SECURITY ASSESSMENT

In the 2015 Annual Report, the CFIUS identified three national security risks that were not included in past practice, namely: (i) the potential disclosure of substantial pools of personal information; (ii) the potential loss of one of only a few US suppliers; and (iii) the potential loss of US technological advantages.[65] Concerning these three risks, the first one entails that any acquisition of a US business, which comprises a great deal of private information, may pose a national security risk (including in relation to transactions in the financial, healthcare, and insurance sectors). The second one, pertaining to deals where there are few alternative suppliers operating, evidences the relevance awarded by the US government to US supply chain issues. The third risk, comprising the loss of US technological advantages to foreign acquirers that also develop technology, would seem to be the key to pass the FIRRMA, based on which the CFIUS' authority to review transactions was strengthened.[66]

Pursuant to section 721(m)(3) of the Defense Production Act, the CFIUS Annual Reports include an assessment by the US Intelligence Community (USIC) on matters that relate to coordinated strategies by countries or companies to acquire companies in US critical technologies. As an example, in the 2020 Report the CFIUS states that it provided the United States Intelligence Community (USIC) with a list of transactions involving one or more critical technologies that the USIC analysed to determine which transactions, if any, meet this Report's definition of a coordinated strategy.[67]

While the 2012 report indicated that the USIC found coordination among foreign entities 'to acquire companies involved in US critical technologies',[68] the 2014 report acknowledged that the USIC only anticipated a possible 'effort among foreign governments or companies to acquire U.S. companies involved in research, development, or production of critical technologies for which the United States is a leading producer'.[69] This observation was emphasized in the 2015 Annual Report, where the USIC noted that 'foreign governments are extremely likely to use a range of collection methods to obtain critical U.S. technologies'.[70] Based on these findings, which have ranged from 'vague' concerns to

(B) the relationship of such country with the United States, specifically on its record on cooperating in counter-terrorism efforts, which shall draw on, but not be limited to, the report of the President to Congress under section 7120 of the Intelligence Reform and Terrorism Prevention Act of 2004; and
(C) the potential for transhipment or diversion of technologies with military applications, including an analysis of national export control laws and regulations;

    (10) the long-term projection of United States requirements for sources of energy and other critical resources and material; and
    (11) such other factors as the President or the Committee may determine to be appropriate, generally or in connection with a specific review or investigation.'

[65] CFIUS (n 20) 23–24.
[66] The 'loss of emerging technologies and personal information' was added to the list of national security threats.
[67] CFIUS, 'Annual Report to Congress' (CY 2020) 50 https://home.treasury.gov/system/files/206/CFIUS-Public-Annual-Report-CY-2020.pdf (accessed 9 September 2023). 'Coordinated strategy' is defined as a '(plan of action reflected in directed efforts developed and implemented by a foreign government, in association with one or more foreign companies, to acquire U.S. companies with critical technologies'. ibid 60.
[68] William R Vigdor and Daniel J Gerkin, 'CFIUS Annual Report Confirms Recent Trends and Highlights Factors to Be Considered when Notifying Transactions to CFIUS' Lexology (23 January 2018) https://www.lexology.com/library/detail.aspx?g=d1e42bfe-e4cc-4b9a-b40a-6deaeb21a2a4 (accessed 9 September 2022).
[69] CFIUS, 'Annual Report to Congress' (CY 2014) 29 https://home.treasury.gov/system/files/206/CFIUS-Annual-Report-to-Congress-for-CY2014.pdf (accessed 8 September 2022).
[70] CFIUS (n 20) 31.

2.4 ENFORCEMENT RECORD   51

'severe' concerns in a matter of only three years, it is not surprising that the scope of the CFIUS expanded over the years culminating in the FIRRMA and on the increase in the number of CFIUS cases between 2015 and 2020, a trend unlikely to be reversed.

Between 2015 and 2017, the Annual Reports of the CFIUS showed an increased scrutiny of semiconductor deals. In 2015, at least two semiconductor-related transactions with Chinese parties were 'cleared' by the CFIUS,[71] followed by adverse outcomes for Chinese acquirers in 2016 and 2017, and a strong setback in 2017 with President Trump's blocking of the proposed acquisition of Lattice Semiconductor Corporation by a US-headquartered private equity fund whose sole investor was owned and controlled by the Chinese government.

Furthermore, the CFIUS approach illustrates the increasing use of mitigation measures, which comprise:

> [c]onditions as restricting which persons can access certain technologies/information, establishing procedures regarding US government contracting, establishing corporate security committees to oversee classified or export-controlled products or technical data, requiring divestments of critical business units, providing periodic monitoring reports to the US Government regarding national security issues, or giving the US Government the right to review future business decisions that implicate national security.[72]

Given the growth in the imposition of the above-mentioned mitigation measures, it is likely that 'an increasingly stringent review process will result in more companies backing off of transactions that encounter resistance from the committee'.[73] The outcome of such a trend could end up being the diversion of incoming FDI and lead to an exclusion of particular countries.

The chapter turns now to discussing some seminal cases in the CFIUS enforcement record that will shed light on the approach the CFIUS takes in assessing specific national security issues. As the CFIUS does not publish its decisions, it is challenging for an outside observer critically to assess its assessment approach, and thus the chapter focuses on the most important issues from a small sample of cases where some information as to the analysis conducted by the CFIUS was made public.

2.4.2 Analysis of Some Seminal Cases

After reviewing the structure and scope of the CFIUS and the procedure in assessing foreign investments, this section will present some of the main CFIUS investigations in

---

[71] Namely, OmniVision Technologies(acquired by a consortium composed of Hua Capital Management Co Ltd, CITIC Capital Holdings Ltd, and GoldStone Investment Co Ltd) and Integrated Silicon Solution (acquired by Uphill Investment Co).
[72] Husisian (n 46) 69–70.
[73] ibid 70.

52 NATIONAL SECURITY ASSESSMENT

order to showcase the approach the CFIUS follows in assessing national security concerns and the measures the CFIUS has taken to address them.

A review of the CFIUS enforcement record portrays three clear observations. The first is the increasing number of CFIUS notifications over the last few years. The second observation is the increasing severity of concerns that the CFIUS has identified which led to the FIRRMA Act strengthening the CFIUS' remit. The third observation is that the CFIUS has been approving a larger number of cases with mitigations. In addition, the CFIUS enforcement record illustrates an increased scrutiny of semiconductor deals, particularly for Chinese acquirers as well as a tendency for more transactions that are notified to the CFIUS, to require lengthier investigations and mitigation conditions in order to be approved.[74] We should forewarn the reader that the information regarding the concerns to national security concerns identified by the CFIUS, as well as the discussions between the parties involved and the Committee, are confidential in nature. Therefore, the reasoning behind every case is limited. Confronted with this issue, we have relied on outside sources or assumptions from the information available.

2.4.2.1 Verio—NTT Communications

One of the first important cases that the CFIUS assessed was in the telecommunications sector. The envisaged transaction was the acquisition of Verio—a US company that operates websites for businesses and provides Internet services—by NTT Communications—a Japanese telecommunications company.[75] The FBI instigated the lengthy CFIUS review that took place in 2000. The CFIUS' intervention led to a fall in Verio's stock price as a result of uncertainty in the market regarding the outcome of the transaction. Concerns also arose related to the fact that the majority interest of the Japanese government in the acquiring company could grant the former access to information regarding surveillance that was being conducted on email and other web-based traffic crossing Verio's computer system.[76] Actually, certain [US] government officials even 'expressed deep reservations that NTT's ownership of Verio's extensive telecommunications would raise foreign espionage risks by giving the Japanese state-controlled company access to US wiretapping activities'.[77]

Notwithstanding the concerns raised by the transaction, the CFIUS recommended President Clinton not to intervene in the process.[78] The POTUS decided not to intervene, claiming that all national security concerns related to the merger had been resolved.[79]

---

[74] William R Vigdor and Daniel J Gerkin, 'CFIUS Annual Report Confirms Recent Trends and Highlights Factors to Be Considered when Notifying Transactions to CFIUS' *Lexology* (23 January 2018) https://www.lexol ogy.com/library/detail.aspx?g=d1e42bfe-e4cc-4b9a-b40a-6deaeb21a2a4 (accessed 9 September 2022).

[75] The case also passed through the FTC's jurisdiction, who ordered for an early termination of the merger review, given that the 'waiting period' ended, on June 14, 2000 https://www.ftc.gov/enforcement/premerger-notif ication-program/early-termination-notices/20003430 (accessed 15 November 2022).

[76] James K Jackson, 'The Committee on Foreign Investment in the United States (CFIUS)', CRS Report RL33388 (19 February 2016).

[77] 'Clinton OK's NTT/Verio Deal' *CNN Money* (23 August 2000) https://money.cnn.com/2000/08/23/deals/ntt_verio/.

[78] ibid.

[79] ibid.

It has been reported that some members of the CFIUS met with NIT and Verio representatives to discuss the concerns raised by the deal, in particular, the possibility that the Japanese enterprise could had access to intercepted communications whose content could expose the espionage activities carried out by the United States.[80] The White House also reported that the non-intervention decision of President Clinton was grounded on the results shown by the 'thorough' investigation completed by the CFIUS, albeit neither was indication about the details of the investigation nor about how the merging parties addressed the purported concerns.[81] Hence, even if the lack of information does not allow us to make further reflections, it confirms the opaqueness of the process.

2.4.2.2 SoftBank—Sprint Nextel

A few years after *Verio—NTT Communications*, in 2013, the CFIUS reviewed and approved another transaction in the telecommunications sector. SoftBank filed to acquire Sprint Nextel for US$21.6 billion.[82] The CFIUS found that there were no unresolved national security issues associated with the proposed acquisition,[83] but required that 'SoftBank and Sprint enter into a National Security Agreement with the Department of Defense, the Department of Homeland Security and the Department of Justice (the "USG Parties")'.[84] The national security issue that was addressed through this agreement was that '[w]ithout US ownership and control of Sprint, SoftBank's reliance on Chinese equipment manufacturers raise[d] significant national security concerns'.[85] The National Security Agreement addressed this problem and comprised, inter alia, that (i) SoftBank and Sprint had to appoint an independent member for Sprint's new board of directors, which had to be approved by the USG Parties; (ii) when Sprint either obtained operational control of Clearwire[86] or consummated its proposed acquisition of Clearwire, USG Parties had a one-time right to require the former to remove certain equipment deployed in the latter's network; and (iii) the USG Parties had the right to review and approve certain network equipment vendors and managed services providers of Sprint, as well as of Clearwire, once the former completed its proposed acquisition.[87] Since Clearwire relied on the Chinese firm Huawei for equipment and for cell

---

[80] 'No National Security Threat Seen in NTT's Proposed Purchase of Verio' *Los Angeles Times* (24 August 2000) https://www.latimes.com/archives/la-xpm-2000-aug-24-fi-9539-story.html (accessed 9 September 2022).

[81] ibid.

[82] Given that the 'waiting period' ended, the FTC ordered an early termination of the merger review on 6 December 2012. See https://www.ftc.gov/enforcement/premerger-notification-program/early-termination-noti ces/20130159 (accessed 15 November 2022).

[83] SEC, Form 8-K dated 29 May 2013, Sprint Nextel Corporation, Commission file number 1-04721 https://www. sec.gov/Archives/edgar/data/101830/000119312513238554/d545797d8k.htm (accessed 15 November 2022).

[84] ibid.

[85] Michael J de la Merced, 'SoftBank and Sprint Win National Security Clearance for Deal' *DealBook* (28 May 2013) https://dealbook.nytimes.com/2013/05/28/softbank-and-sprint-said-to-win-national-security-clearance-for-deal/ (accessed 15 November 2022).

[86] Clearwire was a telecommunications operator which provided mobile and fixed wireless broadband communications services to retail and wholesale customers in the US, Belgium, and Spain. After being acquired by Sprint Nextel, it changed its name to Sprint Corporation.

[87] Since Clearwire relied on the Chinese firm Huawei for equipment and for cell tower base stations, SoftBank agreed to remove Huawei as a supplier when the acquisition of Sprint was finalized. See also SEC, Form 8-K dated 29 May 2013, Sprint Nextel Corporation.

54 NATIONAL SECURITY ASSESSMENT

tower base stations, SoftBank agreed to remove Huawei as a supplier when the acquisition of Sprint was finalized.

2.4.2.3 Smithfield Foods—Shuanghui International Holdings

In the food sector, also in 2013, a Hong Kong-based company that owns a variety of businesses in the food and logistics sectors—Shuanghui International Holdings Ltd— proposed to acquire the world's largest hog producer and pork processor, US company Smithfield Foods, for US$4.7 billion, in the largest acquisition of a US firm by a Chinese company up to that time.

The significance of this case is due to the public interest attributed to 'food security'. The National Strategy for Critical Infrastructures and Key Assets[88] identified the latter as a fundamental part of the country's core infrastructure, which makes the assurance of its safety a high priority.[89] Even though the meat industry is not as sensitive as the natural resources one, the transaction still received much criticism from politicians. For instance, while the review by the CFIUS was taking place, the US Senate Committee on Agriculture, Nutrition, and Forestry held a hearing where several concerns regarding the transaction were raised, including those about the security and safety of food supplies in the country, the potential impact of the transaction on jobs and food prices, and the restrictions on reciprocal investment opportunities into China.[90] Iowa Senator Chuck Grassley expressly pointed out that 'the deal might further consolidate the agriculture industries ... [since] it will be more difficult for market participants to buy pork products with a fair price ... [and] consumers [will have] fewer choices and higher costs'.[91]

The fact that Smithfield was going to be a vertically integrated company not only raised concerns related to the effect of the merger in 'different markets and different parts of the food production infrastructure in ways that might not have been considered in a CFIUS review',[92] but it also provided a 'future competitor with the necessary resources to mount a competitive challenge to other U.S. food producers'.[93] Reportedly, the transaction also raised two more national security concerns. First, as Smithfield was a direct supplier to the US Department of Defence and other governmental agencies, there were fears that sensitive information about location and members of the staff

---

[88] 'The National Strategy for the Physical Protection of Critical Infrastructure and Key Assets establishes a foundation for building and fostering the cooperative environment in which government, industry, and private citizens can carry out their respective protection responsibilities more effectively and efficiently. Moreover, this document identifies a clear set of national goals and objectives and outlines the guiding principles that will underpin the efforts to secure the infrastructures and assets vital to national security, governance, public health and safety, economy, and public confidence.' https://www.hsdl.org/?abstract&did=1041 (accessed 15 November 2022).

[89] The National Strategy for the Physical Protection of Critical Infrastructure and Key Assets (February 2003) 36.

[90] Francis J Aquila and others, 'Sullivan & Cromwell discusses Shuanghui International's CFIUS Clearance for its Purchase of Smithfield Foods' *CLS Blue Sky Blog* (20 September 2013) https://clsbluesky.law.columbia.edu/2013/09/20/sullivan-cromwell-discusses-shuanghui-internationals-cfius-clearance-for-its-purchase-of-smithfield-foods/ (accessed 30 April 2023).

[91] Chanting Chen, 'A National Security Study of the Shuanghui-Smithfield Case' (2017) DEStech Transactions on Social Science Education and Human Science http://dx.doi.org/10.12783/dtssehs/hsmet2017/16534.

[92] Congressional Research Service (n 12) 46.

[93] ibid.

could had been exposed.[94] Secondly, the fact that some Smithfield premises were located near military units created some worries.[95] The CFIUS unconditionally approved the transaction, even in view of the unreserved resistance from Congress. Despite the limited reasoning provided to the public when reviewing deals under its authority given that the review in itself and discussions with interested parties are confidential, the CFIUS has stated that the analysis aimed at establishing which assets constitute critical infrastructure takes place on a case-by-case basis.[96] Given the approval decision, it is evident that on this occasion the involved target market -food supply- did not fall within these sectors. In any case, Shuanghui gave assurances that it 'will not import any product from China into the U.S.'.[97] In addition, it vowed not to modify or worsen the working conditions of Smithfield's employees and not to close any of their facilities and locations, among other pledges.[98] These commitments do not seem to address the above purportedly national security concerns which can only imply they were not considered by the CFIUS as important for national security.

2.4.2.4 ChemChina—Syngenta

Chinese state-owned enterprise (SOE) ChemChina proposed to acquire Syngenta—an agrochemical Swiss company—in 2016 for US$43 billion. This created turmoil among US law-makers and groups of farmers, since they feared for a Chinese SOE being in a position to influence the country's food supply.[99] As US Senator Chuck Grassley, chairman of the US Senate Judiciary Committee[100] stated, '[t]he fact that a state-owned enterprise may have yet another stake in US agriculture is alarming'.[101]

The CFIUS cleared the transaction, but Syngenta refused to provide details to the public as to the envisaged requested mitigating measures imposed on the parties, stating it was 'not disclosing the details of the agreement with CFIUS ... [since] mitigation measures are not material to Syngenta's business'.[102] This emphasizes the secrecy of the CFIUS' decision-making process and assessment, and creates uncertainty amongst foreign investors as well as uncertainty in the legal and business community.

---

[94] Ziad Haider, 'China Inc. and the CFIUS National Security Review' *The Diplomat* (5 December 2013) https://thediplomat.com/2013/12/china-inc-and-the-cfius-national-security-review.

[95] ibid.

[96] ibid.

[97] ibid.

[98] Alston & Bird, 'Shuanghui Wins CFIUS Approval of Smithfield Acquisition: Company's Careful Approach to U.S. Government Validated' (September 2013) https://www.alston.com/-/media/files/insights/publications/2013/09/iclient-alerti-shuanghui-wins-cfius-approval-of-sm/files/view-client-alert-as-pdf/fileattachment/smithfield-cfiuseng.pdf (accessed 9 September 2022).

[99] Michael Shields and Greg Roumeliotis, 'U.S. clearance of ChemChina's Syngenta deal removes key hurdle' *Reuters* (22 August 2016) https://www.reuters.com/article/us-syngenta-ag-m-a-chemchina-approval-idUSKCN10X0DS (accessed 15 November 2022).

[100] On 5 October 2021, Senators Tommy Tuberville, Cynthia Lummis, Roger Marshall, and Rick Scott introduced the Foreign Adversary Risk Management (FARM) Act, which would add the secretary of agriculture as a member of CFIUS, whose last action took place in Senate in May 2021. See FARM Act, s 2931 https://www.congress.gov/bill/117th-congress/senate-bill/2931/cosponsors?r=1&s=5 (accessed 9 September 2022).

[101] Shields and Roumeliotis (n 99).

[102] 'Syngenta Says Won't Disclose Details of CFIUS Clearance, Any Mitigation Measures Not Material to Its Business' *Reuters* (22 August 2016) https://www.reuters.com/article/syngenta-ag-ma-chemchina-measureschina-n/syngenta-says-wont-disclose-details-of-cfius-clearance-any-mitigation-measures-not-material-to-its-business-idUSZ8N135028 (accessed 15 November 2022).

56 NATIONAL SECURITY ASSESSMENT

In April 2017, the FTC cleared the acquisition,[103] imposing on the buyer to divest three types of pesticides from its portfolio that were manufactured by Adama Agricultural Solutions Ltd, an Israeli-based ChemChina subsidiary. The FTC was of the view that the proposed merger would be detrimental to competition in the US markets for the three following pesticides: (1) the herbicide paraquat, (2) the insecticide abamectin, and (3) the fungicide chlorothalonil.[104] The concerns were raised because Syngenta was the owner of the branded version of these pesticides with significant market shares in the United States, while ADAMA was the first or second-largest generic supplier of the same pesticides in the country.[105] In short, the FTC was concerned that the merger would 'eliminate the direct competition' between the merging parties.[106] Hence, American Vanguard Corp. was set to acquire the pesticides, although the terms of this transaction were not disclosed.[107]

2.4.2.5 Chicago Stock Exchange—Chongqing Casin Enterprise Group

In 2016, the CFIUS was asked to intervene once again in a merger where the Chinese government was involved. The case related to the envisaged acquisition of the Chicago Stock Exchange by the Chinese-led consortium Chongqing Casin Enterprise Group for a value of about US$22 million.[108] Since the ties between the acquirer and Chinese government officials could grant China's government influence over US equity markets, some Congress members sent a letter to the US administration expressing their concerns regarding how such influence could potentially enhance the acquirer's ability to manipulate the markets to the advantage of Chinese companies or the Chinese economy.[109]

Although the CFIUS approved the merger by the end of 2016, the US Securities and Exchange Commission (SEC), an agency that reviews proposed mergers involving exchanges to ensure they observe federal regulations and appropriately self-monitor their brokerage members, was requested by the concerned members of the Congress to block the acquisition.[110] After a lengthy review period and under its authority to oversee the deal, the SEC blocked the transaction given that the 'lack of information on the would-be buyers threatened the ability to properly monitor the exchange after the deal'.[111] The SEC stated that among the key unanswered questions that largely influenced the

---

[103] FTC, 'China National Chemical Corporation and others' Decision and Order, Docket No C-4610 (16 June 2017) https://www.ftc.gov/legal-library/browse/cases-proceedings/1610093-china-national-chemical-corporation-et-al-matter.

[104] ibid.

[105] ibid.

[106] ibid.

[107] Schwartz and Mammen (n 36).

[108] Congressional Research Service (n 12) 48.

[109] Josh Rogin, 'Congress Wary of National Security Implications of Chinese Deal for Chicago Stock Exchange' *Chicago Tribune* (17 February 2016) https://www.chicagotribune.com/business/ct-congress-chicago-stock-exchange-sale-20160217-story.html.

[110] On antitrust grounds, however, the DOJ signed off in November 2016, finding that the deal did not violate any antitrust laws. See https://www.houstonchronicle.com/business/article/In-brief-Chinese-group-buying-Chicago-exchange-6811059.php (accessed 15 November 2022).

[111] John McCrank, 'SEC Blocks Chicago Stock Exchange Sale to China-Based Investors' *Thomson Reuters* (16 February 2018) https://uk.reuters.com/article/us-sec-chicagostockexchange/sec-blocks-chicago-stock-exchange-sale-to-china-based-investors-idUKKCN1G000H (accessed 15 November 2022).

prohibition decision were the origins of funding, the relationship between upstream investors and the determination of the 'ultimate owners'.[112] In this context, it seems that the SEC's decision was not grounded on national security concerns but rather on how challenging it would have been, in practice, to monitor the merged entity, which appears to be a justifiable decision. At the same time, it casts doubts about the accuracy of the CFIUS's approval decision given the uncertainties around key aspects such as the identity of the investors, a critical aspect that under its review should have not been ignored and left unchallenged. This case is another example of the divergence between governmental bodies with authority to oversee the same transaction.

2.4.2.6 Alibaba—MoneyGram

In the financial services sector, the CFIUS decided to block the proposed acquisition of MoneyGram International—a worldwide provider of financial services—by Ant Financial, a Chinese company owned by the Alibaba Group in 2018.[113] In this case, the CFIUS intervened even though MoneyGram does not operate in the defence sector nor does it deal with critical infrastructure. Instead, the concern lay with the potential risk that Ant Financial could have access to sensitive personal and financial information of American citizens after the takeover.[114] The concern was amplified by the fact that some of the MoneyGram outlets are located inside or close to US military installations, which are frequently used by members of the army, their relatives, and defence contractors.[115] Besides accessing their identities, the higher risk was to expose their financial difficulties and, therefore, put them in jeopardy.[116] One additional concern related to the importance of money transfer services in tackling money laundering, terrorism, and financial crimes. It was thought that once MoneyGram was in hands of the acquirer, the government would lose this significant investigative and enforcement tool.[117]

The parties tried to address the concerns that the CFIUS had raised in relation to the envisaged transaction and offered various commitments largely orientated to alleviate the concerns that data could be used to identify US citizens.[118] Notwithstanding their intention to mitigate national security, approval 'was denied because the Chinese government holds a 15% stake in Ant Financial, and it was feared the data held by

---

[112] Thomas Heath, 'Chinese Investors Blocked from Buying a U.S. Stock Exchange' *The Washington Post* (16 February 2018) https://www.washingtonpost.com/business/capitalbusiness/chinese-investors-blocked-from-buying-a-us-stock-exchange/2018/02/16/c0adbfe4-134f-11e8-9065-e55346f6de81_story.html (accessed 11 September 2022)

[113] Notwithstanding the fact that the merger obtained antitrust clearance in the US. See http://ir.moneygram.com/news-releases/news-release-details/moneygram-and-ant-financial-enter-amended-merger-agreement (accessed 15 November 2022).

[114] John P Barket and others, 'CFIUS Scrutiny of Foreign Investment Intensifies with Broadening Scope' *Arnold & Porter* (24 January 2018) https://www.arnoldporter.com/en/perspectives/advisories/2018/01/cfius-scrutiny-of-foreign-investment-intensifies.

[115] ibid.

[116] ibid.

[117] ibid.

[118] Greg Roumeliotis, 'U.S. blocks MoneyGram sale to China's Ant Financial on national security concerns' *Reuters* (2 January 2018 https://www.reuters.com/article/us-moneygram-intl-m-a-ant-financial/u-s-blocks-moneygram-sale-to-chinas-ant-financial-on-national-security-concerns-idUSKBN1ER1R7> accessed 12 September 2022

58   NATIONAL SECURITY ASSESSMENT

MoneyGram could be used by the Chinese government to target activists, journalists, and others'.[119] This case marks an era in which aspects such as personal data, initially perceived as unrelated to national security, have become one of the most guarded and preserved assets. It also shows that the US government would exert all its powers to prevent American citizens becoming vulnerable to countries seen as rivals by making their private data unreachable to the latter.

2.4.2.7 Aleris—Zhongwang

In the defence industry, Zhongwang USA LLC, an investment firm majority-owned by the founder of China Zhongwang Holdings Limited, cancelled its planned acquisition of US aluminium maker Aleris Corp. for US$2.33 billion, announced in August 2016, after failing to receive approval on national security grounds.[120] The involved parties have agreed as an initial deadline to their deal 31 August 2017, being subsequently extended to 15 September and then 29 September 2017.[121] Aleris produced specialized alloys used by the defence industry. Its research and technology were so critical to US economic and national security interests that the US Commerce Department initiated an investigation to determine whether an import of aluminium imports from either China or any other country could compromise US national security. The Commerce Secretary Wilbur Ross also explained that the investigation was needed not just because high-purity aluminium is required to build some combat aircrafts, but because the metal had become scarce after several local smelter factories had been forced to close, negatively impacting the extraction of the metal.[122]

In July 2017, the CFIUS raised some concerns about the deal, having extended the scheduled merger deadline to allow for additional discussions. After fifteen months of waiting for the CFIUS' approval, and since the agency continued to raise national security concerns with the merger, the parties withdrew their request for approval.[123] There is no evidence that the merging parties offered any remedies to mitigate the national security concerns raised by the CFIUS. The only information available in that regard is contained in a statement released by Zhongwang USA in which an unidentified person indicated that 'Through the proposed acquisition, the Company was committed to preserving American jobs and investing substantial funds into Aleris, beyond the

---

[119] Olga Torres and Jonathan Creek, *United States: 2018 Trends For CFIUS Reviews* (Mondaq 2018) http://www.mondaq.com/unitedstates/x/675886/Inward+Foreign+Investment/2018+Trends+For+CFIUS+Reviews (accessed 15 November 2022).

[120] However, it did obtain the antitrust clearance. Since the 'waiting period' ended, the FTC ordered an early termination of the merger review on 13 October 2016 https://www.ftc.gov/enforcement/premerger-notification-program/early-termination-notices/20161823 (accessed 15 November 2022).

[121] Joe Deaux, 'Aleris Keeps Door Open to Takeover by Chinese Aluminium Baron' *Bloomberg UK* (1 September 2017) <https://www.bloomberg.com/news/articles/2017-09-01/aleris-says-it-extends-merger-agreement-with-zhongwang-usa?leadSource=uverify%20wall (accessed 13 September 2022); 'Zhongwang and Aleris Further Extend Their Merger Deal', *AlCircle* (16 September 2017) https://www.alcircle.com/news/zhongwang-and-aleris-further-extend-their-merger-deal-28741 (accessed 13 September 2022).

[122] 'Aleris, Zhongwang USA Scrap Merger after Regulatory Snag' *Reuters* (13 November 2017) https://www.reuters.com/article/us-aleris-m-a-zhongwangusa-idUSKBN1DD1PP (accessed 13 September 2022).

[123] Aleris Reports Second Quarter 2017 Results. See https://www.sec.gov/Archives/edgar/data/1518587/000151858717000029/a2q17earningsrelease.htm (accessed 15 November 2022).

purchase price'.[124] In this case the government dealt with the concerns raised by the transaction through an elongated process, forcing its termination by the parties. Such lengthy processes erode trust in the review system. If such delays become a common practice, it could lead to a wave of scepticism among investors, so the next question is whether the government would be able to restore their confidence in a welcoming investment environment.

2.4.2.8 Cree—Infineon

The CFIUS was reluctant to grant clearance on the grounds of national security concerns, in the proposed acquisition by German chip-maker Infineon Technologies AG of US LED lighting-maker Cree's Wolfspeed Power unit. Notably, the latter 'makes devices using gallium nitride, a sensitive powdery compound that can have military applications', which has been the reason for 'US blocking acquisitions in the past'.[125] According to a press release issued by Cree, 'Cree and Infineon have been unable to identify alternatives which would address the national security concerns of the ... (CFIUS), and as a result, the proposed transaction will be terminated'.[126]

Although the parties did not specify the nature of the national security concerns, it was argued that the main reason for the CFIUS' concerns related to the Chinese ability to obtain Cree technology via the German acquirer.[127] Even though Infineon is based in Germany, it has significant engineering and manufacturing resources in China.[128]

2.4.2.9 NavInfo—HERE

Showing the comprehensive scope of US national security review process, in 2017 the CFIUS withheld another approval to a merger involving the Chinese gigantic Tencent, the Beijing-based digital map and software provider NavInfo Co. and the Singapore state-owned firm GIC, which had intended and later desisted from jointly acquiring a 10 per cent share of the digital mapping service and software company HERE International BV.[129] The acquired entity, owned by BMW, Daimler AG, and VW's Audi business and whose core business relates to the development of high-resolution maps to enable autonomous driving,[130] operates and has assets in the US. The acquisition of the 10 per cent stake in HERE would have allowed the acquirers to nominate a board

---

[124] 'Merger Agreement Between Zhongwang USA and Aleris Called Off after 15 Months' *Aluminium Insider* (14 November 2017) https://aluminiuminsider.com/merger-agreement-zhongwang-usa-aleris-called-off-15-months/ (accessed 13 September 2022).

[125] Christoph Steitz and Liana B Baker, 'Infineon, Cree Warn U.S. Might Block Wolfspeed Deal' *Reuters* (9 February 2017) https://www.reuters.com/article/uk-cree-m-a-infineon-technol-idUKKBN15O053.

[126] Cree, Press Release, Ex-99.1, Form 8-K (16 February 2017) SEC Filing.

[127] Steitz and Baker (n 125).

[128] Maury Wright, 'Cree Cancels Wolfspeed Deal with Infineon Based on US Government Concerns' *Leds Magazine* (22 February 2017) https://www.ledsmagazine.com/leds-ssl-design/article/16700750/cree-cancels-wolfspeed-deal-with-infineon-based-on-us-government-concerns (accessed 15 November 2022).

[129] Chris Duckett, 'Tencent and NavInfo Buy into Here Maps and Form Chinese Joint Venture' *ZDNET* (28 December 2016) https://www.zdnet.com/article/tencent-and-navinfo-buy-into-here-maps-and-form-chinese-joint-venture/ (accessed 15 September 2022). See HERE Press Release, 'HERE Expands into China; Provides Update on Shareholders' (26 September 2017).

[130] Eric Auchard, 'Chinese Drop Investment in Maps Firm HERE after U.S. Resistance' *Thomson Reuters* (2017) https://uk.reuters.com/article/us-china-autos (accessed 15 November 2022).

60 NATIONAL SECURITY ASSESSMENT

director, apparently an employee from NavInfo, and a member of the strategic advisory committee, presumably someone from Tencent.[131] Further, and according to an announcement made by the acquirers, their plan also included the creation of a 50/50 joint venture between HERE and Navinfo with the aim of providing mapping services in China, permitting HERE the use of Navinfo's data, another transaction also subject to approval.[132] Allegedly, the possibility that foreigners could exert some control over HERE precipitated the CFIUS' intervention.[133]

This rejection is characterized as an indication of the Trump administration's caution toward Chinese acquisitions.[134] US analysts familiar with the CFIUS had acknowledged that '[y]ou get the sense that this US administration would just rather have these transactions fall off, just run out the clock on the transactions', which can explain the trend of the CFIUS in leaving recent Chinese transactions 'in limbo' instead of explicitly requesting mitigation measures or recommend the POTUS to prohibit it.[135] Indeed, the announcement of the transaction was made in April 2016 and in September 2017 the involved parties announced the withdrawal.[136]

NavInfo official statements stated that there had been changes in the CFIUS' approach after the latest US elections 'at a time when China-US relations have been strained by Mr. Trump's harsh rhetoric against Chinese trade',[137] stating that the CFIUS continuously required them to change their application and revealed that 'even the emails they gave us were very vague, and just mentioned "national security reasons"'.[138] As we saw above, this is not the first time a transaction has been withdrawn after having raised national security concerns to which the CFIUS has responded with a prolonged review. This is neither the first time foreign investors question whether the US can ensure a transparent and reliable investment environment.

2.4.2.10 Ekso—Zhejiang & Shaoxing

Ekso Bionics Holdings (Ekso) a manufacturer of robotic mechanical suits, 'exoskeletons',[139] partnered with Zhejiang Youchuang Venture Capital and Shaoxing City Keqiao District Paradise Sillicon Intelligent Robot Industrial Investment Partnership (Zhejiang & Shaoxing), with the purpose of extending the exoskeletons market in

---

[131] Tang Shihua, 'Regulatory Delays Push NavInfo to Terminate Acquisition of Stake in Map Services Firm HERE' (28 September 2017) https://www.yicaiglobal.com/news/regulatory-delays-push-navinfo-to-terminate-acquisition-of-stake-in-map-services-firm-here (accessed 14 September 2022).

[132] Duckett (n 129).

[133] Tang (n 131).

[134] Chris Reiter and David McLaughlin, 'Chinese Bid for Stake in Mapping Firm Denied by U.S. Panel' *Bloomberg* (27 September 2017) https://www.bloomberg.com/news/articles/2017-09-26/chinese-bid-for-stake-in-here-maps-denied-by-u-s-security-panel (accessed 15 November 2022).

[135] Auchard (n 130).

[136] Tang (n 131)

[137] Yuan Yang, 'Chinese Bid for Mapping Company Falls at US Hurdle' *Financial Times* (27 September 2017) https://www.ft.com/content/6f0e519c-a33f-11e7-9e4f-7f5e6a7c98a2.

[138] ibid.

[139] Exoskeletons can be used to help people with mobility issues and can be used to help soldiers carrying heavier weapons while moving faster. See David Wang and others, 'CFIUS Extends Its Reach to Order the Termination of Ekso Bionic's Role in Joint Venture in China' *Paul Hastings* (10 June 2020) https://www.paulhastings.com/insights/client-alerts/cfius-extends-its-reach-to-order-the-termination-of-ekso-bionics-role-in-joint-venture-in-china (accessed 1 November 2022).

China and the Asian markets.[140] According to the terms of the deal, Ekso would license its manufacturing technology in return for a 20 per cent ownership position, and the Chinese partners would contribute about US$90 million in cash.[141] The Department of Defence and the Treasury Department made some inquiries about the joint venture resulting in a voluntary notice to the CFIUS in December 2019, although the products involved did not fall within the national security regulations. In May 2020, after imposing some interim measures, the CFIUS announced that the security concerns were insurmountable and as a result requested the termination of Ekso's role in the joint venture.[142] It has been reported that Ekso's claims that the CFIUS did not have jurisdiction to review the transaction considering that the transaction did not involve a foreign investment in a US business, Ekso did not transfer any rights or control, and its role in the joint venture consisted of know-how and a non-exclusive license to manufacture its technology, were not enough to prevent the termination order from the CFIUS.[143]

Some commentators seem to support Ekso's claims by indicating that the application of US export control laws would have been more appropriate in this case than the CFIUS' intervention.[144] It has also been indicated that according to Ekso, the joint venture did not have the power to appoint members of Ekso's board and that according to the CFIUS regulation a transaction solely involving the license of intellectual property to a foreign entity is not considered an acquisition of control.[145] However, it appears that the CFIUS treated the deal as covered by the pilot programme, which granted it jurisdiction to screen it.[146] This case illustrates that the power to review suspicious transactions is not confined to just types of assets, control, market shares, or acquisition of US companies, and it could simply rest on the possibility of disclosure of information. This approach reveals that the scope of reviewing the national security implications of foreign investments in the US is wide, covering various types of business models, structure of transactions/FDI, and can be targeted to foreign acquirers from specific jurisdictions. The CFIUS' extensive jurisdiction and intense scrutiny could be used as an effective tool to respond to economic and (geo)political tensions, but at the

---

[140] Press Release, 'Ekso Bionics Announces CFIUS Determination Regarding China Joint Venture' (20 May 2020) https://www.globenewswire.com/news-release/2020/05/20/2036681/0/en/Ekso-Bionics-Announces-CFIUS-Determination-Regarding-China-Joint-Venture.html (accessed 1 November 2022).

[141] ibid.

[142] ibid.

[143] David Wang and others, 'CFIUS Extends Its Reach to Order the Termination of Ekso Bionic's Role in Joint Venture in China' *Paul Hastings* (10 June 2020).

[144] https://www.clearytradewatch.com/2020/06/cfius-blocks-joint-venture-outside-the-united-states-releases-2018-2019-data-and-goes-electronic/ (accessed 1 November 2022).

[145] Section § 800.302(f)(7) of the CFIUS regulation provides that: '§800.302 Transactions that are not covered control transactions. (f) Examples: (7) Example 7. Same facts as the example in paragraph (f)(6) of this section, except that Corporation X, a U.S. business, has developed important technology in connection with the production of armoured personnel carriers. Corporation A seeks to negotiate an agreement under which it could be licensed to manufacture using that technology. Assuming no other relevant facts, neither the proposed acquisition of technology pursuant to that license agreement, nor other actual acquisition, is a covered control transaction.' See also Marquardt, Kaniecki, and Kurcab (n 144).

[146] § 801.302 'Transactions that are pilot program covered transactions ... (b) ... Corporation A will be provided access to material non-public technical information in the possession of Corporation B to which Corporation A did not previously have access.'

same time this also creates the risk for national security assessment being used as a tool for political aims that will not be related to national security concerns.

The case law discussed above allows us to draw the following implications. The scope of intervention of the CFIUS covers a wide variety of sectors, including telecommunications, food, financial services, defence industry, and technology. In some of the cases analysed here, the US government showed concerns that the Chinese government could have attained security and safety advantages at its disposal, even if in some of the reviewed transactions a Chinese entity was not directly involved, and even if the involved parties did not operate in the defence sector or did not deal with critical infrastructure which are the sectors explicitly identified as important for the national security in the US. Although approval has been given in some of the cases discussed above, it seems that another successful strategy used to effectively prohibit transactions, has been the lengthy timelines, which led to parties withdrawing their intended transactions after waiting for a decision for considerable periods of time. A recurrent theme is the secrecy that surrounds the assessment process and its outcomes, in which it seems that neither the parties nor the public are entitled to information on the process, or the considerations that led to the decision, making the CFIUS's review unpredictable at times. Finally, we should also emphasize the impact that a CFIUS investigation has on the share price of both the acquirer and the target. A CFIUS investigation, even more so a protracted one, is likely to cause downward pressure on the share prices of the parties involved, which can lead to transactions failing because of this knock-on impact on the share prices.

2.4.2.11 Magnachip

In this operation, Wise Road Capital, a Chinese private equity firm, agreed indirectly to acquire Magnachip Corp., a New York Stock exchange (NYSE) listed company with operations in Asia, for US$1.4 billion. The latter designs and manufactures analogue and mixed signal semiconductors.[147]

However, in December 2021, Wise Road Capital, and Magnachip Corp., announced that they had to abandon their planned merger in the face of CFIUS disapproval.

Even if is it well established that the CFIUS views the semiconductor sector as a very sensitive sector from a U.S national security perspective, here again, the parties believed that a CFIUS review was not mandatory or recommended because of Magnachip's limited US presence. In this context, they did not notify the transaction. However, a few months later, the CFIUS blocked the operation concluding that the deal posed 'risk to national security' and that the party failed to adequately mitigate the identified risks'[148]. This case highlights the fact that the Committee pays more attention to non-notified transactions which could present risks for national security.

---

[147] Chase D Kaniecki, William S Dawley, and Pete Young, 'CFIUS Threatens to Block Magnachip Deal; Shows Willingness to Interpret Its Jurisdiction Broadly' *Cleary Gottlieb* (15 December 2021).

[148] Damely Perez and Kimberly Shi, 'Back to the Future: The Committee on Foreign Investment in the United States (CFIUS) Scuppers Another Semiconductor Transaction' *Clifford Chance* (11 January 2022).

This case exemplifies the fact that the CFIUS has broad discretion in interpreting its rules and is willing to use that discretion as needed in order to review transactions in which it may have a substantive interest. In the case of Magnachip, the transaction involves China and semiconductors, both of which are hot buttons for the CFIUS.[149]

2.4.3 Transactions Blocked by US Presidents

In addition to the de facto prohibitions of the CFIUS, due to harsh mitigation conditions or lengthy reviews, as these were assessed above, the POTUS has the authority to prohibit transactions. The book will turn now to the analysis of the handful of transactions that the POTUS has intervened in and prohibited since 1990.

2.4.3.1 George H. W. Bush administration

President Bush stated in March 1990's Report on National Security Strategy of the US, that his turn to lead the country happened in an era where 'the international landscape [was] marked by change that [was] breath-taking in its character, dimension, and pace'.[150] In this report, he emphasized that an 'enduring element' of the US strategy 'has been a commitment to a free and open international economic system'[151] and added that the US should 'never forget the vicious circle of protectionism that helped deepen the Great Depression and indirectly fostered the Second World War'.[152] He noted that his administration was committed to work with other countries to 'promote the prosperity of the free market system' and to 'reduce barriers that unfairly inhibit international commerce'.[153] It is against this backdrop that the following case should be read.

2.4.3.1.1 *China National Aero-Technology Import and Export Corp.*

President Bush exercised for the first time the power that was granted to the 'head of state' under the so-called Exon-Florio provision (introduced in 1989) to block the foreign purchase of an American company. The case was brought to public attention when he ordered China National Aero-Technology Import and Export Corp. (CATIC) to divest all of their interest in MAMCO Manufacturing Co. of Seattle (MAMCO), a company which manufactures metal components for commercial aircraft, because there was credible evidence that led him to believe that, in exercising its control of MAMCO, CATIC might take action that would threaten to impair the national security of the US.[154]

---

[149] Jonathan Gafni, 'Thoughts on CFIUS's Review of Wise Road-Magnachip' *Linklaters* (14 September 2021).

[150] George HW Bush, *National Security Strategy of the United States*, Historical Office, Office of the Secretary of Defence (March 1990) preface v https://history.defense.gov/Portals/70/Documents/nss/nss1990.pdf?ver=2014-06-25-121138-080 (accessed 15 November 2022).

[151] ibid 1.

[152] ibid.

[153] ibid.

[154] Presidential Order (1 February 1990) 55 FR 3935.

64   NATIONAL SECURITY ASSESSMENT

Being the very first instance of a US President blocking a transaction, one would expect a detailed account of the reasoning behind the decision. The ambiguous language used by the CFIUS, the President, his spokesman, and administration officials, alongside the secrecy that surrounds the CFIUS decision-making process, did not provide sufficient clarity on the circumstances that comprised such 'impair[ment] to the national security'. What we can surmise is that there was a concern 'that CATIC could use MAMCO as a base for intelligence activities in the US, getting access to Boeing plants' and that CATIC might use the 'purchase as a front to penetrate into other, more promising areas of security'.[155] In addition, it was publicly known by that time that CATIC had already violated US export regulations[156] in the past, when it purchased General Electric aircraft engines for the Chinese military.[157] So, it seems that the problem with the approach to national security concerns is, in principle, not the absence of in-depth review from the authorities, but rather the lack of clarity to the wider public about the justification for the approach and decision taken.

2.4.3.2 Barack H. Obama administration

The Obama administration decided to avoid the winding path of interfering with the CFIUS' approach, and let most matters be resolved at the Committee level, even though the number of CFIUS filings increased significantly during both of his terms.[158] Evidence of such an approach was embodied in the Congress' request for the US Government Accountability Office (GAO) to prepare a report regarding the CFIUS process, where it specifically noted that the stance towards Chinese acquirers should be focused on 'a strategic rather than overt national security threat'.[159] As a consequence of such attitude, only two deals were either called off by the parties (the takeover of Aixtron, a semiconductor company, by FGC, a Chinese firm) or required divestments by Obama (Chinese SOE Ralls Corp, which was required to divest wind farm assets located near a defence facility). The chapter discusses these cases in detail below.

2.4.3.2.1 Ralls Corporation (2012)

In the middle of Obama's second term election campaign against Republican Mitt Romney, who was accusing him of being soft on China,[160] Obama blocked a privately owned Chinese company from building wind turbines close to a Navy military site in Oregon due to national security concerns. According to his order, there was 'credible evidence' that led him to believe that Ralls Corporation might take action that

---

[155] Working Papers, Review of Foreign Acquisitions under the Exon-Florio Provision, Section of Antitrust Law, Drafting Committee Lawrence R Fullerton and Christopher G Griner (American Bar Association Section of Antitrust Law 1992) 152.

[156] US export regulations are also relevant in the context of transactions reviewed by the CFIUS. Discussing in detail the US export regulations fall outside the scope of the analysis in this chapter.

[157] ibid.

[158] For instance, in the period from 2012 to 2014, the CFIUS reviewed sixty-eight potential acquisitions involving China, whereas in the three years before the FINSA enactment there were only four. Husisian (n 46) 69.

[159] ibid.

[160] Rachelle Younglai, 'Obama Blocks Chinese Wind Farms in Oregon over Security' Reuters (29 September 2012) https://www.reuters.com/article/us-usa-china-turbines-idUSBRE88R19220120929.

threatened to impair the national security of the US through the exercise of control over the target assets.[161]

According to the Obama administration, Ralls Corp had been installing wind turbines by Sany Group originating from China wind turbine generators by Sany Group, and by the time of the deal[162] had four wind farm projects that were within or in the vicinity of restricted air space at a naval weapons system training facility.[163] The company explained that only one of their four wind farms was in the alleged restricted airspace, and that the CFIUS never suggested a remedy to address the specific national security issue, ie only divest interest in the particular windfarm that was at the root of the national security concern.[164] Also, they stated that there were other wind farms in the same area operated by foreign persons/entities (from Denmark and Germany),[165] which may incite criticism that the prohibition based on the national security concerns was targeted against Chinese acquirers in particular. In response, the Treasury Department accepting to mitigate these criticisms stressed that the President's decision 'was not a precedent for other investments from China or any other country'.[166]

An interesting development in this case was that Ralls filed a lawsuit against the CFIUS for 'ordering it to stop all construction and operations at its projects while the government panel completed its investigation and finalized its recommendation to Obama',[167] comprising the only lawsuit against a CFIUS decision until that time. In 2014, Ralls won its appeal, since the DC Circuit accepted that the CFIUS failed to provide Ralls with 'an opportunity to rebut ... unclassified, non-privileged information',[168] hence 'violating Ralls' due process rights'.[169] The settlement between the US government and Ralls in October 2015 was a suitable choice for both parties. Although Ralls achieved great success when the DC Circuit sided with the company, some commentators argued that there was a chance for the US government to win if the litigation went further and the DC Circuit judgment was appealed.[170] Nevertheless, it seems that the CFIUS was also conscious that any extended litigation

---

[161] Presidential Order (28 September 2012).

[162] 'Ralls opted not to undergo CFIUS review before the international investment, as is usually done by foreign companies, but instead waited until after the transaction had closed to voluntarily file with CFIUS.' See Judy Wang, 'Ralls Corp v CFIUS: A New Foreign Direct Investments to the US' (2016) 54 Columbia Journal of Transnational Law 30, 31.

[163] Younglai (n 160).

[164] ibid.

[165] ibid.

[166] ibid.

[167] ibid.

[168] Stephen Heifetz, 'Ralls and U.S. Government Settle only CFIUS Suit in History' Lexology (14 October 2015) https://www.lexology.com/library/detail.aspx?g=a7cadd6a-eae5-4fe6-b6bf-57d4622ffa6d (accessed 16 September 2022).

[169] ibid.

[170] 'The US Government's position on the merits ... seemingly was undented. Neither the district court nor the appeals court indicated any interest in second-guessing the Executive Branch's national security views. With a little more give on "process", it appeared the US Government might ultimately prevail in forcing divestment without compensating Ralls.' See Heifetz (n 168).

66 NATIONAL SECURITY ASSESSMENT

could have in principle risked the Committee's remit to impose mitigation conditions for the approval of transactions.[171]

2.4.4 A Brief Historical Overview

2.4.4.1 Aixtron (2016)

Even though there was a tendency present in the CFIUS reviews during the Obama administration towards a positive stance to Chinese acquirers,[172] this changed in the years 2016–2017, and the prospects for deals involving Chinese acquirers to be cleared on national security grounds started to deteriorate.[173]

In 2016, the Department of Commerce issued a report stating that the US government was concerned about how focused Chinese acquirers were on closing the relative gap to the US in their capabilities on semiconductors, and emphasizing that the US should be more protective of its technology and manufacturing of semiconductors, since they were essential for US national security. In this context, in 2016 Obama prohibited the acquisition of Aixtron SE, a German semiconductor company with a US subsidiary, by a Chinese SOE in Germany, Grand Chip Investment GmbH.[174] Also, the CFIUS called off the sale of Philips NV's Lumileds, a manufacturer of lighting components and LEDs (a form of semiconductor), to a consortium that included several Chinese firms.[175] In another case in the semiconductor sector, Xiamen San'an Integrated Circuit Co Ltd had to abandon the envisaged merger with GCS Holdings, which would have brought Global Communications Semiconductors, LLC (GCS Holdings' wholly owned subsidiary in the US) into the San'an Group of companies, and a US-based semiconductor chip manufacturer, Fairchild Semiconductor International, had to reject an acquisition offer from two Chinese firms (China Resources Microelectronics Ltd and Hua Capital Management Co Ltd) due to the CFIUS' concerns.[176]

Obama's decision to block the Aixtron deal (Fujian Grand Chip's, FGC, takeover of the German company and its US subsidiaries[177]) came amidst expectations that his successor, Donald Trump, might adopt an even more hostile attitude towards Chinese investment in the US with both Democrats and Republicans in Congress calling for a broadening of the CFIUS' mandate.[178] Notably, by the time of the Aixtron decision, the CFIUS was focused on the scrutiny of (i) investments in the high-tech sector, particularly in the market for semiconductors (especially when the company's technology has military applications) and (ii) investments involving Chinese acquirers (it is noteworthy that the three presidential actions under the CFIUS up to that point had involved Chinese acquirers).[179]

---

[171] ibid.
[172] Husisian (n 46) 69.
[173] Sonsini Goodrich & Rosati (n 51).
[174] ibid.
[175] ibid.
[176] ibid.
[177] Presidential Order (2 December 2016).
[178] Schwartz and Mammen (n 36).
[179] Until December 2019.

Alongside the German authorities, the US national security authorities (ie the CFIUS) had jurisdiction to review the transaction, because of Aixtron's US subsidiary, Aixtron. On 18 November 2016, Aixtron stated publicly that the CFIUS had informed the parties of their national security concerns regarding the envisaged transaction, and had advised the parties to abandon the deal under the threat of referring the case to President Obama with a recommendation to prohibit the transaction.[180] It is noteworthy that the CFIUS order includes any assets of Aixtron that are not owned by the US business, but could be within the US, and could also include assets outside the US that are used in the activities of the US business.[181]

The POTUS adopted the recommendation of the CFIUS[182] to which China's Foreign Ministry commented that there were ' "groundless accusations" against Chinese firms by the United States and lamented the "politicization" of what it said was a commercial takeover'.[183] Despite the national security risks being 'groundless' according to China's Foreign Ministry, and the fact that 'President Obama's Executive Order d[id] not elaborate on specific national security concerns',[184] there was indeed a justification provided for the prohibition. The US Department of the Treasury issued a statement that:

> the national security risk posed by the transaction relates, among other things, to the military applications of the overall technical body of knowledge and experience of Aixtron, a producer and innovator of semiconductor manufacturing equipment and technology, and the contribution of Aixtron's US business to that body of knowledge and experience.[185]

The statement also made reference to Aixtron's business as a manufacturer of 'Metal-Organic Chemical Vapor Deposition (MOCVD) systems used to build compound semiconductor materials'.[186] Aixtron also manufactures gallium nitride, which has military applications, and was used 'to upgrade US and foreign-owned patriot missile defense systems'.[187] Thus, the CFIUS was concerned with the transfer of know-how to China.[188] Furthermore, Obama went beyond the usual approach that US presidents have taken when prohibiting a transaction, and required the acquirer through its executive order to:

---

[180] Michael T Gershberg and Justin A Schenck, 'President Obama Blocks Chinese Acquisition of Semiconductor Manufacturer Aixtron' *Fried Frank International Trade and Investment Alert* (8 December 2016) https://www.friedfrank.com/uploads/siteFiles/Publications/FINAL%20-12-8-2016-ITI%20Alert-President%20Obama%20Blocks%20Chinese%20Acquisition%20of%20Semiconductor1.pdf (accessed 30 April 2023).

[181] ibid 2.

[182] David McLaughlin, 'Obama Blocks Chinese Takeover of Aixtron as U.S. Security Risk' *Bloomberg* (2 December 2016) https://www.bloomberg.com/news/articles/2016-12-02/obama-blocks-chinese-takeover-of-aixtron-as-u-s-security-risk (accessed 15 November 2022).

[183] Maria Sheahan, 'China's Fujian Drops Aixtron Bid after Obama Blocks Deal' *Thomson Reuters* (8 December 2016) https://www.reuters.com/article/us-aixtron-m-a-fujian/chinas-fujian-drops-aixtron-bid-after-obama-blocks-deal-idUSKBN13X16H (accessed 15 November 2022).

[184] Gershberg and Schenck (n 180) 2.

[185] ibid.

[186] ibid.

[187] Sheahan (n 183)

[188] Gershberg and Schenck (n 180) 2.

68 NATIONAL SECURITY ASSESSMENT

[f]ully and permanently abandon the proposed acquisition of not just the US business ... but also 'any asset of Aixtron or Aixtron, Inc. used in, or owned for the use in or benefit of, the activities in interstate commerce in the US of Aixtron, Inc., including without limitation any interest in any patents issued by, and any interest in any patent applications pending with, the United States Patent and Trademark Office.[189]

There is an increasing level of Chinese investment in the US, with particular interest in the US semiconductor industry that keeps raising national security concerns by the CFIUS and has led to tougher scrutiny. Moreover, the trend is for companies to reject offers from Chinese investors, since the results of the CFIUS' analyses is now more likely to be adverse to the transaction. For instance, this was the case of Fairchild Semiconductor International, a US-based semiconductor chip manufacturer, who rejected an acquisition offer from Chinese investors in 2016[190] 'because of what it said was an 'unacceptable level of risk' that the CFIUS would reject the deal'.[191]

2.4.4.2 Donald Trump administration

During his presidential campaign, President Trump recurrently stated that incoming FDIs should be viewed through a national security prism, and he appeared to focus particularly on Chinese investors, whom he even accused of taking US employees' jobs.[192] These views were consistent with those of Republicans in Congress, who were looking forward to reinforce US government review of transactions with a potential national security impact on the US.[193] During his campaign there were 'indications that the new administration will favour an informal 'reciprocity' test for foreign investment—i.e. that countries that do not allow a comparable investment in the same sector would not see CFIUS approvals'.[194] These comments have particular importance for China, since it is a country that usually restricts investments from US investors.[195]

The increasing prominence of the CFIUS as a potential obstacle that, combined with a healthy US investment climate, was leading to an increased number of CFIUS reviews.

---

[189] ibid.

[190] Diane Bartz and Liana B Baker, 'Fairchild Rejects Chinese Offer on U.S. Regulatory Fears' https://www.reuters.com/article/us-fairchild-semico-m-a/fairchild-rejects-chinese-offer-on-u-s-regulatory-fears-idUSKCN0VP1O8 (accessed 15 November 2022).

[191] Gershberg and Schenck (n 180) 2.

[192] Ana Swanson, 'Trump Blocks China-Backed Bid to Buy U.S. Chip Maker' *New York Times* (13 September 2017) https://www.nytimes.com/2017/09/13/business/trump-lattice-semiconductor-china.html (accessed 9 September 2023).

[193] Husisian (n 46) 69.

[194] ibid.

[195] 'Roughly two dozen sectors in China—construction, mining, banking, insurance, and so on—remain effectively off-limits to American investment, because the Chinese government protects its domestic companies through regulations and financial subsidies. Even in sectors that technically allow foreign investment, discriminatory industrial policies tilt the playing field in favor of Chinese firms. Until this changes, Washington would be justified—even obligated—to limit Chinese investment in the U.S. market.' See Jennifer M Harris, *Writing New Rules for the U.S.-China Investment Relationship* (Council on Foreign Relations 2017) 1 https://www.cfr.org/sites/default/files/report_pdf/Discussion_Paper_Harris_China_OR.pdf (accessed 15 November 2022). See also Covington & Burling LLP, 'CFIUS and Foreign Direct Investment Under President Donald Trump' (2016) https://www.cov.com/-/media/files/corporate/publications/2016/11/cfius_and_foreign_direct_investment_under_president_donald_trump.pdf (accessed 15 November 2022).

Prohibitions of transactions were infrequent (although this trend started to change slightly for Chinese investments in US technology), and concerns about Chinese access to bulk data on US citizens were more prevalent.[196] The President on the one hand stated publicly his reaffirmation of support for inward foreign investment and, on the other hand, he also expressed support for the FIRRMA, which expanded the CFIUS' jurisdiction, and expanded the criteria by which the CFIUS assesses national security concerns.[197] However, Wolin explains that 'there has been further development of the idea that transactions that originate in certain geographies or that involve certain kinds of technology will be scrutinized very carefully ... those perspectives began during the Obama Administration'.[198] So what Trump proposes 'is not a sea change. It is more of a movement further down that path'.[199]

2.4.4.2.1 Lattice Semiconductor (2017)

In a sector where the US government has become increasingly wary of US technology firms being acquired by Chinese entities,[200] and in a move that could signal more aggressive scrutiny of China's investors' deal-making ambitions,[201] Trump blocked Chinese private equity firm Canyon Bridge Capital Partners LLC from purchasing Lattice Semiconductor Corp., a US-based company that manufactures programmable logic chips used in communications, computing, as well as industrial and military applications, on grounds of national security.[202]

Regardless of Lattice's efforts to address any outstanding national security concerns, the administration was not convinced.[203] The White House explained that it prevented the envisaged acquisition on the one hand because the US government relies on the target company's products (the semiconductor industry is a vital one for the US), and on the other given the raised concerns over the acquirer's close ties to China, since the investment group included China Venture Capital Fund Corporation, which was owned by state-backed entities.[204] In a press release, the CFIUS Chairman and Secretary of the Treasure Steven T. Mnuchin indicated that the transaction offered the following four main national security concerns: (i) 'the potential transfer of Lattice's intellectual property to Canyon Bridge', (ii) 'the role of the Chinese government in the transaction', (iii) 'the importance of the semiconductor supply chain to the US government', and (iv) 'the

---

[196] Sonsini Goodrich & Rosati (n 51).

[197] Wolin (n 25).

[198] 'For example, the Obama Commerce Department put out a report in 2016 saying the US government was quite concerned about the extent to which the Chinese government was focused on closing the gap relative to the US in their basic set of capabilities around semiconductors, essentially saying the US ought to be more protective of its technology and manufacturing advantage in semiconductors, which can be relevant to national security. This line of thinking has to some extent further intensified, in terms of the range of sensitive technologies and capabilities that give the US pause.' Ibid.

[199] Ibid.

[200] Former US President Obama released a report prior to leaving office in January that warned that China's ambitious push to expand its domestic chip production could threaten the semiconductor industry.

[201] Swanson (n 192).

[202] Presidential Order (13 September 2017).

[203] Swanson (n 192).

[204] ibid.

70   NATIONAL SECURITY ASSESSMENT

US government's use of Lattice products'.[205] As shown, this prohibition, the fourth one ever issued by a US President under the Exon-Florio amendment, emphasizes the US government's significant concerns about Chinese investment in the US, especially in technology manufacturers.[206]

2.4.4.2.2 Qualcomm (2018)

In a year where the US blocked the US$1.2 billion sale of money transfer firm MoneyGram to China's Ant Financial, the digital payments arm of Alibaba,[207] and Trump announced that he would implement tariffs on foreign steel and aluminium companies in order to lead to the manufacturing of those commodities in the US,[208] the President blocked a planned takeover of chipmaker Qualcomm by Singapore-based rival Broadcom[209] on grounds of national security.[210] Despite his executive order invoking 'credible evidence' that the proposed US$140 billion deal threatened to impair the national security of the US,[211] with no further details provided, commentators opined that 'there were concerns the takeover could have led to China pulling ahead in the development of 5G wireless technology [since] [t]he deal would have been the biggest technology sector takeover on record'.[212] Notably, Qualcomm's takeover would have created the world's third-largest maker of microchips, behind Intel and Samsung. Although there were arguments that this was an attempt by President Trump to 'sharpen his nationalist knife',[213] a deal between Qualcomm and Broadcom could have given Huawei the opportunity to solidify its position in the market—a development US politicians wanted to prevent given their ongoing security concerns around Chinese telecom firms doing business with US carriers.[214] In fact, it was stated by sources close to the CFIUS that the US military was concerned that within ten years Huawei 'would essentially be a dominant player in all of these technologies', which would leave the American carriers with no other choice but buying Huawei equipment.[215] This case

---

[205] Michael Gershberg and Justin Schenck, 'President Trump Blocks Chinese Acquisition of Lattice Semiconductor Corporation' *Harvard Law School Forum on Corporate Governance and Financial Regulation* (24 September 2017) https://corpgov.law.harvard.edu/2017/09/24/president-trump-blocks-chinese-acquisition-of-lattice-semiconductor-corporation/ (accessed 15 November 2022).

[206] John B Bellinger III and others, 'New Presidential Order Blocking Chinese Acquisition of Semiconductor Firm Flags a Trend of Heightened CFIUS Review of Chinese Investments' *Arnold & Porter* (22 September 2017) https://www.arnoldporter.com/en/perspectives/publications/2017/09/new-presidential-order-blocking (accessed 15 November 2022).

[207] The CFIUS requested mitigation measures that the parties were unwilling to offer. See https://www.bbc.co.uk/news/business-42549537 (accessed 9 November 2022).

[208] Matthew Renda, 'Trump Blocks Tech Company Merger Citing National Security' *Courthouse News Service* (12 March 2018) https://www.courthousenews.com/trump-blocks-tech-company-merger-citing-national-secur ity/ (accessed 15 November 2022).

[209] Broadcom had grown through acquisitions, but was deemed to be weaker on R&D. See 'Trump Blocks Broadcom's Bid for Qualcomm on Security Grounds' *BBC* (13 March 2018) https://www.bbc.co.uk/news/busin ess-43380893.

[210] Presidential Order (12 March 2018).

[211] BBC (n 209).

[212] ibid.

[213] James Moore, 'Trump Blocks $140bn Tech Mega Merger: An Example of Nasty Nationalism or Simple Pragmatism? It Might Be Both' *Independent* (13 March 2018) https://www.independent.co.uk/news/business/comment/donald-trump-qualcomm-broadcom-merger-block-protectionism-regulation-us-a8253306.html.

[214] BBC (n 209).

[215] Reuters (n 45).

raised concerns in a context where 5G is considered a crucial asset[216] for the US economy.[217]

As has been common practice in executive orders, the US President did not provide a detailed rationale for his decision. However, a letter from the Treasury Department calling for a review of the transaction explained that the administration was concerned about Broadcom's relationships with other foreign companies, and 'strongly hinted that those companies of interest are based in China'.[218] The letter also highlighted that Broadcom had reduced spending on R&D of the businesses it acquires, a practice that would most likely make Qualcomm less innovative. This envisaged scenario would in turn be beneficial to Chinese businesses in terms of the development of the technology for the next generation of mobile phones (ie 5G).[219]

In addition to national security concerns this envisaged takeover raised serious antitrust concerns as well.[220] Alongside the weakening on innovation, the transaction could possibly lead to competition harm, as in a more concentrated market firms may have greater incentives to raise prices of existing products as well as reduce product choice or quality.

2.4.4.2.3 StayNTouch, Inc. (2020)

By executive order on 6 March 2020, President Trump prohibited Beijing Shiji Information Technology Co Ltd (and together with its wholly owned subsidiary Shiji (Hong Kong) Ltd, Beijing Shiji), a Chinese public company, from acquiring any ownership in StayNTouch, Inc. (StayNTouch) or any of StayNTouch assets. The latter develops technology platforms used by hotels. On the other hand, Shiji Group is specialized on software for hotels, restaurants, and retail stores.

This executive order followed a seven-month review initiated by the CFIUS and came more than a year after the acquisition.[221] It suggested that there was credible evidence that the purchaser 'might take action that threatens to impair the national security of the United States'[222] without specifying the threat. It ordered the Chinese company to divest from StayNTouch, a US company that makes cloud-based hotel management software, and its assets, including customer data, within 120 days.[223]

---

[216] According to Mario Morales, vice president of enabling technologies and semiconductors at global research firm IDC.

[217] BBC (n 209). The US government is dependent on Qualcomm, and its role in developing communications systems for the military. See 'Trump Was Right to Block a Merger' *New York Times* (14 March 2018) https://www.nytimes.com/2018/03/14/opinion/trump-qualcomm-merger.html (accessed 15 November 2022).

[218] *New York Times* (n 217).

[219] ibid.

[220] In fact, according to US Research Company Gartner: 'if the Broadcom-Qualcomm merger had gone through, just three companies—Samsung, Intel, and Broadcom—would have controlled more than 36 per cent of the global market for chips'. ibid.

[221] Olivier J Borgers, 'Foreign Investment Review, USA' *McCarthy Tétrault LLP* (2 February 2022).

[222] Donald Trump, Order Regarding the Acquisition of Stayntouch Inc by Beijing Shiji Information Technology Co Ltd (6 March 2020).

[223] ibid.

72 NATIONAL SECURITY ASSESSMENT

2.4.4.2.4 *Infineon (2020)*

US national security officials had recommended that President Donald Trump block German chipmaker Infineon Technologies AG's proposed US$10 billion deal to buy Cypress Semiconductor Corps. Indeed, according to officials, this operation might have posed a risk to national security, although no clear explanations were exposed.[224] However, on 9 March 2020, Infineon Technologies AG and Cypress Semiconductor Corp., the two parties to the transaction, announced that the CFIUS had cleared the operation.

This case highlights the intensifying concerns about foreign investment in the semiconductor sector. Indeed, Infineon is based in a NATO ally (Germany) but the CFIUS has been scrutinizing the transaction for more than eight months.[225] However, on the other hand, the Infineon case proves that the United States is still open to foreign investment even in a very sensitive sector such as the semiconductor one.

2.4.4.3 Joe Biden administration

For the first year since 2016, no Presidential decisions were issued in 2021 and 2022.[226] However, President Biden has recently signed a new executive order to 'ensure robust reviews of evolving national security risks by the Committee on Foreign Investment in the United States'. This is the first ever presidential directive defining national security factors that the CFIUS must consider when reviewing and evaluating transactions.[227]

From the above-mentioned analysis of the cases blocked by US presidents, four conclusions can be drawn. First, the number of occasions where a US President has exercised their right to block a transaction has been limited, namely to just five so far. Secondly, a common theme is the lack of detailed information about the reasons that supported each prohibition. Thirdly, the second term of Obama's administration signalled an increase in the US government's concern about transactions that have a direct or indirect Chinese government nexus. Fourthly, during President Trump's administration the national security concerns in relation to acquirers representing Chinese interests seem to have become more prevalent.

2.4.5 National Security Concerns and State-Owned Enterprises (SOEs)

One of the recurring national security concerns raised by CFIUS assessments is the threat imposed by 'the growing international presence and investment activity of firms

---

[224] Saleha Mohsin, David McLaughlin, and Jenny Leonard, 'Trump Advised to Halt Infineon Deal Amid China Security Risk' *Bloomberg* (6 March 2020) https://www.bloomberg.com/news/articles/2020-03-05/trump-is-warned-on-security-risk-from-infineon-deal-for-cypress (accessed 15 November 2022).

[225] Harry Clark, 'President Trump Orders Divestment of U.S. Company; CFIUS Clears Semiconductor Transaction' *Orrick* (13 March 2020) https://www.orrick.com/en/Insights/2020/03/President-Trump-Orders-Divestment-of-US-Company-CFIUS-Clears-Semiconductor-Transaction (accessed 15 November 2022).

[226] CFIUS, 'Annual Report to Congress' (CY 2021) https://home.treasury.gov/system/files/206/CFIUS-Public-AnnualReporttoCongressCY2021.pdf (accessed 15 November 2022) 15.

[227] Farhad Jalinous and others, 'Biden Issues First-Ever Presidential Directive Defining National Security Factors for CFIUS to Consider in Evaluating Transactions' *White & Case* (19 September 2022) https://www.whitecase.com/insight-alert/biden-issues-first-ever-presidential-directive-defining-national-security-factors (accessed 15 November 2022).

that are owned or controlled by foreign governments'.[228] As opposed to ten years ago, where only one or two SOEs were found 'at the top of the league table',[229] they now 'account for over a fifth of the world's largest enterprises'.[230]

Notably, since China is the world's second-largest economy after the US,[231] particular focus has been placed on Chinese SOEs' activities, since, if one considers China's holdings foreign exchange reserves that amounted to US$3.061 trillion by March 2020,[232] this 'enable[s] China to expand its foreign investments by acquiring companies and other assets abroad'.[233] China has acquired 'foreign technologies and know-how to advance these objectives as well as to further its national security interests',[234] while exploiting investment opportunities in different countries.

However, from the standpoint of the recipient country of the incoming FDI, China's presence 'may also entail risks [which] may embrace broad national interests, sensitive and newly emergent technologies, and the natural resources of countries receiving China's investments'.[235] Because of such risks, SOEs' activities predictably find resistance in the US for political, national, security and economic reasons.[236] Evidence of this is the view from former White House chief strategist Stephen K. Bannon, who stated in very colloquial language in Wolf's (2018) latest book prologue that:

> China's everything. Nothing else matters. We don't get China right, we don't get anything right. This whole thing is very simple. China is where Nazi Germany was in 1929 to 1930. The Chinese, like the Germans, are the most rational people in the world, until they're not. And they're gonna flip like Germany in the thirties. You're going to have a hypernationalist state, and once that happens you can't put the genie back in the bottle.[237]

In the US, Republicans in Congress have demanded that the GAO should determine whether CFIUS reviews 'have effectively kept pace with the growing scope of foreign acquisitions in strategically important sectors in the US',[238] while specifically singling

---

[228] Congressional Research Service (n 12) 28. The growing is such that, by 2010–2011, from the Forbes Global 2000 list of the world's largest 2000 public companies, 204 have been identified as majority SOEs in that business year, with ownership spread across thirty-seven different countries. China leading the list with seventy SOEs. Przemyslaw Kowalski and others, 'State-Owned Enterprises: Trade Effects and Policy Implications' (2013) OECD Trade Policy Paper No 147, 6 https://www.oecd-ilibrary.org/docserver/5k4869ckqk7l-en.pdf (accessed 15 November 2022).

[229] OECD, 'Ownership and Governance of State-Owned Enterprises: A Compendium of National Practices' (2018) 4 https://www.oecd.org/corporate/ca/Ownership-and-Governance-of-State-Owned-Enterprises-A-Compendium-of-National-Practices.pdf (accessed 15 November 2022).

[230] ibid.

[231] KL Alex Lau, Angus Young, and YN Hong, 'Merger Control in China under the Anti-Monopoly Law: A Competition Regime in Transition' (2016) 37(9) Comparative Law 285, 285.

[232] CGTN Global Business, 'China's Foreign Exchange Reserves Remain Stable' (8 July 2019) https://news.cgtn.com/news/2019-07-08/China-s-foreign-exchange-reserves-remain-stable-Ian6GuDliE/index.html (accessed 15 November 2022).

[233] Charles Wolf Jr and others, *China's Expanding Role in Global Mergers and Acquisitions Markets* (RAND 2011) 6 https://www.rand.org/pubs/monographs/MG1162.html (accessed 15 November 2022).

[234] ibid 27.

[235] ibid 2.

[236] ibid 5.

[237] Michael Wolff, Fire and Fury (Little Brown 2018) Prologue.

[238] Husisian (n 46) 72.

74 NATIONAL SECURITY ASSESSMENT

out Chinese and Russian SOEs' investments as causes of concern.[239] Based on public information, in the last nine years for which the CFIUS has published its Annual Reports, Chinese investors appear to have been the most significant source of CFIUS filings[240] in the years 2013, 2014, 2015,[241] 2016, 2017, and 2018,[242] and the second biggest contributor in 2019, 2020, 2021,[243] and 2022.[244]

We discuss below some important transactions that involve Chinese SOEs in order to assess how the CFIUS has approached them.

2.4.5.1 LENOVO—IBM (2005)

In 2005, and despite some national security concerns, the CFIUS approved the acquisition of IBM's personal computing division by LENOVO, a partially state-controlled company.[245] Moran has asserted that possible threats such as the leakage of sensitive technology, infiltration, espionage and disruption were unlikely to arise given the characteristics of the relevant market, such as the number of participants in the production of PCs—more than a dozen—and the lack of dominance from any of them. In his view, the number of choices at the disposal of buyers and the unlikelihood that Lenovo could have influenced access to PC supplies can explain the CFIUS' approach.[246]

2.4.5.2 CNOOC—UNOCAL (2005)

In June 2005, the Chinese Offshore Oil Corp (CNOOC) bid for US oil company UNOCAL. The latter's total production was less than 1 per cent of domestic oil consumption and 70 per cent of its assets were gas reserves in Asia.[247] The Congress immediately opposed the deal arguing, inter alia, that China will gain access to 'cavitation' technology—a process where oil is drilled for in deep water—enabling the Chinese state 'to do nuclear tests underground and to mask them so we would not ever be able to detect them'.[248] Such opposition resulted in a non-binding resolution and a call for an instant thorough review of the possible transaction by the CFIUS given that a Chinese state-owned energy company exercising control of critical US energy infrastructure

---

[239] See Letter from Robert Pittenger to Hon Gene L Dodaro (15 September 2016) 1.

[240] For instance, *Chemchina—Syngenta* and *Lattice Semiconductors* (both filed in 2016) and *Global Eagle Entertainment/HNA* (filed in 2017) could be mentioned among some of the filings from Chinese investors with the greatest impact on the media. See CFIUS (n 67).

[241] In all, 21 out of 97 total filings in 2013; 24 out of 147 in 2014; 29 out of 143 in 2015. See CFIUS (n 20) 16–17.

[242] 54 out of 172 total filings in 2016; 60 out of 237 in 2017; 55 out of 229 in 2018. See CFIUS, 'Annual Report to Congress' (CY 2018) 20–21 https://home.treasury.gov/system/files/206/CFIUS-Public-Annual-Report-CY-2018.pdf (accessed 15 November 2023).

[243] 25 out of 231 total filings in 2019; 17 out of 187 in 2020; 44 out of 272 in 2021. See CFIUS (n 229) 32–33.

[244] 36 out of 286. See CFIUS (n 62) 39–41.

[245] Arik Hesseldahl, 'Lenovo's Global Rise Began with IBM PC Deal a Decade Ago' *Vox* (30 January 2014) https://www.vox.com/2014/1/30/11622894/lenovos-global-rise-began-with-ibm-pc-deal-a-decade-ago (accessed 16 September 2022).

[246] Theodore H Moran, 'Toward a Multilateral Framework for Identifying National Security Threats Posed by Foreign Acquisitions: With Special Reference to Chinese Acquisitions in the United States, Canada, and Australia' (2014) 7(1) China Economic Journal 39, 44.

[247] Genevieve Ding, 'The CNOOC Bid for Unocal and US National Security: Was the Political Outcry in Congress Justified?' https://sites.duke.edu/djepapers/files/2016/10/Ding.pdf (accessed 9 November 2022).

[248] House of Representatives Democratic Leader Nancy Pelosi (30 June 2005) Pelosi Statement on Amendment to Block Chinese Bid to Acquire Unocal http://www.house.gov/pelosi/press/releases/June05/unocal.html (accessed 9 November 2022).

and energy production capacity could threaten US national security.[249] After concerns that the transaction would not get the approval, CNOOC withdrew its bid.[250]

This case represents another example of a transaction that was withdrawn in light of a possible regulatory roadblock by the CFIUS. While there is no public evidence provided to underpin any of the political, economic or national interest concerns shown by Congress, the reality is that at the time of the proposal twenty-one countries had oil for export in volumes greater than UNOCAL's entire production.[251] In addition, there was significant advancement in discovery and production of oil that would have had a positive impact in energy markets (US included) and global energy consumers.[252] In short, it may be the case that Congress overstated the national security threats posed by the takeover, and its position portrayed a protectionist stance towards Chinese SOEs.

2.4.5.3 BAIN—3Com/HUAWEI Technologies Co (2007)

In 2007, Bain Capital Partners LLC, an international private investment firm, intended to buy 3Com, a leading US hardware and software network company, for US$2.2 billion. At the time of this transaction, 3Com had already formed a joint venture with Huawei in China—H3C. Huawei would acquire a 16.5 per cent minority shareholding on 3Com as well.[253] In March 2008, BAIN abandoned the deal as a result of opposition due to national security concerns. The possible threats consisted of (i) the interest that Huawei would acquire (16.5 per cent), which, however, seemed insufficient to enable the Chinese government to influence how 3Com goods and services were offered; (ii) leakage of sensitive technologies or other capabilities to Chinese users that they would not otherwise have access to, even though many of the products produced by 3Com were already produced in China; and, (iii) potential capability for infiltration, surveillance, or sabotage of US interests.[254]

These transactions involving SOEs, reveal the approach of the US government to transactions involving US assets by entities that are owned directly or indirectly by the Chinese government. The US approach has led to the withdrawal of two transactions due to the hostility shown by the US government grounded on national security concerns.

Based on the CFIUS enforcement record and approach to the assessment of national security concerns, commentators have noted that '[R]epublicans in Congress have been trying for years to alter the scope of the CFIUS review process and are likely to view the election of Mr Trump as an opportunity to enact this agenda.'[255] The book discusses below some of the most recent concerns of Congress in relation to the CFIUS remit, and the proposed legislation to address these concerns.

---

[249] US Congress, House 2005, H Res 344 https://www.congress.gov/bill/109th-congress/house-resolution/344 (accessed 9 November 2022).
[250] Ding (n 246).
[251] Moran (n 246) 45.
[252] ibid.
[253] ibid 46.
[254] ibid 47.
[255] ibid 6.

76 NATIONAL SECURITY ASSESSMENT

2.5 Proposals for Changes to the CFIUS

The strengthening of the scope of the CFIUS was being advocated for quite some time prior to the FIRRMA coming into effect.

These concerns have focused on: (1) the increase in foreign investment activity by Chinese state-owned companies (which will be addressed at a later stage); (2) the perception that such investment is part of a government-coordinated approach that serves official strategic purposes; and (3) on the fact that investments from Chinese companies are receiving government support, which entitles them to an 'unfair' competitive advantage over other private investors.[256]

Consequently, there are several amendments to the CFIUS remit that have been put forward. The amendments aim to broaden the scope of the review and also its mandate to adopt a more holistic approach in the assessment of transactions. In addition, a mandatory filing process is being put forward. Furthermore, the proposals include leveraging access to the US market to gain reciprocal access in foreign markets; applying penalties to foreign firms that receive subsidized financing or preferential domestic regulations; and discriminating among foreign investors based on membership in certain organizations.[257]

2.5.1 National Defence Authorization Act for Fiscal Year 2018, HR 2810[258]

This Act became Public Law No 115-91[259] and enables the Secretary of Defence to offer recommendations to agencies in order to improve the effectiveness of the interagency vetting of foreign investments that could impair the national security of the US.[260] It also establishes a process for enhancing the ability of the Defence Department to analyse and monitor foreign investments in the defence industrial base[261] and allows for the development of a programme to assess the feasibility of increasing the capability of the defence industrial base to support production needs to meet military requirements and the manufacturing and production of emerging and commercial technologies.[262] Finally, it allows for the 'exemption of organizations whose ownership or majority control is based in a country that is part of the national technology and industrial base from one or more of the foreign ownership, control, or influence requirements of the

---

[256] Congressional Research Service (n 12) 36.

[257] ibid 39. Notably, greenfield investments are also not covered by the CFIUS, so there is a gap in coverage that Congress could seek to fill by amending the statute. However, it does not currently seem to be a priority on the Congress' agenda. The book will discuss these amendments only to the extent that they are relevant for the discussion herein.

[258] The measure was signed by President Trump on 12 December 2017, and designated PL 115-91.

[259] Pub L No 115-91 (2017).

[260] HR2810, National Defence Authorization Act for Fiscal Year 2018, s 1069.

[261] ibid s 1071.

[262] ibid s 1711.

National Industrial Security Program'.[263] Moreover, the Act requires the Commander of the Air Force Space and Missile Systems Center to establish and maintain a watch-list of contractors under the criteria of 'security or foreign ownership and control issues'.[264]

2.5.2 Foreign Investment and Economic Security Act of 2017, HR 2932

This Act shall 'alter the composition of CFIUS and require a "net benefits" (cost-benefit) test, as part of a CFIUS national security review of a proposed foreign investment transaction'.[265] Such test provides that the President 'shall' consider the overall effects on the level of economic activity in the US and the effect of the proposed investment transaction on productivity, industrial efficiency, technology transfers, product innovation, and competition within the US and with other countries.[266] Thus, the scope of the analysis is expanded by introducing an additional criterion in the assessment of the national security risks that a transaction may pose. This Act grants the net benefit test an important role in determining whether a transaction can be approved from a national security perspective.

2.5.3 Section 616: The Food Security is National Security Act of 2017

This Act will include the Secretaries of Agriculture and Health and Human Services as permanent members of the CFIUS and, by doing so incorporate the impact of foreign investment in the food and agriculture systems on national security, as part of the CFIUS criteria for its assessment of a transaction.[267]

2.5.4 Section 1722: The True Reciprocity Investment Act of 2017

This Act requires the CFIUS to consider the reciprocity of foreign investment; this is if an investor's home country would allow a reciprocal investment of US interests in the

---

[263] ibid s 1712.

[264] HR2810, National Defence Authorization Act for Fiscal Year 2018, s 1612.

[265] Congressional Research Service (n 12) 39. The last recorded action of this proposal took place on 23 June 2017, when it was referred to the Subcommittee on Digital Commerce and Consumer Protection. See https://www.congress.gov/bill/115th-congress/house-bill/2932/all-actions (accessed 16 September 2022).

[266] Congressional Research Service (n 12) 39.

[267] ibid. The last recorded action of this proposal took place on 14 March 2017, when it was read twice and referred to the Committee on Banking, Housing, and Urban Affairs https://www.congress.gov/bill/115th-congress/senate-bill/616/all-actions (accessed 16 September 2022). On 5 October 2021, Senators Tommy Tuberville, Cynthia Lummis, Roger Marshall, and Rick Scott introduced the Foreign Adversary Risk Management (FARM) Act, which would add the secretary of agriculture as a member of the CFIUS, whose last action took place in Senate in May 2021. See FARM Act, s 2931 https://www.congress.gov/bill/117th-congress/senate-bill/2931/cosponsors (accessed 9 September 2022).

78 NATIONAL SECURITY ASSESSMENT

same industry.[268] This proposal is just an attempt to widen the scope of considerations to be considered by the CFIUS when reviewing deals under its authority.

2.5.5 Section 2987/HR 5515: The Foreign Investment Risk Review Modernization Act of 2018 (FIRRMA)

The FIRRMA represents a comprehensive revision of the foreign investment review process under the CFIUS, modifying the Act's defensive approach into a more assertive role that emphasizes US economic, as well as national security interests.[269] This piece of legislation, which was incorporated and enacted as part of the 2019 National Defense Authorization Act, addresses concerns arising from certain foreign non-controlling investments involved with critical technology, critical infrastructure, or sensitive personal data[270] and real estate transactions that previously fell outside the CFIUS' jurisdiction.[271] Before all regulations executing the FIRRMA were issued, two sets of interim regulations implementing certain provisions were adopted, one mainly related to administrative rules[272] and the other, known as the pilot programme, that authorized the CFIUS to review certain transactions involving foreign persons and critical technology companies and which required mandatory declarations.[273]

Besides broadening the scope of transactions subject to the CFIUS's review, this Act introduces some changes aiming to make the assessment process more effective. One of the most significant developments of the reform was that it successfully overcame the ambiguity about the confinement of the CFIUS' authority. It is important to say that, before the FIRRMA, the Committee could not review any transaction in which there was not a sufficient transfer of control of the local enterprise to a foreign investor. Under section 1703 of the FIRRMA, the term 'covered transactions' now encompasses both controlling and non-controlling foreign investments.[274] The FIRRMA also modified the exceptions for certain real estate transactions in airports and maritime ports[275] and

---

[268] The last recorded action of this proposal took place on 2 August 2017, when it was read twice and referred to the Committee on Banking, Housing, and Urban Affairs. See https://www.congress.gov/bill/115th-congress/senate-bill/1722/text (accessed 16 September 2022).

[269] Congressional Research Service (n 12) 1–2.

[270] Known as TID US business and by which the FIRRMA now provides some examples of these types of transactions.

[271] https://home.treasury.gov/system/files/206/Summary-of-FIRRMA.pdf (accessed 9 November 2022).

[272] Department of the Treasury, Office of Investment Security, Billing Code 4810-25-P, 31 CFR Part 800, RIN 1505-AC60, 'Provision Pertaining to Certain Investments in the United States by Foreign Persons'.

[273] 31 CFR Part 801: Pilot Program to Review Certain Transactions Involving Foreign Persons and Critical Technologies https://www.law.cornell.edu/cfr/text/31/part-801 (accessed 15 November 2022). The interim provisions contained in the pilot programme remained in effect until final CFIUS regulations were implemented or before 13 February 2020. If a transaction was subject to the pilot programme, the parties had to submit to CFIUS either (i) a mandatory declaration of the transaction according to 31 CFR §801.402; or (ii) a notice of the transaction according to 31 CFR § 801.501, including the supplemental information required by 31 CFR § 801.503.

[274] FIRRMA, s 1703, § (A)(i)(ii), which stipulates: '(A) IN GENERAL.—Except as otherwise provided, the term 'covered transaction' means- (i) any transaction described in subparagraph (b)(i); and (ii) any transaction described in clauses (ii) through (v) of subparagraph (B) that is proposed, pending, or completed on or after the effective date set forth in section 1727 of the Foreign Investment Risk Review Modernization Act of 2018.'

[275] FIRRMA, s 1703, § (A)(i)(ii), which provides: '(B) TRANSACTIONS DESCRIBED.- A transaction described in this subparagraph is any of the following: (i) Any merger, acquisition, or takeover that is proposed or

refined the geographic coverage relating to certain military installations.[276] Of great importance also are the improvements brought by the interim regulations. Among them are the introduction of the definition of 'principal place of business',[277] the revision of the definition of 'substantial interest',[278] the adjustment of the treatment of genetic data within the definition of 'sensitive personal data',[279] and, in the realm of real estate transactions, the application of exempted rules by certain 'excepted investors' from certain 'excepted foreign estates'.[280] Such an exemption is not absolute though, as even if a foreign person meets the modified criteria to qualify as an 'excepted investor', the CFIUS shall retain authority to review a transaction that could result in foreign control of any US business.[281]

Pursuant to the FIRRMA, while the CFIUS continues as a voluntary review process, there are two categories of foreign investment where mandatory filing is required: (i) investments by an investor (subject to certain exemptions) in certain TID[282] business involved with critical technologies; and (ii) certain investments by foreign investors with substantial government ownership (subject to certain exemptions) in any TID US business.[283] In light of the recent expansion of the CFIUS's authority, it seems that almost any foreign person or entity is potentially within its regulatory reach. Hence, the FIRRMA strengthens the role of the CFIUS by, on the one hand, providing clarity to some considerations that are relevant for its assessment and, on the other hand, by clarifying the criteria of what would be considered an 'excepted investor', while maintaining its power to assess all transactions involving foreign acquirers and US domestic assets.

Before turning to the examination of the CFIUS enforcement activity, it is important to note that in 8 June 2021 the Strategic Competition Act of 2021 was approved by the US Senate, expanding the scope of the CFIUS even further by reviewing certain gifts made to, and contracts made with, US higher education institutions concerning foreigners.[284]

---

pending after August 23, 1988, by or with any foreign person that could result in foreign control of any United States business, including such a merger, acquisition or takeover carried out through a joint venture. (ii) Subject to subparagraphs (C) and (E), the purchase or lease by, or a concession to, a foreign person of private or public real estate that- (II)(aa) is, is located within, or will function as part of, an air or maritime port; or (bb)(AA) is in close proximity to a United States military installation or another facility or property of the United States that is sensitive for reasons relating to national security.'

[276] https://home.treasury.gov/system/files/206/Final-FIRRMA-Regulations-FAQs.pdf (accessed 9 November 2022).

[277] 85 FR 3160, stating that: '§ 800.232 now provides a definition of a party's "principal place of business" as the "primary location" where an entity's management directs, controls, or coordinates the entity's activities, or, in the case of and investment fund, where the fund's activities and investments are primarily directed, controlled, or co-ordinated by or on behalf of the general partner, managing member, or equivalent.'

[278] 85 FR 57125, indicating that: 'The substantial interest analysis as revised in the proposed rules at § 800.244(b) is appropriately focused on the interest held in the general partner, managing member, or equivalent when such general partner, managing member, or equivalent primarily directs, controls, or coordinates the activities of the entity rather than in all cases where an entity simply has a general partner, managing member, or equivalent.'

[279] 85 FR 3158.

[280] 85 FR 3162. The provision has identified Australia, Canada, and the UK as 'excepted foreign estates', given their robust intelligence sharing, and defence industrial base integration mechanisms with the US.

[281] ibid.

[282] TID businesses stand for US businesses with critical technologies, critical infrastructure, and personal data.

[283] FIRRMA, s 1706, § (v)(IV)(bb)(AA)(cc).

[284] The US Innovation and Competition Act, s 138. This provision responds to concerns that China is exploiting the open research and development of US higher education institutions. See https://www.foreign.sen

80 NATIONAL SECURITY ASSESSMENT

In September 2022, President Biden issued the executive order on ensuring robust consideration of evolving national security risks by the CFIUS. This is the first time in the Committee's history that a president has directed the CFIUS to prioritize certain national security risks when reviewing covered transactions.[285] Until now, the national security factors that form the CFIUS' mandate have been defined by Congress in the Defense Product Act of 1950 and more recent legislation including the Foreign Investment Risk Review Modernization Act of 2018.

This executive order will not change the Committee's review process or legal jurisdiction; it mostly provides details on existing factors and adds new national security factors. Specifically, the executive order requires the CFIUS to consider five national security factors in its review: domestic supply capacity and supply chain resilience, US technological leadership in critical sectors, aggregate industry investment trends, cybersecurity risks, sensitive data on US persons.[286] The new executive order also highlights the CFIUS' increasing attention to the cumulative threat posed by a pattern of investment by a specific foreign investor. Thus, it confirms this ongoing trend by the Committee of viewing transactions in a broader investment context.[287]

Lastly, the executive order aligns closely with the policy goals of the recently enacted Creating Helpful Incentives to Produce Semiconductors (CHIPS) Act,[288] which is aimed at reducing US dependence on Chinese critical technologies by implementing an industrial strategy to revitalize domestic manufacturing, create well-paid American jobs, strengthen American supply chains, and accelerate the industries of the future.[289]

2.6 Concluding Remarks

The first part of this book has focused on the national security concerns in assessing M&A transactions, showing a spectrum of the CFIUS's decisions in diverse industries including telecommunications, food, financial services, the defence industry, and technology. The CFIUS' enforcement record and the trend in assessing national security concerns illustrates the US government's determination to safeguard US industries

---

ate.gov/imo/media/doc/DAV21598%20-%20Strategic%20Competition%20Act%20of%202021.pdf (accessed 17 September 2022).

[285] Michael J Lowell and others, 'Executive Order Directs CFIUS to Expand Review of National Security Factors' *Reed Smith Client Alerts* (5 October 2022) https://www.reedsmith.com/en/perspectives/2022/10/executive-order-directs-cfius-to-expand-review-of-national-security-factors (accessed 15 November 2022).

[286] Executive Order 14083, 87 FR 57369.

[287] Kirkland & Ellis, 'President Biden Issues First-Ever Directive to CFIUS on National Security Considerations in Transactions' (21 September 2022) https://www.kirkland.com/publications/kirkland-alert/2022/09/cfius-executive-order.

[288] CHIPS Act, Pub L No 117-167 (2022).

[289] Joe Biden, The White House, 'Fact Sheet: CHIPS and Science Act Will Lower Costs, Create Jobs, Strengthen Supply Chains, and Counter China' (9 August 2022).

from risks to US national security raised by acquisitions of US domestic assets by foreign acquirers.

In the assessment of the CFIUS regime the book discussed how the scope of this agency has expanded to the point where now almost any foreign person or entity is potentially within its regulatory reach. In spite of its increased powers, the transparency of the process appears to remain restricted, a shortfall that has been subject to criticism among the parties and scholars. Some M&A transactions have been blocked, while others have been withdrawn by the parties after clear signs of opposition combined with long waiting assessment periods. The analysis has also shown that even if the number of transactions that have been blocked remains relatively low, the assessment process would be improved if the parties and the public were provided with a more detailed perspective of the CFIUS rationale for its decisions.

What is of paramount importance is for the US national security regime to provide certainty to the investment as well as the legal community on the transparency and clarity of their approach to transactions that can raise national security concerns. Otherwise, the regime runs the risk of providing excuses for the adoption and furtherance of industrial strategies, which will be an unwelcome outcome.

Among the public interest considerations in the US merger regime, the approach to national security discussed above, and the approach to public interest considerations in regulated sectors are the most significant considerations for many US regulatory agencies. After reviewing the national security regime in the US and the impact this has on transactions involving foreign acquirers of US assets, the book turns now to the assessment of public interest considerations in regulated sectors and how such assessment converges or diverges from the competition assessment that the antitrust agencies conduct. We will review the legislative framework for several regulated sectors in the US and discuss the scope of the public interest standard, its application, and how transactions have been assessed when the competition considerations had to be balanced with public interest considerations.

3

Public Interest Assessment and the Federal Communications Commission (FCC)

3.1 The Federal Communications Commission (FCC)

The telecommunications sector has been one of the sensitive sectors in most economies globally. At the same time, it is only one of the most heavily regulated ones in most jurisdictions. As the OECD states in its Report on Regulatory Reform in the US:[1]

The telecommunications industry has seen significant regulatory reform in OECD countries in recent years. Twenty-three OECD countries now have unrestricted market access to all forms of telecommunications, including voice telephony, infrastructure investment and investment by foreign enterprises, compared to only a handful only a few years ago. The success of the liberalisation process depends on the presence of a transparent and effective regulatory regime that enables the development of full competition, while effectively protecting other public interests. There is a need to promote entry in markets where formerly regulated monopolists remain dominant and to consider elimination of traditionally separate regulatory frameworks applicable to telecommunications infrastructures and services, and to broadcasting infrastructures and services'.

The chapter will start with a discussion of the composition of the Federal Communications Commission (FCC) and the relevant regulatory framework before discussing some of the seminal case law that will show the approach the FCC takes in applying its public interest test and how this approach compares with the one antitrust authority takes pursuant to its competition standard. The chapter will also discuss some implications that arise from comparing the role and practice of the regulator and that of the competition authority.

---

[1] OECD, 'Report on Regulatory Reform in the United States: Regulatory Reform in the Telecommunications Industry' (1999) 5 https://www.oecd.org/regreform/2506672.pdf (accessed 14 November 2022).

3.1.1 Composition and Legislation

The FCC is an independent US government agency led by five commissioners who are appointed by the President and confirmed by the US Senate.[2] According to the Communications Act of 1934[3] (Communications Act), the FCC has the authority to review telecommunications mergers involving the transference of carrier authorizations, radio licences, and submarine cable landing licences, which compels merging parties to obtain prior approval before proceeding. In particular, section 310(d) of the Communications Act, which imposes limits to the holding and transfer of licences, provides that:[4]

> [n]o construction permit or station license, or any rights thereunder, shall be transferred, assigned, or disposed ... to any person except upon application to the [FCC] and upon finding by the [FCC] that the public interest, convenience, and necessity will be served thereby.

In addition to the Communications Act, sections 7 and 11 of the Clayton Act[5] give authority to the FCC to object to acquisitions of 'common carriers engaged in wire or radio communications or radio transmissions of energy ... where ... the effect of such acquisition may be substantially to lessen competition, or to tend to create a monopoly'.[6] Similarly, the Electronic Code of Federal Regulations,[7] Title 47—Telecommunication Chapter I—establishes that the FCC has jurisdiction to assess the following five multiple ownership:[8] (i) the radio sub caps, 47 CFR § 73.3555(a), which restricts the number of amplitude modulation (AM) and frequency modulation (FM) stations a company can own in a single market; (ii) the local television ownership cap, 47 CFR § 73.3555(b), which prohibits ownership of two of the top four television stations in a market; (iii) the radio-television cross-ownership cap, 47 CFR § 73.3555(c), which bans ownership of more than two commercial TV stations and one commercial radio station, with some exceptions; and (iv) the newspaper/broadcast cross-ownership rule, 47 CFR § 73.3555(d), which proscribes common ownership of a newspaper and television or radio station in the same market.

---

[2] The President also selects one of the commissioners to serve as chairman. See Federal Communications Commission, 'What We Do' https://www.fcc.gov/about-fcc/what-we-do (accessed 14 November 2022).

[3] Pub L No 73-416, 48 Stat 1064. As amended, 47 USC § 214, § 310, §§ 34–39.

[4] As amended, 47 USC § 310(d).

[5] The Clayton Act was passed in 1914 with the aim to reinforce the Sherman Act, and s 7 of the Clayton Act was envisaged as an effective tool for preventing anticompetitive mergers. In relation to the substantive assessment of merger and acquisitions, its primary provision is s 7 of the Clayton Act (5 USC § 18) which prohibits acquisitions of assets or stock where 'the effect of such acquisition may be substantially to lessen competition, or to tend to create a monopoly'.

[6] 15 USC § 21(a), 18 (1994).

[7] The e-CFR is a currently updated version of the Code of Federal Regulations that is presented in an organized manner in a single publication; see Office of the Federal Register, 'About the Electronic Code of Federal Regulations' https://www.archives.gov/federal-register/cfr/about-ecfr (accessed 18 November 2022).

[8] Electronic Code of Federal Regulations (e-CFR), 47 CFR § 73.3555 https://www.law.cornell.edu/cfr/text/47/73.3555 (accessed 15 November 2022).

3.1 THE FEDERAL COMMUNICATIONS COMMISSION (FCC)

At this juncture, it is important to indicate that in the communications sector common ownership[9] and cross-ownership of assets are frequent. The Department of Justice (DOJ) and the Federal Trade Commission (FTC) define common ownership as 'the simultaneous ownership of stock in competing companies by a single investor, where none of the stock holdings is large enough to give the owner control of any of those companies'.[10] In relation to the possible anti-competitive effects of common ownership, the literature has mentioned that they can appear in the form of price increases, executive compensation or voting rights,[11] and that they also raise the 'possibility of active efforts to coordinate the decisions of competitors by or through common owners'.[12] A similar point was made by the European Commission in *Dow—DuPont* (Case M.7932), whereby common ownership could trigger possible coordinated effects by facilitating the common owners' aligning of their incentives.[13]

3.1.2 Filing Instructions and Process Overview

In the telecommunications sector, the Federal Communications Commission (FCC), the DOJ, and the FTC have the jurisdiction to review mergers and acquisitions. The DOJ and the FTC have consented to a 'clearance process' (also known as a Memorandum of Understanding) whereby, based on their past expertise and experience, these two agencies agree upon deliberation which one will review a transaction. Almost all mergers related to common carriers (that is most media and telecommunications transactions) are reviewed by the DOJ, and the FTC is responsible for cable and various deals involving companies that produce or circulate media content.[14] It is also important to remember that in the media sector the review of mergers by FCC is limited to companies that have FCC licences: wireline and wireless telecommunications providers, cable system operators, and broadcasters.[15]

---

[9] Common ownership does not necessarily grant control. For an elaborate analysis of common ownership see José Azar and Xavier Vives, 'General Equilibrium Oligopoly and Ownership Structure' (2021) 89(3) Econometrica 999; José Azar and Xavier Vives, 'Revisiting the Anticompetitive Effects of Common Ownership' (2022) ECGI Finance Working Paper 827/2022 https://ssrn.com/abstract=3805047; José Azar, Martin C Schmalz, and Isabel Tecu, 'Anticompetitive Effects of Common Ownership' (2018) 73 Journal of Finance 1513; José Azar, 'Portfolio Diversification, Market Power, and the Theory of the Firm' (2016) http://papers.ssrn.com/abstract=2811221; Martin C Schmalz, 'Common-Ownership Concentration and Corporate Conduct' (2018) 10 Annual Review of Financial Economics 413.

[10] OECD, 'Hearing on Common Ownership by institutional investors and its impact on competition:– Note by the United States' (2017) DAF/COMP/WD(2017)86, 2 https://one.oecd.org/document/DAF/COMP/WD(2017)86/en/pdf (accessed 15 November 2022).

[11] ibid 7.

[12] ibid 3.

[13] *Dow—DuPont* (Case M.7932) C(2017) 1946, Annex 5 to the Commission Decision, 3.

[14] James R Weiss and Martin L Stern, 'Serving Two Masters: The Dual Jurisdiction of the FCC and the Justice Department Over Telecommunications Transactions' (1998) 6 CommLaw Conspectus 195, 209; Andrew J Schwartzman, 'How the Department of Justice, Federal Trade Commission and Federal Communications Commission Regulate Media Company Acquisitions' *Benton Institute for Broadband & Society* (4 January 2016) https://www.benton.org/blog/how-department-justice-federal-trade-commission-and-federal-communications-commission-regulate (accessed 14 November 2022).

[15] See Communications Act of 1934, § 2(a), 48 Stat 1093 (1934). Companies can avoid an FCC review by not incorporating transactions where licences are involved. As an illustration, in the AT&T—Time Warner merger, Time Warner divested its Atlanta television station and surrendered the wireless and earth station licences used by

The FCC review process starts with the filing of an application by the merging parties, which, once in order and accepted, is announced in a public notice with the purpose of receiving public comments or opposition, for which thirty days are usually provided.[16] If comments or opposition take place, the applicants have between ten and fifteen days to respond to them, and seven days later commentators can also provide a response (these times can be shorter or longer depending on the complexity of the case).[17] The FCC does not have a statutory deadline to make a final decision; instead, it has a voluntary deadline of 180 days for deciding on a merger.[18] An important feature that also needs to be highlighted is that the FCC does not need to go to court to block a merger as the FTC and DOJ would; the FCC can deny the transfer of the licence under request.[19]

Likewise, the process through which the FCC, under sections 7 and 11, seeks to block a transaction, under a standard that is equivalent to that of the DOJ,[20] starts with a complaint followed by a hearing, in which the Attorney General and other stakeholders can testify.[21] The FCC can issue an order requesting the defendant to terminate and abstain from completing the intended transaction, as well as to dissociate itself of the stock or other interest that has been illegitimately acquired.[22] Nonetheless, it has been noted that the FCC has not used this power, as under the Communications Act their reviews in the public interest standard 'necessarily subsumes and extends beyond the traditional parameters of review under the antitrust laws'.[23]

If, under the Hart-Scott-Rodino Act (HSRA, enacted in 1976 with the aim of introducing significant changes to the merger enforcement regime such as the removal of the obligation to prove anti-competitive conduct to prohibit a merger under section 7 of Clayton Act),[24] the merging parties need to notify the antitrust agencies of the transaction, the latter have thirty days to decide whether to challenge the merger after a second request.[25] If a second request takes place the FTC/DOJ has twenty days to

---

HBO, CNN, and other networks. See Meredith Senter and Erin E Kim, 'Recent Trends in Media Industry Mergers and Acquisitions' *Lexis Practical Guidance J* (19 December 2017); See also Schwartzman (n 14).

[16] FCC, 'Overview of the FCC's Review of Significant Transactions' https://www.fcc.gov/reports-research/guides/review-of-significant-transactions (accessed 12 November 2022).

[17] FCC (n 16).

[18] This decision timeline is not frequently adhered to. See FCC (n 16); see also Victoria Peng, 'Astroturf Campaigns: Transparency in Telecom Merger Review' (2016) 49 University of Michigan Journal of Law Reform 525, 528; Donald J Russell and Sherri Lynn Wolson, 'Dual Antitrust Review of Telecommunications Mergers by the Department of Justice and Federal Communications Commission' (2002) 11 George Mason Law Review 143, 149–50.

[19] William E Kovacic, Petros C Mavroidis, and Damien Neven, 'Merger Control Procedures and Institutions: A Comparison of the EU and US Practice' (1 February 2014) Robert Schuman Centre for Advanced Studies Research Paper No 2014/20 (2014) 10 https://ssrn.com/abstract=2397870 (accessed 15 November 2022).

[20] 15 USC §§ 18, 21(a).

[21] Weiss and Stern (n 14) 198.

[22] ibid.

[23] ibid; see also William J Rinner, 'Optimizing Dual Agency Review of Telecommunications Mergers' (2009) 118 Yale Law Journal 1574.

[24] 15 USC § 18.

[25] 15 USC § 18a(b)(1)(B). If the DOJ takes no action during these thirty days the initial period expires automatically; see 15 USC §§18a(a), (b)(2).

decide to challenge the merger,[26] in which case it must file a suit in court and secure an injunction,[27] with the aim of blocking the transaction, which, according to section 7 of the Clayton Act, may 'substantially ... lessen competition, or ... tend to create a monopoly'.[28] If a feasible remedy is available the competition agency and the parties may discuss a settlement resulting in a consent decree.[29] The focus of this review is to determine whether the proposed transaction would hamper present or prospective competition in a way that harms consumers by assessing market shares, possible adverse effects, entry barriers, and merger-specific efficiencies.[30] Traditionally, the FCC waits until the antitrust agency has completed the review to provide its own conclusion.[31] Further review of the competitive effects of the transaction is sometimes required from state public utility commissions (PUCs). PUCs regulate various sectors, among them telecommunications, the members of the PUCs are appointed by the governor of the respective state and, as a rule, PUCs are entrusted with guaranteeing that through regulation utilities are provided to customers at efficient levels and reasonable prices.[32] It is also possible that the FCC requests information from local franchising authorities (LFAs) to elaborate further on the competitive effects of transactions involving cable operators and cable television services. According to the Communications Act, LFAs regulate cable operators and cable television services by awarding or denying the required cable franchises and setting the franchise fees.[33] This chapter examines the dual review process carried out by the DOJ or the FTC and the FCC.

3.2 The 'Public Interest' Standard

The FCC 'is perhaps the most notorious implementer of any statutory public interest standard on the books'.[34] According to Title 47 of the Code of Federal Regulations (CFR), concentrations in the communications and media sector should adhere to the 'public interest, convenience, and necessity' standard.[35] This provision emerged as a result of Congress' intention to protect American business and culture by giving the authority to review any licence transfer to the FCC that enjoys unequivocal expertise

---

[26] ibid § 18a(e)(1). The parties may not complete the transaction until thirty days after they have observed the requests for the submission of extensive documentation and information. See 15 USC § 18 a(e)(2).

[27] ibid § 18a(f). See also Weiss and Stern (n 14) 199.

[28] 15 USC § 18.

[29] Lawrence M Frankel, 'The Flawed Institutional Design of U.S. Merger Review: Stacking the Deck against Enforcement' (2008) Utah Law Review 159, 169. The judicial review of a consent decree is under the Tunney Act, where the role of the judge is not to examine if other remedies were suitable or if some social or political interests were affected by the merger. See 15 USC § 16(b)–(h). See also Russell and Wolson (n 18).

[30] See Department of Justice, Statement of Joel I Klein, 'Consolidation in the Telecommunications Industry' (24 June 1998) https://www.justice.gov/archive/atr/public/testimony/1806.pdf (accessed 13 November 2022).

[31] Harold Feld, 'The Need for FCC Merger Review' (2000) 18 Commercial Law 24.

[32] Russell and Wolson (n 18) 144. See also Sam Feder and Christine Sanquist, 'Communications: Regulation and Outsourcing in the United States: Overview' Thomson Reuters Practical Law (1 January 2018) https://uk.practical law.thomsonreuters.com/6-620-5752?transitionType=Default&contextData=(sc.Default)&firstPage=true (accessed 24 October 2022).

[33] Communications Act of 1934, Title VI, s 621(b)(1) and s 621(a)(1).

[34] Jodi L Short, 'In Search of the Public Interest' (2023) 40 Yale Journal of Regulation 759, 795.

[35] 47 USC § 310(d).

88 PUBLIC INTEREST ASSESSMENT AND THE FCC

in the industry.[36,37] Under this public interest standard, the FCC questions whether the proposed licence transfer would violate any provisions of the communications statutes or the FCC's rules or impede the enforcement of the communications acts or their objectives, and whether it would 'promise ... to yield affirmative public benefits'.[38]

The content of the FCC's public interest concerns is broad and varied. It has been described as comprising 'the effects of the proposed transaction on universal service, national security, spectrum efficiency, technological innovation, and diversity of views and content'.[39] Other factors also include whether the transaction would potentially affect the quality of the communication services or it could result in the provision of new services to consumers.[40] Interestingly, in the media sector, considerations such as the number of potential independently owned opinions in a market and the effect of the merger on the amount of minorities and women who may be able to own media assets are also integrated.[41]

In her study of the notion of public interest, Short identified sixty-one different public interest standards in Title 47 (the Communications Act alone 'contained no fewer than eighty').[42] She analysed a corpus of sixty decisions issued between 1943 and 2019 and concluded that the FCC's understanding of public interest has been grounded consistently in the Communications Act and in its judicial interpretations.[43] Looking at the justifications used either to approve or to oppose a transaction, efficiency-related arguments were the most common (168 mentions); procedural values accounted for 59 mentions; substantive values were cited 118 times, with a preference for those based on the statutory text (72 mentions) over non-statutory ones (46 mentions). Amongst the individual justifications, applicant qualifications (43 mentions) and access to telecom services (22 mentions) were most frequently invoked, followed by national security (11 mentions). Oddly enough, content diversity and commitment to public service only received 7 and 8 mentions, respectively.[44]

The applicants carry the burden of demonstrating that their proposed transaction is in favour of the public interest.[45] In addition, they need to show that the merger is not

---

[36] Peng (n 18).

[37] Cable Television Consumer Protection and Competition Act of 1992, Pub L No 102-385, 106 Stat 1460 (1992), and Telecommunications Act of 1996, Pub L No 104-104, 110 Stat 56 (1996).

[38] Rinner (n 23), quoting *SBC—Ameritech*, 14 FCC Rcd 14712, 14737–38 (1999) (emphasis added); Christopher S Yoo, 'Merger Review by the Federal Communications Commission: Comcast-NBC Universal' (2014) 45(3) Review of Industrial Organization 295.

[39] Weiss and Stern (n 14) 198.

[40] FCC Blog, Jon Sallet, General Counsel, *FCC Transaction Review: Competition and the Public Interest* https://www.fcc.gov/news-events/blog/2014/08/12/fcc-transaction-review-competition-and-public-interest (accessed 16 November 2022).

[41] Schwartzman (n 14). See also Lili Levi, 'Reflections on the FCC's Recent Approach to Structural Regulation of the Electric Mass Media' (2000) 52 Federal Communications Law Journal 581, 590.

[42] Short (n 34) 795, 836.

[43] ibid 803.

[44] ibid 801.

[45] Jon Sallet, General Counsel, 'FCC Transaction Review: Competition and the Public Interest' *FCC Blog* (2014) https://www.fcc.gov/news-events/blog/2014/08/12/fcc-transaction-review-competition-and-public-interest (accessed 10 November 2022); AT&T Inc & Bellsouth Corp Application for Transfer of Control, 22 FCC Rcd 5662 (2007) (Mem Op and Order) http://hraunfoss.fcc.gov/edocs_public/attachmatch/FCC-06-189A1.doc (accessed 15 November 2022) (indicating that '[t]he Applicants bear the burden of proving, by a preponderance of evidence, that the proposed transaction, on balance, serves the public interest'). See also Peng (n 18).

expected appreciably to reduce competition or that 'any likely anti-competitive effect is more than offset by other benefits'.[46] Usually, the merging parties and the FCC negotiate concessions or commitments to address the Commission's concerns, and merger-specific efficiencies such as 'cost-reductions, productivity enhancements, or improved incentives for innovation'[47] are considered before the FCC issues an order.[48] If the parties disagree with the order they can appeal it under a deferential standard.[49] In exceptional circumstances, if the FCC is unable to conclude that the proposed transaction serves the public interest, a formal adjudicatory hearing before an administrative law judge (ALJ) is scheduled,[50] where the parties need to demonstrate that the transaction is aligned with the public interest.[51] After the hearing, the FCC makes a decision considering the conclusion reached by the ALJ, and the parties can appeal the FCC's decision pursuant to a deferential standard.[52]

In procedural terms, when the FCC conducts its own antitrust analysis it starts by defining the relevant geographic and product market and then the current and potential participants in the relevant market; next, it assesses the merger's effects on competition in the relevant market, and the merger-specific efficiencies, just as the DOJ and the FTC do.[53] Unlike the FTC/DOJ, the FCC focuses its analysis on potential rather than actual competition threats,[54] and considers as part of the competitive effect analysis whether the merger will facilitate its ability to regulate.[55] Yet, if the antitrust analysis conducted by the FCC seems to fall outside the scope of the traditional competition policy exercised by the antitrust agencies, under the public interest standard such an approach has been described as being even 'more amorphous and wide-ranging',[56] as the next section will explore in more detail.

---

[46] Frankel (n 29) 201.

[47] Rachel E Barkow and Peter W Huber, 'A Tale of Two Agencies: A Comparative Analysis of FCC and DOJ Review of Telecommunications Mergers' (2000) University of Chicago Legal Forum 29, 44.

[48] Frankel (n 29) 201.

[49] *SBC Commc'ns Inc v FCC* 56 F3d 1484, 1490 (DC Cir 1995), stating that the review scope of an FCC order is 'only to determine whether is arbitrary, capricious, and abuse of discretion, or otherwise not in accordance with law'; see also Frankel (n 29) 176.

[50] 47 USC § 309(e). See also FCC, *Memorandum Opinion and Order in the Matter of Entercom Communications and CBS Radio Seek Approval to Transfer Control of and Assign FCC Authorizations and Licenses* (MB Docket No 17-85, 2017).

[51] Frankel (n 29) 202.

[52] See *FCC v RCA Communications* 346 US 86, 91 (1953), where the Supreme Court indicated that: 'Congress has charged the courts with the responsibility of saying whether the Commission has fairly exercised its discretion within the vaguish, penumbral bounds expressed by the standard of "public interest". It is our responsibility to say whether the Commission has been guided by proper considerations in bringing the deposit of its experience, the disciplined feel of the expert, to bear on applications for licenses in the public interest.'

[53] Barkow and Huber (n 47) 45.

[54] Rinner (n 23) 1575; Barkow and Huber (n 47) 45.

[55] Barkow and Huber (n 47) 46.

[56] Frankel (n 29) 201.

3.3 Challenges of Concurrent Jurisdiction

One common criticism of the concurrent jurisdiction between the FCC and the FTC/DOJ is that the merger review is an resource demanding duplicative process and adds an unnecessary delay. In relation to the expenses, it has been indicated that merging parties endure substantial expenses in responding to coinciding requests for information by both agencies, paying legal fees, providing interminable pages of documents, responding to comments and depositions, and attending meetings.[57] The shared jurisdiction has also signified that while an average merger requires between two and four months to be decided, in the telecommunications sector it takes between nine and twelve months, albeit the FCC has a 180-day voluntary deadline that is rarely observed.[58]

Another, and perhaps the most prevalent criticism of this dual review, is that the agencies pursue different purposes; in particular, it has been argued that the unlimited scope of review under the 'ill-defined' public interest test[59] seeks the development of regulatory purposes through the evaluation of factors envisioned to deal with case-specific issues that are 'important at the time'.[60] Flynn has asserted that federal agencies, the FCC included, have been shaping their findings to support their substantive policies by presenting them as the plain result of neutral legislative fact-finding.[61] Such an approach differs from the FTC/DOJ antitrust review, the aim of which is to determine whether a transaction may substantially lessen the competition,[62] an attitude that seems to be more predictable and through which the antitrust agencies bear the burden of proof.[63] This discrepancy has led to contradictory decisions, bringing uncertainty among the merging parties who do not know what to expect, particularly from the FCC's malleable public interest assessment.[64]

It has also been argued that, given the procedural and substantive flexibility offered by the public interest standard, the FCC has abused its power negotiating voluntary

---

[57] Weiss and Stern (n 14) 206; Damien Geradin and Michel Kerf, *Controlling Market Power in Telecommunications, Antitrust vs Sector-specific Regulation* (OUP 2003) 116; Philip J Weiser, 'Reexamining the Legacy of Dual Regulation: Reforming Dual Merger Review by the DOJ and the FCC' (2008) 61(1) Federal Communications Law Journal 167, 170 https://www.repository.law.indiana.edu/fclj/vol61/iss1/11.

[58] Peng (n 18); Erin M Reilly, 'The Telecommunications Industry in 1993: The Year of the Merger' (1994) 2 CommLaw Conspectus 95, 108.

[59] Weiser (n 57) 169.

[60] Barkow and Huber (n 47) 35, 48 (indicating that the Commission is entitle to examine a merger based on its compatibility with the broad aims of the 1934 and 1996 Acts, such as 'deregulatory national policy framework'); Rinner (n 23) 1577; Peter W Bradbury and James A Champy, 'Corporate Acquisition of Broadcast Facilities: The "Public Interest" and the Antitrust Laws' (1967) 8 BCL Review 903, 909 http://lawdigitalcommons.bc.edu/bclr/vol8/iss4/6 (accessed 15 November 2022).

[61] Joan Flynn, 'The Costs and Benefits of Hiding the Ball: NLRB Policymaking and the Failure of Judicial Review' (1995) 75 BUL Review 387, 405.

[62] 15 USC § 18.

[63] Rinner (n 23) 1573; Peng (n 18).

[64] Weiss and Stern (n 14) 205–207; Christopher Y Soo, 'Merger Review by the Federal Communications Commission: Comcast-NBC Universal, University of Pennsylvania Carey Law School, 1543, 1549-7' (2014) 45 Review of Industrial Organization 295 https://scholarship.law.upenn.edu/faculty_scholarship/1543 (accessed 12 November 2022).

agreements and conditions, which are frequently unrelated to the mergers (although the FCC has repeatedly affirmed that its conditions are transaction-specific)[65] and forced, and which also escape judicial review.[66] The FCC's awareness of the merging parties' desire to close deals quickly has facilitated the imposition of heavy conditions, and these are usually unchallenged for the following four reasons.[67] First, they are not agency action. Secondly, as the agency is a specialized body it is unlikely that the court will challenge its fact-findings. Thirdly, the judicial review would focus on determining whether the application of the policy in the case under review was appropriate, rather than examining the validity of the policy itself, and, fourthly, the urgent need to have approval would prevent merging parties from seeking lengthy judicial reviews.[68]

The validity of these criticisms has been evaluated by some authors, who have recognized the importance of two bodies looking thoroughly at the same transaction from different perspectives, especially a specialized body that has extensive knowledge of the industry, a factor that greatly complements the antitrust agency's review,[69] does not add unnecessary delays, and allows the implementation of the policies required to ensure the development of new technologies and prevent market failure.[70] Similarly, it has been mentioned that the agencies work in close cooperation, consulting extensively to coordinate their reviews and to create remedies that are consistent and comprehensive.[71] In this context, the next part examines some seminal cases with the aim of establishing whether the above concerns are justified or whether, indeed, the advantages of a dual review outweigh the concerns.

3.4 Enforcement Record

Table 3.1 shows that, between 2008 and 2022, on average 2.6 major mergers were concurrently reviewed every year by the FCC and the antitrust agencies. In 2011, seven applications were filed, followed by six in 2013 and four in 2008. In terms of types of decisions, out of a total of thirty-nine applications, thirty-six were approved by the FCC and the antitrust agencies, and two were withdrawn, which signifies that, between 2008 and 2022, most of the mergers were cleared. It is also noticeable that the FCC conditioned the approval of a majority of them (thirty-one out of the thirty-six approved).

---

[65] See 47 USC §§ 214(c), 303(r) (allowing the FCC to impose conditions on licence transfers and authorizations). See also *CenturyLink—Level 3* 32 FCC Rcd 9581 (11)https://www.fcc.gov/document/fcc-approves-centuryl ink-level-3-transaction 6.

[66] Rinner (n 23). See also Levi (n 40) 615–16, who has argued that 'such "voluntary" action is always suspect as effectively coerced'; Weiser (n 57) 168–69.

[67] Barkow and Huber (n 47) 69–71.

[68] Flynn (n 61) 413–17.

[69] Feld (n 31) 24; Weiser (n 57) 198.

[70] Feld (n 31) 24.

[71] OECD, 'Public Interest Considerations in Merger Control: Note by the United States' (2016) DAF/COMP/WP3/WD(2016)10, 5–6 http://www.oecd.org/officialdocuments/displaydocument/?cote=DAF/COMP/WP3/WD(2016)10&docLanguage=En (accessed 15 November 2022).

92 PUBLIC INTEREST ASSESSMENT AND THE FCC

Table 3.1 Major transactions concurrently reviewed by the FCC and the antitrust agencies (2008-2022)

Year	Number of filed applications	Approved by the FCC	With conditions from the FCC	Withdrawn	Approved by the antitrust agencies
2008	4	4	4	0	4
2009	2	2	2	0	2
2010	2	2	2	0	2
2011	7	6	5	1	6
2012	2	2	2	0	2
2013	6	6	6	0	6
2014	3	3	2	0	3
2015	2	2	1	0	2
2016	3	3	2	0	3
2017	2	2	2	0	2
2018	1	0	0	1	0
2019	2	2	2	0	2
2020	0	0	0	0	0
2021	1	1	1	0	1
2022	2	1	0	1	2
TOTAL	39	36	31	3	37

Source: data available on the FCC's website.[*]

[*]https://www.fcc.gov (accessed 3 October 2023).

3.4.1 Analysis of Some Seminal Cases

We shall discuss below some of the most important cases that the FCC has assessed. The chapter will present the FCC's approach to public interest considerations especially in cases where competition considerations and/or a competition investigation by the DOJ/FTC had to be considered as well.

3.4.1.1 Transactions where FTC/DOJ and FCC diverged on the remedies needed to clear a transaction

The first cluster of cases includes those in which the antitrust agency either did not have any concerns or did have some but these were addressed with some remedies. Instead, the FCC had multiple concerns over the same transaction and imposed a significant number of conditions which, on some occasions, were different to the ones the competition agency imposed.

3.4.1.1.1 Bell Atlantic—NYNEX
In April 1996, Bell Atlantic Corporation (Bell Atlantic) and NYNEX Corporation (NYNEX) pronounced their decision to merge. Bell Atlantic was a local telephone

company that served about 18 million customers in six eastern states from Virginia to New Jersey and NYNEX served about 20 million customers with local telephone services from New York to Maine.[72] The transaction would create the biggest local telephone company with a presence in thirteen states, 39 million lines, US$53 billion in assets, and US$3.4 billion in projected annual revenues.[73] On 24 April 1997, the DOJ announced that after a thorough analysis of the merger it had decided 'not to challenge the transaction, having concluded that the merger does not violate the antitrust laws'.[74] This position was shared by the thirteen state commissions, which also reviewed and cleared the transaction.[75]

In contrast, the FCC was concerned about the loss of potential competition, non-price discrimination against long-distance carriers, reduction of regulatory enforcement, and the absence of public interest,[76] issues that were alleviated once the parties committed to multiple conditions, which led to approval on 14 August 1997.[77] The conditions related (i) to the facilitation of the implementation of 'unbundled network elements' (UNEs)[78] obligations in favour of new local carriers; (ii) to publishing frequent reports aimed at revealing any possible discrimination or poor performance in the supply of UNEs affecting competing carriers, and (iii) to establishing rates for interconnection and UNEs grounded on economic costs.[79] In its decision, the FCC clarified that even if a transaction meets the criteria of the existing rules it is possible that it impedes the policies of the Communications Act,[80] adding that the merger 'on balance will enhance and promote, rather than eliminate and retard, competition'.[81] Indeed, some of the commitments reflected this approach as they were orientated to facilitate the entry and expansion of other firms.[82] One pitfall of forcing merging parties seeking approval to engage in significant voluntary concessions is that, in practical terms, this undermines the legality of the merger control process undertaken by the FCC.[83] The problem is that the unfettered authority of the FCC in negotiating conditions (one must bear in mind that the FCC does not observe a statutory deadline to make a final decision and

---

[72] Steven R Brenner, 'Potential Competition and Local Telephone Service: The Bell Atlantic-NYNEX Merger' in John E Kwoka Jr and Lawrence J White, *The Antitrust Revolution* (OUP 2003) 73, 77.

[73] Weiss and Stern (n 14).

[74] United States Department of Justice, Antitrust Division Statement Regarding Bell Atlantic—NYNEX Merger (24 April 1997) https://www.justice.gov/archive/opa/pr/1997/April97/173at.htm (accessed 23 October 2022).

[75] Brenner (n 72) 77.

[76] ibid 78.

[77] Weiss and Stern (n 14).

[78] An incumbent telephone company allowing new local carriers the use of lines that connect customers to the local network and the use of local switches, is an illustration of unbundled network elements (UNEs) obligations. See Brenner (n 72) 76.

[79] Brenner (n 72) 93.

[80] *Bell Atlantic—NYNEX*, 12 FCC Rcd 19985 (1997) paras 29–36.

[81] ibid 157.

[82] Brenner (n 72) 93–94. In this case, the FCC determined the use of a particular methodology for establishing the prices at which the merging parties would provide unbundled networks elements to competitors despite that the Eighth Circuit in the *AT&T v Iowa* case had ruled that the Commission did not have authority to regulate methodologies to be used for pricing determinations. See Russell and Wolson (n 18) 154.

[83] Bryan N Tramont, 'Too Much Power, Too Little Restraint: How the FCC Expands Its Reach through Unenforceable and Unwieldy Voluntary Agreements' (2000) 53 Federal Communications Law Journal 49, 54–55.

94 PUBLIC INTEREST ASSESSMENT AND THE FCC

the judicial review is limited in nature) is what appears to spawn the willingness of the merging parties to accept extensive conditions.

To sum up, Bell Atlantic—NYNEX is proving the risk of contradictory decisions between the DOJ and the FCC in reviewing the same transaction. While for the DOJ the transaction did not raise any concerns, it did raise concerns for the FCC. Such a contradiction can mitigate the predictability and the efficiency of the assessment and decision-making process. Another shortfall was the length of the procedure coupled with the imposition of severe wide-ranging commitments in the name of the public interest, which could not have been obtained otherwise.

3.4.1.1.2 SBC—Ameritech

In July 1998, Ameritech Corporation (Ameritech) and SBC Communications, Inc. (SBC) filed an application for licence transfer approval, whereby SBC would own all of the stock of Ameritech and 57.5 per cent of the pre-merger stakeholders of SBC, and 42.5 per cent of the pre-merger stakeholders of Ameritech would own SBC.[84] The combined company would serve over 55.5 million local exchange access lines (31.9 per cent of the country's total access lines), have more than 200,000 employees, and a turnover of more than US$45 billion in annual revenues.[85] Ameritech was a local exchange carrier (LEC) serving Illinois, Indiana, Michigan, Ohio, and Wisconsin with more than 20 million exchange access lines and more than US$17.1 billion in revenue; it was also present in cellular, personal communications services (PCSs), paging, security, cable television, internet access, alarm monitoring, and directory publishing services.[86] SBC was an LEC serving Arkansas, Kansas, Missouri, Oklahoma, and Texas with over 35.7 million exchange access lines and over US$28.7 billion in excess revenue. It also provided wireless, internet access, cable television, interexchange (long distance) directory publishing services, PCSs, and paging services.[87]

The FCC focused its analysis on three main competitive harms. First, it was concerned that the applicants would not enter each other's territories after the merger. Secondly, the FCC stated that one important way to ensure the Communication's Act objectives was by comparing the practices of the carriers. Thus, it warned that as the merger would reduce the number of regional Bell operating companies (RBOCs) its ability to benchmark them against one another would be diminished. Further to this argument, the FCC noted that the combination of two large incumbent LECs would expand the incentive of coordination among the remaining rivals. Thirdly, the combined entity would have an incentive to discriminate against competitors in the delivery of advanced services, exchange services, and circuit-switched local exchange services.[88]

---

[84] ibid *SBC—Ameritech* (n 38) para 30.
[85] ibid para 31.
[86] ibid paras 6–7.
[87] ibid paras 9–10.
[88] William J Kolasky, 'The FCC's Review of the Bell Atlantic/NYNEX and SBC/Ameritech Mergers: Regulatory Overreach in the Name of Promoting Competition' (2001) 68 Antitrust Law Journal 771, 790.

In relation to the loss of competition (the first concern), the DOJ shared the same view after establishing that the merger would prevent Ameritech from offering bundled wireline and wireline local exchange services in the St. Louis area, where no other firms other from SBC and Ameritech were able to do so, and that the merger would increase the levels of concentration in the provision of wireless mobile telephone services in some overlapping markets.[89] But while for the DOJ the divestiture of one of the two cellular telephone systems in each of the overlying markets was enough to mitigate the harm, for the FCC it was not.[90]

Relative to the rest of FCC's concerns, the DOJ did not anticipate any harm in terms of benchmarking or discrimination. Thus, the parties tried to convince the FCC of the possible efficiencies, such as annual costs savings of US$1.42 billion and better options to compete in other regions. Both claims were rejected because the FCC was uncertain that the costs savings would be passed on to consumers and there was a possibility that the parties could enhance their ability to compete on their own.[91] Therefore, the FCC imposed thirty conditions, among them being that SBC had to enter thirty out-of-region markets within thirty months of closing the merger or face fines of up to US$40 million for each market, or a total US$1.2 billion across all markets[92] and performance measurements in twenty categories with self-imposed payments of US$1.25 billion over three years to the US Treasury for a shortfall.[93] It is no surprise that this transaction was described as one that was 'worth billions of dollars'.[94] Likewise, the terms of the Commissioner Powell in his partial dissent were not a revelation when he stated that the FCC 'places harms on one side of a scale and then collects and places any hotchpotch of conditions—no matter how ill-suited to remedying the identified infirmities—on the other side of the scale'.[95]

The SBC—Ameritech case illustrates the disparities between the DOJ and the FCC in assessing the same transaction. It also shows that the competition review standard applied by the antitrust agency is more objective and certain, while the competition and public interest standards used by the FCC can lead to less accurate assessment of the impact of the transaction on competition. Similarly, it exemplifies how intrusive and onerous commitments can be under a public interest standard. In this case, a year after the application was filed, the Commission sent a letter to the applicants informing them of the serious concerns it had about the transaction and telling them to expect a full hearing if the required conditions were not met.[96] The assessment process of this case also questions the efficiency and transparency of this dual review process.

---

[89] *United States v SBC Communications and Ameritech Corp* Competitive Impact Statement (16 April 1999) https://www.justice.gov/atr/case-document/competitive-impact-statement-186 (accessed 24 October 2022).
[90] ibid.
[91] Kolasky (n 88).
[92] *SBC—Ameritech* (n 38).
[93] Kolasky (n 88) 799–800; *SBC—Ameritech* (n 38) 15,000.
[94] Tramont (n 83) 54–52.
[95] *SBC—Ameritech* (n 38), 15,197 (Statement of Commissioner Powell, concurring in part and dissenting in part).
[96] Barkow and Huber (n 47) 44, 65.

3.4.1.1.3 AT&T—TCI

In July 1998, AT&T Corp (AT&T) announced its US$31.6 billion offer to acquire Telecommunications, Inc. (TCI). AT&T was the largest provider of mobile wireless telephone services in the United States with almost 9 million customers and revenues of approximately US$52 billion. TCI was the second largest operator of cable television systems nationally with revenue of approximately US$7.5 billion and was the owner of nearly 23.5 per cent of the stock of Sprint PCS's mobile wireless telephone business (Sprint), with approximately US$975 million in revenue.[97] AT&T and Sprint operate wireless networks at the national level.[98]

The DOJ approved the transaction after the applicants agreed to transfer Sprint's stock to an independent trustee before closing the merger and AT&T committed to compete aggressively against Sprint until the consummation of the divestiture.[99] The FCC also approved the transaction, imposing the same spectrum cap condition already decided by the DOJ, and adding AT&T's obligation to adopt a programme for allocation to Liberty Media Group stakeholders the economic profits of its possession of the Sprint stock.[100] An important aspect that deserves attention is that the FCC imposed the same divestiture condition previously decided by the DOJ. An issue that was highlighted by Commissioner Harold Furchtgott-Roth's statement, related to the FCC's excessive analysis, goes beyond its expertise and authority and duplicates the analysis of the DOJ.[101] But' most importantly, Furchtgott-Roth's statement questioned the FCC's authority to review mergers extensively and, in his opinion, FCC should focus on the transfer of licences and authorizations, excluding aspects such as corporate restructuring, stock purchases, and corporate personnel. He added that in the AT&T and TCI transaction, the licences were not even identified because the Commission simply rushed to examine the merger. Adding that the FCC's open-ended approach to the issues it assesses through merger review is rather another lever of regulatory control.[102]

In this case, it is uncertain why the FCC imposed a remedy that had already been agreed by the DOJ. What is clear is that the lack of communication between the review bodies amplifies the costs that merging parties need to endure as they need to observe an excessive number of conditions resulting from this unjustified dual review. In addition, the case illustrates that the merger parties need to be ready to prove that the merger will not frustrate or undermine the vast plans of the FCC, a standard difficult to satisfy.

---

[97] Department of Justice Press Release, 'Justice Department Approves AT&T Corp's Merger with TCI after Companies Agreed to Divestiture' (30 December 1998) https://www.justice.gov/archive/atr/public/press_releases/1998/2139.htm (accessed 25 October 2022).

[98] ibid.

[99] ibid.

[100] Federal Communications Commission, Report No CS 99-2 (17 February 1999) https://transition.fcc.gov/Bureaus/Cable/News_Releases/1999/nrcb9002.html (accessed 15 November 2022).

[101] AT&T—TCI, Memorandum Opinion and Order, CS-Docket 98-178, Commissioner Harold Furchtgott-Roth's statement, Appendix.

[102] ibid.

3.4.1.1.4 Bell Atlantic—GTE

In October 1998, Bell Atlantic Corporation (Bell Atlantic) and GTE Corporation (GTE) requested approval to transfer the control of licences and lines from GTE to Bell Atlantic. GTE was the nation's largest independent incumbent LEC, serving twenty-eight states with more than 26 million access lines, and a provider of wireless, internet access, and directory publishing services.[103] Bell Atlantic was a primary incumbent LEC in thirteen states, serving more than 43 million local exchange access lines, providing cellular, personal communications services (PCSs), paging, internet access, and directory publishing services.[104] According to the merger plan, GTE would remain as a wholly owned subsidiary of Bell Atlantic, approximately 43 per cent of the shares of Bell Atlantic would be held by the shareholders of GTE, and the board of directors would be equally integrated by members of the merging firms.[105]

The DOJ in its review identified that the transaction would reduce competition in the markets for wireless mobile telephone services in thirteen main trading areas (MTAs), ninety-six metropolitan statistical areas (MSAs), and fifteen rural service areas (RSAs).[106] As a result, on 9 December 1999, the DOJ filed a proposed final judgment, requiring the divestiture of wireless assets in ninety-six overlapping markets and requested provisional measures to diminish any risk of competitive harm that could arise until their completion.[107] The transaction also required the approval of twenty-eight states.[108] The FCC approved the merger after imposing certain conditions to address the following three potential public interest harms: (1) that the merger would reduce the prospect of competition by removing one of the most important potential participants in the local telecommunications market within Bell Atlantic's region; (2) that the reduction in the number of incumbents would negatively impact the ability of the Commission to benchmark their practices, therefore increasing the costs of regulation; and (3) that the newly combined entity would have an augmented incentive to discriminate against its rivals.[109] After considering that the transaction did not yield public interest benefits and did not support the implementation of the rules contained in the Communications Act, the Commission conditionally approved it.[110]

The FCC also used this case to develop its competition doctrine. According to the FCC:

---

[103] *Bell Atlantic—GTE*, 15 FCC Rcd 14032 (2000) paras 1, 6–7.

[104] ibid paras 10–11.

[105] ibid para 13.

[106] *United States v Bell Atlantic Corp and Others* Civil Action No 1:99CV01119, Final Judgment (DDC filed 9 December 1999) https://www.justice.gov/atr/case-document/motion-entry-final-judgment-1 (accessed 30 October 2022).

[107] On 7 May 1999, the United States filed the original complaint in this proceeding, which challenged a 28 July 1998 merger agreement between Bell Atlantic and GTE. On 21 September 1999, Bell Atlantic and Vodafone entered into a partnership agreement to combine the wireless businesses of Bell Atlantic, Vodafone, and GTE. On 6 December 1999, the United States filed a motion for leave to file a Supplemental Complaint and to add Vodafone as a defendant to this action. The motion was granted by the court, and the Supplemental Complaint was accepted as filed on 9 December 1999. See *United States v Bell Atlantic Corp and Others* (n 102).

[108] *Bell Atlantic—GTE* (n 103) para 16.

[109] ibid para 5.

[110] ibid para 25.

98 PUBLIC INTEREST ASSESSMENT AND THE FCC

[a] merger between an existing market participant and a firm that is not currently a market participant, but that would have entered the market but for the merger, violates antitrust laws if the market is concentrated and entry by the nonparticipant would have resulted in de-concentration of the market or other pro-competitive effects.[111]

The analysis includes as the most significant participants those firms already dominant and 'those that are more likely to enter in the near future, in an effective manner, and on a large scale once a more competitive environment has been established'.[112] However, such a doctrine has been described as speculative, lacking economic and factual support.[113] Some authors have indicated that the application of this doctrine by which competition concerns arise in cases where the acquired firm is not unique in the market, and has not decided to enter it either, becomes excessively conjectural.[114] This view was shared by Commissioner Powell, who described the apparent harms identified by the Commission as speculative and exaggerated.[115] However, this approach is in line with the one the DOJ and the FTC would take in a competition context.

It is important also to mention that it took almost two years for the FCC to clear the merger. Such a delay, combined with the number and extent of the voluntary commitments obtained from the merging parties, generated some discontent. The applicants tried to convince the FCC about the benefits of the merger; in particular, they argued that the merger would permit them to offer a package of services to large business customers in twenty-one out-of-region cities eighteen months after the merger took place.[116] According to the FCC, a merger was not necessary to obtain such benefits.[117] As a result, the merging parties engaged in a long negotiation process that resulted in numerous non-merger specific conditions, which were similar in nature to those negotiated in the SBC—Ameritech deal.[118] Commissioner Powell, who in his statement had previously indicated his disagreement with the harms foreseen by the Commission, went further in relation to the negotiated commitments, arguing that: 'I would be very hesitant to subject the public to these harms and would instead disapprove the merger, rather than try to offset it with commitments that are wholly unrelated to the harms.'[119]

This transaction exemplifies the shortfalls of the dual review between the DOJ and the FCC, in particular that the duplicative analysis creates a tension between the standards for merger review. While for the DOJ the analysis of the competitive effects is more factual, objective, supported in economic analysis, and less predictive, for the FCC it is more suppositional, a fact that undoubtedly adds uncertainty to the process and can

---

[111] ibid para 98.
[112] ibid.
[113] Russell and Wolson (n 18) 152.
[114] Phillip E Areeda and Herbert Hovenkamp, *Antitrust Law: An Analysis of Antitrust Principles and Their Application* (Wolters Kluwer Law 1996) 1118.
[115] *Bell Atlantic—GTE* (n 103) Commissioner Michael K Powell's statement.
[116] ibid para 219.
[117] ibid para 220–25.
[118] Barkow and Huber (n 47) 52, 64, 79.
[119] *Bell Atlantic—GTE* (n 103) Commissioner Michael K Powell's statement.

affect the fate of a transaction, allowing mergers to be cleared that otherwise would have been blocked. Another important point to note is the length of the FCC process, which offers an opportunity to impose commitments that are distant from the nature of the merger, under a review standard that seeks, among other things, to overreach regulatory purposes in the name of promoting competition.

3.4.1.1.5 Verizon—MCI

In February 2005, MCI, Inc. (MCI), a major provider of internet backbone and Verizon Communications, Inc. (Verizon), one of the largest RBOCs with a significant presence in wireless telephony, announced MCI would become a wholly owned subsidiary of Verizon.[120] This merger generated opposition among competitors, who claimed that the merger would increase concentration in wireline connections, and the public.[121] The transaction was conditionally approved by the DOJ and the FCC. Both reviewing bodies believed that in certain premises where Verizon and MCI were the only competitors the merger would affect the market for Type I wholesale special access services. The DOJ addressed this concern by issuing limited divestitures, which the FCC found enough to alleviate its own concerns.[122] In addition, the FCC concluded that the transaction would not have anti-competitive effects in the retail enterprise, mass market, internet backbone, wholesale interchange, and international markets.[123]

Even though the FCC indicated that the remedy imposed by the DOJ was enough to counteract the possible harms of the transaction and that no other competition issues were identified, a broad range of voluntary commitments were negotiated with the parties. Among them were fixed rates for special access services, the supply of unbundled network elements, broadband distribution, internet backbone networks, and adherence to the FCC's neutrality policy codes.[124] Commissioner Abernathy described these conditions as a 'failure to appreciate the degree to which the market has changed', adding that some were unnecessary and had been created to address unknown and hypothetical issues whose effects would instead generate market distortions.[125] Abernathy's view coincides with the position shown by the DOJ, whereby the transaction would benefit consumers given the current competition, evolving technologies, the changing regulatory setting, and remarkably large merger-specific efficiencies.[126]

The analysis of this case provokes some reflections about the real need for commitments 'voluntarily' offered by the merging parties. If the remedy imposed by the DOJ

---

[120] Verizon—MCI, 20 FCC Rcd 18433, para 1.

[121] A quick search on the FCC's Electronic Comment Filing System at https://www.fcc.gov/ecfs/search/search-filings/results?q=(proceedings.name:(%2205-75%22))(accessed 3 October 2023) reveals that more than 8,000 comments have been filed in this case.

[122] United States v Verizon Communications, Civil Action No 1:05CV02103, Final Judgment (DDC filed 27 October 2005) https://www.justice.gov/atr/case-document/final-judgment-165 (accessed 28 October 2022); See also Verizon—MCI (n 120) paras 2, 35.

[123] Verizon—MCI (n 120) para 3.

[124] Warren G Lavey, 'Telecom Globalization and Deregulation Encounters US National Security and Labor Concerns' (2007) 6 Journal of Telecommunications & High Technical Law 121, 150.

[125] Verizon—MCI (n 120) Commissioner Kathleen Q Abernathy.

[126] Ilene Knable Gotts and Philipp Hoffmann, 'Back to the Future: Will Telecommunications and Entertainment Service Providers Be Permitted to Converge Globally' (2007) 8 Business Law International 308, 322.

100 PUBLIC INTEREST ASSESSMENT AND THE FCC

was enough to alleviate the concerns of the FCC in relation to access to services, and since no other issues were identified in other markets, and the DOJ accepted the efficiencies of the merger, why were an important number of commitments negotiated? Perhaps the answer resides in Commissioner Abernathy's statement. But other factors undoubtedly play a role, as repeatedly seen in the cases examined throughout this chapter. It is the inability of the merging parties to resist the leverage the FCC enjoys in these negotiations.

3.4.1.1.6 Comcast—NBCU

In December 2009, Comcast Corporation (Comcast) and NBC Universal (NBCU) announced that Comcast would acquire a controlling interest in NBCU. At the time of the transaction, Comcast participated in the development, management, and operation of cable systems, and the delivery of programming content, and was the owner of television stations such as the Golf Channel, E! Entertainment Television, and the Style Network, among others. NBCU was a media and entertainment business present in a television group, film production, and distribution network, various theme parks, digital media operations, broadcast television networks (NBC and Telemundo), and broadcast television stations.[127] Before the transaction, NBCU was a provider of video programming to Comcast, which was then distributed to consumers by the latter.[128] The merger was a vertical one, considering that NBCU was a strong provider of video programming with a small presence in video distribution, and Comcast was an important video distributor with just 3.3 per cent participation in the video programming network.[129] In horizontal terms, the merging companies were providers of video programming through broadcast and cable networks, respectively, and distributors of video programming through broadcast television stations (NBCU) and cable operators (Comcast).[130] In short, the transaction signified a horizontal integration in video programming and video distribution, and a vertical integration in the distribution chain.

While the DOJ did not raise any concerns in relation to the horizontal effects of the transaction, the FCC, despite the small revenue of the merging parties in the video programming market (NBCU 14 per cent, Comcast 2 per cent), was worried that the combined company would harm the market.[131] Such a concern was addressed by a remedy, which was imposed to deal with the vertical concerns of the transaction.[132] In relation to the vertical effects, both reviewing agencies agreed that it was possible that in the distribution market the merged entity would increase the prices for NBCU's programming, deny access to them, or reduce access to the Comcast broadband network to its competitors, a concern that was not mitigated by the apparent efficiencies alleged by

---

[127] Thomas Curtin, 'Achieving the Franchise: The Comcast—NBC Universal Merger and the New Media Marketplace' (2010) 19 CommLaw Conspectus 149, 152.

[128] William Rogerson, 'Vertical Mergers in the Video Programming and Distribution Industry: The Case of Comcast-NBCU' in John E Kwoka Jr and Lawrence J White (eds), *The Antitrust Revolution* (OUP 2013).

[129] Yoo (n 38) 9.

[130] ibid 7.

[131] ibid 15–16.

[132] Federal Communications Commission, FCC 11-4, Docket No 10-56, para 146.

the applicants.[133] However, the DOJ focused its analysis on the potential disadvantage that the online video programming distributors (OVDs) would face, and the FCC assessment included OVDs as well as the multi-channel video programming distributors (MVPDs).[134] Almost a year after the transaction was filed, the parties received approval, conditional on programming availability to OVDs and MVPDs, and an arbitration process in the case of price increases.[135] In addition, the FCC negotiated with Comcast—NBCU more than 100 commitments that were not merger-specific,[136] contrary to what some scholars had anticipated, that 'the merger should and likely will pass with few conditions'.[137]

This case illustrates the contradictory conclusions reached by the DOJ and the FCC in relation to the horizontal effects of the transaction. Regarding the vertical effects of the merger, even if there was a consensus, the focus was different. The case also shows the lengthy procedure, but most importantly the disproportionate number of commitments that were negotiated, which differed from the limited number that was expected by the legal community. In this sense, Comcast—NBCU validates the criticism that the FCC frequently negotiates wide-ranging 'voluntary commitments'. Nonetheless, in 2016, Donald Trump declared in relation to the media market that if elected, he 'would look at breaking up Comcast's acquisition of NBC Universal' as 'Deals like this destroy democracy', a view that seems to encourage the persistence of stringent merger reviews and cumbersome negotiations in the telecommunications sector.[138]

3.4.1.1.7 Sinclair—Tribune

On 28 June 2017, Sinclair Broadcast Group (Sinclair) and Tribune Media Company (Tribune) filed applications seeking to transfer control of Tribune subsidiaries to Sinclair. According to the merger plan, Sinclair would acquire Tribune through a merger of a newly formed subsidiary of Sinclair with and into Tribune, followed by Tribune merging with and into Sinclair's wholly owned subsidiary, Sinclair Television Group (STG), with STG as the surviving company. Specifically, the applicants sought the FCC's consent to transfer control of Tribune's 'full-power broadcast televisions stations, low-power television stations, and TV translator stations to Sinclair'.[139] According to the application, Sinclair owned or operated 173 broadcast television stations, consisting of 528 channels, in eighty-one markets, with affiliations with all major networks, and was the largest local news provider in the US. Tribune, in turn, owned or operated forty-two broadcast television stations in thirty-three markets, also with affiliations with all major networks, and owned cable network WGN America, digital multicast network Antenna TV and WGN-Radio. Although the

[133] Rogerson (n 128) 3.
[134] ibid 59.
[135] ibid 3.
[136] Yoo (n 38) 33.
[137] Curtin (n 127) 178.
[138] Emily Stephenson, 'Trump Vows to Weaken U.S. Media "Power Structure" if Elected' *Reuters* (22 October 2016) https://www.reuters.com/article/usa-election/trump-vows-to-weaken-u-s-media-power-structure-if-elected-idUSL1N1CS08H.
[139] *Sinclair Broadcast Group—Tribune Media Company*, 33 FCC Rcd 6830 Hearing Designation Order (2018).

102 PUBLIC INTEREST ASSESSMENT AND THE FCC

merging parties admitted that: 'the combined company would reach 72 per cent of US television households and would own and operate the largest number of broadcast television stations of any station group ... [also] the combined company would have a national audience reach in excess of the FCC's current regulations,'[140] they expressed their intention to take any action necessary to comply with the FCC's rules in order to obtain its approval.[141]

The transaction was severely opposed by the public and several stakeholders, including cable and satellite operators, trade associations, mobile phone companies, independent programmers, and public interest organizations.[142] The FCC was also suspicious about the veracity of three proposed operations that instead of transferring broadcast television licences in Chicago, Dallas, and Houston directly to Sinclair, proposed to transfer them to other entities. Particularly, it was uneasy about the proposal whereby Sinclair would transfer a station to an individual without prior experience in broadcasting, who served as chief executive officer (CEO) of a company in which Sinclair had some vested interests, subject to a price below market value and with the option to buy back the station in the future. Although the parties withdrew this and the other two operations, for the FCC any other related transaction involving Sinclair would be vitiated with misrepresentation, 'lack of candor' and therefore raised concerns whether they will be aligned with the public interest.[143] The applicants offered some other divestiture options, a few of them also subject to negotiation with the DOJ (eg St. Louis station), but the FCC was dissatisfied with them. In the end, the FCC did not approve the merger, referring the case to an administrative law judge,[144] stating that it was 'unable to find ... that grant of the applications would be consistent with the public interest,'[145] and placing special emphasis on the 'broadcast ownership rules', which justified the court hearing according to section 309(d) of the Communications Act.[146]

In September 2018, Tribune sued Sinclair for breach of contract and in January 2020 Sinclair settled with Nexstar Media Group (which had bought Tribune in late 2019).[147] Finally, in March 2019, almost two years after the application was filed, Administrative Judge Jane Halprin decided not to proceed with the FCC's claim as the transaction

---

[140] ibid.

[141] ibid.

[142] Meredith Senter and Erin E. Kim, 'Recent Trends in Media Industry Mergers and Acquisitions' *LexisNexis Practical Guidance Journal* (19 December 2017) https://www.lexisnexis.com/lexis-practice-advisor/the-journal/b/lpa/archive/2017/12/19/recent-trends-in-media-industry-mergers-and-acquisitions.aspx (accessed 15 November 2022).

[143] *Sinclair Broadcast Group—Tribune Media Company* (n 139).

[144] ibid.

[145] ibid.

[146] Under s 309(d) of the Act, '[i]f a substantial and material question of fact is presented or if the Commission for any reason is unable to find that grant of the application would be consistent [with the public interest, convenience, and necessity]', it must formally designate the application for a hearing in accordance with s 309(e) of the Act.

[147] Under the terms of the settlement, Sinclair will pay Nexstar US$60 million and will transfer control of WDKY-TV in the Lexington, Kentucky, market; see Daniel Uria, 'Sinclair Agrees to Pay $48M Civil Penalty to Settle FCC Probe into Tribune Deal' *UPI* (6 May 2020) https://www.upi.com/Top_News/US/2020/05/06/Sinclair-agrees-to-pay-48M-civil-penalty-to-settle-FCC-probe-into-Tribune-deal/2941588818179/ *UPI* (accessed 15 November 2022).

had already been terminated.[148] An important lesson that can be drawn from this case is that the impression the FCC had that the merging parties tried to deceive it into thinking that the potential buyers of some stations were real, when in its view they were not, led to the conclusion that the merger was against the public interest. This posture suggests that whenever the FCC has a sense that a merger application is grounded on misleading or incomplete information then this circumstance amounts to another consideration that can be used to decide whether a transaction observes the public interest or not. It is also noteworthy that the administrative law judge's decision came two years after the application (a delay that can often lead to the failure of a transaction), whereas in similar instances before the FTC the judgment usually comes within a matter of months.

The examination of the above cases has shown that there is a need to assess the effectiveness of a concurrent merger review and the application of a public interest review as well as a competition assessment review. The ability of the FCC to have leverage on the parties leads to them having to accept an array of conditions in order to complete their transaction. In this respect, two important considerations stand out: first, whether this approach is efficient; and, secondly, whether it is time to revisit the merger control rules in the telecommunications sector in the US.

3.4.1.2 Transactions where FTC/DOJ and FCC converged on the assessment
The next group of merger cases illustrates either some form of coordination and a degree of convergence between the antitrust agency and the regulator or some degree of convergence in their conclusions, although in some cases the analysis could have been more distinctive between the agencies.

3.4.1.2.1 AOL—Time Warner
In 2000, America Online (AOL) was a provider of interactive services, web brands, internet technologies, and electronic commerce, and Time Warner (Time Warner), a worldwide media and entertainment company, requested approval to transfer control of certain licences and authorizations to a new combined company, AOL Time Warner.[149] The transaction value was US$183 billion.[150]

The FTC found that the merger would harm competition in the residential internet access marketplace and imposed conditions on the merging parties, requiring them to allow access to Time Warner's cable plant to unaffiliated internet service providers (ISPs), compelling them not to discriminate against unaffiliated content, and requesting AOL Time Warner to market AOL's digital subscriber line (DSL) services in the same manner and at the same retail price in Time Warner cable areas as in other areas, and to

---

[148] David Shepardson, 'U.S. Judge Drops Hearing into Sinclair after Failed Tribune Merger' *Reuters* (5 March 2019) https://www.reuters.com/article/us-sinclair-ma-tribune-media-fcc/u-s-judge-drops-hearing-into-sinclair-after-failed-tribune-merger-idUSKCN1QM2G4 (accessed 15 November 2022).

[149] *AOL—Time Warner*, 16 FCC Rcd 6547 paras 1, 27, 36.

[150] Mark Leibovich, 'AOL to Acquire Time Warner in Record $183 Billion Merger' *The Washington Post* (11 January 2000) https://www.washingtonpost.com/archive/politics/2000/01/11/aol-to-acquire-time-warner-in-record-183-billion-merger/92bdb300-0f48-4dfd-ae7e-38d9aec6417a/ (accessed 25 October 2022).

104   PUBLIC INTEREST ASSESSMENT AND THE FCC

hold distinct Road Runner, a cable ISP, from AOL's ISP service until AOL Time Warner had an unaffiliated ISP on all AOL Time Warner cable systems.[151]

The FCC approved the transaction subject to conditions aiming to address the following four concerns: (i) that AOL Time Warner might be able to discriminate against unaffiliated ISPs in terms of the rates, terms, and conditions of access; (ii) AOL could enhance its dominance in the high-speed access market by obtaining preferential carriage rights for AOL on the facilities of other cable operators; (iii) AOL could dominate the next generation of advanced instant messaging (IM)-based applications; and, (iv) AOL could discriminate against the interactive television (ITV) services of unaffiliated video programming networks.[152]

The approval order imposed the following conditions to address the above four issues. Contractual terms and negotiations between AOL Time Warner and unaffiliated ISPs were a necessary requirement to address the first issue. In order to address the second issue, AT&T was prevented from giving AOL exclusive carriage or preferential terms, conditions, and prices. In order to remedy the third issue FCC imposed interoperability conditions between AOL Time Warner NPD-based applications and those of other providers to solve the third issue; and, it relied on the arrangements contained in the FTC Consent Agreement designed to halt the ability and incentive of AOL Time Warner to discriminate against the 'ITV' services of unaffiliated video programming networks.[153]

This case has been questioned for a number of reasons. First, the FCC overlooked the fact that AOL did not have any granted licences, implying a lack of jurisdiction to review the transaction, which was overcome by assessing the transaction as AOL acquiring Time Warner instead of the other way round.[154] Secondly, it was claimed that the FCC imposed conditions without analysing whether there was a relationship between the transaction, the nature of the competitive harm, and the remedy.[155] In particular, it was argued that the order to make IM-based applications interoperable was not based on a proper competition analysis, to the extent that Commissioner Powell in his dissenting statement referred to this remedy as 'flawed'.[156] This view was shared by Commissioner Furchtgott-Roth, who indicated that the 'Commission has speculated about as yet undeveloped facts that are only tangentially related to license usage, and then applied to that conjecture a standard of review that is virtually unknowable ex ante'.[157] Finally, the IM interoperability order was perceived as a regulatory decision

---

[151]   *AOL—Time Warner* (n 149) para 17.

[152]   ibid para 18.

[153]   ibid.

[154]   Weiser (n 57) 170–71. See also Commissioner Furchtgott-Roth, who in his dissenting assessment stated that: 'The overwhelming bulk of this document has little, if anything, to do with the proposed transferee's use of the CARS licenses that are the jurisdictional object of this proceeding. Instead, the Order focuses on the transferee's various lines of internet business, including instant messaging and interactive television.' *AOL—Time Warner* (n 149) Commissioner Harold Furchtgott-Roth's statement.

[155]   Weiser (n 57) 171.

[156]   *AOL—Time Warner* (n 149) Commissioner Michael K Powell. See also Philip J Weiser, 'Internet Governance, Standard Setting, and Self-Regulation, Northern Kentucky Law Review' (2001) 28(4) North Kentucky Law Review 842; Weiser (n 57) 170–71.

[157]   *AOL—Time Warner* (n 149), Commissioner Harold Furchtgott-Roth's statement.

that was insufficiently supported, surrounded by practical implementation issues that forced its revocation two years later.[158] This point echoes what some call a market facilitator who uses its merger review powers to accommodate the needs of all the business players present in the telecommunications sector overseen by it, regardless of not having been affected by the transaction.[159]

Although in this case there was not a marked contradiction between the decisions made by the FTC and the FCC, the analysis of the possible harms and the required remedies was different. The analysis of the FCC was predictive in nature and therefore the imposition of its remedies insufficiently grounded, forcing the revocation of the interoperability solution that had initially been enforced. But perhaps the most important observation is that two Commissioners in their statements cast doubt about the authority and the quality of the FCC's review analysis.

3.4.1.2.2 News Corp—DirecTV

In 2003, General Motors Corporation (GM), Hughes Electronics Corporation (Hughes), and the News Corporation Limited (News Corp) obtained conditional approval to transfer control of various licences and authorizations related to the telecom sector, including direct broadcast satellite (DBS)[160] and fixed satellite space station, earth station, and terrestrial wireless authorizations held by Hughes and its wholly- and majority-owned subsidiaries to News Corporation.[161] The transaction would result in News Corp holding a de facto controlling interest over Hughes and its subsidiaries, including DirecTV Holdings LLC (DirecTV), a wholly-owned subsidiary of Hughes, which provides DBS services in the United States, as well as Hughes Network Systems (HNS), a facilities-based provider of very small aperture terminal (VSAT) network systems, and PanAmSat Corporation (PanAmSat), a global facilities-based provider of geostationary-satellite orbit fixed satellite services (FSS).[162]

DirecTV was one of two US national DBS providers and the second major US MVPD.[163] News Corp held cable and broadcasting programming interests, including Fox broadcast network, television broadcast stations, cable networks, and a broadcast network.[164] The proposal raised concerns about the possible vertical effects of the transaction in the distribution of programming interests such as FX, Fox news, and regional sports channels, where the new combined company could exploit its ownership to the detriment of its competitors.[165]

---

[158] Weiser (n 57) 171; Weiser (n 152). It is important to mention that Commissioner Powell in his statement expressed the concern 'that our license transfer process continues to pull the Commission away from its core responsibilities and competencies'. *AOL—Time Warner* (n 149) Commissioner Michael K Powell.

[159] Levi (n 40) 606.

[160] DBS is the acronym used in the United States to describe the domestic implementation of the satellite service known internationally as the broadcasting satellite service (BSS). See 47 CFR § 25.201.

[161] *GM—Hughes—News Corp*, 19 FCC Rcd 473 para 1.

[162] ibid para 2.

[163] Knable Gotts and Hoffmann (n 126).

[164] *GM—Hughes—News Corp* (n 161) para 7; Knable Gotts and Hoffmann (n 126) 327.

[165] Weiser (n 57) 172.

106   PUBLIC INTEREST ASSESSMENT AND THE FCC

In particular, the FCC considered that the new entity would have the incentive to exclude or increase the fees for its programming for its MVPD's rivals and could impose restrictions or exert pressure in terms of withholding of regional sports networks (RSNs) programming.[166] In order to address the identified concerns, the parties committed to not discriminate against unaffiliated programming services, to make all MVPDs national and regional programming services available non-exclusively and without discriminatory terms, and to creating a neutral arbitration panel to solve disputes over the terms and conditions of carriage of RSNs.[167]

An aspect that deserves attention is that the DOJ issued a statement supporting the FCC's conditions, indicating that there had been consultation among them, and that the DOJ had helped the FCC. In the end, the DOJ did not impose its own conditions.[168] Contrary to what happened in AOL—Time Warner, the regulator and the competition agency coordinated their assessments and avoided the unnecessary imposition of similar in nature remedies. This approach favours the efficiency of the process and the burden of satisfying the multiple requests that the merger parties bring to bear.

3.4.1.2.3 AT&T—DirecTV
In June 2014, AT&T entered into an agreement with DirecTV whereby DirecTV would merge with and into a wholly owned subsidiary of AT&T. The new DirecTV would be the owner of the stock of the subsidiaries of the pre-transaction DirecTV, and the subsidiaries would continue to hold the FCC licences they held prior to the envisaged transaction.[169] In July 2015, the FCC approved the transaction subject to conditions.[170]

As explained by the FCC, in order to ensure that the envisaged transaction 'serves the public interest, convenience, and necessity', it had engaged in an arduous analysis of the potential harms and benefits that the transaction would create.[171] The applicants (ie AT&T and DirecTV) had to prove that the transaction would serve the public interest and that the balance would be positive.[172]

Since under the 'public interest authority' the FCC can impose 'conditions to confirm specific benefits or remedy specific harms likely to arise from transactions',[173]

---

[166] Knable Gotts and Hoffmann (n 126) 327.

[167] ibid.

[168] Department of Justice, Justice Department Will not Challenge News's Corp.'s acquisition of Hughes Electronics Corp, Press Release (19 December 2003) https://www.justice.gov/archive/opa/pr/2003/December/03_at_714.htm (accessed 25 October 2022).

[169] AT&T—DirecTV, 30 FCC Rcd 9131 (2015) para 7.

[170] ibid.

[171] ibid.

[172] ibid 9.

[173] ibid 11. Also see SBC Communications Inc and AT&T Corp Applications for Approval of Transfer of Control, Memorandum Opinion and Order, 20 FCC Rcd 18290, 18303 19 (2005); Applications of AT&T Wireless Services Inc and Cingular Wireless Corporation for Consent to Transfer Control of Licences and Authorizations and others, Memorandum Opinion and Order, 19 FCC Rcd 21522, 21545–46 43 (2004); Applications of Nextel Partners Inc Transferor, and Nextel WIP Corp and Sprint Nextel Corporation, Transferees, for Consent to Transfer Control of Licences and Authorizations, Memorandum Opinion and Order, 21 FCC Rcd 7358, 7361 9 (2006); Applications of AT&T Inc and CellCo Partnership d/b/a Verizon Wireless for Consent to Assign or Transfer Control of Licences and Authorizations and Modify a Spectrum Leasing Arrangement, Memorandum Opinion and Order, 25 FCC Rcd 8704, 8747 101 (2010). The agreement set out that, after consummation, Cablevision

AT&T—DirecTV was (i) required to expand its deployment of high speed, fibre optic broadband internet access service to 12.5 million customer locations; (ii) prohibited from using discriminatory practices to disadvantage online video distribution services and had to submit its internet interconnection agreements for an FCC review; and (iii) made to offer broadband services to low-income consumers at discounted rates.[174]

The FCC concluded that the

> [n]ewly combined entity will be a more effective multichannel video programming distributor competitor, offering consumers greater choice at lower prices ... the combined AT&T-DIRECTV will increase competition for bundles of video and broadband, which, in turn, will stimulate lower prices ... benefiting consumers and serving the public interest ... This is, in other words, a bet on competition.[175]

Soon after the FCC approved the deal, the DOJ announced that it would not challenge AT&T's acquisition of Direct TV. The federal agency stated that after a lengthy investigation it concluded that the transaction did not raise any significant competitive concerns. An important element contained in the press release was the recognition that the DOJ inquiry availed itself of twinning collaboration with the FCC. The DOJ also reported that the commitments covered in the FCC order had the potential to benefit millions of subscribers.[176]

3.4.1.2.4 Altice—Cablevision

In September 2015, Cablevision (a US corporation) and Altice (a Dutch company) entered into an agreement by means of which Altice would acquire all the shares of Cablevision.[177,178] The parties filed to the FCC, pursuant to the Communications Act, seeking approval for the transfer of control of Cablevision and certain subsidiaries to Altice. In May 2016, the FCC declared that the transaction was in the 'public interest' and noted that Altice had vowed to invest in upgrading Cablevision broadband. Previously, on 4 November 2015, the DOJ had granted early termination of the waiting period under the HSR Act.[179]

Notably, according to section 308(b) of the Communications Act, amongst the factors that the FCC should take into consideration for its public interest assessment a key

---

would ultimately be majority owned and controlled by Patrick Drahi, a citizen of Israel (approximately a 60.45 per cent interest through his indirect ownership interest in Altice). *Altice—Cablevision*, 31 FCC Rcd 4365 (2016).

[174] Press Release, FCC Grants Approval of AT&T-DirecTV Transaction *FCC News* (2015) https://www.fcc.gov/document/fcc-grants-approval-attdirectv-transaction.

[175] *AT&T—DirecTV* (n 169).

[176] Department of Justice, 'Justice Department Will Not Challenge AT&T's Acquisition of Direct TV' (21 July 2015) https://www.justice.gov/opa/pr/justice-department-will-not-challenge-atts-acquisition-directv (accessed 25 October 2022).

[177] The agreement set out that, after consummation, Cablevision would ultimately be majority owned and controlled by Patrick Drahi, a citizen of Israel (approximately a 60.45 per cent interest through his indirect ownership interest in Altice).

[178] *Altice—Cablevision* (n 173) 3.

[179] ibid 1–2.

108   PUBLIC INTEREST ASSESSMENT AND THE FCC

one is to consider whether the applicant has the necessary 'citizenship, character, and financial, technical, and other qualifications'. As stated in the Memorandum Opinion and Order, the *Altice—Cablevision* transaction satisfied these qualification requirements.[180]

Third parties raised concerns regarding the financing of the transaction and whether it required the applicants to assume too much debt, which would have 'harmful effects on network investment, service quality, and jobs for the post-transaction Cablevision'.[181] However, the FCC found that the transaction was likely to result in 'tangible benefits for customers' and concluded that, 'on balance, the benefits outweigh any potential public interest harms'.[182] It found that, apart from the unpredictable market risks that surround any transaction, the buyer had demonstrated that it had the requisite financial capabilities to hold and use these FCC licences and authorizations in the public interest.[183] Thus, as can be observed, the FCC takes into account the financial stability of the parties in order to assess whether they are fit for the transaction and for the 'public interest' overall, and in this case it found that the transaction was not likely to result in financial instability for Cablevision or reduce its ability to invest in network infrastructure, concluding that 'Altice is likely to have the financial resources necessary to maintain and improve the Cablevision network'.[184]

Other factors that the FCC analyses when assessing a deal under the 'public interest' test are employment issues, and whether job cuts may arise from the transaction. In *Altice—Cablevision*, the FCC determined that there was not a 'public interest harm associated with a loss of employment',[185] since Altice was not financing its acquisition through job cuts; nor had it identified these to achieve cost savings.[186]

In relation to quantifiable and transaction-specific benefits created by a transaction, the FCC usually 'asks whether the benefit likely will be accomplished in the absence of the proposed transaction and whether the benefit will flow through to consumers and accrue to the public interest'. Even though the FCC did not quantify the potential benefit to consumers and did not rely on such benefits in determining whether the

---

[180] In this regard, the FCC made reference to its conclusion in a previous decision, *Suddenlink—Altice* order, 30 FCC Rcd 14358, para15, where it stated that: 'No commenter has raised substantive concerns regarding Altice's qualifications to provide service, and we find no evidence in the record that Altice is unqualified to hold Commission authorizations. Other than the ordinary market risks that accompany any business transaction, there is no evidence in the record indicating that this transaction will be likely to result in financial harms or distress that would compromise Altice's ability to maintain and improve broadband and other services in the Suddenlink service territory... there is persuasive evidence in the record that Altice will bring operational expertise, scale, and resources to enable it to maintain and accelerate service offerings for Suddenlink's customers. Further, no commenters raised concerns regarding Altice's character or technical qualifications.'

[181] *Altice—Cablevision* (n 173) 6.

[182] ibid 7.

[183] See *Verizon—Frontier* order, 25 FCC Rcd at 5981–83, para 19, where it is stated that: '[a]lthough the Commission has a responsibility to consider the financial qualifications of the transferee, it is not the Commission's role to substitute its business judgment for that of the applicants or the market; rather, the relevant question here is whether Frontier has the requisite financial qualifications to hold and use these Commission licenses and authorizations in the public interest'.

[184] *Altice—Cablevision* (n 173) 13.

[185] ibid 13–14.

[186] ibid 13–14.

transaction was in the public interest.[187] It concluded that, overall, the transaction was likely to result in some benefits to consumers, thereby serving the public interest.[188]

3.4.1.2.5 *Nexstar—Media General*

In 2016, Nexstar, a Delaware corporation that owns, operates, or services broadcast television stations in sixty-two metropolitan areas and Media General, a Virginia corporation that owns, operates, or services broadcast television stations in forty-eight metropolitan areas, entered into an agreement. According to that agreement, Nexstar would acquire all outstanding shares of Media General, which were valued at approximately US$4.6 billion,[189] which gave rise to an application before the FCC, seeking its consent to the long form transfer of control of twenty-eight licence subsidiaries of Media General to Nexstar.[190] In January 2017, the FCC conditionally approved the transaction. On 15 September 2016, the FTC granted early termination under the Hart-Scott-Rodino Act Premerger Notification Programme and, on 14 September 2016, the DOJ entered into a consent decree with the applicants, requiring Nexstar to divest seven broadcast stations to proceed with the deal.[191] The DOJ was concerned that, after the merger, the existing head-to-head competition between Nexstar and Media General would be eliminated resulting in higher prices for broadcast television spot advertising in each of the designated market areas (DMAs) and higher licensing fees for the retransmission of broadcast television programming to MVPDs in each of the DMA markets.[192] The FCC agreed with the concerns expressed by the DOJ with regard to effects on retransmission, as well as with the remedies imposed by the federal agency to ameliorate them.[193]

The parties claimed that the proposed transaction would produce 'operational efficiencies and economies of scale that would be reinvested in programming, providing tangible benefits to viewers'.[194] The FCC, in turn, indicated that the examination of the alleged claims will follow four steps: (i) each alleged benefit must be transaction specific. This means it must be likely to occur because of the transaction, but unlikely to be realized by other practical means having less anti-competitive effect; (ii) each claimed benefit must be verifiable; therefore, applicants have the burden of providing sufficient evidence to support each claimed benefit to enable the FCC to verify its likelihood and magnitude; (iii) the FCC calculates the magnitude of benefits net of the cost of achieving them; and (iv) the FCC will make sure that the benefits flow to consumers and do not solely benefit the merging parties.[195]

---

[187] ibid 20–21.

[188] ibid 23–24.

[189] Nexstar, 'Nexstar Broadcasting Obtains Federal Communications Commission Approval for Media General Acquisition' https://www.nexstar.tv/nexstar-broadcasting-obtains-federal-communications-commission-approval-for-media-general-acquisition/ (accessed 15 November 2022).

[190] *Nexstar—Media General* 32 FCC Rcd 183 (2017) 3.

[191] 81 Red Reg 63206 (14 September 2016) https://www.govinfo.gov/content/pkg/FR-2016-09-14/pdf/FR-2016-09-14.pdf.

[192] ibid 63206–63207.

[193] *Nexstar—Media General* (n 190) 14.

[194] ibid 10.

[195] ibid 11.

110   PUBLIC INTEREST ASSESSMENT AND THE FCC

These factors resemble the criteria that the FTC and DOJ take into account in the assessment of efficiencies that arise from a merger/acquisition.[196] As is also explained in the decision, the FCC applies a 'sliding scale approach' to evaluate benefit claims, through which if potential harm appears to be substantial and likely, the applicants should demonstrate a higher degree of magnitude and likelihood of the claimed benefits.[197] After applying the four-step method described above, the FCC concluded that the merging parties have sufficiently demonstrated how the merger would generate public interest benefits. Specifically, the FCC accepted that the viewers of Nexstar would have access to reporting from Media General's Washington, D.C. news bureau. The FCC admitted that the establishment of a new bureau demands high investment costs, a reason why the merger was the most likely option for Nexstar to operate in the capital market and to allow its viewers enjoying the content offered by Media General.[198] The FCC also conceded that the same reasoning was applicable in other states where Nexstar had stations but not in the capital markets, or reporters but with limited news presence. In these states, the FCC agreed that the viewers of the combined entity would have access to more and better-quality content.[199] Although the FCC concurred with these claim benefits, it disregarded a number of others. For instance, it contended that the merger was not required to offer new and diverse programming to viewers. It also clarified that even if the merging parties were able to achieve cost savings, they were mostly fixed costs unlikely to result in benefits for consumers (eg lower prices).[200] Once the FCC had found that the proposed divestments were sufficient to comply with the local and national ownership rules,[201] the merger was cleared.

In this case the FCC largely relied on the analysis of the anti-competitive effects carried out by the DOJ and on the measures adopted by the antitrust agency to mitigate them. The focal point of the FCC assessment was to determine whether the transaction would serve the public interest, convenience, and necessity standard. The regulator carefully examined all the alleged claims and, in each case, provided a reasoning about when the purported benefit served the public interest or not. It was established that when the merger is the only means by which viewers can access broader and better-quality content, then merging parties can expect that the FCC sees such a benefit as being in line with the public interest. According to the views expressed by the FCC in this case, the same is not true when the same benefit can be obtained without the merger or when the gain does not flow to consumers. This is a similar approach followed by competition authorities in the consideration of efficiencies in merger assessment. The

---

[196] 'Many mergers produce savings by allowing the merged firms to reduce costs, eliminate duplicate functions, or achieve scale economies. Firms will often pass merger-specific benefits on to consumers in the form of lower prices, better products, or more choices. The agencies are unlikely to challenge mergers when the efficiencies of the merger prevent any potential harm that might otherwise arise from the proposed merger.' https://www.ftc.gov/tips-advice/competition-guidance/guide-antitrust-laws/mergers/entry-efficiencies (accessed 15 November 2022).

[197] *Nexstar—Media General* (n 190) 11.

[198] *Altice—Cablevision* (n 173) 13.

[199] ibid 12.

[200] ibid 13.

[201] ibid 15–16.

efficiencies need to lead to benefits to consumers as one of the three cumulative criteria for efficiencies to be accepted as sufficient to lead to the clearance of a transaction.

3.4.1.2.6 CenturyLink—Level 3

CenturyLink (CenturyLink) and Level 3 Communications (Level 3) sought approval to transfer control of some licences and authorizations from Level 3's operating subsidiaries to CenturyLink.[202] The combination of CenturyLink and Level 3's facilities-based networks and services formed a business telecommunications player worth about US$50 billion, whose goal was to expand its presence internationally, to enter into cloud services, and to compete with the giants AT&T and Verizon.[203] Before the merger, the value of CenturyLink was about US$16 billion and US$19 billion debt, and the value of Level 3 was almost US$20 billion and US$10 billion in debt, and CenturyLink funded the transaction through about US$24 billion in shares and cash, and Level 3's debt.[204]

On 27 October 2017, the FCC approved the transaction after concluding that its remedies and those imposed by the DOJ were enough to alleviate the harms and that the transaction served the public convenience and necessity.[205] The FCC found that the merging parties were the only fibre providers in ten specific locations that had been prevented from increasing their prices for five years in that area following the consolidation of the transaction.[206] The remedies imposed by the DOJ consisted of the newly combined company divesting its fibre and other assets in specific metropolitan statistical areas, as well as twenty-four strands of dark fibre that linked thirty sets of cities throughout the country.[207] Approval was also obtained from the board of directors and shareholders of both companies, state public utility commissions, and pertinent local governments and municipalities.[208]

Among the four claimed public interest benefits of the merger, the FCC agreed with two: that the merger would better enable the created enterprise to compete against larger incumbents and that the newly-combined complementary fibre facilities would benefit the public interest by increasing its range and capacity.[209] The FCC could not measure whether continuity in experienced leadership and success in prior acquisition integration would enhance the entity's capacity to accomplish its deal intentions and also rejected the claim about financial projections.[210]

---

[202] *CenturyLink—Level 3*, 32 FCC Rcd 9581.

[203] Colm Gorey, 'Merger Between CenturyLink and Level 3 Could Create a $50 bn Giant' *siliconrepublic* (28 October 2016) https://www.siliconrepublic.com/companies/centurylink-level-3-merger (accessed 19 October 2022).

[204] Nic Fildes, 'Level 3 Brings the Global Internet to CenturyLink' *Financial Times* (31 October 2016) https://www.ft.com/content/8276fab0-9f65-11e6-86d5-4e36b35c3550 (accessed 19 October 2022).

[205] *CenturyLink—Level 3* (n 65) 3.

[206] ibid 13.

[207] ibid 5. See also Mari Silbey, 'DOJ Blesses CenturyLink, Level 3 Merger … with Conditions' *LightReading* (10 March 2017) https://www.lightreading.com/services/broadband-services/doj-blesses-centurylink-level-3-merger-with-conditions/d/d-id/736908 (accessed 19 October 2022).

[208] *CenturyLink—Level 3* (n 65) 4.

[209] ibid 25–27.

[210] ibid 27–28.

112 PUBLIC INTEREST ASSESSMENT AND THE FCC

It is noteworthy that in this case the FCC showed a very relaxed approach, imposing conditions that responded to the Commission's intention to make clear that it 'will not be using them as a vehicle to extract extraneous concessions from parties'.[211] Nonetheless, considering the size of the transaction and the overlapping markets in which the applicants were present, this approach was criticized. Indeed, Commissioner Mignon L. Clyburn expressed the same concern in his dissenting statement: 'A $34 billion merger between two major companies providing business data services in a highly- concentrated market. One would think that a transaction of this magnitude would trigger market-based conditions to mitigate potential public interest harms. However, the only condition imposed in this item is short-term price controls on 10 buildings nationwide'.[212]

In relation to the public benefits factors that were accepted by the FCC in this case, one could argue that if we accept the unequivocal assumption that mergers increase the market power of the parties, enabling them to compete better in the market, most transactions will fulfil the public interest test. Ordinarily, we would expect merging parties to increase their market power after the merger. Nevertheless, there is insufficient empirical evidence showing a positive correlation between mergers and acquisitions and their effect on market power or their efficiency effects.[213] Hence, the FCC's proposition, attractive because of its simplicity, does not hold up to a more rigorous confrontation with empirical facts. In addition, given the limited reasoning presented by the FCC in this regard, it is unclear how the alleged benefit would effectively reach the consumers.

3.4.1.2.7 T-Mobile—Sprint

In April 2020, the FCC approved the merger between T-Mobile US and Sprint Corporation, the third and fourth largest national wireless carriers in the US. T-Mobile sought to take control of the licences and authorizations held by Sprint. The DOJ conditioned the approval to the divestment of some assets, in particular, the sale of Boost Mobile to DISH Network Corporation (DISH) to facilitate DISH's expansion in order to make it a stronger competitor.[214] The FCC found that the merger would be likely to create upward pricing pressure and reduce competition, resulting in commitments such as to build a world-leading nationwide 5-G Network, to provide high-speed 5G services to rural areas, to divest Boost Mobile, and some pricing commitments.[215]

Although the FCC and the DOJ had cleared the transaction, fourteen State Attorneys General challenged the transaction. A US district judge accepted that Sprint was

---

[211] See ibid, Statement of Commissioner Brendan Carr; see also ibid, Statement of Chairman Ajit Pai.

[212] ibid 36.

[213] Bruce A Blonigen and Justin R Pierce, 'Evidence for the Effects of Mergers on Market Power and Efficiency' National Bureau of Economic Research, Working Paper 22750 (October 2016) https://www.nber.org/system/files/working_papers/w22750/w22750.pdf (accessed 23 September 2022).

[214] United States v Deutsche Telekom AG, No 19-cv-02232 (DDC 26, July 2019) ECF No 2-2 (DOJ Proposed Final Judgment) (requiring, inter alia, (a) divestiture of Sprint's prepaid assets to DISH Network; (b) transfer of certain spectrum licences to DISH Network; and (c) entry into a mobile virtual network operator (MVNO) agreement between DISH Network and New T-Mobile). See also T-Mobile—Sprint, Memorandum Opinion and Order, FCC-19-103, WC-Docket No 18-197, para 12.

[215] T-Mobile—Sprint, Memorandum Opinion and Order, FCC-19-103, WC-Docket No 18-197, appendix G.

dealing with severe financial difficulties,[216] and gave the green light to the deal in a ruling that went against the State Attorney General who had opposed the transaction, arguing that the company would have continued as a potential competitor without the merger.[217] As a result of the transaction, Deutsche Telekom AG would be the single largest shareholder and would control the new company.[218]

The next transaction is one of the few cases where the FCC decided not to review the transaction and the DOJ challenged it. Interestingly, the FCC supported the position of the antitrust authority before the courts.

3.4.1.2.8 AT&T—Time Warner

In 2016, AT&T and Time Warner announced their plans to merge. The combination of Time Warner—one of the largest media and entertainment companies in the world and owner of some of the most popular brands such as TNT, TBS, CNN, and HBO—with AT&T—the nation's biggest wireless and telecommunications company, would, according to the parties, improve the experience of consumers, content creators, distributors, and advertisers in the media and entertainment industry.[219] It would also allow the newly merged entity to compete more effectively against Facebook and Google by collecting usage data about its viewers and therefore having a stronger digital advertising arm.[220] While the FCC decided not to review the transaction even though dozens of FCC licences were involved, the DOJ, focusing on the impact of the case on competition, on 20 November 2017 filed a request before the US District Court for the District of Columbia to enjoin the proposed merger. The DOJ claimed that AT&T would have the power to increase its rival's prices and the incentive to exclude competitors from the live content.[221] In relation to price concerns, the federal agency explained that once AT&T gained control over Time Warner, it could coerce other cable companies to pay extra for the rights to the channels and programmes held by the latter.[222] With respect to the fear of harming rivals, the DOJ indicated that the transaction would increase the possibility that AT&T would act unilaterally or in coordination with Comcast-NBCU

---

[216] Matthew Perlman, T-Mobile, 'Sprint Beat State-Led Merger Challenge' https://www.law360.com/articles/1242797 (accessed 10 November 2022). The judicial decision indicated that 'telling of severe financial, operational, and marketing difficulties, Sprint experiences the highest rate of loss customer it has gained ... Because of its poor past performance and uncertain future prospects, Sprint has considered merging with T-Mobile and various carriers on multiple occasions'. See *United States District Court Southern District Court of New York and Others v Deutsche Telekom AG and Others*, 19 Civ 5434 (VM) https://www.theverge.com/2020/2/12/21134278/sprint-tmobile-merger-court-ruling-opinion-decision-explainer-carriers-antitrust.

[217] https://www.cnet.com/news/t-mobile-and-sprint-are-one-what-you-need-to-know-about-the-mobile-mega-merger/ (accessed 10 November 2022).

[218] https://www.fcc.gov/transaction/t-mobile-sprint (accessed 15 November 2022).

[219] See AT&T, 'AT&T Completes Acquisition of Time Warner Inc.' (15 June 2018) https://about.att.com/story/att_completes_acquisition_of_time_warner_inc.html (accessed 27 October 2022).

[220] Brian Fung and Tony Romm, 'AT&T and the Government Face off in Court Today: Here's Everything You Need to Know' *The Washington Post* (19 March 2018) https://www.washingtonpost.com/news/the-switch/wp/2018/03/19/att-and-the-government-face-off-in-court-today-heres-everything-you-need-to-know/ (accessed 27 October 2022).

[221] Hadas Gold, 'Appeals Court Backs AT&T Acquisition of Time Warner' *CNN Business* (27 February 2019) https://edition.cnn.com/2019/02/26/media/att-time-warner-merger-ruling/index.html (accessed 1 November 2022).

[222] See AT&T (n 219); Fung and Room (n 220).

114 PUBLIC INTEREST ASSESSMENT AND THE FCC

to diminish MVPDs and to use HBO channels to retain or attract new customers while preventing rival distributors from accessing it.[223] As the District Court denied the request[224] the DOJ decided to appeal the decision, arguing that the District Court 'clearly erred when it found the merger was unlikely to have an anti-competitive effect', a position that was supported by the FCC, albeit its initial resistance to review the case under its own authority.[225]

The Court of Appeal upheld the District Court's decision. It confirmed that the vertical transaction was beneficial given the advantages of sharing complementary data, which is vital in online streaming services.[226] It also observed that the existence of an arbitration agreement in case of pricing or contract dispute, joined by the fact that the market was dynamic, factors that were ignored by the government, prevented any risk of price increase.[227] The Court of Appeals added that any concern that the merger would harm rivals in the MVPD market should be dismissed considering that this market was already in decline as a result of the increasing use of subscription video on demand services (SVDOs), as indicated by the District Court's ruling.[228] Further, it also accepted the District Court's view that the DOJ failed to demonstrate that AT&T would prevent the use of HBO to its rivals. It was also noted that even if Time Warner enjoyed attractive content and an advertising catalogue, it did not have direct contact with its customers through which to explore their preferences, a restraint that its competitors in the two markets for advertising and content creation, Google and Netflix, did not face.[229] Thus, the merger would allow Time Warner to use 'AT&T's consumer relationships, consumer data, and large wireless business' and challenge its rivals.[230]

An important implication arising from this case is that it took more than a year for the DOJ to investigate and to decide on challenging the merger. So, if one potential solution to making the merger control process in the media sector more efficient was to remove the dual system review between the regulator and the antitrust agencies, this case does not support such a reform, as the antitrust process itself can take a significant amount of time. Another aspect that deserves attention was the decision of the regulator not to intervene under its own authority, yet it supported the DOJ's claims,

---

[223] See Thomson Reuters Practical Law, 'Key Findings from the AT&T-Time Warner Merger Decision' (15 June 2015) https://uk.practicallaw.thomsonreuters.com/w-015-2754?transitionType=Default&contextData=(sc.Default)&firstPage=true (accessed 27 October 2022).

[224] *United States of America v AT&T Inc and Others*, Civil Case No 17-2511 (RJL) (12 June 2018) https://ecf.dcd.uscourts.gov/cgi-bin/show_public_doc?2017cv2511-146 (accessed 14 November 2022).

[225] See   https://arstechnica.com/tech-policy/2018/08/fcc-says-court-made-error-in-approval-of-atttime-warner-merger/ (accessed 12 November 2022). FCC supported the DOJ's appeal before the Court of Appeals, pointing out an error made by the US District Court of Columbia: Judge Richard Leon in his ruling against the DOJ said he was 'hesitant to assign any significant evidentiary value' to previous statements that AT&T and AT&T-owned DirecTV made to the FCC, since these—which were made in the years prior to the AT&T—Time Warner merger—supported the DOJ's case that a merged entity could raise the price of programming. Also note that those AT&T statements were made as part of the FCC's 2010 review of the Comcast—NBCUniversal merger.

[226] Gregory P Luib and Mike Cowie, 'Big (But Not Bad) Data and Merger Efficiencies' (28 January 2020) https://www.lexology.com/library/detail.aspx?g=3712daef-e9df-4584-83c3-ccfe465ea0f4 (accessed 12 November 2022).

[227] Gold (n 221).

[228] See Thomson Reuters, Practical Law (n 223); see also Gold (n 221).

[229] Gold (n 221).

[230] ibid.

3.4 ENFORCEMENT RECORD 115

signalling that this type of cooperation seems possible and perhaps less costly for all the agencies, as well as the parties themselves.

One final remark relates to the stance shown by the courts. In both instances, in the District Court and in the Appeal Court, the DOJ's claims were rejected. One wonders whether, had the FCC challenged the merger, its claims would also have been rejected by the courts entirely. Until recently,[231] non-horizontal mergers did not seem to cause concerns in the US antitrust regime,[232] as they did in the EU one. This approach has recently changed with the FTC and the DOJ working on the issuance of new guidelines for the assessment of non-horizontal mergers.

The examination of the cases in this section has shown that the FCC and the DOJ took a more consensual approach in reviewing the deals. With some exceptions, such as in the AOL—Time Warner case where the agencies shared some concerns, in practice they were grounded on different theories of harm that ultimately resulted in the imposition of divergent remedies. It was reassuring to observe close collaboration between them, seeing them agreeing on the types of measures to be adopted and relying on those already adopted by their counterparts. This pragmatic approach mitigates the unjustified duplication of effort observed in cases analysed in the previous section, in which the merging parties faced prolonged and costly procedures and at times contradictory decisions that can be difficult to reconcile. However, one remaining concern in the merger review process in the telecommunications sector in the US is the inherent difficulty of charting the scope of application of the public interest test.

3.4.1.2.9 Nexstar—Tribune

As previously mentioned, shortly after the Sinclair—Tribune deal fell through, Nexstar managed to acquire Tribune and its forty-one television stations in 2019. Despite some discrepancies, the regulatory hurdles were still there and were comparable. According to the local television ownership rule, a single entity is prevented in principle from owning two top-four television stations in the same DMA; as a result of the transaction, Nexstar would end up controlling two stations in thirteen DMAs, and two top-four stations in eleven DMAs.[233] Furthermore, pursuant to the national television ownership rule, a single entity is only allowed to own television stations reaching—in total—up to 39 per cent of all the television households in the US. The acquisition of Tribune would take Nexstar over the limit, although the company had planned several divestitures to fall back into line with both rules.

---

[231] See Steven C Salop, 'Invigorating Vertical Merger Enforcement' (May 2018) 127 Yale Law Journal 1962. See Federal Trade Commission, Federal Trade Commission and Justice Department Seek to Strengthen Enforcement against Illegal Mergers' https://www.ftc.gov/news-events/news/press-releases/2022/01/federal-trade-commiss ion-justice-department-seek-strengthen-enforcement-against-illegal-mergers (accessed 15 November 2022).

[232] See Michael H Riordan and Steven C Salop, 'Evaluating Vertical Mergers: A Post-Chicago Approach' (1995) 63 Antitrust Law Journal 513; Robert H Bork, *The Antitrust Paradox* (The Free Press 1978) 225; Robert H Bork and others, 'The Goals of Antitrust: A Dialogue on Policy' (1965) 65 Columbia Law Review 363.

[233] 34 FCC Rcd 8436, 8438.

116   PUBLIC INTEREST ASSESSMENT AND THE FCC

Arguing in light of the public interest standard, Nexstar claimed that the transaction would enhance its ability to deliver high-quality content to local communities. In particular, the unlocked efficiencies—estimated at US$160 million in the first post-merger year—would allow it to expand its local services, and better exploit the synergies between its own news bureaux and local stations, raising the level of its journalistic programming. Secondly, they would free up resources for further investment on the technological side.[234] However, several petitioners raised the concern that the merger would harm the public interest by enabling the new entity to charge more for retransmission fees, to the detriment of distributors and consumers.[235]

The agency did not accept the petitioners' argument, both because the planned divestitures would have left the bargaining position of the individual television stations unchanged and, more importantly, because higher retransmission rates are not 'necessarily a public interest harm'.[236] However, the FCC accepted the notion that better access to news bureaux is a public interest benefit, as confirmed by its own long-standing decisional practice, and embraced a similar view while assessing the applicant's investment goals. It thus concluded that the transaction was indeed in the public interest. We might summarize the case by pointing out that Nexstar learnt from Sinclair's mistakes, and took them into account by topping the deal with a credible divestiture plan, which eventually secured approval.[237]

However, while its interaction with the FCC was reasonably smooth, dealing simultaneously with the DOJ required more time and rather more formality, as it necessitated a consent decree, which was filed in July 2019[238] and was finalized in February 2020.[239] Procedure aside, there are a few differences between the FCC's reasoning and the DOJ's reasoning. First, the latter obviously was not as invested in the public interest considerations which made up a major argument for the former. Secondly, as regards the competition concerns, the DOJ went beyond the FCC's analysis of retransmission rights and discussed the transaction's effects on the advertising market, with an approach that was firmly grounded in a traditional understanding of the primacy of broadcasting advertising, in line with the agency's own decisional practice,[240] but that for the very same reason raised more than a doubt.[241]

3.4.1.2.10 Verizon—TracFone

Just like in Nexstar—Tribune, in Verizon—TracFone the FCC and the antitrust agencies (here the DOJ) can be said to have eventually converged in their assessments, but following two wildly different approaches: the DOJ was content with a superficial

---

[234] ibid 8442.

[235] ibid 8445.

[236] ibid 8450–51.

[237] Jenna Ebersole, 'Nexstar's Tribune Deal Sets Up Smoother Regulatory Process than Sinclair's Bid' *M-Lex* (5 December 2018) https://content.mlex.com/#/content/1047451.

[238] 84 FR 41738.

[239] *United States v Nexstar Media and Tribune Media*, Case 1:19-cv-02295-DLF (DDC 2 February 2020).

[240] cf *United States v Ray and Graycom*, Case 1:18-cv-02951 DDC (5 June 2019); 33 FCC Rcd 12349.

[241] Ebersole (n 233).

examination of the matter and granted the parties an early termination under the HSRA,[242] while the FCC embarked on a lengthy review and eventually authorized the transaction with a range of conditions. The main reason why this in-depth analysis was needed in light of the public interest standard but not of the competition standard has to do with the fact that TracFone, the mobile operator being acquired by Verizon, was providing its services to around 1.7 million Lifeline customers at the time of the deal.[243] Lifeline is a programme funded by the US federal government to enable the most vulnerable people in society to access telecommunications services at a subsidized price,[244] hence the necessity to take into account that there was a non-commercial, social dimension to the issue. Besides this 'potential to cause some public interest harms', the FCC was also concerned with the possibility that Verizon, in its capacity as wholesale provider, might have an incentive to raise costs for the mobile virtual network operators competing with TracFone.

Before the merger, TracFone served about 20 million prepaid mobile customers under several brand names; in September 2020, Verizon agreed to purchase the business from its parent company América Móvil at a valuation of over US$6 billion in a cash-and-stock transaction. According to the applicants, the acquisition would generate substantial benefits by making Verizon's technologies and compatible devices more easily available to the underserved. The FCC analysed the transaction's effects on competition and concluded that both unilateral and coordinated effects appeared unlikely,[245] but could not reach the same conclusion about vertical effects unless specific remedies were introduced. As regards the deal's effects on the public interest, moreover, there was a likelihood that Lifeline members in particular could be harmed by the new entity. These negative effects could only be partially offset by positive effects such as the elimination of double marginalization or the access to more advanced devices and technologies.

Among the extensive remedies attached to the deal, Verizon committed to keep offering TracFone's Lifeline services in the same service area for seven years, and to provide devices or sims free of charge to existing customers, when needed to switch to Verizon's network; to honour TracFone's existing MVNO agreements—including outside Verizon's own mobile network—and rate plans, as well as to keep serving its customers for three years; to grant to the MVNOs under contract with it the option to renew on a monthly basis on the same terms and for up to three years; and to arrange for some reporting obligations to be carried out for seven and a half years, including by an independent compliance officer.

---

[242] FTC, *Early Termination Notices*, Transaction No 20201618 (24 November 2020) https://www.ftc.gov/enfo rcement/premerger-notification-program/early-termination-notices/20201618.

[243] FCC, *Verizon—TracFone*, GN Docket No 21-112 (19 November 2021) 2.

[244] FCC, 'Lifeline Program for Low-Income Consumers' https://www.fcc.gov/general/lifeline-program-low-inc ome-consumers.

[245] *Verizon—TracFone* (n 243) 21–22.

118   PUBLIC INTEREST ASSESSMENT AND THE FCC

3.5 Some Implications of the Analysis

The analysis presented in this chapter has shown that the antitrust agencies and the FCC engage in different assessments of telecommunications mergers. The antitrust agencies focus their analyses on determining whether the transaction may substantially reduce competition, resulting in decisions that usually respond to just this principle and in remedies that only seek to address the harm on competition. The FCC, in contrast, applies a substantive merger analysis that entails broad aims. Under the public interest test the FCC includes a multitude of additional factors that fall outside traditional antitrust issues. For instance, the Bell Atlantic—NYNEX[246] case illustrates that the reduction of regulatory enforcement was one of the worries that the transaction raised in the FCC's view.

Another example of the wide scope of the FCC was observed in AOL—Time Warner.[247] In this case, the FCC clearly stated that one of the main goals of a merger is to positively promote competition, rather than to potentially lessen it, which is the principle that governs the standard of review of the antitrust agencies. Thus, judging from this case, the FCC appears to put an emphasis of merger synergies in its assessment, whereas antitrust authorities focus on the consumer harm. In this case, the FCC imposed a remedy in the form of instant messaging (IM) interoperability aiming to favour the rivals of the new entity. This remedy led to accusations that FCC was acting as a market facilitator. This approach to remedies was also observed in the Bell Atlantic—NYNEX[248] case, in which the merging parties committed to providing detailed monitoring reports to their competitors and accepted other obligations[249] in order to facilitate the entry and expansion of other firms. Similarly, in SBC—Ameritech[250] the applicants guaranteed to offer discounts to their rivals on the purchase of residential unbundled local loops.[251]

In Bell Atlantic—NYNEX[252] the DOJ and thirteen states raised no concerns, but despite this, the FCC raised many concerns that were alleviated after the parties submitted remedies.[253] In SBC—Ameritech,[254] the DOJ was concerned about the loss of competition, which was resolved with a divestiture remedy; such a concern was also shared by the FCC, for whom the remedy was not enough, imposing more than thirty additional

---

[246] *Bell Atlantic—NYNEX* (n 80).

[247] *AOL—Time Warner* (n 149).

[248] *Bell Atlantic—NYNEX* (n 80).

[249] Such as the facilitation of the implementation of 'unbundled network elements' (UNEs) obligations in favour of new local carriers; the publication of frequent reports aimed at revealing any possible discrimination or poor performance in the supply of UNEs affecting competing carriers, and the establishment of rates for interconnection and UNEs grounded on economic costs. See Brenner (n 72) 93.

[250] *SBC—Ameritech* (n 38)

[251] Kolasky (n 88) 801.

[252] *Bell Atlantic—NYNEX* (n 80).

[253] Such as the facilitation of the implementation of 'unbundled network elements' (UNEs) obligations in favour of new local carriers; the publication of frequent reports aimed at revealing any possible discrimination or poor performance in the supply of UNEs affecting competing carriers, and the establishment of rates for interconnection and UNEs grounded on economic costs. See Brenner (n 72) 93.

[254] *SBC—Ameritech* (n 38).

3.5 SOME IMPLICATIONS OF THE ANALYSIS   119

conditions with large monetary penalties for non-compliance. In AT&T—TCI[255] the DOJ approved the transaction subject to a divestiture. The FCC, imposed additional conditions such as those affecting the transfer of non-radio licence assets in order to ensure that the merger would not frustrate or undermine the FCC's policies.[256]

In Bell Atlantic—GTE,[257] while the DOJ requested the divestiture of wireless assets in some overlapping markets, the FCC under the 'potential competition doctrine' identified possible public interest harm, which resulted in a two-year review process, and non-merger specific conditions to address 'speculative and exaggerated' concerns, as Commissioner Powell said. In Verizon—MCI[258] the DOJ approved the transaction conditioned to some divestitures, which the FCC found adequate; however, even if the FCC did not identify other concerns, a broad range of commitments were negotiated confirming the unfettered power exerted by the FCC. In Comcast—NBCU[259] the DOJ did not find a single concern, but for the FCC the transaction was so likely to harm the market that a year after the application was filed over one hundred commitments were negotiated. In AT&T—DirecTV[260] the DOJ announced that it would not challenge the transaction but the FCC approved the transaction conditionally.[261]

It is evident that the merging parties are compelled to offer a variety of commitments to obtain FCC's approval. The above analysis reflects such a tendency, as while for the DOJ some transactions have not raised any concerns, for the FCC the opposite has been the case. A similar disparity has been observed in terms of remedies. While merger specific remedies have been enough to overcome the anti-competitive concerns of the DOJ, a broad variety of non-merger specific commitments have been conceded by parties, with the aim of obtaining the FCC's approval. The inclination is so evident that in CenturyLink—Level 3[262] the FCC tried to mitigate it by endorsing the remedies already agreed with the DOJ, and by clarifying that the FCC 'will not be using them as a vehicle to extract extraneous concessions from parties'.

The examination of the cases has also revealed that the antitrust agencies and the FCC do not usually consult each other as a standard practice or coordinate their assessment. This is at odds, for example, with the competition regime in the UK, whereby the UK competition authority (CMA) will consult the telecommunications regulator (OFCOM) on the assessment of a merger transaction. The exceptions are NewsCorp—DirecTV[263] and AT&T—DirecTV,[264] where the respective statements from the DOJ indicated that discussions between the DOJ and the FCC had taken place and that they

---

[255] *AT&T—TCI*, Memorandum Opinion and Order, CS-Docket 98-178.
[256] ibid, Commissioner Harold Furchtgott-Roth's statement, Appendix https://transition.fcc.gov/Speeches/Furc htgott_Roth/Statements/sthfr906.html (accessed 21 September 2022), indicating that the FCC conclusory asserted that 'the face of some merger applications may reveal that the merger could not frustrate or undermine our policies'.
[257] *Bell Atlantic—GTE* (n 103)
[258] *Verizon—MCI* (n 120).
[259] Federal Communications Commission, FCC 11-4, Docket No 10-56.
[260] *AT&T—DirecTV* (n 169).
[261] ibid.
[262] *CenturyLink—Level 3* (n 65).
[263] *GM—Hughes—News Corp* (n 161).
[264] *AT&T—DirecTV* (n 169).

120   PUBLIC INTEREST ASSESSMENT AND THE FCC

closely assisted each other. The analysis has also revealed that in cases where the anti-trust agency did not have any concerns, such as in Comcast—NBCU,[265] the merging parties had to wait over a year to obtain clearance from the FCC. The same delay was observed in SBC—Ameritech,[266] where a year after the application was filed the merging parties received a letter from the FCC warning them that in the absence of commitments a hearing would occur. The FCC's assessment timeline seems to be longer than the FTC/DOJ one in a number of cases.

3.6 Concluding Remarks

The purpose of this chapter was to analyse some seminal cases with the aim of verifying whether the criticisms that the dual review of telecommunications mergers by the FCC and the DOJ has raised are valid. Thus, we note that the multiple agency review has proven to be costly, lengthy, and cumbersome. Our examination has also established that often the assessments conducted by the antitrust agencies and the FCC on the same transactions are divergent. The competition analysis carried out by the DOJ is more objective, subject to a detailed judicial review, more predictive, and the antitrust agencies bear the burden of proving the anti-competitive effects of the transaction. By contrast, the competition and the public interest standards used by the FCC appear broad, more ambiguous, onerous, and cumbersome.

In addition, the chapter has identified that the FCC is not subject to a statutory deadline to make a final decision. One important implication of this feature is that the FCC has exploited this vulnerability in the public interest's defence. This vulnerability involves the merging parties' willingness to accept any conditions due to their need to close the deals and due to their lack of bargaining power. Introducing a deadline to decide on transactions would be an appropriate step to moderate the vulnerabilities that have emerged in the absence of an assessment timeframe. We would also expect the merger procedures before the FCC to be shortened. This chapter has shown that FCC assessment can frequently be unduly prolonged, and that the remedies imposed could be less intrusive. As the analysis has demonstrated, this has not always been the case. The hope is that a well-defined merger procedure under the authority of the regulator will illuminate trade-offs between public interest and certainty, thus helping to steer decision-makers and merging parties towards a more efficient merger assessment regime in this sector.

The challenges created by this dual review process could be addressed in different ways, for instance, by promoting close cooperation between the antitrust agencies and the FCC, ie by them consulting extensively with each other in order to coordinate their reviews and devising remedies that are both consistent, appropriate, and proportionate to the harm the transaction is likely to create.

---

[265] Federal Communications Commission, FCC 11-4, Docket No 10-56.
[266] *SBC—Ameritech* (n 38).

We will propose another solution to this challenge. Like the DOJ and the FTC, the FCC assesses the merger's effects on competition[267] but, unlike the federal agencies, the FCC does not have the expertise in conducting this type of analysis.[268] A model in which the competition analysis of a merger is confined only to the antitrust agencies and the public interest to the regulator presents a double advantage: it reduces the risks of having erroneous competition assessments from the regulator and enhances predictability and certainty. It has also been suggested that jurisdiction should be given to just one authority, with the possibility of requesting an opinion from other relevant agencies.[269] This is the approach followed by the UK competition regime. What seems imperative is a reform that can lead to a more transparent, efficient, predictable, and fair process. If the US government does not address the issues provoked by this concurrent merger review, the result will be more conflicted decisions between the federal antitrust agencies and the FCC.

---

[267] Barkow and Huber (n 47) 45.

[268] Rinner (n 23) 1575; Barkow and Huber (n 47) 45.

[269] For further discussion about the possible institutional designs to overcome the issues created by this dual review see David A Curran, 'Rethinking Federal Review of Telecommunications Mergers' (2002) 28 Ohio NU Law Review 747.

4

Public Interest Assessment and the Federal Energy Regulatory Commission (FERC)

4.1 The Federal Energy Regulatory Commission (FERC)

The Presidential Policy Directive 21[1] emphasized that the US energy sector acts as a very important enabler for all critical sectors of the US economy. The energy infrastructure is divided into three interrelated segments: electricity, oil, and natural gas. The majority of electricity is generated by combusting coal, followed by nuclear power plants, and by combusting natural gas. Less than 10 per cent of the energy is generated by hydroelectric plants, oil, and renewable sources.[2] There is a significant dependence of the energy sector on the transportation sector, mainly on the railroad that was analysed in the previous chapter as well as rail itself and other modes of transport that will be analysed in the next chapter.

The Federal Energy Regulatory Commission (FERC or Commission) regulates interstate transmission of electricity, natural gas, and oil. It also regulates hydropower projects and natural gas terminals.[3] As will be shown below, its powers have expanded over the years and are evidence of the importance of the energy sector for the US economy.

The chapter will start with a discussion of the composition of the FERC and the relevant regulatory framework before discussing some of the seminal case law that will show the approach the FERC takes in applying its assessment test and how this approach compares with that which the antitrust authority takes pursuant to its competition standard. The chapter will also discuss some implications that arise from assessing the role and practice of the regulator and the competition authority.

4.1.1 Composition and Legislation

The FERC is an independent agency that was established on 1 October 1977 by the Department of Energy Organization Act, replacing the Federal Power Commission

---

[1] The Presidential Policy Directive (PPD) on Critical Infrastructure Security and Resilience advances a national unity of effort to strengthen and maintain secure, functioning, and resilient critical infrastructure. See https://obamawhitehouse (accessed 18 November 2022). See further archives.gov/the-press-office/2013/02/12/presidential-policy-directive-critical-infrastructure-security-and-resil (accessed 18 November 2022).

[2] See https://www.cisa.gov/energy-sector (accessed 18 November 2022).

[3] See https://www.usa.gov/federal-agencies/federal-energy-regulatory-commission (accessed 18 November 2022).

124 PUBLIC INTEREST ASSESSMENT AND THE FERC

(FPC). The FPC was established in 1920 by the Federal Water Power Act and had the authority to license hydroelectric power projects. Its authority was extended by the Federal Power Act of 1935,[4] including in relation to the regulation of electric utilities' wholesale rates and transactions. It was then further expanded by the Natural Gas Act, which granted jurisdiction to the FPC over wholesale sales and the transportation of natural gas in interstate commerce by pipeline firms.[5] The majority of the powers under the Federal Power and Natural Gas Act were transferred to the FERC. The Commission is constituted of five members appointed by the President with the advice and consent of the US Senate, each of whom has a four-year term of office, and one of whom is designated by the President to serve as chairman.[6]

The FERC has jurisdiction to review transactions involving public utilities under section 203(a)(1) of the Federal Power Act, which provides that:

> No public utility shall sell, lease, or otherwise dispose of the whole of its facilities subject to the jurisdiction of the Commission ... without first having secured an order of the Commission authorizing it to do so ... [I]f the Commission finds that the proposed ... [transaction] will be consistent with the public interest, it shall approve the same.[7]

According to section 203(a)(1),[8] the FERC enjoys jurisdiction to oversee the following transactions where authorization is required, before a public utility can:[9]

(A) sell, lease, or otherwise dispose of the whole of its facilities subject to the jurisdiction of the Commission, or any part thereof of a value in excess of $10,000,000;

(B) merge or consolidate, directly or indirectly, such facilities or any part thereof with those of any other person, by any means whatsoever;

(C) purchase, acquire, or take any security with a value in excess of $10,000,000 of any other public utility;

(D) purchase, lease, or otherwise acquire an existing generation facility—

   (i) that has a value in excess of $10,000.000; and

   (ii) that is used for interstate wholesale sales over which the Commission has jurisdiction for ratemaking purposes.[10]

The FERC also has jurisdiction to overview transactions by holding companies under section 203(a)(2). This provision requires prior authorization when a holding

---

[4] Public Utility Act, Pub L No 74–333, 49 Stat 803 (1935).
[5] Federal Energy Regulatory Commission/1979 Annual Report, FERC-0063, 1.
[6] ibid 3.
[7] 16 USC § 824b(a) (2000).
[8] The Energy Policy Act of 2005 (EPAct 2005) increased the jurisdictional dollar from US$50,000 to US$10,000,000 and added acquisitions by public utilities of certain existing generating facilities and certain transactions by holding companies. See Pub L No 109–58, 119 Stat 594 (2005) (codified at 42 USC §§ 15801–16524 (2012)).
[9] 16 USC § 824b(a)(1).
[10] 16 USC § 824b(a)(1)(A)–(D).

4.1 THE FEDERAL ENERGY REGULATORY COMMISSION (FERC) 125

company in a holding company system that includes a transmitting utility or an electric utility may 'purchase, acquire, or take any security with a value in excess of $10,000,000 of, or, by any means whatsoever, directly or indirectly, merge or consolidate with, a transmitting utility, an electric utility company, or a holding company in a holding company system that includes a transmitting utility, or an electric utility company.[11]

Prior to proceeding with the analysis below, we need to present the definition of some terms that will be used in this chapter. First, a 'holding company' traditionally is 'any company that directly or indirectly owns, controls, or holds, with power to vote, 10 per cent or more of the outstanding voting securities of a public-utility company or of a holding company of any public-utility company' that owns or operates facilities used for (a) 'the generation, transmission, or distribution of electric energy for sale' or (b) 'the distribution at retail ... of natural gas for heat, light, or power.[12] Secondly, a 'holding company system' is 'a holding company, together with its subsidiary companies.[13] Thirdly, a 'transmitting utility' is 'an entity that owns, operates, or controls facilities used for the transmission of electric energy: (a) in interstate commerce; or (b) for the sale of electric energy at wholesale.[14] Fourthly, an 'electric utility' is 'a person or Federal or State agency that sells electric energy.[15] Fifthly, an 'electric utility company' is a company that 'owns or operates facilities used for the generation, transmission, or distribution of electric energy for sale.[16] Sixthly, a 'public utility' is 'any person who owns or operates facilities used for the transmission of electric energy in interstate commerce or the sale of electric energy at wholesale in interstate commerce but does not include the United States, a state or any agency, authority, or instrumentality of, or any corporation that is wholly owned by, the United States or any state.[17]

The most common transactions filed at the FERC are under section 203(a)(1)(A), in which a public utility transfers to another person a facility, eg an electric transmission line. In such a case, the FERC's jurisdiction over the physical facility begins if it is used for wholesale sales or the transmission of electric energy in interstate commerce.[18] Likewise, under this section the transfer of 'paper facilities', such as tariffs or contracts, requires the FERC's consent. The same provision is also applicable to change-in-control deals involving direct or indirect transfers of proprietary ownership interests in public utilities (eg stock or membership interests).[19] Seeking to reduce the number of applications under section 203(a)(1)(A), the FERC has established that some transactions are exempt from pre-approval and are known as 'blanket authorizations', for which filing

---

[11] ibid § 824b(a)(2).

[12] ibid § 824b(a)(6); 42 USC § 16451(5), (7), (8), (14) (2012); 18 CFR § 33.1(b)(4).

[13] 42 USC § 16451(9).

[14] 16 USC § 796(23) (2012).

[15] ibid § 796(22).

[16] 42 USC § 16451(5).

[17] 16 USC § 824I.

[18] See Hugh E Hilliard, 'FERC, May I: When Is FERC Authorization Needed for Transfer of Public Utility Assets and Equity Interests in Public Utilities' (2013) 34 Energy Law Journal 151, 155.

[19] See ibid 157. The FERC presumes that less than 10 per cent of the voting securities of a public utility does not amount to a transfer of control. See Federal Power Act section 203 Supplemental Policy Statement, FERC Stats & Regs 31.253 (2007), 120 FERC 61,060 at 27 (2007), 72 FR 42,277, clarified, 122 FERC 61,157 (2008).

an application is not necessary.[20] A further exemption was introduced in March 2019 regarding a *de minimis* threshold of US$10 million in utility mergers, meaning that only those above the threshold will be subject to prior approval.[21]

Few applications relate to section 203(a)(1)(B) consisting of the transfer of, or electric interconnection to, a public utility in which the transferred facilities merge with the transmission facilities of the acquiring public utility.[22] Regarding section 203(a)(2), which refers to holding company transactions, it is important to indicate that the Energy Policy Act of 2005 (EPAct 2005) partly replaced section 9(a)(2) of the Public Utility Holding Company Act of 1935 (PUHCA 1935),[23] broadening the FERC's scope to holding companies whose only interests in public-utility companies are in exempt wholesale generators (EWG),[24] qualifying facilities (QFs),[25] and foreign utility companies (FUCOs).[26] EPAct 2005 also revoked the authority of the Securities and Exchange Commission (SEC), which was responsible for implementing PUHCA 1935, to oversee mergers and other transactions of public utility holding companies. Before the enactment of EPAct 2005, the FERC had some authority over some holding company activities, but the statute extended this authority to include the oversight of holding companies that were removed from SEC oversight. The substantive standard applied by the FERC to assess applications under section 203(a)(1)—public utilities—and section 203(a)(2)—holding companies—is the public interest standard. The focal point of this standard is to assess the effects of the transaction on competition, rates, and regulation, and on preventing cross-subsidization.[27] In the utility sector, the jurisdiction to review mergers is shared between the FERC (under a public interest standard), the SEC (under a 'public interest or for the protection of investors and consumers' standard),[28]

---

[20] For further analysis about blanket authorizations see Hilliard (n 18) 164. See also 18 CFR § 33.1(c), § 33.1(c) (12)–(16).

[21] See https://www.gibsondunn.com/congress-clarifies-statutory-thresholds-for-ferc-merger-approvals/ (accessed 15 November 2022); Gavin Bade, 'FERC Moves to Narrow Jurisdiction over Utility Mergers after FPA Changes' https://www.utilitydive.com/news/ferc-moves-to-narrow-jurisdiction-over-utility-mergers-after-fpa-changes/543236/ (accessed 15 November 2022), Dockets Nos RM19-4-000, RM-19-13-000, RM-18-15-000 https://www.ferc.gov/media/news-releases/2019/2019-1/02-21-19.asp#.Xr5mbi2ZOu4 (accessed 15 November 2022).

[22] Hilliard (n 18) 169.

[23] PUHCA 1935 required holding companies to register with the US Securities and Exchange Commission (SEC), imposed certain substantive restrictions and procedural requirements to companies that owned more than 10 per cent of the voting securities or that exercised a controlling interest over electric and/or gas public utilities. See the Repeal of the Public Utility Holding Company Act of 1935 (PUHCA 1935) and Its Impact on Electric and Gas Utilities https://www.everycrsreport.com/reports/RL33739.html (accessed 6 November 2022).

[24] An exempt wholesale generator has been defined as 'a person who is engaged directly or indirectly through one or more affiliates exclusively in the business of owning or operating all or part of a facility for generating electric energy and selling electric energy at wholesale'. See *Law Insider* https://www.lawinsider.com/dictionary/exempt-wholesale-generator (accessed 1 October 2022).

[25] Qualifying facilities 'means generating facilities that meet the criteria specified by the FERC in 18 CFR Part 292 Subpart B'. See *Law Insider* https://www.lawinsider.com/dictionary/qualifying-facilities (accessed 1 October 2022).

[26] Foreign utility company 'means any company that own or operates facilities that are not located in any state and that are used for the generation, transmission, or distribution of electric energy for sale or the distribution at retail or natural or manufactured gas for heat, light, or power'. See *Law Insider* https://www.lawinsider.com/dictionary/foreign-utility-company (accessed 1 October 2022).

[27] Hilliard (n 18) 177. The Securities and Exchange Commission was created in 1934 by the Security and Exchange Act of 1934, conferring on it authority to review public utility acquisitions and mergers (15 USC § 79(i)) and some publicly listed companies under section 14(a) of the Exchange Act and Regulation (17 CFR.24.14a-1–240.14b-2).

[28] 15 USC § 79(j).

the Federal Trade Commission (FTC) or the Department of Justice Antitrust Division (DOJ) (both under a competition standard),[29] and the states. A review merger by one agency does not prevent a review by others, and clearance by one does not exclude a challenge by the others. Finally, if parties fail to request approval when it is needed, the FERC can impose civil penalties as well as conditions such as an order to unravel the consummated transaction or to disgorge revenues received under wholesale electric sales contracts transferred through unauthorized transactions.[30]

Another important aspect to be considered is that the sale of electricity is controlled by federal and state governments.[31] Seeking to reduce the nation's dependence on oil and gas, as well as to encourage the advance of alternative energy sources, Congress enacted the Public Utility Regulatory Policy Act of 1978 (PURPA) requiring electric utilities to bid to buy electric energy from energy producers that fulfil detailed criteria, designating 'a qualifying facility' as an energy producer that meets such criteria.[32] Likewise, the PURPA gave authority to the FERC to enact the applicable purchase rates rules with the aim of ensuring that the rates are 'just and reasonable to the electric consumers of the electric utility and in the public interest'.[33] At the same time, the PURPA prohibits rules that would 'provide for a rate which exceeds the incremental cost to the electric utility of alternative electric energy'.[34]

In relation to the natural gas sector, the industry was traditionally seen as a natural monopoly and, as such, it was thought that it would function most efficiently with only one supplier in each region.[35] The industry was also subject to rigorous regulatory control, which resulted in shortages, especially in the 1970s, that forced the enactment of the Natural Gas Policy Act (NGPA) in 1978, which aimed to incentivize an increase in the natural gas supply by gradually deregulating prices.[36] Further deregulation took place in 1989, when Congress, through the Natural Gas Wellhead Decontrol Act, removed all residual price controls, which were described as an 'outdated, inaccurate relic from a period of stringent economic regulation'.[37]

Thus, the natural gas sector became one of the first deregulated industries in the US. Amongst the many provisions that were introduced was Order 636, issued in 1992 by

---

[29] Garry A Gabison, 'Dual Enforcement of Electric Utility Mergers and Acquisitions' (2017) 17(2) Journal of Business & Securities Law 11, 13–14. The DOJ usually reviews mergers that involve electric utilities or electricity and natural gas utility companies, where the main effect is on electricity markets. The FTC traditionally reviews proposed transactions involving securities acquisitions by natural gas companies or by oil and petroleum companies. See OECD, 'Directorate for Financial and Enterprise Affairs Competition Committee, Independent Sector Regulators—Note by the United States' DAF/COMP/WP2/WD/(2019)18 (22 November 2019) 5 https://www.ftc.gov/system/files/attachments/us-submissions-oecd-2010-present-other-international-competition-fora/oecd-independent_sector_regulators_us.pdf (accessed 11 November 2022).

[30] Enforcement: Civil Penalties, FERC.GOV http://www.ferc.gov/enforcement/civil-penalties.asp.

[31] 16 USC § 824(a). The wholesale of electric energy is defined as 'the sale of electric energy for resale'; see 16 USC § 824(d).

[32] 16 USC § 824a-3(a)(2). See also Sandeep Vaheesan, 'Market Power in Power Markets: The Filed-Rate Doctrine and Competition in Electricity' (2013) 46 University of Michigan Journal of Law Reform 921, 926.

[33] 16 USC § 824a-3(b).

[34] ibid.

[35] David Balto and James Mongoven, 'Deregulation and Merger Enforcement in the Natural Gas Industry' (2001) 69(2) Antitrust Law Journal 527, 532–33.

[36] 15 USC §§ 3301–32. See also Balto and Mongoven (n 35) 532–34.

[37] 15 USC § 3301.

128 PUBLIC INTEREST ASSESSMENT AND THE FERC

the FERC to restructure the sector.[38] An important feature of this package of reforms was that the FERC retained the authority to review mergers in the natural gas industry[39] or any change in control of facilities and services.[40] Therefore, parties seeking to merge need to obtain a 'certificate of public convenience and necessity', which is granted after the FERC applies a 'public interest standard', that includes an analysis of the competitive impact of the transaction. Another important development is that the role played by the antitrust agencies in the review of merger cases in the natural gas industry has been clarified by the Supreme Court, which stated that even if the FERC has approved a merger the antitrust agencies can seek to submit the approval decisions to judicial review.[41]

4.1.2 Filing Instructions and Process Overview

In procedural terms, there are some aspects that are unique to the FERC's proceedings. First, while the DOJ and the FTC must keep collected information strictly confidential under the Civil Investigative Demand and the Hart-Scott-Rodino Antitrust Improvements Act, the FERC is not subject to the same obligation.[42] This is because the FERC merger applications need to observe the Freedom of Information Act (FOIA Act).[43] The issue is that under the FOIA Act and with the aim of ensuring due process, third parties, whose intervention in the regulatory approach is significant, are entitled to request such information to validate applicants' analysis, with the assurance that it will be kept confidential. Additionally, the FERC's rules provide that, once a merger application is filed, all parties to the proceedings must be present during the respective Commission meetings.[44] Thus, in the FERC's regulatory process the parties can seek the disclosure of sensitive business information.[45] Secondly, the FERC cannot request information from non-parties and, thirdly, unlike the antitrust federal agencies, the FERC can block mergers that are inconsistent with the public interest without resorting to the courts.[46]

In its Merger Policy Statement, the FERC adopted the DOJ/FTC 1992 Horizontal Merger Guidelines as its basic framework for assessing the competition effects of proposed mergers.[47] The methodology that the FERC applies for evaluating mergers is mostly based on Appendix A of the Merger Policy Statement (also known as Appendix

---

[38] 57 FR 15,267 (16 April 1992); Order 636-B, 57 FR 57,911 (8 December 1992).

[39] Section 7(c) NGA.

[40] 15 USC §§ 717–717z.

[41] 369 US 482 (1962).

[42] See Revised Filing Requirements under Part 33 of the Commission Regulations, 94 FERC § 61289 (2001).

[43] 18 CFR § 388.112 (2017).

[44] Diana L Moss, 'Antitrust Versus Regulatory Merger Review: The Case of Electricity' (2008) 32(3–4) Review of Industrial Organization 241, 246.

[45] ibid. See also Milton A Marquis, 'DOJ, FTC, and FERC Electric Power Merger Enforcement: Are There too Many Cooks in the Merger Review Kitchen' (2002) 33 Loyola University Chicago Law Journal 783, 785.

[46] American Bar Association (ABA) Antitrust Law Section, *Energy Antitrust Handbook* (3rd edn, ABA Book Publishing 2017) 109.

[47] See FERC, Policy Statement Establishing Factors the Commission Will Consider in Evaluating Whether a Proposed Merger Is Consistent With the Public Interest (Merger Policy Statement), 61 FR 68595.

4.1 THE FEDERAL ENERGY REGULATORY COMMISSION (FERC) 129

A analysis).[48] In theory, the FERC has adopted the 1992 Horizontal Merger Guidelines in their entirety; in practice, it focuses on only two factors: defining relevant markets and performing market share calculations.[49] Some commentators have indicated that the choice made by the FERC to focus the merger analysis on just these two factors of the 1992 Horizontal Merger Guidelines fails to ensure an accurate analysis, as it is necessary to use all of the assessment factors contained in the antitrust federal agencies Guidelines[50] to obtain a precise notion of the anti-competitive effects that might arise from a proposed merger.[51]

According to the Appendix A Analysis, the merger application needs to be accompanied with information concerning relevant product, geographic markets, and market share calculations.[52] These calculations use the Herfindahl–Hirschman Index (HHI) contained in the Appendix A Analysis, which mirrors those of the 1992 Horizontal Merger Guidelines: unconcentrated post-merger market,[53] moderately concentrated post-merger market,[54] and highly concentrated post-merger market.[55] If post-merger the transaction is unconcentrated, the FERC does not inquire further into the merger's potential effect on competition.[56] By contrast, if the HHI levels of the transaction raise significant competitive concerns, the merging parties, instead of providing an analysis about competitive effects, entry, and efficiencies, can propose remedies. A transaction would be approved if the market power of the merged entity was 'within acceptable thresholds or satisfactorily mitigated'.[57] The fact that remedies are contemplated regardless of possible efficiencies or entry likelihood has been criticized[58] because it could lead to the imposition of unnecessary remedies for mergers that do not raise any anti-competitive concerns.[59]

As mentioned above, the applicants provide an analysis of the effects of the transaction, and the FERC usually relies almost completely on the applicants' assessment. The FERC may question the parties' analysis by requesting additional data, and third parties can submit their own analysis. However, commentators have argued that this approach does not lead to the same accuracy as an 'in-house' analysis, which is the

---

[48] See Merger Policy Statement, 68606.

[49] Darren Bush, 'Electricity Merger Analysis: Market Screens, Market Definition, and Other Lemmings' (2008) 32(3–4) Review of Industrial Organization 263, 268.

[50] U.S. Department of Justice and U.S. Federal Trade Commission, Horizontal Merger Guidelines (1992) http://www.usdoj.gov/atr/public/guidelines/hmg.htm (accessed 18 November 2022).

[51] Bush (n 49) 268.

[52] See Merger Policy Statement, 68607–68609.

[53] If the post-merger HHI is below 1,000, the merger is unlikely to have adverse competitive effects regardless of the change in HHI. See Merger Policy Statement, 68609.

[54] If the post-merger HHI ranges from 1,000 to 1,800 and the change in HHI is greater than 100, the merger potentially raises significant competitive concerns. See Merger Policy Statement, 68609.

[55] If the post-merger HHI exceeds 1,800 and the change in the HHI exceeds 50, the merger potentially raises significative competitive concerns; if the change in HHI exceeds 100, it is presumed that the merger is likely to create or enhance market power. See 1992 Horizontal Merger Guidelines, 41558, and Merger Policy Statement, 68609.

[56] US Federal Energy Regulatory Commission (2000) 60. The Merger Policy Statement indicates that if a merger does not meet the safe harbour concentration levels, the FERC can set a trial-type hearing. See Merger Policy Statement, 68606.

[57] Merger Policy Statement, 68597.

[58] Moss (n 44) 247.

[59] Bush (n 49) 270.

130   PUBLIC INTEREST ASSESSMENT AND THE FERC

approach followed by the DOJ and the FTC in merger cases.[60] Another aspect that reduces the correctness of the substantive competitive test used by the FERC—described in the Appendix A Analysis—is the lack of clear parameters to define relevant markets. Thus, if merging parties do not have clear indications about how a relevant market should be properly defined and because the FERC usually bases its merger conclusions on the relevant market analysis provided by the parties, then the inevitable result is that the regulatory merger control is inadequate.[61]

During the filing process parties seeking to merge under section 203 file an application together with a competitive analysis screen (CAS), as well as the data used to perform the CAS. This information will be publicly available.[62] Next, a public notice is issued and a sixty-day comment period starts, allowing third parties to comment on the merger.[63] Thereafter, the FERC has 180 days to complete its merger review, a period that can be extended to a total of 360 days.[64] If the Commission concludes that the merger does not meet the public interest standard provided in section 203, the merger is either prohibited[65] or conditionally approved.[66]

The DOJ and the FTC share jurisdiction in the electricity sector, and their competition inquiry takes into account a number of factors other than just concentration levels.[67] According to some size thresholds,[68] parties need to submit a notification form under the Hart-Scott-Rodino Antitrust Improvements Act (HSR Act) to the antitrust agency.[69] If the DOJ considers that the transaction violates section 7 of the Clayton Act,[70] it must file a suit to block the merger;[71] alternatively, it can enter into a consent decree with the parties to remedy any harm arising from the transaction. It has been indicated that the DOJ's review merger process is longer than the FERC's process, as an investigation can take from about nine up to eighteen months for more complex deals.[72] In a case where the FTC decides to challenge the approval of a merger, it must

---

[60] Moss (n 44) 249.

[61] ibid 250.

[62] Merger Policy Statement, 68606–10.

[63] ibid 68600.

[64] Federal Power Act, 16 USC § 824(b)(5) (2011).

[65] Merger Policy Statement, 68597, 68606.

[66] ibid 68597, 68610.

[67] Section 7 of the Clayton Act, 15 USC § 18 (2011). A merger violates s 7 if its effect 'may be substantially to lessen competition, or to tend to create a monopoly'.

[68] 15 USC § 18a(a). See Federal Register, 'Revised Jurisdiction Thresholds for Section 7A of the Clayton Act' Vol 87 No 10 FR 3541, 2022–01214 (23 February 2022); and Federal Register, 'Revised Jurisdiction Thresholds for Section 8 of the Clayton Act' Vol 87 No 15 FR 3540, 2022–01215 (24 January 2022).

[69] 16 CFR § 801–803.10(b), 15 USC § 18a; Marquis (n 45) 785.

[70] Section 7 of the Clayton Act was conceived as an effective tool for preventing anti-competitive mergers: 38 Stat 730 (1914). The original version of s 7 of the Clayton Act indicated that: '[N]o corporation engaged in commerce shall acquire, directly or indirectly, the whole or any part of the stock or other share of capital of another corporation engaged also in commerce where the effect of such acquisition may be to substantially lessen competition between the corporation whose stock is so acquired and the corporation making the acquisition, or to restrain such commerce in any section or community, or tend to create a monopoly in any line of commerce.'

[71] 15 USC § 18 (2011). The DOJ may also challenge a transaction as an unreasonable 'restraint of trade' under s 1 of the Sherman Act: 15 USC § 1.

[72] Mark J Niefer, 'Explaining the Divide Between DOJ and FERC on Electric Power Merger Policy' (2012) 33 Energy Law Journal 505, 527.

seek a preliminary injunction in the federal district court[73] and then a permanent injunction through its administrative court.[74]

So far, some differences have been identified between the antitrust agencies' and the FERC's respective approaches when examining the anti-competitive effects of mergers in wholesale electricity markets. These include the following aspects. First, even if both of these bodies use the Horizontal Merger Guidelines issued by the DOJ and the FTC, the analysis of the FERC is largely based on market concentration, while the antitrust agencies apply a more comprehensive analysis in which other factors such as efficiencies, entry, and anti-competitive effects are examined. Secondly, the FERC relies extensively on the merging parties' analysis, while the antitrust agencies perform their own in-house analysis. Thirdly, the FERC does not issue so-called second requests, while the antitrust agencies can issue them to parties and non-parties (including testimonies, interrogatories, documents, etc.).[75] Fourthly, before the FERC's proceedings third parties play a significant role, while before the DOJ/FTC they do not have an equally formal role. Fifthly, the antitrust agencies keep the information strictly confidential, while the FERC cannot ensure the same treatment. Sixthly, the FERC has the authority to reject a merger, while the DOJ/FTC need to go to the courts to block them. Finally, before the FERC applicants bear the burden of proving that the proposed merger is consistent with the public interest, while the antitrust agencies are obliged to demonstrate that the transaction will substantially reduce competition. So not only who bears the burden of proof differs between the two processes, but the standard of assessment varies as well.

4.2 The 'Public Interest' Standard

We have seen that in the electricity sector merging parties carry the burden of demonstrating that their transaction is aligned with the public interest. Thus, in 1963 when the Federal Power Commission reviewed the merger between the California Electric Power Company and the Southern California Edison Company it established that the proposed transaction would be consistent with the public interest by examining the following non-exclusive factors, commonly known as the Commonwealth Edison factors, that informed merger review from 1968 to 1996:

1. the merger's likely impact on the applicants' operating costs and the rate levels[76] of the combined company;
2. the merger's effect on competition;

---

[73] Federal Trade Commission Act § 13(b), 15 USC § 53(b) (1994).

[74] ibid.

[75] According to the Hart-Scott-Rodino Antitrust Improvements Act of 1976, the federal agency has thirty days after the notification of the proposed transaction to investigate and resolve whether the merger can proceed or whether a second request for information should be issued: 15 USC § 18a(b), (e).

[76] To promote the public interest obligation, the Federal Power Commission sought to ensure that the proposed transaction would not raise regulated electricity rates or that it would result in lower rates for wholesale customers. See Robert J Graniere and Robert E Burns, 'Mergers and Acquisitions: Guidelines for Consideration by State

3. the reasonableness of the purchase price;
4. whether the acquiring firm had coerced the target firm into acceptance of the merger;
5. the merger's effect on federal and state regulation; and
6. the contemplated accounting treatment of the merged entity.[77]

In 1996, when the FERC revisited its merger policy by incorporating the core aspects of the merger guidelines of the federal antitrust agencies, as discussed above, it also narrowed the scope of its public interest test to the evaluation of mergers' effects on competition, rates and regulation.[78] In its Merger Policy Statement, the FERC explained that the public interest standard has broader implications than the antitrust standard of review as '[w]e recognize that there may be unusual circumstances in which, for example, a merger that raises competitive concerns may nevertheless be in the public interest because customer benefits (such as the need to ensure reliable electricity service from a utility in severe financial distress) may clearly compel approval'.[79] It also highlighted that: '[w]hile in the past we had focused only on increases in market power, we no longer believed that we could find any merger to be consistent with the public interest, whether or not the merger created increased market power, unless the merging utilities provided open access'.[80]

In consequence, the six Commonwealth Edison factors were replaced by the following three factors: (i) effect on competition; (ii) effect on rates; and (iii) effect on regulation.[81] Then, the Energy Policy Act of 2005 included a cross-subsidization factor as part of the public interest standard,[82] providing that a transaction should 'not result in cross-subsidization of a non-utility associate company or the pledge or encumbrance of utility assets for the benefit of an associate company, unless the Commission determines that [it] will be consistent with the public interest'.[83] However, some commentators have argued that this cross-subsidization factor has not been clearly defined.[84]

Public Utility Commissions' (1996) The National Regulatory Research Institute (NRRI) Research Paper No 96–35, 4 https://pubs.naruc.org/pub/FA85F516-C5E6-33A2-5146-F46AF91A43F4 (accessed 11 November 2022).

[77] Commonwealth Edison Co, 36 FPC 927, 932 (1966). See also John T Miller Jr, 'A Needed Reform of the Organization and Regulation of the Interstate Electric Power Industry' (1970) 38(4) Fordham Law Review 653. The contemplated accounting treatment refers to the examination of how the accounting of the merger entity would be served and the establishment of possible concerns afterwards. See Merger Policy Statement, 68604.

[78] Marquis (n 45) 784. Regarding the effect on regulation, in the Commonwealth merger decision, the Federal Power Commission was initially concerned with ensuring that there was not a regulatory gap (Commonwealth, 36 FPC at 931). Once the FERC had reviewed its merger policy in 1996, the concern expanded to the effectiveness of the state and federal regulation stemming from the transfer of authority from one regulatory jurisdiction to another or issues associated with cost allocation. See Merger Policy Statement, 68604, 68618.

[79] Merger Policy Statement, 68597.

[80] ibid 68598.

[81] In relation to the effect on regulation the Merger Policy Statement indicated that: 'If the state lacks ... authority and raises concerns about the effect on regulation, we may set the issue for hearing; we will address these circumstances on case-by-case basis.'

[82] Energy Policy Act of 2005, Pub L No 109–58, 1289, 119 Stat 594, 982–83 (2005), codified as 16 USC § 824b(a)(4).

[83] 16 USC § 824b(a)(4).

[84] Scott Hempling, 'Inconsistent with the Public Interest: FERC's Three Decades of Deference to Electricity Consolidation' (2018) 39 Energy Law Journal 233, 272.

The public interest standard also contemplates other factors such as the maintenance of service quality and reliability, consumer choice, and limited price increases.[85] The public interest standard applied by the FERC to transactions under section 203(a)(2) is similar to the one applied to mergers under section 203(a)(1);[86] that is, the assessment focuses on the effects of the transaction on competition, rates, and regulation, and on inhibiting cross-subsidization between entities with captive customers subject to cost-based rate regulation and affiliated companies that are not subject to cost-based regulation.[87] The FERC's approach also highlights that if a transaction could have adverse effects on competition, and if the additional factors examined do not mitigate or counterbalance the adverse competitive effects of the transaction, it can impose remedies in order to approve the transaction, as will be demonstrated further below.[88]

According to a recent analysis by Jodi Short, 'FERC has been the most transparent and consistent of the agencies studied' as 'the agency explicitly sets forth the factors it will consider in its public interest analysis in almost all cases, and those factors remain remarkably stable over the sample's eight decades'.[89] In particular, the FERC has 'consistently grounded its public interest analysis in the broad purposes of its enabling statutes'.[90] As regards the most frequent justifications employed, just as in the case of telecommunications, efficiency tops the ranking (266 mentions), followed by other statutorily required factors such as transaction financing considerations (159 mentions) and the potential impact on the ability of regulators to monitor the merged entity (78 mentions). Procedural considerations received 68 mentions, while substantive values obtained only 40, half of which pertained to the risk of cross-subsidization.[91] Short emphasizes some peculiarities in the FERC's approach to public interest: the virtual absence of labour and environmental considerations; the minimal attention devoted to quality and access; and the substantial rejection of cost-benefit analysis.[92]

4.3 Challenges of Concurrent Jurisdiction

The existence of multiple agencies reviewing the same merger has resulted in inconsistent procedures and decisions between the regulator and the federal antitrust

---

[85] Moss (n 44) 241.

[86] 16 USC § 824b (2000).

[87] Cost-based rates are grounded on the cost of service of the supplier as opposed to market-based rates in which companies have the authority to sell energy at market-based rates. The FERC has stated its concern that 'a franchised public utility and an affiliate may be able to transact in ways that transfer benefits from the captive customers of the franchised public utility to the affiliate and its shareholders' and '[w]here a power seller with market-based rates makes power sales to an affiliated franchised public utility, the concern is that such sales could be made at a rate that is too high, which would give an undue profit to the affiliated entity at the expense of the franchised public utility's captive customers'. See Federal Register Vol 73 No 41 (29 February 2008) 11014 https://www.govinfo.gov/content/pkg/FR-2008-02-29/pdf/E8-3820.pdf (accessed 18 November 2022).. Hilliard (n 18) 177.

[88] FERC, 18 CFR pt 2 (Docket No RM96-6-000) 'Inquiry Concerning the Commission's Merger Policy under the Federal Power Act: Policy Statement Order No 592 Policy Statement' (issued 18 December 1996) 6.

[89] Jodi L Short, 'In Search of the Public Interest' (2023) 40 Yale Journal of Regulation 759, 805.

[90] ibid 806–807.

[91] ibid 809.

[92] ibid 810–11.

134 PUBLIC INTEREST ASSESSMENT AND THE FERC

enforcers. As an illustration, while the antitrust agencies include several factors in the competitive analysis of a transaction, the FERC has been criticized for focusing on market concentration alone and for ignoring other relevant aspects such as potential entry, efficiencies, and the anti-competitive effects of the transaction, which is the reason why the regulator can arrive at a different conclusion from that of the antitrust agency.[93] This embedded approach of confining merger review analysis to a static analytical approach that focuses only on market shares and HHI levels carries the risk of permitting transactions despite the competition issues they may raise. In the electricity industry it is not uncommon for firms with less than a 10 per cent market share to own a significant percentage of uncommitted capacity in the relevant market. In such a case, small market shares might understate the market power that the firm may have, unless additional indicators like capacity excess are also taken into consideration. Consequently, the FERC's approach has been described by some commentators as 'short-sighted',[94] because some of the main features of the electricity sector are not considered by this market concentration focused approach, such as elasticity of demand, volatility in spot prices, and short-term limits on generation and capacity.[95] Therefore, the merger analysis performed by the FERC should put less emphasis on market shares and more on other evidence such as capacity, brand, customer switching/inertia, and vertical integration in order to predict the competitive effects of a merger.

The FERC has also been criticized for relying heavily on the applicants' economic analysis, which one would expect to be subjective and biased, an aspect that also affects the soundness of its decisions. Additionally, some commentators have indicated that the public interest applied by the FERC is ill-defined, and that because the Federal Power Act (FPA) is an economic regulatory statute, any analysis derived from it requires an assessment of economic performance in terms of structure, conduct, and performance, which the FERC has failed to provide after thirty years of approvals.[96]

Another important divergence between the regulator and the competition agencies that has been identified is the type of remedies that are imposed, an aspect that is problematic considering that while the DOJ and the FTC prefer the imposition of structural remedies,[97] the FERC is inclined to impose behavioural remedies, and in the end the merging parties need to conform with both, which results in enhanced costs for them.[98] There are also some differences in procedural terms, and it has been suggested that the information collected during the FERC's proceedings should be subject to strict confidentiality (as is the case with the DOJ and the FTC) and that the regulator

---

[93] FERC, 'Comment of the Staff of the Federal Trade Commission' 1 https://perma.cc/X7DL-AMUV.

[94] See Gabison (n 29) 44.

[95] Jeremiah D Lambert, *FERC's Shortfall as Market Regulator in Energy Companies and Market Reform: How Deregulation Went Wrong* (Pennwell Corporation 2006) 109.

[96] Hempling (n 84) 268–70.

[97] The DOJ Remedies Policy Guide indicates that: 'Structural remedies are preferred to conduct remedies in merger cases because they are relatively clean and certain, and generally avoid costly government entanglement in the market. A carefully crafted divestiture decree is simple, relatively easy to administer, and sure to preserve competition. A conduct remedy, on the other hand, typically is more difficult to craft, more cumbersome and costly to administer, and easier than a structural remedy to circumvent.' See USDOJ 2004, s 3.1.

[98] Moss (n 44) 254–57.

should have the power to issue second requests seeking to obtain evidence from parties and third parties (as is the case with the DOJ and the FTC). Since the competition assessment that is performed by the federal antitrust agencies is more detailed and based on an extensive amount of data as well as on a rigorous analysis, unsurprisingly their review process takes longer than the FERC's.

The varying procedures and potentially divergent decisions observed above need to be resolved with the aim of reducing the overall costs to the merging parties and the uncertainty of outcomes. Some analysts have endorsed the view that the primary authority to solve merger cases in the electricity market should be given to the antitrust agencies, with the assistance of the FERC as an expert adviser; nonetheless, other commentators have expressed that it would be preferable if the FERC had exclusive jurisdiction.[99] Whatever the chosen agency, the most important goal must be to introduce reforms that minimize the unnecessary duplicative and inconsistent merger review processes that prevail in this sector.

4.4 Enforcement Record

The FERC classifies change of ownership into three different types. A merger is a transaction where two or more entities combine their portfolio and convert into a new single entity. An acquisition or disposition refers to the transfer of assets where the single entities involved do not cease to exist but their different portfolios are altered post-transfer.[100] To illustrate when a disposition takes place, we will use the ITC Holdings Corp (ITC) and Entergy Corporation (Entergy) transaction as a case study.[101] In this case, the transaction involved, among other things, the move of a 'significant number of employees' from Entergy to ITC. These employees had stock in Entergy that had to be divested as they were moving to ITC. Such a divestiture of their stock was subject to FERC disposition approval.[102] At the same time, the transaction also concerned the acquisition of Entergy transmission assets by ITC. Thus, this case study allows us to see the difference between a disposition and an acquisition according to the FERC's classification.

An important aspect is that the Energy Information Administration (EIA) applies a different classification approach for mergers, resulting in disparity between the EIA

---

[99] Niefer (n 72) 535.

[100] Gabison (n 29) 20. Section 203(a)(1) of the Federal Power Act (FPA) provides, in pertinent part, that: 'No public utility shall, without first having secured and order of the Commission authorizing it to do so—(A) sell, lease or otherwise dispose of the whole of its facilities subject to the jurisdiction of the Commission, or any part thereof of a value in excess of $10,000,000; (B) merge or consolidate, directly or indirectly, its facilities subject of any other person, or any part thereof, that are subject to the jurisdiction of the Commission and have a value in excess of $10,000,000, by any means whatsoever; (C) purchase, acquire, or take any security with a value in excess of $10,000,000 of any other public utility; or (D) purchase, lease or otherwise acquire an existing generation facility—(i) that has a value in excess of $10,000.000; and (ii) that is used for interstate wholesale sales and over which the Commission has jurisdiction for ratemaking purposes.'

[101] ITC Corporation & Entergy Corporation, 143 FERC § 61,256 (2013).

[102] ibid.

136   PUBLIC INTEREST ASSESSMENT AND THE FERC

Table 4.1 Mergers reviewed by the FERC related to electric utility companies (2007–2022)

Year	Authorized mergers	Denied mergers	EIA reported mergers
2022	3	1	8
2021	1	0	8
2020	1	0	7
2019	2	0	7
2018	4	0	12
2017	2	0	15
2016	5	0	14
2015	1	0	27
2014	2	0	11
2013	1	0	9
2012	3	0	13
2011	4	0	14
2010	3	0	11
2009	1	0	12
2008	4	0	16
2007	4	0	33
TOTAL	41	1	217

Source: Data in the first two columns are the author's elaboration based on FERC, 'Mergers and Sections 201 and 203 Transactions' https://www.ferc.gov/electric/general-information/mergers-and-sections-201-and-203-trans actions (accessed 3 October 2022); Gabison (n 29) 21; Scott Hempling, *Regulating Mergers and Acquisitions of U.S. Electric Utilities: Industry Concentration and Corporate Complication* (Edward Elgar Publishing 2020) 38–40; and the FERC eLibrary, https://elibrary.ferc.gov/. Data in the third column are from Energy Information Administration (EIA), 'Annual Electric Power Industry Report, Form EIA-861 detailed data files' https://www.eia. gov/electricity/data/eia861 (accessed 3 October 2023);

Notes: FERC, 'Mergers and Sections 201 and 203 Transactions' last updated in FY 2016; EIA data for 2022 were released in August 2023. Pursuant to EIA, the early release is provided for the express purpose of providing immediate access to individual utility data for analysts who use this type of information. The data has not been fully edited and is inappropriate for aggregation, such as to state or national totals. Also, in some cases, data for a certain number of utilities has been excluded from this early release pending further data validation.

reports and the data reported by the FERC.[103] Table 4.1 shows the major mergers reviewed by the FERC between 2007 and 2022 and the outcome of those procedures. it is noteworthy that the first ever prohibition decision was issued in 2022.[104]

4.4.1 Analysis of Some Seminal Cases

Although the FERC has tried to align its competition standard analysis with that of the FTC and the DOJ, the FTC has been critical of the FERC's approach, indicating that it

---

[103] Gabison (n 29) 21.
[104] *Liberty Utilities—Kentucky Power—AEP Kentucky Transmission Company*, 181 FERC 61,212 (15 December 2022).

is outdated and that it only focuses on market definition without assessing other factors that might indicate dynamic competition such as substitutability.[105] In fact, as we shall see in the analysis of the FERC's enforcement record below, this divergence between the authorities' assessment approach has led to contradictory decisions for the same transaction.[106] This section discusses some seminal cases in the FERC's enforcement record with the aim of identifying the most significant substantive aspects in assessing merger applications.

The assessment of the following cases exhibits the scope of the public interest standard, its application, and the views of the courts in this respect.

4.4.1.1 Transactions assessed by the sectoral regulator

4.4.1.1.1 PacifiCorp—UP&L

In August 1987, PacifiCorp and the Utah Power and Light Company (UP&L) announced their intention to merge in a deal valued at almost US$2.2 billion, which would create one of the largest amalgamations of electric utilities at that time, serving around 1.2 million customers in seven Western states.[107] The analysis of this case illustrates two important features that characterize the merger review activity in this sector. First, the parties can escape review from some agencies; for instance, the SEC did not have jurisdiction over this merger because PacifiCorp, owner of Pacific Power & Light (PP&L), presented PP&L and UP&L as separate corporate divisions, as part of a strategy to avoid the SEC's oversight, pursuant to the PUHCA's exemption.[108] Secondly, the FERC, under the public interest standard, has historically accepted benefits that are not merger-specific, and which in fact could be attained without the merger.[109]

Reportedly, the post-merger cost savings were US$505 million, arising from power supply benefits and non-power supply benefits. The power supply benefits related to the combination of the winter-peaking demand for electricity enjoyed by PacifiCorp in Oregon and Wyoming, and the summer-peaking system held by UP&L, while the non-power benefits came from consolidation of administrative functions and the removal of duplicative functions.[110] Opponents of the merger claimed that the alleged benefits were unrelated to the transaction and that they would have been obtained contractually.[111] This argument was shared by some commentators, who explained that even if the alleged benefits were largely reduced after the regulator made the approval conditional on opening the transmission lines to outside users,[112] the applicants did

---

[105] Gabison (n 29) 28.

[106] In American Electric Power Company and Central and West Corporation such a situation took place. Gabison (n 29) 35.

[107] Richard W Stevenson, 'Pacificorp, Utah Power to Merge' *The New York Times* (14 August 1987) https://www.nytimes.com/1987/08/14/business/pacificorp-utah-power-to-merge.html (accessed 18 November 2022).

[108] Dennis Ray and others, 'Electric Utility Mergers and Regulatory Policy' (1992) National Regulatory Research Institute (NRRI) Paper No 92–12, 21 https://ipu.msu.edu/wp-content/uploads/2016/12/Ray-Electric-Utility-Mergers-92-12-June-92.pdf (accessed 18 November 2022).

[109] Hempling (n 84) 276.

[110] Dennis Ray and Howard Thompson, 'Fifty in Five: The Prospects for Merger in the Electric Utility Industry' (1990) 2 Journal of Regulatory Economics 111, 117.

[111] Hempling (n 84) 276.

[112] It has been reported that, since the merger of PacificCorp/UP&L, the FERC has required that the merged firm provide its competitors with equal access to its transmission lines. This condition, however, has become

138 PUBLIC INTEREST ASSESSMENT AND THE FERC

not withdraw the proposal as their real motivation was to achieve stockholder gains by exerting market power.[113] The lack of an adequate definition of the public interest standard has allowed parties to further their own commercial interests through consolidation.[114]

Consequently, the FERC responded to the claims by saying that 'the possibility of achieving a particular benefit through a contractual arrangement does not diminish the cost saving associated with that benefit.[115] It added that, under section 203 the FERC was not expected to launch an inquiry revolving around rates alone; in its words, a 'rate-case type inquiry' but rather a 'more generalized inquiry and cross-examination regarding the types of savings and efficiencies that might be achieved through merger.[116] This consideration implies that applicants do not need to demonstrate that the alleged benefits of the transaction will extend to consumers. Furthermore, it suggests that virtually almost any gain is deemed to be aligned with the public interest, even if consumers are deprived of any resulting benefits, as would be the requirement under an efficiency analysis conducted by antitrust authorities. The approach followed by the FERC has been described as an 'amorphous net merger benefits' scenario.[117] To ensure that the claimed benefits are not overvalued, it is essential that they be confined to gains demonstrating a high likelihood of being passed on to consumers and that they should not be considered in cases where the benefits simply accrue to the merging parties. A further virtue of adopting a stricter analysis of the benefits that a merger would probably generate is to avoid arbitrary decisions that are not based on a well laid out analytical approach. Lastly, merging parties should be compelled to show the causal link between the merger and the purported benefits.

4.4.1.1.2 Northeast Utilities—Public Service Company of New Hampshire

On 28 January 1988, the Public Service Company of New Hampshire (PSNH), an electric utility, a wholesale service provider, and the largest ownership share of Seabrook Unit No 1—a nuclear generating facility—filed a voluntary bankruptcy petition that was approved by the court.[118] Northeast Utilities (NU), a holding company, proposed to merge with PSNH and to buy and operate all of its power facilities so that, after the merger, PSNH would be a wholly-owned subsidiary of NU and would transfer its ownership interest in Seabrook to a newly formed NU subsidiary—North Atlantic Energy Corporation (North Atlantic).[119] The transaction was conditionally approved by the FERC, arguing that the transaction would bring about various benefits, among which

---

unnecessary as FERC's Order 888 demands open transmission access for wholesale customers. See Graniere and Burns (n 76) 5.

[113] Ray and Thompson (n 110) 119.
[114] Hempling (n 84) 268.
[115] 45 FERC 61095, 61191–61192 (1989).
[116] ibid 61298.
[117] Hempling (n 84) 263.
[118] Northeast Utils Serv Co v FERC, 993 F 2d 937 (1st Cir 1993).
[119] ibid.

was that PSNH would emerge from bankruptcy as a viable utility on a solid financial footing, 'even if those benefits would have been achieved by other means'.[120] This decision was challenged by a group of public and private electric utilities, state commissions, state agencies, independent power producers, co-generators, and electric end users, who claimed, among other things, that the FERC had erred by stating that the benefits of the merger outweighed its costs.[121]

The first aspect that deserves consideration is that the court initiated the judicial review of the merger approval by noting the great deference that is given to the FERC:

> [w]e defer to the agency's expertise, particularly where the statute prescribes few specific standards for the agency to follow, so long as its decision is supported by 'substantial evidence' in the record and reached by 'reasoned decision-making', including an examination of the relevant data and a reasoned explanation supported by a stated connection between the facts found and the choice made.[122]

A second important aspect is that the court explained that the public interest standard does not compel the Commission 'to analyze proposed mergers under the same standards that the [DOJ] ... must apply', given that an administrative agency is not obliged to 'serve as an enforcer of antitrust policy in conjunction' with the DOJ or the FTC.[123] At the same time, the Court recognized that '[a]lthough the Commission must include antitrust considerations in its public interest calculus under the FPA, it is not bound to use antitrust principles when they may be inconsistent with the Commission's regulatory goals ... [I] ndiscriminate incorporation of antitrust policy into utility regulation "could undercut the very objectives the antitrust laws are designed to serve" '[124] and confirmed that '[a] lthough antitrust considerations may be relevant [in determining the public interest], they are not determinative'.[125] Thus, the decision was upheld in this respect.

The analysis of this case illustrates the great deference enjoyed by the FERC from the courts, the subordination of the competition standard to the public interest one, and that the concept of benefits under the public interest is a very broad one.

The next cluster of cases comprises those approved by the federal agency and the regulator but with diverging remedies.

4.4.1.2 Transactions with diverging remedies between the FERC and the DOJ

4.4.1.2.1 American Electric Power Company—Central and South West Corporation

In December 1997, American Electric Power (AEP), the largest utility in the Midwest, made public its intention to acquire Central & South West Corporation (CSW), a large utility in the Southwest, for a total of US$6.44 billion, a transaction that would

---

[120] 56 FERC at 61994–96.
[121] *Co v FERC* (n 118) citing *Electricity Consumers Resource Council v FERC*, 747 F 2d 1511, 1513 (DC Cir 1984).
[122] ibid.
[123] ibid.
[124] ibid.
[125] 410 US 373, 93 S Ct 1028 (1973).

create America's third largest diversified electric utility and would allow the acquirer to expand its presence in Oklahoma, Texas, Arkansas, and Louisiana, where CSW used to serve almost 1.7 million customers through four electric utilities.[126] After a long investigation, in 2000, the DOJ approved the transaction without any remedies.[127] In parallel, the FERC spent three years on its own investigation and arrived at quite the opposite conclusion, which resulted in the imposition of diverse remedies, among which were the divestiture of 550 MW of generating capacity,[128] and to vest control over their transmission lines through a FERC-approved regional transmission organization (RTO), whose strong structure would promote retail access and reduce the need for FERC oversight.[129] One must bear in mind that an RTO is the result of a collaborative process by which public utilities and non-public utilities that own, operate, or control interstate transmission facilities decide to form an RTO.[130] Such a cooperation from regional participants, in the view of the FERC, allows the RTO and its members to improve their structure, operations, market support, and existing level of transmission system and to deliver services tailored to the specific needs of each region.[131]

The FERC found that, based on the conventional method of charging for transmission services used by the parties seeking to merge, the projected merger would create an excessively concentrated market. Therefore, the FERC requested that the merging parties 'amend the pricing formula to adopt the rate that the seller could have charged if it could have sold the power elsewhere. This will satisfy the principle of holding the selling company harmless, but will not result in a price above market for the buying company'.[132] Similarly, and under the presumption that if the relevant markets were kept under reasonable levels of concentration the expected anti-competitive effects would disappear, the FERC asked the merged firm to join an independent system operator (ISO).[133]

An important development shown by this case was the type of remedy that was imposed, which has encouraged entities without previous participation in the electric

---

[126] 'AEP to Acquire Central & South West' *Los Angeles Times* (23 December 1997) https://www.latimes.com/archives/la-xpw-1997-dec-23-fi-1568-story.html (accessed 18 November 2022).

[127] American Bar Association, 'Report on Electric Merger Review by the Section of Antitrust Law to the Antitrust Modernization Commission' (17 July 2006) 7 http://www.americanbar.org/content/dam/aba/administrative/antitrust_law/comments_electric-powermergers.authcheckdam.pdf (accessed 18 November 2022).

[128] ibid.

[129] FERC, 'Regional Transmission Organizations' Order No 2000, Docket No RM99–2–000 (20 December 1999) http://www.ferc.govnews/rules/pages/RM99-2A.pdf (accessed 18 November 2022); see also FERC, 'Final Rule to advance the formation of Regional Transmission Organizations (RTOs)' 18 CFR pt 35, Docket No RM 99–2-000; Order No 2000, 95–96 (20 December 1999) https://www.ferc.gov/sites/default/files/2020-06/RM99-2-000.pdf (accessed 2 October 2022).

[130] FERC, Final Rule to Advance the Formation of Regional Transmission Organizations (RTOs).

[131] ibid.

[132] *American Electric Power Company and Central and South West Corporation*, 90 FERC 61242, 61799 (15 March 2000).

[133] Richard J Pierce Jr, 'Mergers in the Electric Power Industry' in Peter C Carstensen and Susan Beth Farmer (eds), *Competition Policy and Merger Analysis in Deregulated and Newly Competitive Industries* (Edward Elgar Publishing 2005) 19. Pierce defines an ISO as an entity that 'controls all of the transmission lines owned by its members and operates a competitive wholesale market in the area covered by those lines'.

market to enter it by acquiring divested utility assets, eg financial entities.[134] The imposition of such a remedy makes one wonder whether selecting third parties to access a very complex market with the purpose of addressing some issues of which they neither have the knowledge nor the experience, is an effective approach. A second insight provided by this case involves the delay in the procedures. It took three years for the FERC to reach a final decision, which would imply a thorough analysis. Even under the assumption that the length of time is correlated with analytical rigour, three years is nonetheless a lengthy period from a transactional perspective and possibly longer than any completed transaction that went through such a lengthy merger control assessment by the antitrust authorities. One final point refers to the overlapping jurisdiction between the DOJ and the FERC which does not appear to lead to a streamlined assessment process. Even if in principle two different tests are applied, a competition standard by the federal agency and a public interest standard by the regulator, in substantive terms both refer to the effects of the merger on competition. Hence, the oversight of the regulator does not complement that of the antitrust agency. Furthermore, this dual merger control structure does not provide for constructive collaboration between the antitrust authority and the regulator either. On the contrary, the competition agency needs to defer to the regulator for the final decision on a transaction.

4.4.1.2.2 Pacific Enterprises—Enova

Pacific Enterprises was a holding company owner of the Southern California Gas Company (SoCalGas), a major supplier of delivered gas services to gas-fired generators in southern California, serving approximately 4.7 million customers and around 12,500 MV.[135] Enova Corporation (Enova) was a holding company, proprietor of the San Diego Gas and Electric Company (SDG&E), which served almost 700,000 gas and 1.2 million electric customers through its own large number of gas-fired generators (SDG&E was a customer of SoCalGas).[136] The applicants filed a merger plan, arguing that the transaction would bring significant ratepayer savings (almost US$1 billion expected over ten years) as a result of the operating synergies between the utility subsidiaries.[137] Approval was also required from the DOJ, the SEC, the California Public Utilities Commission (CPUC), and the California State Attorney General.

The FERC used the DOJ 1984 Horizontal Merger Guidelines as a legal framework to review this merger. In doing so, it identified four concerns: the restriction of access to inputs, an increase in input costs, the facilitation of collusion, and the evasion of regulation. The FERC focused its analysis on the first two issues, leaving the examination of the circumvention of regulation to the CPUC and ignoring collusion as part of

---

[134] Michael T Burr, The Utility Sector: A Wall Street Takeover? *Fortnightly Magazine* (January 2004) https://www.fortnightly.com/fortnightly/2004/01/utility-sector-wall-street-takeover (accessed 10 November 2022).

[135] Shawn Bailey, 'Merger Market Power Analysis: Pacific Enterprises and Enova Corporation' (1999) 8(1) Utilities Policy 51.

[136] ibid 51–52; see also Tim Brennan, '"Vertical Market Power" as Oxymoron: Getting Convergence Mergers Right' Resources for the Future Discussion Paper 01–39 (August 2001) 3.

[137] Bailey (n 135) 52.

142   PUBLIC INTEREST ASSESSMENT AND THE FERC

the assessment.[138] Considering that the merger combined the extensive electric generation capacity operated by SoCalGas and the accompanying income for generation assets owned by SDG&E, multiple intervenors refused the deal. The most recurrent concern was that the newly merged entity would have the ability to control its storage and transport operations to impact the dispensed price of gas to California generators, and hence the price of power in the wholesale electric market.[139] The FERC started the examination by establishing delivered gas as the upstream product and energy as the downstream market. This was followed by a market concentration analysis, in which the FERC found that SoCalGas was a dominant supplier in the upstream market and served more than 60 per cent of the capacity downstream.[140]

Next, the FERC concluded that:

[o]n the whole, circumstances in the upstream delivered gas and downstream wholesale electricity markets indicate that the merged company could potentially raise input costs to competing generators, therefore resulting in higher wholesale prices. Under the circumstances of this case, [the FERC] believes that the proportion of economic capacity served by SoCalGas is still high enough to effectively limit wholesale power customers' alternatives to economic capacity not served by SoCalGas.[141]

To address the FERC's concerns, the transaction was approved subject to the following conditions. First, SoCalGas was compelled not to share any information with SDG&E about the latter's competitors as a result of the supply connection with them. Secondly, SoCalGas had to observe some rules to prevent it from discriminating against SDG&E's competitors. Thirdly, the rules covered possible discrimination against gas marketers and electric gas customers. Finally, SoCalGas was obliged to publish an electronic bulletin board with gas prices that were applicable to SDG&E when the latter was buying all of its supplies for electricity generation from SoCalGas.[142]

In parallel, in March 1998, the DOJ filed a complaint and proposed a consent order to alleviate the competition concerns that emerged from the transaction.[143] The antitrust agency found that SDG&E was the only provider of natural gas transportation services to plants in southern California, the only provider of gas natural storage services in California, and the owner of low-cost generators.[144] So, after defining the relevant market as the 'provision of electricity in California during high demand of periods', and by looking at the applicants' entire portfolio, the DOJ concluded that the newly merged entity would have the ability to reduce the supply of natural gas with the

---

[138] Brennan (n 136) 4.
[139] Bailey (n 135) 51.
[140] Brennan (n 136) 5.
[141] FERC, 'Order Conditionally Approving Disposition of Facilities, Dismissing Complaint as Moot, and Denying Request for Consolidation' Enova Corporation and Pacific Enterprises, Docket No EL97–15-001 (25 June 1997) III.C.1.d.
[142] Brennan (n 136) 6.
[143] *United States v Enova Corp* No 98-cv-583 (DDC) (filed 9 March 1998).
[144] ibid.

aid of increasing the cost of gas-powered generators and the whole cost of electricity from gas-powered generators during peak periods.[145] As a result, the DOJ imposed a condition requiring the divestiture of certain natural gas-fired generation units, which, according to some commentators, would have been enough to eradicate 'the ability of the merged company to foreclose rival generators from access to gas transportation'.[146] Thus, the behavioural remedies imposed by the FERC were unnecessary as the divestment remedy imposed by the DOJ would address the FERC's concerns as well.

On the one hand, this case confirms that the FERC prefers the imposition of behavioural remedies—in this case the disclosure of information—while the DOJ prefers structural divestments. On the other hand, this dual review imposes higher costs for the merging parties and can be an inefficient process where remedies (with the risk of being overlapping or conflicting) are imposed by multiple agencies. It seems that, in order to overcome such a shortfall, close cooperation in substance and process between the regulator and the antitrust agency is required or perhaps a legal reform is imperative. In addition, it is pertinent to see that the DOJ delineated the relevant market around peak times, an aspect that is not contemplated in the market concentration approach applied by the FERC, which compromises the soundness of the FERC's findings, as has been argued by some commentators.[147]

4.4.1.2.3 Dominion—CNG

In 1999, Dominion Resources (Dominion) offered to purchase Virginia Natural Gas (VNG), a subsidiary of Consolidated Natural Gas (CNG), for US\$5.3 billion.[148] VNG held more than 70 per cent of all electric power generation capacity in Virginia and was the main distributor of natural gas in south-eastern Virginia.[149] Dominion supplied electricity in Virginia and North Carolina, and generated electricity in the country.[150] For the FTC, the proposal raised the concern that the control over VNG would give Dominion the ability to increase the cost of entry into the electric power generation market and production in south-eastern Virginia. Such a concern was based around there being high barriers to entry into the natural gas market in the area, that the extension of the existing pipeline would be costly and time-consuming, and that the adjacent pipelines did not have excess capacity. To address the issue, Dominion was required to divest VNG, with the acquirer being subject to the FTC's approval, and if a fit purchaser was not found, VNG would have had to be spun off to its shareholders.[151]

The analysis of the FERC concluded that the gas and electricity markets relevant to the merger were highly concentrated, and that after the merger the new entity would have the incentive to increase the costs of its rivals and prevent entry into the electricity

---

[145] Balto and Mongoven (n 35) 567.
[146] Moss (n 44) 257.
[147] Lambert (n 95) 109.
[148] Balto and Mongoven (n 35) 562.
[149] ibid.
[150] Brennan (n 136) 6.
[151] Dominion Resources, FTC Docket C-3901 (9 December 1999).

144 PUBLIC INTEREST ASSESSMENT AND THE FERC

market.[152] To mitigate these concerns, the new entity was compelled not to share sensitive information with Dominion about its competitors, according to the FERC's Standards of Conduct for interstate pipeline operations.[153] Once again, this case reflects the disparity between the antitrust and regulatory remedies and how merging parties need to comply with both structural and conduct-based remedies.

4.4.1.2.4 Exelon—PSEG

On 20 December 2004, Exelon Corporation (Exelon) and Public Service Enterprise Group (PSEG) agreed to merge in a deal that would create one of the largest electricity companies in the US by combining assets of US$79 billion and annual revenues of US$27 billion.[154] Both companies sold wholesale electricity in different regions. Particularly in central and eastern Pennsylvania, New Jersey, Delaware, the District of Columbia, and parts of Maryland and Virginia the merged entity would have more than 35 per cent of the electric generating capacity after the merger, and in the northern New Jersey and Philadelphia regions more than 45 per cent.[155] According to the DOJ, the proposed merger would eliminate competition between the applicants and would give them the incentive to increase wholesale electricity prices for a significant number of residential, commercial, and industrial customers in the areas in violation of section 7 of the Clayton Act by substantially reducing competition.[156]

The DOJ concluded that the incentive to increase prices resulted from combining Exelon's low-cost generating units with PSEG's high-cost generating units, as the merged firm would find it profitable to withhold selected output, forcing customers to buy the more expensive units to meet demand, and that such growth in revenue would outweigh the cost of withholding capacity.[157] The DOJ's analysis pointed out that in the Mid-Atlantic—an area affected by the merger and home to the largest transmission grid in the country—the latter was run by PJM Interconnection (PJM), a private, non-profit organization whose members are transmission line owners and generation owners, among others, and whose role included supervising the auctions for the sale and purchase of wholesale electricity. Absent transmission constraints, PJM aimed to minimize generation costs by prioritizing the lowest offers.[158] However, the DOJ found that Exelon and PSEG owned capacity in PJM, specifically in two distinctive markets: PJM East and PJM Central-East, where the sale of electricity was geographically constrained. It was established that after the merger Exelon would own almost 49 per cent of the generating capacity in PJM East and approximately 40 per cent in PJM Central-East, moving from 29 per cent and 19 per cent, respectively.[159] In its statement, the DOJ explained that 'in both

---

[152] Brennan (n 136) 7.
[153] ibid.
[154] *United States of America v Exelon Corporation and Public Service Enterprise Group Incorporated* 71 FR 49477 (23 August 2006).
[155] ibid.
[156] ibid.
[157] ibid 49487.
[158] ibid 49478.
[159] ibid.

geographic markets the merged firm would own low-cost baseload units that provide incentive to raise prices, mid-merit units that provide incentive and ability to raise prices, and certain peaking units that provide additional ability to raise prices in times of high demand'.[160] In addition, the DOJ indicated that entry would not be timely, likely, and sufficient to offset the incentive and ability of the merged firm to exercise market power.[161]

After fifteen months of intense scrutiny, more than nine million pages of documents, a significant number of depositions and interviews, and extensive analysis of the competitive effects of the transaction, including the vertical issues associated with the amalgamation of the electric and gas assets of the merging firms, the parties finally reached a consent decree in which the DOJ required the divestiture of fossil-fuel electric generating stations with a full volume of almost 5,600 megawatts, the largest divestiture in the energy sector at that time.[162] The DOJ clarified that even if the required divestitures maintained their market shares at their pre-merger levels, the main objective of such a measure was to prevent the merging parties from withholding output, and therefore the generating units that would have significantly enhanced the ability profitably to suppress output were subject to divestiture.[163]

The competitive analysis carried out by the FERC was radically different from that of the DOJ and took only four months. The FERC focused its assessment exclusively on market shares and levels of concentration, leaving aside the analysis of any expected conduct resulting from the increase in market power.[164] Thus, using the safe harbour thresholds contained in the Merger Policy Statement, the FERC found that even if the concentration levels in the market as a result of the transaction would infringe the safe harbour thresholds in certain periods, the parties' proposed remedies were adequate to address these concerns and clear the merger, and an administrative hearing was not necessary.[165] Seeking to reduce the resulting concentration level, the applicants offered the divestiture of generating units meeting 6,600 MW of capacity (including nuclear, mid-merit, and peaking, but without specific indication of the units to be divested) and bidding all capacity into the daily market at a price of zero.[166] In its final decision, the FERC explained that limiting the competitive analysis of the merger just to the examination of the concentration levels was enough to anticipate the potential exercise of market power without further scrutiny. It stated:

> We are not convinced by arguments that Applicants should have analyzed the merger's effect on their ability and incentive to harm competition by engaging in strategic

---

[160] ibid.

[161] ibid 49487–49488.

[162] Public Service Enterprise: 'Exelon and PSEG Announce Agreement with U.S. Department of Justice' *MarketScreener* (22 June 2006) https://m.marketscreener.com/quote/stock/PUBLIC-SERVICE-ENTERPRISE-13969/news/Public/Svc-Ent-Exelon-and-PSEG-Announce-Agreement-with-U-S-Department-Of-Justice-216 003/ (accessed 7 November 2022).

[163] *United States of America v Exelon and PSEG* (n 154) 49488.

[164] Bush (n 49) 271.

[165] Niefer (n 72) 518.

[166] Bush (n 49) 272.

146   PUBLIC INTEREST ASSESSMENT AND THE FERC

bidding (which is a form of unilateral market power). The Commission's analysis focuses on a merger's effect on competitive conditions in the market. That is, we look at the merger's effect on the concentration of the relevant market, as measured by the HHI ... [T]he Merger Guidelines recognize that the HHI, does, in fact, convey information about the likelihood of the unilateral exercise of market power.[167]

This case clearly illustrates how the DOJ and the FERC apply different approaches when analysing the competitive effects of a merger. The focal point of the public interest standard applied by the FERC is to assess the effects of the merger on competition, rates, and regulation. Despite the FERC using the Horizontal Merger Guidelines 1992 issued by the DOJ and the FTC as the assessment framework, the FERC relies entirely on concentration levels to predict the likely competitive effects of a merger and is satisfied with the respective analysis presented by the parties and the remedies offered by them.[168] On the contrary, the DOJ's analysis in the above-mentioned case used concentration levels as a starting point, covering a wider range of aspects, such as geographic restraints, entry barriers, and evidence related to the composition of Exelon's and PSEG's generation portfolio. This inclusive analysis underpinned a unilateral effects theory of harm which anticipated the possibility that the merged entity would withhold mid-merit and peaking units to the advantage of the combined firm's baseload units.

In terms of remedies, there are also some divergences between the FERC and the DOJ. As the FERC is inclined to derive its conclusions from looking at concentration levels alone, parties seeking to merge know in advance that they need to offer remedies that will reduce concentration to pre-merger levels.[169] Nevertheless, it has been indicated that these unsuitable types of remedies will not prevent merged firms from exercising market power.[170] In contrast, remedies that are negotiated with the DOJ are tailored according to the harm arising from every transaction, and as a result the merging parties need to be ready to satisfy specific, unexpected, and challenging measures. The fact that the parties need to offer commitments to different agencies in relation to the same transaction and theory of harm (eg competition theory of harm) can be a heavy burden that demands an alignment of policies or institutional reform. Similarly, after observing the in-depth competitive analysis that the DOJ applies, the question arises as to whether the duplicative and incomplete competitive analysis that the regulator employs is in any way necessary or beneficial, or if it contributes to the uncertainty and high costs associated with the merging parties having to prepare two separate merger reviews.

---

[167]   138 FERC 61,167, at 131.

[168]   The methodology that the FERC applies for evaluating mergers is mostly based on its Merger Policy Statement—Appendix A (Appendix A Analysis). In theory, the FERC has entirely adopted the 1992 Horizontal Merger Guidelines; in practice, it focuses on only two factors: defining relevant markets and performing market share calculations.

[169]   See the ABA's report indicating that the FERC 'has approved divestitures designed to lower the offending HHI thresholds without inquiring whether any divestiture is actually necessary or, if so, which specific generating units, if any, would be most suitable for divestiture based on identifiable competitive concerns': American Bar Association (n 127) 6.

[170]   Bush (n 49) 272.

4.4.1.2.5 Duke—Progress

In April 2011, Duke Energy Corporation (Duke) and Progress Energy (Progress) started proceedings aimed at obtaining approval for a deal that would consist of Progress becoming a wholly owned subsidiary of Duke.[171] Duke was one of the largest electric power holding companies in the US, serving almost 4 million customers in the south-east and mid-west and Progress was an energy company generating more than 22,000 megawatts and serving about 3.1 million customers in the Carolinas and Florida through two major electric utilities.[172] The applicants promised that the transaction would have considerable benefits, among which were significant investments orientated towards replacing old infrastructure with little impact on customers, and with this promise they hoped to obtain approval from the SEC, the Kentucky Public Service Commission, the FERC, the Nuclear Regulatory Commission, the DOJ, the South Carolina Public Service Commission, and the Federal Communications Commission.[173]

Interestingly, while for the DOJ the proposed transaction did not raise any concerns and therefore remedies were not imposed, for the FERC the significant anti-competitive effects stemming from the transaction in the wholesale electric markets rendered the imposition of a considerable number of remedies necessary.[174] In light of the FERC's CAS and based on the applicants' analysis, the Commission concluded that the deal would negatively impact the price of the electric service as the parties would exercise monopoly market power, particularly in the North Carolina area where the merged firm did not have electric retail competitors.[175] Among the main proposed mitigation measures to counteract the negative effects caused by the post-merger concentration levels that the FERC suggested was the divestiture of some power plants, the construction of transmission lines, the sale of capacity and energy, and the transfer of rights to generated electricity.[176] After some negotiations, the FERC was finally convinced that the agreed remedies sufficiently addressed the competition harm of the transaction, so the applicants formally accepted them and, on 2 July 2012 the merger was completed by the parties.[177]

This case elucidates the dissenting approaches between the DOJ and the FERC in examining the competitive effects of a transaction. Considering the extensive analysis of the antitrust agency finding that this transaction was unproblematic, the conclusion that arises is that if the FERC had looked at aspects such as efficiencies or entry barriers

---

[171] Kathleen O'Nan, 'Duke Energy, Progress Energy make regulatory filings for merger approval' *Carolina Public Press* (5 April 2011) https://carolinapublicpress.org/1821/duke-energy-progress-energy-make-regulatory-filings-for-merger-approval-carolina/ (accessed 9 November 2022).

[172] ibid.

[173] ibid.

[174] Duke Energy Corporation & Progress Energy Inc, 139 FERC, 61,194, 13 (2012).

[175] Arthur Adelberg and others, 'Report of the Competition & Antitrust Committee' (2013) 34 Energy Law Journal 313, 321; 'FERC Imposes Conditions on Proposed Duke-Progress Merger' *National Law Review* (3 January 2012) https: www.natlawreview.com/article/ferc-imposes-conditions-proposed-duke-progress-merger (accessed 9 September 2020).

[176] Duke Energy Corporation & Progress Energy Inc (n 174).

[177] Duke Energy Press Release, 'Duke Energy, Progress Energy Complete Merger' (2 July 2012) https://news.duke-energy.com/releases/duke-energy-progress-energy-complete-merger (accessed 3 October 2022).

148   PUBLIC INTEREST ASSESSMENT AND THE FERC

as the DOJ did, it is likely that the anti-competitive effects of the deal would have been mitigated and the imposition of demanding remedies that the merging parties had to agree to would not have been necessary. But until an alignment in the assessment of transactions between the antitrust agencies and the FERC takes place, such inconsistencies will persist.

4.4.1.2.6 Exelon—Constellation

In 2011, Exelon Corporation (Exelon) and Constellation Energy Group (Constellation) sought approval of a deal that would have resulted in a new entity possessing more than 30,000 MW of generation in the PJM market,[178] combined assets of US$72 billion, and revenues of US$33 billion.[179] The merging companies were selling wholesale electricity in Delaware, Illinois, Kentucky, Maryland, Michigan, New Jersey, North Carolina, Ohio, Pennsylvania, Tennessee, Virginia, West Virginia, and the District of Columbia. On 9 March 2012, the FERC approved the merger subject to some divestitures and other mitigation measures such as divesting MW capacity, not to sell to identified entities,[180] and to bid energy, capacity, and ancillary services at cost-based rates, among other things, aimed at addressing the horizontal market power concerns.[181] Such concerns emerged from the applicant's own opinions on the relevant geographic markets and the increase in market shares. The merging parties offered the following measures: plant divestitures, fixed price sales contracts, and to bargain all free capacity at capped prices.[182] Third parties opposed the offered measures, alleging, among other things, that the applicants' own analysis was inaccurate and that as a result the subsequent remedies were inappropriate.[183] The FERC, after agreeing additional commitments with the applicants and based on its own analysis of the merger (as it was settled with the intervenor American Antitrust Institute), confirmed that the initial remedies were adequate, and that no vertical issues were foreseen.[184]

In the meantime, on 21 December 2011, the DOJ filed a complaint claiming that the projected deal would substantially reduce competition in the provision of wholesale electricity, in violation of section 7 of the Clayton Act.[185] The DOJ found that the merger would enhance Exelon's ability to withhold low-cost generating capacity and increase prices in PJM Mid-Atlantic North and PJM Mid-Atlantic South by increasing its share of higher-cost capacity in those markets, and that entry in such areas would not be

---

[178] PJM Interconnection (PJM) is a private, non-profit organization, whose members are transmission line owners and generation owners, among others, who administer the transmission grid including the oversight of auctions for sale and purchase of wholesale electricity. See USDOJ 2006, 6.

[179] *United States v Exelon Corp* 2012 WL 3018030 (DDC 23 May 2012) (No 1:11-cv-02276), 76 FR 81,528 (28 December 2012) https://www.justice.gov/atr/case-document/file/495416/download (accessed 14 November 2022).

[180] The identified entities are: American Electric Power Company; First Energy Corporation; GenOn Energy Inc; Edison International; Dominion Resources Inc; Public Service Enterprise Group Incorporated; Calpine Corporation; and PPL Corporation. See Exelon Corporation, 138 FERC 61,167 at 27 (2012).

[181] ibid 2.

[182] ibid 51–53.

[183] ibid 64–67.

[184] ibid 103, 95, 97, 113.

[185] *United States v Exelon Corp* (n 179).

timely, likely, and sufficient to counteract the predicted price increase.[186] Concurrently with the complaint, the DOJ filed a proposed final judgment in which the defendants were required to divest three generating plants located in PJM Mid-Atlantic North and PJM Mid-Atlantic-South: Brandon, Wagner, and Crane power plants (accounting for 2,600 MW), seeking to maintain competition for wholesale energy in these geographic markets by allowing one or more independent competitors to acquire them.[187]

In this case, as was also seen in Exelon—PSEG, the DOJ's analysis included aspects other than just the concentration levels. In particular, the examination of the shared range of generating capacity that the merged company would enjoy, in conjunction with the particularities of the two geographic markets that would be affected by the merger, such as densely populated areas and congested transmission lines, as well as the entry analysis, led the DOJ to be concerned about the harm of the transaction in the market. This rigorous analysis contrasts with the FERC's review, which was largely based on the applicants' analysis and on their proposed remedies. Considering that the regulator based its findings entirely on the information provided by the applicants, the American Antitrust Institute, acting as intervener, demanded that the FERC conduct its own analysis. Interestingly, the new assessment presented by the regulator reflected the analysis of the initial report submitted by the applicants. This heavy reliance on the applicants' analysis and on concentration levels alone to derive conclusions about the anti-competitive effects of the merger, which departs markedly from the analysis conducted by the DOJ, suggests that the review process conducted by the FERC is inaccurate and may not address the harm the transaction causes. Such an assumption matches the findings of a study that proposes that market concentration is an inadequate predictor of market power in the electricity markets.[188]

4.4.1.2.7 Dominion—SCANA and SCE&G

On 23 February 2018, Dominion Energy (Dominion), SCANA Corporation (SCANA), and South Carolina Electric & Gas Company (SCE&G), under sections 203(a)(1) and 203(a)(2) requested authorization from the FERC for a transaction whereby SCANA and SCE&G would become wholly owned subsidiaries of Dominion.[189] Dominion was an energy company that supplied, delivered, and processed energy, and SCANA was a holding company whose dealings included regulated electric and natural gas utility operations, telecommunications, and other non-regulated business.[190] The transaction was expected to deliver energy to around 6.5 million customers, and to increase its electric transfer and distribution lines.[191] Approval was also required from the shareholders

---

[186] 76 FR 81,530-81,531 (28 December 2011).

[187] 76 FR 81,531-81,534 (28 December 2011).

[188] Paul Twomey and others, 'A Review of the Monitoring of Market Power: The Possible Role of FSOs in Monitoring for Market Power Issues in Congested Transmission Systems' (2005) MIT Center for Energy and Environmental Policy Research Working Paper No 05–002 http://web.mit.edu/ceepr/www/publications/worin gpapers/2005-002.pdf (accessed 18 November 2022).

[189] FERC, 'Order Authorizing Disposition and Merger' Docket No EC18–60–000 (12 July 2018) 1.

[190] ibid.

[191] See Dominion Energy Press Release, 'Dominion Energy/SCANA Merger Receives FERC Approval' (13 July 2018) https://news.dominionenergy.com/2018-07-13-Dominion-Energy-SCANA-Merger-Receives-FERC-Approval (accessed 21 October 2022).

of SCANA, the Georgia Public Service Commission, the FTC under the HSR Act, the public service Commissions of South Carolina and North Carolina, and the Nuclear Regulatory Commission.[192] The FTC permitted early termination of the thirty-day waiting period, indicating a lack of concerns.[193]

According to the applicants' findings, which were adopted entirely by the FERC, the proposed transaction would not have any unfavourable effect on horizontal competition as, after applying the delivered priced test (DPT), the market concentration level changes would range from no change to one HHI point. The applicants also indicated that in those areas where Dominion and SCANA would enter and SCE&G was already present, the generating capacity was under long-term contract to SCE&G.[194] In relation to vertical restraints, it was said by the merging parties that, despite an overlap in the south-east where Dominion owned interstate pipeline capacity and SCANA had located generation capacity, given the small participation in the transmission of gas by Dominion, combined with open access and the inability to withhold capacity or restrict services to raise prices, such an overlap would not create adverse effects.[195] Likewise, the applicants did not foresee any adverse impact on wholesale power rates,[196] or on regulation and did not envisage any cross-subsidization.[197]

On 12 July 2018, the FERC approved Dominion's bid to acquire SCANA and SCE&G, stating that 'the combination of the two companies is consistent with the public interest and is authorized'.[198] On 1 January 2019, the transaction, valued at more than US$14 billion, was completed.[199] The most prominent feature of this approval is that the FERC cleared the deal solely on the ground of the analysis provided by the applicants, for whom the transaction obviously satisfied the four factors that are part of the public interest test review.[200]

4.5 Some Implications of the Analysis

The examination of the regulatory framework under which the FERC applies its authority to review mergers, which contrasts with the provisions that guide the approach to merger enforcement of the antitrust agencies, can lead to some interesting conclusions about the

---

[192] See Dominion Energy Press Release (n 191).

[193] Chris Galford, 'Dominion Energy Merger with SCANA Receives FERC Approval' *Daily Energy Insider* (17 July 2018) https://dailyenergyinsider.com/news/13664-dominion-energy-merger-with-scana-receives-ferc-approval/ (accessed 15 November 2022).

[194] FERC, 'Order Authorizing Disposition and Merger' (n 189) 2–3.

[195] ibid 3.

[196] The applicants voluntarily committed to hold customers harmless from costs related to the proposed transaction, including prior to and five years after the consummation of the proposed transaction, by which they will adopt appropriate accounting controls and procedures to track them. See FERC, 'Order Authorizing Disposition and Merger' (n 189) 3.

[197] ibid 3–5.

[198] See Dominion Energy (n 191).

[199] See Saad A Sulehri, 'Dominion, SCANA Close Merger' *S&P Global* (2 January 2019) https://www.spglobal.com/marketintelligence/en/news-insights/trending/Qw7lje92dBpkkIQqfbTvAA2 (accessed 2 November 2022).

[200] The four factors are: effects on competition, rates, regulation, and cross-subsidization.

advantages and disadvantages of each agency's review process. This section has studied some seminal cases with the aim of assessing the approach of each agency. For instance, it has been confirmed that the FERC relies heavily on the applicants' analysis to derive its own findings, as seen in Exelon—Constellation,[201] and Dominion—SCANA,[202] whereas the DOJ conducts an extensive competition analysis.

The analysis of Exelon—PSEG,[203] Progress—Duke,[204] and Exelon—Constellation[205] has also established that the anti-competitive effects analysis applied by the FERC focuses solely on concentration levels, which has led to the design of mitigation measures seeking only to maintain concentration at pre-merger levels. This approach differs markedly from the anti-competitive effects analysis followed by the antitrust agencies, in which aspects such as geographic restraints, entry barriers, and potential entry are assessed to determine the impact on competition. This was clearly observed in Exelon—Constellation[206] and Exelon—PSEG,[207] where the remedies imposed by the DOJ were targeted at anticipating a possible abuse of the market power after the merger.

Another aspect that has been reaffirmed is that the public interest concept lacks a clear definition, resulting in a variety of aspects being accepted by the FERC as 'benefits', even if they are not merger related. The FERC's approach has been supported by the courts, as was the case in Northeast—PSNH.[208] Likewise, the analysis of the cases has shown that the differences between the approaches to assessing a merger's competitive effects has resulted in inconsistent outcomes. This was the case in AEP—CSWC,[209] where the DOJ approved the transaction without remedies, while the FERC imposed numerous remedies, including the divestiture of 550 MW of generating capacity. Similarly, in Progress—Duke,[210] the DOJ cleared the merger without remedies, while the FERC imposed significant mitigation measures such as the construction of some transmission expansion projects and the sale of capacity and energy under agreements with certain unaffiliated sellers, among others.

The case law analysis has shown that the DOJ prefers the imposition of structural remedies and the FERC behavioural ones (as in Exelon—PSEG,[211] Pacific—Enova,[212] Dominion—CNG,[213] and Exelon—Constellation[214]). Besides the fact that the parties must abide by all types of remedies, they need to observe some that are unnecessary, as seen in Pacific—Enova, where the remedies imposed by the DOJ were sufficient to mitigate the same concerns expressed by the FERC, and thus its behavioural remedies

---

[201] *United States v Exelon Corp* (n 179).
[202] FERC, 'Order Authorizing Disposition and Merger' (n 189).
[203] 71 FR 49,477 (23 August 2006).
[204] Duke Energy Corporation & Progress Energy Inc (n 174) 13.
[205] *United States v Exelon Corp* (n 179).
[206] ibid.
[207] 71 FR 49,477 (23 August 2006).
[208] 56 FERC 61,994–96.
[209] FERC, 'Regional Transmission Organizations' (n 129).
[210] Duke Energy Corporation & Progress Energy Inc (n 174) 13.
[211] 71 FR 49,477 (23 August 2006).
[212] FERC, 'Order Conditionally Approving Disposition of Facilities, Dismissing Complaint as Moot, and Denying Request for Consolidation, Enova Corporation and Pacific Enterprises' (n 141).
[213] Dominion Resources, FTC Docket C-3901 (9 December 1999).
[214] *United States v Exelon Corp* (n 179).

were redundant. This shortcoming imposes additional burdens on merging parties, which suggests that the DOJ and the FERC should reach some degree of consensus with the aim of diminishing the likelihood of duplicative or inconsistent remedies. Furthermore, it would be advisable for the FERC to include efficiencies as part of its review, which might result in fewer remedies or more accurate remedies being identified as necessary to address the harm a transaction can induce.

4.6 Concluding Remarks

Although in the cases discussed in this chapter the public interest is a recurrent topic, its definition seems to be very narrow, and the decisions have not contributed to its further development and clarity. Aspects such as cross-subsidization have been used to provide examples of what could constitute a public interest benefit, and yet the scope remains uncertain. It is vital to provide a clear definition of what should be understood as a public benefit and what factors count as benefits. Likewise, if this duplicative agency review process remains, it is considered that the effects on competition should be removed as a factor to be examined under the public interest standard and be left to the DOJ, considering that in the overlapping decisions between the DOJ and the FERC, additional burdens on the merging parties are imposed. Otherwise, if jurisdiction to review the competitive effects of a merger continues to be shared, it is necessary to align the assessment methods and merger policies to achieve consistent outcomes. In particular, it is important to reconsider the FERC's dependence on the applicants' analysis.

Another alternative to make the entire process more efficient and predictable consists in giving exclusive merger control jurisdiction to the antitrust agencies, which are better suited to conduct the review, and using the FERC as an expert advisory agency in the process. In our opinion, the approach used by the antitrust agencies to assess the competitive effects of a merger is more comprehensive, as it includes a wider range of factors that lead to a more accurate assessment of the harm. Similarly, the antitrust agencies have more efficient means to collect sufficient data to reach their respective decisions.

5

Public Interest Assessment and the Surface Transportation Board (STB)

5.1 The Surface Transportation Board (STB)

The Surface Transportation Board (STB) is the US regulatory agency for surface transportation, and in particular for freight rail, although it does deal with certain passenger rail transport related issues as well such as the intercity bus lines.[1]

STB was one agency encouraged—although not required—to take action to protect or enhance competition by President Biden's executive order of 9 July 2021.[2] These actions consisted of:

- commencing or continuing a rule-making to strengthen regulations pertaining to reciprocal shipping;
- consider rule-makings pertaining to any other relevant matter of competitive access, including bottleneck rates, interchange commitments, or other matters;
- ensure that passenger rail is not subject to unwarranted delays and interruptions in service due to host railroads' failure to comply with statutory requirements for passenger rail access and preferential use of facilities, and 'vigorously enforce' the new on-time performance requirements that took effect on 1 July 2021;
- consider a carrier's fulfilment of its responsibilities relating to Amtrak's statutory rights to host railroad tracks when determining whether a proposed merger/acquisition is consistent with the public interest.[3]

In August 2022, it was reported that the Surface Transportation Board was considering aggressive new rule-making to force railroads to share tracks and improve competition.[4] Earlier in the year, in April 2022, the Surface Transportation Board, voted to

---

[1] 'The agency has jurisdiction over railroad rate, practice, and service issues and rail restructuring transactions, including mergers, line sales, line construction, and line abandonments. The STB also has jurisdiction non-energy pipelines, household goods carriers' tariffs, and rate regulation of non-contiguous domestic water transportation (marine freight shipping involving the mainland United States, Hawaii, Alaska, Puerto Rico, and other U.S. territories and possessions).' Surface Transportation Board, 'About STB' https://www.stb.gov/about-stb/ (accessed 15 November 2022).

[2] EO 14036, 'Protecting Competition in the American Economy' (9 July 2021) § 5(n).

[3] Congressional Research Service, *The Surface Transportation Board (STB): Background and Current Issues* (January 2022) 13 https://crsreports.congress.gov/product/pdf/R/R47013 (accessed 15 November 2022).

[4] Ted Mann, 'Railroad Regulator Turns Up Heat on Industry to Fix Shipping Delays' *WSJ* (21 August 2022) https://www.wsj.com/articles/railroad-regulator-turns-up-heat-on-industry-to-fix-shipping-delays-11661090581 (accessed 15 November 2022).

propose an update of its emergency service rules, which enable it to compel railroads to address issues of delayed and adequate service.[5]

The chapter will discuss the relevant legislation for the railroad industry and the composition and process before the STB. It will also discuss the enforcement record of STB and the assessment of the public interest test in assessing M&A transactions in the sector (and throughout the chapter we will use the words mergers, acquisitions, and transactions interchangeably), trying to identify areas of convergence and divergence with the FTC/DOJ.

5.1.1 Composition and Legislation

The railroad industry was first regulated by the Interstate Commerce Act 1887 (ICA),[6] which established the Interstate Commerce Commission (ICC) to enforce it, and the trucking sector was regulated in 1935 through the Motor Carrier Act (MCA), giving the ICC the authority to oversee entry and rates.[7] Until 1920, railroad companies did not require approval to merge, but after the crisis in rail transportation experienced during the First World War, the Transportation Act of 1920 amended section 5(2)54 of the ICA, shifting from a federal regulation regime largely focused on rates to a more expansive jurisdiction in which the ICC received exclusive jurisdiction to review and approved railroad mergers, according to a public interest standard. The changes also included a railroad consolidation plan for the entire country to be established by the ICC.[8] Furthermore, the 1920 amendment gave authority to the ICC to dispense merging parties from observing the antitrust laws under the 'implied immunity doctrine'.[9] This doctrine emerged from the need to address inconsistencies between statutes,[10] and was originally invoked in court, in the 1890s, by railroad companies alleging that as the Sherman Act was a general statute while the ICA was specific, a reverse by implication should take place,[11] thus insulating railroad companies from antitrust rules.

---

[5] Ted Mann, Railroad Regulators Propose Rule Change to Get Freight Moving' *WSJ* (22 April 2022) https://www.wsj.com/articles/railroad-regulators-propose-rule-change-to-get-freight-moving-11650650593 (accessed 15 November 2022).

[6] 24 Stat 379 (1887), as amended, 49 USC §§ 12–27 (1958). The enactment of the ICC and the Sherman Antitrust Act in 1890 sought to protect the public against the abuses of the railroads by price-fixing and predatory pricing. See Frank Dobbin, 'Railroads' in Glenn R Carroll and Michael T Hannan (eds), *Organizations in Industry: Strategy, Structure, and Selection* (OUP 1995) 59, 82–83.

[7] Samuel Best, Paul Teske, and Michael Mintrom, 'Terminating the Oldest Living Regulator: The Death of the Interstate Commerce Commission' (1997) 72(12) International Journal of Public Administration 2067.

[8] Transportation Act of 1920, 41 Stat 456 (1920), providing that the ICC had to develop a master plan for consolidation of all railroads into a 'limited number of systems', in which 'competition shall be preserved as fully as possible and wherever practicable the existing routes and channels for trade and commerce shall be maintained'. Thus, railroads had to conform with the consolidation plan in proposing any future unifications.

[9] 41 Stat 482.

[10] See J F Burrows, 'Inconsistent Statutes' (1976) 3 Otago Law Review 601, 607–15.

[11] See Barak Orbach, 'The Implied Antitrust Immunity' (2014) Arizona Legal Studies Discussion Paper No 14–16, 6 http://ssrn.com/abstract=2447718 (accessed 15 November 2022). In *Gozlon-Peretz v United States* 498 US 395, 406 (1991) it was explained that the reverse by implication principle takes place when 'A specific provision

5.1 THE SURFACE TRANSPORTATION BOARD (STB)   155

In 1940, section 5 of the ICA was reworded by stating that the ICC should approve those transactions that 'will be consistent with the public interest'.[12] Thus, the reform eliminated the mandate of the ICC to formulate a national plan for consolidation of railroads and to approve only those that were aligned with that preconceived plan. Hence, the ICC had the authority to approve, deny or modify a proposed transaction, and the standard it used was that the transaction involving railroads alone was against the public interest.[13] Likewise, the 1940 reform adapted the ICC's authority to grant immunity to merging parties from the operation of the antitrust laws and it was preserved 'insofar as may be necessary to carry into effect the [approved] transaction'.[14] A further reform took place regarding the authority that the ICA gave to the ICC to set minimum rates on goods that were part of the railroads' total tonnage.[15]

These reforms illustrate that the nation's railroads were subject to a complex system of federal and state regulation in which a high level of interventionism played an important role in controlling entry, consolidation, and pricing, that with time was weakened by a deregulation drive and resulted in the abolition of the ICC. The change was elicited by the railroads' desire to establish their own rates allowing them effectively to compete with other forms of transportation such as motor carriers or water carriers of bulk commodities. Thus, in 1948 the Reed-Bulwinkle Act introduced rate fixing by rate-bureaus, subject to approval by the ICC, where each member of the bureau had the right to make rate proposals according to their interests at bureau meetings.[16] In 1976, following one of the worst financial crises in the history of the railways, the Railroad Revitalization and Regulatory Reform Act (4R Act) was enacted,[17] which introduced some flexibility in the rates mandated by the ICC and a track/service reduction in routes required by the ICC regardless of their traffic potential.[18]

Then, a major deregulation of the railroads and trucking in 1980[19] led to the adoption of freight rail agreed charges and services rather than published tariffs, and to the termination of the ICC and the creation of the Surface Transportation Board (STB) fifteen years later.[20] In 2015, the Surface Transportation Board Reauthorization Act of 2015 (STB Reauthorization Act) made the STB a fully independent agency, no longer part

---

controls over one of more general application', an interpretation that was repeated in *Morales v Trans World Airlines Inc* 504 US 374, 385 (1992), whereby 'It is a commonplace of statutory construction that the specific governs the general'.

[12] 54 Stat 906 (1940), as amended 49 USC § 5(2)(b) (1958).

[13] Robert G Bleakney Jr, 'The Interstate Commerce Commission' (1970) 11 Boston College Law Review 785, 791.

[14] 54 Stat 908-09 (1940), as amended 49 USC § 5(11) (1958).

[15] Carl H Fulda, *Competition in the Regulated Industries: Transportation* (Little, Brown & Co 1961) 283–305.

[16] 62 Stat 472 (1948), 49 USC § 5(b) (1958). See Carl H Fulda, 'Antitrust Aspects of Recent Transportation Mergers' (1964) 48 Minnesota Law Review 723, 740.

[17] Pub L No 94-210, 90 Stat 31.

[18] The literature has identified excess route capacity as one of the most important problems that have contributed to the financial crisis in the railroad sector. See Michael R Crum and Benjamin J Allen, 'U.S. Transportation Merger Policy: Evolution, Current Status, and Antitrust Considerations' (1986) 13(1) International Journal of Transport Economics 41, 42.

[19] The Motor Carrier Act of 1980, and the Staggers Act of 1980. See Douglas W Caves, Laurits R Christensen, and Joseph A Swanson, 'The Staggers Act, 30 Years Later' (2010) 33 Regulation 28, 30.

[20] See ICC Termination Act of 1995 (ICCTA), Pub L No 104-88, 109 Stat 803 (codified in scattered sections of 49 USC (2006)). Under ICCTA, the economic regulation of the freight rail industry was transferred to the STB. See

of the US Department of Transportation.[21] The Reauthorization Act also increased the number of the members of the STB board from three to five, who are appointed by the President of the US and confirmed by the Senate, each of whom has a five-year term of office.[22] The board's chairman is selected by the President from among the members.[23]

Nowadays, the STB has exclusive jurisdiction to review and approve railroad mergers,[24] as well as to grant antitrust immunity to certain transactions approved by the STB under 49 USC § 11321 such as consolidations, mergers, acquisitions, leases, trackage rights, pooling agreements, and agreements to divide traffic.[25] The STB can also grant immunity to certain rate-related agreements approved under 49 USC § 10706.[26] The goal of this immunity, as explained by the current Chairman of the Surface Transportation Board, Charles Nottingham, is 'to protect the national and public interest in ensuring the free flow of interstate commerce by preventing parties that do not want to see an increased rail presence in their communities from blocking or delaying those transactions with hundreds of individual suits in every local jurisdiction affected by the transaction.'[27] Aiming to review the appropriateness of these types of transactions, the STB applies a 'public interest' standard,[28] examining considerations such as sufficiency of revenue, adequacy of transportation to the public, and the protection of the rail carrier employees affected by the merger.[29] In 2001, a revised merger rule was adopted, imposing a sounder competitive effects analysis and increasing the burden on major merger applicants, in an attempt to mitigate the massive consolidation of railroads observed in the past.[30]

---

also John C Spychalski, 'From ICC to STB: Continuing Vestiges of US Surface Transport Regulation' (1997) 31(1) Journal of Transport and Policy 131, describing that according to ICCTA the STB has jurisdiction to scrutinize rail transport (Part A); motor carriers, motor carrier freight brokers, water carriers, and freight forwarders (Part B); and pipeline transport (Part C).

[21] STB Reauthorization Act of 2015, Pub L No 114-110 (2015).

[22] ibid. See also Surface Transportation Board, Board Members https://prod.stb.gov/about-stb/board-memb ers/ (accessed 15 November 2022).

[23] 49 USC § 1301.

[24] 49 USC § 10501(b)(2).

[25] 49 USC §§ 10501(b), 10706, 11321(a).

[26] 49 USC § 10706(a)(5).

[27] See Testimony of Charles D Nottingham, Chairman of the Surface Transportation Board before the Senate Judiciary Committee, Subcommittee on Antitrust, Competition Policy and Consumer Rights, at a Hearing Entitled 'An Examination of S. 772, the Railroad Antitrust Enforcement Act' (3 October 2007) https://www.judici ary.senate.gov/imo/media/doc/Nottingham%20Testimony%20100307.pdf (accessed 24 September 2022).

[28] 49 USC § 11324.

[29] ibid.

[30] Railroad Acquisition, Control, Merger, Consolidation Project, Trackage Rights, and Lease Procedures, 49 CFR § 11.80.1 (2010). It was reported that, over three decades, the number of major railroad operators was reduced from fifty-six to seven by 2001. See Leslie Picker, 'Regulations, Doubts and Concerns May Thwart Railway Mergers' The New York Times (20 December 2015) https://www.nytimes.com/2015/12/21/business/dealbook/regu lations-doubts-and-concerns-may-thwart-railway-mergers.html (accessed 5 November 2022). The chairwoman of the STB, Linda J Morgan, during the first hearing session (STB's New Merger Rules before the Subcommittee of Surface Transportation and Merchant Marine of the Committee on Commerce, Science, and Transportation United States Senate, One Hundred Seventh Congress (28 June 2001)), indicated that 'because of the small number of remaining large railroads, the fact that rail mergers are no longer needed to address excess capacity in the rail industry, and the transitional service problems that have accompanied recent rail mergers, future merger applicants will be required to bear a heavier burden to show that a major rail combination is consistent with the public interest. This shift in policy, the Board noted, will place greater emphasis in the public interest assessment on enhancing competition, while ensuring a stable, balanced, and reliable rail transportation system in a way that

5.1 THE SURFACE TRANSPORTATION BOARD (STB)   157

The STB is also responsible for reviewing and approving mergers, acquisitions, leases, and any other means of transferring control of motor carriers of passengers.[31] The 'public interest' is the standard of review applied to review these types of transactions, and it includes the examination of factors such as adequacy of transportation to the public, total fixed charges resulting from the proposed transactions and impact on employment.[32] The STB has the power to exempt the parties involved in a motor carriers transaction from observing the antitrust laws and any other state or local law, if that is necessary to 'carry out the transaction, hold, maintain, and operate property, and exercise control or franchises acquired through the transaction'.[33] In short, the STB has the authority to grant antitrust immunity in three distinctive transportation areas: rail, intercity buses and truck services, and it not only reviews proposed mergers, but also resolves railroad rate and service disputes, and investigates rail service matters of regional and national significance,[34] such as fertilizer shipment delays, rail car supply issues that impact grain shipments, or extensive congestion at strategic interchange points.[35]

5.1.2 Filing Instructions and Process Overview

The STB has formalized its approval process of transactions in the railroad sector. Prior approval from the Board is required when two or more railroads seek to consolidate through a merger or joint-control arrangement.[36] Here it is important to remember that by law the STB has the authority to invalidate conflicting state or federal laws, including antitrust laws, to the extent necessary for the interested parties to carry out the merger transaction.[37] Thus, carriers may choose to file an application under 49 USC §§ 11323–25 or to seek an exemption from the full application procedure under 49 USC § 10502. There are four types of transactions proposed under 49 USC 11323 involving more than one carrier by railroad: major, significant, minor, and exempt.[38] A major transaction involves two or more class I railroads.[39] A *significant* transaction is a transaction not involving the control or merger of two or more class I railroads that is of regional or national transportation significance. A transaction not involving the control or merger of two or more class I railroads is not significant if a determination

---

accounts for smaller railroads, ports, and passenger and commuter services'. https://www.govinfo.gov/content/pkg/CHRG-107shrg88970/html/CHRG-107shrg88970.htm (accessed 15 November 2022).

[31] 49 USC § 14303.

[32] 49 USC § 14303(b).

[33] 49 USC § 14303(f).

[34] Surface Transportation Board, 'Overview of the STB' https://www.stb.gov/stb/about/overview.html (accessed 10 November 2022); STB Reauthorization Act of 2015 (n 21) § 12(a).

[35] 81 FR 90233.

[36] 49 USC §§ 11323–25.

[37] See Orbach (n 11) 6.

[38] 49 CFR §1180.2.

[39] 49 CFR §1180.2(a). For regulatory purposes, railroads are classified as Class I, II, or III, based on their annual operating revenues: Class I (US$250 million or more), Class II (less than US$250 million but more than US$20 million), and Class III (US$20 million or less). See STB FY Annual Report https://prod.stb.gov/wp-content/uploads/files/docs/annualReports/Annual%20Report%202017.pdf (accessed 5 November 2022).

158   PUBLIC INTEREST ASSESSMENT AND THE STB

can be made either that the transaction clearly will not have any anti-competitive effects, or that any anti-competitive effects of the transaction will clearly be outweighed by the transaction's anticipated contribution to the public interest in meeting significant transportation needs. A transaction not involving the control or merger of two or more class I railroads is significant if neither such determination can clearly be made.[40] A minor transaction involves more than one railroad and cannot be classified as major, significant, or exempt.[41] A non-exhaustive list describes the types of transactions that are exempt, which are subject to the 49 USC 10502 requirements.[42] This provision states that, where appropriate and in accordance with the law, the board can remove or reduce regulatory requirements to facilitate approval processes for stakeholders if the transaction is not needed to implement the rail transportation policy of 49 USC 10101; and is of limited scope or unnecessary to protect shippers from market abuse.[43]

The classification of a transaction into major, significant, minor, and exempt determines the procedure which will be followed in relation to the timeline and the filing requirements. The STB review timeline starts three to six months before the filing of the official application. In major proceedings, parties need to file the original and twenty-five copies of all documents, and in significant and minor proceedings the original and ten copies shall be filed.[44] The parties need to submit a pre-filing notice, propose a procedure schedule, propose the use of a voting trust, and submit additional information if required. For major transactions, the merging parties also need to submit a statement of waybill in which they must indicate that the totality of their traffic tapes will be available to any interested party.[45] The procedural schedule adopted by the STB establishes the timing of the various steps in the assessment process. Once the schedule has been prepared, the parties submit the official application and no later than thirty

---

[40] 49 CFR § 1180.2(b).

[41] 49 CFR § 1180.2(c).

[42] 49 CFR § 1180.2(d). The following categories of transactions are exempt: '(1) Acquisition of a line of railroad which would not constitute a major market extension where the Board has found that the public convenience and necessity permit abandonment. (2) Acquisition or continuance in control of a non-connecting carrier or one of its lines where (i) the railroads would not connect with each other or any railroads in their corporate family, (ii) the acquisition or continuance in control is not part of a series of anticipated transactions that would connect the railroads with each other or any railroad in their corporate family, and (iii) the transaction does not involve a class I carrier. (3) Transactions within a corporate family that do not result in adverse changes in service levels, significant operational changes, or a change in the competitive balance with carriers outside the corporate family. (4) Renewal of leases and any other matters where the board has previously authorized the transaction, and only an extension in time is involved. (5) Joint projects involving the relocation of a line of railroad which does not disrupt service to shippers. (6) Reincorporation in a different State. (7) Acquisition of trackage rights and renewal of trackage rights by a rail carrier over lines owned or operated by any other rail carrier or carriers that are: (i) based on written agreements, and (ii) not filed or sought in responsive applications in rail consolidation proceedings. (8) Acquisition of temporary trackage rights by a rail carrier over lines owned or operated by any other rail carrier or carriers that are: (i) based on written agreements, (ii) not filed or sought in responsive applications in rail consolidation proceedings, (iii) for overhead operations only, and (iv) scheduled to expire on a specific date not to exceed 1 year from the effective date of the exemption. If the operations contemplated by the exemption will not be concluded within the 1-year period, the parties may, prior to expiration of the period, file a request for a renewal of the temporary rights for an additional period of up to 1 year, including the reason(s) therefor. Rail carriers acquiring temporary trackage rights need not seek authority from the Board to discontinue the trackage rights as of the expiration date specified under 49 CFR 1180.4(g)(2)(iii). All transactions under these rules will be subject to applicable statutory labor protective conditions.'

[43] 49 USC § 10502(a).

[44] 66 FR 32586.

[45] ibid.

days the STB must accept it as complete or reject it as incomplete (if this is the case, the applicants may re-submit). Within twelve months of the application being accepted, the evidentiary record closes for a major transaction; within 180 days for a significant transaction; and within 105 days for a minor one. No later than ninety days after the evidentiary proceedings are over, the STB issues its final decision in major and significant transactions, and no later than forty-five days in minor transactions.[46]

Under the full exemption procedure, once an interested party has filed a full exemption application, the board has ninety days to decide whether to begin an appropriate class exemption proceeding, and in such a case, it must be completed within nine months after it is begun. If the class exemption is granted, the board needs to specify the period during which it will be effective.[47]

The interplay between the federal agencies and the STB in a concurrent merger review is as follows, the former acts as a commenting party, but the latter has the power to approve mergers despite DOJ opposition. If the antitrust agency is concerned with an impact on competition in the post-merger rail market, it can file statements opposing the transaction[48] and can challenge the decision in court if in its view the STB has given little importance to competition considerations.[49] In other words, the antitrust agency submits the potential anti-competitive effects analysis to the STB, which can embrace or dismiss it. In parallel, the ICC/STB in order to determine whether the transaction is consonant with the public interest, it counterbalances the possible anti-competitive and other detrimental effects against the likely effects of the merger.[50]

Based on the Horizontal Merger Guidelines issued by the federal agencies and in the context of the railroad industry, elements such as private carriage, other modes of transportation, and whether the transportation of specific commodity groups are part of distinctive markets are taken into consideration in the determination of the product market.[51] In terms of the geographic market, the assessment will establish whether the market is regional or national and if certain routes such as river segments or city pairs should be included. In addition, the DOJ will look at demand and supply substitution, as well as at the Herfindahl-Hirschman Index post-merger concentration levels.[52] Although the ICC/STB relies upon the federal agencies' merger guidelines, its application differs markedly both in terms of the determination of the relevant market and the identification of potential anti-competitive effects. In particular, the potential anti-competitive adverse effects are usually underestimated by the regulator or alleviated with the imposition of questionable conditions, as we will see throughout this chapter.

---

[46] ibid. See also Surface Transportation Board, 'Major Railroad Mergers and Consolidations' https://www.stb.gov/stb/industry/merger.html (accessed 10 November 2022).

[47] 49 USC § 10502(b)(g). This provision indicates that the board cannot relieve a rail carrier of its duty to protect the interest of employees.

[48] 49 USC §§ 11321–11328.

[49] Willian H Tucker and John H O'Brien, 'The Public Interest in Railroad Mergers' (1962) 42 Boston University Law Review 160

[50] Crum and Allen (n 18) 70.

[51] ibid 73; Stan Kaplan, 'Rail Transportation of Coal to Power Plants: Reliability Issues' CRS Report RL34186 (26 September 2007) 14.

[52] Crum and Allen (n 18) 73.

5.2 The 'Public Interest' Standard

This railroad sector has observed distinctive periods in which the aims of and approach to public policy considerations towards mergers has developed: (1) from 1890 to 1903, the goal was to preserve competition among the nation's railroads; (2) between 1904 and 1920 mergers were prohibited, in an attempt to protect consumers against excessive railroad rates; (3) in the period 1920 to 1960 consolidation was promoted;[53] (4) voluntary mergers consistent with the public interest were permitted under the Transportation Act of 1940;[54] and (5) after 1965, there was a nationalization process, which resulted in the passenger rail service being separated from the freight service and nationalized, and carriers were allowed to leave unprofitable routes and to restructure by merging.[55]

Initially, the ICC authorized those mergers that were 'in the public interest'[56]—exempting them from the antitrust laws[57]—or when the 'public interest' was promoted by the merger.[58] During the period from 1920 to 1940 there was no definition of the 'public interest' concept.[59] In 1933, Congress passed the Emergency Railroad Transportation Act, dictating that the Commission should consider the promotion of the public interest when approving mergers.[60] Then, the Transportation Act of 1940 included as part of the 'public interest' considerations, inter alia, the sufficiency of the transportation service for the public,[61] the total fixed charges resulting from the proposed merger,[62] and the interests of the carrier employees affected.[63]

Later, in 1976, the 4R Act was issued incorporating a wider set of public interest considerations such as the needs of rail transportation; the effect on rail and intermodal competition; the environmental impact; the cost of facility rehabilitation; the rationalization of the system; the impact on shippers, consumers, and railroad employees; the effect on communities; and whether the transaction would improve the rail service.[64]

---

[53] As an illustration, the Annual Report of the ICC (1958) 58, expressly promoted consolidation by indicating that: 'One of the results of the recent recession and its accompanying adverse effect upon railroad earnings was to increase interest in railroad unification which, it is generally recognized, offer great opportunities for substantial operating economies, with resulting improvement of railroad earnings.'

[54] Charles F Philips Jr, Railroad Mergers: Competition, Monopoly and Antitrust (1962) 19(1) Washington & Lee Law Review 1, 21 https://scholarlycommons.law.wlu.edu/wlulr/vol19/iss1/2/; J Roger Edwards Jr, 'Railroad Mergers' (1964) 18 Southwestern Law Journal 439, 441 https://scholar.smu.edu/smulr/vol18/iss3/5.

[55] Congress responded to the losses in freight and passenger by creating the National Railroad Passenger Corporation (Amtrak) and Conrail, see Dobbin (n 6) 80.

[56] Former s 5(2) of the ICA, enacted as a part of the Transportation Act of 1920 (28 February 1920) ch 91 § 407, 41 Stat 48.

[57] Transportation Act of 1920, 41 Stat 456 (1920).

[58] Former s 5(6) of the ICA, enacted as a part of the Transportation Act of 1920 (28 February 1920) ch 91 § 407, 41 Stat 48.

[59] Tucker and O'Brien (n 49) 178.

[60] 48 Stat 211 (1933).

[61] 54 Stat 906 (1940), 49 USC § 5(2)(c)(1) (1958).

[62] ibid.

[63] ibid.

[64] 44R Act of 1976, § 403. The intention of the Congress with this provision was to instruct the ICC to encourage 'efforts to restructure the [rail industry] on a more economically justified basis' and reflects that it is 'intended to encourage mergers, consolidations, and joint use of facilities that tend to rationalize and improve the Nation's rail

Next, the Staggers Rail Act of 1980 added as a public interest consideration 'whether the proposed transaction would have an adverse effect on competition among all carriers in the affected region'.[65] Currently, the assessment of transactions in this sector is based on federal statutes,[66] the STB's railroad merger regulations,[67] and the 2001 Major Rail Consolidation Procedures.[68] All federal statutes regarding the consolidation, merger, and acquisition of control involving rail carriers providing transportation are included in Title 49 of the US Code.[69] In particular, the US Code states that '[w]hen an application is filed with the Board [the STB], [it] shall notify the chief executive officer of each State in which property of the rail carriers involved in the proposed transaction is located and shall notify those rail carriers',[70] who needs to examine the following five factors:

(1) the effect of the proposed transaction on the adequacy of transportation to the public;
(2) the effect on the public interest of including, or failing to include other rail carriers in the area involved in the proposed transaction;
(3) the total fixed charges that result from the proposed transaction;
(4) the interest of rail carrier employees affected by the proposed transaction; and
(5) whether the proposed transaction would have an adverse effect on competition among rail carriers in the affected region or in the national rail system.[71]

In terms of those mergers that do not involve large railroads, the STB will approve those unlikely to decrease competition substantially, create a monopoly, or restrain trade in freight surface transportation in any US region, and whose public interest outweigh anti-competitive effects by providing important transportation needs for consumers.[72] This is a similar approach to the assessment of efficiencies that the antitrust agencies take into account in balancing a substantial lessening of competition. In balancing the benefits of a transaction in the rail sector against any competitive harm, conditions can be imposed to alleviate the harm.[73] Therefore, the STB has the authority to impose conditions that are necessary[74] and to monitor them for a period of up to five years following the merger.[75]

system'. See Paul Stephen Dempsey, 'Antitrust Law and Policy in Transportation: Monopoly is the Name of the Game' (1987) 21 Georgia Law Review 505, 554.

[65] Staggers Rail Act of 1980, s 228(a)(2).
[66] 49 USC § 11321 ff.
[67] 49 CFR § 1180.
[68] 66 FR 32582.
[69] 49 USC §§ 11321–11328.
[70] 49 USC § 11324 (a).
[71] 49 USC § 11324 (b).
[72] Antitrust Enforcement Improvement Act of 2000, Hearing Before the Committee on the Judiciary House of Representatives, HR 4321, Serial No 117 (12 September 2000) 55.
[73] Union Pacific—Control and Merger—Southern Pacific Rail, Finance Docket No 32760 (UP—SP), Decision No 44 (12 August 1996) 98–99.
[74] Surface Transportation Board, 'Major Railroad Mergers and Consolidations' https://web.archive.org/web/20190710195818/https://www.stb.gov/stb/industry/merger.html (accessed 30 April 2023).
[75] ibid.

The public interest standard requires that, in order to 'ensure balanced and sustainable competition in the railroad industry',[76] the STB can only approve transactions that are consistent with this standard,[77] in particular 'when substantial and demonstrable gains in important public benefits—such as improved service and safety, enhanced competition, and greater economic efficiency—outweigh any anticompetitive effects, potential service disruptions, or other merger-related harms'.[78] Additionally, the 2001 Major Rail Consolidation Procedures[79] specify that the parties need to demonstrate the benefits that the transaction will bring in terms of public interest that could offset the possible negative effects of the merger, such as competitive harm or service disruptions.[80] As stated in *Missouri-Kansas-Texas R Co v United States*, 'the Act's single and essential standard of approval is that the [Board] find the [transaction] to be 'consistent with the public interest'.[81]

The legislative evolution notwithstanding, Short's analysis of thirty-five decisions issued by the ICC between 1999 and 1923 concluded that 'the ICC has been explicit and broadly consistent in defining the public interest'. In particular, looking at the criteria introduced by the Transportation Act of 1940, the adequacy of transportation to the public received twenty-eight mentions; the possible inclusion of other rail carriers received twenty-seven mentions; the total fixed charges and the interest of employees both received twenty-six mentions. The fifth factor, the adverse effect on competition, was formally introduced by the Staggers Act of 1980, although 'this statute merely codified the ICC's longstanding practice'.[82] The ICC's interpretation of the notion of public interest relied heavily on cost-benefit analysis, as expressly acknowledged in seventeen decisions, as well as in the 1981 Policy Statement.[83] In terms of justifications, efficiency was the most widely used (199 mentions), and statutory substantive values—while much less common—received as much attention (seventy-four mentions) as procedural concerns (sixty mentions) and non-statutory substantive values (fourteen mentions) combined.[84]

---

[76] 49 CFR § 1180.1(a).

[77] 49 USC § 11324(c).

[78] 49 CFR § 1180.1(c).

[79] STB Docket EP 582 (Sub-No 1).

[80] The STB stated that, because of the small number of remaining Class I railroads, the fact that rail mergers are no longer needed to address excess capacity in the rail industry, and the transitional service problems that have accompanied recent rail mergers, future merger applicants will be required to bear a heavier burden to show that a major rail combination is consistent with the public interest. This shift in policy, the board noted, will place greater emphasis in the public interest assessment on enhancing competition, while ensuring a stable, balanced, and reliable rail transportation system in a way that accounts for smaller railroads, ports, and passenger and commuter services. In STB Press Release, 'Surface Transportation Board Issues New Rules Governing Major Railroad Mergers & Consolidations' (2001) https://www.stb.gov/newsrels.nsf/29d1486804c22b1785256e59005e7e87/ 72ac2e784ae07a3485256a680050e630?OpenDocument (accessed 15 November 2022).

[81] *Missouri-Kansas-Texas Ry Co v United States* 632 F 2d 392, 395 (5th Cir 1980), 451 US 1017 (1981).

[82] Jodi L Short, 'In Search of the Public Interest' (2023) 40 Yale Journal of Regulation 759, 786–87.

[83] ibid 789–90.

[84] ibid 793.

5.3 Challenges of Concurrent Jurisdiction

Sectoral regulators have extensive expertise on the issues that affect the sector itself (eg capacity constraints, market structure constraints, etc.), but they usually have less expertise on competition law related issues.[85] The rail regulator has no extensive exposure to competition assessment of mergers. This is primarily because the application of competition laws has been overlooked, and the concerns raised by antitrust agencies have been frequently ignored. This was due to two important factors. The first is the policy to protect the rail industry from other types of transportation, which has resulted in the creation of consolidated rail systems with the aim of offsetting decades of excessive interventionism. The second is, as we will see below, the disproportionate deference that courts offer to the sectoral regulator when reviewing its merger decisions.[86]

A change in the policy on assessing the competition impact of transactions in this sector would render the analysis of the competitive harm of a transaction a relevant factor and the judicial review would strictly scrutinize whether, under the antitrust laws, its assessment has been appropriate, and hold the regulator responsible for inaccurate competition assessment where relevant. It could be advisable for the antitrust agency to be the decision maker on the competition assessment of a merger and the regulator providing its expert opinion since the latter lacks expertise in competition and its decisions have been biased in favour of the railroad carriers, as we will see further below. Otherwise, the role played by the antitrust agency will continue to be subordinate to the sectoral regulator and the interaction between competition and regulation will remain unbalanced.

Another aspect that requires a radical reform is the excessive protection that incumbents enjoy from the antitrust immunity granted through 'paper barriers' and 'refusal to deal' conducts. Paper barriers are limitations that the seller inflicts on the buyer or lessee of a short line restricting its capacity to deliver traffic to any other connecting railroad, specifically, to competitors of the former Class I parent line. These prohibitions on some occasions are indefinite.[87] Refusals to deal refer to the ability of railroads to refuse to deal with competing railroads concerning the traffic of captive shippers.[88] A shipper is captive when is served by a single railroad.[89] A possible modification would be the imposition of time and scope limitations to these types of antitrust immunities, and to transfer the authority to grant them to the antitrust agencies which could be better placed to review the justifications for such exemptions critically. As some commentators have argued, the STB has been protecting incumbents by accepting their

---

[85] Peter C Cartensen, 'Replacing Antitrust Exemptions for Transportation Industries: The Potential for a "Robust Business Review Clearance"' (2011) 89 Oregon Law Review 1059, 1097.

[86] *Southern Pacific Transp Co v ICC* 736 F 2d 708 (DC Cir 1984).

[87] Russell Pittman, 'The Economics of Railroad Captive Shipper Legislation' (2010) 62 Admin Law Review 919, 927–930; Cartensen (n 85) 1081.

[88] See Pittman (n 87).

[89] P V Garrod and W Miklius, '"Captive Shippers" and the Success of Railroads in Capturing Monopoly Rent' (1987) 30(2) The Journal of Law & Economics 423 http://www.jstor.org/stable/725503 (accessed 15 November 2022).

164 PUBLIC INTEREST ASSESSMENT AND THE STB

justifications for the continuation of antitrust immunity without embarking on a critical assessment of their arguments and more importantly of the impact of their conduct in the relevant markets.[90]

5.4 Enforcement Record

Table 5.1 examines the STB's enforcement record of rail mergers and consolidations between 2007 and 2016. In terms of applications, there has been a small number of filings (ten), a somewhat larger number of grants (thirteen), and just two denials. Likewise, thirty-five petitions for exemption were filed,[91] out of which thirty-three[92] were granted and eight were denied. The highest enforcement activity related to notices of exemption from any enforcement action with 148 filings, 145 approvals and just four denials.[93] In all these enforcement activities, the total number of grants was almost the same as the total number of applications, with a very low number of denials.

5.4.1 Analysis of Some Seminal Cases

The chapter continues with an examination of the main case law of the ICC/STB. The analysis will assess the application of the public interest standard and the competition standard. In doing so, the next group of cases show how the tensions in the application of these approaches has resulted in divergence between the regulator and the antitrust authority. This divergence, as we sought to explain in the previous section, does result largely from the weaker position of the antitrust authority whose role is confined simply to provide a non-binding comment about the potential anti-competitive effects of the merger. Whereas the regulator, who does not have expertise in competition matters, has the authority to decide a merger applying a public interest standard that includes, among other things, the analysis of the anti-competitive effects of the merger. Paradoxically, as the examination of the following cases illustrate, the regulator can disregard the competition concerns transactions may give to. One significant consequence of this dichotomy is the approval of mergers without a proper competition scrutiny leading to high levels of concentration. That result is indeed what the next section discusses.

---

[90] Cartensen (n 85).

[91] The Surface Transport Board indicates that 'Where a merger or acquisition involves only Class II or III railroads whose lines do not connect with each other, carriers need only follow a simple notification procedure to invoke a class exemption at 49 CFR § 1180.2(d)(2).' See Surface Transportation Board, FY 2017 Annual Report 15 https://www.stb.gov/wp-content/uploads/files/docs/annualReports/Annual%20Report%202017.pdf (accessed 29 September 2023).

[92] This number includes some cases carried over from the previous year.

[93] ibid. With regard to Table 5.1, this is the most recent data available on the STB website. Although there is some data about FY 2017, the information is not presented in a similar manner as in previous years. The FY 2017 Annual Reports notes that thirteen merger and consolidation matters were decided by the board. See Surface Transportation Board, FY 2017 Annual Report 15 https://www.stb.gov/wp-content/uploads/files/docs/annual Reports/Annual%20Report%202017.pdf (accessed 29 September 2023).

Table 5.1 Rail mergers and consolidations (2007–16)

Year	Applications					Petitions for Exemption					Notices of Exemption				
	Filed	Granted	Denied	Dismissed	Pending	Filed	Granted	Denied	Dismissed	Pending	Filed	Granted	Denied	Dismissed	Pending
2016	1	2	1			3	2			1	15	17	1		
2015	1	2	1			4	6	3			18	16	2	1	1
2014				1		5	4			3	17	16			1
2013	1	2			1	6	6	1	1	1	15	15			
2012	N/A	N/A	N/A	N/A	N/A	N/A	N/A	N/A	N/A	N/A	N/A	N/A	N/A	N/A	N/A
2011	1	2				3	4	1			21	21	1	1	
2010	2	1			1	4	2	1		1	13	15			3
2009		2		3		4	4				19	18			2
2008	3	1				5	4	2			15	13		1	
2007	1	1				1	1				15	14		1	
TOTAL	**10**	**13**	**2**	**3**	**3**	**35**	**33**	**8**	**1**	**6**	**148**	**145**	**4**	**4**	**7**

Source: STB Annual Reports.[*]

[*]STB—Annual Reports https://prod.stb.gov/about-stb/agency-materials/annual-reports/ (accessed 4 October 2023). This is the most recent data available on the STB website. Although there is some data about FY 2017, the information is not presented by STB in a similar comprehensive manner as in previous years. The FY 2017 Annual Reports notes that thirteen merger and consolidation matters were decided by the board. See Surface Transportation Board, FY 2017 Annual Report 15 https://www.stb.gov/wp-content/uploads/files/docs/annualReports/Annual%20Report%202017.pdf (accessed 29 September 2023).

5.4.1.1 Divergence in the approach of STB and DOJ

5.4.1.1.1 Pennsylvania Railroad—New York Central Railroad

In the 1960s, the railroad passenger and freight market in parts of the United States were mainly Pennsylvania Railroad (PR) and New York Central Railroad (NYR). At that time, the railroad industry was facing insurmountable difficulties given the strong competition from trucks, airlines, and interstate highways, as a result of the outstanding construction of airports and the Interstate Highway System mostly funded by the government, combined with a reduction in passenger numbers due to the emergence of commuting by car.[94] The situation was aggravated by the ICC's reluctance to allow freight and passenger rate increases and the rejection of the railroad's requirement to abandon non-profit branch lines.[95] Faced with this factual context, in January 1962 the two companies decided to merge in an attempt to overcome their financial difficulties. The merger was initially approved by the ICC in April 1966, and finally approved by the Supreme Court on 31 January 1968, resulting in the largest corporate transaction at that time (Penn Central), in spite of strong opposition from unions, states, cities and railroads and the initial opposition from the DOJ.[96]

As Commissioner Tuggle noted at the Annual Convention of the National Association of Railroad Commissioners in 1960: 'In conclusion and for the record, I want to say that the ICC stands ready, willing and able—and I might add, anxious, to give thorough and sympathetic consideration to any merger proposals under section 5.' The hearing of this merger lasted more than a year, and a few years passed before a final decision was issued.[97] The approval of the deal became uncertain as on 1 October 1963 the DOJ and the White House, in a joint statement, opposed the merger, affirming that it would 'eliminate a vast amount of beneficial rail competition', 'endanger the service ... prospects ... and existence' of small railroads, and 'preclude more balancing restructuring' of railroads in the East.[98]

The ICC's approval of this merger needs to be seen within the following context: the Transportation Act of 1920 exempted the railroads from the enforcement of antitrust laws, competition was just one more factor used to evaluate whether a proposal was in the public interest, and the relevant provisions did not specify how to assess the competitive effects of the merger.[99] This approach was confirmed in the ICC decision that followed: 'While there may be some lessening of competition as a result of the proposed merger, we do not regard the fact as of controlling importance.'[100] Thus, in an attempt to

---

[94] Jerry W Jordak, 'Penn Central: Fifty Years Later' (31 January 2018) http://railfan.com/penn-central-fifty-years-later/ (accessed 7 November 2022).

[95] ibid.

[96] Marc Ivaldi and Gerard McCullough, 'Welfare Trade-offs in U.S. Rail Mergers" (2010) Toulouse School of Economics Working Paper Series 10-196, 7 https://www.tse-fr.eu/sites/default/files/medias/doc/wp/io/10-196.pdf (accessed 7 November 2022); Jordak (n 94).

[97] W N Leonard, 'Issues of Competition and Monopoly in Railroad Mergers' (1964) 3(4) Transportation Journal 6.

[98] ibid 9.

[99] A study from the Bureau of Transport Economics and Statistics of the ICC, reported that: 'Without detailed analysis, it cannot be stated that a workable consistent method of appraising the degree, impact, and desirability of competition between railroads can be developed for use in pending and proposed merger cases.' See Leonard (n 97).

[100] Norfolk & Western Ry, Merger, 307 ICC 40, 440 (1959).

provide some guidance to the ICC in relation to the importance of competition considerations and to inspect competitive rate abuses, in 1962 a bill was introduced making section 7 of the Clayton Act applicable to future rail mergers and imposing a temporary moratorium on railroad mergers 'involving a line with US$200 million or more in assets where the Commission found that the merger tend to lesser competition or might tend toward monopoly'.[101] However, the proposal did not receive support by the Senate Judiciary Committee causing its expiration.[102]

Against this context, it is noteworthy that the DOJ urged the immediate consummation of the merger before the Supreme Court after realizing that it would be 'in the public interest', showing a departure from its initial position of opposing the proposal.[103] Hence, the strongest opposition came from different cities in the state of Pennsylvania, namely Scranton, Shapp, and Moosic, which alleged that the combined revenue of the two entities, the fact that they were direct competitors in thirty-two urban areas where no other rail facilities were available, and that the two railroads operated at 160 common points or junctions would have anti-competitive effects.[104]

The Supreme Court, in its approval decision of the PR/NYR merger, affirmed the approach that 'competition is merely one consideration' and endorsed the ICC's analysis with respect to the lessening of competition, whereby strong competition would remain after the merger from other railroads and that the following factors would act as a restraint upon the new merged entity: 'The power of shippers to direct the routing, the availability of numerous routes in a dense network of interline routes, the influence of connecting carriers in preventing a deterioration in service on the joint routes in which they participate, the growing strength of the N & W and C & O-B & O systems, all stand to provide a check against any abuse of economic power by the merged applicants.'[105] Finally, the ICC conditioned the approval upon the acquisition of the bankrupt New York, New Haven, and Hartford Railroad by the new merged entity.[106]

However, not long after the merger was finally approved, on 21 June 1970, Penn Central filed for bankruptcy protection under section 77 of the Bankruptcy Act. A combination of different circumstances resulted in this outcome: (i) operational difficulties such as the incompatibility between the computer systems of the two merged companies, which made the exchange of information about freight cars and shipments impossible; (ii) the large amount of money that had been invested to reach an agreement with the unions; (iii) the already perilous financial position of New Haven; (iv) a decline in revenue; and (v) poor organizational decisions.[107] As a consequence, the

---

[101] Section 3097, introduced 3 April 1962. See also 'New National Transportation Policy Asked', CQ Almanac 1962 https://library.cqpress.com/cqalmanac/document.php?id=cqal62-1325203 (accessed 25 November 2022).

[102] Section 3097 (13 October 1962) 87th Congress.

[103] 389 US 486 (1968).

[104] 389 US 486 (1968).

[105] 389 US 486 (1968). N&W stands for Norfolk & Western, C&O for Chesapeake & Ohio, B&O for Baltimore & Ohio.

[106] Richard Salvato, 'Penn Central Transportation Company (New York, Pennsylvania, and Long Island Railroads)' New York Public Library Records 1796–1986, 7 https://www.nypl.org/sites/default/files/archivalcoll ections/pdf/penncentral.pdf (accessed 15 November 2022).

[107] Jordak (n 94).

168 PUBLIC INTEREST ASSESSMENT AND THE STB

government created Amtrak, seeking to gain control of all long distance passenger services in the country,[108] and nationalized Penn Central through the creation of Conrail, a government corporation that acquired this and other bankrupt railroads, which, at a later stage, was bought by CSX and Norfolk Southern.[109]

The analysis of this case reveals that mergers do not always constitute an immediate solution to financial issues, particularly if between the merging parties there are irreconcilable operational and managerial disparities. It also shows that competition was not a factor that it was not given much attention and was only one consideration of not great importance as confirmed by the Supreme Court. Instead, in assessing the merger both the ICC and the Supreme Court gave overriding weight to the policy of protecting the public interest, in particular, the protection of employment. Finally, it casts doubt on the ICC's argument that the growing strength of the new railroad companies would prevent a deterioration in service, given that soon after the merger Penn Central and many other companies collapsed, necessitating government intervention.

5.4.1.1.2 Seaboard Air Line—Atlantic Coast Line

On 22 July 1960, Seaboard Air Line Company (Seaboard) and Atlantic Coast Line (Atlantic), two profitable companies whose lines were parallel and competing in the south, filed a merger proposal that would create a US$2 billion business, which amounted to double the revenue of its closest competitor in the area, controlling Louisville and Nashville.[110] The merger was approved by the ICC, despite strong opposition from the DOJ, which stated that the proposed transaction would 'flagrantly contravene' the antitrust laws because it would 'destroy the vigorous competition' that existed between the two lines. The DOJ added that the merger would 'jeopardize the existence of several small railroads' in the southeast, injure some communities and shippers who could be left with a reduced rail service, and 'impair adequate transportation'.[111]

For the ICC, even if the merging parties served 121 common points in a six-state area and had almost 54 per cent of the total distance in the affected area, the transaction did not raise any concerns. Similarly, in Florida the new merged entity would own almost 81 per cent of the rail mileage, and after the transaction competition would cease between the merging parties in one-third of their collective total capacity, yet for the ICC: 'the reduction of rail competition caused by the proposed merger will not be substantial'.[112] The ICC based its view on the proposition that competition from other modes of transport had increased, making intramodal competition insignificant. In the words of the Commission: 'motor carriers are increasing their long-haul business and are capable of handling practically any type of commodity'.[113] It highlighted that 'it is

---

[108] Geoffrey H Doughty, Jeffrey T Darbee, and Eugene E Harmon, *Amtrak: America's Railroad* (Indiana University Press 2021) 52–57.

[109] Conrail, 'A Brief History of Conrail' (2003) https://web.archive.org/web/20101121075513/http://conrail.com/history.htm (accessed 15 November 2023).

[110] Leonard (n 97) 5–15, 6; Edwards (n 54).

[111] Philips (n 54) 2–3.

[112] Edwards (n 54) 463.

[113] Seaboard Air Line Railroad—Control—Atlantic Coast Line Railroad, Finance Docket No 21215, Decision (2 December 1963) 60.

not realistic to insist that intramodal rail competition must be preserved in all places, at all times and under all circumstances'.[114]

Additionally, the ICC supported its competition approach in the *McLean Trucking v United States* case, which was the first case to deal directly with the antitrust law exemption, whereby the Supreme Court held that the Commission was not obliged to undertake extensive application of the antitrust laws in merger cases,[115] and 'has no power to enforce the Sherman Act as such. It cannot decide definitely whether the transaction contemplated constitutes a restraint of trade or an attempt to monopolize which is forbidden by that Act'.[116] Equally, the ICC, through its decision, clarified that bankruptcy is not an indispensable factor in approving mergers.[117] Finally, as a condition, the new merged company was obliged to open the Jacksonville gateway to the Southern Railways and its associates to 'mutual switching'.[118] Mutual switching occurs when an 'incumbent carrier transports a shipper's traffic to an interchange point, where it switches the cars over to the competing carrier. The competing carrier pays the incumbent carrier a switching fee for bringing or taking the cars from the shipper's facility to the interchange point or vice versa'.[119] Some commentators have noted that, in former transactions, the STB has traditionally imposed the same condition with the prevailing aim of safeguarding competing carriers.[120]

The ICC's approval decision of the Seaboard—Atlantic case was reviewed by a three-judge District Court, who found that the analysis of the anti-competitive effects was defective because the Commission had not determined whether the proposal violated section 7 of the Clayton Act by reference to the relevant product and geographic markets. This decision from the District Court was appealed, and subsequently annulled by the Supreme Court, which argued that the District Court had erred in its analysis of the McLean case, clarifying that there is 'little doubt that the Commission is not to measure proposals for [acquisitions] by the standards of the antitrust laws' and that the Commission had been authorized by Congress to approve the merger of railroads if it had adequate evidence that such a merger would be 'consistent with the public interest'.[121]

Edwards has contended that the *McLean* case does not support the *Seaboard— Atlantic* case, as the District Court claimed, because in *McLean* the issue was about the weight to be placed on the effects on competition, while in the *Seaboard—Atlantic* merger case the issue was about what method was used to assess them (product and

---

[114] ibid 152. Commissioner Webb in his dissent statement held that there was 'no adequate substitute for intramodal rail competition for the principal commodities carried by the applicants and thus, no reason to believe that the foundation of applicant's prosperity is not secure'.

[115] Neil McEwen, 'The Role of Antitrust Law in Railroad Mergers: A Case Study: The Great Northern and Northern Pacific Merger' (1964) 41 North Dakota Law Review 44.

[116] *McLean Trucking Co v United States* 321 US 67 (1944).

[117] Pierre R Bretey, 'Merger Progress Slow but Sure' (1965) 21(2) Financial Analysts Journal 65, 66.

[118] ICC, 'Rail Merger Study' (1977) Rail Services Planning Office Issue Paper No 1, 44.

[119] 81 FR 51150.

[120] Bretey (n 115).

[121] *Seaboard Air Line Ry Co v United States* 382 US 154 (1965).

170   PUBLIC INTEREST ASSESSMENT AND THE STB

geographic relevant markets). He has added that the public interest is a 'nebulous term' that was used by the ICC to allow the integration of prosperous competing businesses.[122]

The examination of this case confirms how little importance competition law has had in reviewing rail mergers and the permissive policy approach that facilitates consolidation under an amorphous public interest standard. Likewise, a significant development in this case was that the Commission maintained that rail and truck services are almost interchangeable in order to justify its approval, a proposition that was clearly retracted in Southern Pacific—Santa Fe, as will be seen in more detail below. It is also important to note that in this case the size of the merging parties, their market shares, the elimination of competition, and the increase in dominance were found to be trivial by the ICC, who described the opposition from the DOJ based on these factors as overstated. In this case, while the DOJ objected to the merger for competitive reasons, it had to defer to the ICC for the final decision. Another interesting point is the deference that the Supreme Court showed towards the authority of the Commission in exempting the application of antitrust laws. Lastly, it appears that the ICC had a cluster of conditions that were regularly imposed on railroad mergers, adapted to an extent to the specific context of the case.

5.4.1.1.3 Great Northern—Northern Pacific (The Northern Lines)

Great Northern Railway Co. (GN) and the Northern Pacific Railway Co. (NP), and three of their affiliates, the Pacific Coast Railroad Co., the Chicago, Burlington & Quincy Railroad Co. (Burlington), and the Spokane, Portland & Seattle Railway Co. (SP&S) filed a plan to merge, which was conditionally approved by the ICC in 1967.[123] GN and NP were the main competitors in the Northern Lines' area, accounting for a large amount of traffic.[124] The ICC argued that there were a number of public benefits deemed to be enough to counteract the anti-competitive effects of the transaction. There would be savings of US$40 million per year, no jobs would be removed and the need for new jobs would be lost, consolidation would result in a more efficient routing of travel, unnecessary facilities would be closed, and there would be a better claims service with the presence of a strong competitor (Milwaukee).[125] A three-judge District Court reviewed this approval decision, concluding that the findings were supported by substantial evidence and that the ICC had correctly applied the legal principles.[126]

The Court's decision was appealed to the Supreme Court by the DOJ which, among others, strongly opposed the transaction, contending that the significant elimination of competition between two financially healthy railroads would lead to a harm on competition unless there were significant transportation needs to be met or there

---

[122] Edwards (n 54) 467–69.
[123] 396 US 491 (1970).
[124] ibid.
[125] ibid. See also Mark D Perreault and Nancy S Fleischman, 'Loss of Rail Competition an Issue in the Proposed Sale of Conrail to Norfolk Southern: Valid Concern or Political Bogeyman' (1986) 34 Cleveland State Law Review 413, 424.
[126] 396 US 491 (1970).

were important public benefits arising beyond the normal savings and efficiencies originating from a merger.[127] The Supreme Court affirmed the Court's decision based on the following findings: (1) that the approval, subject to conditions, was substantiated on evidence that measured the competitive effects of the merger against its benefits; (2) that based on the *McLean Trucking* case, ICC had the authority to determine whether consolidation would contribute to the application of transportation policies even if the number of competitors was reduced; (3) that the benefits of the transaction were supported by the required volume of evidence; and (4) that with the enactment of the Transportation Act of 1940 Congress sought 'to facilitate merger and consolidation in the transportation system'. Thus, it was incorrect to conclude that the approval of mergers was just confined to 'situations where weak carriers are preserved by combining with those that are strong'.[128]

This case illustrates that the DOJ's concerns did not play a significant role before the ICC or the courts. It also raises the questions of whether the alleged savings allegedly created by the merger would effectively benefit customers, and if in fact the alleged benefits were over and above the usual benefits that any merger would create. While there is often an acute difficulty in identifying those legitimate interests that merit accommodation within the competition framework, in this case the ICC and the courts seem to have overcome such a complexity in a flexible, and perhaps simplistic manner, accepting the preservation of jobs and unsupported economic savings claims, among others, as aligned with public interest considerations. One implication of assuming that such public interest considerations constitute issues worthy of recognition in antitrust law enforcement, is that it renders their verification somehow irrelevant. Finally, the decision of the Supreme Court clearly shows that consolidation in the rail sector, which inevitably induces market power increase, follows a policy that was well supported by the ICC and the judiciary.

5.4.1.1.4 Union Pacific—Missouri Pacific—Western Pacific

Union Pacific announced its intention to acquire Missouri Pacific and Western Pacific railroads, becoming the third-largest system in the US linking the Middle West, Southwest, and Pacific Coast and carrying grain, coal, and some other commodities between Chicago and the Pacific Coast extending southward to the Gulf of Mexico.[129] The approval of this transaction confirms the ICC's tendency to protect railroad incumbents against other forms of competition such as motor, air, and water transportation. It also shows how irrespective some concerns expressed by its own office of Special Counsel that 'the merger would reduce competition among railroads in the Middle West', that were shared by the DOJ, and opposition from Southern Pacific, the ICC sent ahead to approve the transaction.[130]

---

[127] ibid.

[128] ibid.

[129] Ernest Holsendolph, '3 Railroads Given Approval by ICC to Merge in West' *New York Times* (14 September 1982) https://www.nytimes.com/1982/09/14/business/3-railroads-given-approval-by-icc-to-merge-in-west.html (accessed 12 November 2022).

[130] ibid.

172   PUBLIC INTEREST ASSESSMENT AND THE STB

On 20 October 1982, the ICC issued its final approval decision, although conceding that the transaction would have significant adverse competitive effects on rail transportation of transcontinental traffic and on rail transportation in the Midwest. Seeking to confront the reduction in the number of railroad competitors in the Middle West, the ICC imposed some conditions including open route and labour protection, and stressed that the public benefits from the transaction would counteract the potential negative effects created by the elimination of competition. In particular, the ICC concluded that the creation of a single-system service would improve the operation in terms of efficiency and reliability, and that the transaction would bring public savings of US$47 million annually.[131] The DOJ was successful in requesting the imposition of conditions to mitigate the competitive issues that would be created on some routes by the proposed merger.[132] Thus, additional competition conditions were imposed on the new merged entity. The latter was required to transfer some trackage rights[133] to Denver & Rio Grande Railroad between Pueblo, Colorado, and Kansas City; Missouri-Kansas-Texas received access to St. Louis from Kansas City; and St. Louis Southwestern railroads received rights on various routes. The ICC also included 'the minimum protections to be afforded those employees affected by a consolidation, absent a voluntarily negotiated agreement.[134]

Southern Pacific appealed the ICC's approval decision, which was upheld by the Court of Appeals, District of Columbia Circuit. One of the main issues examined in this appeal was whether the proposed consolidation was consistent with the public interest considering that in the view of the petitioner, the conceded anti-competitive effects of the merger outweighed any public benefits that the merger could produce.[135] The Court disagreed with the petitioner's view, affirming that 'the Commission is required to give anticompetitive effects not merely substantial but dispositive weight. We think that the Commission properly recognized that while competition is a "major factor" in its calculus, its "primary inquiry" is still to be conducted under the terms of the Interstate Commerce Act'. The Court continued by stating that, based on the *McLean Trucking* case, the Commission had never sat 'as an antitrust court [to determine] compliance with the Clayton Act, or related antitrust acts', that the ICC had properly balanced the serious anti-competitive effects of the merger against the benefits, and that 'we owe the Commission substantial deference in reviewing its decisions.[136] The Court emphasized the clear derogation of competition concerns in favour of the public interest in the assessment of rail consolidation.

---

[131] Union Pacific—Control—Missouri Pacific & Western Pacific 366 ICC 459 (1982) 487, 533, 642.

[132] William F Baxter, 'Antitrust Division' (1982) Attorney General Annual Report 133, 137.

[133] Trackage rights have been defined as 'the right by which one railroad company operates trains in scheduled service over tracks owned and used by another railroad company'. See Illinois Compiled Statutes, 35ILCS200-Sec 11-70 (e)/Property Tax Code https://ilga.gov/legislation/ilcs/ilcs4.asp?DocName=003502000H Art%2E%2B12%2BDiv%2E%2B1&ActID=596&ChapterID=8&SeqStart=32400000&SeqEnd=33200000 (accessed 26 September 2022).

[134] Union Pacific—Control—Missouri Pacific & Western Pacific (n 131) 619.

[135] *Southern Pacific Transp Co v ICC* (n 86).

[136] ibid.

This case further illustrates the ICC's intense focus on remedies that were imposed somewhat by default in any approved transaction that aimed at the protection of labour and competing carriers. It also reveals that the ICC was biased in favour of rail consolidation of single-system lines to safeguard them against alternative modes of transportation, regardless of the competitive harm that could be caused by 'collateral damage' on competition dynamics. This view has also been voiced by Senator Larry Pressler, who noted that:

> Mergers proliferate. Since the passage of Staggers, the number of major railroads has declined from 12 to 8 ... As major railroads continue to consolidate, many of the marginal lines become increasingly threatened ... Mergers and abandonments will certainly create more captive shippers who are forced to rely upon one rail line.[137]

At the same time, it raises the question of whether the judicial review of the ICC's decisions has been a mere box-ticking process, where the extent of deference that is given to the regulator renders irrelevant the application of antitrust laws in cases involving mergers by railroads. Likewise, this broad approach of dissolving competition concerns by adopting a public interest approach has enhanced the discretion of the regulator in approving mergers without a detailed assessment of the transactions on competition in the relevant markets.

5.4.1.1.5 Union Pacific—Southern Pacific

The 1996 merger between Union Pacific Corporation and Southern Pacific Rail Corporation railroads, approved by the STB despite strong objections from the DOJ, was a milestone in the history of the railroad industry.[138] In its decision, the STB concluded that the merger would be in the public interest, since it found that the leasing by the merged entity of rights to its track to its competitor Burlington Northern and Santa Fe Railway (BNSF, the other large railroad in the West),[139] would suffice to address the monopoly position of Union Pacific/Southern Pacific in a number of markets,[140] and that there would be important service improvements and efficiencies arising from the merger. Moreover, the merger would allow Southern Pacific Rail Corporation, which was financially weak at that time, to 'become part of a large, financially healthy rail

---

[137] Oversight of the Staggers Rail Act of 1980: Hearings Before the Subcomm. On Surface Transportation of the Senate Comm. on Commerce, Science, and Transportation, 99th Congress, 1st Session, 30–31 (1985). (Statement of Senator Pressler).

[138] Jennifer Pucci, 'Antitrust Law or "Public Interest" Standard? An Analysis of the Surface Transportation Board's Approval of the Union Pacific Southern Pacific Merger' (2006) University of Virginia School of Law, 3 https://govinfo.library.unt.edu/amc/public_studies_fr28902/regulated_pdf/060518_Pucci_student_paper_Regulated.pdf (accessed 15 November 2022).

[139] 'Applicants claim that the merger will generate annual quantified public benefits in excess of US$750million, and that a merged UP—SP will be more competitive and efficient, and better able to compete with BNSF.' See UP—SP (n 73) 15–16.

[140] Pucci (n 138).

174   PUBLIC INTEREST ASSESSMENT AND THE STB

system and thereby be in a position to sustain efficient operations and maintain a viable level of investment in its plant'.[141]

Among the public interest justifications, the parties argued that the proposed merger would allow them

> [t]o combine [their] separate routes and to create new routes; to improve operations through terminals, and to avoid delay by eliminating interchanges and combining traffic volumes into new trains and new blocks; to improve service ... through technological support and access to capital; to improve equipment utilization and availability; and to consolidate yards and functions.[142]

The DOJ expressed strong opposition, arguing that the transaction would lead to an increase in market concentration and prices and would also enhance the possibility of collusion post-merger. The STB dismissed all of the concerns based on the apparent above-mentioned benefits, because there was no evidence of previous collusion among the merging parties, and the assumption that the parties would manage prices appropriately.[143] Some commentators have criticized the approach of the STB, contending that the benefits were not merger specific (as the DOJ repeatedly argued), that its decision was biased to such an extent that even if both authorities used the same methodologies to review the anti-competitive effects of the transaction the outcomes would be divergent, and that the deference towards the merging parties was rather contrary to the public interest.[144]

The STB (and its predecessor ICC)[145] have stated that through their enforcement practice they always ensure that transactions are consistent with the public interest,[146] which 'necessarily involves an examination of the public benefits that will result from the transaction',[147] such as cost reductions, cost savings, and service improvements.[148] In spite of the STB confidently predicting such benefits, congestion problems arose,

---

[141] Denis A Breen, *The Union Pacific/Southern Pacific Rail Merger: A Retrospective on Merger Benefits* (FTC 2004) https://www.ftc.gov/sites/default/files/documents/reports/union-pacific/southern-pacific-rail-merger-retrospective-merger-benefits/wp269_0.pdf (accessed 15 November 2022).

[142] See UP—SP (n 73) 15–16.

[143] Pucci (n 138).

[144] ibid.

[145] It has also been asserted that under the public interest standard ICC has favoured competitors of the merging parties, limiting the foreseeable benefits of the transaction https://www.justice.gov/archive/atr/public/testimony/0056.pdf 4 (accessed 15 November 2022).

[146] Section 11344(b)(1)(A). Also, the STB has to assess sometimes the special public interest factors. 'The Board is also required ... to make special, narrowly focused public interesting findings (where applicable) on the following aspects of any major rail consolidation; (1) a guaranty or assumption of the payment of dividends or of fixed charges, or an increase of total fixed charges ...; (2) rail acquisition of motor carriers ...; and (3) inclusion of other rail carriers located in the area'. See UP—SP (n 73) 100–101.

[147] See ibid 99.

[148] 'Cost reductions are public benefits because they permit a railroad to provide the same level of rail services with fewer resources. An integrated railroad can realize additional benefits by capitalizing on the economies of scale, scope, and density, which stem from expanded operations. Cost savings in rail consolidations can come from a variety of sources, including elimination of interchanges, internal reroutes, more efficient movements between the two merging parties, reduced overhead, and elimination of redundant facilities'. See ibid.

making it necessary in 1998 to take emergency measures to ameliorate them;[149] however, the congestion issues reappeared in 2003–2004.[150] Additionally, the DOJ's concerns in relation to increases in rate levels were evident soon after the merger, which led to the renegotiation of some transportation contracts.[151] Nonetheless, a study conducted by Breen concluded that the efficiencies that the merging parties had alleged were eventually realized,[152] although some authors recommend the adoption of a cautious approach in relation to the competitive harm of these types of mergers, at least in the short term.[153]

The above case has illustrated the tensions that can arise when jurisdiction is shared between antitrust agencies and sectoral regulators. Similarly, it has illustrated the competition related risks in the application of a 'public interest' standard that emerges from the subjectivity that surrounds the assessment of such transactions, and how the decisions of regulators can be driven by policies that might differ from the objectives pursued by competition authorities. It is unclear in what way a regulator can advocate the goals of competition enforcement by focusing on (wide and vague) public interest grounds without risking its impartiality. Also, the assessment of mergers without adopting or at least considering a competition lens leads to higher levels of discretion from the regulator. On a more positive note, the Union Pacific–Southern Pacific case has also contributed to the analysis of 'public interest considerations' by providing greater clarity on the examples of what these considerations encompass, i.e. traffic efficiencies, service improvements, efficient operations, new routes, and fewer delays, all of which would in principle benefit consumers.

5.4.1.1.6 Peter Pan—Greyhound

On 20 May 1997, Peter Pan Bus Lines (Peter Pan) and Greyhound Lines (Greyhound) requested approval for an operations and revenue pooling agreement for their motor passenger and express transportation service between New York and Washington D.C., via New Jersey, Turnpike, and Interstate Highway 95, under 49 USC 14302.[154] Peter Pan is a Class I regional bus and Greyhound is a Class I nationwide bus carrier. The former operates thirteen daily trips between New York City and Washington and fourteen daily return trips, and the latter operates twenty-three southbound and twenty northbound trips, most of them daily.[155] The applicants claimed that the pooling of

---

[149] ibid; Union Pacific—Control and Merger—Southern Pacific, Finance Docket No 32760 Sub-No. 21 (UP—SP Oversight) Decision No 12 (31 March 1998) 63 Fed Reg 16,628.

[150] Donald G Avery and Kendra A Ericson, 'Railroad Mergers: A Coal Shipper's Perspective' The Transportation Antitrust Update (ABA) (October 2004) 10. This is consistent with a broader point of Pittman, who has indicated that 'the UP—SP combination resulted in dramatic and expensive problems for shippers in some areas of the country'. See Russell Pittman, 'Railway Mergers and Railway Alliances: Competition Issues and Lessons for Other Network Industries' (2009) 10(3) Competition and Regulation in Network Industries 262.

[151] Avery and Ericson (n 150) 11.

[152] Denis A Breen, 'The Union Pacific/Southern Pacific Rail Merger: A retrospective on Merger Benefits' (2004) 3 Review of Network Economics 283.

[153] Clifford Winston, Vikram Maheshri, and Scott M Dennis, Long-Run Effects of Mergers: The Case of U.S. Western Railroads (2011) 54(2) The Journal of Law & Economics 275, 302.

[154] 62 FR 46400.

[155] STB, Docket No MC-F-20908 (21 April 1998).

176 PUBLIC INTEREST ASSESSMENT AND THE STB

operations would result in the elimination of excess bus capacity, a decrease in journeys during off-peak times and an increase during peak times, and the elimination of restrictions on tickets sold from both companies. Finally, greater financial capacity would allow them to acquire technologically advanced coaches.[156]

The DOJ opposed the agreement, stating that Peter Pan and Greyhound were the only bus lines providing transportation between New York City and Washington, and that the deal would create a monopoly between those points. It added that the other available modes of transportation were more expensive, which was why they could not be included in the same product market, and stressed that it would be difficult for other bus companies to enter the market.[157] The applicants disagreed with the DOJ's position and offered counterarguments that were embraced by the STB, which, in a brief rather than succinct analysis, concluded that the applicants were able to demonstrate that the proposed agreement was in the public interest by offering a more frequent and flexible bus service, by reducing the excess capacity and by rationalizing the prevailing level of service on this route.

The STB indicated that the DOJ had failed to explain why the market between New York City and Washington was so unique that no other bus companies would be able to enter it or why other modes of passenger transportation would not restrain the ability of the applicants to raise fares above competitive levels. Thus, approval was given after the STB noted that the concern about the way in which the applicants might behave was based on predictions only, and that even if the DOJ were right, there was nothing that the STB could do to remedy any anti-competitive behaviour that might occur. Therefore, the STB imposed a condition to the applicants who were required to submit data to the STB every six months for a three-year period about the fares charged on the route between New York and Washington, and if unjustified increases were observed the STB would re-examine the authorization of the agreement.[158]

In this case, it is noticeable that the reduction of excess capacity was still seen as a good reason to approve the merger between the carriers, an argument that has been previously used by the ICC in the Northern Lines case[159] and now by the STB. Another noteworthy aspect is that the STB did not take into account a market study from the DOJ that supported the latter's opposition to the transaction, and that throughout the STB's analysis and decision a detailed assessment of product and geographic market definition was also absent. Finally, it is interesting and, in our view, surprising to see that the STB admitted that the behaviour of the firms was unpredictable and that, in consequence, there was nothing that the agency could do.

5.4.1.1.7 CSX/NS Acquisition of CONRAIL
The Consolidated Railroad Corporation (Conrail) resulted from merging the majority of Penn Central and major sections of the lines of Central New Jersey, Lehigh Valley, Lehigh & Hudson, Pennsylvania-Reading Seashore, and Ann Arbor Railroads with

---

[156] ibid.
[157] ibid.
[158] ibid.
[159] 396 US 491 (1970).

small portions of the Reading and Erie-Lacka-wanna Railroads.[160] Once Conrail was privatized, two of the three residual Class I carriers, CSX and Norfolk Southern, were involved in a bidding battle to acquire it. They decided to acquire Conrail jointly, and to distribute its traffic and rail lines between themselves.[161] On 23 June 1997, CSX and Norfolk Southern filed their application to acquire Conrail, including the partition of most of Conrail's assets and operations.[162] DOJ urged STB to impose some conditions to protect the coal transportation market, after claiming that competition in such a market would descend from two to one, and that in two geographic markets, the transaction would create a monopoly (Indiana and Maryland). DOJ added that unless conditions were imposed, consumers and electric utilities located in the areas affected by the transaction would endure an increase in rates and requested that CSX allow Norfolk Southern the use of its tracks to handle coal shipments in Indiana and Maryland.[163]

Some other opponents to the transaction (over 140 parties filed applications in the proceedings)[164] argued that the alleged benefits of the transaction were unlikely, and that the high purchase price paid by the acquirers would force them to increase rates in order to recover their investment.[165] In particular, the Department of Agriculture advocated the imposition of conditions after predicting potential rate increases to agricultural shippers and receivers of goods, adverse effects that were not balanced by the apparent benefits of the transaction that 'are often elusive, if not illusory'.[166] At the same time, the shipping community expressed concerns about potential rate increases and reduction in competition.[167]

However, contrary to the arguments advocated by challengers, STB was convinced by the merging parties that the benefits of the transaction in terms of service improvements and efficiencies were valid and sufficient to address the alleged harm on competition. Therefore, the merger was approved with some conditions such as mutual switching, agreements with third parties to improve efficiency and service, and measures to address safety and passenger concerns, as well as agreements with trade unions, to alleviate the alleged insignificant competitive concerns that were identified by the STB, for whom the combination '[w]ill be end-to-end and not parallel. It has been our experience that end-to-end restructurings of this kind rarely result in a diminution of

---

[160] See 45 USC §§ 701–748 (1974). See also Dempsey (n 64) 565; Perreault and Fleischman (n 125) 429.

[161] Senate Hearing 105-514, Conrail Merger Implications, Before a Subcommittee of the Committee on Appropriations United States Senate https://www.govinfo.gov/content/pkg/CHRG-105shrg47739/html/CHRG-105shrg47739.htm (accessed 15 November 2022). See also https://www.stb.gov/stb/environment/key_cases_conrail.html (accessed 15 November 2022).

[162] https://www.stb.gov/stb/environment/key_cases_conrail.html.

[163] Department of Justice Press Release, 'Justice Department Urges Surface Transportation Board to Impose Conditions on CSX/Norfolk Southern Acquisition of Conrail' (27 February 1998) https://www.stb.gov/stb/environment/key_cases_conrail.html (accessed 15 November 2022).

[164] Railroad Transportation (1998) ABA Sec Public Utilities Commission & Transp Annual Report 279 (1998) 282.

[165] Avery and Ericson (n 148) 12. See also Ang and Boyer, indicating that the acquisition of Conrail by CSX and Norfolk Southern 'was the most expensive rail acquisition in history, with CSX and Norfolk paying US$10.2 billion for Conrail'. James Ang and Carol Boyer, 'Finance and Politics: Special Interest Group Influence During the Nationalization and Privatization of Conrail' (2000) Department of Finance College of Business Florida State University.

[166] Finance Docket 33388, Comments of the United States Department of Agriculture (21 October 1997) 13, 15 https://www.ams.usda.gov/sites/default/files/media/STB_10-21-97.pdf (accessed 15 November 2022).

[167] Railroad Transportation (1998) ABA Sec Public Utilities Commission & Transp Annual Report 279 (1998).

178 PUBLIC INTEREST ASSESSMENT AND THE STB

competition'.[168]

Following the CSX and NS acquisition of Conrail the new merged entity experienced congestion and service issues.[169] In addition, it did not achieve the expected cost savings from the expected efficiencies and there was a major increase in coal shipments rates.[170] The described rate increase took place in spite of an agreement between the merging parties and the National Industrial Transportation League (NITL) that was announced in December 1997, that included rate freezes for aggregate shippers at the existing level for five years, arbitration clauses that dissatisfied customers can use in case of contractual disputes, and the enactment of a shipper advisory council to improve the communications between customers and the carriers.[171] Yet, it appears that this agreement was insufficient to contain the coal rate litigation initiated years later by two large coal shippers.[172] In the aftermath, the CSX/NS merger left only two main railroads in the East, some customer service complaints, and a number of litigation cases.

Our analysis has questioned the level of scrutiny when evaluating the alleged efficiencies under the public interest standard, as it seems from the case law that the scope is so wide that a range of multiple factors can be interpreted as public interest benefits. This substantive test, in which a breadth of public interest considerations can be integrated into the assessment makes the test opaque and leaves the protection to competition to the discretion of the enforcers. Therefore, the likelihood of convincing the regulator of benefits generated by a merger, even if they are not merger-specific or do not reach consumers, is very high. Also, it appears that the STB in assessing the merging parties' envisaged efficiency gains, is inclined to overstate them. This tendency, however, has the potential to erode the credibility of the competence of the STB to assess mergers based on a public interest standard. In consequence, it is advisable to consider whether the assignment of merger control assessment powers involving railroads and other regulated carriers to any of the antitrust federal agencies might be more appropriate given their expertise and that the substantive standard they rely on is solely based on an economic assessment of competitive effects.

5.4.1.1.8 Canadian Pacific—Kansas City Southern

This is a fairly complex case, both from a factual and legal perspective, with lots of moving parts and several peculiar twists. Starting with the standard of review: since the merger at hand is a major merger, namely a merger concerning at least two Class I railroads, the relevant statutory provision instructs the STB to approve the transaction if

---

[168] CSX & Norfolk Southern—Control and Operating Leases/Agreements—Conrail, Finance Docket 33388, Decision No 89 (23 July 1998) 50, 250–51.

[169] See Salvatore Massa, 'Surface Freight Transportation: Accounting for Subsidies in a "Free Market"' (2000–2001) 4 Legislation and Public Policy 331, 332. See also VM Bier and others, 'Effects of Deregulation on Safety: Implications Drawn from the Aviation, Rail, and United Kingdom Nuclear Power Industries' NUREG/CR-6735, US Nuclear Regulatory Commission Office of Nuclear Regulatory Research (August 2001) 11. Expressly, it was indicated that 'because there was so much [duplication] of service and routing ... Even though it took two years to develop a safety integration plan, they are still having many problems'.

[170] Avery and Ericson (n 150) 12. See also Pittman (n 150).

[171] Railroad Transportation (1998) ABA Sec Public Utilities Commission & Transp Annual Report 279 (1998).

[172] Avery and Ericson (n 150).

'consistent with the public interest'.[173] However, for major mergers involving KCS, the standard of review is set by the pre-2001 policy statement, meaning that it does not require the transaction to promote competition positively, but merely demands that any harms to competition be outweighed by public benefits.[174] Moreover, the pre-2001 policy puts a special emphasis on operating efficiencies and cost savings.[175]

The deal was bound to create a single-line service connecting Canada and Mexico passing through the Midwest and the South of the US, facilitating the exchange of goods. Despite being—as already noted—a merger between two Class I railroads, it concerned the two smallest ones, and even the merged entity remains smaller than its Class I counterparts. Nonetheless, it will be better positioned to compete with them, and it gathered the support of almost 1,000 third parties, between shippers, smaller railroads, and rail suppliers.[176]

The STB provided a detailed treatment of the public benefits arising from the transaction, whether qualitative (expanded market opportunities for shippers, a reduction in carbon emissions, increased competition, and easier access to energy and supply chains) or quantitative (cost savings, quantified in US$173 million; increased revenue for US$889 million once the transaction has been fully implemented; 1,000 jobs, 800 of them in the US; and an expanded capacity). However, that does not mean that the competition analysis was neglected—quite the opposite. In terms of vertical effects, the parties argued persuasively that the transaction involved a so-called end-to-end merger, meaning that there are no overlaps or duplications—in other words, no harm to competition. A thorough environmental assessment—the final page count amounted to 5,000—was also requested and prepared: among the findings, it was estimated that the merger could shift 64,000 truckloads from road to rail per annum.

Following this exhaustive evaluation, the STB concluded that the merger was indeed 'consistent with the public interest' and that it would not negatively affect competition, nor the quality of transportation services available to the public, nor the interests of workers.[177] It did attach, however, a wide range of conditions, some mostly obvious ('keep getaways open' and safety requirements), some somewhat arbitrary.[178] It is important to point out that some of the remaining Class I railroads tried to hijack the process by requesting 'conditions and other remedies that appear aimed at protecting their own traffic'.[179]

In the context of our analysis, the behaviour of the DOJ in the present case raises some questions. The DOJ submitted to the STB a first set of comments back in 2021, focusing on a few substantive issues—including the perhaps excessive reliance on voting

---

[173] 49 USC § 11324(c).

[174] Canadian Pacific Railway—Control—Kansas City Southern Railway, Finance Docket 36500 (Canadian Pacific—Kansas City Southern) Decision No 35 (15 March 2023) 18.

[175] ibid.

[176] ibid 21.

[177] ibid 172.

[178] ibid 12–13.

[179] ibid 4.

trusts, which affects the independence of the shareholders, typically at a time when the STB's assessment is still underway.[180] In January 2023, however, they submitted a second set of comments, prompted at least in part by an applicant's remark, in order to emphasize that nothing should be read into the DOJ's absence from the STB's hearing in September 2022, certainly not an absence of interest: 'The Antitrust Division's commentary here and in its previous comment should in no way imply that the Antitrust Division lacks concern or support the transaction.'[181] Nevertheless, the tone of the DOJ's new comments appeared very different from the first set. This could be explained in several ways—personnel changes at the DOJ might have plaid a role, or the way the proceedings had developed in those two years might have caught someone at the DOJ off guard. Surprises are not over yet, by the way—just as the manuscript for this book reaches the publisher, railroad competitor Union Pacific announced they are appealing the STB's decision.[182]

The next cluster of cases shows that, despite arriving at the same conclusion, the regulator and the antitrust agency grounded their decisions on contrasting analyses.

5.4.1.2 Convergence in the approach of STB and DOJ but using contradictory analysis

5.4.1.2.1 Averitt Express and others—Pooling Agreement

On 31 December 2007, Averitt Express (Averitt), DATS Trucking Inc (DATS), Lakeville Motor Express (Lakeville Motor), Land Air Express of New England (Land Air), Pitt Ohio Express LLC (Pitt Ohio), Canadian Freightways (CF), and Epic Express (Epic Express) collectively filed a pooling agreement application in accordance with 49 USC 14302.[183] The applicants who transported general commodities across different points in the United States, proposed the creation of a network—Reliance Network—with the intention of coordinating their information technology, administrative functions, sales, marketing, and operations. The parties argued that their agreement would facilitate the movement of freight between the carriers, and customers would be better served and supported.[184] The parties also advocated that they would continue competing with each other, that other carriers could enter into similar agreements, that the intended agreement would allow them to compete with the national carriers, and that by reducing the number of truck movements there would be a reduction in congestion, emissions and fuel consumption.[185]

---

[180] Canadian Pacific Railway—Control—Kansas City Southern Railway Canadian National Railway—Control—Kansas City Southern Railway, Finance Docket 36514, DOJ Comments I (12 April 2021) 3–4 https://www.justice.gov/media/1141206/dl?inline (accessed 15 September 2023).

[181] Canadian Pacific Railway—Control—Kansas City Southern Railway, Finance Docket 36500, DOJ Comments II (24 January 2023) 4 https://www.justice.gov/media/1273856/dl?inline (accessed 15 September 2023).

[182] 'Union Pacific Asks Federal Appellate Court to Overturn CPKC Merger' Competition Policy International (8 May 2023) https://www.competitionpolicyinternational.com/union-pacific-asks-federal-appellate-court-to-overturn-cpkc-merger.

[183] Averitt Express Inc, STB Docket No MC-F-21023, 2008 WL 258338 (Surface Transp Bd (31 January 2008).

[184] ibid.

[185] ibid.

The board approved the agreement after finding that the transaction was not of great significance for the railroad market, as it involved a small number of regional motor carriers and a small movement of shipments. Also, competition would not be restrained given the existence of a large number of carriers operating in the areas served by the applicants, and there was a possibility for other carriers to engage in similar network agreements. In terms of rates, STB was satisfied that the rates would be established independently between the originating carrier and the customers, and that the revenues would be divided between the participants, using an agreed formula. The agreement was authorized for a term of five years, renewable for one-year periods in the absence of dissent from a participating member.[186]

Following authorization from the STB, the members of the joint venture requested clearance from the DOJ. The reason for this request rested on the fact that the immunity granted by the STB would last five years with the possibility of a renewal, while the clearance of the DOJ would not be time-limited unless explicitly cancelled.[187] The DOJ assessment affords us the opportunity to examine the DOJ's review of the agreement and to contrast it with that of the STB. As indicated earlier, the representatives of the joint venture sent a written request to the DOJ asking authorization under the review procedure 28 CFR § 50.6, which the federal agency responded through a letter nine months after. The DOJ noted that the applicants had claimed that some aspects of the pooling agreement such as services, traffic, and revenues, had received authorization from STB, and explained that further activities beyond those already approved by the STB were required to make the collaboration successful. As a result, they created a Supplemental Agreement that provided for geographic limitations on the participants' operations and for nationwide or multi-regional pricing.[188]

In relation to the collaborative pricing provision, the applicants indicated that for the Reliance Network to be able to compete effectively with nationwide less-than-truckload (LTL)[189] carriers, it was necessary for the members to be entitled to communicate with each other in cases where shipments originated from more than one operating region so as to determine acceptable pricing levels. That communication would be restricted only to those events so price shipments originating and ending within the same region would be determined independently by the respective carrier.[190] Regarding the geographic limitations on participants' operations, the supplemental agreement postulated that if a member carrier wanted to operate outside its functional region, it had to obtain consent from the other members of the alliance. The justification for this restriction was that the nationwide service through the Reliance Network was only possible if

---

[186] ibid.

[187] Cartensen (n 85) 1085.

[188] Letter from Molly S Boast, Acting Assistant Attorney General, US Department of Justice, to James R Weiss (8 September 2009) https://www.justice.gov/sites/default/files/atr/legacy/2009/09/08/249806.pdf (accessed 18 November 2022).

[189] Less-than-truckload (LTL) 'allows multiple shippers to share space on the same truck'. This option is cost-efficient as companies pay only for their portion of trailer space. See CH Robinson, --, 'Truckload vs. Less than Truckload: What's the Difference?' *FreightQuote* https://www.freightquote.com/blog/less-than-truckload-vs-truckload-freight-whats-the-difference/ (accessed 28 November 2022).

[190] Boast (n 188).

182   PUBLIC INTEREST ASSESSMENT AND THE STB

each member were confident that they would not be competing against their network partners in their own historically serviced area.[191]

Continuing with the justifications for the geographic restraints, the applicants argued that together they had far less than 20 per cent of the total domestic motor carrier LTL shipments, that each carrier held fewer than 8 per cent of the shipments within its own region, and that the combined market share of the joint venture would be less than 20 per cent in each of the separate geographic areas in which the applicants operated. Additionally, the applicants maintained that the agreement would achieve many procompetitive efficiencies, which could only be obtained through the coordination of their information technology, operations, sales and marketing efforts, and administration, and by sharing key information about customers' lists and other confidential information.[192] The DOJ accepted the arguments offered by the applicants, and stated that the supplemental agreement was necessary and unlikely to harm competition, as the members of the joint venture were not competitors within their respective regions and their market shares were not significant. Nonetheless, DOJ warned that caution was needed to prevent collaborative rate-setting between members that might become future competitors and reserved the right to start enforcement action if required.[193]

This case offers a vital insight into how inefficient this dual regulatory process is. Our analysis of both STB and DOJ assessments illustrates that the arguments presented before the two agencies were quite similar, considering that the supplemental agreement filed before the DOJ did not cover aspects beyond the scope of STB's authorization. Hence, it is likely that the only or main motivation behind filing the clearance requests before the DOJ was to obtain unlimited time immunity. One needs to bear in mind that the immunity granted by the STB lasts five years with a renewal whereas that of the DOJ does not have a time limit. Moreover, given the wide scope of the immunity granted in terms of time limit, a more in-depth analysis of the applicants' claims should be required. This is illustrated by the fact that in order to obtain the STB's approval, the carriers gave assurance that they would continue competing against each other, an argument that was accepted by STB, while in order to obtain the DOJ's clearance the carriers pledged that they would not compete with their network partners.[194]

5.4.1.2.2 *Canadian Pacific—Norfolk Southern*

In spring 2016, Canadian Pacific Railway Limited (Canadian Pacific) made public its intention to acquire Norfolk Southern Railway Company (Norfolk Southern), and in connection with this transaction, on 2 March 2016, Canadian Pacific filed a petition for

---

[191] ibid.
[192] ibid.
[193] ibid.
[194] Regarding the geographic limitations on participants' operations, the supplemental agreement postulated that if a member carrier wanted to operate outside its functional region, it had to obtain consent from the other members of the alliance. The justification for this restriction was that the nationwide service through the Reliance Network was only possible if each member was confident that they would not be competing against their network partners in their own historically serviced area.

a declaratory order from STB, requesting the use of a voting trust pending STB's review of the transaction.[195] Voting trust measures have traditionally been used as strategies to preserve the independence of acquiring and target firms during the ongoing assessment of a transaction before the ICC and STB.[196] On 8 April 2016, the DOJ urged the STB to deny the voting trust, claiming that it threatened to modify the competitive dynamics between the two railroads in a way that could not be rectified if the STB rejected the merger.[197]

The DOJ explained that the voting trust would align the business strategies of the companies, adding that because Canadian Pacific proposed to put itself into the trust and to put the current Chief Executive of Canadian Pacific in control of Norfolk Southern, it would facilitate the implementation of the desired changes of the potential acquirer, which the antitrust agency considered as contrary to public interest. It added that Norfolk Southern had developed independent plans to increase efficiency by cutting costs that might be prevented once Canadian Pacific took control during the ongoing merger review. At the same time, the DOJ argued that this pre-merger tactic could irreversibly modify the relationship between Norfolk Southern and its customers and employees, as in their eyes the existence of Norfolk Southern would be blurred. It also highlighted that once Canadian Pacific accessed information about customers, contracts, pricing, and long-term and short-term plans, it would use this to its advantage to the detriment of its competitors. It underlined that, if eventually the merger were to be denied, the strategic decisions of the companies would already have been implemented to some degree, without the possibility of divestments addressing the harm on competition. Finally, it noted the existence of other mechanisms capable of ensuring the self-governance of the firms intended to be acquired without curtailing competition such as the negotiation of break-up fees, divestiture, and material adverse change clauses.[198]

On 11 April 2016, Canadian Pacific withdrew its petition, indicating that 'its Board of Directors voted unanimously to cease efforts to pursue discussions with Norfolk Southern regarding a business combination'.[199] This case exemplifies how the strong opposition from the DOJ influenced the decision of the applicants to terminate the underlying merger agreement, as the following statement of the Chief Executive of Canadian Pacific confirms: '[W]ith no clear path to a friendly merger at this time, we will turn all of our focus and energy to serving our customers and creating long term value for C.P. shareholders.'[200]

---

[195] Canadian Pacific Railway—Petition for Expedited Declaratory Order, Finance Docket No 36004, Decision 13 April 2016.

[196] Russell Pittman, 'The Strange Career of Independent Voting Trusts in U.S. Rail Mergers' (2017) 13(1) Journal of Competition Law & Economics 89.

[197] Canadian Pacific (n 195) Reply of the DOJ (8 April 2016).

[198] ibid.

[199] ibid.

[200] Leslie Picker, 'Canadian Pacific Ends Bid for Norfolk Southern' The New York Times (11 April 2016) https://www.nytimes.com/2016/04/12/business/dealbook/canadian-pacific-ends-bid-for-norfolk-southern.html (accessed 12 November 2022).

184   PUBLIC INTEREST ASSESSMENT AND THE STB

In order to present a wide spectrum of STB and DOJ assessment approaches on the same transactions, we discuss next one of the relatively few cases where the regulator and the antitrust authority adopted the same analysis and reached the same outcome. Analysing this convergence between the STB and the DOJ can illustrate how the two agencies can follow a homogenous approach in some exceptional cases.

5.4.1.2.3 Southern Pacific—Santa Fe

In September 1983, the Atchison, Topeka, and Santa Fe Railway (Santa Fe) and Southern Pacific Transportation Company (Southern Pacific) proposed to merge, which would have created the third largest railroad in the western US.[201] However, the ICC rejected the envisaged merger by a vote of four to one, a decision at odds with 'a 20-year history of approving major railroad mergers'.[202] The concerns were grounded on whether the public benefits were outweighed by 'adverse effects so great they cannot be remedied, thus requiring denial'.[203] These adverse effects were related to the reduction in competition in some areas of the West and Southwest of the country. These concerns were shared by the DOJ, which also announced its opposition to the merger.[204] The main concern of the DOJ was that the merging parties were the only two remaining systems in the southwest US, and they were two out of the three rail carriers in California and the Midwest,[205] so this transaction would have created dominance on a heavy traffic route.

In this case, Professor J. Baumol rendered testimony before the ICC asserting that the rail industry itself was a contestable market. For him, other modes of transportation like trucks were close competitors of railways, capable of restraining the market power of the latter. He added that 'the availability of close competitive option, particularly if that role is played by contestable barges or trucks, is all that is needed for tight constraint of pricing by the merged railroad, and for effective preclusion of all exercise of market power'.[206] In his view, given the supposedly contestable nature of the railways, it was plausible to expect the realization of pricing and operational efficiencies by the end-to-end mergers.[207] Baumol's theory was rejected by the ICC. As explained by Shepherd, trucks and railroads have different cost profiles that might not satisfy the needs of the customer.

---

[201] Russell W Pittman, 'The Santa Fe/Southern Pacific Merger Proposal' (1990) 39 The Journal of Industrial Economics 25.

[202] Reginald Stuart, 'ICC Bars Santa Fe Merger' The New York Times (25 July 1986) https://www.nytimes.com/1986/07/25/business/icc-bars-santa-fe-merger.html (accessed 15 November 2022).

[203] Sallie Gaines, 'ICC Rejects Rail Merger' Chicago Tribune (25 July 1986) https://www.chicagotribune.com/news/ct-xpm-1986-07-25-8602230520-story.html (accessed 15 November 2022).

[204] Pittman (n 196).

[205] The two roads provided the only rail service along the 'southern corridor' between southern California, through Arizona and New Mexico, to Texas and the Gulf ports., and they were two of only three rail carriers between California and the Midwest. See Pittman (n 196) 26.

[206] Verified Statement of William J Baumol before the Interstate Commerce Commission, Finance Docket No 30,400, Southern Pacific Transportation Company; Merger: The Atchison, Topeka, and Santa Fe Railway Company and Southern Pacific Transportation Company 20–21 (March 1984).

[207] An 'End-to-end' merger involves 'two or more carriers that serve separate regions and connect with each other at relatively few points'. See Scott M Dennis, 'Economic Analysis of an End-to-End Railroad Merger' (1988) 1177 Transportation Research Record 6 https://onlinepubs.trb.org/Onlinepubs/trr/1988/1177/1177-002.pdf (accessed 28 September 2022). For interesting comments on Baumol's theory see William B Tye, 'Some Subtle Pricing Issues in Railroad Regulation: Comment" (1984) 11(2–3) International Journal of Transport Economics 207.

They also have different aspects that affect customer choice such as speed, length of haul, time, type of products, and volume of shipments, which make contestability ineffective.[208] This position was advocated by the ICC in the Coal Rate Guidelines,[209] in which it stated that: '[T]he railroad industry is recognized to have barriers to entry and exit and thus is not considered contestable for captive traffic.'[210]

One thing that is striking about this merger is that the ICC had approved similar transactions in the past, one of which led to the creation of the single rail system of the Burlington-Northern[211] in the northwest, and another one led to the United Pacific[212] across the middle of the west, so this denial was unusual. According to some commentators, the ICC was 'desperate to retain its power by proving to Congress that it could regulate even-handedly, and decided the Santa Fe was not to be'.[213] In particular, some authors have indicated that the ICC sought to shift from a permissive policy approach where mergers were approved as a matter of usual practice to one that was tougher.[214] As we discussed above, the ICC was terminated in 1995, thus, as this merger was filed in 1983, at a time when the accuracy of and the approach of the ICC in transactions involving railroads and other regulated carriers was scrutinized by Congress, such a move comes as little surprise. Indeed, in an exceptional manner the ICC found that the public interest benefits that justified the approval of so many transactions in the past decades, in this case were insufficient to offset the anti-competitive effects. Additionally, the reduction in competition became an important consideration that until then the ICC had effectively relegated to a mere secondary concern, incapable of tramping the public interest considerations. Another important feature to be highlighted is the fact that the parties filed the proposal on 22 November 1983, and a decision was issued three years later, on 10 October 1986, which denotes how inefficient the process was.[215]

In order to complete the detailed assessment of the STB's and the DOJ's enforcement approach we discuss below a transaction in which the DOJ albeit acting as a decision-maker, unsuccessfully tried to oppose the transaction.

5.4.1.2.4 Norfolk Southern—Conrail

In 1970, after Penn-Central filed for bankruptcy in the context of an adversely affected financial industry, characterized by excess capacity and high rail rates, Congress responded by passing the Emergency Rail Services Act 1970, which generated US$125 million dollars in loan guarantees.[216] The increasing number of bankruptcies

---

[208] William G Shepherd, 'Potential Competition Versus Actual Competition' (1990) 42 Administrative Law Review 5, 32.

[209] The Coal Rate Guidelines were developed by the STB to evaluate the reasonableness of the Stand-Alone Cost rates charged by railroads. See Federal Register vol 66, no 48 (12 March 2001).

[210] Coal Rate Guidelines, Nationwide, 1 ICC 2d 520 (1985).

[211] 396 US 491 (1970).

[212] UP—SP (n 73).

[213] Lawrence H Kaufman, *A Ghost of Mergers Past at the STB* (JOC.COM 2000) https://www.joc.com/ghost-mergers-past-stb_20000314.html (accessed 15 November 2022).

[214] Tenpao Lee, C Philip Baumel, and Patricia Harris, 'Market Structure, Conduct and Performance of the Class I Railroad Industry, 1971–1984' (1987) 26 Transportation Journal 54.

[215] https://www.justice.gov/archive/atr/public/testimony/0056.pdf (accessed 21 November 2022).

[216] Dempsey (n 64) 565; Perreault and Fleischman (n 125) 430.

186   PUBLIC INTEREST ASSESSMENT AND THE STB

triggered the enactment of the Regional Rail Reorganization Act of 1973 (3R Act), providing for more federal subsidies and loan guarantees, and the creation of the Consolidated Railroad Corporation (Conrail). The latter resulted from merging the majority of Penn Central and major sections of the lines of Central New Jersey, Lehigh Valley, Lehigh & Hudson, Pennsylvania-Reading Seashore, and Ann Arbor Railroads with small portions of the Reading and Erie-Lacka-wanna Railroads.[217]

After the creation of Conrail, the government invested around US$7 billion until finally, in 1981, it reached profitability, moving from US$39.2 million in 1981 to US$313 million in 1983.[218] The combination of the improved performance of Conrail and Reagan's ideology of privatizing state owned companies, resulted in its sale. Under the Northeast Rail Service Act (NERSA) reforms took place to make the purchase of Conrail more appealing,[219] and, in June 1984, following a Department of Transport purchase invitation, Norfolk Southern made a bid of US$1 billion, which was increased a few months later to US$1.2 billion, and was filed with the DOJ for antitrust assessment.[220] Considering that 85 per cent of Conrail's stock was held by the government, approval from Congress was required as well. Another important feature was that NERSA established that if Conrail were fragmentedly sold, DOJ would act as commentator, but it did not refer to what the involvement of the DOJ would be if the company was sold as a whole. Unexpectedly, Conrail was sold as a whole and as a result, the DOJ did not just act as a commentator -as is the case with every transaction that proceeds before the ICC—but as a decision-maker pursuant to the Clayton Act.[221] Accordingly, as part of a formal notification and assessment process before the DOJ, a large amount of information was requested from Norfolk Southern between 1984 and early 1985 and the DOJ concluded that competition would be adversely affected in more than one hundred markets in thirty-nine counties and twenty-one states, and that there would be enhanced concentration, leading to market power.[222]

Seeking to mitigate its concerns, the DOJ informed the DOT that approval would be given subject to sufficient divestitures allowing the enhancement of competition in certain markets and the connection of some of them with the main eastern and western intersection points.[223] While a tense negotiation process took place between

---

[217] See 45 USC §§ 701–748 (1974). See also Dempsey (n 64) 565; Perreault and Fleischman (n 125) 429.

[218] See 45 USC §§ 701–748 (1974). See also Dempsey (n 64) 565.

[219] 45 USC §§ 761–767c, §§ 1101–1116. It (1) allowed Conrail to abandon unprofitable lines of track; (2) created a government-fund severance program to enable Conrail to perpetually reduce the size of its labour force; (3) spared Conrail from liability for state taxes; (4) moved commuter service to local and regional authorities; (5) abolished full crew laws; (6) eliminated Conrail's liability for wage guarantees; and (7) permitted cash settlements to idle employees in exchange for compensation to idle employees. *See* James S Ang and Carol Boyer, 'Finance and Politics: Special Interest Group Influence during the Nationalization and Privatization of Conrail' Department of Finance College of Business Florida State University (2000), DOI: 10.2139/ssrn.251413 https://www.researchgate.net/publication/228253386_Finance_and   _Politics_Special_Interest_Group_Influence_during_the_Nationalization_and_Privatization_of_Conrail#read (accessed 15 November 2022). Robert E Gallamore and John R Meyer, *The Brief, Mainly Happy Life of Conrail, 1976–1999 in American Railroads* (Harvard UP 2014) 210.

[220] Perreault and Fleischman (n 125) 434–35 (1985–1986).

[221] ibid 435.

[222] Dempsey (n 64) 566; See also Letter from J Paul McGrath to Elizabeth H Dole (29 January 1985).

[223] ibid.

the applicant and the DOJ in relation to the conditions, the Senate approved the US$1.2 billion offer but the House eschewed it, forcing Norfolk Southern to increase the bid to US$1.9 billion, which later, in August 1986, it withdrew.[224] Commentators have indicated that the DOJ considered this case as a good opportunity to stress its views on competitive dynamics in the railroad market, something that it had unsuccessfully attempted to do before Congress over previous years, the courts and the ICC. However, it has been highlighted that the DOJ underestimated the existence of an embedded national policy that supports consolidation of rail carriers as a key means to preserve the rail transportation system.[225] On 26 March 1987, Conrail became a privatized company.[226]

5.4.1.2.5 CSX—Pan Am Railway

The recent decision in the case of CSX—Pan Am provides an example which clearly illustrates how the different views held by the STB and the DOJ, in this instance regarding the effectiveness of behavioural and structural remedies, can pan out and point to quite different outcomes, even when the tension between the two institutions doesn't concern the standard of review, properly understood. Indeed, what's especially interesting about this analysis is the fact that, while the STB eventually did look at public interest criteria, it did so for the sake of comprehensiveness, almost in a formulaic way, having already determined that this merger should be authorized based on competition considerations alone.

On 1 July 2021—having already seen their applications rejected twice: once for classifying the transaction as 'minor', and once for failing to provide the required amount of information—CSX Corporation and CSX Transportation (collectively CSX) and Pan Am Railways (Pan Am) submitted an amended application to the STB, seeking approval for CSX to acquire Pan Am, as well as for several related transactions.[227] The applicants maintained that, by integrating an 'under-resourced' regional railroad within the CSX network, the deal would be beneficial to shippers and local consumers alike. Furthermore, CSX had taken steps and entered negotiations with third parties to prevent the risk of competitive harm. For instance, at the time of the merger, CSX and Pan Am ran two parallel lines between Albany and Boston; the Pan Am line was owned by a joint venture with Norfolk Southern Railway (NSR) and operated by a Pan Am subsidiary. It follows that, after the merger and in the absence of specific remedies, CSX would end up operating this second line too and controlling its infrastructure, albeit not by itself. Under the NSR Settlement Agreement, however, NSR could force CSX to sell its

---

[224] ibid 566–67.

[225] Perreault and Fleischman (n 125) 439.

[226] James Sterngold, '85% U.S. Stake in Conrail Sold for $1.6 Billion' *New York Times* (27 March 1987) https://www.nytimes.com/1987/03/27/business/85-us-stake-in-conrail-sold-for-1.6-billion.html (accessed 15 November 2022).

[227] CSX—Control and Merger—Pan Am Railway, Financial Docket 36472 (CSX—Pan Am) Decision No 9 (14 April 2022).

188 PUBLIC INTEREST ASSESSMENT AND THE STB

shares for a pre-determined price at any point over the following seven years, either to itself or to a different party.

The DOJ took issue with this commitment and with the other behavioural remedies—the 'complicated contractual arrangements'—offered by the parties, not just because they appeared inadequate to address the worsened competitive conditions produced by the acquisition itself, but because they would cause, according to the agency's assessment, issues of their own. On the one hand, as a part owner, CSX might be able to distort the joint venture's business decisions, including investment choices, regardless of its formal commitment to recuse itself from the relevant discussions.[228] On the other hand, the notion that CSX could opportunistically choose to prevent the joint venture from investing in its lines seems to overlook the fact that even prior to the merger Pan Am subsidiaries were already lagging behind on this front.[229]

This was a key argument leading the STB to determine that the transaction would not bring about a substantial lessening of competition, once the commitments had been taken into account.[230] On this point, the disagreement between the STB and the DOJ could not be more relevant and meaningful. The DOJ put forward the divestiture option, based on the assumption that 'structural remedies tend to be cleaner, more efficient, more durable, and easier to enforce, and they reduce the likelihood of ongoing entanglement that can further harm competition'.[231] The STB, however, did not accept the conclusion that 'divestiture would provide a superior alternative to both the more narrowly tailored commitments made by CSX and the other railroads here, which are targeted to address specific competitive concerns, and the Board's continued oversight'.[232]

Having declared that the merger was not going to produce a substantial lessening of competition, the STB was not legally required to assess whether the anti-competitive effects of the transaction could be outweighed by public interest consideration; however, it did examine the matter nonetheless,[233] and it identified a number of possible benefits: beyond the already mentioned increased ability to finance maintenance and new capital investment, additional marketing opportunities for shippers, environmental benefits, and the capacity to offer 'more competitive routings for propane ... a vital commodity to the New England region' were all mentioned.[234]

5.5 Some Implications of the Analysis

The analysis of the above-mentioned seminal cases, which were decided in different periods of time and by different regulators (ICC/STB), leads to some interesting conclusions. Undoubtedly, the usual competition analysis that is seen in merger enforcement

---

[228] ibid 11.
[229] ibid 14.
[230] ibid 20.
[231] STB, Docket No FD 36472 (n 227) DOJ Comments 3.
[232] ibid 20.
[233] ibid 21.
[234] ibid 22.

5.5 SOME IMPLICATIONS OF THE ANALYSIS   189

in both unregulated and regulated markets is absent in the railroad sector, a trend that has been prevalent in the last sixty years. Thus, aspects such as market power, dominance, and the reduction or elimination of competition, which in other sectors would impede the integration of undertakings, do not have the same determinative relevance in the rail sector. For instance, Penn Central,[235] Seaboard—Atlantic,[236] the Northern Lines,[237] UP—Missouri & Western,[238] and the UP—SP[239] merger cases were characterized by leading to integrated strong competitors with significant market positions.

In all of these cases, DOJ showed concern in relation to the harm of the transactions on competition in the markets and, in some cases, strong opposition, which was discounted by the ICC/STB, which argued that competition would not be substantially affected, that intramodal competition was insignificant in the light of other modes of transportation (*Seaboard—Atlantic*),[240] and that there was no evidence of previous anti-competitive investigations that could lead to inferring that the merging parties would behave unlawfully again (*UP—SP*).[241]

Another common theme was the number and scope of benefits that ICC/STB accepted in these transactions, in particular the economic savings (Northern Lines[242] and UP—Missouri & Western[243]), which, if seen as beneficial for the merging parties, were instinctively presumed to be beneficial for the customers as well. Similarly, the analysis has identified some additional recurrent benefits accepted by ICC/STB, such as better use of equipment, consolidation of yards (UP—SP[244]), a reduction of excess capacity (Peter Pan—Greyhound,[245] Northern Lines[246]) and greater financial stability (Peter Pan/Greyhound). While all these benefits have been characterized by various commentators, third parties and the DOJ as non-merger specific, they were considered to be merger-specific by the ICC/STB and the courts on appeal. Moreover, the ICC/STB considered that those benefits were enough to counterbalance the anti-competitive effects created by the respective mergers, which in the view of the ICC/STB were often overstated by the antitrust agency. Unsurprisingly, the public interest has been described as a vague term used by the ICC to allow the integration of prosperous, competing businesses.

Another important feature that has also been illustrated following the examination of the above cases is that the approach used in the *McLean Trucking* case has repeatedly been used by the ICC to emphasize that it is not obliged to undertake a detailed application of the antitrust laws in transactions (as was shown in Penn Central,[247] Seaboard/

---

[235] 389 US 486 (1968).
[236] Seaboard—Atlantic (n 113) 60.
[237] 396 US 491 (1970).
[238] UP—Missouri & Western (n 131).
[239] UP—SP (n 73).
[240] Seaborn—Atlantic (n 113) 60.
[241] UP—SP (n 73).
[242] 396 US 491 (1970).
[243] UP—Missouri & Western (n 131).
[244] UP—SP (n 73).
[245] STB, Docket No MC-F-20908 (21 April 1998).
[246] 396 US 491 (1970).
[247] 389 US 486 (1968).

190   PUBLIC INTEREST ASSESSMENT AND THE STB

Atlantic,[248] Northern Lines,[249] and UP/Missouri/Western[250]). In addition to fully embracing this approach, the courts have also recognized that the regulator deserves extensive deference, having clearly stated that 'we owe the Commission substantial deference in reviewing its decisions', as indeed was the case in Penn Central, Northern Lines, and UP/Missouri/Western.[251] Furthermore, the analysis of the cases has revealed a steady trend of the regulator in relation to the imposition of the same type of conditions, which in most cases have consisted of open route protection for other carriers and job retention (as was shown in Penn Central,[252] Seaboard/Atlantic,[253] Northern Lines,[254] and UP/Missouri/Western[255]).

Although in most of the transactions that were analysed herein, the ICC/STB has not accepted the opposition shown by the DOJ in its decision-making, the ICC has exceptionally adopted DOJ's concerns and prohibited the Southern Pacific/Santa Fe merger[256]—after a long streak of approving railroad transactions—by rejecting the contestability test previously used to justify the approval of Seaboard/Atlantic.[257] A similar case was Canadian Pacific/Norfolk Southern,[258] where, after strong opposition from DOJ, the applicants withdrew the use of the voting trust petition, an approach that was mirrored in Norfolk Southern/Conrail,[259] in which the former withdrew the bid to acquire the latter. In both cases, it is uncertain whether in the absence of the withdrawal of the applications, ICC/STB would have denied the petitions and thus prohibit the transactions based on the concerns expressed by the DOJ. What remains clear is a need to shift the long-standing public policy approach orientated to the consolidation in the railroad sector based on argumentation that the railroad sector competes with other modes of transportation. This consolidation approach that has been promoted in Congress and is well safeguarded by the ICC/STB and the courts, has resulted in a sector where the application of the antitrust laws in assessing transactions is inadequate and ineffective.

5.6 Concluding Remarks

This chapter has shown the immense consolidation drive of the North American railway sector, with a particular reduction in the number of Class I railroads. The DOJ

---

[248] Seaborn—Atlantic (n 113).
[249] 396 US 491 (1970).
[250] UP—Missouri &Western (n 131).
[251] ibid; *McLean Trucking Co v United States* 321 US 67 (1944); *Minneapolis & St Louis Ry v United States* 361 US 173 (1959).
[252] 389 US 486 (1968).
[253] Seaborn/Atlantic (n 113).
[254] 396 US 491 (1970).
[255] UP—Missouri & Western (n 131).
[256] Interstate Commerce Commission, Finance Docket No 30,400 (March 1984).
[257] Seaborn—Atlantic (n 113).
[258] STB Canadian Pacific (n 193).
[259] Perreault and Fleischman (n 125) 434–35.

has unsuccessfully raised serious competition related concerns about the transactions analysed herein, but in spite of these, ICC/STB have approved most of them. This phenomenon corresponds to a philosophy that has been nurtured by Congress[260] and implemented by the ICC and the STB, consisting of the consolidation of rail systems. Nonetheless, the approach to assessing public policy considerations in the rail sector has signified that the competition principles are discounted when reviewing rail mergers at the expense of a prevailing 'public interest' standard that is much wider than the respective competition standard (substantial lessening of competition).

We advocate a merger review that balances public interest considerations and the promotion of competition. Perhaps it would be advisable to grant the authority for approval of transactions to the DOJ as well (based on a competition standard), given its expertise in competition and the lack of any incentives in protecting the economic interest of the members of this industry. If this reform is unattainable, the current enforcement regime should give more weight to the concerns of the DOJ and immunity should be restricted to those cases that do not raise any competition harm after careful assessment. Such a shift offers one advantage: The limited intervention of the ICC and the STB to block transactions while completely ignoring the risks of consolidation on the competitive dynamics in the market. In this chapter, we have confirmed that this failure is largely driven by the ICC/STB's mistaken perspective that two competitors are adequate to ensure a competitive market and that consolidation can be beneficial for the railroad sector. One final remark: the level of deference that courts concede to the ICC/STB should be revisited and a strict judicial review scrutiny should take place instead.

---

[260] The Transportation Act of 1920, 41 Stat 456 (1920), provides that 'the ICC had to develop a master plan for consolidation of all railroads into a "limited number of systems", in which "competition shall be preserved as fully as possible and wherever practicable the existing routes and channels for trade and commerce shall be maintained". Thus, railroads had to conform with the consolidation plan in proposing any future unifications.

6

Public Interest Assessment and the Department of Transportation (DOT)

6.1 The Department of Transportation (DOT)

The Department of Transportation (DOT) has the authority to promote competition in the airline industry. This industry has become heavily consolidated in the last few decades. The statistics illustrate this point particularly well. In 1978, a deregulation process took place in the United States when, prior to that, there were more than 400 airlines operating across the country.[1] Currently, there are four airlines—Southwest, Delta, American, and United—controlling nearly 70 per cent of the domestic market.[2] To emphasize this point, after looking at some segmented markets, it has been found that a single airline controls the market in 40 of the 100 largest airports,[3] and one or two airlines control the majority of seats in 93 of the top 100 airports.[4]

It has been argued that the approval of a significant number of M&As has driven this consolidation process.[5] As a result, in July 2021, President Biden issued an executive order directing the DOT to address consumer protection issues, in particular, 'ensuring that consumers are not exposed or subject to advertising, marketing, pricing, and charging of ancillary fees that may constitute an unfair or deceptive practice, or an unfair method of competition'.[6] Most important, the DOT was directed to further define 'unfair' and 'deceptive' practices and to coordinate with the Department of Justice to ensure competition in air transportation.[7] Being one of the most affected industries by the

---

[1] Bill Hethcock, 'How Mergers Have Driven Consolidation of the Airline Industry' *Dallas Business Journal* (6 April 2017) https://www.bizjournals.com/dallas/news/2017/04/06/how-mergers-have-driven-consolidation-of-the.html (accessed 12 October 2022).

[2] ibid; see also Niraj Chokshi, 'Frontier and Spirit Airlines Plan to Merger' *The New York Times* (7 February 2022) https://www.nytimes.com/2022/02/07/business/frontier-spirit-airlines-merger.html (accessed 12 October 2022).

[3] David Koenig and Scott Mayerowitz, 'U.S. Airports Increasingly Dominated by 1 or 2 Carriers' *USA Today* (15 July 2015) https://eu.usatoday.com/story/todayinthesky/2015/07/15/us-airports-increasingly-dominated-by-1-or-2-carriers/30152927/ (accessed 12 October 2022).

[4] ibid.

[5] See Lucile S Keyes, 'The Regulation of Airline Mergers by the Department of Transportation' (1988) 53 Journal of Air Law and Commerce 737, 750; Hethcock (n 1); Kevin Kinder, 'Friendly Skies or Turbulent Skies: An Evaluation of the U.S. Airline Industry and Antitrust Concerns' (2018) 91 Southern California Law Review 943.

[6] The White House, 'Executive Order on Promoting Competition in the American Economy' (9 July 2021) https://www.whitehouse.gov/briefing-room/presidential-actions/2021/07/09/executive-order-on-promoting-competition-in-the-american-economy/ (accessed 12 October 2022).

[7] ibid.

194 PUBLIC INTEREST ASSESSMENT AND THE DOT

Covid-19 pandemic but also one that has received immense financial support from the US government in the tune of US$50 billion,[8] the Biden administration considered it is high time for the DOT to address some of the competition and consumer issues the air industry faces.

The chapter will start with a discussion of the composition of the DOT and the relevant regulatory framework before discussing some of the seminal case law that will show the approach the DOT takes in applying its assessment test and how this approach compares with the one the DOJ takes pursuant to its competition standard. The chapter will also discuss some implications that arise from assessing the role and practice of the regulator and how that compares and contrasts with the competition authority.

6.1.1 Composition and Legislation

The DOT was established in 1966,[9] and its first official day of operation was 1 April 1967.[10] The DOT is responsible for keeping the public travel safe, increase their mobility, and ensure that the transportation system conduce to economic growth.[11] Likewise, the DOT performs an advisory[12] role to the DOJ in regard to airline mergers and acquisitions[13] and enjoys exclusive jurisdiction to approve foreign air traffic agreements.[14] The head of the Department is the Secretary, who is appointed by the President, with the advice and consent of the Senate.[15] Among the main responsibilities of the Office of the Secretary (OST) is the negotiation and implementation of international transportation agreements and the declaration of the fitness of the US airlines.[16] The DOT operates through different bureaus, one of which is the Federal Aviation Administration (FAA), whose main obligation is to supervise the safety of civil aviation.[17] Other bureaus include, the National Highway Traffic Safety Administration (NHTSA), the Office of Inspector General (OIG), the Federal Highway Administration (FHWA), the Pipeline and Hazardous Materials Safety Administration (PHMSA), the Federal Motor Carrier Safety Administration (FMCSA), the Federal Railroad Administration (FRA), the Great Lakes St. Lawrence Seaway Development Corporation (GLS), the Federal Transit Administration (FTA), and the Maritime Administration (MARAD).[18]

---

[8] Kate Gibson, 'Airlines Still Owe Travellers Billions in Refunds for Flights Cancelled in 2020' CBS News (2 December 2021) https://www.cbsnews.com/news/airlines-owe-billions-refunds-cancelled-flights-2020/ (accessed 12 October 2022).

[9] Pub L No 89-670 (15 October 1966) s 3(a).

[10] DOT, 'About DOT' https://www.transportation.gov/about (accessed 13 November 2022).

[11] DOT, 'U.S. Department of Transportation Administrations' https://www.transportation.gov/administrations (accessed 4 October 2022).

[12] See 15 USC 21 and 15 USC 18.

[13] Section 7 of the Clayton Act, 15 USC 18, prohibits mergers and stock acquisitions whose effect 'may be substantially to lessen competition, or to tend to create a monopoly' in a relevant market.

[14] International Air Transportation Act of 1979, Pub L No 96-192, 94 Stat 35 (1980).

[15] Pub L No 89-670 (n 9) s 3(a).

[16] DOT, 'U.S. Department of Transportation Administrations' https://www.transportation.gov/administrations (accessed 4 October 2022).

[17] ibid.

[18] ibid.

6.1 THE DEPARTMENT OF TRANSPORTATION (DOT)   195

In relation to its role in dealing with airline mergers, it is important to highlight that even if the DOT merely advises the DOJ, it has a de facto merger-blocking power.[19] This is because under 49 U.S.C. 41102, the DOT must issue a certificate allowing airlines to operate at a domestic and international level.[20] Also, it approves any transfer of operating certificates to another carrier. As we will see later, the DOT grants authorization when the transfer of a certificate is 'consistent with the public interest'.[21] Interestingly, the authorization takes place after the Secretary has discussed the effects of the transfer on 'competition in the domestic airline industry',[22] among other things. Similarly, the airlines can be exempted from these conditions if their request align with the public interest.[23] Moreover, their certifications can be suspended or revoked if the DOT determines that it is 'in the public interest to do so'.[24]

The Civil Aeronautics Act of 1938[25] gave authority to the Civil Aeronautics Board (CAB)[26] to approve mergers or acquisitions that were consistent with the public interest and unlikely to create a monopoly position that would restrain competition.[27] Although competition was one factor that the Board took into account under the public interest standard, this factor did not receive any distinctive weight.[28] At this point, the industry was highly regulated by the CAB, which decided on routes, frequencies and fares.[29] Subsequently, the Airline Deregulation Act of 1978[30] introduced two antitrust tests and retained the public interest.[31]

The first antitrust test, known as the 'Sherman Act' test,[32] prohibited any transaction that may result in a monopoly in the air transportation industry in any region of the United States.[33] The second, the 'Clayton Act' test,[34] proscribed any transaction, '[t]he effect of which in any region of the United States may be substantially to lessen competition, or to tend to create a monopoly, or which in any other manner would be in restraint of trade, unless the Board finds that the anti-competitive effects of the proposed transaction are out-weighed in the public interest by the probable effect of the transaction in meeting significant transportation conveniences and needs of the public, and unless it finds that such significant transportation conveniences and needs may

---

[19] 49 USC 41105; DOT, 'How to Become a Certified Air Carrier' (September 2012) 28 https://www.transportation.gov/sites/dot.dev/files/docs/Certificated_Packet_2012_final.pdf (accessed 4 October 2022).

[20] 49 USC 41102.

[21] 49 USC 41105(a).

[22] 49 USC 41105(b)(2).

[23] 49 USC 40109(c).

[24] 14 CFR § 298.53.

[25] Civil Aeronautics Act of 1938, Pub L No 75-706, 52 Stat 973, repealed by Federal Aviation Act of 1958, Pub L No 85-726, 72 Stat 31, codified as amended at scattered sections of 49 USC.

[26] The Sunset Act of 1984 gave the authority to review mergers to the DOT from 1 January 1985, which also marked the end of CAB.

[27] 52 Stat 1001–02.

[28] The Civil Aeronautics Act determined that the board 'may, upon its own initiative or upon complaint by an air carrier', investigate competition. ibid 1002–03.

[29] John Q Mulligan, 'The End of Prosecutorial Discretion for Airlines: The DOJ's Challenge to AMR/US Airways Merger' (2013) 13 Issues Aviation Law & Policy 31, 34.

[30] Pub L No 95-504, 92 Stat 1705 (1978) (codified as amended at scattered sections of 49 USC app).

[31] 49 USC §1384 (Supp II 1978).

[32] Sherman Act, 15 USC 1–7 (1982).

[33] 49 USC app 1378(b)(1)(A) (1982).

[34] Clayton Act, 15 USC 12–27 (1982).

196 PUBLIC INTEREST ASSESSMENT AND THE DOT

not be satisfied by a reasonably available alternative having materially less anticompetitive effects'.[35] The Deregulation Act of 1978 also introduced two important provisions. It established that the opponents of a transaction carried the burden of proving its anti-competitive effects while the parties carried the burden of demonstrating that the transaction satisfied the transportation conveniences and needs of the public and that no other less anti-competitive alternative was available.[36] Likewise, antitrust immunity could be granted to ensure the public interest.[37]

The Sunset Act of 1984 provided that the authority to review mergers initially transferred to the DOJ would be given to the DOT from January 1, 1985, which also marked the end of the CAB.[38] But then, in 1988, seeking greater enforcement, Congress transferred the antitrust authority[39] back to the DOJ.[40] However, section 411 of the Federal Aviation Act preserved the jurisdiction of the DOT to stop 'unfair or deceptive practice[s] or unfair method[s] of competition'.[41] The implication is that, under section 411, the DOT enjoys the authority to prohibit anti-competitive behaviour despite Congress having explicitly transferred its enforcement authority under section 7 of the Clayton Act to the DOJ. Thus, in relation to airline mergers and acquisitions, the DOT, under the Clayton Act,[42] performs its own competitive analysis, which is delivered to the DOJ in an advisory capacity,[43] exercises authority over slot controls[44] and route transfers to alleviate competition concerns,[45] and conducts 'fitness' reviews to ensure that an air carrier proposing to undergo substantial change in ownership, operations or management is still fit to operate under its existing authority.[46] In practice, as explained

[35] 49 USC app 1378(b)(1)(B) (1982).
[36] 49 USC app 1378(b)(1)(B) (1982).
[37] 49 USC app 1384.
[38] 49 USC app 1551(b)(1)(C), and 49 USC app §1551(b)(1)(c) (Supp III 1985).
[39] The CAB Sunset Act of 1984, Pub L No 98-444, 98 Stat 1704 vested the Department of Transportation with supervision over airline mergers until the end of 1988. At that time, merger supervision became the responsibility of the Department of Justice. See Daniel Gifford and Robert T Kudrle, 'U.S. Airlines and Antitrust: The Struggle for Defensible Policy Towards a Unique Industry' (2017) 50 Indiana Law Review 539.
[40] CAB Sunset Act of 1984 (n 39). In the report to the ABA House of Delegates supporting enactment of legislation transferring antitrust enforcement of airline mergers from the DOT to the DOJ, it was indicated that '[t]he result of transferring airline merger jurisdiction to DOJ would be that transactions that raise serious competitive problems will receive a more thorough review, while transactions that do not present such problems will be permitted to proceed more expeditiously'. See Mark Crane, 'The Future Direction of Antitrust' (1987) 56(3) Antitrust Law Journal 3.
[41] See 49 USC 41712 (1994), authorizing the DOT to investigate and prohibit any unfair or deceptive practice or an unfair method of competition of an air carrier, foreign air carrier, or ticket agent.
[42] Section 7 of the Clayton Act, 15 USC 18, prohibits mergers and stock acquisitions whose effect 'may be substantially to lessen competition, or to tend to create a monopoly' in a relevant market.
[43] See 15 USC 21 and 15 USC 18.
[44] 49 USC 40103 gives authority to the DOT/Federal Aviation Administration to assign the use of airspace to ensure its efficient use and modify or revoke a slot assignment when required in the public interest. See also 49 USC 40101, Title 49, that instructs the DOT and the Federal Aviation Administration (FAA), in carrying out aviation programmes, to incorporate certain established factors, plus additional factors that may be examined in the Secretary or FAA Administrator's discretion, as being in the public interest, including furthering airline competition.
[45] US Department of Transportation Notice of Practice Regarding Proposed Airline Mergers and Acquisitions, No 80,011, 80 Fed Reg 2468-69 (proposed 16 January 2015).
[46] The involved air carrier needs to provide the data indicated in § 204.3 to support its application, these data must be submitted in cases where: '(1) The proposed change required new or amended authority, or (2) The change substantially alters the factors upon which its latest fitness finding is based, even if no new authority is required.' The data is reviewed by the DOT's Air Carrier Fitness Division). See14 CFR 204.5. See also 49 USC § 41110 (an air carrier must 'continue to be fit, willing, and able to provide the transportation authorized by its certificate').

6.1 THE DEPARTMENT OF TRANSPORTATION (DOT) 197

above, the DOT has the power to approve or disapprove airline mergers. Equally, it retains exclusive jurisdiction to approve and immunize foreign air services agreements.[47]

The DOT maintains that when there is a transfer of an airline's routes, such a transaction needs its approval.[48] In doing this, the DOT verifies that the transfer is consistent with the public interest. Its assessment is conveyed to the relevant House and Senate Committees[49] with an analysis that includes the viability of each carrier involved in the transition; the competition in the domestic airline industry; and the trade position of the United States in the international transportation market.[50]

In relation to foreign air transportation agreements, they can consist of moving passengers across two or more carriers on the same itinerary (interlining), allowing customers to buy a single ticket that involves two different airlines (code sharing), or sharing gates or baggage facilities.[51] The level of cooperation between carriers can be higher if they share revenues and costs, and jointly set prices and schedules.[52]

It is also important to note that many countries have imposed restrictions on the foreign ownership of airlines. In the US a domestic carrier must be a US entity[53] and foreign airlines cannot take part in the domestic market.[54] Furthermore, an airline is a US citizen if it has US citizens as two-thirds of its board or has at least 75 per cent of its voting interest owned by US citizens.[55] Additionally, US and foreign airlines are considered competitors as the law precludes them from entering a parent-subsidiary association; therefore, any price, revenue or schedule coordination would be considered illegal.[56] Moreover, the DOT demands the existence of an open skies agreement (OSA), which allows bilateral aviation rights negotiations that include factors such as flight frequency, and fares for the service,[57] before granting immunity to applicant carriers wanting to create a joint venture or alliance.

Under 49 USC §§ 41308–41309 the DOT engages in a two-step analysis to decide on an alliance agreement. Firstly, the DOT needs to establish whether the alliance agreement 'substantially reduces or eliminates competition'. Assuming it does, there are two possible outcomes: (i) to reject the proposal, or (ii) to approve it if is deemed 'necessary to meet a serious transportation need or to achieve important public benefits' and

---

Certificate authority refers to the authority to provide air transportation granted by the Secretary of Transportation in the form of a certificate of public convenience and necessity under 49 USC 41102 or an all-cargo air transportation certificate to perform all-cargo air transportation under 49 USC 41103.

[47] International Air Transportation Act of 1979, Pub L No 96-192, 94 Stat 35 (1980).

[48] 49 USC 41105 (2009).

[49] Senate Committee on Commerce, Science and Transportation, and House Committee on Transportation and Infrastructure.

[50] 49 USC 41105 (2009).

[51] United States Government Accountability Office, Report to Congressional Requesters, International Alliances: Greater Transparency Needed on DOT's Efforts to Monitor the Effects of Antitrust Immunity (March 2019) 3, 4 https://www.gao.gov/assets/700/697690.pdf (accessed 3 July 2022).

[52] ibid 6.

[53] 49 USC Appendix 1301 (1994).

[54] See 49 USC Appendix 1508(b) (1992).

[55] 49 USC 40102(15) (1994).

[56] Charles N W Schlangen, 'Differing Views of Competition: Antitrust Review of International Alliances' (2000) 1 University of Chicago Legal Forum 413, 417.

[57] ibid 543–46.

there is no less anti-competitive alternative.[58] Once an agreement has been authorized subject to those considerations, it is exempted from the antitrust laws.[59] Opposing third parties are required to demonstrate that the agreement is anti-competitive and the merging parties are required to show that it provides public benefits.[60] Secondly, if the DOT concludes that the alliance agreement does not provide adverse competition effects and is consistent with the public interest, then it is approved. In this case, the antitrust laws exemption is granted only 'to the extent necessary to allow the person to proceed with the transaction specifically approved by the order and with any transaction necessarily contemplated by the order'.[61]

6.1.2 Filing Instructions and Process Overview

The review process of antitrust immunity (ATI) for a cooperative agreement observes the Administrative Procedure Act (APA), which means that the process should be open to the public for comments. The process starts with an application, which is reviewed by the DOT and has the power to request additional information. Once the application is completed, a public comments period starts.[62] The applicants can request confidential treatment of some of the information provided.[63] The DOT undertakes the competition and public interest analysis, the provisional findings of which are published for comments from interested parties. The DOT publishes then a final order approving or disapproving the agreement,[64] no later than the last day of the sixth month that begins after the date the matter was submitted,[65] a deadline that is, however, not always observed.[66]

6.1.2.1 Assessment of Alliances
The DOJ and the DOT coordinate the alliance reviews, whereby the former provides comments to the latter, and if the DOJ has concerns, it can seek to block the agreement in the federal court or to discuss a consent decree with the applicants,[67] while the DOT

[58] 49 USC 41309(b).

[59] 49 USC 41308(c).

[60] 49 USC 41309(c)(2).

[61] 49 USC 41309(b), 41308(b).

[62] DOT Order 2008-11-8, Expanded Star Application, Docket DOT-OST-2008-0234- 0067, issued 12 November 2008.

[63] See eg DOT Notice Providing Access to Documents, Expanded Star Application, Docket DOT-OST-2008-0234-0006, issued 24 July 2008 (access only permitted to those filing an affidavit under 14 CFR 302.12 stating that: '(1) the affiant is counsel for an interested party or an outside independent expert providing services to such a party; (2) the affiant will use the information only for the purpose of participating in this proceeding; and (3) the affiant will disclose such information only to other persons who have [also] filed a valid affidavit'. ibid 1–2).

[64] United States Government Accountability Office, Report to Congressional Requesters, International Alliances – Greater Transparency Needed on DOT's Efforts to Monitor the Effects of Antitrust Immunity (March 2019) 7 https://www.gao.gov/assets/700/697690.pdf (accessed 3 July 2022).

[65] 49 USC 41710 (2009).

[66] DOT Order 2009-7-10, 21.

[67] United States General Accounting Office, Aviation Competition, Proposed Domestic Airline Alliances Raise Serious Issues, GAO/T-RCED-98-215 (4 June 1998) 6 https://books.google.co.uk/books?id=hgg6A QAAMAAJ&pg=PA6&lpg=PA6&dq=DOJ+and+DOT+merger+reviews&source=bl&ots=bIwDdnvMEQ&sig= ACfU3U2SpXCtwqbgHUXlAzDe2MhFlwcEWw&hl=es&sa=X&ved=2ahUKEwivqZzu0sXqAhX0lFwKHeu

can issue a cease-and-desist order based on a recommendation from an administrative law judge.[68] The DOJ's review standard of an alliance is the same as that applied to examine domestic airline mergers, while the main focus of the DOT is to scrutinize foreign-policy related factors, such as the attainment of a more open global aviation regime.[69] Although both agencies analyse whether the members of the alliance would be able to exert market power according to the Clayton Act test,[70] the DOT generally leaves to the DOJ the detailed economic analysis of the relevant market, and, in the end, the DOT enjoys the exclusive authority to decide whether to grant or deny immunity.[71] The DOT's competitive analysis evaluates whether the alliance: '(1) would significantly increase market concentration; (2) whether it would cause competitive harm; and (3) whether new entry into the market would be timely, likely, and sufficient either to deter or to discipline the potential competitive harm'.[72] Once immunity has been granted, the DOT may request the alliance's members to re-submit their application for a renewed review.[73]

6.1.2.2 Assessment of Mergers

The review process of airline mergers starts with a proposal under the Hart-Scott-Rodino Antitrust Improvements Act (HSR)[74] requirements with the aim of determining whether the proposed merger will create or enhance market power. If the DOJ does not request additional information, the parties can close the proposed transaction.[75] The DOJ can issue a Second Request, which triggers a final thirty-day waiting period that begins once it is certified that the applicants have complied with the request to a large extent.[76] During the waiting period the parties and the DOJ can discuss any anti-competitive concerns that the transaction induces and possible remedies to overcome them; it is also possible to extend the period to facilitate the negotiations.[77] If the DOJ finds the merger anti-competitive and the remedies offered by the parties insufficient, it must obtain a court order to prohibit it.[78]

The DOJ follows a five-part assessment to identify possible antitrust concerns. First, it defines the product and geographic markets in which the merging firms operate

---

ZAGkQ6AEwD3oECAYQAQ#v=onepage&q=DOJ%20and%20DOT%20merger%20reviews&f=false (accessed 11 July 2022).

[68] ibid.
[69] Schlangen (n 56) 419.
[70] Order to Show Cause, 7, Delta Air Lines Inc, DOT-OST-2015-0070 (Department of Transportation, November 2016).
[71] Schlangen (n 56).
[72] Order to Show Cause (n 70) 9.
[73] 14 CFR 303.06 (2018).
[74] 15 USC 18.
[75] 15 USC 18a(b).
[76] 16 CFR 803.20 (2009).
[77] United States Government Accountability Office, Airline Industry, Potential Mergers and Acquisitions Driven by Financial and Competitive Pressures, GAO-08-845 (July 2008) 34 https://www.gao.gov/assets/280/278891.pdf (accessed 6 November 2022).
[78] 15 USC 18a(f).

(city-pairs in the case of airlines)[79] and establishes whether there would be a significant concentration increase. Secondly, it studies possible adverse effects such as higher prices or output restrictions in each city-pair market. Thirdly, it examines the potential entry of other airlines and whether they would counteract any anti-competitive effects (factors such as whether the potential entrant has a hub in one of the city-pairs of concern, or whether there is a shortage of slots or gates are part of the analysis). Fourthly, it verifies alleged efficiencies that are merger specific. Fifth, it determines whether, in the absence of the merger, one of the merger firms would fail and therefore exit the market.[80] As an example of the latter scenario in the EU, in 2013, the European Commission approved a merger based on a failing firm claim in which two Greek Airlines, Olympic and Aegean, sought a combination after the Greek sovereign debt crisis provoked by the global financial crisis of 2007–2008.[81] Although in 2011 the European Commission did not accept the failing firm defence claim,[82] in 2013 when the merging parties submitted again the proposal, the merger was approved because the economic conditions of the parties had worsened due to the Greek economic crisis, and absent the merger Olympic would have exited the market.

The DOT conducts its own analysis and submits its views to the DOJ accompanied by the relevant data that has been used to underpin its findings. Once the transaction has been cleared, the DOT undertakes additional economic and safety reviews and issues the respective authorizations that every airline requires to start operations. As we have indicated above, these authorizations give a de facto major enforcement power to the DOT.[83] Thus, the Office of the Secretary[84] assesses whether the applicants have enough financial resources to operate the new airline, the disposition to comply with regulations, and the administrative capability (economic authorization), and the Federal Aviation Administration (FAA)[85] certifies that the new airline complies with all federal safety standards (safety authorization).[86]

---

[79] City pair 'means two cities or other locations between which any Air Carrier offers scheduled service, whether domestic or international and whether or not non-stop or direct'. See *Law Insider* https://www.lawinsider.com/dictionary/city-pair (accessed 6 October 2022). As an illustration, in the Northwest/Republic merger the DOJ identified ninety-seven city pairs that would be affected by the transaction, including twenty-six Minneapolis-St Paul (MSP) and twelve Detroit city pairs in which Northwest and Republic provided a non-stop service, among the other city pair routes departing from these two hubs. See Keyes (n 5).

[80] United States Government Accountability Office (n 77).

[81] Case No COMP/M.6796 *Olympic/Aegean II*, Commission Decision of 9 October 2013.

[82] Case No COMP/M.5830 *Olympic/Aegean*, Commission Decision of 26 January 2011.

[83] 49 USC 41105; US Department of Transportation, 'How to Become a Certified Air Carrier' (September 2012) 28 https://www.transportation.gov/sites/dot.dev/files/docs/Certificated_Packet_2012_final.pdf (accessed 4 October 2022).

[84] 49 USC 41104.

[85] 49 USC 44702.

[86] United States Government Accountability Office, 'Airline Industry, Potential Mergers and Acquisitions Driven by Financial and Competitive Pressures' GAO-08-845 (July 2008) 34–35 https://www.gao.gov/assets/280/278891.pdf (accessed 12 November 2022).

6.2 The 'Public Interest' Standard

The DOT incorporates a number of non-competition related considerations for passenger and cargo flights as part of its public interest standard, including:[87] safety; improving relations between air carriers; encouraging fair wages and working conditions; developing and maintaining a sound regulatory system; encouraging air transportation through secondary or satellite airports; maintaining a complete and convenient system of continuous scheduled interstate air transportation throughout the US; promoting, encouraging, and developing civil aeronautics; strengthening the competitive position of air carriers to ensure equality with foreign competitors; and, ensuring that consumers, including those in small communities and rural and remote areas, have access to an affordable, regularly scheduled air service.[88]

Furthermore, the public interest test incorporates a number of competition related considerations. Hence, the text below only refers to the pertinent parts of the legal provision:[89]

(6) placing maximum reliance on competitive market forces and on actual and potential competition—

    (A) providing the necessary air transportation system; and

    (B) encouraging efficient and well-managed air carriers to earn adequate profits and attract capital, considering any material differences between interstate air transportation and foreign air transportation.

(9) preventing unfair, deceptive, predatory, or anti-competitive practices in air transportation.

(10) avoiding unreasonable industry concentration, excessive market domination, monopoly powers, and other conditions that would tend to allow at least one air carrier or foreign air carrier unreasonably to increase prices, reduce services, or exclude competition in air transportation.

(13) encouraging entry into air transportation markets by new and existing air carriers and the continued strengthening of small air carriers to ensure a more effective and competitive airline industry.

In relation to the assessment of the public interest benefits of code-share relationships, which is a very prevalent feature in the airline sector, the DOT takes into account expansion of services and fare options in its analysis.[90] Likewise the DOT, when evaluating international airline alliances (IAAs or alliances) in light of the public interest standard, takes into account factors such as 'the availability of a variety of

---

[87] Included in s 40101 https://www.law.cornell.edu/uscode/text/49/40101 (accessed 18 November 2022).
[88] Included in s 40101 https://www.law.cornell.edu/uscode/text/49/40101 (accessed 18 November 2022).
[89] ibid.
[90] US Department of Transportation, 'Code Sharing' https://www.transportation.gov/policy/aviation-policy/licensing/code-sharing (accessed 18 November 2022).

202 PUBLIC INTEREST ASSESSMENT AND THE DOT

air service, maximum reliance on market forces, the avoidance of unreasonable industry concentration, and opportunities for the expansion of international services.[91] The DOT has enlarged the public considerations by taken into account aspects such as 'double marginalization, cost and operational efficiencies, expanded networks, improved coordination and services, increased capacity, aligned frequent flyer benefits,[92] increased levels of service and lower fares.[93] Furthermore, it has recognized the US foreign policy as a fundamental public benefit[94] and international comity as an additional consideration.[95] Equally, the DOJ and the DOT, when evaluating the validity of the claims about the benefits that the alliance brings to the public, consider how much new traffic can be generated by minimal additions to the frequency of the flights, how many more destinations can be created, and whether the partners would continue to compete with one another on price.[96]

The unprecedented outbreak of domestic airline consolidation in the US during the late 1980s and early 1990s offers a good opportunity to assess how the public interest standard has been applied.[97] As an illustration, Clougherty has examined the reasons that constantly ensured high levels of merger approvals.[98] More specifically, the author looks at the political forces that surrounded the merger review process, which rendered concerns related to market power in the domestic US markets irrelevant. He notes that transactions leading to stronger airlines which could compete internationally received strong support from private stakeholders, such as the members of the industry who displayed significant lobbying efforts, and public entities, the author has referred to them as political forces. In his view, the DOT embraced such a political stance. This approach shows how in practice the public interest standard was applied: the adverse competitive effects of the transaction in the domestic markets were offset by the stronger competitive position internationally of the merged domestic air carriers.

Turning our focus to the allocation of gates and slots, this falls within the remit of the DOT,[99] which according to Gifford and Kudrle, has been the source of competitive imbalances between incumbents and low-cost carrier airlines (LCCs).[100] Gates and slots at major airports are limited, difficult to replicate, and necessary for LCCs to compete. Paradoxically, as noted by Dempsey, the DOT under its public interest standard has

---

[91] European Commission and US Department of Transportation, 'Transatlantic Airline Alliances: Competitive Issues and Regulatory Approaches' 3 (2010).

[92] Order to Show Cause (n 70) 7.

[93] Schlangen (n 56) 424.

[94] William Gillespie and Oliver M Richard, 'Antitrust Immunity and International Airline Alliances' (2011) Economic Analysis Group Discussion Paper No 11-1, 5 https://www.justice.gov/atr/antitrust-immunity-and-international-airline-alliances (accessed 7 October 2022)

[95] 49 USC 41309(b)(1)(A).

[96] United States General Accounting Office (n 67) 13.

[97] Brueckner and Spiller have reported that from 1985 to 1989 the US antitrust authorities approved the totality of mergers reviewed. See Jan Brueckner and Pablo Spiller, 'Competition and Merger in Airline Networks' (1991) 9 International Journal of Industrial Organization 323.

[98] Joseph A Clougherty, 'A Political Economic Approach to the Domestic Airline Merger Phenomenon' (2002) 36 Journal of Transport Economics and Policy 27, 37 https://www.jstor.org/stable/20053891 (accessed 18 November 2022).

[99] 49 USC 41714 (2012).

[100] See Gifford and Kudrle (n 39) 573.

granted antitrust enforcement immunity to some alliances resulting in a restricted use of slots and gates by LCCs.[101] This explains why the DOJ in few cases, as we will explore in more detail later in this chapter, has ordered gate and slots transfers from incumbent carriers to LCCs seeking to stimulate competition. Occasionally, the imposition of this type of remedy has been mirrored by the DOT.

6.3 Challenges of Concurrent Jurisdiction

It has been critically questioned whether approved airline alliances have indeed been beneficial for consumers.[102] Under the public interest test the regulator often applies a presumption according to which any impact brought about by an airline alliance is deemed as aligned with the public interest standard, even including those generated by the inherent nature of such alliances, as we will see in the *AA—TACA*[103] and *Continental—United—Star* cases.[104] This approach implies that parties can relatively straightforwardly satisfy the public interest test. Unsurprisingly, commentators have argued that the standard of review applied by the DOT, specifically regarding airline alliances, tends to benefit parties at the expense of competition.[105]

It has also been debated whether the DOT possesses enough expertise to deal with antitrust policy and enforcement issues. This lack of (extensive) expertise in competition analysis has negative implications not just for the competition assessment of the deals that is carried out by the DOT but also for the application of the public interest standard. The result has been that, notably, since 2003, the DOT and the DOJ have had contradictory positions in a number of cases in the sector.[106] In particular, as the analysis of some seminal cases will show, the concerns expressed by the DOJ are ignored by the DOT. Since this review system gives ultimate merger approval authority to the DOT, it would be advisable for DOT to work closely with the DOJ in assessing the competition effects of transactions.

In relation to airline mergers, the DOJ has been critical of the DOT's approach. According to the latter's approach, merger opponents need to show not just that the transaction would increase the levels of concentration but also that it would be

---

[101] Paul Stephen Dempsey, 'Carving the World into Fiefdoms: The Anticompetitive Future of International Aviation' (2002) 27 Annals of Air and Space Law 260, 261, 292 https://ssrn.com/abstract=2699211.

[102] See Gillespie and Richard (n 94). In their assessment they have noted that: 'The evidence supports the normal antitrust presumption that eliminating or substantially reducing competition through merger or collaboration enhances the market power of the remaining suppliers and leads to higher prices, harming consumers.'

[103] Department of Transportation, Final Order, American Airlines Inc and the TACA Group Reciprocal Code-Share Services Proceeding, Docket OST-96-1700,134, 1 (20 May 1998).

[104] Department of Transportation, Final Order, Joint Application of Air Canada, the Austrian Group, British Midland Airways Ltd, Continental Airlines Inc, Deutsche Lufthansa AG, Polskie Linie Lotnicze Lot SA, Scandinavian Airlines System, Swiss International Air Lines Ltd, Tap Air Portugal, and United Air Lines Inc, Docket OST-2008-234, 1 (10 July 2009).

[105] Peter Carstensen, 'Replacing Antitrust Exemptions for Transportation Industries: The Potential for a "Robust Business Review Clearance"' (2011) 89 Oregon Law Review 1059, 1090.

[106] W Robert Hand, 'Continental Joins the (All)Star Alliance: Antitrust Concerns with Airline Alliances and Open-Sky Treaties' (2011) 33 Houston Journal of International Law 641, 675–76.

204 PUBLIC INTEREST ASSESSMENT AND THE DOT

anti-competitive.[107] In this regard, it has been noted that the DOT since 1978 has approved almost every application on the ground that the merger opponents were unable to demonstrate a reasonable possibility of substantial reduction of competition.[108] The DOJ has also emphasized that the review process under the antitrust rules is more accurate to assess airline mergers than the standard that the DOT applies.[109] It has been also suggested that in light of the significant enforcement authority that the DOT enjoys in the airline industry, its function should be restricted to the analysis of non-competition matters allowing for the leading role for merger review to be played by the antitrust authorities.[110]

6.4 Enforcement Record

Between 1993 and 2017, the DOT adjudicated 38 applications involving a US and foreign carrier(s), granting immunity in thirty-one cases.[111] A large number of these immunities remain active across today, as can be seen in Table 6.1.[112]

Between 1985 and 1987, a period when the DOT had the authority to review mergers, a total number of nine proposals were filed and approved by the DOT, while three of them were opposed by the DOJ.[113] The DOT does not keep official records of airline mergers and acquisitions activity.[114] In relation to code-sharing applications, by 2011 out of fifty-seven proposals, the DOT denied just one.[115] This trend consisting of a high number of approvals has raised some concerns among commentators who question the level of scrutiny that the DOT exercise over these transactions.[116]

6.4.1 Analysis of Some Seminal Cases

Below, we present some of the most important cases the DOT and the DOJ have independently or concurrently assessed. We draw out some interesting implications of

---

[107] Keyes (n 5) 741.

[108] ibid.

[109] United States General Accounting Office, Airline Competition, DOT's Implementation of Airline Regulatory Authority (June 1989) 32–33 https://www.gao.gov/assets/150/147932.pdf (accessed 11 November 2022).

[110] Diana L Moss, 'The American Antitrust Institute, Regulated Industries: Before the Antitrust Modernization Commission' (5 December 2005) https://govinfo.library.unt.edu/amc/commission_hearings/pdf/Moss_Statement.pdf (accessed 31 October 2022).

[111] United States Government Accountability Office, 'International Air Alliances: Greater Transparency Needed on DOT's Efforts to Monitor the Effects of Antitrust Immunity' GAO-19-237 (March 2019) 17 https://www.gao.gov/assets/700/697690.pdf (accessed 27 October 2022). Last update available at time of manuscript submission was data as of 30 October 2019.

[112] One single agreement can include a number of immunities such as fares and flight frequencies.

[113] Steven A Morrison and Clifford Winston, 'Enhancing the Performance of the Deregulated Air Transportation System' in Martin Neil Baily and Clifford Winston (eds), Brooking Papers on Economic Activity: Microeconomics 1989 (Brookings Institutions 1989).

[114] See Airlines for America, Data & Statistics, 'U.S. Airline Mergers and Acquisitions' (12 April 2022) https://www.airlines.org/dataset/u-s-airline-mergers-and-acquisitions/ (accessed 12 October 2022).

[115] Carstensen (n 105).

[116] ibid.

6.4 ENFORCEMENT RECORD 205

Table 6.1 Department of Transportation: List of Antitrust Immunity Cases

	Case	Filed	Issued	Conditions
1	American—Finnair	04/04/02	30/07/02	None
	American—British Airways—Iberia—Finnair—Royal Jordanian	15/08/08	20/07/10	Transfer four slot pairs to competitors (10 years)
2	American—Japan Airlines	12/02/10	10/11/10	None
3	American—Qantas	26/02/18	03/06/19	None
4	Northwest—KLM	09/09/92	11/01/93	None
	Delta—Air France—Alitalia—Czech Airlines			Removed by Order 2008-5-32
	Delta—Korean Air—Air France—Alitalia–Czech Airlines			
	Delta—Northwest—Air France—KLM—Alitalia—Czech Airlines			Removed by Order 2002-1-6
	Delta—Virgin Atlantic—Air France—KLM—Alitalia	08/04/13	23/09/13	
5	Delta—Aeromexico	31/03/15	14/12/16	
6	Delta—LATAM	08/07/20	30/09/22	Remove constraint, 10-year expiration and self-assessment
7	United—Lufthansa	29/02/96	20/05/96	Carve-outs imposed for US point-of-sale non-stop O&D traffics in the Chicago–Frankfurt and Washington–Frankfurt markets
	United—Lufthansa—SAS			
	United—Air Canada			
	United—Austrian—Lufthansa—SAS			
	United—BMI—Austrian—Lufthansa—SAS			
	United—Lufthansa—Air Canada—SAS—Austrian—BMI—LOT—Swiss—TAP			
	United—Lufthansa—Air Canada—SAS—Austrian—BMI—LOT—Swiss—TAP			
8	United—Air New Zealand	17/12/99	03/04/01	Excludes all local US POS, time-sensitive travellers (unrestricted coach, business, or first-class fares): Los Angeles–Auckland, Los Angeles–Sydney
9	United—Copa	22/12/00	03/05/01	None
10	United—Asiana	03/01/03	14/05/03	None
11	United—All Nippon Airways	31/03/10	10/11/10	None
12	SAS—Iceland Air	13/04/00	13/10/00	None

Source: Department of Transportation, 'DOT Aviation Anti-Trust Immunity Cases', https://www.transportation.gov/office-policy/aviation-policy/dot-aviation-anti-trust-immunity-cases (accessed 30 September 2023).

206   PUBLIC INTEREST ASSESSMENT AND THE DOT

the approach that the two agencies took based on their separate standards, the public interest one (that includes some competition considerations)[117] and the competition one (substantial lessening of competition). Also, the study of some cases enables us to explore how the DOT and the DOJ have conducted their respective competition analysis, as well as to offer some observations on the two approaches. First, we will examine some merger and acquisition decisions, then some antitrust immunity alliances and finally some slot transactions.

6.4.1.1 Transactions where the DOT and the DOJ diverged on the outcome
The next section covers cases in which there has been a concurrent jurisdiction between the antitrust authority and the regulator, whose views have been conflicting.

6.4.1.1.1 Northwest—Republic
In January 1986, Northwest Orient Airlines (Northwest) announced the acquisition of Republic Airlines (Republic) in a US$884 million deal that would create the nation's third largest airline with 298 airplanes and more than 30,000 employees, serving almost 100 cities in the US.[118] The merger was approved by the DOT despite objections from the DOJ. The DOJ identified ninety-seven city-pairs that would be affected by the transaction, including twenty-six Minneapolis–St. Paul (MSP) and twelve Detroit city-pairs in which Northwest and Republic provided a non-stop service, among the other city-pair routes departing from these two hubs.[119] The DOJ claimed that the replication of some of the applicants' hubs was necessary to discipline competition in certain MSP city-pairs, but given the scarcity of capacity this measure was difficult to achieve.[120] In the words of the DOJ, this was an issue regarding the 'economics of hubbing', which is referred to as a type of barrier to entry.[121]

Borenstein has explained that the economics of hubs offer a great advantage to airlines that operate in their own hub airports as they can serve passengers from diverse origins and diverse destinations with just one large plane covering all the itineraries, i.e. multi-stop routes between one point of origin and destination. Due to these economies of density and the likely cost efficiency these routes can be offered at relatively low prices. Frequent-flyer miles programmes enhance the advantage these airlines can have from network effects. He adds that those airlines that operate routes outside their own

---

[117] Such as placing maximum reliance on competitive market forces and on actual and potential competition; providing the necessary air transportation system; encouraging efficient and well-managed air carriers to earn adequate profits and attract capital, considering any material differences between interstate air transportation and foreign air transportation; preventing unfair, deceptive, predatory, or anti-competitive practices in air transportation; avoiding unreasonable industry concentration, excessive market domination, monopoly powers, and other conditions that would tend to allow at least one air carrier or foreign air carrier unreasonably to increase prices, reduce services, or exclude competition in air transportation; encouraging entry into air transportation markets by new and existing air carriers and the continued strengthening of small air carriers to ensure a more effective and competitive airline industry. See 49 US Code 40101.

[118] Douglas B Feaver, 'Merger Planned by Northwest and Republic' *The Washington Post* (24 January 1986) https://www.washingtonpost.com/archive/politics/1986/01/24/merger-planned-by-northwest-and-republic/8e86f3e9-999d-4ad4-b0bf-93e456d03f2d/ (accessed 16 October 2022).

[119] Keyes (n 5) 750.

[120] ibid.

[121] Panel Discussion: Market Power and Entry Barriers (1988) 57 Antitrust Law Journal 701, 711.

hubs cannot offer such similar routes structure and thus less competitive frequencies, prices, loyalty programmes, and that given the limited capacity of the airports, the lack of hubs is an effective barrier to entry which can lessened competition in the market.[122]

The DOT's position when a strong carrier has a strong hub is that the analysis of barriers to entry needs to include aspects such as feeds from other hubs, connecting services, and code sharing, which serve to discipline the dominant carriers in terms of fares and services; this differs from the position adopted by the DOJ, for whom the presence of a hub is a barrier that is almost impossible to overcome.[123] In addition, the DOT considers that the airline sector is a contestable market that is subject to 'hit and run' before incumbents can react, without incurring sunk costs.[124] The DOJ has refuted this argument, stating that it is very likely that the hub carrier possesses information that is necessary to operate, as well as the ability to establish how much and what space an entrant can enjoy, and that even if the new entrant offers lower fares, pre-existing frequent flyer programmes or business travellers may make this strategy ineffective.[125] Kahn has also refuted the contestability theory sustained by the DOT. In his opinion, it has become more difficult for genuinely new firms to enter the airline industry because of the traditional practices implemented by dominant carriers, together with the development of new methods such as computerized reservation systems (CRSs).[126] Kahn adds, 'if contestability were perfect, there would be no need for antitrust laws at all'.[127]

Another central issue is that the DOT has found that merger opponents do not demonstrate that new entrants are unable to establish new hubs in all MSP points; in other words, what the DOT requires from the opponents to the transaction is a 'factual basis that allows us to evaluate entry conditions, to assess possible impediments to entry, and to weigh these factors against various pro-competitive factors that we know, from experience and from the record, are operative in most airlines'.[128] Commentators have noted that this obligation to prove entrance likelihood is very challenging as is the burden of proof on third parties rather than the regulator.[129] Interestingly, after this merger a study from Borenstein showed a price increase of 9.5 per cent from 1985 to 1987 across eighty-four routes, including Northwest/Republic's hub of MSP,[130] and a reduced service between city pairs.[131] This finding was confirmed by more empirical evidence showing that prices rose in Minneapolis due to a scarcity of gate space,

---

[122] Severin Borenstein, 'The Dominant-Firm Advantage in Multiproduct Industries: Evidence from the U.S. Airlines' (1991) 106 Quarterly Journal of Economics 1237.

[123] Panel Discussion (n 122) 705.

[124] ibid 711; Charles F Rule, 'Merger Enforcement Policy: Protecting the Consumer' (1987) 56 Antitrust Law Journal 739, 742.

[125] Panel Discussion (n 122) 713.

[126] Alfred E Kahn, 'Deregulatory Schizophrenia' (1987) 75 California Law Review 1059, 1063.

[127] ibid 1067.

[128] Keyes (n 5) 752. See Northwest-Republic Acquisition Case, DOT Docket No 43,754.

[129] Keyes (n 5) 753.

[130] Matthew Weinberg, 'The Price Effects of Horizontal Mergers' (2008) 4 Journal of Comparative Law & Economics 433, 440.

[131] Severin Borenstein, 'Airline Mergers, Airport Dominance, and Market Power' (1990) 80 American Economic Review 400.

208 PUBLIC INTEREST ASSESSMENT AND THE DOT

implying that Northwest did not need to worry about new entry, as the DOJ had anticipated but the opponents had failed to demonstrate.[132]

This case illustrates marked disparities between the regulator and the antitrust agency around critical issues such as entry barriers and the burden of proving them. The post-merger data shows that the DOT should not have ignored the concerns expressed by the DOJ and explains why, in 1988, Congress decided to return the authority to review this type of mergers to the antitrust agency. At the same time, it questions the extent to which opponents are expected to demonstrate the anti-competitive effects of proposed mergers, a task that is sometimes difficult to fulfil, even for the authorities that have expertise in, and experience with antitrust.

6.4.1.1.2 Ozark—TWA

In February 1986, it was reported that Trans World Airline (TWA) would purchase up to 2.2 million shares of Ozark Holdings (Ozark) common stock for about US$250 million, making TWA the sixth largest airline.[133] The DOJ opposed the transaction, stating that it would eliminate the existing competition in the hub city of St. Louis and result in prices and services being adversely affected.[134] On this occasion, the DOT again dismissed the concerns expressed by the antitrust agency and approved the merger after finding that it was not likely to lessen competition and that other competitors 'will prevent the merged carriers from exercising market power'.[135] Additionally, the DOT supported its decision on the basis that the airline industry was changing so rapidly that any predictions about the merger's effects would be inconsistent.[136]

In response to the DOT's position about the likelihood of entry, the DOJ asserted that the concept of ease of entry is very elusive and that many merger decisions rest on this factor (as with the Ozark—TWA case).[137] It clarified that the key point is not just to establish if entering the market is feasible within a two-year period, but whether it is likely if prices go up 5 or 10 per cent.[138] In this particular case, the DOJ's concern was based on the fact that Ozark and TWA, as hub operators at St. Louis, competed non-stop on thirty city pair routes (nineteen of which did not have other non-stop services) and in forty-one other city pairs where one of them—not both—operated non-stop.[139] However, the DOT confirmed the prior position shown in Northwest/Republic, that non-hub services could have a disciplinary impact on competition and that airline

---

[132] Andrew N Kleit, 'Competition without Apology: Market Power and Entry in the Deregulated Airline Industry' (1991) 14 Regulation 68, 74. See also Gregory J Werden, Andrew S Joskow, and Richard L Johnson, 'The Effects of Mergers on Economic Performance: Two Case Studies from the Airline Industry' (1991) 12(5) Managerial & Decision Economics 341.

[133] TWA-Ozark Acquisition Case, DOT Order No 86-9-29, 2 (12 September 1986). See also John Crudele, 'TWA to Buy Ozark in Bid for More Traffic' The New York Times (28 February 1986) ytimes.com/1986/02/28/business/twa-to-buy-ozark-in-bid-for-more-traffic.html (accessed 16 November 2022).

[134] Richard V Butler and John H Houston, 'Merger Mania and Airline Fares' (1989) 15 Eastern Economic Journal 7.

[135] Reginald Stuart, 'Company News: TWA-Ozark Merger is Approved' New York Times (13 September 1986).

[136] Butler and Houston (n 134).

[137] Panel Discussion (n 122) 709.

[138] ibid.

[139] Keyes (n 5) 753.

6.4 ENFORCEMENT RECORD 209

markets are contestable, and recognized that 'the basic industry assets, airplanes, are highly mobile and that entry barriers are low'.[140]

In light of these two opposing interpretations, a post-merger assessment found that the transaction resulted in a small fare increase of 1.5 per cent and a significant service reduction,[141] which is consistent with the prediction presented by a previous study suggesting that the routes jointly served by TWA and Ozark would see a fare increase of about 1.3 per cent as a result of the removal of an actual competitor.[142] The results also confirmed the concern raised by the DOJ to the DOT that the elimination of competition at St. Louis hub would result in higher fares to and from that hub.[143] Some authors have explained that a possible reason why this merger did not show a higher increase in prices, as seen in Northwest/Republic, is because the St. Louis market was facing a low demand period.[144] In the end, these results seem to endorse the view that 'the DOT was over-tolerant of airline merger activity'[145] and that it would have been advisable for the DOJ's recommendation to have been incorporated by the DOT.

The next section includes mergers that have only been assessed by the antitrust agency. The purpose of such an examination is to assess how the competition standard was applied in these cases and whether any discernible divergence can be observed compared to the transactions discussed above where both the competition authority and the sectoral regulator assessed the same transaction.

6.4.1.2 Transactions on slot allocation where there is convergence between the DOT and the DOJ

The next cases illustrate some convergence between the regulator and the antitrust authority in relation to the importance of slots and the effects that they have on ensuring competitive markets.

6.4.1.2.1 Delta—US Airways slot swap

In August 2009, US Airways and Delta announced that they would exchange a number of slots at La Guardia Airport (LGA) and Ronald Reagan National Airport in Washington (DCA).[146] According to Delta, the transaction would increase its capacity from sixteen to twenty-seven gates and from 148 to 272 daily departures after the deal was completed.[147] The sale of slots at LGA required a waiver from a 2006 FAA Order, which prohibited the permanent sales of LGA slots.[148] The FAA proposed to grant the

---

[140] ibid 753, 761.

[141] Paul A Paulter and Robert P O'Quinn, 'Recent Empirical Evidence on Mergers and Acquisitions' (1993) 38 Antitrust Bulletin 741, 759–760.

[142] Butler and Houston (n 134) 15.

[143] Rule (n 124) 742.

[144] Weinberg (n 130).

[145] Gifford and Kudrle (n 39) 570–71; Catherine A Peterman, 'The Future of Airline Mergers after the US Airways and American Airlines Merger' (2014) 79(4) Journal of Air Law and Commerce 781, 798–801.

[146] James Barron, 'Delta to Increase Service at La Guardia' The New York Times (12 August 2009) https://www.nytimes.com/2009/08/13/nyregion/13laguardia.html (accessed 30 October 2022).

[147] ibid.

[148] 71 FR 77854.

210   PUBLIC INTEREST ASSESSMENT AND THE DOT

waiver conditionally by requesting the applicants to divest twenty slot pairs at LGA and twenty-four pairs at DCA to a new entrant and incumbent carriers, a proposal that was supported by the DOJ.[149]

The DOJ found that the proposal: (i) would reduce competition at LGA and DCA resulting from the decrease in the number of available slots, slot hoarding, and disincentives to sell or lease them; and (ii) would reduce competition between Delta and US Airways. In particular, the DOJ was concerned that the proposed transaction would increase the share of LGA slots held by Delta from 24 to 49 per cent, and the share of DCA slots held by US Airways from 44 to 54 per cent.[150] Therefore, the DOJ concluded that the FAA's proposal would be in the public interest by making slots available for other carriers, facilitating entry at LGA and DCA, increasing competition and lowering fares for consumers.[151] In consequence, US Airways and Delta reformed their agreement by offering the divestiture of some slots (different from those requested by the FAA) that in May 2010 was rejected by the FAA, granting the petition subject to the conditions initially imposed.[152]

In August 2010, US Airways and Delta appealed the joint decision issued by the DOT/FAA to the D. C. Court, arguing that both the DOT and the FAA lacked authority to review effects on competition.[153] In January 2011, the case was held in 'pending settlement', and in May 2011, a new agreement was announced under which Delta would acquire 132 slot pairs at LGA from US Airways and US Airways would acquire forty-two slot pairs at DCA from Delta, the rights to operate additional daily service to Sao Paulo in 2015, and Delta would pay US Airways US$66.5 million in cash. The applicants offered the divestiture of sixteen slot pairs at LGA and eight slot pairs at DCA to airlines with limited or no service at those airports.[154] In October 2011, the FAA finally approved the transaction, after being convinced by the merging parties that the market conditions had changed since the first proposal was filed and that the remedies were enough to mitigate any concerns.[155] The DOJ concluded its investigation in relation to the transfer of slots at LGA and announced that it would continue its investigation 'with a focus on the increase in US Airways' share and use of slots at Reagan National and the resulting decrease in Delta's share of slots at this slot-constrained airport, at which passengers pay among the highest fares in the country'.[156]

---

[149] United States Department of Justice, 'Comments on Grant of Petition with Conditions' Docket FAA-2010-0109, 2–3 (24 March 2010) https://www.justice.gov/sites/default/files/atr/legacy/2010/04/14/257463.pdf (accessed 30 October 2022).

[150] ibid 4–5.

[151] ibid 2–3.

[152] J Bruce McDonald, 'Delta and USAIR Convince DOT to Approve LaGuardia-Reagan Slot Swap, and DOJ Continues to Investigate at National' *Mondaq* (10 February 2012) https://www.mondaq.com/unitedstates/aviation/164270/delta-and-usair-convince-dot-to-approve-laguardia-reagan-slot-swap-and-doj-continues-to-investigate-at-national (accessed 30 October 2022).

[153] *Delta Air Lines Inc and US Airways Inc v FAA and DOT* No 10-1153, Doc 1259764, 3 (DC Cir 2010). The parties voluntarily dismissed the case in May 2011.

[154] Delta Air Lines, 'Delta, US Airways Announce New Agreement to Transfer Flying Rights in New York and Washington D. C.' (23 May 2011) https://news.delta.com/delta-us-airways-announce-new-agreement-transfer-flying-rights-new-york-and-washington-dc (accessed 30 October 2022).

[155] McDonald (n 152).

[156] Department of Justice, 'Justice Department Statement on US Airways/Delta Airlines Acquisition of Slots at Washington's Reagan National and New York's Laguardia Airports' (11 October 2011) https://www.justice.gov/

6.4 ENFORCEMENT RECORD   211

This case has shown an initial convergent analysis between the DOT and DOJ in relation to the importance of slots in the air operation and the effects that they have on competition. It has also shown that this process could become prolonged and cumbersome. In addition, it has illustrated that even if both agencies had a similar understanding of the review process, at the end the DOJ partially departed from the DOT's final decision by underlining that although working closely, 'the two agencies act under substantially different statutory and regulatory frameworks'.[157] Nevertheless, as these airlines extract dominance from gate and slots control,[158] which are tools to impede entry or expansion and to generate considerable economic rents for their slot-holdings, it would be advisable for these two agencies to continue working closely in reviewing slot transactions.

6.4.1.2.2 United Airlines—Delta (Newark slots)

In July 2015, United decided to purchase from Delta twenty-four take-off and landing slots at Newark airport for US$14 million, and later in November 2015 the DOJ filed a lawsuit in the District Court of New Jersey opposing the acquisition.[159] The DOJ argued that Newark serves over 35 million passengers domestically and internationally each year, that an airline must have slots to be able to serve at Newark, that passengers using Newark airport pay among the highest fares in the country, that United was the monopoly non-stop provider to 139 of the 206 destinations served non-stop from Newark, that it already controlled 902 (73 per cent) slots at Newark, and after the acquisition it would control 75 per cent, and that United was not using all of the slots.[160]

In April 2016, the FAA, after conducting a capacity and operational performance review at the New York City area airports, decided to remove slot controls at Newark.[161] As a consequence, United informed about the termination of the slot lease agreement subject of litigation in the District Court of New Jersey.[162] According to the DOJ, this was the third attempt from United to acquire more slots at Newark since 2010.[163] In this case, both agencies through different mechanisms reached a similar understanding that resulted in the abandonment of the intended transaction.

opa/pr/justice-department-statement-us-airwaysdelta-airlines-acquisition-slots-washingtons-reagan (accessed 30 October 2022).

[157] ibid.

[158] Justin Bachman, 'Forget about Airline Mergers: Now It's All About Trading Airport Slots' *Bloomberg* (16 June 2015) https://www.bloomberg.com/news/articles/2015-06-16/forget-about-airline-mergers-now-it-s-all-about-trading-airport-slots (accessed 30 October 2022).

[159] *United States v United Continental* No 2:33-av-00001 (DNJ 2015) https://www.justice.gov/opa/file/792401/download (accessed 29 October 2022).

[160] ibid.

[161] 81 FR 19861–3.

[162] The decision states that: 'On April 5, 2016, Defendant United Continental Holdings, Inc ("United") informed Plaintiff United States of America that on April 4, 2016, United terminated the Slot Lease Agreement dated June 16, 2015, (the "Agreement") that is the subject of this litigation.' *United States v United Continental* (n 159).

[163] Department of Justice, 'Antitrust Division Blocks United Airline's Attempt to Bolster Its Monopoly at Newark Airport' (5 May 2016) https://www.justice.gov/atr/division-operations/division-update-2016/division-blocks-united-monopoly-newark (accessed 29 October 2022).

6.4.1.3 Transactions assessed solely by the DOJ

6.4.1.3.1 Delta Air Lines—Northwest Airlines Corporation

Between 2001 and 2005, US passenger airlines lost US$60 billion.[164] Douglas Steenland—CEO of Northwest Airlines in 2008—stated that 'consolidation was necessary to stabilize'.[165] He added that for years 'the public was in essence being subsidized by airline employees through wage cuts and through the shareholders, through loss of their equity'.[166] It was in this context that Delta Air Lines (Delta) and Northwest Airlines (Northwest) decided to merge. Northwest was strong financially but was lagging in relation to employee culture and passenger service, while Delta's finances were in poor shape, but it had a very strong employee culture and was well regarded by its customers.[167]

In 2009, the DOJ approved the Delta—Northwest merger, which was valued at US$2.6 billion and created the world's biggest airline at the time,[168] since the transaction was found to be 'likely to produce substantial and credible efficiencies that will benefit US consumers and is not likely to substantially lessen competition'.[169] The DOJ explained in its decision that the merger would result in efficiencies such as cost savings in airport operations, information technology, supply chain economics, and fleet optimization. It also added that the merger would benefit consumers, who would also benefit from the improved service resulting from the combination of complementary aspects of the airlines' networks.[170]

The Delta—Northwest merger differed from the two transactions that followed, United—Continental and American—US Air, as its approval did not require the merging parties to divest any gates or slots.[171] In United—Continental and American—US Airways the DOJ argued that only through ensuring the divestment of slots and gates at key airports would the benefits reach consumers, as the low-cost carriers would be encouraged to increase quality and decrease fares.[172]

Furthermore, as will be shown below, when assessing United—Continental in 2010, and American—US Airways in 2013, the DOJ did not focus on the 'potential competition issues between and among the merger participants'.[173] One of the most plausible explanations for such an approach, according to Gifford and Kudrle, is that the DOJ

---

[164] According to Airlines for America, an industry trade and lobbying group.

[165] Leslie Josephs, 'We Wanted to Go First. Here's What's Different in the Decade since Delta's MERGER with Northwest Upended the Airline Industry CNBC (7 April 2018) https://www.cnbc.com/2018/04/07/a-decade-after-deltas-northwest-merger-upended-the-airline-industry.html (accessed 18 November 2022).

[166] ibid.

[167] ibid.

[168] Martin Moylan, 'Justice Department Approves Northwest-Delta Merger' MPR NEWS (8 November 2016) http://www.mprnews.org/story/2008/10/29/northwest_delta_merger_ approved (accessed 18 November 2022).

[169] Statement of the Department of Justice's Antitrust Division on Its Decision to Close Its Investigation of the Merger of Delta Air Lines Inc and Northwest Airlines Corporation (29 October 2008) https://www.justice.gov/archive/opa/pr/2008/October/08-at-963.html (accessed 18 November 2022).

[170] ibid.

[171] Instead, it 'rested on an increase in consumer valuation of likely changes by the two merging parties on the apparent assumption that they were not imminently likely to engage in more competitive behaviour towards each other'. Gifford and Kudrle (n 39) 570.

[172] ibid 570–71; Peterman (n 145).

[173] Gifford and Kudrle (n 39) 565.

'does not consider the major airlines as potential competitors' in each other's routes.[174] Another important aspect that deserves attention is that in Delta—Northwest the DOJ presumed that consumers would benefit from the transaction.

6.4.1.3.2 *United—Continental*

In May 2010, UAL Corporation's United Airlines (United), the third largest carrier in the US by revenue, and Continental Airlines (Continental), the fourth largest carrier in the US by revenue, announced their decision to merge in a deal worth US$3.2 billion that would result in expected annual revenues of US$29 billion and savings of almost US$1 billion over the three years after the transaction.[175] United shareholders would own 55 per cent of the combined equity value and Continental shareholders the remaining 45 per cent.[176] In August 2010, the DOJ approved the deal subject to some conditions.[177] The agency's main concern was that the transaction would result in an overlap on a number of routes, particularly between United's hub airports and Continental's hub at Newark airport, which could be alleviated by leasing some slots and other assets at Newark to Southwest, a low cost carrier.[178]

Contrary to what we observed in Delta—Northwest, where remedies were not imposed, on this occasion the transaction triggered some remedies. However, these were minimal compared to those imposed a few years later in American—US Airways. In this case, the DOJ's decision not to challenge the merger meant that it ignored the issues raised by the Government Accountability Office, whose report alerted them to the fact that the merger would surpass Delta's in scope, and lead to the largest workforce in the US airline industry as well as a considerable number of overlaps in airport-pair combinations.[179] As part of the approval decision in a later case, the American Airlines—US Airways merger, the DOJ indicated that the remedial measure adopted in United—Continental to transfer thirty-six slots, three gates and other facilities to Southwest resulted in fares that were 27 per cent lower between Newark and St. Louis, and 15 per cent lower between Newark and Houston, as well as to a traffic increase for certain routes.[180] Another study showed that on some routes after the merger there was a fare decrease of 3–4 per cent.[181]

---

[174] ibid.

[175] Aaron Smith, 'United and Continental to Merge' *CNN Money* (3 May 2010) https://money.cnn.com/2010/05/03/news/companies/United_Continental_merge/ (accessed 15 November 2022).

[176] DOJ Press Release, 'United Airlines and Continental Airlines Transfer Assets to Southwest Airlines in Response to Department of Justice's Antitrust Concerns' 3 (27 August 2010) https://www.justice.gov/opa/pr/united-airlines-and-continental-airlines-transfer-assets-southwest-airlines-response (accessed 15 November 2022).

[177] ibid.

[178] ibid.

[179] United States Government Accountability Office, 'Airline Mergers: Issues Raised by the Proposed Merger of United and Continental Airlines' (27 May 2010) 12–15 https://www.gao.gov/assets/130/124803.pdf (accessed 15 November 2022).

[180] *United States v US Airways Grp Inc* 38 F Supp 3d 69 (DDC 2014) (No 1:13-CV-01236) ECF No 148 https://www.justice.gov/atr/case-document/file/514516/download [https://perma.cc/492D-JC7Y].

[181] Dennis W Carlton and others, 'Are Legacy Airline Mergers Pro- or Anti-Competitive? Evidence from Recent U.S. Airline Mergers' (2018) 1 International Journal of Industry Organization 3.

214 PUBLIC INTEREST ASSESSMENT AND THE DOT

The consumer welfare generated by the allocation of slots and gates to a low cost carrier (LCC) appears to have been at the forefront of the DOJ's thinking in the approval of this merger, which in its view would have a pro-competitive effect in terms of price decreases. This position was reiterated in American—US Airways, as we will see next. However, it seems that this position has been disputed, as some data has shown that after United and Continental merged, the fare for travel between Houston and Chicago was 57 per cent higher than three years earlier.[182] Similarly, some other commentators have indicated that it was premature to claim that by strengthening the position of LCCs the airline industry would observe fare decreases.[183] Regardless of the validity of such arguments, the more interesting question to contemplate is that the likely strengthening of LCCs balanced the DOJ's concerns in relation to the increased concentration post-merger.

6.4.1.3.3 American—US Airways

In February 2013, US Airways Group (US Airways) and American Airlines' parent company, AMR Corporation (AMR), announced their plans to merge their operations with the aim of creating the world's largest airline: American Airlines (AA).[184] In August 2013, the DOJ, six State Attorneys and the District of Columbia indicated that they were going to challenge the proposed deal as it would substantially lessen competition and result in 'passengers paying higher airfares and receiving less service'.[185] According to them, it was necessary to consider the following five topics: (1) an increase in market concentration; (2) the applicants did not need the merger to achieve their objectives; (3) a reduction in the number of competing airlines; (4) the government's duty to protect smaller airlines; and (5) the policy to protect consumers.[186]

Before examining how these concerns were addressed, it is important to explore previous deals with similar characteristics that did not receive the same level of concern from the DOJ. In April 2008, Delta Airlines (the third largest airline in the US) announced its intention to acquire Northwest airlines (the fifth largest airline in the US), creating the largest airline at the time.[187] Despite the predictions that the deal would be thoroughly scrutinized given its size, in October 2008, the DOJ closed its investigation

---

[182] Courtney D Lang, 'The Maverick Theory: Creating Turbulence for Mergers; (2014) 59 St Louis University Law Journal 257, 258.

[183] Peterman (n 145) 806.

[184] Genevieve Shaw Brown, 'What the US Airways and American Airlines Merger Means for Travelers' abcNEWS (14 February 2013) https://abcnews.go.com/Travel/us-airways-american-airlines-merger-means-travelers/story?id=18411484 (accessed 14 November 2022). According to the deal, 'AMR's stakeholders will own 72% of the new company and US Airways' stakeholders the remaining 28%'. See Antu Augustine, 'World's Largest Airlines? Proposed Merger of US Airways–American Airlines' (12 September 2013) https://ssrn.com/abstract=2338566 (accessed 18 November 2022).

[185] DOJ, 'Justice Department Files Antitrust Lawsuit Challenging Proposed Merger Between US Airways and American Airlines' (13 August 2013) https://www.justice.gov/opa/pr/justice-department-files-antitrust-lawsuit-challenging-proposed-merger-between-us-airways-and (accessed 14 November 2022).

[186] United States v US Airways Grp Inc (n 180) Complaint 13.

[187] Chris Isidore, 'Delta Acquires Northwest in $3.1 B deal' CNN Money (15 April 2008) https://money.cnn.com/2008/04/14/news/companies/delta_northwest/index.htm?eref=rss_travel (accessed 14 November 2022).

after finding that the proposed merger was likely to produce substantial and credible efficiencies that 'will benefit U.S. consumers and is not likely to substantially lessen competition'.[188] In August 2010, as discussed above, United and Continental also received approval from the DOJ, on the condition that they transfer a few airport slots at Newark Liberty Airport to Southwest Airlines.[189] Finally, in 2011, the DOJ argued that, despite some overlaps on certain non-stop routes, the merger between Southwest Airlines and AirTran was not likely substantially to lessen competition[190] (similar overlap concerns were also present in United and Continental, resulting in some slots being transferred to Southwest).[191] Some scholars have indicated that the losses generated since the 9/11 attacks combined with excess capacity within the US domestic market explain this consolidation phenomenon in the airline sector.[192]

Another important development that needs to be considered is that in 2002 and 2004 US Airways filed for bankruptcy and, in 2011, American Airlines declared bankruptcy.[193] Against this backdrop, it seemed unlikely that American—US Airways would give rise to any concerns; yet this was not the case.[194] The DOJ claimed that the merger was not necessary to ensure the viability of the two airlines. Another concern was the increase in market concentration, which was criticized by some commentators, who indicated that the DOJ's inaction in Northwest—Delta and United—Continental had forced US Airways and AA to remain 'viable competitors in a shrinking competitive landscape that the DOJ allowed to exist'.[195] Interestingly, from the perspective of fare increases, a study conducted by Kim and Singal using data from fourteen airline mergers from the mid-1980s noted that fares were significantly increased when airlines in bankruptcy were involved.[196] Opponents of the DOJ's decision also argued that interfering in the American Airlines—US Airways transaction would have made it difficult for the merging parties to compete under equal conditions with the 'super-Delta' and 'super-United', whose creation had already been blessed by the antitrust agency.[197]

---

[188] DOJ Press Release, 'Statement of Department of Justice's Antitrust Division on Its Decision to Close Its Investigation of the Merger of Delta Airlines Inc and Northwest Airlines Corporation' (29 October 2008) https://www.justice.gov/archive/opa/pr/2008/October/08-at-963.html (accessed 14 November 2022).

[189] DOJ Press Release (n 176).

[190] DOJ Press Release, 'Statement of the Department of Justice Antitrust Division on Its Decision to Close Its Investigation of Southwest's Acquisition of Airtran' (26 April 2011) https://www.justice.gov/opa/pr/statement-dep artment-justice-antitrust-division-its-decision-close-its-investigation (accessed 14 November 2022).

[191] Jordan T Sawyer, 'Unexpected Turbulence: An Examination of External Factors that Influenced the DOJ's Intensive Review of the American Airlines/US Airways Merger and Its Potential Impact on Future Mergers' (2015) 80 Journal of Air Law and Commerce 595, 605.

[192] Mulligan (n 29).

[193] Sawyer (n 191).

[194] Marilyn Geewax, 'DOJ Suit Seen Delaying, Not Killing Big Airline Merger' NPR (13 August 2013) stating that: 'Given that other airline mergers were approved, this was a surprise', University of Richmond transportation economist George Hoffer said. Other major carriers already have been allowed to combine forces, so 'it's illogical to oppose this merger. This move comes a day late and a dollar short'. https://www.npr.org/2013/08/13/211729 307/doj-suit-seen-delaying-not-killing-big-airline-merger?t=1594650320557&t=1594804557488 (accessed 14 November 2022).

[195] Lang (n 182) 258.

[196] Ehan H Kim and Vijay Singal, 'Mergers and Market Power: Evidence from the Airline Industry' (2003) 83 American Economic Review 549–.

[197] Sawyer (n 191) 611.

216 PUBLIC INTEREST ASSESSMENT AND THE DOT

The DOJ was also concerned about the reduction in the number of major domestic airlines from five to four, which would increase the chances of coordination given the similarity of the business models.[198] It is worth emphasizing that this concern did not emerge in previous transactions, although at that time the airline industry was equally highly concentrated.[199] To mitigate the concentration concern, the DOJ ordered US Airways and AA to divest a number of slots (required for take-off and landing) and gates (required to fly in and fly out): all 104 air carrier slots at Reagan National Airport; thirty-four slots at La Guardia International Airport; and two gates each at Boston Logan Airport, Chicago O'Hare airport, Dallas Love Field, Los Angeles International Airport, and Miami International Airport.[200] And, seeking to protect the small airlines and consumers, the DOJ stated that the slots and gates had to go to 'low cost carrier airlines' (LCCs) as a way to enhance system-wide competition in the airline industry with more choices and more competitive airfares for consumers.[201] Finally, a few days before the scheduled trial date, the parties and the DOJ reached a settlement.[202]

This departure from the prior DOJ position was predictable in light of the following two main factors. First, President Obama, during his campaign in 2007, announced that, if elected, he would 'direct [his] administration to reinvigorate antitrust enforcement' and that his goal was that antitrust agencies would 'step up review of merger activity and take effective action to stop or restructure those mergers that are likely to harm consumer welfare, while quickly clearing those that do not'.[203] Secondly, in 2010 the DOJ and the FTC published a revised version of the Merger Guidelines, developing the concept of a maverick firm, which is a firm that has 'a greater economic incentive to deviate from the terms of coordination than do most of [its] rivals'[204] and that 'plays a disruptive role in the market to the benefit of consumers'.[205] According to this framework, the DOJ treated US Airways as a maverick firm considering that it was a smaller airline that was used to offering low fares called 'advantage fares'.[206] These two factors explain the approach the DOJ took in the American Airlines—US Airways merger.

The DOJ's decision to challenge this merger reveals that levels of antitrust enforcement are a reflection of political priorities. Prior to Obama's administration, there was low merger enforcement that allowed the consolidation of large airlines. This was then

---

[198] *United States v US Airways Grp Inc* (n 180) Complaint 13.

[199] Lang (n 182) 275.

[200] DOJ Press Release, 'Justice Department Requires US Airways and American Airlines to Divest Facilities at Seven Key Airports to Enhance System-wide Competition and Settle Merger Challenge' (12 November 2013) https://www.justice.gov/opa/pr/justice-department-requires-us-airways-and-american-airlines-divest-facilities-seven-key (accessed 14 November 2022).

[201] ibid.

[202] Peterman (n 145) 172.

[203] Lang (n 182) 259.

[204] US Department of Justice and Federal Trade Commission, 'Horizontal Merger Guidelines' § 2.12 (1992) https://www.justice.gov/sites/default/files/atr/legacy/2007/08/14/hmg.pdf (accessed 15 November 2022).

[205] ibid § 2.1.5. The benefit derives from the ability or incentive that a maverick firm has to constrain price increases, particularly if the firm: (1) 'threatens to disrupt market conditions with a new technology or business model'; (2) has an 'incentive to take the lead in price cutting'; (3) has 'the ability and incentive to expand production rapidly using available capacity'; or (4) 'has often resisted otherwise prevailing industry norms to cooperate on price setting or other terms of competition'.

[206] Lang (n 182) 275–76; Mulligan (n 29).

6.4 ENFORCEMENT RECORD   217

shifted to a more aggressive approach in the Obama administration. This trend signifies that merging parties need to include as part of their merger plan the current administration's antitrust policies. The decision also shows that the DOJ reflected on the overall trend observed before this merger, which allowed the consolidation of big airlines without significant agency resistance. In this sense, it could be said that the assessment of American Airlines—US Airways was overly harsh or that the assessment of the earlier mergers was lenient.

6.4.1.4 International Airline Alliances with Antitrust Immunity

The following section presents transactions in which there have been opposing views between the competition agency and the regulator in assessing international (cross-border) airline alliances. As discussed above, the DOJ in its assessment of airline alliances it follows the same approach and standard as that applied to domestic airline mergers, while the main focus of the DOT is to scrutinize foreign-policy related factors, such as the attainment of a more open global aviation regime.[207]

6.4.1.4.1 Delta—Swissair—Sabena—Austrian Airlines alliance

In September 1995, Delta Air Lines (Delta), Swissair, Swiss Air Transport Company Ltd (Swissair), Sabena SA, Sabena Belgian World Airlines (Sabena), and Austrian Airlines (Austrian) jointly filed an application for approval of an alliance.[208] The DOJ's assessment was that the alliance would eliminate existing competition, that the ability of connecting services between New York and Geneva, Zurich, Brussels, and Vienna would not discipline the fares of the applicants for non-stop services for time-sensitive travellers, and that entry by other airlines into these markets was improbable.[209] Although the members of the alliance had already signed an OSA,[210] the DOJ argued that such a factor was not enough to reassure entry, particularly in New York, which was a city hub for Delta.[211] In addition, the DOJ claimed that New York was an unprofitable market, which was resulting in airlines leaving the market rather than entering and that the low number of passengers made entry questionable.[212] The DOJ also suggested that incumbent airlines such as Delta had the ability to bring supra-competitive prices to competitive levels, which constituted a considerable barrier for a new entrant.[213]

The DOT declined to adopt the totality of the DOJ's recommendations arguing that the loss of competition elicited by the alliance was irrelevant and that, by contrast, this cross-border cooperation agreement embraced a long-term international aviation

---

[207] Schlangen (n 56) 419.
[208] DOT, Joint Application of Delta Air Lines NC, Swissair, Swiss Air Transport Company Ltd, Sabena SA, Sabena Belgium World Airlines, and Austrian Airlines, for approval of and Antitrust Immunity for Alliance Agreements Pursuant to 49 USC §§ 41308 and 41309, Order 96-6-33, Docket OST-95-618-47 (17 June 1996).
[209] ibid.
[210] We noted above that the DOT requires the existence of an Open Skies Agreement (OSA), which allows negotiations on bilateral aviation rights that include issues such flight frequency, and fares, before granting immunity to international (cross-border) applicant carriers wanting to create a joint venture or alliance.
[211] Schlangen (n 56).
[212] Comments of the Department of Justice on Order to Show Cause, Delta—Swissair—Sabena—Austrian, Docket OST-95-618-39, 17 (28 May 1996).
[213] ibid 18.

218 PUBLIC INTEREST ASSESSMENT AND THE DOT

policy of great importance.[214] In balancing both, the DOT found that carving out New York would prevent the alliance from being implemented, which would endanger the pro-consumer and procompetitive effects of the proposed alliance.[215] This conclusion was grounded on the announcement made by the applicants that the agreement would be withdrawn if New York was carved out.[216] Therefore, New York-Brussels, Geneva, Vienna, and Zurich, and some other city pair markets received approval and thus antitrust immunity, as, according to the DOT, barriers to entry were not foreseen and the transaction was in the public interest.[217]

In this case we observe that the DOT did not present a detailed analysis of the reasons that would have refuted the serious concerns expressed by the DOJ in particular, in relation to the New York hub. Instead, the decision, in a very restricted way, suggested that entry was possible, and that the agreement was required by the public interest. One could argue that it seems that the announcement from the applicants about their intention to abandon the transaction if New York was carved out, was very persuasive in that regard. Nevertheless, an in-depth assessment by DOT of the anti-competitive effects suggested by the DOJ would have been a more defendable approach than a dismissal of the concerns based mainly on the parties' announcement about the divestment of the NY hub.

6.4.1.4.2 American Airlines—TACA

American Airlines (AA) and the TACA Group (TACA) jointly requested authorization to engage in reciprocal code-share services.[218] Costa Rica, El Salvador, Guatemala, Honduras, Nicaragua, and Panama were members of the TACA Group.[219] In December 1997, the DOT issued a show cause order summarizing its preliminary conclusions of the agreement. Accordingly, the DOT indicated that the agreement would advance important public benefits, such as lower costs and an enhanced service for US and international consumers, and invited comments on that order.[220] The DOJ, prior to expanding on its comments, clarified that their purpose was to establish whether the proposed code-sharing agreement would promote competition rather than to assess the likelihood that the agreement would violate the antitrust laws.[221] In light of this position, the DOJ indicated that the claimed benefits of the agreement were small and that the agreement posed some risks to competition that should be weighed in the public interest.[222]

---

[214] Delta—Swissair—Sabena—Austrian (n 208).

[215] ibid.

[216] Answer of Joint Applicants to Comments on Order to Show Cause, Joint Application of Delta Air Lines Inc, Swissair Ltd, Sabena SA, Austrian Airlines AG, Docket OST-95-618-44, 6–7.

[217] Delta—Swissair—Sabena—Austrian (n 208).

[218] DOT, Final Order, American Airlines, Inc and the TACA Group Reciprocal Code-Share Services Proceeding (n 103) 1.

[219] ibid.

[220] ibid.

[221] Comments of the United States Department of Justice on the Order to Show Cause, 'American Airlines Inc and the TACA Group Reciprocal Code-Share Services Proceeding' Docket OST-96-1700-99, 2 (28 January1998).

[222] ibid.

In particular, the DOJ was very concerned about the risk of harm due to the overlapping non-stop Miami–Central American city pairs, where the members of the agreement had combined market shares of between 88 per cent and 100 per cent.[223] The concern was also based on the fact that AA and TACA operated overlapping non-stop flights on almost all routes between Miami, the main Latin American hub in the US, and Central American gateway cities.[224] Under these largely horizontal networks, the DOJ affirmed that the code-share agreement had little potential to create pro-competitive effects and promote the public interest, and posed a relatively high risk to competition.[225] In relation to the benefits of the agreements, the DOJ indicated that the code-share service would represent a very small expansion of American's existing network, urging the DOT 'to give little weight to the parties proffered efficiencies and resulting claims of expanded networks and seamless service in the U.S.–Central American market'.[226]

On this occasion, the DOT once again disregarded the DOJ's opposition and granted antitrust immunity, stating that 'unless there are adverse competitive impacts that cannot be mitigated so as to promote the consumer benefits to be gained by open skies, total rejection of cooperative arrangements provided for under an open skies regime has the potential to frustrate, if not cancel, the overall benefits available through an open-skies regime'.[227] Some scholars have noted that the immunity granted in this case, in the Delta—Swissair—Sabena—Austrian Airlines alliance, and in some others, represented a 'heightened public benefits standard' that the DOT justified by finding that it was in the public interest and allowed 'airlines with small market shares to combine their networks and become more effective in competing against larger airlines'.[228] This trend shown by the DOT in granting immunity during the 1990s under the public benefits approach has been described as nothing more than a 'copy and paste' exercise, and the discrepancies between the DOT and the DOJ as a dispute between 'antitrust evidentiary standards' versus 'international aviation competition policy' positions,[229] a dispute in which the DOT's position prevailed.

6.4.1.4.3 Continental—United—Star

In July 2009, the DOT granted immunity and the conditional approval of alliance agreements that added Continental to the existing alliance involving Air Canada, Austrian, BMI, LOT, Lufthansa, SAS, Swiss, TAP, and United, and approval of an integrated joint venture agreement called Atlantic Plus—Plus (A++) involving Air Canada, Continental, Lufthansa, and United, which provided for the four parties to engage in joint pricing, sales and marketing, and revenue sharing for the transatlantic routes

---

[223] ibid.

[224] ibid.

[225] ibid.

[226] ibid.

[227] Final Order, American Airlines-TACA Group, Docket OST-96-1700-134, 15 (20 May 1998).

[228] Kinder (n 5) 974–75; Volodymyr Bilotkach and Kai Huschelrath, 'Antitrust Immunity for Airline Alliances' (2011) 7 Journal of Competition Law & Economics 335, 361.

[229] Hubert Horan, 'Double Marginalization and the Counter-Revolution Against Liberal Airline Competition' (2010) 37 Transportation Law Journal 251, 256.

220   PUBLIC INTEREST ASSESSMENT AND THE DOT

encompassed by the agreement.[230] The DOT concluded that the transaction did not substantially reduce or eliminate competition, it was not adverse to the public interest, and it was required by the public interest,[231] in spite of the DOJ's concerns that underpinned its recommendation to deny the requested immunity and instead grant a more restricted exemption.[232]

According to the DOJ, the proposed transaction would eliminate competition between certain Star alliance members—particularly between United and Continental in the domestic and non-transatlantic international markets—leading to higher fares and resulting in harm to certain international routes, where entry was unlikely. In addition, the DOJ suggested that the international alliance would facilitate coordination among United and Continental in terms of pricing, capacity planning, and entry and exit decisions regarding domestic operations outside the scope of the immunity. Furthermore, the DOJ, contrary to the findings of the DOT, considered that the applicants had not demonstrated why immunity was necessary to achieve the claimed benefits of the transaction, disregarded the applicant's assertion that they would not move forward without immunity, described as 'exaggerated' the concerns about significant litigation risks in the absence of immunity that were alleged by the applicants, indicated that the parties had 'inflated' the benefits of inter-alliance competition, and rejected the argument that the transaction would advance open skies. Therefore, the DOJ recommended carving out the following routes: Houston–Calgary, Houston–Toronto, Cleveland–Toronto, NYC–Halifax, NYC–Ottawa, NYC–Stockholm, NYC–Copenhagen, NYC–Lisbon, and NYC–Zurich, and maintaining some others. It also advocated for a more cautious and detailed analytical scrutiny before granting unrestricted immunity.[233]

The DOT was not persuaded by the concerns expressed by the DOJ, as in the DOT's view: (i) refusing immunity undermines the credibility of the US with its international partners, preventing the signature of more Open Skies agreements and the maintenance of the already existing.[234] (ii) a 'metal-neutral'[235] benefit-sharing arrangement is more beneficial than a simple code-sharing because it allows the maximization of joint revenues and gives more options to passengers in terms of fares and routes,[236] (iii) the proposed transaction showed significant benefits, inter alia: fare combinability, a reduction of double marginalization, economies of density, reduced costs, monetary benefits for frequent flyers, and the enhancement of efficiencies through sharing best practices

---

[230] Department of Transportation, Final Order (n 104); see also Comments of the United States Department of Justice on the Show Cause Order, Joint Application of Air Canada, the Austrian Group, British Midland Airways Ltd, Continental Airlines Inc, Deutsche Lufthansa AG, Polskie Linie Lotnicze Lot SA, Scandinavian Airlines System, Swiss International Air Lines Ltd, Tap Air Portugal, and United Air Lines Inc, Docket OST-2008-234, 6 (26 June 2009).

[231] Department of Transportation, Final Order (n 104) 3.

[232] Comments of the United States Department of Justice on the Show Cause Order, Docket OST-2008-234, 2 (26 June 2009).

[233] Comments of the United States Department of Justice on the Show Cause Order, Docket OST-2008-234 (26 June 2009).

[234] Department of Transportation, Final Order (n 104) 11.

[235] ibid, indicating that metal-neutral is a type of airline alliance where parties disregard who operates the 'metal' (aircraft) or collect revenue on a given itinerary.

[236] ibid 13–14.

and commercially sensitive data,[237] (iv) a reduction from four to three city pair markets or from three to two did not offer any risk of a substantial reduction in competition,[238] (v) the applicants were able to demonstrate that by sharing risks and optimizing the joint network, consumers would have more travel options, shorter travel times, and reduced fares at the margin, and this was likely to speed up the insertion of new capacity worldwide,[239] (vi) the restriction of the global granting of immunity could undermine 'greater service benefits for consumers'.[240]

Horan has asserted that given the number of benefits that the DOT listed as a result of this transaction, the public benefit standard has been reduced to a worthless process where any applicant can meet such an arbitrary rule, whereby it is enough to demonstrate that one consumer will benefit regardless of detrimental effects in other markets.[241] It has also been argued that some of the above factors DOT took into account are 'automatically' a result from an alliance agreement. Hence, unsurprisingly when Continental joined the Star alliance there was an expansion of Star's routing options, online service, and financial performance. As a practical matter, it seems that in future any market specific analysis will be unnecessary given that essentially any cross-border alliance will most likely 'automatically' meet the requirements of the regulator in relation to the ensuing benefits in the market.[242] This of course is a non-defendable approach of the DOT in its role as guarantor of the effective operation of the airline market(s) in the US.

Undoubtedly, this case represents a clear clash between the DOT's and the DOJ's standards of merger enforcement, in which the proclaimed protection of international aviation policies and international negotiations appeared to prevail to competition concerns. Such prevalence suggests that the DOT tends to favour airline alliances and neglects the DOJ's objections.[243] Perhaps the gap between these two agencies could be narrowed if the DOT clarified and restricted the scope of the public interest test and if more weight was given to the findings of the antitrust agency. This approach might also address criticisms that the decisions of the DOT are biased.

The examination of the next case is significant as it shows a policy shift of the DOT in assessing cross-border alliances.

6.4.1.4.4 *Delta—Aerovias de Mexico SA de CV*
In December 2016, the DOT granted conditional antitrust immunity to the alliance agreement between Delta Air Lines (Delta) and Aerovias de Mexico SA de CV (Aeromexico), allowing them to operate a joint venture (JV) between the US and Mexico.[244] The DOT found that the agreement would have anti-competitive effects at

---

[237] ibid 15–16.
[238] Department of Transportation, Final Order, Docket OST-2008-234 at 18 (10 July 2009).
[239] ibid.
[240] ibid.
[241] Horan (n 230) 278.
[242] ibid.
[243] Schlangen (n 56) 439–40.
[244] Department of Transportation, Final Order, Joint Application of Delta Air Lines Inc and Aerovias de Mexico SA de CV, Docket OST-2015-0070, 1 (14 December 2016).

New York City's John F. Kennedy International Airport (JFK) and Mexico City's Benito Juarez International Airport (MEX) airports due to infrastructure constraints, and at MEX, due to the absence of a slot regime aligned with international standards.[245] The concern of the DOT rested to a large extent on the fact that two-thirds of all domestic, and one-third of all international passengers in Mexico departed or landed at MEX, where the joint applicants controlled approximately 50 per cent of MEX slots, which they could use to their advantage to impede entry.[246]

Although the DOT identified that the proposed alliance would have substantial public benefits such as broader connectivity between the US and Mexico, improved network coordination, reduced travel times, and improved efficiency, it ordered the following remedial measures: (1) the divestiture of twenty-four slot pairs at MEX and four slot pairs at JFK to LCCs; (2) a limited duration of immunity to five years; (3) the elimination of exclusivity clauses in the alliance agreements; (4) annual reports of the alliance's public benefits and commercial development; (5) origin and destination data reports; (6) removal from IATA tariff determination that involves the discussion of fares, rates or charges applicable between the United States and any countries whose airlines have been or are subsequently granted antitrust immunity, or renewal of, to participate in similar alliance activities with a US airline(s); and (7) the responsibility to obtain approval for any common branding.[247] The DOT explained that the eligibility of LCCs to receive the divested slots at MEX was the most efficient way to discipline the dominant position of the joint applicants at MEX by introducing sufficient competition.[248] Another important feature of the DOT's decision was that the DOT limited the grant of immunity to five years in spite of the applicant's claims that immunity was usually granted for much longer, and that the time limit would have a negative impact on their ability to make long term investments.[249] Nonetheless, the DOT maintained that as the airline industry changes constantly, it was necessary to retain the authority to review the Antitrust Immunity (ATI) and to establish whether more divestitures were necessary.[250]

Through this case the DOT communicated a policy shift by granting immunity with multiple conditions that had never been seen before. It is important to highlight that the resistance from the joint applicants against the five-year ATI limit condition based on the concern that it would impede long term investments was proved to be speculative. Indeed, after the immunity was granted Delta invested more than US$620 million in acquiring additional shares of Grupo Aeromexico.[251] In relation to the restricted condition to divest slots only to LCCs, this raised some criticism, namely that by doing

---

[245] ibid.
[246] ibid.
[247] ibid.
[248] ibid.
[249] ibid.
[250] ibid.
[251] Morgan Durrant, 'Delta Successfully Completes Cash Tender Offer for Additional Shares of Grupo Aeromexico' Delta News Hub (13 March 2017) https://news.delta.com/delta-successfully-completes-cash-tender-offer-additional-shares-grupo-aeromexico (accessed 23 October 2022).

so the DOT was 'picking winners and losers' within a framework that ignores competitive realities.[252] This approach had been adopted much earlier when United and Continental were asked to transfer some slots to Southwest, a measure that at that time was seen as orientated towards protecting competitors rather than competition.

6.4.1.4.5 *American Airlines—JetBlue*

Between July and October 2020, American Airlines and JetBlue submitted to the DOT a number of joint venture agreements that taken together were meant to replicate on the domestic stage the model of international alliances which American Airlines pursued. Under the name Northeast Alliance (NEA), the scheme included—among other things—interline, code-sharing, and revenue sharing. The DOT reviewed the NEA framework and negotiated some commitments with the parties: for instance, they undertook to abide by specific communication protocols in order to limit the potential for collusion, to provide the DOT regularly with information regarding the Alliance's performance, and to divest several slots (some upfront, some only conditionally, in case the parties failed to hit their capacity targets). The agreement between the parties and the DOT was finalized in January 2021.

The DOJ's reaction to the agreement was not nearly as relaxed; in September of the same year, the government filed a strong-worded complaint to block it, by shedding light on its most controversial featured.[253] Under their umbrella agreement, the parties would coordinate 'on all aspects' of network planning at the four north-eastern airports most directly concerned by the agreement; and according to the Mutual Growth Incentive Agreement, they would pool their revenues and share them so that each participant would earn equal revenues. The Department claimed that this would remove any incentive for the parties to compete with each other on price, both in the relevant areas and throughout the country, and would enable them to reduce capacity without any appreciable consequences.[254] In other words, the alliance 'effectively operates like a merger in domestic markets that have either Boston or JFK/LaGuardia, as an endpoint'.[255]

The considerable difference in the interpretation of the agreement by the DOT and by the DOJ is not the only point of interest of the case: a few days after the DOJ filed its complaint, the DOT seized the opportunity to explain its own choices and to chart a different path going forward. It did so by releasing an unusual document titled 'Clarification of Departmental Position on American Airlines-JetBlue Airways Northeast Alliance Joint Venture'[256], which aims to convey two messages: first, that the Department's prerogatives don't grant it the authority to 'approve or disapprove agreements submitted for review' under Section 41720, so much that the concessions extracted from the parties should be regarded as an uncontroversial success. Secondly,

---

[252] Kinder (n 5) 985.
[253] *United States and Others v American Airlines and JetBlue Airways* Case 1:21-cv-11558 (D Mass 2021).
[254] ibid § 26.
[255] ibid § 49.
[256] 86 FR 53401.

the Department 'intends to defer to the DOJ, as the primary enforcer of Federal anti-trust laws, to resolve antitrust concerns with respect to the NEA. The Department be-lieves that it would be inefficient and unhelpful to have two concurrent proceedings and therefore intends to defer any independent action until the DOJ antitrust litigation has concluded'.

The 'Clarification' does not say explicitly whether this wait-and-see attitude is to be understood as a one-off occurrence or a new policy. But a hint that it might be the latter comes from another, even more recent, case: the proposed acquisition of Spirit Airlines by JetBlue. On the very same day that the DOJ challenged the merger in court,[257] the DOT published a statement[258] to clarify that it did support the DOJ's effort, and that it planned to deny the exemption application submitted by the two airlines to be al-lowed to operate under common ownership prior to deal being finalized.[259] Should the DOT follow through with this deferential approach towards the DOJ, the merger control system in the airline sector might be about to get an informal but much needed clarification and simplification.

6.5 Some Implications of the Analysis

This section examined five merger and acquisition enforcement decisions, two of which were decided by the DOT and three by the DOJ. This analysis relates to a sector that has moved from being strictly regulated to being completely liberalized, it has been affected by the effect of the 9/11 terrorist attacks and is one of the industries that has been most impacted by Covid-19. Over time the airline sector has been characterized by a con-solidation trend. This tendency prompted policies that try to align business interests with national strategic ones. In this challenging balancing exercise, our analysis shows that there is little room for competition concerns to be properly assessed and/or to be taken into consideration. This phenomenon has led to the consolidation of big airlines, for example the Delta—Northwest,[260] United—Continental,[261] and American—US Airways[262] outcomes.

Some notorious examples of this consolidation approach were seen in the Northwest—Republic[263] and Ozark—TWA[264] cases, in which the DOT estimated that the airline sector is a contestable market, entry barriers are low, and non-hub services

---

[257] *United States and Others v JetBlue Airways and Spirit Airlines* Case 1:23-cv-10511 (D Mass 2023).

[258] DOT, 'USDOT Statement on the Justice Department's Lawsuit to Block Proposed JetBlue-Spirit Merger' (7 March 2023) https://www.transportation.gov/briefing-room/usdot-statement-justice-departments-lawsuit-block-proposed-jetblue-spirit-merger.

[259] David Shepardson, 'U.S. rejects JetBlue, Spirit Exemption Request, Citing Lawsuit' (24 March 2023) https://www.reuters.com/business/aerospace-defense/us-transportation-dept-denies-jetblue-spirit-exemption-request-citing-doj-2023-03-24.

[260] Statement of the Department of Justice's Antitrust Division on Its Decision to Close Its Investigation of the Merger of Delta Air Lines Inc and Northwest Airlines Corporation (n 169).

[261] DOJ Press Release (n 176).

[262] *United States v US Airways Grp Inc* (n 180) Complaint 13.

[263] Northwest-Republic Acquisition Case, DOT Docket No 43,754.

[264] TWA-Ozark Acquisition Case, DOT Order No 86-9-29, 2 (12 September 1986).

6.5 SOME IMPLICATIONS OF THE ANALYSIS   225

such as code-sharing serve as hub options. Such an approach was reinforced by requiring the merger opponents to demonstrate that the transaction would increase levels of concentration and would be anti-competitive. The DOJ was consistently opposing these arguments, however, when the DOJ regained the authority to review the mergers, the pattern of protecting airlines did not change. It was noted that 'the post-2008 crisis period has seen four major mergers approved by the DOJ', which created a significant cumulative increase in concentration[265] and 'look very questionable in light of its own [the DOJ's] merger guidelines'.[266] In the Delta—Northwest[267] case, despite the size of the operation, the DOJ found that the merger was beneficial in terms of cost savings in airport operations, supply chain economies, and fleet optimization, among others, that a presumption that such benefits would benefit consumers was established and the transaction was approved without conditions. Later, in United—Continental,[268] the concerns about overlapping routes between United's hub airports and Continental's hub at Newark airport were mitigated by transferring some slots and other assets at Newark to Southwest, an LCC, this time under the presumption that such a measure would bring price decreases resulting in consumer welfare.

In American—US Airways,[269] the DOJ was concerned with the reduction in the number of airlines and an increase in market concentration, aspects that in Delta—Northwest[270] and United—Continental[271] were seen as advantageous. In terms of city pair markets and according to the horizontal merger guidelines, 460 of them should have been treated as concentrated since as a result of that merger their Herfindahl–Hirschman Index would exceed 2,500 and the merger would raise the index by over 200 points.[272] Arguably, 'the airline industry's unique characteristics support a merger analysis that differs in critical ways from traditional merger analysis', given that it creates network effects.[273] Thus, the DOJ's approach was that mergers between largely non-overlapping airline networks can generate a significant consumer surplus without offsetting price effects due to complementarities between the operation and the scope for cost rationalization.[274] In the end, the transaction was approved with multiple conditions.

Likewise, the analysis of some airline alliance cases has illustrated a big gap between the DOT's and the DOJ's approaches. According to the DOT's approach, every airline

---

[265] 'The airline industry shows a four-firm national concentration level based on airline passenger miles of about seventy percent while four-firm concentration based on the shares of all domestic ticketed passengers is close to eighty percent.' See Fiona Scott Morton and others, 'Benefits of Preserving Consumers Ability to Compare Airline Fares' (2015) 1 Travel Technical Association 35https://skift.com/wp-content/uploads/2015/05/CRA.TravelTech. Study_.pdf (accessed 18 November 2022).

[266] Gifford and Kudrle (n 39) 539.

[267] Statement of the Department of Justice's Antitrust Division on Its Decision to Close Its Investigation of the Merger of Delta Air Lines Inc and Northwest Airlines Corporation (n 169).

[268] Department of Justice Press Release (n 176).

[269] *United States v US Airways Grp Inc* (n 180) Complaint 13.

[270] Statement of the Department of Justice's Antitrust Division on Its Decision to Close Its Investigation of the Merger of Delta Air Lines Inc and Northwest Airlines Corporation (n 169).

[271] Department of Justice Press Release (n 176).

[272] *United States v US Airways Grp Inc* (n 180) Complaint at Appendix A.

[273] Gifford and Kudrle (n 39) 577.

[274] ibid.

226 PUBLIC INTEREST ASSESSMENT AND THE DOT

alliance inherently involves a great number of benefits that do not seem to be clear for the DOJ. For instance, in AA—TACA[275] and Continental—United—Star,[276] the DOT listed numerous benefits that the DOJ considered to be non-significant, overstated, or untested. Equally, while the DOJ was concerned about the anti-competitive effects of the agreements, for the DOT they were minor (Delta—Swissair—Sabena—Austrian Airlines alliance[277]) or less important than losing credibility in the international arena (Continental—United—Star[278]). It has also been illustrated that when applicants argued that they would cease the application if a particular remedy were to be imposed, this served as an effective persuasion mechanism to DOT. This was the case in the Delta—Swissair—Sabena—Austrian Airlines alliance,[279] where despite the DOJ's concerns over the divestment of the New York hub, the DOT compromised its decision by stating that this divestment would prevent the implementation of the alliance. Given this lenient approach, it was a surprise to observe the reservations shown by the DOT in Delta—Aerovias Mexico[280] in terms of the anti-competitive effects derived from the significant number of slots that the applicants had in JFK and MEX airports, and the number or remedies that were imposed, among which were the divestiture of slots and the time limitation of the immunity.

The analysis of these airline alliances leads to the following two conclusions. First, the efforts of the DOJ in analysing the potential anti-competitive effects and possible remedies to mitigate them were pointless, as the DOT had a biased view that these alliances were beneficial per se. Secondly, for the DOT the protection of international aviation policies and international negotiations is the core of merger enforcement, in which competition does not play a main role. These two conclusions reveal that the review system favours the interest of the parties.

Having seen some decisions related to slot transactions, it could be said that it is encouraging to observe that the DOJ and the DOT recognize that a proper use of slots is in the public interest as they facilitate entry, increase competition, and promote lower fares for consumers (Delta—Us Airways slot swap[281]). In the United—Delta case,[282] it was promising to see these two bodies working closely even if at the end there was a disparity. It is though paradoxical if the two agencies could not reach a common understanding when reviewing a few transactions as shown in this chapter.

---

[275] Department of Transportation, Final Order, American Airlines, Inc and the TACA Group Reciprocal Code-Share Services Proceeding (n 103).
[276] Department of Transportation, Final Order (n 104) 1.
[277] DOT, Joint Application (208).
[278] Department of Transportation, Final Order (n 104) 1.
[279] DOT, Joint Application (n 208).
[280] Department of Transportation, Final Order, Joint Application of Delta Air Lines, Inc. and Aerovias de Mexico, S. A. DE C.V., Docket OST-2015-0070 at 1 (December 14, 2016).
[281] United States Department of Justice(n 149) 4–5.
[282] *United States v United Continental* (n 159).

6.6 Concluding Remarks

M&A are an important tool to ensure an efficient air transport system. So far, merger enforcement has facilitated the consolidation of market power and has protected large airlines. It is hard to predict the future of the airline industry, but we propose the following recommendations to create a more efficient review process: regardless of the agency in charge of making the approval decisions, it is important that the benefits of the transactions are assessed in detail, that entry is deemed likely rather than speculative, that the remedies are appropriate and closely monitored, and that the standards of review are consistent.

In relation to airline alliances, while they can bring to their members economies of scale, scope, and density; cost reduction; and revenue growth,[283] it is unclear whether those agreements provide real benefits to consumers.[284] Even if these types of arrangements do not involve a proper transfer of ownership, they have led to an increase in market power. Alliances, that have been assessed and are immune to antitrust enforcement, have also led to harm to competition by adopting conducts, such as refusing to code-share with LCCs, rejecting the participation of LCCs in interline traffic, and limiting the use of airport facilities (eg slots and gates).[285] Aside from the benefits that airline alliances provide to their members and to the international air transportation policy goals that are consolidated through them, such as credibility from international partners and with that the possibility of signing new cross-border agreements,[286] there is still one important aspect that deserves attention: competition. Even if an airline alliance has been granted immunity by the DOT under the public interest standard, this does not imply that the airlines that comprise the alliance are still competing on the merits as any other two airlines outside the alliance (or indeed any other two companies in any market) would. Therefore, it is important to reconcile the benefits that cross-border agreements can offer at a national and international level and mitigate the risks posed by granting antitrust immunity.

In sum, we advocate a policy in which competition principles play a fundamental role and more weight should be given to the analysis of the DOJ, whether the DOJ becomes the primary agency for the assessments of M&As, slot transactions and alliances or it still shares the assessment of transactions with the DOT.[287] Moreover, we consider that the best possible way to tackle the application of inconsistent assessment approaches leading to contradictory decisions in this concurrent system of merger enforcement

---

[283] Rigas Doganis, *The Airline Business in the Twenty-first Century* (Routledge 2001) 71.

[284] Dempsey (n 101) 250. United States Government Accountability Office, 'International Air Alliances: Greater Transparency Needed on DOT's Efforts to Monitor the Effects of Antitrust Immunity' 14 (March 2019) https://www.gao.gov/assets/700/697690.pdf (accessed 27 October 2022).

[285] Dempsey (n 101).

[286] Department of Transportation, Final Order, Docket OST-2008-234 at 11 (1 July 2008).

[287] See eg Carstensen (n 105) 1103–104 who proposes a presumption against immunity in those cases where the DOJ objects an agreement on competitive basis. In such a case, he adds, the DOT would then have the obligation to defend that the public interest outweighs the competitive risks. Otherwise, the DOJ should have the capacity to challenge the agreement as an antitrust infringement.

would be to remove the authority from the DOT to review the anti-competitive effects of the transactions and bestow it solely to the DOJ. This withdrawal of antitrust assessment powers from the DOT is based on its limited expertise in competition analysis compared to the DOJ. Hence, the antitrust agency should have the ultimate decision making power while the DOT, as a sectoral expert, should decide on non-competition concerns and act in a confined advisory role in the DOJ's competition assessment. Such an approach is followed in the UK and is based on clear demarcation lines of the respective remit and scope of the regulator and the competition authority, as well as on a close cooperation modus operandi that involves information exchange and reciprocal analytical assistance (eg by sharing the analysis or contributing to the analysis of each other). This concurrent jurisdiction model has the potential to offer better quality decisions in a more efficient manner.

7

Public Interest Assessment and the Federal Reserve Board (FRB), the Office of the Comptroller of the Currency (OCC), and the Federal Deposit Insurance Corporation (FDIC)

7.1 The Regulators

The banking sector has undergone a radical transformation over the past decades. Technological advancements have led to structural changes in the market. The sector has seen the appearance of intermediaries—white-label banks—which offer regulated financial services such as payment and advisory services.[1] Physical branches have in turn been replaced by online banking, in which the emergence of financial technology (FinTech) has been staggering. As part of this transition, it is remains unclear whether traditional banks have embraced and accompanied the structural change.

Another legitimate question is whether the existing concurrent merger jurisdiction shared between the banking regulators and the antitrust agencies, with their respective standards of review and procedures, reflect the structural transformation trends. This question is especially pertinent for a nation that has witnessed the consolidation of 70 per cent of its banks over the past four decades. Is this the result of mergers being approved without proper scrutiny and without assurances that consumer welfare takes priority? President Biden in his Executive Orden on Promoting Competition in the American Economy has noted that no single banking merger application has been denied in the last fifteen years, urging the banking regulators and the Department of Justice to update the guidelines on banking mergers 'to provide more robust scrutiny of mergers'.[2]

---

[1] OECD, 'Digital Disruption in Banking and its Impact on Competition' (2020) http://www.oecd.org/daf/comp etition/digital-disruption-in-financial-markets.htm (accessed 18 November 2022).

[2] White House, 'Fact Sheet: Executive Order on Promoting Competition in the American Economy' (9 July 2021) https://www.whitehouse.gov/briefing-room/statements-releases/2021/07/09/fact-sheet-executive-order-on-promoting-competition-in-the-american-economy/ (accessed 18 November 2022)

230   PUBLIC INTEREST ASSESSMENT AND FRB, OCC, AND FDIC

Hence, the purpose of this chapter is to offer an overview of the merger review process in the banking sector and to try to answer these questions by examining case law. The chapter will start with a discussion of the composition of the banking regulators, the FRB, OCC and FDIC, and the relevant regulatory framework before discussing some of the seminal case law that will show the approach they take in applying their assessment tests and how these approaches compare with the one antitrust authorities take pursuant to their competition standard. The chapter will also discuss some implications that arise from assessing the role and practice of the banking regulators and the competition authority.

7.1.1 Composition and Legislation

The Federal Reserve Board (FRB) was given jurisdiction to review acquisitions[3] of bank stock by means of the Clayton Antitrust Act of 1914.[4] Then, in an attempt to control bank mergers, the National Bank Consolidation Act of 1918 designated the Office of the Comptroller of the Currency (OCC) to oversee mergers between state and national banks.[5] The Banking Act of 1933 gave authority to the board of governors of the Federal Reserve Board (FRB) to assess mergers between member banks, while the Federal Deposit Insurance Act of 1950 conferred to the Federal Deposit Insurance Corporation (FDIC) the power to supervise mergers between non-member banks.[6] Nevertheless, it has been indicated that two main aspects influenced the absence of merger enforcement during the first half of the twentieth century: (1) the above-mentioned rules did not provide a clear competitive criterion about how to assess mergers;[7] and (2) the lack of interest from the DOJ to get involved in the review process.[8] This led to a significant merger movement where almost 2,600 banks merged, most of them without approval by the respective agencies.[9] This phenomenon forced Congress to enact the Bank Merger Act of 1960, establishing a federal supervisory regime for bank mergers.[10]

According to the Bank Merger Act of 1960, before merging, approval was required from the Office of the Comptroller of the Currency (OCC) for national banks,[11]

---

[3] In this chapter the terms 'merger' and 'acquisition' are used interchangeably.

[4] 38 Stat 730–32, 734 (1914), as amended, 15 USC §§ 17–19, 21 (1958).

[5] National Bank Consolidation Act of 1918, Pub L No 65-240, 40 Stat 1043, 1043–44 (codified as amended at 12 USC §§ 215–215b (2018)).

[6] Banking Act of 1933, ch 89, Pub L No 73-66, 48 Stat 162 (codified as amended in scattered sections of 12 USC); Federal Deposit Insurance Act of 1950, Pub L No 81-797, § 2, 64, Stat 873, 892 (codified as amended at 12 USC § 1828(c)).

[7] Benjamin J Klebaner, 'Federal Control of Commercial Bank Mergers' (1962) 37(3) Indiana Law Journal 290. Casson and Burrus have indicated that '[n]either ... [the National Bank Consolidation and Merger Act of 1918 or the Federal Deposit Insurance Act] contained any provisions relating to any standards to be applied by the respective agencies in determining the competitive aspects of the banking combinations.' See Joseph E Casson and Bernie R Burrus, 'Federal Regulation of Bank Mergers' (1969) 18 American University Law Review 677, 682.

[8] Jeremy C Kress, 'Modernizing Bank Merger Review' (2020) 37 Yale Journal on Regulation 435, 444. Kress noted that there was also a belief that banks were exempted from the Clayton and Sherman Antitrust Acts.

[9] ibid.

[10] Bank Merger Act, Pub L No 86-463, 74 Stat 129 (1960) (codified as amended at 12 USC § 1828(c)).

[11] A national bank in the United States 'is a chartered financial institution that is a member of the Federal Reserve System. In most cases, it is owned and operated by private individuals ... The main difference between national and

from the Federal Reserve Board (FRB or the board) for state member banks, and the Federal Deposit Insurance Corporation (FDIC) for non-member banks. Likewise, the Act provided three indicators that the agencies had to examine during the merger review: (1) the effect on competition; (2) the convenience and needs of the community to be served; and (3) the financial conditions of the banks seeking to merge, as well as the general character[12] and fitness of their management.[13] An additional development took place not long after the Bank Merger Act of 1960 was enacted. The Supreme Court clarified that banking mergers were also subject to the federal antitrust rules, which led to oversight from the DOJ after decades of DOJ's lack of intervention.[14] Later in 1966, the Bank Merger Act of 1960 was amended with the aim of unifying the regulatory framework applied by the antitrust agencies and the banking agencies.[15] This unification was provoked by the high number of conflicting outcomes between the antitrust agencies and the banking agencies, as it was the case in almost one-third of the mergers approved in 1960.[16]

The 1966 amendment explained that the convenience and needs factor included in the Bank Merger Act of 1960, referred usually to the ability of the banking system to 'provide banking services essential to the full development of the economy, to full employment and full production'.[17] At the same time, the reform added that agencies should examine not just the financial and managerial resources of the merging parties, but 'the future prospects of the existing and proposed institutions'.[18] Another important development was that the reform highlighted that in every merger case the convenience and needs of the community to be served should be satisfied regardless of the competitive effects of the transaction.[19] Later, in 1977, through the Community Reinvestment Act (CRA) another factor was included requiring the agencies to study the effects of the proposed merger on underserved populations.[20] The review was also expanded by adding the 'risk to the stability of the United States banking or financial

---

state banks is that the former belongs to the Federal Reserve while the latter do not'. See 'The National Bank History and Purpose' https://study.com/learn/lesson/national-bank-history-purpose.html (accessed 13 October 2022).

[12] The general character of a bank refers to the bank's core business plan. Any change in the general character of a bank requires permission of the board, for instance, if the bank wants to become primarily internet-focused or to concentrate solely on subprime lending or leasing activities. See Board of Governors of the Federal Reserve System, 'Guidance Regarding Significant Changes in the General Character of a State Member Bank's Business and Compliance with Regulation H' (2002) SR 02-9 https://www.federalreserve.gov/boarddocs/srletters/2002/sr0209. htm (accessed 28 November 2022).

[13] 12 USC § 1828(i)(4). For an interesting analysis of management attributes in banks, see Linda V Ditchkus, Gregory E Sierra, and Brad J Reed, 'The Role of Managerial Prudence in Bank Loans Loss Provisioning' (2011) 23(4) Journal of Managerial Issues 447.

[14] See *United States v Philadelphia National Bank* 374 US 321, 335–49 (1963). See also *United States v First National Bank & Trust Co of Lexington*, 376 US 655, 672–73 (1964).

[15] Pub L No 89-356, 80 Stat 7 (codified as amended in 12 USC § 1828(c) (2018)).

[16] Klebaner (n 7).

[17] HR Rep No 89-1179, 5 (1965).

[18] 12 USC § 1828(c)(5).

[19] ibid. This amendment signifies that the convenience and needs criteria is an independent consideration separate from the competitive analysis.

[20] Community Reinvestment Act of 1977, Pub L No 95-128 § 804, 91 Stat 1111, 1148 (codified at 12 USC § 2903 (2018)).

system' as one more consideration.[21] At this juncture, it is important to indicate that banks used to avoid oversight from the banking agencies by turning or reincorporating themselves as holding companies, which induced Congress in 1956 to enact the Bank Holding Company Act (BHCA) providing that bank holding companies seeking to merge should request pre-approval by the Federal Reserve, whose standard is similar to the Bank Merger Act examined earlier.[22]

Two more bank industry laws are relevant for the regulation of financial institutions mergers or acquisitions: the Home Owners' Loan Act (HOLA),[23] that refers to acquisitions of control of savings associations or savings and loan holding companies, including any company that directly or indirectly controls a savings association; and the Change in Bank Control Act (Control Act),[24] that governs the direct or indirect acquisition of control of any depository institution, different from a transaction covered by the BHCA, the BMA, or the HOLA, such as an acquisition by an individual, corporation, partnership, trust, association, joint venture, pool, syndicate, or site proprietorship. Likewise, important steps towards deregulation took place in the 1990s with the enactment of the Riegle-Neal Interstate Banking and Branching Efficiency Act (Riegle-Neal Act) in 1994, later amended in 1997, permitting commercial banks to function with full/unrestricted/unlimited freedom across state lines.[25]

7.1.1.1 Federal Reserve Board (FRB)

The Federal Reserve System is the central bank of the United States.[26] The FRB is run by seven members, or 'governors', who are nominated by the President and confirmed by the Senate, serving a fourteen-year term.[27] The board is responsible for reviewing mergers and acquisitions of companies that are subject to the BHCA,[28] as well as in circumstances where the acquirer is a state bank that is a member of the Federal Reserve System. A simple majority vote is required to render a decision,[29] having the possibility of delegating such a task to the Federal Reserve Bank if the transaction does not induce important competitions or other concerns.[30] The delegation criteria do not apply when '(i) the merger or acquisition would raise the HHI by 200 points or more to a

---

[21] 12 USC § 1828(c)(5).

[22] 12 USC § 1842(c).

[23] 12 USC §§ 1461–1700.

[24] 12 USC § 1817(j).

[25] Riegle-Neal Amendments Act, Pub L No 105-24, 111 Stat 238 (1997).

[26] Board of Governors of the Federal Reserve System, 'About the Federal Reserve System' https://www.federal reserve.gov/aboutthefed/structure-federal-reserve-system.htm (accessed 28 November 2022).

[27] ibid.

[28] 12 USC §§ 1242(c)(3)–(4).

[29] Board of Governors of the Federal Reserve System, 'FAQs: How do the Federal Reserve and the US Department of Justice, Antitrust Division, analyze the competitive effects of mergers and acquisitions under the Bank Holding Company Act, the Bank Merger Act and the Home Owners Loan Act?' https://www.federalreserve. gov/bankinforeg/competitive-effects-mergers-acquisitions-faqs.htm (accessed 21 November 2022).

[30] ABA Section of Antitrust Law, *Bank Mergers and Acquisitions Handbook* (2006) 9. There are twelve Federal Reserve Banks operating within particular geographic areas that link the Federal Reserve System with the private sector through their directors, who are appointed by their respective banks (6) and by the Federal Reserve Board (3); see Board of Governors of the Federal Reserve System, 'About the Federal Reserve System' (n 26).

7.1 THE REGULATORS   233

level of 1800 or higher in any local banking market in which the parties to a transaction have overlapping operations, or (ii) the merger or acquisition would increase the post-transaction market share for the acquiring firm to more than 35 percent in any overlapping market.'[31] The FRB also needs to ensure compliance of the merged entity with the CRA, which includes[32] lending (loans for small businesses, small farms, and community development loans), investment, and service tests.[33]

7.1.1.2 Office of the Comptroller of the Currency (OCC)

The OCC supervises around 1,200 national banks, federal savings associations, and federal branches and agencies of foreign banks, ensuring that they operate safely and that fair access and fair treatment is provided to customers.[34] The OCC is led by the Comptroller of the Currency, who is appointed by the President with the consent of the Senate. In reviewing mergers under the provision 12 CFR 5.33,[35] the agency examines the capital level of the new entity, the observance of the respective regulations, the safety and soundness of the transaction, and the effects on the shareholders, depositors, other creditors, and consumers.[36] In addition to these factors, the OCC also examines the effect on competition, the financial and managerial resources and future prospects of the new entity, the probable effects on the convenience and needs of the community served, the effectiveness of the applicants' money laundering policies, the risk to the stability of the U.S. banking and financial system, concentration levels, and the performance of the merging parties in helping to meet the credit needs of the relevant communities, including low and moderate income (LMI) neighbourhoods pursuant to 12 USC 2903(a)(2).[37]

7.1.1.3 The Federal Deposit Insurance Corporation (FDIC)

The FDIC is an independent agency of the federal government that was created in 1933, whose mission is to preserve stability and public confidence in the financial system.[38] The FDIC is funded by premiums that banks and savings associations pay for deposit

---

[31] Board of Governors of the Federal Reserve System, 'FAQs' (n 29).

[32] Board of Governors of the Federal Reserve System, 'Electronic Applications and Applications Filing Information' https://www.federalreserve.gov/supervisionreg/afi/cra.htm (accessed 21 November 2022). See also Federal Financial Institutions Examination Council's (FFIEC), 'Examination Procedures: Overview' https://www.ffiec.gov/cra/exam_overview.htm (accessed 15 November 2022).

[33] Board of Governors of the Federal Reserve System, 'Electronic Applications' (n 32). Service tests vary in scope depending on the size of the institution. As part of the service test, 'the availability and effectiveness of a bank's systems for delivering retail banking services and the extent and innovativeness of its community development services' are assessed; see 12 CFR § 25.24 and, for more information, Office of the Comptroller of the Currency, 'Comptroller's Handbook: Community Reinvestment Act Examination Procedures' (June 2018) https://www.occ.treas.gov/publications-and-resources/publications/comptrollers-handbook/files/cra-exam-procedures/index-cra-examination-procedures.html (accessed 14 October 2022).

[34] Office of the Comptroller of the Currency, '2022 Annual Report' https://www.occ.treas.gov/publications-and-resources/publications/annual-report/files/2022-annual-report.html (accessed 20 November 2022).

[35] Office of the Comptroller of the Currency, 'Comptroller's Licensing Manual: Business Combinations' (July 2018) 2 https://www.occ.gov/publications-and-resources/publications/comptrollers-licensing-manual/files/bizcombo.pdf (accessed 21 November 2022).

[36] ibid.

[37] ibid.

[38] Federal Deposit Insurance Corporation (FDIC), 'What We Do' https://www.fdic.gov/about/what-we-do/ (accessed 28 October 2022).

insurance coverage.[39] The agency is led by a board of five directors, including the Comptroller of the Currency and the Director of the Consumer Financial Protection Bureau, who are appointed by the President and confirmed by the Senate.[40] Section 18(c) of the Federal Deposit Insurance Act (FDIA)—also known as the Bank Merger Act[41]—stipulates that prior approval is required before any insured depository institution may: (1) merge or consolidate, with purchase or otherwise acquire the assets of, or assume any deposit liabilities of, another insured depository institution if the resulting institution is to be a non-member bank, or (2) merge or consolidate with, assume liability to pay any deposits or similar liabilities of, or transfer assets and deposits to a non-insured bank or institution.

The FDIC cannot approve transactions that would result in a monopoly, would limit trade or the effect of which may be substantially to lessen competition, unless such an anti-competitive effect is outweighed by a public interest of the community to be served.[42] As an illustration, the FDIC may approve a transaction aiming at preventing the breakdown of one of the institutions involved.[43] Before approval, the FDIC should also examine the financial and managerial resources and prospects of the existing and proposed institutions, the convenience and needs of the community to be served, and the efficacy of each insured depository institution involved in contesting money-laundering activities, including in overseas branches.[44]

7.1.2 Filing Instructions and Process Overview

As was indicated above, once the DOJ reinvigorated its role in banking merger reviews, there was significant discrepancy in the approach of the banking agencies and the DOJ, with regard to the types of transactions that should be assessed.[45] Seeking to reach some consensus, the banking agencies and the DOJ in 1995 jointly published a 'merger screens' system,[46] similar to the Herfindahl–Hirschman Index (HHI)[47] in the US horizontal merger guidelines introduced in 1982[48] that helps to identify transactions that do not incur significant adverse effects on competition. Screen A covers transactions in areas with fewer than 10,000 people, with an HHI post-merger not higher than 1,800

---

[39] ibid.

[40] ibid.

[41] 12 USC 1828(c).

[42] FDIC Statement of Policy on Bank Merger Transactions 73 FR 8870.

[43] ibid.

[44] ibid.

[45] US General Accounting Office, 'Bank Merger Process Should Be Modernized and Simplified' (1982)GAO-82-53, 10 https://www.gao.gov/assets/140/138428.pdf (accessed 18 November 2022).

[46] US Department of Justice, 'Bank Merger Competitive Review: Introduction and Overview' (1995 Banking Guidelines) https://www.justice.gov/atr/bank-merger-competitive-review-introduction-and-overview-1995 (accessed 14 November 2022).

[47] The Herfindahl-Hirschman Index (HHI) is a tool to measure market concentration. For a good explanation see Charles R Laine, 'The Herfindahl-Hirschman Index: A Concentration Measure Taking the Consumer's Point of View' (1995) 40(2) Antitrust Bulletin 423; and Donald I Baker and William Blumenthal, 'Demystifying the Herfindahl-Hirschman Index' (1984) 19(2) Mergers and Acquisitions 42.

[48] US Department of Justice, *1982 Merger Guidelines* https://www.justice.gov/archives/atr/1982-merger-guidelines.

points, and an increase of less than 200 points. These are unlikely to be subjected to a further review. Screen B covers transactions exceeding the 1,800/200 rule and such transactions would be subject to a more detailed assessment.[49] In September 2020, the DOJ invited comments from the public aimed at establishing whether the 1995 joint guidelines between the federal agency and the banking regulators merit some updates. Later, in December 2021, the DOJ sought additional comments on Bank Merger Competitive Analysis.[50]

In relation to proceedings before the OCC, the merging parties can contact the agency seeking guidance about the transaction through exploratory calls or meetings, followed by prefiling meetings or discussions. Once the application is filed, the OCC starts its review by ensuring that all relevant information has been provided and, if required, additional information can be requested. Then a public comment period on applications starts. Next, the OCC will decide on the fifteenth day after the end of the public comment period under an expedited review or within sixty calendar days from the filing or the publication of the public notice under a standard review.[51]

As regards the filing procedure before the FRB in relation to bank mergers, bank service providers[52] and change in control transactions, the parties seeking to merge must file their applications accompanied by the required information. Also, applications involving bank mergers under section 18 (c) of the FDIA need to observe some publication requirements consisting of three notices in local newspapers[53] (no publication is required in relation to bank service company transactions). Although the Bank Holding Company Act and the Community Reinvestment Act do not provide a stage for public comments, the FRB considers all written public comments and schedules hearings at its discretion. The processing times for bank mergers and bank service company transactions is within thirty to sixty days after receipt of the application, a period that can be extended by the FRB, and for change in control it is sixty days, with a similar possibility of extension. Every type of transaction has a different consummation period that must be observed.[54]

As indicated above, some screens have been established for the purpose of the approval authority that the board of governors delegates to the relevant Reserve Bank. These screens use deposits as a proxy, the concentration of which is measured by the HHI index and the calculation of which provides some insights about possible anti-competitive effects. In this regard, the FRB has clarified that the first HHI calculations

---

[49] Office of the Comptroller of the Currency, 'Comptroller's Licensing Manual: Business Combinations' (n 35) 59–60.

[50] US Department of Justice, 'Antitrust Division Banking Guidelines Review: Public Comments Topics & Issues Guide' (17 December 2021) https://www.justice.gov/atr/antitrust-division-banking-guidelines-review-public-comments-topics-issues-guide (accessed 28 October 2022).

[51] Office of the Comptroller of the Currency, 'Comptroller's Licensing Manual: Business Combinations' (n 35) 28–31.

[52] The expression 'bank service provider' refers to a company or person that performs services for a banking organization that are subject to the Bank Service Company Act (12 USC 1861–1867).

[53] See Board of Governors of the Federal Reserve System, 'Electronic Applications and Applications Filing Information' https://www.federalreserve.gov/supervisionreg/afi/smfilings.htm (accessed 28 October 2022).

[54] ibid. For transactions involving changes in the general character of a State Member Bank's Business, Domestic Branches, Emergency Applications, Membership, addition or changes in Directors or Senior Executive Officers and Premises Acquisition see the particular filing requirements.

take into account the deposit shares of the depository institutions in a local banking market. It has also made clear that different weight in computing market shares is allocated depending on whether the deposits of all institutions have a commercial bank charter[55] (100 per cent weight) or whether they have a thrift charter (50 per cent weight).[56] The FRB considers that the use of deposits as a proxy is a rational choice as a great number of consumers and small businesses have deposit accounts, and also because some institutions exert their lending capacity based upon deposit shares of the depository institutions in a local banking market.[57] So, the FRB includes the products and services denoted by the term commercial banking, does not include internet banking in the calculation of local market shares as it is not possible to establish the location of those depositors, and applies particular rules when dealing with bank record deposits at a central office or with government deposits.[58] Based on commuting patterns, shopping patterns, and other information required to establish where consumers could turn for services, the FRB has divided the whole country into twelve districts and each district has predefined banking markets.[59] Thus, in the district of Chicago, for instance, the research department of the Federal Reserve Bank of Chicago has delineated local geographic markets within the following states: Illinois, Indiana, Iowa, Michigan and Wisconsin. Subsequently, every state has an identified market area with its respective counties, whereby Illinois has thirty-six defined markets with their respective counties (eg the Burlington market comprises Henderson County, Illinois and Des Moines County, Iowa).[60]

In order to assess whether a transaction can lead to competition harm in the market, the FRB would assess a number of factors: (1) attractiveness of the market for entry and ease of market entry; (2) number and quality of remaining competitors; (3) market shares of competitors; (4) the effects of a consolidated market; (5) likelihood of business failure; and 6) any other factors that parties consider would be suitable to mitigate the structural effects of a transaction in the post-merger market.[61] When the mitigation factors do not alleviate the competition concerns, FRB can request the divestment of branches.[62] It should be noted that these factors are similar to the ones taken into account by the DOJ in its competition assessment of transactions.[63]

---

[55] Official document permitting a banking company to commence business as a bank.

[56] Board of Governors of the Federal Reserve System, 'FAQs' (n 29). Barron's Business Dictionaries define 'thrift institution' as 'a generic name for savings banks and savings and loan associations' (Dictionary of Business Terms) and as a 'depository financial institution whose primary function is promoting personal savings (thrift) and home ownership through mortgage lending. Thrift institutions hold most of their assets in mortgages and collect most of their deposits from consumers, savings and loan associations savings banks, and credit unions are all considered thrift institutions' (Dictionary of Banking Terms, https://www.allbusiness.com/barrons_dictionary/dictionary-thrift-institution-4942755-1.html, accessed 19 October 2022).

[57] Board of Governors of the Federal Reserve System, 'FAQs' (n 29) § 10.

[58] ibid.

[59] Brian W Smith and Laura R Biddle, 'Is the Bank Merger Regulatory Review Process Ripe for Change?' (2005) 18(3) Bank Accounting & Finance 10. See also Board of Governors of the Federal Reserve System https://www.federalreserve.gov/supervisionreg/afi/market_info.htm (accessed 11 November 2022).

[60] Federal Reserve Bank of Chicago, 'Banking Market Definitions for Illinois' https://www.chicagofed.org/banking/banking-markets-definitions/illinois (accessed 11 November 2022).

[61] Board of Governors of the Federal Reserve System, 'FAQs' (n 29) § 8.

[62] Smith and Biddle (n 59) 10.

[63] Board of Governors of the Federal Reserve System, 'FAQs' (n 29) § 8.

Simultaneously, the DOJ conducts an independent competition review of the proposed transaction, and if it concludes that the transaction raises competition concerns, it might bring a court action under the antitrust laws within thirty days after the FRB's approval.[64] One of the main differences in analysis between the FRB and the DOJ is that the latter considers two separate product markets: the individual consumers and the business consumers (ie small and medium-sized businesses). In contrast, the FRB jointly considers commercial banking products and services, resulting in broader relevant markets and lower concentration levels. In relation to divestitures, it has been noted that the DOJ carefully chooses the specific asset/s and the potential buyers, while merging parties have some more leeway to choose the affected assets or the possible buyers when the remedial action is overseen by the FRB.[65]

In relation to the notification process before the FDIC, once the relevant information has been filed and reviewed for compliance with the relevant regulation, the application will be processed, and the agency will make a final decision once the merging parties have provided proof that the notice of the proposed transaction has been published in a newspaper of general circulation according to the pre-established requirements set out in the law.[66] It is important to note that such a publication is not required under section 303.64 of the FDIC rules which are applicable to some transactions eligible for an expedited procedure.[67] The geographic market(s) includes the areas in which the offices to be acquired are located, the areas from which those offices gain the main share of their loans, deposits, or other business, and the areas where existing and potential customers will be impacted. The relevant product market includes the banking services presently offered by the merging parties and those that the new merged entity will offer, as well as substitutable services offered by other types of competitors, such as depository institutions, securities firms, or finance companies.[68] Once the relevant market is defined, the competitive effects analysis will focus on establishing the types and extent of existing competition and whether the proposed transaction would eliminate, reduce, or enhance it.[69]

The FDIC uses different methodologies to assess the respective markets. Thus, in some cases the analysis includes deposit and loan totals, the number and volume of transactions, contributions to net income, among others.[70] In terms of concentration levels, the FDIC usually approves transactions the HHI of which is 1,800 points or less, or if it is above 1,800 points, where the increase is less than 200 points from the

---

[64] ibid §§ 8–9.

[65] Smith and Biddle (n 59) 10.

[66] 12 CFR 303.65. See also 12 CFR 303.7.

[67] 12 CFR 303.64, stating that: 'The FDIC will process an application using expedited procedures if: (i) Immediately following the merger transaction, the resulting institutions will be "well-capitalized" pursuant to subpart H of part 324 of this chapter, as applicable; and (ii) (A) All parties to the merger transaction are eligible depository institutions as defined in § 303.2(r); or (B) The acquiring party is an eligible depository institution as defined § 303.2(r) and the amount of the total assets to be transferred does not exceed an amount equal to 10 percent of the acquiring institution's total assets as reported in its report of condition for the quarter immediately preceding the filing of the merger application.' See also 12 CFR 303.2.

[68] 73 FR 8870.

[69] ibid.

[70] ibid.

pre-merger HHI. Additionally, factors such as barriers to entry will be considered, including electronic banking, and whether the transaction would create a stronger and a more efficient institution.[71] Regarding the public interest standard, the FDIC may approve those proposed transactions that are anti-competitive if that is the least adverse option to a possible failure of an insured depository institution.[72]

Moving to the analysis of the prudential factors, the FDIC has stated that it would be unlikely that transactions where the new entity will not meet capital standards, keeps weak or unsatisfactory management, or whose earnings prospects are doubtful, be approved.[73] The convenience and needs factor would be satisfied if the transaction benefits the general public through higher lending limits, new or expanded services, reduced prices, etc.[74] Finally, in reviewing the anti-money laundering consideration the FDIC would examine the suitability of the involved institutions' programmes, policies, and procedures created for that purpose.

The DOJ has jurisdiction to review bank merger transactions in conjunction with the banking regulators.[75] In the banking sector, merging parties do not need to file notifications under the Hart-Scott-Rodino (HSR) Act;[76] instead, they do need to file the application with the respective banking agency who will send copies of it to the DOJ for reviewing the competitive effects of the proposed transaction. Considering that the assessment of the DOJ is not under the HSR Act, it cannot issue a second request for information. In case more information is required, it needs to start a civil investigative demand.[77] If the two authorities reach different conclusions,[78] the banking statutes provide for an automatic stay of any transaction that the DOJ intends to challenge by suing before the Federal District Court.[79] Applicants will be given an opportunity to submit comments to the FDIC in relation to the assessment of the impact of the transaction on competition.[80]

Usually, the competitive effects analysis applied by the DOJ in the banking area focuses on market shares and market concentration, giving less weight to factors such as entry or efficiencies.[81] Thus, the DOJ would be concerned if after the merger the HHI is above 1,800, or if the transaction would cause an HHI increase of more than 200 points. In relation to the geographic market, the DOJ examines the specific areas affected by the transaction in question whereas the banking agencies have pre-established

---

[71] ibid.

[72] ibid.

[73] ibid.

[74] ibid.

[75] ABA Section of Antitrust Law (n 30) 1.

[76] Pub L 94-435. The HSR Act applies to mergers of non-banking assets.

[77] A civil investigative demand is a tool that the US government uses to obtain documents and information to establish possible violations of the False Claims Act. The government has the power to require any person or entity to 'produce documents, answer written interrogatories or give oral testimony' (31 USC § 3733). See also Brian Irving, 'How to Respond to a Civil Investigative Demand' *Lexology* (12 April 2022) https://www.lexology.com/library/detail.aspx?g=a44a809d-fbe6-41f4-9d75-ffb1b66e6f7f (accessed 19 October 2022).

[78] ABA Section of Antitrust Law (n 30) 1.

[79] ibid.

[80] FDIC, 'Application Procedures Manual' 4–12 https://www.fdic.gov/regulations/applications/resources/apps-proc-manual/section-04-mergers.pdf (accessed 6 November 2022).

[81] ABA Section of Antitrust Law (n 30) 2.

metropolitan areas that are used as their relevant geographic markets. In terms of the product markets, the DOJ analysis includes a wider range of products and services while the banking regulators rely entirely on the traditional banking services.[82]

At the same time, the Gramm-Leach-Bliley Act of 1999 (GLBA), that amended the Hart-Scott-Rodino Antitrust Improvements Act of 1976 (HSRA), also gave jurisdiction to the FTC to review the competitive effects of transactions in which certain merging companies have competing non-bank subsidiaries. According to this provision, transactions that involve financial activities that do not require FRB approval must be filed under the HSRA if certain thresholds are met. The statutory thirty-day waiting period remains the same, with the possibility of a second request of information for another thirty days once all the information has been received.[83] State agencies through the federal and/or state antitrust laws can also review the effects of a/the merger on competition, assessing factors such as consumer protection and employment.[84] Furthermore, they have the right to challenge the merger decisions.[85]

7.2 The 'Public Interest' Standard

This concept was initially used in 1908, when New York City, in response to the Bank Panic of 1907—one of the most acute financial crises in the United States before the Great Depression[86]—enacted the Banking law of New York in which it was stated that banks that did not promote 'public convenience and advantage' should not be established.[87] Hence, this legislation sought to prevent the occurrence of a similar predicament from happening again.[88] In 1920, the service to the community was included as a factor to be examined when a bank applied for a charter, considering their quasi-public nature.[89] It was in 1935 that the community convenience and needs concept was initially introduced by the federal banking statutes,[90] which provided that '[t]he factors to be enumerated in the certificate required under section 1814 of the title and to be considered by the board of Directors under section 1815 of this title shall be the following: [t]he convenience and needs of the community to be served by the bank'.[91]

---

[82] ibid.

[83] Smith and Biddle (n 59) 12.

[84] ibid.

[85] ibid 14.

[86] For a proper background about the Bank Panic of 1907 see Jon Moen and Ellis W Tallman, 'The Bank Panic of 1907: The Role of Trust Companies' (1992) 52(3) Journal of Economic History 611.

[87] NY Laws 1908, Ch 125, § 5.

[88] Pierre Jay, 'Recent and Prospective State Banking Legislation' (1909) 23(2) Quarterly Journal of Economics 233.

[89] See the 'Instructions of the Comptroller of the Currency Relative to the Organization and Powers of National Banks' (1920) 115 https://babel.hathitrust.org/cgi/pt?id=osu.32435016480709 (accessed 27 April 2023).

[90] 'The Federal Deposit Insurance Corp. was created in 1933 as an amendment to the Federal Reserve Act (June 13, 1933, 48 Stat. 162). The phrase did not appear in the statute at that time. The Federal Reserve Act was amended by the Banking Act of 1935 (49 Stat. 684), in which the phrase first appeared. The FDIC was removed from the Federal Reserve Act in 1950 and made a separate act to be known as the Federal Deposit Insurance Act, Pub. L. 86-230. See 12 USC § 1811.' See Warren L Dennis, 'The Community Reinvestment Act of 1977: Defining Convenience and Needs of the Community' (1978) 95 Banking Law Journal 693, 704.

[91] 12 USC § 1816.

240   PUBLIC INTEREST ASSESSMENT AND FRB, OCC, AND FDIC

Later, during the 1960s, banks started to adhere to the convenience and needs of the 'communities' principle in the areas where they were registered and functioning, as a strategy to support and defend their envisaged consolidation trend.[92]

Equally, the Supreme Court recognized the importance of the public interest standard by stating that this was 'the ultimate test imposed' in a bank merger application.[93] The relevance of applying the public interest standard was also stressed in 1977 by Senator William Proxmire, who presented the S. 406 bill in Congress affirming that 'a public charter conveys numerous economic benefits and in return it is legitimate for public policy and regulatory practice to require some public purpose'.[94] Following the statement, he compared a bank charter to 'a franchise to serve local convenience and needs', and suggested that it was fair for benefits to accrue to the public. This belief that financial institutions have responsibilities to the public, which surpass the obligation to maintain their own solvency and profitability, represent the evolving change in the way that the US Congress viewed the banking system and the role of the government in overseeing it.[95]

It is important to remember that the Bank Merger Act of 1966[96] had already prohibited transactions that substantially lessen competition, create a monopoly, or restrict trade unless the anti-competitive effects of the transaction are '[o]utweighed in the public interest by the probable effect of the transaction in meeting the convenience and needs of the community to be served'[97] and stressing that '[i]n every case, the responsible agency shall take into consideration ... the convenience and needs of the community to be served'.[98] In the *Bank of New Bern v Wachovia Bank & Trust Co* case, the convenience and needs concept was assessed through the following considerations: (1) whether existing banks provide a full complement of banking services at competitive rates and fees; (2) whether there is a need for specialized services not presently available; (3) leadership and participation in economic growth of community by management of existing banks; (4) composition of population and prospects for future growth; (5) nature and strength of economy and its prospects for growth; (6) extent to which competition will stimulate economy and make for more healthy banking business; and (7) extent to which entry of new bank has public support in the community.[99]

Thus, seeking to improve the above-mentioned traditional convenience and needs criteria and to ensure a safe and sound banking operation among low and moderate-income neighbourhoods, in 1977 the Community Reinvestment Act (CRA) was

---

[92] Joseph Moore, 'Community Reinvestment Act and Its Impact on Bank Mergers' (1997) 1 NC Banking Institute 412, 419–20.

[93] *United States v Third National Bank in Nashville* 390 US 171, 184 (1968).

[94] '123 Cong. Rec. S1202 (daily edn 24 January 1977). The Community Reinvestment Act, 12 USC §§ 2901– 2905, provides that "regulated financial institutions have a continuing and affirmative obligation to help meet the credit needs of the local communities in which they are chartered," and directs the federal financial supervisory agencies to "assess" an institution's record of meeting these needs in the examination process and to "take such records into account" in evaluating applications for charter, insurance, branching, relocation, merger, or acquisition of shares requiring approval under the Bank Holding Company Act of 1956.' See Dennis (n 90) 693–94.

[95] ibid.

[96] The 1966 amendment to the Bank Merger Act 1960.

[97] 12 USC § 1828 (c)(5)(B).

[98] 12 USC § 1828(c)(5).

[99] See *Bank of New Bern v Wachovia Bank & Trust Co NA*, 353 F Supp 643 (EDNC 1972).

enacted. The CRA's initiative tried to remedy the customary discrimination suffered by low-income communities whose access to and enjoyment of the benefits of credit markets had been restricted.[100] Pursuant to this Act, the insured depository institutions are obliged to keep a record of how they are helping communities by satisfying their credit needs; a record that is used by the three agencies when reviewing mergers and acquisitions.[101] Of great importance, CRA neither provides a definition of the communities or credit needs concepts nor indicates how it would be enforced.[102] In addition, this governmental intervention has been described as redundant considering that, as a general rule, banks profit from serving the communities,[103] expensive because of the high associated compliance costs, and inadequate given that if the root cause of the issues lies in racial discrimination or lack of wealth, a redistribution policy like the CRA would not be able to address them.[104] By contrast, others have claimed that the implementation of the CRA has expanded the access to credits to low- and moderate-income, and minority borrowers at a fairly low cost, by addressing information externalities issues, coordinating bank lending and encouraging banks and thrifts to provide credit services to these groups, an achievement that would not have been possible otherwise.[105] Notably, '[t]he parties to the transaction [bank mergers] bear the burden of proving this "public-interest defence"'.[106]

In general terms, the public interest assessment includes the following three considerations: (1) the convenience and needs of the community to be served,[107] that could be assessed by looking at the increase in access to credit, lending limits, and specialized banking services;[108] (2) compliance with fair lending and other consumer protection laws; and (3) CRA records showing the levels of credit needs satisfaction amongst communities. These considerations serve to offset the anti-competitive effects of the proposed transactions, and the convenience and needs of the community factor is an independent consideration that must be examined in every merger case. Regrettably, there are still some reservations among some scholars around the convenience and needs criteria, who consider it as ill-defined and whose analysis lacks any statutory principles.[109] One implication is that, the argument continues, the banking agencies have created a process in which comments from the public are received as a way to remedy the absence of clear concepts. In doing so, the result is that even if those

---

[100] Michael S Barr, 'Credit Where It Counts: The Community Reinvestment Act and Its Critics' (2005) 80(2) New York University Law Review 513, 515–16.

[101] See https://www.ffiec.gov/cra/history.htm (accessed 21 November 2022)

[102] Richard D Marsico, 'A Guide to Enforcing the Community Reinvestment Act' (1993) 20 Fordham Urban Law Journal 165. Marsico describes the standards that have been created by the regulators and how they have been enforcing the CRA.

[103] Lawrence J White, 'The Community Reinvestment Act: Good Intentions Headed in the Wrong Direction' (1993) 20 Fordham Urban Law Journal 281, 282.

[104] Barr (n 100) 534–60; Michael Klausner, 'Market Failure and Community Investment: A Market-Oriented Alternative to the Community Reinvestment Act' (1995) 143 University of Pennsylvania Law Review 1561.

[105] Barr (n 100) 534–60.

[106] *United States v First City National Bank of Houston* 386 US 361, 366 (1967).

[107] 12 USC § 1828(c)(1)(2).

[108] Dennis (n 90) 710.

[109] Smith and Biddle (n 59) 14.

242 PUBLIC INTEREST ASSESSMENT AND FRB, OCC, AND FDIC

comments do not have the capacity to influence a prohibition decision, they have the power to extend the review process and, therefore, force the negotiation of unrelated conditions from merging parties urged to close their deals.[110]

7.3 Challenges of Concurrent Jurisdiction

The shared jurisdiction among multiple regulators creates at times a convoluted assessment process as well as uncertainty with respect to process and outcomes. As an illustration, in spite of the existence of a jointly developed HHI market screens, it has been reported that the DOJ and the banking agencies diverge on how to apply it, which has resulted in the definition of dissimilar relevant markets in their respective assessments.[111] Some commentators have indicated that such a contradiction stems from the fact that traditionally the banking agencies have considered deposits to determine market shares while the DOJ has included both deposits and commercial loans.[112] Additionally, the DOJ has affirmed that small and medium-sized businesses are part of the same relevant product market, whose needs such as payroll, collection, disbursement services, etc., may not be satisfied by small banks, an approach that has been dismissed by the banking regulators.[113] Similarly, discrepancy also exists in relation to the definition of geographic markets as the banking agencies have pre-established areas[114] whereas for the antitrust agencies the delineation depends on the specific case.[115] Indeed, regulators and the courts in some of the seminal cases that will be analysed below, have repeatedly sustained that the geographic market for the cluster of banking products and services is local in nature.[116]

Likewise, the use of the public interest standard in the banking sector has received some criticism among scholars. For instance, Benston has argued that it is in the public interest to promote competition in the banking sector rather than applying protective rules that prevent it. In his words:

---

[110] ibid 13.

[111] Kress (n 8) 450.

[112] ibid.

[113] Jonathan M Rich and Thomas G Scriven, 'Bank Consolidation Caused by the Financial Crisis: How Should the Antitrust Division Review "Shotgun Marriages?"' *The Antitrust Source* (1 December 2008) https://www.morg anlewis.com/-/media/files/publication/outside-publication/article/richscrivenbankconsolidationshotgunmar riagesdec08.pdf (accessed 26 April 2023).

[114] As explained above, based on commuting patterns, shopping patterns, and other information required to establish where consumers could turn for services, the FRB has divided the whole country into twelve districts and each district has predefined banking markets.

[115] According to the DOJ: '[S]ome have questioned why we, in some cases, have not used the Fed's pre-defined markets ... [W]e will depart from the Fed's regions where the market realities suggest we should. Moreover, unlike the Fed, which views banks as providing a cluster of services, we view banks as multi-product firms. As a result, we sometimes have to use different geographic market definitions for each of the products we examine.' See Robert E Litan, Deputy Assistant Attorney General, Antitrust Div, US Department of Justice, Address before the Antitrust Section of the ABA: Antitrust Assessment of Bank Mergers (6 April 1994) https://www.justice.gov/atr/speech/antitrust-assessment-bank-mergers (accessed 30 October 2022).

[116] First Union Corp 84 Fed Res Bull 489, 491–92 (1988).

7.3 CHALLENGES OF CONCURRENT JURISDICTION 243

[t]he issue of protecting the public has become confused with (1) protecting the institutions which comprise the financial structure, and (2) regulating rather routine operations instead of policy matters that affect the financial health of the institution ... The
elimination of all competition could hardly be in the public interest, even if the financial stability of the institution were improved.[117]

He added that since agencies have a strong motivation to prevent banks from failing,
their reviews have discouraged banks from innovating and competing, which leads to
the needs of the customers being neglected.[118] It has also been argued that the term convenience and needs of the community has been wrongly understood as the economic
attainments of the bank rather than the satisfaction of the community's credit needs, a
reason why the concept has been depicted as a term of 'art' in banking law.[119] In consequence, some commentators have claimed that the banking regulators usually approve
the majority of merger applications under the presumption that they protect the public
interest even if there is little evidence provided to support that argument.[120] Yet, the
type of evidence that is considered sufficient to obtain approval often refers to a minimal consumer acquiescence,[121] to the point that it has been assumed that by protecting
the structure of financial institutions, the public is unequivocally protected.[122] As a result, it can be argued that the public interest standard has been applied in a manner that
unduly favours the merging parties.[123]

Wilson went further and noted that in a period of five years the analysis of the public
interest standard applied by the banking regulators has been oversimplified. The underlying idea of his observation is that regulators have not exercised a rigorous assessment of the public interest. In consequence, he asserts, typically the regulators report
that the merger satisfies the public interest standard by merely referring to the fact, that
'the regulator considered the issue', without providing any explanation or supporting
empirical analysis.[124] Another criticism is that the ambiguity of the convenience and
needs of the community standard, combined with the ability that third parties have
to provide adverse comments during the review process and to challenge merger applications, have enabled regulators to secure commitments from merging parties
which are unwilling to endure an extended review or a litigation process, that are not

---

[117] George J Benston, 'Savings Banking and the Public Interest' (1972) 4(1–2) Journal of Money, Credit and
Banking 133, 203.

[118] ibid 203–204.

[119] Dennis (n 90) 709. See also Mehrsa Baradaran, Banking and the Social Contract (2014) 89 Notre Dame Law
Review 1283, 1338 https://digitalcommons.law.uga.edu/fac_artchop/942 (accessed 18 November 2022).

[120] Benston (n 117); Warren (n 90) 709; Baradaran (n 119); Kress (n 8) 476.

[121] The public interest is met when the three following factors are observed: (1) the convenience and needs of
the community to be served; (2) compliance with fair lending and other consumer protection laws; and (3) CRA
records showing the levels of credit needs satisfaction amongst communities. 12 USC §§ 1828(c)(1)–(2).

[122] Benston (n 117) 203.

[123] Kress (n 8) 476.

[124] Mitria Wilson, 'Protecting the Public's Interests: A Consumer-Focused Reassessment of the Standard for
Bank Mergers and Acquisitions' (2013) 130 Banking Law Journal 350, 372.

244 PUBLIC INTEREST ASSESSMENT AND FRB, OCC, AND FDIC

Table 7.1 Federal Reserve Merger and Acquisition Applications (2011–2023)

	Submitted	Approved	Withdrawn	Denied
2011	237	194	43	0
2012	269	226	43	0
2013	230	190	40	0
2014	273	248	25	0
2015	300	279	21	0
2016	273	245	28	0
2017	253	238	15	0
2018	200	190	10	0
2019	206	190	16	0
2020	158	144	14	0
2021	190	184	6	0
2022	166	155	11	0
2023	58	46	12	0

Source: Banking Applications Activity Semiannual Reports[*]
Note: 2023 data refers to the first half of the year

[*]https://www.federalreserve.gov/publications/semiannual-report-on-banking-applications-activity.htm (accessed 3 October 2023); see also Kress (n 8) 456.

merger related, inter alia, the funding of community development initiatives or lending commitments.[125]

The contradictory approaches between the antitrust agencies and the regulators and the lack of clarity in substantive and procedural terms about the public interest standard question the effectiveness and reliability of the current enforcement process. In addition, it has been reported that since 1985 the DOJ has not challenged a bank merger, which denotes that its role is not very prominent in the merger review process and according to critics adds more doubt about the robustness of the enforcement process.[126] The next part provides some statistics aiming to show the trends in terms of approvals and prohibitions among the FRB, FDIC, and OCC.

[125] Smith and Biddle (n 59) 13–14. LaWare has described how community groups were able to secure lending commitments from merging parties whose deals were announced in 1991, after threatening CRA disputes against them. In the NCNB and C&S/Sovran case, NCNB approved US$10 billion; in the Chemical Bank and Manufacturers Hanover Trust Company case, Chemical approved US$750 million; and in the Bank of America and Security Pacific, the Bank of America approved US$12 billion. See John P LaWare, 'Member, Board of Governors of the Federal Reserve Systems, Statement Before the House Comm. on Banking, Fin., and Urb. Affairs (Sept. 24, 1991)' (1991) 77 Federal Reserve Bulletin 932.

[126] Kress (n 8) 453; Aaron C Stine and Eric D Gorman, 'Ebbing the Tide of Local Bank Concentration: Granting Sole Authority to the Department of Justice to Review the Competitive Effects of Bank Mergers' (2012) 62 Syracuse Law Review 405, 417. See also Litan (n 115). Litan has explained that the low challenge rate responds to the fact that: 'In many cases, the banks involved in these mergers have not competed with each other and thus have not posed antitrust risks. In most of the others where the banks have competed against each other, it was clear that the market would continue to be competitive even after the merger.'

7.4 Enforcement Record

Table 7.1 shows that between 2011 and 2023 the FRB did not issue any prohibition decisions. The statistics illustrate that from 2014 until 2023 the tendency was that at least 90 per cent of the merger proposals are approved every year by the FRB, culminating in an approval rate of 97 per cent in 2021. In terms of withdrawals, it is interesting to observe that there was a significant number of removals during 2011 and 2013, accounting for more than forty per year, although the quantity of withdrawals was lower between 2014 and 2022. Interestingly, in the first half of 2023 we observe both a reduction in the number of applications submitted (down to forty-six from eighty-seven at the same point in time in 2022) and an increase in the number of applications withdrawn (up from four to twelve, and from 5 per cent to 21 per cent in relative terms). It is still premature to say whether this is just a fluke or an early signal of a new trend.

As mentioned above, the inclination shown by the banking regulators to approve mergers has received continuous criticism. Here, it is pertinent to examine the terms of the recent Memorandum issued by the House Financial Services Committee on 27 November 2019, in preparation for the hearing to question whether bank regulators are effectively overseeing the nation's banks. The section regarding bank mergers and acquisitions indicates that:

> Concerns have been raised about federal financial regulators rubber stamping prior merger and acquisition applications. For example, based on data provided by the Federal Reserve, from January 1, 2006 through December 31, 2017, over 3,800 merger applications were submitted to the agency. During this eleven-year period, however, the Federal Reserve did not reject any merger application.[127]

Another criticism, discussed by Kress, is that banking regulators have contributed to the lack of prohibition decisions as they alert the parties about the weaknesses of their proposal, which has resulted in voluntary withdrawals.[128] As Tables 7.2 and 7.3 indicate, the FDIC and the OCC present a similar approval tendency.

Between 2012 and 2022, the FDIC did not issue any prohibition decisions in relation to merger applications. Also, as Table 7.2 shows, a significant share of requests was withdrawn in the last few years (17, or 13 per cent, in 2022; and 20, or 14 per cent, in 2020).[129]

---

[127] United States, House of Representatives (4 December 2019) Subject: 'Oversight of Prudential Regulators: Ensuring the Safety, Soundness, Diversity, and Accountability of Depository Institutions?' (27 November 2019) https://financialservices.house.gov/uploadedfiles/hhrg-116-ba00-20191204-sd002.pdf (accessed 4 November 2022).

[128] Kress (n 8) 455–56.

[129] The FDIC website, as part of the application process strongly recommends a pre-filing meeting between the applicant and the appropriate regulatory agencies to discuss filing requirements and other relevant matters, which sometimes result in informal rejections or parties deciding not to apply. See https://www.fdic.gov/regulations/applications/resources/apps-proc-manual/section-04-mergers.pdf (accessed 4 November 2022).

246 PUBLIC INTEREST ASSESSMENT AND FRB, OCC, AND FDIC

Table 7.2 FDIC Merger and Acquisition Applications (2012–2022)

	Approved	Returned/Withdrawn	Denied
2012	140	N/A	0
2013	142	17	0
2014	144	12	0
2015	139	7	0
2016	125	9	0
2017	110	8	0
2018	141	9	0
2019	126	4	0
2020	141	20	0
2021	189	9	0
2022	134	17	0

Source: FDIC website, Merger Decisions: Annual Reports to Congress.[*]

[*] FDIC, Merger Decisions: Annual Report to Congress https://www.fdic.gov/bank/individual/merger/ (accessed 18 September 2023). See also https://www.fdic.gov/regulations/applications/actions.html (accessed 3 October 2023).

The same trend is present in the number of merger application approvals issued by the OCC as Table 7.3 shows. It is also observed that the number of conditionally approved decisions has gradually decreased, moving from eight in 2011 to one, two, four, one, and one in 2018, 2019, 2020, 2021, and 2022, respectively.

Table 7.3 Office of the Comptroller Merger and Acquisition Applications (2011–2022)

	Received	Approved	Conditionally approved	Denied
2011	70	43	8	0
2012	98	86	6	0
2013	92	90	8	0
2014	102	98	8	0
2015	75	61	5	0
2016	78	64	5	0
2017	63	67	3	0
2018	52	57	1	0
2019	51	42	2	0
2020	36	37	4	0
2021	46	43	1	0
2022	36	30	1	0

Source: Office of the Comptroller of the Currency, Annual Reports.[*]

[*] https://www.occ.gov/publications-and-resources/publications/annual-report/index-annual-report.html (accessed 4 October 2023).

7.4.1 Analysis of Some Seminal Cases

During the period from 1980 to 1998 the US experienced an unprecedented number of bank mergers, amounting to 'approximately 8,000 mergers, involving US$2.4 trillion in acquired assets'.[130] Furthermore, research conducted by the Federal Reserve in that period, indicates that 'mergers reduced the number of banks overall ... and that retail electronic banking has, in the short run, actually reduced rather than increased competition'.[131] The next section examines some of the most relevant merger cases the banking regulators and the federal antitrust agency have concurrently assessed. Our intention is to derive some implications of the approach followed by each of them and to identify any convergence or divergence. Through this analysis we observe the extent to which the anti-competitive concerns expressed by the DOJ have been regularly dismissed by the banking regulators, how the assessment of post-merger HHI levels have produced conflicting decisions between the reviewers, and how the vagueness of the public interest test applied by the banking regulators has ended in questionable approval decisions.

The assessment presents the approach of regulators in their decisions dating back to the 1960s that has underpinned the approval tendency referred to earlier and illustrates the contradictory views between the antitrust agency and the sectoral regulator. The DOJ does not seem to play a prominent role because its competition concerns are dismissed by the regulators and the DOJ has not challenged these transactions.

7.4.1.1 Transactions decided by the sectoral regulators

7.4.1.1.1 Community Bankshares—Citizens

Community Bankshares (Community), a bank holding company, requested approval from the FRB to acquire Citizens Financial Corporation (Citizens) and its subsidiary bank, the Citizens State Bank of Cortez (Citizens State Bank). Community was the seventeenth largest depository organization in Colorado, and Citizens was the 103rd.[132] The board approved the transaction after confirming the position established during the 1960s that, 'in defining a geographic market the board and the courts have consistently found that the relevant geographic market for analysing the competitive effects of a proposal must reflect commercial and banking realities and should consist of the local area where customers can practicably turn for alternatives'.[133]

In this case, the FRB insisted on defining the relevant geographic market as local by nature. The approval decision recounted that the board interviewed some bankers who confirmed that all local banks found the cities of Cortez and Durango to constitute

---

[130] 'During the merger period, the number of banks in the United States declined from 14,381 in 1984, to 8,697 banks in 1998.' See Susan Lott, *Bank Mergers and the Public Interest* (The Public Interest Advocacy Centre 2005) 39 https://www.piac.ca/wp-content/uploads/2014/11/piac_bank_merger.pdf (accessed 18 November 2022).

[131] ibid.

[132] *Community Bankshares Inc* 93 Fed Res Bull C59 (2007).

[133] *United States v Philadelphia National Bank* (n 14), and many other decisions were cited to support the position.

248   PUBLIC INTEREST ASSESSMENT AND FRB, OCC, AND FDIC

separate markets, that at times during winter, commuting between these two cities was difficult, that there was insufficient evidence about economic integration of the counties, and that banks located in each city did not have many customers from the other city. This decision illustrates that the approach of banking regulators to merger assessment since the 1960s did not evolve, even though banking markets had significantly changed since. This is because geographic restrictions in the United States have undergone a radical transformation over the past decades. According to the historical approach, banks were banned from operating beyond their home state,[134] then during the 1970s some states lifted this restriction by allowing operation across state borders,[135] and, finally, in 1994 the restriction was completely abolished.[136] More recently, the successive technological transformations have introduced certain major aspects of structural change that include a shift from physical presence to online banking.[137] In sum, this case study, that was decided in 2007, has shown that the regulator has disregarded the realities that have unleashed several legal reforms and new ways to compete. Hence, recourse to preserve narrow and unrealistic approaches in defining geographic markets does not appear to be the best response.

7.4.1.1.2 First Financial Bancorp—MainSource Financial Group

In 2018, the FRB approved the proposed merger of First Financial Bancorp (First Financial) and MainSource Financial Group (MainSource) under section 3 of the Bank Holding Company Act of 1956 (BHC) and under section 18(c) of the Federal Deposit Insurance Act and section 9 of the Federal Reserve Act. In this case, the FRB considered the number of competitors that would remain in each banking market; the relative share of total deposits in insured depository institutions in each market that the acquirer would control (market deposits); the concentration levels of market deposits and the increase in these levels; other features of the relevant markets; and the commitments proposed by the acquirer to divest four of its branches.[138]

Focusing on the consideration of convenience and needs of the communities being served, the board evaluated the 'reports of examination of the CRA performance of First Financial Bank and MainSource Bank; the fair lending and compliance records of both banks; the supervisory views of the Federal Reserve Bank of Cleveland and other federal regulatory agencies; confidential supervisory information; and information provided by First Financial'.[139] Its conclusion was that the convenience and needs factor

---

[134] Jeremy C Kress, 'Solving Banking's "Too Big to Manage" Problem' (2019) 104 Minnesota Law Review 171, 180–81.

[135] ibid 181–82.

[136] See Riegle-Neal Interstate Banking and Branching Efficiency Act of 1994 https://fraser.stlouisfed.org/files/docs/historical/congressional/riegle-neal-interstate-banking-1994.pdf?utm_source=direct_download (accessed 27 October 2022).

[137] Narcisa Monsteanu and others, 'Digital Technologies' Implementation within Financial and Banking System during Socio Distancing Restrictions: Back to the Future' (2020) 11(6) International Journal of Advanced Research in Engineering and Technology 307; Mohamad Hannan, Mohammad Rahman, and Mohamad Main Uddin, 'E-Banking: Evolution, Status and Prospect' (2007) 35(1) Cost and Management Journal 1 hhtps://ssrn.com/abstract=2371134 (accessed 18 November 2022).

[138] Federal Reserve System, FRB Order No 2018-07, 7.

[139] ibid 17.

7.4 ENFORCEMENT RECORD   249

was consistent with approving the transaction.[140] One aspect that deserves attention is that in many orders issued by the FRB, approving bank mergers, the wording in relation to the 'competition' and 'convenience and needs' considerations is similar, which begs the question if a case-by-case analysis takes place or whether it is just a simple 'rubber-stamping' process.[141]

7.4.1.1.3 *Philadelphia National Bank—Girard Trust Corn*

The Philadelphia National Bank (Philadelphia) entered into an agreement to acquire Girard Trust Corn Exchange Bank (GTCEB). Approval was required from the Office of the Comptroller of the Currency. After consummation, the new entity would have controlled 36 per cent of the deposits in the Philadelphia metropolitan area, and the four largest banks in the area (including the merged bank) would have accounted for almost 77 per cent of the deposits in the same area.[142] In spite of receiving adverse reports from the FRB, the Attorney General, and the FDIC, on 24 February 1961, the Comptroller approved the merger.[143] The DOJ filed its complaint and, after trial, the District Court held that section 7 of the Clayton Act was not applicable to the transaction, a decision that was appealed.[144]

The Supreme Court overturned the decision of the District Court, indicating that bank mergers were subject to section 7 of the Clayton Act and that the Bank Merger Act of 1960 did not remove bank mergers from the application of the antitrust laws. It further added that the proposed merger violated section 7 of the Clayton Act, and that the argument presented by the merging parties whereby a larger bank was needed in the Philadelphia area to encourage the economic development of the commercial sector in the area was unsupported.[145] Another important development introduced by the Supreme Court was the definition of the relevant market. It was held that the correct product market was the cluster of products and services denoted by the term commercial banking[146] and that the geographic market was the area in which bank customers

---

[140] ibid 22. In most of the merger cases where the board deems complied the convenience and needs standard, it offers the same arguments and wording. In this sense, see Federal Reserve System, Orders Approving the Merger of Robertson Holding Company LP, Unified Shares LLC, and Commercial Bancgroup Inc, FRB Order No 2017-36 (15 December 2017) https://www.federalreserve.gov/newsevents/pressreleases/files/orders20171218b1.pdf (accessed 18 November 2022); Synovus Financial Corp and Synovus Bank Columbus, FRB Order No 2018-25 (7 December 2018) https://www.federalreserve.gov/newsevents/pressreleases/files/orders20181207b1.pdf (accessed 18 November 2022); Ozarks Inc, FRB Order No 2016-11 (28 June 2016) https://www.federalreserve.gov/newseve nts/pressreleases/files/orders20160628b1.pdf (accessed 28 November 2022).; and Cadence Bancorporation, FRB Order No 2018-26 (7 December 2018) https://www.federalreserve.gov/newsevents/pressreleases/files/orders201 81207a1.pdf (accessed 18 November 2022), among many others.

[141] See FRB Order No 2019-06 (11 March 2019); FRB Order No 2019-05 (6 March 2019); FRB Order No 2019-04 (27 February 2019); FRB Order No 2019-03 (5 February 2019); FRB Order No 2019-02 (23 January 2019); FRB Order No 2019-01 (10 January 2019); among many others https://www.federalreserve.gov/newsevents/pressrelea ses.htm (accessed 18 November 2022).

[142] William T Lifland, 'The Supreme Court, Congress, and Bank Mergers' (1967) 32(1) Law and Contemporary Problems 15, 20 https://scholarship.law.duke.edu/lcp/vol32/iss1/3.

[143] ibid.

[144] ibid.

[145] *United States v Philadelphia National Bank* (n 14).

[146] The Supreme Court underpinned its finding on the following argument: 'Some commercial banking products or services are so distinctive that they are entirely free of effective competition from products or services of other financial institutions; the checking account is in this category. Others enjoy such cost advantages as to be

250 PUBLIC INTEREST ASSESSMENT AND FRB, OCC, AND FDIC

found it viable to do their banking business.[147] The Supreme Court judgment became the standard that for decades was applied by the banking regulators and the courts, who had shown some reluctance to adopt a more accurate approach that reflected the current state of the financial services market.[148] Although in 2002, the Supreme Court in the *Ring v Arizona*[149] case admitted that precedent is not 'sacrosanct', it remains unclear whether the approach instituted by the Philadelphia National Bank would ever be completely reversed.[150]

On the contrary, the DOJ has departed numerous times from the Philadelphia National Bank Court's precedent. The agency has argued that it

> does not adhere to the Federal Reserve Board's 'cluster-of- services' product market. Rather, the DOJ disaggregates the product cluster into its constituent components and defines a different geographic market for each of the component product markets and type of customers using those products. Thus, the DOJ asserts that retail depositors, small businesses, middle-market businesses, and large corporations demand different banking products and access those products across different geographic distances.[151]

Regrettably, the statistics show that since the enactment of the Bank Merger Act of 1960 and through 1965, 97 per cent of the merger applications were approved by the banking regulators, while the DOJ found anti-competitive effects in 58 per cent of them. It is noteworthy that less than 1 per cent were challenged in the courts.[152] The same tendency was observed during the 1966–72 period, where the approval rate was 96.8 per cent, and the DOJ foresaw anti-competitive effects in 51 per cent of them.[153] The next case exemplifies the permissive approach applied by the regulators and the unsuccessful attempt by the DOJ to find support from the courts.

---

insulated within a broad range from substitutes furnished by other institutions ... Finally, there are banking facilities [*sic*] which, although in terms of cost and price they are freely competitive with the facilities [*sic*] provided by other financial institutions, nevertheless enjoy a settled consumer preference, insulating them to a marked degree, from competition; this seems to be the case with saving deposits.' See ibid 356–57.

[147] Lifland (n 142) 20.

[148] Edward Pekarek and Michela Huth, 'Bank Merger Reform Takes an Extended Philadelphia National Bank Holiday' (2008) 13(4) Fordham Journal of Corporate & Financial Law 595, 665–68.

[149] *Ring v Arizona* 536 US 584, 608 (2002).

[150] Pekarek and Huth (n 148) 665–68. See also Christopher E Rhodes Jr, 'Back to Basics: The Principles of Bank Merger Review' (2020) 25 North Carolina Banking Institute 273, 281 https://scholarship.law.unc.edu/ncbi/vol25/iss1/10, stating that the merger test introduced by the Philadelphia National Bank case stands as 'it exists today'.

[151] Constance K Robinson, Director of Operations, Antitrust Division, US Department of Justice, Address before the Association of the Bar of the City of New York (30 September 1996) http://www.usdoj.gov/atr/public/speeches/1004.htm.

[152] Samuel Richardson Reid, 'Legislation, Regulation, Antitrust, and Bank Mergers' (1975) 92 Banking Law Journal 6, 13.

[153] ibid 15.

7.4.1.2 Transactions where the sectoral regulators and the DOJ diverged

7.4.1.2.1 National Bank of Commerce—Washington Trust Bank

National Bank of Commerce (NBC), a national banking association located in Seattle, a wholly owned subsidiary of Marine Corporation (Marine) announced its intention to acquire Washington Trust Bank (WTB), a state bank with headquarters in Spokane. NBC had 107 branch banking offices—none of them in the Spokane Metropolitan area—total assets of US$1.8 billion, total deposits of US$1.6 billion, and total loans of US$881.3 million. Marine was the second largest banking organization with headquarters in Washington. WTB was the eighth largest banking organization in Spokane, with seven branch offices, total assets of US$112 million, total deposits of US$95.6 million, total loans of US$57.6 million, and controlling 17.4 per cent of the forty-six commercial banking offices in the Spokane metropolitan area.[154] In February 1971, the applicants requested approval from the Comptroller of the Currency, by which NBC, as the post-acquisition bank, would operate the banking offices of WTB as branches of NBC.[155]

On 24 September 1971, the Comptroller approved the transaction, largely grounded on the view that the transaction would add to the convenience and needs of bank customers in Spokane by passing to them services not formerly offered by WTB.[156] The DOJ opposed the transaction and challenged its legality under section 7 of the Clayton Act by considering that it would lessen competition in three ways:

> [b]y eliminating the prospect that NBC, absent acquisition of the market share represented by WTB, would enter Spokane de novo or through acquisition of a smaller bank, and thus would assist in deconcentrating that market over the long run; by ending present procompetitive effects allegedly produced in Spokane by NBC's perceived presence on the fringe of the Spokane market; and by terminating the alleged probability that WTB as an independent entity would develop through internal growth or through mergers with other medium-size banks into a regional or ultimately state-wide counterweight to the market power of the State's largest banks'.[157]

The trial Court dismissed the DOJ's complaint after finding that the merger would substantially increase competition in commercial banking in the Spokane metropolitan area; that it would not have inherent anti-competitive effects; that there was no reasonable indication that, absent the merger, NBC would enter the market in the reasonably foreseeable future; and finally that the government failed to demonstrate the existence of a bank different from WTB available for acquisition by NBC.[158]

On appeal to the Supreme Court, the latter accepted the findings of the trial Court; particularly, it agreed that the relevant product market was the business of commercial banking (and the cluster of products and services denoted thereby), which for

---

[154] *United States v Marine Bancorporation Inc* 418 US 602 (1974).
[155] ibid.
[156] ibid.
[157] ibid.
[158] ibid.

252 PUBLIC INTEREST ASSESSMENT AND FRB, OCC, AND FDIC

the Supreme Court was 'in full accord with [its] precedents'.[159] At the same time, the Supreme Court rejected the suggestion made by the DOJ that the geographic market was the state of Washington in which WTB had its largest portion of services, stating that the appropriate geographic market was the area in which the acquired firm was an actual, direct competitor, describing as 'speculative' the potential competition doctrine applied by the antitrust agency.[160] This case evidences the opposite approaches applied by the antitrust agencies and by the banking regulators, the latter supported by the courts,[161] in terms of definition of relevant markets that predictably resulted in different outcomes. Banking regulators have insistently been asked to leave behind the idea that banking markets are unique and insulated, by instead embracing a more pragmatic view that incorporates the realities of such an evolving market.[162]

7.4.1.2.2 First National State Bancorporation (FNSB Central—South)

First National State Corporation (Bancorporation) was a bank holding company whose headquarters were located in Newark, Essex County, New Jersey, with the First National State Bank of Central Jersey (FNSB Central) as one of its subsidiaries, an operating banking business within the state of New Jersey. First National Bank of South Jersey (South) was a national banking association, that by 1979 was the sixteenth largest commercial banking organization in New Jersey, and the largest bank in Atlantic County.[163] In January 1978, South and FNSB Central entered into a merger agreement, by which approval was requested from the Comptroller of the Currency (Comptroller). The merger application was also submitted to the FRB, the FDIC, and the DOJ. All these three agencies agreed that the transaction would have adverse effects on competition. Despite these reports, the Comptroller approved the transaction subject to the divestiture of certain banking offices.[164]

The DOJ filed a complaint seeking to enjoin the merger approval between FNSB Central and South claiming that, notwithstanding the divestitures, the transaction would (1) eliminate substantial direct competition between South and Bancorporation in the Atlantic City, Hammonton, and Atlantic County commercial banking markets; (2) eradicate Bancorporation as a potential competitor in these three markets; (3) exclude Bancorporation as a perceived potential competitor in such markets; (4) foster concentration or embed Bancorporation as the dominant bank in the relevant markets; and (5) trigger other mergers and consolidations in the relevant markets.[165] The court dismissed the arguments of the complaint and instead agreed with the defendant bank's position that the geographic relevant market was the area of effective competition or actual overlap between the merging parties and that the divestitures were

---

[159] ibid.

[160] ibid.

[161] It has been reported that the DOJ has lost most of the merger cases brought to trial. See Rich and Scriven (n 113) 3–4.

[162] Pekarek and Huth (n 148) 664–68.

[163] *United States v First National State Bancorporation* 499 F Supp 793 (DNJ 1980).

[164] ibid.

[165] ibid.

enough to outweigh any anti-competitive effects of the merger.[166] Further, the court found that entry by larger bank companies significantly increases competition in local markets and that the relevant markets were already competitive because the rates and fees charged by the different commercial banks in the relevant markets were varied.[167] Thus, after emphasizing that commercial banking was the relevant line of commerce, the court approved the merger.

On appeal, the Supreme Court confirmed the findings of the trial court that the business of commercial banking was the correct line of commerce, in accordance with the Philadelphia National Bank precedent, that the relevant market was the area of competitive overlap between the parties seeking to merge, that the remedies imposed by the Comptroller were sufficient to counterbalance the possible anti-competitive effects arising from the proposed transaction, and that they would serve as an incentive for other banks to enter the relevant markets. Likewise, it rejected the entrenchment antitrust theory of the DOJ, which in the Court's view is applicable '[w]here an acquiring firm's market power, existing capabilities, and proposed merger partner are such that the merger would produce an enterprise likely to dominate the target market'.[168] The Supreme Court noted that two of the largest banks in the state had recently entered the geographic market and that the barriers to entry were low, making significant consolidation in the market to be unlikely. In sum, it found that the merger as conditioned by the Comptroller was pro-competitive and that it was not in violation of section 7 of the Clayton Act.[169]

The examination of this case shows another unsuccessful attempt by the DOJ to block a banking regulator-approved merger. Equally, it exemplifies the consistent use by the banking regulators and the courts of an old-fashioned approach in the determination of the relevant product and geographic markets, in which regulators[170] and the courts have been reluctant to include other services in market definition that for bank retail customers are fully competitive alternatives such as thrifts.[171] Yet competition from

---

[166] ibid.

[167] The Court indicated that: '[T]he overwhelming weight of the evidence establishes that each of the markets is competitive. This ultimate finding stems from numerous subsidiary findings regarding the reliability of concentration ratios as evidence of the competitiveness of markets, the historical trend toward deconcentration in the relevant markets, competition from thrift institutions, loan activity as an alternative measure of market power, future pro-competitive trends in the areas, the required divestitures, and actual evidence of pro-competitive behaviour.' See ibid. See also Michael E Friedlander and John H Slayton, 'Determination of the Relevant Product Market in Bank Mergers: A Time for Reassessment?' (1981) 36(4) The Business Lawyer 1537, 1550.

[168] United States v Marine Bancorporation (n 154).

[169] United States v First National State Bancorporation (n 163).

[170] In 2005, the General Counsel of the Board of Governors of the Federal Reserve System, Scott G Alvarez, in his statement before the Antitrust Modernization Commission, admitted that 'the Federal Reserve ha[s] not found persuasive evidence to alter the general framework for analyzing bank mergers and acquisitions', adding that 'the courts have consistently held that arguments for changing these long-standing product and geographic market definitions must be based on persuasive economic and, to date, have found such persuasive evidence to be lacking'. http://www.amc.gov/commission_hearings/pdf/Alvarez_Statement.pdf (accessed 18 November 2022).

[171] The Board of Governors of the Federal Reserve System, in the Supporting Statement for the Survey to Obtain Information on the Relevant Market in Individual Merger Cases (FR 2060; OMB No 7100-0232), acknowledged that: 'Since the Connecticut decision, numerous changes in bank regulation, technology, and economy have raised questions regarding the traditional definition of locally limited commercial banking. The most notable of these changes are: thrift institutions are now permitted to offer the majority of banking products, including transaction accounts and commercial loans.' https://www.federalreserve.gov/reportforms/formsreview/FR2060_20070 530_omb.pdf (accessed 23 October 2022).

thrift institutions has been used by the regulators and the courts to demonstrate that the markets are competitive.[172] Specifically, it has been observed that some mergers have been approved albeit market concentration levels were significantly increased after the merger. In the view of the Federal Reserve Board, 'the presence of active competition from thrifts and other financial institutions in the market' were enough to counteract its anti-competitive effects.[173] Moreover, with the emergence of Fintech firms offering investment advice, saving products and loans, some observers debate whether it is still fit for purpose to apply such a narrow product and geographic market definitions in which banks would be isolated from these new and growing types of competition.[174] It also confirms that the differing merger review methodologies between the DOJ and the regulators (and the courts), which have been observed since the 1960s, remained intact in the 1980s, resulting in diverging decisions.

7.4.1.2.3 First National Bank of Logan—Zions First National Bank

First National Bank of Logan, Utah (FNBL) and Zions First National Bank (Zions), the former with deposits of US$53.7 million and the latter of US$1 billion, requested approval to merge. While the Comptroller authorized the transaction, the DOJ found it in violation of section 7 of the Clayton Act.[175] The DOJ claimed that in Cache County, in which Logan is the largest city, the market was already highly concentrated, a reason why Zions that enjoyed 28 per cent of Logan's market should be forbidden to acquire FNBL.[176] The DOJ underlined that Zions had to be forced to enter the market through de novo entry, that a merger should not diminish the opportunity to enter the market by this means, and that losing that type of future competition constituted an antitrust violation.[177] In response to the complaint, the Comptroller argued that the purpose of the antitrust regulation is to prevent mergers that significantly lessen competition rather than endorsing those that improve it. In contrast, it was contended by the Comptroller that the application of the potential competition doctrine suggested by the DOJ would be anti-competitive as entrance to the market by new competitors would be prevented.[178] The position of the Comptroller was adopted by the District Court for the

---

[172] See First Bancorporation of NH Inc, 64 Fed Res Bull 967 (1978), in which the Federal Reserve Board found that: 'While the Board continues to view commercial banking as a distinct line of commerce, the Board recognizes that the presence of thrift institutions in the relevant banking market, particularly in New England where thrift institutions have certain expanded lending and deposit-taking powers, is one of the factors that may be taken into account in analyzing the competitive effects of a particular acquisition ... In the instant case, the presence of thrift institutions holding significant amounts of deposits in the Manchester banking market, in the Board's view, lessens the severity of the effects of the proposed transaction on competition in that market.' See also Old Stone Corporation, 62 Fed Res Bull 1055 (1976).

[173] See Elijah Brewer III and others, 'The Price of Bank Mergers in the 1990s' (2000) 24(1) Federal Reserve Bank of Chicago Economic Perspectives 8 https://www.chicagofed.org/~/media/publications/economic-perspectives/2000/epartl1-pdf.pdf (accessed 30 April 2023).

[174] See Saule T Omarova, 'New Tech v New Deal: Fintech as a Systemic Phenomenon' (2019) 36 Yale Journal on Regulation 735, 782–86; Rory Van Loo, 'Making Innovation More Competitive: The Case of Fintech' (2018) 64 UCLA Law Review 232, 238–42; Hilary J Allen, 'Driverless Finance' (2020) 10 Harvard Business Law Review 157.

[175] United States v Zions Utah Bancorporation C79-0769A (D Utah 1980).

[176] ibid.

[177] Office of the Comptroller of the Currency, Report of Operations (1980) https://www.google.co.uk/books/edition/Report_of_Operations/eH5QAQAAMAAJ (accessed 30 April 2023).

[178] Friedlander and Slayton (n 167) 1552.

District of Utah, which found that a de novo entry by Zions could be more obstructive of competition than a merger.[179]

The Court also dismissed the suit based on the evidence offered by the defendants that the market was already highly competitive, accepting a 'sincere desire [by the banks] to obtain business from their competitors', by different means such as advertising and diverse rates.[180] Finally, the Court, as was explained in the *Bancorporation* case above, included the activity of thrifts institutions to establish that the Cache County commercial banking market was competitive, but ignored it as part of the line of commerce.[181] Indeed, from November 1982 through June 1987, thrifts were not measured in HHI calculations but were considered as a main mitigation factor in 87.7 per cent of the markets that presented competitive issues.[182] Once again, the DOJ tried to block an approved merger, but failed to do so.

7.4.1.2.4 Indiana Bancorporation—Financial Incorporated, Fort Wayne, Indiana

Indiana Bancorporation, a single-bank holding company, requested the FRB's approval to merge with Financial Incorporated, Fort Wayne, Indiana (Financial), also a single-bank holding company. Indiana Bancorporation was the thirteenth largest commercial banking organization in Indiana, controlling a subsidiary, Indiana Bank & Trust Company (Indiana B&T), and Financial was the fifteenth largest commercial banking organization in the state, controlling also one subsidiary, Peoples Trust.[183] Both parties operated in the Fort Wayne banking market, where Indiana Bancorporation was the third largest commercial organization with 15.6 per cent of the total of deposits, and Financial was the fourth with 13.5 per cent.[184] The board found that despite the significant size of the financial institutions involved in the transaction, the proposal 'would have no substantial effect on the concentration of banking resources in Indiana'.[185]

Interestingly, the board's approval was supported by the previous approval by the FDIC of the merger between the two subsidiaries of the applicants, Indiana B&T and Peoples Trust. The FDIC concluded that given the financial distress of Peoples Trust, its unpromising prospects, and its ineptitude as a competitor, the anti-competitive effects of the merger were counterbalanced by the possible weight of the proposal in satisfying the convenience and needs of the community to be served. Indeed, for the FDIC the

---

[179] *United States v Zions Utah Bancorporation* (n 175).

[180] ibid.

[181] The Court stated that: 'All of these enterprises have an offer of some kind that affects this commercial banking market. And that is just as much as part of the factual backdrop in which these commercial banks compete as is the population of the number of commercial banks. There was one savings and loan bank institution that would be affected. There are 10 or 12 that would be a factor. And given the significance of their success with deposits and other things in this area, it is a factor that affects the business in question, a background fact. I'm still considering the issue as being limited, commercial banking, the product involved for the area, but this is part of the backdrop of circumstances in which they compete.' See ibid.

[182] Christopher L Holder, 'The Use of Mitigating Factors in Bank Mergers and Acquisitions: A Decade of Antitrust at the Fed' [1993] Federal Reserve Bank of Atlanta Economic Review 36 https://www.atlantafed.org/-/media/Documents/banking/sr/bankapps/holdermarapr93.pdf (accessed 30 April 2023). See also Jan G Loeys, 'Bank Acquisitions: The Mitigating Factors Defense' (1986) 103 Banking Law Journal 427, 433–35.

[183] *Indiana Bancorp*, Fed Res Bull 913 (1983).

[184] ibid.

[185] ibid.

256 PUBLIC INTEREST ASSESSMENT AND FRB, OCC, AND FDIC

probable public benefits, which the merger between Indiana B&T and Peoples Trust would offer, would override the significant adverse effects on competition identified by the DOJ.[186] Thus, the board embraced the convenience and needs considerations debated by the FDIC, specifically, the view that no other less anti-competitive alternative was feasible. In sum, the board concluded that the financial improvement, which the proposal would signify for the applicant, satisfied the convenience and needs of the community to be served.

Three aspects are relevant in this case. First, that the board relied almost entirely on the findings of the FDIC. Second, that the lack of other potential acquirers weighed heavily towards the approval of the merger; and third, that the financial relief of the applicant was seen as beneficial for the community, to such an extent that the concerns about the anti-competitive effects expressed by the DOJ were deemed to be addressed.

7.4.1.2.5 National Bank and Trust Company of Norwich—National Bank of Oxford

In July 1982, National Bank and Trust Company of Norwich (NBT) and National Bank of Oxford (Oxford Bank) requested approval from the Comptroller of the Currency to merge. NBT had total deposits of US$283.962.000 and seventeen offices in Central New York state, seven of them located in Chenango County. Oxford Bank had one office in the village of Oxford, Chenango County, New York, with total deposits of US$16,607.000. On 8 April 1983, the Comptroller, despite the concerns expressed by the DOJ that the proposed transaction would have a 'significantly adverse' effect on competition, approved the deal.[187]

On 6 May 1983, the DOJ filed a civil action seeking to enjoin permanently the granted merger as a violation of section 7 of the Clayton Act. The antitrust agency found that the applicants were direct competitors in two submarkets: (i) the retail banking services (provided to individuals and households) and (ii) the business banking services (including commercial loans), in which just three other depository institutions were significant competitors.[188] Likewise, the antitrust agency found that the effect of the acquisition might substantially lessen competition considering that the existing and potential competition in retail and commercial banking in Chenango county would be permanently eliminated and that concentration in this market would be significantly increased (the HHI in the commercial banking market would increase from 986 to 6181 and from 637 to 4185 in the retail banking market).[189] In the course of the trial, the parties reached a settlement in which the merger was authorized in exchange for some divestments and other measures such as inter alia holding separate the assets and liabilities of Oxford Bank from the assets and liabilities of NBT, and not to transfer managerial staff between the merging parties.[190] This case exemplifies that whilst the divergent perspectives applied by the banking

---

[186] ibid.

[187] *United States v National Bank and Trust Company of Norwich and National Bank of Oxford*, Complaint (ND New York 1983) https://www.justice.gov/atr/case-document/file/988436/download (accessed 30 April 2023).

[188] ibid.

[189] ibid.

[190] *United States v National Bank and Trust Company of Norwich and National Bank of Oxford*, 1984-2 Trade Cases 66,074 (ND New York 1984) https://www.justice.gov/atr/page/file/1100881/download (accessed 15 November 2022).

regulators and the antitrust agency in reviewing the effects on competition of a merger were 'significantly adverse' for the DOJ, they were non-existent for the Comptroller. Such a divergence runs the risk of maintaining an incoherent sector-wide enforcement policy in relation to M&A transactions.

7.4.1.2.6 First Hawaiian—First Interstate of Hawaii

On 11 May 1990, First Hawaiian, Honolulu, Hawaii, and FHI Acquisition Corporation (collectively First Hawaiian) entered into an agreement with First Interstate of Hawaii, Honolulu, Hawaii (FIHI), by which First Hawaiian would purchase 100 per cent of the voting shares of FIHI for approximately US$140 million. First Hawaiian was the second largest commercial banking organization in Hawaii, controlling 32 per cent of total deposits in commercial banking organizations in Hawaii, and FIHI was the fourth.[191] After the merger, First Hawaiian would have 37.3 per cent of the total deposits in commercial banking organizations in Hawaii.[192] In this case, the DOJ defined as product market the commercial lending to small and medium-sized businesses,[193] whereas the FRB used the traditional total deposits approach.[194] This contradiction resulted in the DOJ filing a civil antitrust complaint by considering that the transaction would violate section 7 of the Clayton Act. The DOJ alleged that the transaction would substantially increase concentration levels in a market already highly concentrated and with significant entry barriers, a circumstance that would negatively impact many small to medium-sized commercial customers purchasing banking services in Hawaii.[195] The DOJ found an HHI increase from 440 points to 2,925 after consummation, therefore considered that the proposed transaction was anti-competitive.[196]

Despite the concerns expressed by the DOJ, on 30 November 1990, the FRB approved the transaction after concluding that it would not have 'a substantially anti-competitive effect in any relevant market'.[197] Even if the FRB ordered the divestiture of some assets, the DOJ found that the ability to sell them to the largest banks would not alleviate the competitive concerns, a reason why the parties reached a consent decree agreement where the divestiture of the assets was subject to the approval of the antitrust agency, and included the divestment of the First Hawaiian franchise, which was deemed to be an important competitive asset.[198] This case clearly illustrates that the findings of the

---

[191] *First Hawaiian Inc* 77 Fed Res Bull 52, 52–54 (1991).

[192] ibid 54.

[193] The report submitted by the DOJ was seen by the FRB as being 'based primarily on the determination that lending to small-and medium-sized businesses—rather than the cluster of banking products and services— constitutes the relevant product market, and the State of Hawaii in its entirety constitutes the relevant geographic market'. See ibid 56.

[194] Federal Reserve Bank of Kansas City, Understanding Antitrust Considerations in Banking Proposals https://www.kansascityfed.org/publicat/banking/bankerresources/UnderstandingAntitrusAnalysisv3.pdf (accessed 20 October 2022).

[195] *United States v First Hawaiian Inc*, Competitive Impact Statement (D Hawaii 1991) https://www.justice.gov/atr/file/869766/download.

[196] Stine and Gorman (n 126) 420.

[197] *United States v First Hawaiian Inc* (n 195).

[198] *United States v First Hawaiian Inc* (n 195). See also Janusz A Ordover and Margaret E Guerin-Calvert, 'Bank Mergers and the 1992 Merger Guidelines: The Bank America/Security Pacific Transaction' (2000) 16(2) Review of Industrial Organization 151, 154.

DOJ were completely disregarded by the FRB, that although both agencies used the same Guidelines they arrived at different outcomes, and that while the DOJ imposed specific remedies carefully designed to overcome the competitive concerns offered by the proposed transaction, those considered by the FRB were insufficient given their breadth and lack of in-depth analysis. Another interesting implication of this analysis concerns the extent to which antitrust agencies can redress some anti-competitive effects via consent decrees. Even though in the banking sector the number of merger cases that are litigated is low, this case confirms that parties cannot ignore the complaints filed by the federal agencies. Thus, the antitrust authorities should embrace the notion that they have a critical role to play in enforcing merging rules by, for instance, filing more complaints and negotiating the adoption of suitable remediation action plans. We cannot forget that parties are not inclined to endure prolonged litigation processes that, it can be assumed, influenced the decision of the merging parties, in this case to abide with the DOJ's remedial decision.

7.4.1.2.7 Fleet/Norstar—New Maine National Bank

Fleet/Norstar Financial Group (Fleet) was a bank holding company that operated as a commercial bank within the State of Maine under the name of Fleet Bank of Maine, with total deposits in the State of Maine by December 1990 of US$2.9 billion, which accounted for almost 22 per cent of the total deposits in the state, and around 110 branch offices throughout the State of Maine, and ranked as the largest commercial bank in this market.[199] New Maine National Bank (NMNB) was the fifth largest commercial bank in the State of Maine, with total deposits in the State of Maine by December 1990 of US$959.712 and approximately forty-four branches. On 6 January 1991, the FDIC was appointed as a receiver of the NMNB, so the FDIC requested bids for its purchase on 22 April 1991. Fleet was selected as winner bid of the bridge bank, and therefore on 14 May 1991 requested from the FRB approval for the acquisition of NMNB.[200]

Fleet and NMNB were direct competitors of business banking services to business customers in the Bangor, Pittsfield, and Presque Isle-Caribou markets. Before the merger the concentration levels in these markets were already high, and after the consummation the new bank would rank first with almost 50 per cent of the total deposits in the Bangor market, moving the HHI from 510 to 3,271; it would rank first in the Pittsfield market with approximately 33.4 per cent of total deposits, and a HHI increase from 556 to 2,605; and it would rank third in the Presque Isle-Caribou market with around 20.8 per cent of total deposits, and a HHI increase by 213 to 2,218. In spite of the significant escalation in concentration levels, on 1 July 1991, the FRB approved the transaction.[201] As a result, the DOJ filed a complaint alleging that the transaction violated section 7 of the Clayton Act because actual or potential competition in the

---

[199] *United States v Fleet Norstar Financial Group Inc* (ND Maine 1991) https://www.justice.gov/atr/case-document/file/628521/download.

[200] ibid.

[201] ibid.

7.4 ENFORCEMENT RECORD   259

Bangor, Pittsfield, and Presque Isle-Caribou markets would be consequently eliminated, concentration in these markets would drastically increase, and competition for business banking services in the same markets would be lessened.[202]

Specifically, the DOJ was concerned that the transaction would greatly harm small to medium-sized business customers, considering that one of the only few financial institutions serving these customers would be eliminated, which would result in higher prices for business banking services. The agency also concluded that entry of new competitors or expansion of the existing would be unlikely to occur so as to prevent any anti-competitive effects.[203] The DOJ reached a consent decree with the merging parties consisting of the sale of specific branches in Presque-Isle Caribou, Pittsfield, and Bangor to qualified purchasers.[204]

In this case it has been observed that even if the concerns expressed by the DOJ were totally ignored by the FRB, the antitrust agency was able to impose some remedies. Once again, the antitrust analysis applied by the banking regulator ignored the existence of lending to small and medium-sized businesses as a distinct submarket, which obviously resulted in low concentration levels and unforeseeable anti-competitive effects. Conversely, the DOJ adopted a more realistic approach whereby the use of submarkets increased 'the odds of finding some of those markets overly concentrated or in danger of becoming overly concentrated',[205] the examination of entry barriers allowed the anticipation of possible anti-competitive effects and the imposition of tailored remedies. If the regulator continues to apply this model, often referred to as a 'monolithic adherence to half-century old doctrine',[206] that ignores all the factors contemplated by the antitrust agency, barely any merger would be deemed likely to lead to competition harm and would be cleared subject to appropriate remedies.

7.4.1.2.8 Society—Ameritrust

Society Corporation (Society) was the third largest bank holding company in Ohio and the third largest commercial bank in Cuyahoga county. Society operated 289 full-service banking offices in Ohio and fifty-three in Cuyahoga—representing 16 per cent of total offices. It had also eleven offices in Lake County—constituting 16 per cent of the total offices. Ameritrust Corporation (Ameritrust), was the fifth largest bank holding company in Ohio and the largest commercial bank in Cuyahoga County, controlling 30.3 per cent of the market in Cuyahoga and 14.5 per cent in Lake County. On 12 November 1991, Society and Ameritrust filed a merger application to the FRB.[207] On 13 February 1992, the FRB approved the transaction subject to some divestitures. The DOJ filed a complaint in the time frame, this is within thirty days after the FRB's

---

[202] ibid.
[203] *United States v Fleet Norstar Financial Group Inc* Competitive Impact Statement (ND Maine, 10 July 1991) https://www.justice.gov/atr/case-document/file/628001/download.
[204] *United States v Fleet Norstar Financial Group Inc* (n 199).
[205] Richard Scott Carnell and others, *The Law of Banking and Financial Institutions* (4th edn, Wolters Kluwer 2009) 227.
[206] Pekarek and Huth (n 148) 646.
[207] 56 FR 61251.

260 PUBLIC INTEREST ASSESSMENT AND FRB, OCC, AND FDIC

approval,[208] alleging that the proposed transaction would possibly decrease competition in the delivery of business banking services to small businesses in Cuyahoga and Lake Counties, which would face higher prices. According to the antitrust agency, the merger would enable coordinated behaviour among the leading banks in Cuyahoga County and Lake County, would reduce the number of leading banks in these markets from five to four, would increase concentration levels (in Cuyahoga County the merged entity would have 51 per cent of deposits after merger, and 26 per cent in Lake County), and entry or expansion would not be sufficient to serve small businesses. Therefore, the DOJ predicted that, absent tailored divestitures, the merger would substantially lessen competition.[209]

In consequence, the DOJ requested from both merging parties the divestiture of specific bank offices with their respective deposits of individuals and small businesses, with the clear prohibition to sell them to certain large firms who already had significant competitive presence in the concerned areas.[210] The merging parties agreed to comply with the remedy package, that was approved by the District Court for the Northern District of Ohio on 4 June 1992.[211] In this case, the DOJ obtained the imposition of its proposed divestitures, which were cautiously crafted to preserve the levels of competition in the provision of business banking services to small businesses in Cuyahoga and Lake Counties. Thus, the merging parties had to adhere to commitments imposed by the antitrust agency and the regulator. In particular, those of the regulator included areas which did not show serious competitive restrictions. This situation suggests that a higher level of coordination between the federal agency and the regulator could be intensified. This close coordination may take the form of outright deference to avoid conflicting and burdensome remedies in the same case. In our view, the federal agency is the best-positioned authority to decide and impose remedies. If this is unattainable, further coordination to impose remedies that are coherent with one another would be welcomed.

7.4.1.2.9 First Busey Corporation—Main Street Trust

First Busey Corporation (First Busey), a bank holding company requested the board's approval to merge with Main Street Trust (Main Street) and its subsidiary bank, Main Street Bank & Trust.[212] First Busey was the 33rd largest depository organization in Illinois, controlling deposits of US$1.5 billion, and Main Street was the thirty-sixth largest depository institution in Illinois, controlling deposits of almost US$1.2 billion. Upon consummation, the merged bank would become the twenty-fourth largest depository organization in Illinois, controlling deposits of approximately US$2.7

---

[208] Board of Governors of the Federal Reserve System (n 29).

[209] *United States v Society Corp*, Competitive Impact Statement (ND Ohio, 13 March 1992) https://www.justice.gov/atr/case-document/file/628021/download.

[210] ibid.

[211] *United States v Society Corp* (ND Ohio, 4 June 1992) https://www.justice.gov/atr/case-document/file/628566/download.

[212] 71 FR 76339.

billion.[213] In the Champaign-Urbana banking market, First Busey was the largest depository institution, controlling 27 per cent of deposits, and Main Street Bank & Trust was the second, with 13 per cent of deposits. The DOJ expressed concerns about the possible adverse effects on competition in this area, that resulted in an agreement with the merging parties to divest two branches in Champaign, two in Urbana, and one in Mahomet.[214]

In its announcement, the DOJ explained that: '[T]hese divestitures will ensure that consumers and businesses in the Champaign-Urbana area will continue to enjoy the benefits of competition for their commercial banking and retail banking services.' It also clarified that it would not challenge the merger if the FRB adopted the divestment of the branch offices detailed in the agreement.[215] Subsequently, the board approved the transaction subject to these divestments. As part of the decision, the regulator recognized that the merger between the first and second largest banks in the Champaign-Urbana area raised some concerns, particularly because the rest of the competitors did not have more than 6 per cent of market deposits. The board also found that entry in the market was likely. The divestitures negotiated with the DOJ in combination with the additional conditions imposed by the FRB, in relation to who would be a suitable purchaser of the divested branches, alleviated the board's concerns.[216]

After determining that First Busey received an outstanding rating in its most recent CRA performance and Main Street Bank & Trust received a satisfactory rating, the board concluded that the convenience and needs of the community to be served was consistent with approval.[217] It is unlikely that in the absence of the agreement between the DOJ and the merging parties, a similar remedial package would have been imposed by the FRB. Notwithstanding the speculations, what remains important is that the antitrust agency persuaded the merging parties as well as the regulator about the need to adopt the divestment of five branch offices to resolve its antitrust concerns. One final noteworthy observation relates to the narrow analysis of the convenience and needs standard presented by the FRB, which was solely based on the CRA ratings obtained by the involved banks.

The purpose of examining the following merger cases is to show how the public interest standard is applied (including in particular how the geographic market is determined by the regulator), which will allow us to assess the challenges of a concurrent jurisdiction.

7.4.1.2.10 *Alaska Mutual Bancorporation—United Bancorporation Alaska*

Alaska Mutual Bancorporation (Alaska Mutual) a bank holding company, requested FRB's approval to merge with United Bancorporation Alaska (United), also a bank

---

[213] *First Busey Corporation and Main Street Trust Inc*, 93 Fed Res Bull C90 (2007).

[214] Department of Justice, 'Justice Department Reaches Agreement Requiring Divestitures in Mergers of First Busey Corporation and Main Street Trust, Inc.' Press Release (12 June 2007) https://www.justice.gov/archive/atr/public/press_releases/2007/223869.htm.

[215] ibid.

[216] *First Busey Corporation* (n 213).

[217] ibid.

262 PUBLIC INTEREST ASSESSMENT AND FRB, OCC, AND FDIC

holding company. Alaska Mutual was the second largest commercial banking organization in Alaska, controlling 17 per cent of the total deposits in commercial banks in the state, and United was the fifth largest commercial banking organization in the same state, with a 10.8 per cent of deposits.[218] Approval was granted largely because the merging parties were experiencing financial difficulties, and despite recognizing that the merger would suppress competition between them, the FRB concluded that by avoiding the deterioration of the financial condition of the applicants, the convenience and needs of the community would be significantly enhanced given that Alaska Mutual and United could continue serving their customers.[219]

Additionally, the FDIC's agreement to assist the applicant's recapitalization strategy by making a major capital contribution to it, was seen by the FRB as an important factor in favour of the deal.[220] The reason for this is that the FRB found the combination of the injection of capital from the FDIC with the cost savings stemming from the merger as advantageous. In consequence, the board concluded that the merger was the best possible alternative to overcome the financial problems of the parties seeking to merge.[221] It has been reported[222] that the weak financial condition of the banks was the second major mitigation factor considered by the regulators to justify many mergers with significant escalations in concentration levels. The reasoning relied upon by the regulators was that when a bank did not have the resources to compete adequately, then its market share was not a good indicator of its competitive position[223] and any projections about anti-competitive effects would be speculative.[224] This is an argument that is credible and frequent in competition enforcement cases too. Moreover, in the view of the banking regulators, the financial health of the merging parties satisfied the public interest standard by providing continuous banking services, and preserving employment within the community.[225] But this reasoning does not explain why the public interest assessment seems to prioritize the financial health of the banks rather than that of the communities.

This approach though is not dissimilar to what has occurred in other jurisdictions. Contrary to the other sectors this book focuses on, the financial and banking sector is probably the only one where governments have intervened to sustain the financial viability and stability of the sector and have allowed transactions that have anti-competitive effects.

In the UK the HBOS—Lloyds merger is a clear example of the direct and unprecedented intervention of the UK government in the assessment of mergers amidst a financial crisis. Prior to this merger, the financial sector was strictly within the remit of the UK Office of Fair Trading ('OFT') and the UK Competition Commission ('CC').[226]

---

[218] *Alaska Mutual Bancorporation*, 73 Fed Res Bull 921 (1987).
[219] ibid.
[220] ibid. See also Holder (n 182) 39.
[221] *Alaska Mutual Bancorporation* (n 218).
[222] Holder (n 182) 39.
[223] Loeys (n 182) 435–37.
[224] Holder (n 182) 39.
[225] ibid.
[226] As of April 2015, the OFT and CC 'merged' into the Competition and Markets Authority (CMA).

In this case the UK government intervened[227] and allowed the merger despite the fact that the merger was capable of giving rise to competition concerns. The merger was cleared on the basis of the bad financial situation of HBOS along with the disadvantages that a failure of a bank entails in terms of consumer confidence.[228] In fact, the government enabled the Secretary of State to decide on the merger and suspend competition rules in order to maintain the general financial stability.

In this case, the UK government introduced an additional public policy consideration providing for the stability of the UK financial system to be introduced as a policy exception, along with national security, to the referral of relevant merger situations to the Competition Commission under section 58 of the Enterprise Act 2002 (Act).[229] If the Secretary of State believes that public interest considerations are relevant in a merger case, he/she may give an intervention notice to the OFT.[230] In such cases, it is the Secretary of State who decides whether a merger should be referred to the CC for investigation once an intervention notice has been given.[231] Lord Mandelson[232] cleared the merger on public interest grounds, rather than follow the conclusion of the OFT and refer the merger to the CC, ranking competition concerns behind financial stability.[233] He argued that the benefits of the transaction for the stability of the UK financial system outweighed the potential for the merger to result in anti-competitive outcomes, which was therefore deemed to be in the public interest.[234]

[227] The UK government could intervene in merger control decisions only in respect to national security and media-related mergers but in this case the government decided to extend the situations where it could intervene by including the category of 'maintaining the stability of the UK financial system' in order to be able to intervene in Lloyds TSB/HBOS.

[228] It has to be stressed though that in the particular case the failing firm defence was not applicable and therefore was not the basis for the clearance of the merger.

[229] The Secretary of State made the final assessment of whether to refer the merger to the UK Competition Commission. In the analysis of the failing firm defence, the OFT recommended reference to the UK Competition Commission but the Secretary of State decided to clear the merger. This unusual procedure could not until then be justified for mergers in the financial industry. In fact, the OFT was the only qualified and independent authority specialized in competition issues. However, when the financial stability of the economy is at stake, it becomes understandable and to an extent necessary for governments to temporarily adopt measures to avoid a deepening of the crisis or the crisis becoming systemic. Summary Record of the discussion on Competition and Financial Markets, DAF/COMP/M(2009)1/ANN2, 10 April 2009, Introduction and Roundtable 1 on Principles: Financial Sector Conditions and Competition Policy, www.oecd.org.

[230] Intervention notices issued in relation to mergers with a national security element are listed at www.berr.gov.uk/whatwedo/businesslaw/competition/mergers/public-interest/nationalsecurity/index.html. Information and documents in relation to the issuing of a intervention notice in respect of the acquisition by BSkyB plc of 17.9 per cent of the shareholding of ITV plc are at www.berr.gov.uk/whatwedo/businesslaw/competition/mergers/public-interest/broadcasting/index.html.

[231] Save where the Secretary of State subsequently decides that there is no relevant public interest consideration, in which case the decision on whether or not to refer the merger to the CC reverts to the OFT under s 56.

[232] He used his powers under the Enterprise Act which contains provisions under which the Secretary of State can intervene on public interest grounds in the merger control process where a merger is subject to review by the OFT. He has the power to decide, on public interest grounds, to clear a merger despite a substantial lessening of competition, or prohibit a merger—or subject it to conditions—even where such measures are not justified by competition concerns alone. Decision by Lord Mandelson, the Secretary of State for Business, not to refer to the Competition Commission the merger between Lloyds TSB Group plc and HBOS plc under s 45 of the Enterprise Act 2002 (31 October 2008 http://www.berr.gov.uk/files/file48745.pdf (accessed 18 November 2022).

[233] BERR, 'Peter Mandelson Gives Regulatory Clearance to Lloyds TSB Merger with HBOS' Press Release 2008/253 (31 October 2008).

[234] There were multiple press articles talking about this unusual involvement of the government in competition law: 'In the UK, at the height of the turmoil in the banking sector last Fall, the British government brokered a merger between the struggling HBOS banking group and its competitor Lloyds TSB, creating a new banking giant—the country's largest bank and mortgage lender' ('Antitrust Implications of the Financial Crisis: A UK and

264 PUBLIC INTEREST ASSESSMENT AND FRB, OCC, AND FDIC

An OECD Report states that the dramatic shift observed in the case of *Lloyds—HBOS* is witness to the extraordinary difficulty of the situation and the consequent subordination of competition concerns to stability concerns, at least in the short run.[235] It is essential to note the important role of competition policy at times of financial crises and to emphasize that competition policy has an increased role to play at such times, bearing in mind that competition authorities and financial regulators do not have contradictory objectives, rather they aim for competitive sustainable financial markets from a different perspective and with different tools at their disposal. But the aim remains the same and it is ever more important at times of financial crises.

7.4.1.2.11 Continental Illinois—Grand Canyon

Continental Bank Corporation and Continental Illinois Bancorp (together Continental Illinois), under section 3 of the BHC Act,[236] requested board's approval to acquire 100 per cent of Grand Canyon State Bank (Grand Canyon). Continental was the second largest commercial banking organization in Illinois, controlling deposits of around US$8.3 billion and dealing with almost 7.8 per cent of total bank deposits in Illinois.[237] Grand Canyon was one of the smaller commercial banking organizations in Arizona, controlling deposits of almost US$14.6 million.[238] After applying the convenience and needs of the communities standard, in particular the responsibilities included in the CRA, on 15 February 1989 the FRB denied the transaction mainly based on the failure by Continental Illinois Bank NA, a subsidiary of Continental Illinois, to comply with the CRA.[239]

The FRB found that the subsidiary did not make sufficient efforts to meet the credit needs of its communities, kept outdated CRA statements for several years including products which were not commonly offered, and did not inform customers of the available products. The FRB concluded that considering the size of the subsidiary and the Chicago area, the overall participation of the bank in 'community development and redevelopment efforts was unsatisfactory'.[240] To address these concerns, the merging parties committed to implement a compliance plan. Nonetheless, the board rejected the proposed commitments arguing that the banking organizations should follow their CRA responsibilities before filing a merger proposal and that commitments cannot serve as a substitute to the CRA's required performance.[241] This was the first time that a bank regulator refused a transaction due to unacceptable performance of a

---

EU View' 23(2) Antitrust 1). Many have even concerned this involvement of the government in the assessment of mergers as 'ripping up Britain's competition law'. See 'HBOS Takeover Fails to End Global Panic on Financial Markets' *The Guardian* (26 September 2008) http://www.guardian.co.uk/business/2008/sep/17/lloydstsbgroup.hbosbusiness2) (accessed 18 November 2022).

[235] Competition and Financial Markets, OECD Report (2009) 32.
[236] 12 USC § 1842.
[237] Continental Bank Corp; 'Continental Ill Bancorp Inc' (1989) 75 Fed Res Bull 304.
[238] ibid.
[239] Craig Ulrich, 'Fair Lending Law Developments' (1990) 45 The Business Lawyer 1807, 1813.
[240] *Continental Bank Corp* (n 237).
[241] ibid.

bank pursuant to CRA.[242] This development responded to Congress' criticism of loose supervision.[243] Two main points accounted for this criticism: (i) the ambiguity of the CRA criteria and assessment, which turned the examination into a vague process, and (ii) the lack of transparency considering that the CRA ratings were unpublished, and that the majority of the institutions, almost by default, received a satisfactory rating.[244] Therefore, beyond the prohibition decision in this case, in April 1989 a joint statement of the Federal Financial Supervisory Agencies regarding the Community Reinvestment Act (1989 Statement) was issued, in which, activities to ensure compliance with the CRA were suggested, such as more efforts to offer higher number of home mortgages, home improvement, and small businesses loans, and more lines of credit to non-profit developers of low-income housing, among others.[245]

A crucial insight provided by this case is that since the adoption of the CRA in 1977, it was not until 1989 that a merger application was denied on the grounds of the institutions' failed performance pursuant to the CRA. Yet, this prohibition decision was a result of pressure by Congress following criticism of negligent oversight.[246] Nonetheless, one cannot ignore that the examination process was afflicted by the application of undefined key concepts such as 'entire community', 'credit needs', and 'low and moderate income neighbourhoods'.[247] Even more, the CRA regulation did not specify how the credit needs requirement should be met, an issue that still remains controversial.

7.5 Some Implications of the Analysis

A wide range of seminal cases have been examined in this section. An aspect that deserves great attention is the decision made by the Supreme Court in the early 1960s in the *Philadelphia—GTCEB*[248] case. Beyond clarifying that bank mergers were subject to section 7 of the Clayton Act, the Supreme court defined the relevant product market as the cluster of products and services denoted by the term commercial banking, and the geographic market as the area in which bank customers found it viable to do their banking business. Despite the fast-changing development experienced by the financial sector, the banking regulators and the courts have for decades adhered to this approach. As an illustration, in the *NBC—WTB*,[249] *FNSB Central—South*,[250] *First Hawaiian—FIHI*,[251] *Fleet—NMNB*,[252] and *Community Bankshares—Citizens*[253] cases,

---

[242] Barr (n 100).
[243] Ulrich (n 239) 1813.
[244] ibid 1811–13.
[245] ibid 1813–15.
[246] ibid 1813.
[247] See Philip C Jackson Jr, 'Member, Board of Governors of the Federal Reserve System, Statement Before the Subcomm. on Fin. Inst. Supervision, Reg. and Ins. of the House Comm. on Banking, Fin. And Urb. Aff.' (26 July 1978), reprinted in 64 Fed Res Bull 631, 632 (1978).
[248] *United States v Philadelphia National Bank* (n 14).
[249] *United States v Marine Bancorporation* (n 154).
[250] *United States v First National State Bancorporation* (n 163).
[251] *First Hawaiian Inc* (n 191).
[252] *United States v Fleet Norstar Financial Group Inc* (n 199).
[253] *Community Bankshares Inc* (n 132).

266 PUBLIC INTEREST ASSESSMENT AND FRB, OCC, AND FDIC

this approach was followed. The opposite approach was followed by the DOJ, which departed from this perspective by instead embracing a more realistic from a consumer substitutability point of view in which sub-markets such as retail banking services, and business banking services were considered separately (as in the *NBT—Oxford Bank*,[254] *First Hawaiian—FIHI*,[255] *Fleet—NMNB*,[256] and *FNSB Central—South*[257] cases). Also, in the *NBC—WTB*[258] case a broader geographic area was taken into account by the DOJ.

Another common theme that the examination of these cases has revealed, is that the anti-competitive concerns expressed by the DOJ have been constantly disregarded by the banking regulators, and sometimes by the courts. This has been the case in the *Philadelphia—GTCEB*,[259] *NBC—WTB*,[260] *FNSB Central—South*,[261] *FNBL—Zions*,[262] *NBT—Oxford Bank*,[263] *First Hawaiian—FIHI*,[264] *Fleet—NMNB*,[265] and *Society—Ameritrust*[266] cases. It has also been noted that a significant increase in concentration levels did not represent any concern for the banking regulators, as was seen in the FNSB Central-South,[267] *FNBL—Zions*,[268] *Indiana Bancorporation—Financial*,[269] *NBT—Oxford Bank*,[270] *First Hawaiian—FIHI*,[271] *Fleet—NMNB*,[272] and *Society—Ameritrust*[273] cases. Indeed, the regulators have repeatedly accepted the activity of thrift institutions, the financial issues of the merging parties and the lack of other less anti-competitive alternatives, as the main mitigation factors that counterbalance the high HHI post-merger levels in merger assessment.

The regulators, besides using the above-mentioned mitigation factors to alleviate the possible anti-competitive effects of the proposed transactions, have also indicated that they serve to satisfy the convenience and needs standard. For instance, in Indiana Corporation—Financial,[274] the board concluded that the financial improvement that the merger would signify for the parties, satisfied the needs of the community. The same reasoning was followed in Alaska Mutual—United,[275] where the FRB recognized that the avoidance of the deterioration of the financial condition of the applicants, fulfilled the convenience and needs standard. This reasoning assumes that as the merger was the best possible alternative to ensure continuous banking services, constant operations

---

[254] *United States v National Bank and Trust Company of Norwich and National Bank of Oxford* (n 187).
[255] *First Hawaiian Inc* (n 191).
[256] *United States v Fleet Norstar Financial Group Inc* (n 199).
[257] *United States v First National State Bancorporation* (n 166).
[258] *United States v Marine Bancorporation* (n 157).
[259] *United States v Philadelphia National Bank* (n 14).
[260] *United States v Marine Bancorporation* (n 157).
[261] *United States v First National State Bancorporation* (n 166).
[262] *United States v Zions Utah Bancorporation* (n 179).
[263] *United States v National Bank and Trust Company of Norwich and National Bank of Oxford* (n 190).
[264] *First Hawaiian Inc* (n 191).
[265] *United States v Fleet Norstar Financial Group Inc* (n 199).
[266] *United States v Society Corp*, Competitive Impact Statement (n 209).
[267] *United States v First National State Bancorporation* (n 166).
[268] *United States v Zions Utah Bancorporation* (n 179).
[269] *Indiana Bancorp* (n 183).
[270] *United States v National Bank and Trust Company of Norwich and National Bank of Oxford* (n 190).
[271] *First Hawaiian Inc* (n 191).
[272] *United States v Fleet Norstar Financial Group Inc* (n 199).
[273] *United States v Society Corp*, Competitive Impact Statement (n 209).
[274] *Indiana Bancorp* (n 183).
[275] *Alaska Mutual Bancorporation* (n 221).

7.5 SOME IMPLICATIONS OF THE ANALYSIS   267

of accessibly located offices and preserving employment within the community, then the public interest standard was fulfilled. Unfortunately, it seems that the presumption followed by the regulators that the financial health of the banks has a strong correlating with benefits for consumers has been overstated. As explained by Baradaran, the banking regulators neither properly scrutinize the claimed benefits nor run any test to determine if they will ever occur.[276] Building on this observation, a study by Markham has presented evidenced about the adverse effects of mergers to the public translated into 'increased loan costs, lower deposit rates, and less small business lending'.[277] The study has emphasized that while the banking regulators keep assuming the purported benefits, they ignore their real detriment to markets and consumers.[278]

Indeed, the Continental Illinois—Grand Canyon[279] case confirms that the convenience and needs standard is ill defined. This case is relevant as for the first time since the enactment of the CRA in 1977, a merger filed in 1989 was prohibited based on the failure to comply with the CRA. However, this denial was the response of the regulator to the criticism of Congress of loose supervision and intervention in M&As. The criticism highlighted the ambiguity of the CRA criteria and assessment,[280] that ratings were unpublished, and that the majority of the banking institutions almost by default obtained a satisfactory rating. The analysis of the CRA standard in First Busey—Main Street[281] and First National—Main Source[282] cases was restricted to the CRA rating from which the regulator assessed parties' compliance, something that has been observed in many other merger decisions where the same wording has been used. This approach affects the soundness of the decision-making process in merger assessment by the regulators.

Finally, in relation to the imposition of remedies, the analysis of the above cases has led us to conclude that those imposed by the DOJ are cautiously tailored to mitigate the specific anti-competitive effects raised by the proposed transaction while those of the regulators are not necessarily well crafted. When we look at the Society—Ameritrust[283] case we find that while the DOJ carefully imposed remedies in the areas affected by the transaction, the regulator forced some obligations in areas unrelated with the impact of the transaction. The First Hawaiian—FIHI case[284] is another good illustration of this situation, in which the merging parties had to conform to the remedies imposed by both the antitrust agency and by the regulator. In some cases, the imposition of divestments has taken place after the DOJ and the merging parties have reached agreements,

---

[276] Mehrsa Baradaran, 'Banking and the Social Contract' (2014) 89 Notre Dame Law Review 1283, 1338 https://digitalcommons.law.uga.edu/fac_artchop/942 (accessed 18 November 2022)

[277] Jesse W Markham Jr, 'Lessons for Competition Law from the Economic Crisis: The Prospect for Antitrust Responses to the "Too Big to Fail" Phenomenon' (2011) 16 Fordham Journal of Corporate & Financial Law 302.

[278] ibid.

[279] *Continental Bank Corp* (n 237).

[280] As mentioned above, in relation to the Continental Illinois- Grand Canyon case, two main points accounted for this criticism: (i) the ambiguity of the CRA criteria and assessment, which turned the examination into a vague process, and (ii) the lack of transparency considering that the ratings were unpublished, and that the majority of the institutions, almost automatically, received a satisfactory rating.

[281] *First Busey Corporation* (n 213).

[282] Federal Reserve System, FRB Order No 2018-07.

[283] *United States v Society Corp*, Competitive Impact Statement (n 209).

[284] *First Hawaiian Inc* (n 191).

268   PUBLIC INTEREST ASSESSMENT AND FRB, OCC, AND FDIC

as was seen in the NBT—Oxford Bank,[285] Society—Ameritrust,[286] and First Busey—Main Street[287] cases.

7.6 Concluding Remarks

After analysing the regulatory framework, the standards of review, and the case law in the banking sector, a key deduction is that the review of transactions in these markets does not give much weight to the anti-competitive effects commonly seen in other sectors, but instead focuses on the convenience and needs analysis standard. Nevertheless, it is unclear how the factors that are examined to ensure the convenience and needs of the consumers, such as the financial health of the target firm, the lack of other potential acquirers or the presence of fragmented competition, could counteract concerns that arise based on a significant reduction of competition as a result of a merger (or an acquisition). In our view, the banking regulators are concerned about the fate of the financial institutions, and the approval of mergers has been used to facilitate their institutions' survival under the notion that communities will undoubtedly benefit from that. On several occasions, the arguments contained in their decisions do not specify, for instance, the direct link between the health of the financial institutions and the welfare of the communities.

Thus, as this chapter has illustrated, in the financial sector the public interest standard overshadows the competition effects standard. The analysis of the seminal cases herein has confirmed the claims that the convenience and needs standard is ill-defined and that the use of the CRA ratings is a poor method to justify that its criteria are satisfied. In a few decisions, it has also been observed that the reasoning that is provided to indicate that the regulators' approval aligns with the public interest standard is insufficient. This chapter has also confirmed that during the last few decades, the banking regulators have shown a clear inclination to approve numerous mergers under the presumption that they are beneficial to the communities. Perhaps, the presumption should be reverted and merging parties should be forced to indeed make great efforts to demonstrate that their proposals will effectively benefit communities. The introduction of such a reversal implies that merging parties need to demonstrate quantifiable or verifiable benefits such as lower costs, better service, strong refund policies, secure data protection measures, effective dispute resolution alternatives, etc. The virtue of this approach is that it would suffice with clarity which applications will successfully serve the communities and which will fail to do that. In this context, it seems that it is time to revisit the concept, scope, and assessment of this public standard.

Given the shortfalls analysed herein in relation to the exiting assessment regime, beyond revisiting the definition and adequate application of the public interest standard,

---

[285] *United States v National Bank and Trust Company of Norwich and National Bank of Oxford* (n 190).
[286] *United States v Society Corp*, Competitive Impact Statement (n 209).
[287] *First Busey Corporation* (n 213).

it is worth considering whether the competition standard should be given priority under the current assessment regime or whether jurisdiction on merger assessment needs to be transferred to the federal competition agencies. This recommendation is grounded on the fact that the DOJ (whose concerns in relation to the impact of transactions on competition have been frequently ignored) has shown a more pragmatic analysis of evolving markets, it has departed from old-fashioned precedents and has imposed tailor made remedies to alleviate the anti-competitive effects created by the mergers and acquisitions in this sector. It may be beneficial to leave the merger assessment in the hands of an agency which does not have a sole interest of protecting the viability of the banks but also considers the impact of banking consolidation on competition in the markets. Transferring jurisdiction to the DOJ would suppress the uncertainty of having multiple reviewing agencies applying different standards of assessment and leading to potentially contradictory decisions and remedies.

By doing so, it would also foster the attainment of a sector-wide coherent enforcement policy. According to this proposal, a single enforcer adopting a single approach would have the potential to overcome the challenges of a multidimensional model in which the application of distinctive standards makes the merger review inconsistent and controversial. Overall, the adoption of a single enforcer does not necessarily entail a merger review without issues. Nonetheless, it offers the advantage of assisting the merging parties with a good understanding of how the merger enforcement will operate by reducing the risks of conflicting requirements, assessments, and outcomes.

Conclusion

In the United States (US), public interest considerations in relation to the impact of mergers and acquisitions (M&A) transactions on the national security of the US as well as on the regulated sectors have been embedded in merger control and corresponding legal frameworks. This book has examined the extent to which the notion of public interest has restricted the regulators' scope of action rather than enabling them to operate as a 'junior varsity Congress'.[1]

In relation to national security, although this concept has not been well defined, it has been used with more frequency to shape regulations aimed at addressing concerns that arose from foreign investment. As the scope of this national security assessment continuously expands, more factors are taken into account in the appraisal. Hence, some of the factors that were initially considered to be relevant to national defence referred to human resources, products, technology, materials, energy supplies, and other critical resources. Then, the potential disclosure of substantial pools of personal information, the potential loss of one of only a few US suppliers in certain sectors, and the potential loss of US technological advantages, were added to the list. More recently, the standard accommodates concerns stemming from certain foreign non-controlling investments involving critical technology, critical infrastructure, or sensitive personal data and real estate transactions that previously fell outside the confines of the Committee on Foreign Investment (CFIUS)'s scrutiny.

This book has shown how, by expanding the scope of the national security test, the number of transactions filed with the CFIUS has significantly increased. We have also analysed to extent to which the US government, with tailored regulation, can impede foreign investment activity targeted not just by types of sectors, but also by the country of origin of the investor. This book has established that a further expansion of the CFIUS' jurisdiction and intense scrutiny facilitates the control of foreign investment rules and represents an effective tool to respond to economic and geopolitical tensions. Nonetheless, this approach entails the risk of being detrimental to the principles of transparency, predictability, and certainty that should govern these types of interventions. What is of paramount importance is for the US national security regime to provide certainty to the investment, as well as the legal community on the transparency

---

[1] *Mistretta v United States* 488 US 361, 427 (1989) (Scalia J, dissenting), cited by Jodi L Short, 'In Search of the Public Interest' (2023) 40 Yale Journal of Regulation 759, 765. According to Short, the agencies employed the standard 'in rational and predictable patterns that comport with rule-of-law values of consistency and transparency' (ibid 766).

272   CONCLUSION

and clarity of their approach to transactions that can raise national security concerns. Otherwise, the regime runs the risk of providing excuses for the adoption and furtherance of industrial strategies, which will be an unwelcome outcome.

Turning to some of the regulated sectors such as energy, telecoms, banking and financial services, rail, and airport transport, the assessment of merger control is shared among different authorities who apply distinctive policies. In this light, this book has sought to deliberate on the overlap in the jurisdictions of antitrust and sector-regulatory authorities. Specifically, regulators have the authority to review such mergers that purportedly intend to translate the consolidation of business into outcomes that extend beyond competition law considerations. Hence, under a public interest standard, regulators—after looking at a wide range of factors—have the ultimate merger authority, whereas the federal antitrust agencies who might have objected to the mergers for competitive reasons had to defer to the regulator for the final decision. The discussions covered the theoretical contentions about including far-fetched considerations as a merger control concern. One initial observation is that this public interest standard is ill-defined, which allows the accommodation of numerous aims that usually are absent under a competition-based analysis. Another observation is that, although sectoral regulators have limited expertise in competition analysis, their authority surpasses that of the antitrust enforcers. A further remark is that this unbalanced approach between the competition and the public interest standard has resulted in a complex, expensive, and inefficient merger review that is difficult to justify.

A good example of the tensions between competition and sector regulators is seen in the railroad industry. This book has revealed that, while the competition concerns expressed by the antitrust authorities have constantly been ignored, the regulator has used the public interest standard to promote railway consolidation and to protect the industry from competing with other modes of transportation such as aeroplanes and trucks (eg Seaboard—Atlantic). In seeking approval, these rail players claim that their mergers will provide a myriad of benefits that—due to the lack of rigorous measurement—usually go uncontested (eg Northern Lines and UP—Missouri—Western). In addition, the regulator tends to impose the same set of conditions on railroad mergers regardless of their appropriateness. All these circumstances, combined with the high level of deference that courts give to the regulator, have resulted in a highly concentrated sector (eg Penn Central, Seaboard—Atlantic, Northern Lines, UP—Missouri—Western). In the end, the prevailing application of this formless public interest standard has placed the protection of competition in the railway sector at the discretion of the regulator.

In the energy sector, the focal point of the public interest standard is to assess the effects of the transaction on competition, rates, and regulation, and on preventing cross-subsidization. Although the regulator and the antitrust agencies look at the anti-competitive effects of the transaction, in doing so, their approach and outcomes are often contradictory. This is because the analysis of the regulator is largely based on market concentration, while the antitrust agencies apply a more comprehensive analysis in which other factors such as efficiencies, entry, and anti-competitive effects are examined (eg Exelon—PSEG, Progress—Duke, and Exelon—Constellation). Additionally, the regulator relies extensively on the merging parties' analysis, while the antitrust agencies perform their own in-house analysis (eg Exelon—Constellation and Dominion—SCANA). Similarly, the regulator has shown a lenient policy towards the types of efficiencies that a merger can achieve (eg Northeast—PSNH). Often, the benefits claimed are overvalued, and the merging parties are not compelled to demonstrate the causal link between the merger and the purported benefits. This book has established that the merger assessment carried out by the regulator can be lengthy. Yet length does not necessarily mean correctness and it is difficult to justify when that imposes excessive costs on merging parties. These costs derive partly from the type and number of remedies imposed: structural from the antitrust authority and behavioural from the regulator (eg Exelon—PSEG, Pacific—Enova, Dominion—CNG, and Exelon—Constellation). It is not necessary to have two authorities examining the effects of the merger on competition, especially when the considerations of the competition expert authority are overshadowed by those coming from a regulator with limited expertise in competition analysis. Indeed, the oversight of the regulator does not complement or exceed that of the federal antitrust agencies.

The airline industry has received similar treatment: the regulator has been overtolerant of merger activity. One important feature that contributes to this tendency is the approach applied by the regulator according to which merger opponents need to show not just that the transaction would increase levels of concentration but also that it would be anti-competitive (eg Northwest—Republic and Ozark—TWA). This burden of proof is so difficult to satisfy that almost any transaction goes unchallenged. At the same time, the concerns expressed by the antitrust authority are ignored. Since this dual review system gives ultimate merger authority to the regulator, the technical expertise of the federal agency is misused. In addition, the application of the public standard in relation to international alliances is so broad that virtually any cross-border agreement involves a great number of benefits (eg the Delta—Swissair—Sabena—Austrian Airlines alliance). However, under the competition standard these benefits become less apparent. The merits of this concurrent merger control model are doubtful as discrepancies between the regulator and the antitrust agency appear to be the rule rather than the exception. Therefore, a model in which the ultimate merger authority lies with the competition expert has the potential to alleviate the inefficiencies of the concurrent model and to improve the decision-making process.

In the telecommunications sector a procedural feature is a determinant aspect of the merger review that is undertaken by the regulator. This is because it does not have a statutory deadline to make a final decision. In substantial terms, an important element is that the applicants carry the burden of demonstrating that their proposed transaction is in the public interest. Furthermore, under the wider public interest standard applied by the regulator, one consideration of the competitive effect analysis, among many others, is whether the merger will facilitate its ability to regulate (eg Bell Atlantic—NYNEX, AT&T—TCI, and SBC—Ameritech). The combination of the procedural and substantive flexibility offered by the public interest standard, and the awareness

274 CONCLUSION

of the merging parties' desire to close the deals quickly, has allowed the imposition of heavy conditions by the regulator and the negotiation of 'voluntary' agreements, which are frequently unrelated to the mergers (eg Bell Atlantic—GTE, Verizon—MCI, Comcast—NBCU, and AT&T—DirecTV). This broader view of what can be evaluated and achieved through a merger has made it difficult for the parties to try to satisfy the unlimited public interest standard applied by the regulator. So, while the competition standard carried out by the antitrust authority is more objective and predictive, the public interest standard has turned merger control into a regulatory tool that promotes intrusive intervention.

In the financial services sector, different regulators and the antitrust agencies share the authority to assess the competitive effects of the proposed transactions. This concurrent jurisdiction has been problematic because the assessment is underpinned by conflicting principles. For instance, while the antitrust agencies examine the specific areas affected by the respective transaction, the banking agencies have pre-established metropolitan areas that are used as their relevant geographic markets. In terms of the product markets, the federal agencies analysis includes a wider range of products and services, whereas the banking regulators rely entirely on the traditional banking services (eg NBC—WTB, FSNB Central-South, First Hawaiian—FIHI, Fleet—NMNB, and Community Bankshares—Citizens). Considering this disparity, the anti-competitive concerns expressed by the antitrust agency have been constantly disregarded by the banking regulators, and sometimes by the courts. In relation to the public interest standard, this book has identified that the regulators have been using it to facilitate the survival of banks facing financial distress under the notion that communities will undoubtedly benefit from merging them (eg Alaska Mutual—United). Indeed, one of the most common themes in the application of the public interest standard is that regulators do not exhibit thorough oversight (eg First Busey—Main Street and First National—Main Source). Put differently, they do not exercise a rigorous confrontation of the public interest with empirical facts. In consequence, banking regulators usually approve most merger applications under the presumption that they protect the public interest even if there is little evidence that it does.

As the book has illustrated, in the regulated sectors a transaction is likely to be assessed under a public interest test by the relevant sectoral regulatory authority and at the same time under the substantial reduction of competition test by the FTC/DOJ. This overlapping assessment approach can lead at times to contradictory outcomes. Furthermore, depending on the sector in question, the outcome of the public interest assessment may supersede that of the competition law assessment, an outcome that in itself can lead to ineffective competitive dynamics in the sectoral market.

In conclusion, a balanced approach must be taken to resolve this conundrum created by this concurrent jurisdiction of antitrust and sectoral regulators in the assessment of M&A transactions. If certain measures are not introduced to mitigate the overlap between authorities, it is very likely that we will continue to witness how these markets become more concentrated. Most importantly, such a divergence will impede the attainment of a sector-wide coherent enforcement policy. As also seen with the national security concerns, this book has established that when deciding to approve or reject a merger under public interest considerations the relevant regulator seems to enjoy unlimited discretion. Whether or not a transaction induces national security or public interest concerns, it is crucial that the parties can predict the outcomes of the authorities' assessments based on the analysis of objective factors, and ones that will be cognizant of the impact of transactions on the competitive dynamics in the markets. In short, more transparency, accountability, and efficiency in the merger review process across the US economy would be advisable and welcomed in ensuring legal certainty and a welcoming investment environment.

Index

For the benefit of digital users, indexed terms that span two pages (e.g., 52–53) may, on occasion, appear on only one of those pages.
Tables and figures are indicated by *t* and *f* following the page number

airline industry *see* DOT

banking sector
  challenges of concurrent jurisdiction 242–44
    contradictory approaches between
      antitrust agencies and regulators 244
    convoluted assessment process and
      uncertainty 242
    criticisms of 242–44, 245
    lack of clarity in substantive and procedural
      terms 244
  composition and legislation of
    regulators 230–34
    FDIC 233–34
    FRB 232–33
    OCC 233
  DOJ 230
    competition assessment of
      transactions 234–35, 236–37, 238–39
    'merger screen's system 234–35
    oversight by 230–31, 234–35
    reviewing bank merger transactions with
      regulators 238
    see also DOJ
  enforcement record *see* banking sector:
    enforcement record and seminal cases
  filing instructions and process
    overview 234–39
    DOJ 234–35, 236–37, 238–39
    FDIC 235, 237–38
    FRB 235–37
    FTC 239
    'merger screens' system 234–36, 242
    OCC 235
    procedure 235
  public interest standard 239–42
    considerations in public interest
      assessment 241–42
    convenience and needs concept 240–41,
      266–67, 268
    historical background 239–40
    importance of 240

    need to revisit application of 268–69
    overshadowing competition effects
      standard 268
    weight given to anti-competitive effects,
      lack of 268
  regulators 229–39
    concurrent merger jurisdiction,
      effectiveness of 229
    need for more robust scrutiny of
      mergers 229
    structural changes in the market 229
banking sector: enforcement record and seminal
  cases 245–65
  House Financial Services Committee
    Memorandum 245
  implications 265–68
    competition standard, need to give priority
      to 268–69
    convenience and needs standard, ill-
      defined nature of 266–67
    definition of relevant product
      market 265–66
    DOJ anti-competitive concerns
      disregarded 266
    mitigation factors, use of 266
    remedies, different approaches
      to 267–68
    whether review jurisdiction should go to
      competition agencies 268–69
  merger applications before FDIC 245
  merger applications before FRB 245
  merger applications before OCC 246
  transactions decided by sectoral
    regulators 247–50
    Community Bankshares–Citizens 247–
      48, 265–66
    First Financial Bancorp–MainSource
      Financial Group 248–49
    Philadelphia National Bank–Girard Trust
      Corn 249–50, 266
  transactions where sectoral regulators and
    DOJ diverged 251–65

278 INDEX

banking sector: enforcement record and seminal cases (*cont.*)

Alaska Mutual Bancorporation–United Bancorporation Alaska 261–64, 266–67
Continental Illinois–Grand Canyon 264–65, 267
First Busey Corporation–Main Street Trust 239–40, 267–68
First Hawaiian–First Interstate of Hawaii 257–58, 265–66, 267–68
First National Bank of Logan–Zions First National Bank 254–55, 266
First National State Bancorporation (FSNB Central–South) 252–54, 265–66
Fleet/Norstar–New Maine National Bank 258–59, 265–66
Indiana Bancorporation–Financial Incorporated, Fort Wayne, Indiana 255–56, 266–67
National Bank and Trust Company of Norwich–National Bank of Oxford 256–57, 265–66, 267–68
National Bank of Commerce–Washington Trust Bank 251–52, 265–66
Society–Ameritrust 259–60, 266, 267–68

CFIUS 2, 3–4, 37–42
composition and legislation 37–39
almost any foreign person potentially within CFIUS' reach 81
broad discretion of CFIUS 63
disclosure of information 39
role and powers of CFIUS 37–38
scope broadened by FIRRMA 38, 52, 68–69, 78–80
covered transactions, nature of 78–79
cross-border mergers 35
delays in process, effects of 58–59, 60, 62
enforcement record *see* CFIUS: enforcement record
evolving national security risks, executive order on 80
Exon-Florio amendment *see* Exon-Florio amendment
filing instructions and process overview 39–42
conditions mitigating threat to national security 40–41
formal assessment 39–41
informal review 39–40, 42, 79
'light filing' process 40
mandatory filing 79
referring transactions to US President 41–42
restricted transparency 81

national security concerns *see* national security concerns
need to provide certainty to investment community 81
proposals for change to *see* CFIUS: proposals for change
US President blocking transactions *see* CFIUS: transactions blocked by US Presidents

CFIUS: enforcement record 43–75
covered notices by sector 47f
covered transactions by acquirer home country 43–44, 45t
covered transactions by sector and year 44–46
covered transactions, withdrawals, and Presidential decisions 46
growth in CFIUS notices filed 43f, 44
increasing number of CFIUS notifications 52
increasing severity of concerns 52
investigations *see* CFIUS seminal cases
lessons from CFIUS national security assessment 49–51
mitigation measures 51, 52
SOEs *see* CFIUS: national security concerns and Chinese SOEs

CFIUS: national security concerns and Chinese SOEs 72–75
BAIN—3Com/ HUAWEI Technologies Co (2007) 75
ChemChina—Syngenta CsS12
CNOOC—UNOCAL (2005) 74–75
LENOVO—IBM (2005) 74
risks from China presence 73

CFIUS: proposals for change 76–80
aim of amendments 76
concerns, nature of 76
FIRRMA, s 2987 78–80
Food Security is National Security Act, s 616 (2017) 77
Foreign Investment and Economic Security Act (2017) 77
National Defence Authorization Act for Fiscal Year 2018 76–77
True Reciprocity Investment Act (2017) 77–78

CFIUS seminal cases 51–63
Aleris—Zhongwang 58–59
Alibaba—MoneyGram 57–58
ChemChina—Syngenta 55–56
Chicago Stock Exchange—Chongqing Casin Enterprise Group 56–57
Cree—Infineon 59
Ekso—Zhejiang & Shaoxing 60–62

INDEX 279

Magnachip 62–63
NavInfo—HERE 59–60
Smithfield Foods—Shuanghui International
Holdings 54–55
SoftBank—Sprint Nextel 53–54
Verio—NTT Communications 52–53
CFIUS: transactions blocked by US
Presidents 63–66
Biden administration 72
Bush administration 63–64
China National Aero-Technology Import
and Export Corp 63–64
historical overview 66–72
Aixtron (2016) 66–68
lack of information about reasons for
blocking 72
limited exercise of right to block
transactions 72
Obama administration 64–68
Ralls Corporation (2012) 64–66
Trump administration 68–72
Infineon (2020) 72
Lattice Semiconductor (2017) 51, 69–70
Qualcomm (2018) 70–71
StayNTouch, Inc. (2020) 71
China
areas of proposed acquisitions
aluminium maker 58–59
computing CsS34
digital mapping 59–60
exoskeletons 60–62
financial services 57–58
food sector 54–56
oil production 74–75
semi-conductors 51, 52, 62–63, 64, 66–68, 69–70
stock exchange 56–57
telecommunications 71, 75
wind farms 64–66
expansion of foreign investments 73
purchases blocked by US President 63–66
restrictions on reciprocal investment
opportunities 54
size of economy 73
SOEs, acquisitions by see CFIUS:
national security concerns and
Chinese SOEs
US stance towards Chinese acquirers 64–72, 75
Clayton Act (1914) 7, 8, 22–23
'Clayton Act' test 195–96, 198–99
DOJ enforcing civilly 19
DOT, and 196–97
historically 7, 22–23, 230

merger control 18, 23–24, 27–28, 33, 86–87, 130–31
private enforcement 25
scope, expansion of 8, 144
vague and broad terms 9–10, 20, 34
wire or radio communications 84
Committee on Foreign Investment in the United
States (CFIUS) see CFIUS
competition law enforcement
achieving efficiency as approach to 1–2
illegality test relying on effect upon
commerce 1–2
politics influencing 1
consumer welfare 214
inefficient competitors, and 1–2
merger control, and 1n.5, 13–14, 216, 229
Sherman Act, and 1n.5, 13–14

defence and military applications 58–59
military units/installations, proximity to 54–55, 57, 64–66
Department of Justice (DOJ) see DOJ
Department of Transportation (DOT) see DOT
diagonal mergers 16–17
digital mapping 59–60
DOJ 2
airline industry
DOJ and DOT approaches, big gap
between 225–26
DOJ and DOT coordinating alliance
reviews 198–99
DOJ critical of DOT's approach 203–4
DOJ's five-part assessment 199–200
DOJ's review standard of alliances 198–99
DOJ's role in airline mergers 194, 195, 196–97
DOT's advisory role to DOJ 194, 195, 196–97
DOT's analysis to DOJ 200
need for DOT to work with DOJ to assess
competition effects 203
transactions assessed solely by
DOJ 212–17
transactions on slot allocation where
convergence between DOT and
DOJ 209–11
transactions where DOT and DOJ diverged
on outcome 206–9
see also DOT
Antitrust Division 19
utility sector, mergers and 126–27
banking sector 230–31
challenges of concurrent jurisdiction see
under banking sector

280 INDEX

DOJ (*cont.*)
  competition assessment of
    transactions 234–35, 236–37, 238–39
  competition concerns dismissed by
    courts 251–55, 259, 266
  competition concerns dismissed by
    regulators 247, 250, 253, 256–58,
    266, 268–69
  differing merger review methodologies
    between DOJ and regulators 253–54,
    255, 256–57, 265–66
  few decisions challenged in courts 244,
    247, 250
  'merger screens' system 234–35
  oversight by 230–31, 234–35
  remedies carefully tailored 267–68
  reviewing bank merger transactions with
    regulators 238
  second requests not permitted 238
  transactions where sectoral regulators and
    DOJ diverged 251–65
  whether jurisdiction on merger
    assessment should be transferred
    to DOJ 268–69
  see also banking sector
electricity energy sector
  challenges of concurrent jurisdiction
    see under FERC
  confidentiality of information 128,
    131, 134–35
  differences with FERC approach 131, 146
  extensive competition analysis 150–51
  factors considered in analysis 131, 146, 151
  in-house analysis 129–30, 131
  mergers in utility sector 126–27
  process of merger reviews 130–31
  second requests 131
  sharing jurisdiction with FTC 130–31
  structural remedies, imposition of 134–35,
    143, 151–52
  tailored remedies 146, 151
  see also FERC
Merger Guidelines *see* Merger Guidelines
merger review assessment *see* merger review
  assessment
railways
  convergence in approach with regulator
    using contradictory analyses 180–88
  convergence in approach with regulator
    using same analyses 184–85, 190
  different views of STB and DOJ pointing to
    different outcomes 160–61
  divergence in approach of STB and
    DOJ 166–80

DOJ as decisionmaker opposing
    transactions 185–87, 190
  immunity, DOJ granting 182
  see also STB
substantial lessening to competition test 3, 4
telecommunications sector 85, 86–87, 89,
    90–91, 118–20
  DOJ challenging merger not reviewed by
    FCC 113–15
  transactions where FTC/DOJ and FCC
    converged on assessment 103–17
  see also FCC
DOT
  airline industry
    alliance agreements, review of 197–98
    antitrust laws exemptions 197–98
    antitrust tests 195–96
    certification of airlines 195
    Civil Aeronautics Board 195, 196–97
    Covid-19 and financial support 193–
      94, 224
    deregulation 193, 195–96
    DOJ role in airline mergers 194,
      195, 196–97
    executive order to DOT on competition
      and consumer issues 193–94
    foreign air transportation
      agreements 196–98
    heavily consolidated 193–94, 202, 216–
      17, 224
    open skies agreements 197, 219,
      220–21
    restrictions on foreign ownership of
      airlines 197
    transfer of an airline's routes 197
  assessment of alliances 198–99
    application process 198
    DOJ and DOT coordinating alliance
      reviews 198–99
    DOJ's review standard of alliances 198–99
    DOT's competitive analysis 198–99
  assessment of mergers 199–200
    DOJ's five-part assessment 199–200
    DOT's analysis to DOJ 200
    DOT's economic and safety
      reviews 198–99
    FAA's safety authorization 200
    negotiations 199
    process for 199
    second requests 199
  challenges of concurrent jurisdiction 203–4
    DOJ critical of DOT's approach 203–4
    need for DOT to work with DOJ to assess
      competition effects 203

INDEX 281

standard of review benefiting parties at expense of competition 203
whether DOT has enough expertise in competition analysis 203
composition and legislation 194–98
bureaus of DOT 194
DOT advisory role to DOJ on airline mergers 194, 195, 196–97
DOT approving/immunizing foreign air services agreements 196–97
DOT's de facto merger-blocking power 195, 196–97, 198–99, 200
establishment of DOT 194
role and functions of DOT 194
enforcement record *see* DOT: enforcement record and seminal cases
filing instructions and process overview 198–200
assessment of alliances 198–99
assessment of merger 199–200
confidentiality 198–99
review process of antitrust immunity open to public 198
public interest standard 201–3, 221
alliances beneficial per se 221, 226
competition related considerations 201
DOT.s non-defendable approach 221
focus on safety, fair wages and working conditions 2–3
international airline alliances, evaluation of 130–31
non-competition related considerations for flights 201
political forces around merger review process 202
public interest benefits of code-share relationships, 201–2
public interest test needs to be clarified and restricted 221
recommendations for more efficient review process 227–28
DOT: enforcement record and seminal cases 204–24
allocation of gates and slots 202–3, 209–11, 213–14, 222
antitrust immunity cases 204, 205*t*
entry barriers 206–9
implications 224–26
consolidation approach, examples of 224–25
DOT and DOJ approaches, big gap between 225–26
DOT's biased view that alliances are beneficial per se 221, 226

DOT's protection of international aviation policies 226
high number of approvals raising concerns 204
little room for competition concerns to be properly assessed 224
mergers between largely non-overlapping airline networks 225
pattern of protecting airlines, no change in 151–52
recognize that proper use of slots in public interest 226
international airline alliances with antitrust immunity 217–24
American Airlines—JetBlue 223–24
American Airlines—TACA 203, 218–19
Continental—United—Star 203, 219–21
Delta—Aerovias de Mexico SA de CV 221–23
Delta—Swissair—Sabena—Austrian Airlines alliance 217–18
transactions assessed solely by DOJ 212–17
American—US Airways 212–13, 214–17
Delta Air Lines—Northwest Airlines Corporation 212–13
United—Continental 212–14
transactions on slot allocation where convergence between DOT and DOJ 209–11
Delta—US Airways slot swap 209–11
United Airlines—Delta (Newark slots) 211
transactions where DOT and DOJ diverged on outcome 206–9
Northwest—Republic 206–8
Ozark—TWA 208–9

electricity energy sector
alternative energy sources, encouragement of 127
classification approach for mergers 135–36
DOJ, and *see under* DOJ
electricity sales controlled by federal and state governments 127
Energy Information Administration (EIA) 135–36
FERC, and *see* FERC
FTC, and *see* FTC
importance of 123
interrelated segments of 123
jurisdiction to review mergers 126–27
natural gas sector 127
deregulation of 127–28
energy infrastructure and energy production 74–75

282 INDEX

Exon-Florio amendment 42
  authority of President to suspend/prohibit
    transactions 38–39, 63, 69–70
  codifying CFIUS process 36
  safe harbour, and 42

FCC: enforcement record and seminal
    cases 91–117
  DOJ challenging merger not reviewed by
    FCC 113–15
  implications 118–20
    agencies engaging in different
      assessments 118
    lack of consultation as standard
      practice 119–20
    need to offer variety of commitments to
      obtain FCC's approval 119
    penalties for non-compliance 118–19
    unfettered power exerted by FCC 119
    wide scope of FCC 118
  major mergers concurrently reviewed by
    FCC/antitrust agencies 91
  transactions where FTC/ DOJ and FCC
    converged on assessment 103–17
    Altice–Cablevision 107–9
    AOL–Time Warner 103–5, 118
    AT&T–DirecTV 106–7, 119–20
    AT&T–Time Warner 113–15
    CenturyLink–Level 3 111–12, 119
    News Corp–DirectTV 105–6, 119–20
    Nexstar–Media General 109–11
    Nexstar–Tribune 115–16
    T-Mobile–Sprint 112–13
    Verizon–TracFone 116–17
  transactions where FTC/DOJ and FCC
    diverged on remedies 103
    AT&T–TCI 96, 118–19
    Bell Atlantic–GTE 97–99, 118, 119
    Bell Atlantic–NYNEX 92, 118–19
    Comcast–NBCU 100–1, 119–20
    SBC–Ameritech 94–95, 118–20
    Sinclair–Tribune 101–3
    Verizon–MCI 99–100, 119
FCC 2, 83–121
  challenges of concurrent jurisdiction 90–91
    agencies pursuing different purposes 90
    agency consultation not standard
      practice 119–20
    closer cooperation between agencies, need
      for 120
    differences in approaches 116–17, 118, 120
    expense and delay 90, 96, 98–99, 119–20
    merger review as resource demanding
      duplicative process 90

  need to assess effectiveness of 103
  negotiating voluntary agreements and
    conditions as abuse of power 90–91
  shortfalls of dual review 98–99
  solution to challenges 121
  competition doctrine, development of 97–98
  composition and legislation 84–85
    common ownership, effects of 85
    FCC role and powers 84, 85–86
  conditions, imposition of 93–94, 95, 96, 97,
    99–100, 104–5, 106–7, 112, 116–17
    length of FCC process, and 98–99
    leverage of FCC, acceptance of conditions
      and 99–100, 101, 103, 120
    penalties for non-compliance 118–19
    unfettered authority of FCC to
      impose 93–94
  enforcement record see FCC: enforcement
    record and seminal cases
  filing instructions and process
    overview 85–87
    blocking transactions, process for 86
    'clearance process' 85
    no statutory deadline to make final
      decision 93–94, 120
    second requests 86–87
    transfer of licence, FCC power to deny 86
  judicial review, limited nature of 93–94
  public interest standard 87–89
    additional factors, inclusion of 118
    antitrust analysis, procedure for 89
    appeals 88–89
    burden of proof 88–89
    concessions or commitments,
      negotiating 88–89
    less accurate assessment of impact on
      competition 95
    misleading or incomplete information,
      and 102–3
    procedural and substantive
      flexibility 90–91
    public interest, convenience, and necessity,
      focus on 2–3, 88
    substantive merger analysis entailing broad
      aims 118
  remedies, imposition of 100–1, 104–5, 106,
    109, 111, 117, 118
    FTC/DOJ and FCC diverging on 92
FDIC
  composition and legislation 230–31,
    233–34
  merger applications before FDIC 245
  procedure before FDIC 235, 237–38
  role and functions 233–34

seminal cases *see* banking sector: enforcement record and seminal cases

see also banking sector

Federal Aviation Administration (FAA) *see under* DOT

Federal Communications Commission (FCC) *see* FCC

Federal Deposit Insurance Corporation (FDIC) *see* FDIC

Federal Energy Regulatory Commission (FERC) *see* FERC

Federal Reserve Board (FRB) *see* FRB

Federal Trade Commission (FTC) *see* FTC

Federal Trade Commission Act (FTCA) 7, 19–22
internal administrative litigation 27, 32–33
merger control 27–28
vague and broad terms 20

FERC: enforcement record and seminal cases 135–50
changes of ownership, types of 135
implications 150–52
additional burdens imposed on merging parties 151–52
DOJ conducting extensive competition analysis 150–51
DOJ preferring structural remedies 151–52
efficiencies as part of review, need to include 151–52
FERC anti-competitive analysis focusing on concentration levels 151
FERC heavily reliant on applicants' analysis 150–51
FERC preferring behavioural remedies 151–52
public interest concept lacking clear definition 151
mergers reviewed by FERC related to electric utility companies 135–36, 136*t*
transactions assessed by the sectoral regulator 137–39
Northeast Utilities—Public Service Company of New Hampshire 138–39, 151
PacifiCorp—UP&L 137–38
transactions with diverging remedies between FERC and DOJ 139–50
American Electric Power Company—Central and South West Corporation 139–41, 151
Dominion—CNG 143–44, 151–52
Dominion—SCANA and SCE&G 149–51
Duke—Progress 147–48, 151

Exelon—Constellation 148–49, 150–52
Exelon—PSEG 144–46, 151–52
Pacific Enterprises—Enova 141–43, 151–52

FERC 123–52
challenges of concurrent jurisdiction 133–35, 140–41
close cooperation in substance and process, need for 143
criticism of FERC's approach 133–34, 136–37
higher costs 143
inconsistent procedures and decisions 133–34, 147–48, 151, 152
need to minimize duplicative and inconsistent merger review 135, 146
need to reduce overall costs and uncertainty of outcomes 135, 146
proposed solution 152
structural and conduct-based remedies, compliance with 143–44
types of remedies imposed 134–35, 146
common transactions filed at FERC 125–26
composition and legislation 123–28
creation of FERC 123–24
holding companies, jurisdiction over 126–27
jurisdiction 124–27
role and functions of FERC 123–24
court's deference to 139
definitions of terms 125
energy sector *see* energy sector
enforcement record *see* FERC: enforcement record and seminal cases
filing instructions and process overview 128–31
blocking mergers without recourse to courts 128
confidentiality of information 128, 131, 134–35
delay 140–41
differences with antitrust agencies' approach 131, 146
disclosure of sensitive business information 128
DOJ and FTC sharing jurisdiction in electricity sector
freedom of information 128
Merger Policy Statement 128–30
parties to be present during Commission meetings 128
second requests, no power to issue 131, 134–35
third parties playing significant role 131
time to complete merger review 130

284 INDEX

FERC (*cont.*)
impact on applicants' operating costs and rate
levels, focus on 2–3
Merger Policy Statement 128–29
FERC relying on parties' assessment 129–
30, 131, 134, 149, 150–51, 152
Horizontal Merger Guidelines, use of 128–
29, 131, 141–42, 146
lack of clear parameters to define relevant
markets 129–30
methodology based on Appendix A
Analysis 128–29
public interest standard 132
relevant information supplied by
parties 129–30
safe harbour thresholds 145
public interest standard 126–27, 131–33
analysis based on market
concentration 131, 133–34, 143,
146, 151
antitrust considerations 139
behavioural remedies, imposition of 134–
35, 143, 151–52
burden of proof in electricity sector on
merging parties 131
Commonwealth Edison factors 131–32
Commonwealth Edison factors,
replacement of 132
cross-subsidization factor as part of 132
evaluation of mergers' effects on
competition, rates and regulation 132
historically accepting non merger-specific
benefits 137, 138, 151
other relevant factors in 133
public interest concept lacking clear
definition 151
food security 54–56
foreign direct investment (FDI) 51, 61–62
China, and 73
increasingly subject to non-competition
scrutiny 35
national security, and 1, 68
support for 68–69
US policy open to 35
Foreign Investment Risk Review Modernization
Act 2018 (FIRRMA) 50–51
broadening scope of CFIUS 38, 52, 68–
69, 78–80
disclosure of information 39
examples of businesses involving national
security considerations 37
'light filing' process 40
FRB
central bank of the US, as 232–33

composition and legislation 230–33
merger applications filed before FRB 245
procedure before FRB 235–37
role and functions 232–33
screens 235–36
seminal cases *see* banking sector: enforcement
record and seminal cases
see also banking sector
FTC 2
banking sector 239
creation and role 19–20, 21–22
electricity energy sector
challenges of concurrent jurisdiction *see
under* FERC
confidentiality of information 128,
131, 134–35
differences with FERC approach 131, 146
factors considered in analysis 131, 146, 151
in-house analysis 129–30, 131
mergers in utility sector 126–27
process of merger reviews 130–31
second requests 131
sharing jurisdiction with DOJ 130–31
structural remedies, imposition of 134–35,
143, 151–52
see also FCC
Merger Guidelines *see* Merger Guidelines
Merger Retrospective Program 28–29
merger review assessment *see* merger review
assessment
structure and composition 21–22
substantial lessening to competition test 3, 4
telecommunications sector 85, 86–87, 89,
90–91, 118–20
transactions where FTC/ DOJ and FCC
converged on assessment 103–17
see also FCC

Hart-Scott-Rodino Antitrust Improvements Act
(1976) 17
acquisitions thresholds, and 26
airline mergers 199
automatic stays 30
banking sector, and 238
confidentiality of information 128
early termination of waiting period 107
notifications under 26–27, 130–31, 239
procedural requirements 26
transformations in merger enforcement
regime 18, 23–24, 25–26, 86–87
Herfindahl–Hirschman Index (HHI) 17, 129,
133–34, 145–46, 266
DOJ, and 238–39
FDIC, and 237–38

INDEX   285

jointly developed HHI market screens 234–35, 242
tool to measure market concentration, as 11
historical overview of US merger control 5–10
  Celler-Kefauver Act 8
  Clayton Act 7–8, 9–10
  evolving and unpredictable judicial
    guidance 6–10, 235–36
  Federal Trade Commission Act 7
  market share presumption doctrine 8–9
  market share presumption doctrine 8–9
  Sherman Act 5–8
hypothetical monopolist test (HMT) 11, 17

institutional setting 19–25
  Antitrust Division (DOJ) *see under* DOJ
  FTC *see* FTC
  private plaintiffs *see* private plaintiffs
  state authorities *see* state authorities
Interstate Commerce Commission (ICC)
    see under STB

judicial review 32–34
  agencies' access to documents and
    testimony 33–34
  anti-competitive decisions, review of 26
  appeals 33–34
  approvals 26–27
  burden of proof 33
  FCC, and 93–94
  FERC, court's deference to 139
  injunctions 26–27, 32–33
  judicial authorization required to block
    mergers 32–33

merger control *see* US merger control
    regime
  achieving efficiency as approach to 1–2
Merger Guidelines 10–17, 128–29
  analysis of efficiency claims 11–12
  competitive effects as core of merger
    analysis 15–16
  decline in merger enforcement 12–13
  DOJ's new merger guidelines 11
  FERC use of 128–29, 131, 141–42, 146
  first non-binding guidelines 10
  FTC and DOJ merger guidelines 13–17
  Herfindahl–Hirschman Index 11
  higher thresholds indicators of potential
    anti-competitive effects 10–11
  hypothetical monopolist test (HMT),
    introduction of 38
  importance of 17
  market share approach 10–11

merger control to advance consumer
    welfare 13–14
merger efficiencies, test for 14
need for consistent regulation of the merger
    review process 10
upward pricing pressure test 15–16
Vertical Merger Guidelines 16–17
merger review assessment 25–34
  clash between aims of antitrust enforcers and
    other policy-makers 34
  judicial review 32–34
  procedural process before FTC/DOJ 25–27
    acquisition thresholds, and 26
    'clearance' procedure 25–26
    internal administrative litigation 27, 32–33
    judicial review *see* judicial review
    second requests 26–27
    shared authority 25–26
    'white papers' 26–27
  settlements 30–32
    asymmetry of information 30–31
    automatic stay triggered by second
      request 30
    effects of consent agreements 31–32
    ending procedure with a consent
      decree 30–31
    negotiation of remedies, reliance on 30
    preferential use of consent decrees,
      statistics on 31–32
  substantive assessment 27–29
    economic-based approach 27–29
    statutes governing merger
      control 27–28
    theories of harm 28–29
money transfer services 57–58

national security assessment 3
  ambiguity and legal uncertainty 38
  CFIUS *see* CFIUS
  concept of national security 36–37
  examples of businesses involving national
    security considerations 37
  FDI, and 1, 68
  geopolitical developments 35–36
national security concerns
  confidential nature of 52, 55, 62
  defence and military applications 58–59
  digital mapping 59–60
  energy infrastructure and energy
    production 74–75
  food security 54–56
  military units/installations, proximity to 54–55, 57, 64–66
  money transfer services 57–58

286 INDEX

national security concerns (*cont.*)
  national security assessment as tool for
    political aims 61–62
  personal data and sensitive information 54–
    55, 57–58, 68–69
  reliance on Chinese equipment
    manufacturers 53–54
  robotic mechanical suits 60–62
  semiconductors 51, 52, 62–63, 64, 66–68,
    69–70, 72
  SOEs, and *see* CFIUS: national security
    concerns and Chinese SOEs
  stock exchanges 56–57
  telecommunications sector 52–54, 70–71, 75
  US government's determination to safeguard
    US industries 80–81
National Strategy for Critical Infrastructures
    and Key Assets 54
natural gas *see* energy sector, mergers and

OCC
  composition and legislation 230–31, 233–34
  merger applications before OCC 246
  proceedings before OCC 235
  role and functions 233
  seminal cases *see* banking sector: enforcement
    record and seminal cases
  see also banking sector
OECD
  Lloyds/ HBOS 264
  Report on Regulatory Reform in
    the US 83
Office of the Comptroller of the Currency
    see OCC

personal data and sensitive information 54–55,
    57–58, 68–69
private plaintiffs 23–25
  challenges to mergers 23–24
  hurdles to private enforcement 24–25
  second requests 23–24, 25
  standing 24
public interest assessment
  challenges of concurrent jurisdiction 90–91
  Department of Transportation *see* DOT
  Federal Communications Commission
    see FCC
  Federal Deposit Insurance Corporation
    see FDIC
  Federal Energy Regulatory Commission
    see FERC
  Federal Reserve Board *see* FRB
  Office of the Comptroller of the Currency
    see OCC

public interest approach of sectoral
    regulators 2–3
public interest standard 87–89
  superseding competition law assessment 3, 4
  Surface Transportation Board *see* STB

railways *see* STB

Securities and Exchange Commission (SEC)
  avoiding SEC review 137
  public utility holding companies, and 126–27
  reviewing mergers involving
    exchanges 56–57
  utility sector, mergers and 126–27
semiconductors 51, 52, 62–63, 64, 66–68, 69–
    70, 72
Sherman Act (1890) 22–23
  consumer welfare, and 13–14
  DOJ enforcing civilly and criminally 19
  expansion of scope of 8
  historically 5–8, 154
  illegality test 2, 6
  merger control 27–28
  rule of reason approach 7
  'Sherman Act test' 195–96
  vague and broad terms 20
SOEs *see* CFIUS: national security concerns and
    Chinese SOEs
SSNIP test 15–16
state authorities 18, 22–23
state-owned enterprises (SOEs) *see* CFIUS:
    national security concerns and
    Chinese SOEs
stock exchanges 56–57
STB 131–32
  actions taken to enhance competition under
    executive order 153
    new rules on sharing tracks and updating
      emergency service rules 153–54
  challenges of concurrent jurisdiction 163–64
    antitrust immunity through paper
      barriers 163–64
    change in policy, need for 163
    need to balance public interest and
      promotion of competition 191
    sectoral regulators, competition law
      experience of 163
    tensions arising from shared
      jurisdiction 175
    whether merger control assessment better
      by antitrust agencies 178, 191
  competition law
    antitrust laws in assessments inadequate
      and ineffective 190

competition analysis in mergers absent in
railroad sector 188–89
competition principles discounted in rail
mergers reviews 190–91
DOJ concerns in relation to
competition 189, 190–91
ICC not obliged to apply antitrust
laws 190–91
little importance of 168, 170, 173,
175, 188–89
railroads exempted from enforcement of
antitrust laws 166–67, 170
composition and legislation 154–57
creation of STB, 155–56
focus on needs of rail transportation 2–3
historical regulation of railroad
industry 154–55
ICC regulating railroad industry 154–55
ICC, termination of 155–56
immunity, STB granting 156, 182
jurisdiction and role 156–57
major deregulation of the railroads and
trucking 155–56
nature of STB 153
consolidations, rail mergers and 164, 190–91
deference to sectoral regulators
extensive nature of 163, 173, 189–90
level of deference, need to revisit 191
enforcement record *see* STB: enforcement
record and seminal cases
filing instructions and process
overview 157–59
authority to grant antitrust immunity 157
authority to invalidate conflicting state or
federal laws 157–58
factors determining product
market 159
federal agencies and STB in concurrent
mergers, roles of 159
formalized approval process 157–58
full exemption procedure 159
review timeline 158–59
types of transactions 157–58
public interest standard 157, 160–62
approval of mergers unlikely to decrease
competition substantially 161
competition law, little importance of 168,
170, 173, 175, 188–89
conditions, imposition of 161, 170,
176, 189–90
development of approach to 160
ICC not obliged to apply antitrust
laws 190–91
mergers 'in the public interest' 160

mergers not always solution to financial
issues 168
merging parties' envisaged efficiency gains,
overstatement of 178
protection of employment, importance
of 168, 171, 173
public benefits 162
railroads exempted from enforcement of
antitrust laws 166–67, 170
reduction of excess capacity 176
wider public interest
considerations 160–61
STB: enforcement record and seminal
cases 164–88
convergence in approach of STB and DOJ
using contradictory analyses 180–88
Averitt Express and others—Pooling
Agreement 180–82
Canadian Pacific—Norfolk Southern 182–
84, 190
convergence in approach of regulator and
DOJ using same analyses
Southern Pacific—Santa Fe 184–85, 190
different views of STB and DOJ pointing to
different outcomes
CSX—Pan Am Railway 187
divergence in approach between STB and
DOJ 166–80
Canadian Pacific—Kansas City
Southern 178
CSX/ NS Acquisition of
CONRAIL 176–78
Great Northern—Northern Pacific
(The Northern Lines) 170–71,
188–90
Pennsylvania Railroad—New York Central
Railroad 166–68, 188–90
Peter Pan—Greyhound 175–76, 189
Seaboard Air Line—Atlantic Coast
Line 168–70, 188–90
Union Pacific—Missouri Pacific—Western
Pacific 171–73, 188–90
Union Pacific—Southern Pacific 173–75,
188–89
DOJ as decisionmaker opposing the
transaction
Norfolk Southern—Conrail 185–87, 190
implications of 188–90
antitrust laws in assessments inadequate
and ineffective 190
competition analysis in mergers absent in
railroad sector 188–89
DOJ concern in relation to
competition 189, 190–91

288   INDEX

STB: enforcement record and seminal cases (*cont.*)
   extensive deference to regulator by courts 189–90
   ICC not obliged to apply antitrust laws 190–91
   number and scope of benefits accepted by regulator 189
   usual competition analysis absent in railroad sector 188–89
Surface Transportation Board (STB) *see* STB

telecommunications sector *see* FCC
transportation
   airlines *see* DOT
   railways *see* STB

unilateral effects 12, 13, 15–16, 146

UPP test (upward pricing pressure test) 15–16, 17
US merger control regime 5–34
   achieving efficiency as approach to 1–2
   Hart-Scott-Rodino Antitrust Improvements Act 17, 18
   historical overview *see* historical overview of US merger control
   institutional setting *see* institutional setting
   Merger Guidelines *see* Merger Guidelines
   merger review assessment *see* merger review assessment
   national security *see* national security assessment
   public interest assessment *see* public interest assessment

Vertical Merger Guidelines 16–17